National Intelligencer Newspaper Abstracts 1844

Joan M. Dixon

HERITAGE BOOKS
2006

HERITAGE BOOKS
AN IMPRINT OF HERITAGE BOOKS, INC.

Books, CDs, and more—Worldwide

For our listing of thousands of titles see our website at
www.HeritageBooks.com

Published 2006 by
HERITAGE BOOKS, INC.
Publishing Division
65 East Main Street
Westminster, Maryland 21157-5026

Copyright © 2005 Joan M. Dixon

All rights reserved. No part of this book may be reproduced or transmitted in any form or by any means, electronic or mechanical, including photocopying, recording or by any information storage and retrieval system without written permission from the author, except for the inclusion of brief quotations in a review.

International Standard Book Number: 978-0-7884-3279-6

NATIONAL INTELLIGENCER NEWSPAPER
WASHINGTON, D C
1844

TABLE OF CONTENTS

Daily National Intelligencer
 Washington, D C, 1844--1

Americans now in Van Dieman's Land--295
Appointments by the President-275-279; 282-283; 285; 286; 319; 374; 527
Army Officers stationed at Fort Gibson, C N--444

Army Orders—326-328
Ass'n of American Geologists & Naturalist—228-229
Biography of John Randolph, of Roanoke, Va--82

Citizens of Pennsylvania—312-314

Commencements: Academy of the Visitation, Gtwn, D C—347-348
                              Columbia College, D C--430
                              Georgetown College, D C—343-344
                              Rittenhouse Academy, Washington-354
                              St Mary's College, Balt, Md—334-336

Contents in cornerstone of Church of the Ascension, Wash-397
Delegates appointed by the Clay Club of Washington—206-209
Delinquent lands in Alleghany Co, Md—166-170

Georgetown Corp, D C-tax sale—93; 414
Illegal voters-Balt City, Md—452-453
Killed and wounded in riots in Phil, Pa—317-318

Late from the African Coast--127
Legacies left by Israel Munson--73
Letter from Jas H McKnight, Washington—529

Local Church Directory, Washington—523-524
Loss of the cutter Vigilant—450
Martha's Vineyard—377-378

Maryland Historical Society Meeting—484
Methodist Episcopal Church clergy--152
Midshipmen—241

Monument to Jos Lovell, Md, U S Army—226-227
Monumental inscription-Mount Auburn—474

i

Mount St Mary's College students--118
Naval Court Martial—19

Naval Surgeons--493
Navy promotions—74-75

Officers of the:　　　Enterprise—20
　　　　　　　　　　Erie—412
　　　　　　　　　　Columbia—351
　　　　　　　　　　Columbus—250
　　　　　　　　　　John Adams--250
　　　　　　　　　　Lawrence--68
　　　　　　　　　　Porpoise--483
　　　　　　　　　　Union--217
　　　　　　　　　　Yorktown—442

Ordinaries & Taverns in Washington City—457-460

Passengers on the steamboat Sydney—63
Postmasters—133-134; 171
Prisons--345

Promotions-Navy—74-75
7th Regt of the U S Infty--369
Spedden vs Spedden-divorce—21

Steamboat Belle of Clarksville disaster--526
Steamboat Lucy Walker disaster—466-467
Steamboat Shepherdess disaster—26-27; 33

Texian prisoners in Mexico—173
Texian prisoners released--196

Washington City-tax sale—409-411
Wounded of the steamer Princeton--108

Index---537

PREFACE
Daily National Intelligencer Newspaper Abstracts
1844
Joan M Dixon

The National Intelligencer & Washington Advertiser is hereafter the Daily National Intelligencer. It was the first newspaper printed in Washington, D C; Samuel H Smith, the originator. The same was transferred to Jos Gales, jr on Aug 31, 1810; on Nov 1, 1812, the paper was under the firm of Jos Gales, sr, & Wm W Seaton. The Library of Congress has microfilm of the paper from the first issue of Oct 31, 1800 thru Jan 8, 1870, the final paper. The Evening Star Newspaper of Jan 10, 1870 reports: The Intelligencer is discontinued: the proprietor, Mr Alex Delmar, says that having lost several thousand dollars, & being in poor health, he has resolved to discontinue its publication.

Included in the abstracts are advertisements; appointments by the President; Hse o/Rep petitions; passed Acts; legal notices; marriages; deaths; mscl notices; social events; tax sales; military promotions; court cases; deaths by accident; prisoners; & maritime information-crews. Items or events which might be a clue as to the location, age or relationship of an individual are copied.

No attempt has been made to correct the spelling. Due to the length of some articles, it was necessary to present only the highlights of same. Chancery and Equity records are copied as written.

The index contains **all** surnames and *tracts of lands/places*. Maritime vessels are found under barge, boat, brig, frig, schn'r, ship, sloop, steamboat, tugboat, yacht or vessel.

ABBREVIATIONS:
AA CO	ANNE ARUNDEL COUNTY
CO	COMPANY/COUNTY
CMDER	COMMANDER
CMDOR	COMMODOR
D C	DISTRICT OF COLUMBIA
ELIZ	ELIZABETH
ELIZA	ELIZA
MONTG CO	MONTGOMERY COUNTY
PG CO	PRINCE GEORGES CO
WASH	WASHINGTON
WASH, D C	WASHINGTON, DISTRICT OF COLUMBIA

BOOKS IN THE NATIONAL INTELLIGENCER NEWSPAPER SERIES: 1800-1805/1806-1810/1811-1813/1814-1817/1818-1820/1821-1823/1824-1826/1827-1829/1830-1831/1832-1833/1834-1835/1836-1837/1838-1839/1840/1841/1842/1843/1844/1845/1846/
SPECIAL: CIVIL WAR 2 VOLS, 1861-1865

Dedicated to the memory of
Andrew J S Dixon, jr b 1891-Gtwn, D C
D 1970-Beth, Md
Mrd 1927
Beulah [Ogle] Dixon b 1891 Fred'k Co, Md
D 1955 PG Co, Md [Parents of Roland C Dixon]

DAILY NATIONAL INTELLIGENCER NEWSPAPER
WASHINGTON, D C
1844

MON JAN 1, 1844
Wm S Staples, s/o the late Capt Staples of Balt, was lost overboard from the vessel **Brig Tweed** on Aug 22. He was assisting in shortening sail while the vessel was scudding in a hurricane.

Tribute of respect: U S brig **Boxer**, Norfolk, Dec 23, 1843. Meeting of the ofcrs of this vessel, was held on board this morning, Lt Commanding Oscar Bullus called to the Chair, & Lt John Rodgers appointed Sec. Tribute to Dr Chas H Broughton, late Assistant Surgeon of this vessel: we sincerely condole & sympathize with his distressed family in their terrible bereavement. We will wear crape on the left arm for 30 days.

Gen Waddy Thompson, the Minister of the U S to Mexico, has forwarded his resignation of that trust, & may be expected to arrive in the U S very shortly.

New store & great attraction. Cheap, cheap, cheap! At the establishment formerly occupied by John Costigan, which has been fitted up in the neatest style, & will keep a constant supply of fresh groceries, hardware, boots & shoes, crockery, china & glass-wares. –S E Smitt

Livery Stable, just completed by the subscriber, on 8th, between D & E sts. –Geo W Young

Mrd: on Thu last, by Rev Septimus Tuston, Mr Henry Olive to Miss Susan Foxwell, all of Wash City.

Died: on Dec 29, 1843, in Wash City, Miss Ann Marche, in her 28th year. She patiently suffered the will of God in her protracted illness, & her redeemed spirit ascended in holy triumph to her God, who gave it.

Died: on Dec 17, 1843, in Morristown, N J, Jacob Mann, in his 68th year. He was the oldest editor in that State. In 1798 he established the "Genius of Liberty," the first paper published in that county. In 1801 he established the "True American" at Trenton. In 1808 he established the "Palladium of Liberty" at Morristown.

Died: on Dec 30, 1843, in Wash City, Mr Simeon Bassett, in his 50th year, leaving a large family & numerous friends to mourn their irreparable loss.

TUE JAN 2, 1844
A vast crowd of persons paid their respects at the President's Mansion on New Year's Day, & were courteously received. Mrs Madison, the wid/o the illustrious President of that name, & Mr Adams, who has in his own person adorned the Presidency, also received the visits of a host of friends.

Mr Jos Tomlinson, of Pittsburg, has contracted to build an iron steamer upon the principle of Lt Hunter's propellers, for Lt John T Laughlin, of the U S Navy, & is intended for a passage boat or the merchant service on the Southern seaboard. It is to be completed in all next summer.

Died: on Dec 20, at the residence of Mr Vincent, near Port Tobacco, Md, Mrs Mary Harris, in her 42nd year, wid/o the late Nathan Harris, of Chas Co, & d/o Horatio Clagett, leaving 6 orphans to lament their irreparable loss.

Died: on Dec 30, 1843, at Alexandria, Chas Pascoe, in his 77th year. [We cannot record this notice without bearing our testimony to the character & worth of the dec'd. His active benevolence, during a long life, made him beloved by the poor & respected by all, whilst the uniform correctness of his intercourse with all his fellow citizens secured their confidence, & will long be remembered by all who knew him. -Gaz]

Died: on Dec 28, 1843, after a brief illness, at the residence of Thos B Barton, in Fredericksburg, Dr Daniel of St Thos Jenifer, s/o the Hon Danl Jenifer. Dr Jenifer was a citizen of Chas Co, Md, & was on a visit to Va when this afflictive dispensation was visited upon his relatives & friends. The dec'd was distinguished from his boyhood for his strict morality & for all the virtues that adorn the character of a gentleman. He died in the faith & in full communion with the Episcopal Church, to which he had been long united.

Trustee's sale: by virtue of a decree of PG Co Court, as court of equity, the undersigned, as trustee, will expose to public sale, at the tavern of Thos Baldwin, in the village of Bladensburg, Md, on Feb 15, 2 tracts of land, called *Fairfax Beall* & *Second Thought*, containing together about 166 acres, on the road leading to Upper Marlboro, & now in the possession of Thos Cator. On said tracts, which adjoin each other, there is a tolerable sized frame dwlg, tobacco house & corn house.
–Eliz Ferrall, Trustee, Bladensburg, Md

Died: on Dec 29, 1843, in Wash City, Miss Eliz S Evans, aged 16 years & 2 months, d/o the late Geo Evans, of Wash City.

We announce the sudden death of the Rev John P Lathrop, Chaplain of the U S Navy, attached to the steamer **Princeton**. Mr Lathrop had entered Mr Godey's bldg, in Chestnut st, & passed into the 3rd story, to procure a visiting card. On descending, he fell in an apoplectic fit, & died in about an hour. -Phil U S Gaz

WED JAN 3, 1844
Gen David Robinson, whose death took place last week, was born in Hardwick, Mass, Nov 11 [old style,] 1754. He was the s/o Saml Robinson, a capt in the old French war, & came to Bennington with his father in Oct, 1761, to a log hut built for the reception of the family in the center of the Centre Village, & on the same spot of ground where he continued to reside 82 years. He married early in life a d/o Capt Stephen Fay, one of the first settlers. He also, in early life, united with the church in this town. As a parent & husband, he was kind & affectionate. He died on Sun, Dec 10, 1843, surrounded by his family & friends, in his 90th year. He was the last of the first settlers of the town & county. The beautiful tract of land in & about Bennington was first discovered by Capt Saml Robinson, on his return march from *Fort George* to Hardwick, A D 1748. He called it the *Promised land*. He applied to Benning Wentworth, Govn'r of N H, & on Jan 3, 1749, & he procured a charter of the township, which he, in honor of the Govn'r, called Bennington. Gen Robinson, with 7 of his brothers, fought in the battle of Bennington, on Aug 16, 1777. He stood close by Gen Stark when he addressed the soldiers. At the close of the war Gen Robinson was appointed constable, which ofc he held 12 or 15 years, when he was appointed sheriff of the county. This ofc he held 22 years, when he was appointed by Pres Madison marshal of the State, which ofc he held for 8 years. He continued during this time to do service in the militia of the state, & rose through all the several grades to that of Maj Gen. This ofc he resigned soon after the close of the last war with Great Britain.

Mrd: on Dec 20, 1843, in Granville Co, N C, by Rev Mr Hines, Dr Otis F Manson, formerly of Richmond, Va, to Miss Mary A S, only d/o Spotswood Burwell, of the former place.

Mrd: on Dec 26, 1843, in Balt, by Rev Dr Roberts, Mr Jas H Speakes, of Washington, to Miss Harriet J Hultz, of Balt.

Mrd: on Dec 18, 1843, in New Orleans, by Rev Theodore Clapp, A T Pickrell, formerly of Gtwn, D C, to Justine, d/o Henry Lockett, of that city.

The Hon J A Pearce, U S Senator elect from Md, is detained at home by severe sickness in his family. -Balt Patriot

Black & White smithing in general: at his old stand on C st, between 10th & 11th sts, opposite Carusi's Saloon. –C Buckingham

Hse/o Reps: 1-Ptn of Maj Jas Smith, of Indiana, for a pension & lands for military services rendered as a spy in the West up to the treaty of Greenville. 2-Ptn of Edw J Forstall, on behalf of Messrs Hope & Co. of Amsterdam, & others, bond-holders of the Bank of Pensacola, praying for relief. 3-Ptn of Manuel Culget, formerly Naval Ofcr at New Orleans, for refunding to him of certain moneys paid into the Treas under an erroneous judgment. 4-Ptn of Larkin Cason & others, of Callaway Co, Missouri, praying the removal of the Circuit Court of the U S for the Missouri district from St Louis to the city of Jefferson.

Senate: Ptn from J Stone & 10 others, stating that from their long confinement in the British prison at Dartmoor, during the late war with Great Britain, their health has become so impaired as to render them unfit to procure their subsistence by daily labor, & therefore ask from Congress a provision for their support. 2-Ptn from Jas Gleason, a manufacturer of frying & bake pans, stating that on several of the articles the duty on the raw material is higher than on the manufactured article, & that such a discriminating duty is in favor of the foreign manufacturer instead of the American. 3-Ptn from John P Skinner, asking reimbursement of money paid by him as surety for a certain pension agent. 4-Ptn from Jacob Ollinger, for a pension. 5-Ptn from citizens of Indiana, in favor of Simon Kenton, for a pension. 6-Ptn from Geo S Gaines, stating he had acted as pension agent for 5 years without receiving any compensation. 7-Mr Upham: take from the files the papers of Robt Day. 8-Cmte on Commerce: reported a bill for the relief of Edw Kennard, with a report, which was ordered to be printed.

THU JAN 4, 1844
Military & Civic Hall at the Washington Assembly Rooms: 3rd Annual Ball on Jan 8, 1844.
Cmte of Invitation & Reception:

Gen R C Weightman	B J Tayman	W A Flaherty
Capt L J Middleton	M J Sheahan	John S Owen
Ensign W I Parham	W M Randolph	Wm Magee
Sergeant John Brannan	Col W W Seaton	John McDermott
	Lt W Monroe Clarke	Saml Pumphrey
Cpl Geo Emerick	Lt E Evans	John Stoddard
M P Mohun	Sergeant Jas L White	
Chas T Iardella	Qrtrmstr John P Coyle	

A sufficient number of servants will be engaged. Tickets $2; to be sold at Gadsby's, Brown's, & Fuller's Hotels; Farquhar & Morgan's Drugstore, 7 Bldgs; Dr Clarke's store, Navy Yard; Kidwell's Drugstore, High st, Gtwn; at Buckingham's Drugstore, Pa ave; & at the door on the evening of the Ball.

Household furniture for sale at auction on Dec 9, by virtue of a deed of trust from Wm B Burger, at his residence on 6th st, between G & H sts. -Robt W Dyer & Co, aucts

Huron Reflector: Mr Patrick & Mr Tucker were killed in Townsend, Huron Co, Ohio, on Dec 23, by the falling of a tree. They had cut a large oak, which in falling struck another tree; the latter, rebounding, came to the ground & crushed the men instantly.

Military & Civic Ball: the Second Annual Ball of the Independent Grays will be held at the Pompeian Hall, Union Hotel, Gtwn, on Jan 16, 1844, being the Anniversary of the formation of the Company.

Managers:

Capt Smith	Capt McClellan	Capt Snyder
Capt Duvall	Capt John Mason, jr	Capt Hawkins
Capt Buckingham	Capt R France	
Capt Tucker	Capt Harkness	

Cmte of Invitation & Reception:

Capt Smith	Robt Wilburn	Saml McAfee
Lt Hill	Wm Herron	Pioneer Bronaugh
Surgeon Lauck	Ensign Kidwell	W T Upperman
A L Settle	Sergeant Garrett	W H Semmes

Cmte on Refreshments:

Lt Kidwell	John Adams	Richd Fullslove
Sergeant Sedgwick	Wm A Waugh	John Conner
Jas A Crow	John Mehegan	

Cmte on Decorations:

Sergeant Ridgway	Wm Spalding	Geo Kell
Jos McLean	Walter Silence	John Newton

Cmte on Music:

Sergeant Garrett	John Calhoun
W Godey	Henry King

Tickets $2, to be had at the Drug Stores of J L Kidwell & G M | J W Sothoron, Gtwn; & at the stores of Farquhar & Morgan & R L Patterson, Washington; & at the door on the night of the Ball. No servants will be admitted, under any circumstances, except those engaged by the Company. Lloyd Williams' Band is engaged.

The Complete Confectioner & Pastry Cook, price 25 cents, giving plain & practical directions for Confectionary, pastry, & baking, together with upwards of 500 receipts for preserves, cakes, comfits, lozenges, ices, liqueurs, sirups, jellies, marmalades, compotes, biscuits, muffins, tarts, pies, etc, by Parkinson, Confectioner, Chesnut st, Phil. Just published & this day received for sale by –F Taylor.

Died: on Dec 14, 1843, at his residence in Cabarras Co, N C, Rev John Robinson, D D: age about 80 years: for more than half a century a distinguished minister of the Gospel in that State. He was of the Presbyterian denomination.

Hse/o Reps:: 1-Ptn of John P Schuyler, of Muncy, Lycoming Co, Pa, praying for relief for wounds received in the late war. 2-Ptn of Jas Carlin & 224 citizens of Indiana, asking for a donation of refuse lands to assist in completing the Wabash & Erie Canal. 3-Ptn of Benj McCammon & 48 citizens of Sullivan Co, Ind, praying a grant of land in the Vincennes land district to improve the navigation of the Wabash river. 4-Ptn of Danl Risinger & 332 other citizens of Knox Co, Ind, asking same as #3.

Meeting of the Friends of Agriculture & Manufactures: held last evening in the Hall of the Hse/o Reps.
Ofcrs appointed:

Hon Levi Woodbury, of N Y, Pres	Hon Thos Clayton, of Dela, V P
Hon Jos Vance, of Ohio, V P	Hon Jacob W Miller, of N J, V P
Hon Wm Wilkins, of Pa, V P	Hon Jas J McKay, of N C, V P
Hon Dixon H Lewis, of Ala, V P	John F Callan, of D C, Sec
Hon Wm D Merrick, of Md, V P	Robt E Horner, of N J, Sec

Mr John S Skinner, of Washington, offered a preamble & resolutions proposing that an exhibition of the products be held in Balt City, Md, next May.

Amasa Sprague, of Cranston, senior partner in the extensive manufacturing house of A & W Sprague, was willfully & cruelly murdered on his farm on Sun last. He was found dead on the earth on his farm: a ball was found to have entered the front & passed out of the back of his head. A pistol was found some distance from his body. Though not an actual resident of our city, his immense business relations led him to be regarded as one of our citizens. His age was about 45, & he was a brother to the Hon Wm Sprague, a U S Senator from R I. –Providence Journal

Sentence of death was passed on Mon last upon Helen Foster, a colored woman, convicted of the murder of a white woman in the Penitentiary last spring. Both were convicts, & Helen was assisted in the crime by another colored woman, whose trial has been continued to the next term. Helen was ordered to be hung on Feb 9 next.

For sale: the subscriber, agent of the guardian of the heirs of Cornelius DeKrafft, dec'd, offers at private sale, the house & lot on E st, nearly opposite the Medical College. It contains 8 rooms, & has a large 2 story porch its whole width in the rear. Inquire of D Saunders.

Senate: 1-Ptn from Hiram March asking remuneration for a sum of money paid by him for an alleged violation of the revenue laws. 2-Ptn of the heirs of John Pettibone, asking remuneration for a patent used by the U S. 3-Ptn from John Thomas & other citizens of Mass, praying indemnification for French spoliations prior to 1800. 4-Bill for the relief of the legal reps of Wm Walker. 5-Bill for the relief of Isaac Ilsley came up on the general orders: postponed until Wed.

The person who lately murdered Mrs Houseman & her child, on Staten Island, N Y, & afterwards fired her dwlg house to conceal the crime, is supposed to have been a sister of the murdered woman's husband, named Polly Bodine, who has borne a very bad character & previously lived in the family. A druggist of N Y named Waite is also suspected of having been concerned in the tragedy. Both have been arrested.

Mrd: on Thu last, by Rev Mr Edwards, Mr Geo H Furtney to Miss Mary E Dowden, all of Wash City.

In Chancery. The Pres & Dirs of the Bank of Metropolis, vs, John A Brackenridge, exc of John Brackenridge, dec'd, & Robt E Kerr, adm of Alex'r Kerr, dec'd. The bill in substance states that the dec'd, John Brackenridge, was in his lifetime, & at the time of his death, indebted to the cmplnts upon his certain promissory note, dated Sep 11, 1840, for $290, payable in 60 days after date, which was discounted by the cmplnts. Brackenridge did execute a certain sealed instrument, whereby he authorized Alex'r Kerr, since dec'd, & whose administrator is the said Robt E Kerr, his successor in ofc, to transfer the said stock to such person as the cmplnts might require. The said note is due & unpaid, except so far as credits have been given thereon for dividends from time to time amounting to $259.52. The bill prays that the said John A Brackenridge, the sole acting exc of the said John, dec'd, may be decreed to pay the said debt by a short day, & that for default of such payment the said stock may be sold; & for general relief. John A Brackenridge does not reside within D C, but in parts beyond the jurisdiction of the Court. The Court orders the said dfndnt, John A Brackenridge, to appear in person or by solicitor, on or before the second Mon in May next. By order of the Court. Test: Coxe & Carlisle, Solicitor for cmplnts. –W Brent, clk

Meeting of the students of the Univ of Va, held on Dec 29, 1843, upon receiving intelligence of the death of Mr Wm F Taliaferro, of Westmoreland Co, on Dec 9, by a fall from his horse, Mr Thos George was called to the chair; Mr J H Saunders appointed sec; when Mr Thos T Fauntleroy, jr, submitted the following remarks: he was, but a year since, a student here. For 12 months up to exactly a week before his death, he had been faithfully engaged in the prosecution of his professional studies. These he had but just completed. We tender to his family, in their affliction, this expression of our earnest sympathy.

FRI JAN 5, 1844
Workboxes, writing desks, boxes of colors, portfolios with lockers, backgammon & chess boards, chessmen, snuffboxes, pocketbooks, penknives & scissors.
–Garret Anderson, between 11th & 12th, Pa ave

Edw McCubbin, Barber & Hair Dresser, Temple of Fashion, #1, 8th st, near Pa ave. He has secured the services of that well known operator in the art, Jas Jefferson: Hairdressing & Shaving.

Senate: 1-Ptn from Geo Whitton, a soldier in the late war, asking a pension. 2-Ptn from Jas Low, a seaman, praying a pension. 3-Ptn from G H McFaddon & others, of the parish of Point Coupee, La, praying for pre-emption rights to certain lands. 4-Ptn of Wm Grant, for a pension. 5-Ptn from John Beercraft, for a pension.

The Button factory of Mr E M Pomeroy, in the center of Wallingford, Conn, was nearly destroyed by an explosion of gas on Mon. –New Haven Courier

The dry goods store of Willett Denike, 245 Spring st, N Y, was consumed by fire on Tue: fire was communicated by an incendiary. The same night, the large machine shop of Robt Hoe & Co, on Gold st, was also consumed by fire, causing a considerable loss of property.

Leonardtown [Md] Herald says that the murder of Mr Francis Knott, a wealthy citizen of this county, shot by one of his own servants in the early part of Nov last, was in the yard of his dwlg. The deed was perpetrated by negro George, a runaway, who had secreted himself behind one of the out-houses near the dwlg. The case was opened on Dec 19, & the Jury found a verdict of guilty of murder in the first degree.

Orphan's Court of Wash Co, D C. Letters of administration de bonis non with the will annexed, on the personal estate of Henry Thompson, late of said county, dec'd. –Rd Dement, admr d b n w a

Hse/o Reps:: 1-Ptn of D W Hopkins & 118 citizens of St Clair & Randolph Counties, Ill, praying that the mail route from Bellville to Fayetteville may be extended to Sparta, Randolph Co. 2-Ptn of the widow & admx of Andrew Lewis, late an ofcr of the U S Army, praying to be reimbursed the cost & charges of a suit instituted against him for responsibility incurred by him in his official capacity. 3-Ptn of Geo W Tripp, praying that a certain pre-emption right in the Columbus land district, Mississippi, may be confirmed to him. 4-Ptn of F E Powers & 199 others, praying a reduction of postage. 5-Memorial of 133 citizens of Illinois, praying an increase of the pension of Isaac Barker, who was wounded in the late war. 6-Nominated as Postmaster: Mr D R McNair, Mr H H Sylvester, Mr John M Johnson, Mr P H Brown, & Mr W J McCormick-present incumbent. On the 3rd ballot, Mr J M Johnson was elected Postmaster to this House.

Wash Corp: Message received announcing the death of Simeon Bassett, a member of the Board of Common Council. He died after a sickness of little more than a week, died at his residence on Capitol Hill, on Sat last, aged 49 years. Deep regrets to his family.

Mrd: on Jan 2, by Rev Jas Brown, Mr Jas E King, jr, formerly of Balt, to Miss Margaret, y/d/o Thos & Sarah Young, of Wash.

Died: on Dec 22, at N Y, Mr Geo H Richards, a deputy inspector of the revenue, in his 53rd year. He was formerly a clerk in the Treas Dept, & resided in Wash City.

Died: on Oct 27 last, in Carracas, South America, Dr Shadrach Nye, for many years a citizen of Nashville, Tenn, & proprietor & publisher of the Nashville Banner. His last illness was but of a few days' duration, & his decease took place at the house of his brother-in-law, Hon A A Hall, Minister resident of the U S near the Gov't of Venezuela.

Died: on Jan 3, in Alexandria, at the residence of Henry Daingerfield, Dr Henry P Daingerfield, in his 62nd year.

For rent, a new frame house with brick basement, on B st south, fronting the mall, between 6th & 7th sts. Inquire of I T Elwood, Merchant Tailor, Pa ave.

For rent, a 3 story brick house on N J ave, adjoining the residence of Col C K Gardner. Apply to J W Hand, Patent Ofc.

22,000 bushels Mercer Potatoes arrived this day at Scott's wharf, Gtwn: for sale on board, or at Mr R Woodward's store, where they will find the subscriber. –Hubbard Swanton, Gtwn [Jan 6 newspaper: same ad is-Hubbard Scranton, Gtwn.]

SAT JAN 6, 1844
Waverley Academy: with a view to the education of his own sons, the subscriber informs that this institution will be continued the ensuing year. –A Keech

Public sale of real estate: by virtue of an order of Montg Co Court, sale on Jan 11, on the premises, the Farm on which Mr Andrew Offutt resided at the time of his death. This land lies about 2 miles above Darnestown, & contains 408 acres: improvements are an orchard, a large brick dwlg-house, kitchen, meat-house, barn, stable, milk-house, & outbldgs. On the same day will be sold a house & lot in Dawsonville-a good stand for a store. On Fri, on the premises, one formerly the residence of Jas Offutt of Wm, containing 138½ acres of land; the other, known as *Hazzy Offutt's farm*, containing 158 1/8 acres . These farms lie contiguous to each other. On the same day, will be offered a small island in the Potomac river, called *Cow Island*: contains about 5 acres of land. For a more particular description of the premises, inquire of the subscribers, or of Messrs John & J W Offutt. –Wm Darne, John H Hilleary, Wm O Chappell, Com'rs

Hse/o Reps:: 1-Ptn of Jonathan Read & 484 other citizens of Ohio, praying for an appropriation for the completion of the Cumberland road. Referred to the Cmte on Roads & Canals. 2-Ptn of Euphemia Dolson & others, widows of ofcrs slain on board of private armed vessels, praying relief. 3-Ptn of Catharine Rinker, of Phil, for a pension on account of the services of her husband in the Revolutionary war.

Orphan's Court of Chas Co, Md. Letters of administraton on the personal estate of Thos H Marshall, late of said county, dec'd. –John H Hardesty, adm of Thos H Marshall

Died: on Jan 4, aged 76, Mrs Sarah Easton, relict of David Easton. Her funeral will be from her late residence, corner of I & 19th sts, today at 3 o'clock.

The Hon Mr Sprague, one of the Senators from R I, has left Wash City for his residence, in consequence of the murder of his brother. [Jan 22 newspaper: the Hon Wm Sprague has been obliged to resign his seat as one of the Senators of the U S from the State of R I, by death of his brother, who was his partner in business.]

$10 reward: strayed or stolen out of the yard of Jas Ford, [colored,] in Washington, a light sorrel mare. I will give the above reward if delivered to me near Piscataway, PG Co, Md. –Wm Bryan of Rd

At the Whig County Convention of Hamilton Co, Ohio, held in Cincinnati on Dec 30, the following were appinted Delegates to the Balt Nat'l Convention from the first Congressional district of Ohio:

Alex'r Mahew	John C Wright	John D Jones
Bellamy Storer	Wm F Harrison	Philip Mann
Jacob Burnett	N G Pendleton	John H Balance
Wm Oliver	Jos Pierce	

The murder of Mr Sprague. The Providence Journal gives some particulars: there were 5 wounds on the body; he was not robbed-$53 in money & a gold watch were left untouched in his pockets. Two foreigners, Nicholas S Gordon & John Gordon, who are brothers, have been arrested on suspicion of having committed the deed. Nicholas has been known to threaten Mr Sprague for defeating his frequent petitions to the town council of Cranston for a license to sell spirituous liquors. They are the only 2 persons who have not visited the house of the dec'd since the murder. A reward of $1,000 has been offered by the family, & $1,000 by a town meeting.

MON JAN 8, 1844
Appointments by the Pres: 1-Green W Caldwell to be Superintendent of the Branch Mint at Charlotte, N C, in the place of Burgess S Gaither. 2-Alex'r Downing to be Surveyor General of Public Lands south of Tenn, in the place of Benj Ludlow.

The barn of Mr Robt Spencer, a few miles south of Fred'k City, Md, was destroyed by fire on Fri last. Several horses, cows, the grain in the barn, & some stacks of hay adjoining, were consumed in the flames.

Wm Brown [alias David Babe] convicted of the murder of Walter A Nicoll, mate of the schnr **Sarah Lavinia**, was sentenced on Wed by Judge Betts to be executed on Mar 7 next. When called on to say why sentence should not be pronounced upon him, he said: "I am innocent of the crime of which I have been found guilty. The capt & mate fell overboard in a controversy between themselves, & if I had the time I could find the cook, for he is alive. The whole people of N Y think me guilty of murder of the cook, but the man is alive, & I could soon show it."

Mrd: on Jan 4, by Rev Mr Samson, Mr Fred'k White to Miss Mary E Jones, all of Wash City.

Mrd: on Dec 26, by Rev Mr Bean, Mr Bernard Gier, of Germany, to Mrs Mary Stepper, of Washington.

Mrd: on Jan 2, at Cedar Hill, Chas Co, Md, by Rev Mr Wilmer, John Tayloe Key, of St Mary's Co, to Mary Eliz, d/o the late Geo Robertson, of Chas Co, Md.

Mrd: on Dec 19, at Pittsburg, Lt Thos J Rodman, U S Army, to Martha, d/o Rev Dr John Black.

Mrd: on Jan 4, in Phil, by Rev W H Odenheimer, Mr Benj Gerhard to Anna, 2nd d/o the Hon John Sergeant.

Died: on Jan 7, Rebecca Gideon, d/o Geo S Gideon, aged 2 years & 5 months. Her funeral will be at 2 o'clock, this afternoon, from her father's residence on 10th st, between D & C sts.

Died: on Jan 3, at Phil, Robt S Tatem, U S Navy, in his 52nd year.

New, Beautiful & Splendid Paris Goods. —C B Thornton, Pa ave, 8 doors west of Brown's Hotel

Dr Thos Pitts, a well-known respectable physician, was killed in N Y on Fri last by the accidental discharge of his gun. He was returning from a shooting excursion in N J, when at the junction of Pearl & Centre sts, in consequence of some jar in crossing the Railroad, his gun went off & lodged the whole in his body, entering below the 5th rib & causing almost instant death. He had formerly been a Methodist minister.

The U S ship of the line **Delaware** & frig **Congress** were at Mahon on Nov 26, & other vessels belonging to the U S Navy were expected. On board one of these vessels in port were 2 colossal statues, one of which represents Christopher Columbus, sculptured in white marble by Persico, who will come to this country with his works.

Fatal accident lately at the mill of Mr Jas W Osborne, by which Francis Marion Magill, formerly of Balt Co, lost his life. The dec'd was stepping over a box containing a conveyer, when by a mis-step he placed his right foot in the box. The pins in the revolving shaft caught his leg at the ankle: his leg had to be amputated, & he died the same evening. –Charlestown [Va] Free Press

Hse/o Reps: 1-Ptn of John H Kleppart & 85 others, citizens of Ohio, praying the abolition of the franking privilege & reduction of the rates of postage. 2-Memorial of John McIntire & 303 others, citizens of Indiana, praying for the appropriation of the unsold lands in the Vincennes land district, towards the completion of the Cross Cut & Central Canal from Terre Haute to Evansville. Also, the memorial of B Royston & 172 others, to the same effect. 3-Ptn of John Shanklin & 150 others, citizens of Indiana, asking a grant of land in the Vincennes district, to assist in completing the Wabash & Erie Canal. 4-Ptn of John B Hawley & 499 others, citizens of Chautauque Co, N Y, praying for the reduction of the rates of postage & the abolition of the franking privilege. 5-Ptn of Jonathan Austin, Geo White, & others, & the ptn of John H Reed & others, praying for the erection of a lighthouse at the mouth of the Cattaraugus Creek, N Y, & for the further prosecution of the unfinished works at that place. 6-Memorial of John C Reed & 61 others, citizens of Laporte, Ind, praying Congress to adopt such efficient measures for the benefit of the colony of Liberia, in Africa, & for the effectual suppression of the African slave-trade, as it may deem consistent with its constitutional powers & duty. 7-Memorial of Hiram Brown & 36 others, citizens of St Joseph, Mich, praying that the shipping & navigation of the Lakes, from Lake Ontario to Lake Michigan inclusive, may be placed under & regulated by the maritime law of the U S. 8-Mr Tibbatts withdrew from the files of the House the ptn of the heirs of Nathl Asby, of Ky, & the same was, on his motion, referred to the Cmte on Revolutionary Pensions.

Trustee's sale: on Feb 7 next, at public auction, by the deed from Duff Green, dated Aug 11, 1835, all that piece of land in Wash City, D C, being part of square 377; with 4 dwlg houses, all in good order & under a reasonable rent to good tenants. The whole must be sold together. Sale in front of the premises on E between 9th & 10th sts, at 4 p m. –A Coyle, trustee -Robt W Dyer & Co, aucts

TUE JAN 9, 1844
Bake-house for rent: near the Centre Market, & in a populous neighborhood. Inquire of Saml De Vaughan.

Supreme Court of the U S, Jan 8, 1844: met at the Court-room in the Capitol. Present, Hon Roger B Taney, Chief Justice, Hon John McLean, Hon Jas M Wayne, Hon John Catron, & Hon John McKinley, Assoc Justices. On motion of the Atty Gen, Wm H Stewart, of Md, was admitted an Atty & Counsellor of this Court.

Bank of Washington: election held on Jan 1: following elected Dirs of the Bank for the ensuing year:

Wm Gunton	Archibald Henderson	Jacob Gideon
Stanislaus Murray	Geo Bomford	John P Ingle
John F Callan	Benj F Middleton	Edw Dyer

Wm Gunton was re-elected Pres, & Francis A Dickins was elected a Dir to fill the vacancy thus created in the Board. –Jas Adams, Cashier

Miss Brochin: Ladies' Fashionable Hair-dresser & Dress-maker: at her residence, on Pa ave, between 9th & 10th sts.

Senate: 1-Ptn from Saml Thompson, asking payment for services rendered as Superintendent of the Custom House in N Y. 2-Ptn from Peter A Carnes, asking for compensation for losses sustained in consequence of irregular orders issued by the War Dept. 3-Ptn from Danl Martin, of Tenn, in favor of the establishment of a naval school. 4-Ptn from Danl C Wilson, late U S Marshal for Delaware, asking an allowance for ofc rent for the period during which he performed the duties. 5-Ptn from A B Quimby, praying that an examination may be made to the boilers of the steam frig **Mississippi**, & into the propriety of dispensing with steam-chimneys in the construction of engines for the use of the navy. 6-Ptn from Wm Easby, surviving partner of Easby & Hanly, asking compensation for hydraulic cement furnished for repair of a bridge over the Pennsylvania ave at 2nd st. 7-Ptn from Thos M Latham, asking compensation to be allowed to the ofcrs & men of the sloop **Marion** for their services & losses for saving the U S troops from a vessel stranded on Tampa Bay in 1837. 8-Ptn from the heirs of Danl Ineheart, to take their papers from file & refer them to the Cmte on Revolutionary Claims. 9-Cmte on Pensions: asking to be discharged from the further consideration of the ptns of Jos Veazie & John Bosworth. Also, adverse reports on the ptns of the widow of Jacob Reddington, the widow of Josiah Gordon, & on the ptn of David Mann. 10-Cmte on Indian Affairs: an adverse report on the claim of Benj Crauford.

The Mormons have recently held a meeting at Nauvoo, at which they resolved that "Jos Smith is not guilty of any charge made against him by the State of Missouri." The city authorities have passed an ordinance directing the imprisonment for life of any person who shall come within the corporate limits of Nauvoo with a legal process for the arrest of Joe Smith, for any offence committed by him in Missouri during the Mormon difficulties. The Prophet Joe declared it his duty, as Lt Genr'l of the Nauvoo Legion & militia of Illinois, to enforce said ordinance.

Yesterday the Pres sent to the Senate the nomination of Mr John C Spencer, to supply the vacancy on the bench of the Supreme Court occasioned by the decease of Judge Thompson.

From Michigan we learn, through a private letter, that on Dec 25 [Christmas] the 2 youngest sons of Gen J W Brown, & nephews of the late Maj Gen Jacob Brown, [U S Army,] were drowned in the River Rai_in, at Tecumseh, Michigan. They left the house of their father, unknown to the family, & went on the ice, some 40 rods from the house, when the eldest, Patterson, in his 13th year, first went through the ice. His little brother, Mason Kirby, in his 11th year, ran to his assistance, & with him found a watery grave. The alarm was given and their father & 2 elder brothers arrived. The eldest brother brought up the body of Patterson. The body of Mason Kirby was also recovered, but in both cases not before life was extinguished.

On Sun last, an alarming fire was discovered in the grocery store of Mr Wm Naylor, at 15th st, nearly opposite St Matthew's Church. Mr Naylor's store & its contents were totally consumed; it was valued at about $3,000, with no insurance. Six other bldgs, including the store occupied by Mr Naylor, belonged to Mr S Brereton: all without insurance. The property was rented by Mr Brereton for about $500 per annum.

The Mechanical Riflemen, under the command of Capt McClelland, had a handsome parade in Wash City yesterday in honor of the Eighth of Jan.

Mrd: on Jan 7, by Rev S G Bulfinch, Mr Henry Ball to Miss Frances H Stone, all of Wash City.

Died: on Jan 5, in Wash City, at the residence of his son, Mr Thos Naylor, in his 59th year, late of PG Co, Md, & for the last 15 years a resident of the District of Columbia.

Died: on Jan 8, Edw, infant s/o Robt W & Mary Eliza Dyer, aged 7 weeks & 2 days. His funeral is today, from their dwlg on H st, between 6th & 7th sts, at 3 p m.

Died: on Dec 24 last, at the residence of his father in Westmoreland Co, Va, Thos Jefferson Hungerford, in his 25th year, after a protracted illness of 20 months, which he bore with manly resignation.

The Columbian Magazine, edited by John Inman, will be published on the first day of every month. Its contributors will be sought for among the ablest & most popular writers in the country; & no efforts will be spared to secure the aid of the most distinguished, such as:

John L Stephens	F G Halleck
J F Cooper	H W Herbert

H T Tuckerman	T S Arthur
J R Chandler	H F Harrington
T C Grattan	H H Weld
J C Neal	W C Bryant
Geo P Morris	J E Paulding
Seba Smith	N P Wilds
W G Simms	John Neal
Epes Sargent	Park Benjamin
Theodore S Fay	R H Dana
Nathl Hawthorne	Rufus Dawes
Mrs Emma C Embury	R W Griswold
Mrs Ann S Stephens	R M Bird
Mrs Seba Smith	Miss Eliza Leslie
Mrs H E Beecher Stowe	Miss C M Sedgwick
Mrs Lydia H Sigourney	Miss Juliet H Lewis
Mrs C W H Esling	Miss Mary Davenant
Mrs Lydia Jane Pierson	Miss Emily Francis
Miss Hannah F Gould	Mrs Mary Clavers
Miss E A Dupuy	Mrs Frances O Osgood
Miss Lucy Austin	Mrs E F Ellet
Miss Sarah Hewett	Mrs Volney E Howard
Miss M A Fairman	Mrs M St Leon Loud
Miss E S Norton	Mrs A M F Annan
Miss Mgt Coxe	Miss Meeta M Duncan
Miss Marion H Rand	Miss Virginia De Forest
H W Longfellow	Miss A S Lindsay
C F Hoffman	Miss C M Keteltas

Hse/o Reps: 1-Ptn of Abner Taylor & Co, & 62 others, & Danl B Stone & 92 others, all merchants of Bangor, Maine, to have Bangor established as a port of entry & clearance. 2-Ptn of Louis Struller for return of duties, etc, improperly paid by Seigert & Struller, of N Y. 3-Ptn of Hiram McNutt & 200 other citizens of Southeast Ohio, praying Congress to make an appropriation for the continuation of the Cumberland road. 4-Ptn of Adam L Mills for payment of moneys withheld from him by the Post Ofc Dept for carrying the U S mail. 5-Ptn of John Boucher, a soldier in the late war, praying arrears of pension. 6-Ptn of Wm McCauley, a soldier in the late war, praying a pension. 7-Ptn of John Francis & !,263 others, citizens of Northern Indiana, praying that Congress at an early day will make adequate appropriation for continuing the construction of the harbor at Michigan City, on Lake Michigan, in Indiana. 8-Ptn of C G Morehouse & 65 other citizens of Indiana & Illinois, praying that the Congress of the U S would grant to the State of Indiana the vacant lands in the Vincennes district, in Indiana, for the continuation of the Wabash & Erie canal from Terre Haute to Evansville, on the Ohio river.

Law Notice. The undersigned, having recently removed from Balt to Phil, informs that as under the old Convention, he will tend to the prosecution of all Claims under the recent Convention with Mexico that may be entrusted to his care. He will also practice in the Supreme Court at Washington & in the Supreme Court of Pennsylvania. –David Hoffman

Wood & chestnut rails for sale: at the subscriber's farm, about 4 miles from the Market-house, on the Washington & Rockville turnpike road. –Henry Ould

For rent: 3 story brick house on Pa ave, between 1st & 2nd sts. Apply to the subscriber on F st, between 12th & 13th sts, or to P Moran at the Railroad Hotel. –G Ennis

For rent: a 2 story brick house on F st, between 13th & 14th sts, containing 12 rooms. Inquire of Jos Abbot.

Circuit Court of Wash Co, D C, sitting in Chancery. Nov Term, 1843. David E Twiggs, cmplnt, vs, Henry D Hunter, John W Hunter, Alex'r Hunter, Benj F Hunter, Isaac J Course & Wilhelmina his wife, Richd B Mason & Mgt his wife, Hezekiah W Scovell, Edw Scovell, a minor, Mgt H Twiggs, Marion R Twiggs, minors, heirs at law of John W Hunter, dec'd, & Richd Wallach, adm of said John W Hunter. Object of the bill is to procure a decree for the sale of certain mortgaged premises in Wash City, in said county, which were on Jul 24, 1838, mortgaged by John W Hunter, late of said county, dec'd, to the cmplnt David E Twiggs. On Jul 24, 1838, the said John W Hunter, dec'd, conveyed certain real estate, which is particularly described in the bill, unto David E Twiggs, by way of mortgage, to secure the payment of $1,100 with interest from said date,w hich was then due & owing from the dec'd, to the cmplnt, in 5 years from the date thereof. That the said John W Hunter hath departed this life, leaving as his heirs at law the said dfndnts. That Henry D Hunter, John W Hunter, Alex'r Hunter, Benj F Hunter, Isaac J Course & Wilhelmina his wife, Richd B Mason & Mgt his wife, Hezekiah W Scovell, Edw Scovell, a minor, Mgt H Twiggs & Marion R Twiggs, minors, reside out of D C. That the dfndnt, Richd Wallach, is adm of said dec'd, John W Hunter. Dfndnts are to appear in this Court in person, by guardian or solicitor, on or before the 2nd Mon of May next, to answer the premises & show cause, if any they have, why a decree ought not to pass as prayed. By order of the Court: -Wm Brent, clk -H May, Solicitor for cmplnt

WED JAN 10, 1844
J F Caldwell, Dental Surgeon, detained by business with Congress, will remain a short time at Mrs Beeler's, C st, in the rear of Gadsby's, where he will operate for any who may call for his services.

David McComas was on Mon elected a Judge of the Genr'l Court of Virginia, to supply the vacancy occasioned by the death of Judge Summers.

Lt Christopher of the Indian navy, who was dispatched from Aden upon a survey of the coast of Africa by Capt Haines, discovered a splendid river to the northward of the river Jub, which he entered & traced for 130 miles. As he advanced the width & depth increased, & according to the report of the natives, [a civil & obliging race,] it continued to do so for the next 400 miles. Lt Christopher named it the "Haines river."

N Y papers: Capt Burrows, cmder of the packet ship **George Washington**, died while on his passage from Liverpool to N Y. He was taken sick of the brain fever 7 days out; recovered, was taken sick again, & died at sea on the 23rd ult. He was much respected both in this country & in England. He had been in command of the **George Washington** for the last 2 years.

Mrd: Jan 9, by Rev Mr Brown, Mr Francis Hayre, of Chas Co, Md, to Miss Catharine Ann Burch, of Wash.

Died: yesterday, after a long & painful illness, Mrs Hannah Larkin, aged about 70 years. Her funeral will be from her late residence on 10th st, between D & E, on Thu, at 2 o'clock.

Ofcr Lounsbury arrived at N Y on Sun, having in his custody Wm Jones, whom he brought on from New Orleans, charged with the willful murder of Jas Doyle in Oct last, by striking him during an election fracas.

On Sat last, whilst the train of cars from Cumberland to Balt was passing between Harper's Ferry & the Point of Rocks, a man named Derr, a supervisor of the road, standing on the outside of the car while it was in motion, in extending his head out to look if all was right, it struck a post & he was much mangled. At last accounts he was doing as well as could be expected, yet fears were entertained of his recovery.

Senate: 1-Ptn from Chas Crocker & others, praying a reduction of postage. 2-Proceedings of a meeting of citizens of New Buffalo, in relation to the construction of a harbor at that place. 3-Ptn from Julius Eldred, for compensation for the removal of the copper rock. 4-Ptn from Jordan L Mott, praying the action of Congress in relation to the exorbitant post ofc rate on an advertising pamphlet. 5-Ptn from E B & S Ward, to be relieved from loss by a contract, which they had been compelled to execute. 6-Ptn from the heirs of Geo Yates, asking commutation. 7-On motion of Mr Huntington, the papers in the case of Wareham Kingsley were taken from the files & referred to the Cmte on Pensions. 8-On motion of Mr Sevier, it was resolved that the papers of F A Kerr be taken from the files & referred to the Cmte on Indian Affairs.

An encounter on Dec 21, near Hornesville, La, between Dr Jewell & Mr Banks Marshall, resulted in the death of Jewell. Marshall also received a ball in his abdomen from the hands of Jewell, & a ball in the shoulder from the hands of a third party named Thos Lewis.

Notice in Chancery. John King, cmplnt, vs, Jas Marshall, adm, & others. All interested in this cause are to attend at the ofc of the undersigned auditor in the City Hall, on Jan 30, 1844, in the distribution of the estate of Geo Webster, dec'd. –Jos Forest, adm

Orphan's Court of Wash Co, D C. In the case of Chas H James, adm of Jas D Woodside, dec'd. Jan 30th appointed for final settlement. –Ed N Roach, Reg/o wills

Hse/o Reps: 1-Mr Smith, of Illinois, will ask leave to introduce the following bills, viz: Bill for the relief of Pierre Menard, the legal rep of Antoine Peltier & Jos Placy. A bill for the relief of David Akenson. 2-Ptn of John M Roseberry, of Mason Co, Va, asking a pension. 3-Ptn of H Havens & Son & others, in relation to a drawback on spirits distilled from foreign molasses. 4-Ptn of Jas Barr, asking for the regular payment of his pension. 5-Ptn & documents of John S Atlee, of Pa, praying that an act may be passed directing the payment of a balance which appears on the Treasury books to have been due to his father as deputy commissary of prisoners in the Revolutionary war. 6-Ptn of Thos H Genin & 122 others, citizens of Belmont Co, Ohio, praying a reduction of the rates of postage, & that the franking privilege be abolished.

Wash Corp: 1-Bill for the relief of Ulysses Ward was rejected. 2-Report of Madame Millet, an Inspectress, on the Infant Schools, giving an account of their institution, management, & requisites of the superintendents. 3-Act for the relief of Nicholas Ferreton; & act for the relief of Wm Creutzfeldt: recommended their indefinite postponement. 4-Cmte of Claims: adverse to the ptn of Wm Dalton. 5-Cmte of Claims: asking to be discharged from the further consideration of the ptns of D W Oyster, of Geo Grymes & Geo T McGlue, of John M Johnson & of Wm Markward, were severally taken up & agreed to.

THU JAN 11, 1844
The Salem Observer announces the death in that city, last week, of Col Jos Peabody, aged 86 years. He was one of the most distinguished & successful merchants of Salem, a man of high & honorable character, & his death will be a loss to the community at large.

Page's improved windmill is an invention calculated to be of immense benefit. One can be seen at my shop in Balt now in successful operation. Price from $50 to $400. –Geo Page, manufacturer, Balt, west Balt st

Wm C Clark, a highly respectable citizen of Greensborough, Choctaw Co, Miss, was shot & instantly killed with a pistol at Carrollton, Miss, on Dec 15, by Jos Lancaster, the publisher of a paper at Middleton, Miss. Mr Lancaster fled to the Sheriff's ofc & was held to bail in the sum of $10,000. The dec'd was a native of Dinwiddie Co, Va. –Louisville Journal

Senate: 1-The bill providing for the adjustment, by arbitration, of the title to the *Pea Patch Island* was taken up. The island was in the Delaware river, 25 or 30 miles below Phil: shown itself above water within the last 70 years; origin was probably a sunken shallop; in 1774 this island contained 194 acres, not 30 or 40 as was heretofore stated; the proprietors in N J took possession of the island; they sold a portion of their title to Mr Gale, who became the sole proprietor of the island: he erected bldgs, establishing fisheries, etc; he had it in his possession for some years, & until the U S sent Gen Bloomfield to examine the island for a site for a fort. An overture for its purchase was made by Gen Bloomfield. He advised the Gov't to embrace the offer made by Mr Gale, to buy the place, at his price, $100,000. In 1814, While Mr Gale was in actual possession, the Gov't forcible disposed him & ejected him from the island. The Gov't remained in possession till 1827. Mr Gale, worn out by legal delays, went to the grave a maniacre & a pauper. His right became invested in his orphan children. They commenced an action in 1836 from a jury in their favor. Case not settled. The Senate then adjourned.

Hse/o Reps: 1-Ptn of Jane Beam, praying for a pension. 2-Memorial of Travis Phillips & 606 other, citizens of Indiana, praying for the armed occupation of Oregon. 3-Memorial of Ebenezer Wheelwright & others, of Newburyport, Mass, asking for redress on account of spoliations by the French prior to 1800. 4-Ptn of Eliz Vandeford, of Salem, wid/o Benj Vandeford, who died on board the ship **Vincennes**, in the Exploring Expedition, asking for a pension. 5-Ptn of Alexis Ward & 33 other citizens of Albion, N Y, for a reduction of postage. 6-Ptn of Joshua Rathbone & 23 other citizens of Orleans Co, N Y, for the completion of Oak Orchard Harbor. 7-Ptn of Nathl Mills & others, heirs of Capt Danl Mills, dec'd, for compensation for his Revolutionary services. 8-Ptn of Francis Stoddard & Jas Taylor, of New Bedford, for payment as clerks in the custom-house at New Beford. 9-Ptn of Andrew Hicks & 65 others, for a light house & buoys at Westport, Mass.

Naval Court Martial now sitting on board the U S ship **Pennsylvania**, at Norfolk:
Capt Stephen Cassin, Pres   Cmder Henry Bruce
Capt Chas W Skinner   Lt Wm Green
Cmder Wm Armstrong   Lt Amasa Paine
Cmder Robt B Cunningham
Members: Jas Hoban, Judge Advocate

Died: on Jan 7, at the residence of her niece, Mrs Updyke, in Loudoun Co, Va, Mrs Mary A Glenn, aged 67, consort of Mr Jas Glenn, of Wash City, after a long & protracted illness.

Died: on Dec 24, at Pensacola, after a short illness, Lt Jas K Bowie, U S Navy.

Died: on Jan 1, near Centreville, Queen Anne's Co, Md, Dr Thos W Hopper.

Obit-died: on Jan 3, at the residence of her husband, Washington Lancaster, in Chas Co, Md, Mrs Anne Causin Lancaster, aged 38 years. She leaves her husband, orphan children, & her brothers. Her last hours were consoled by the administration of the rites of the church within whose pale her life had passed. -C

The U S schnr **Enterprise** was lying off Buenos Ayres on Nov 5. List of her ofcrs:
Jas Muir Watson, Lt Commanding   Edw Bissell, Purser
Chas Hunter, Lt   Jas McClelland, Acting Surgeon
Edw Fitzgerald Beale, Acting Master Danl Noble Johnson, Capt's Clk
Thos Lloyd Dance, John S Maury, Alex'r J Dallas, jr, Jeff H Nones, Chas K Graham, Midshipmen; Geo H Baker, Master's Mate
The **Enterprise** was, for the time being, bearing the broad pennant of Cmdor Danl Turner, who was on a visit of a few weeks duration to Buenos Ayres to investigate the case of the American ship **Herald**, seized some time since by Admiral Brown for trading in contraband goods, & condemned by the Admiralty Court of the Argentine Republic as a legal prize. Cmdor Turner had already succeeded in effecting her release, having had an audience with Govn'r Rosas upon the subject. Cmdor Turner was accompanied by the following ofcrs: Cmder Edw G Tilton, of the ship **Columbus 74**; Lts L Maynard & Henry Cadwalader of do; Fleet Surgeon B F Bache of do; Purser John N Todd of do; Lt Marines E Lloyd West, of do; Cmdor's Sec Jas Fauns, of do; Assist Surgeon John Hastings, of do; Midshipmen Wm H Parker, Wm W Williamson, Edw C Grafton, & G D Chenoworth, of do; with Lt John R Goldsborough, Surgeon Solomon Sharpe, & Acting Master John C Howell, of the frig **Columbia**. The U S ship-of-the-line **Columbus**, Capt Cooper, & U S frig **Columbia**, Capt Shubrick, were lying off Montevideo on Nov 5, ofcrs & crews all well

Polly Bodine confessed to the Staten Island murder & is in confinement at Port Richmond on a charge of murder, robbery, & arson, in having destroyed the lives of the wife & child of her brother, & then robbed & fired his dwlg.

Mrd: on Dec 21, at Portland Manor, residence of Jas Kent, Anne Arundel Co, Md, by the Rev Joshua Morsell, Dr Julius Hall, of Calvert Co, Md, to Miss Jane Contee Kent, & Thos H Kent, of Calvert Co, Md, to Miss Harriet A Kent, dghts of the late Govn'r Kent.

Meeting of the Organization of the Colonization Society of D C: held on Jan 9, in the Presbyterian Church, 4½ st, the Rev Dr Laurie resumed the chair, J H Offley appointed sec of the meeting. The cmte appointed the Rev Mr Gurley, chairman of the cmte. Following were unanimously elected ofcrs of the Society:
Hon Chas B Penrose, Pres.
Vice-Presidents: For Washington-Rev Jas Laurie, D D, Rev Wm Hawley, Rev Jas Knox, Rev John Davis, Messrs Aaron O Dayton, Jacob Gideon, & A Rothwell
For Gtwn-Rev C M Butler, Rev R T Berry, Rev Jas McVean, Messrs Saml McKenney, Anthony Hyde, Wm G Ridgeley, & Jeremiah Orme
For Alexandria-Rev Elias Harrison, Rev Chas B Dana, Rev Jas T Johnston, Messrs Robt Jamieson, Benoni Wheat, John Withers, & Jas Vanzant
Rev R R Gurley, Corr Sec   Jas Adams, Treas
John P Ingle, Rec Sec

Farm for sale: the subscriber wishes to sell the farm on which he now resides, near the turnpike leading from Rockville, Montg Co, to Gtwn, D C: farm contain 300 acres; improvements are a large 2 story brick mansion; a grist & saw-mill, barn, cornhouse, & smokehouse. Apply to the subscriber, whose post ofc is at Rockville, Md. –Jno A Carter

Appointments by the Pres: 1-Jas Magoffin, reappointed Reg of the Land Ofc at St Stephens, Ala. 2-Wm W Stevenson, do, at the Land Ofc at Little Rock, Ark. 3-John J Coleman, do, at Huntsville, Ala. 4-Robt J Hockley, do, at Talahassee, Fla. [All re-appointed.]

FRI JAN 12, 1844
John C Montgomery, Postmaster of the city of Phil, met with a serious accident at Camden on Sun when he stepped into a hole with a piece of iron rail sticking out. He received a terrible wound to his side, but the injury is not considered dangerous.

Mr Saml Coddeback, a wealthy & respectable citizen of Orange Co, committed suicide at his house, near Cuddebackville, last Sat, by shooting himself. He told his wife he intended to kill himself, but she doubted that he would do it. Mr Coddeback said that he had a painful & lingering disease, & that he would rather die than be subject to its ravages. He was probably insane. Many respectable families of this county & Orange were connected with him. –Sullivan [N Y] Watchman

Chas Co Equity Court, Jan 3, 1844. Mary J Spedden vs Jos A Spedden. Suit is to procure a divorce a vinculo matrimonii of Mary J Spedden from her husband Jos A Spedden. In Apr, 1837, the cmplnt, Mary J Spedden, mrd the said Jos A Spedden, & that he has abandoned the cmplnt, & remained absent from the State of Md for 5 years before the filing of the bill in this case, & that Jos A Spedden resides out of the State of Md. Absent dfndnt to appear in this Court on or before Mar 21 next.
–John Stephens

$50 reward for runaway negro woman Eliza, aged about 42 years, who took 2 children with her, a girl about 8 & a boy about 4 years. She was formerly the property of the late Henry Brawner, of Pomonkey; she has a sister & several other relations in Alexandria. –J R Robertson, Port Tobacco, Chas Co, Md

Senate: 1-Ptn from Mrs Downes, wid/o Capt Downes, of the U S schnr **Grampus**, stating her destitute condition, & asking the aid of Congress. 2-Ptn from the legal reps of Harman Blannerhassett, asking compensation for property of their ancestor destroyed by the militia of the U S. Mr Wright said a memorial had been presented at the 2nd session of the 27th Congress from the wid/o Mr Blannerhassett, & a report was in her favor, but she died while the case was pending; & it appeared that the present memorialists relied very much on that report. Mr Wright said he was on the cmte from which that report emanated, yet he was at the time by no means prepared to adopt it. 3-Ptn from the wid/o Abraham Guiles, a soldier of the Revolution, asking a pension. 4-Ptn from the wid/o Wm Barker, a lt in the Revolutionary army, for a continuance of her pension. 5-Ptn of Wm Wynn, praying confimation of a certain title of land in Arkansas. 6-It was ordered that the documents on file in relation to the claim of Geo Duvall be referred to the Cmte on Indian Affairs. 7-Ordered that the papers on the files of the Senate in the case of Francis Vigo be referred to the Cmte on Revolutionary Claims. 8-Cmte of Claims asked to be discharged from the further consideration of the claim of the heirs of Wm Eaton, & that it be referred to the Cmte on Military Affairs. 9-Cmte on the Public Lands, reported a bill for the relief of Geo Davenport, of Rock Island, Ill. 10-Bill for the relief of Edw Kennard was taken up in the Cmte of the Whole: ordered to be engrossed for a 3rd reading, & was afterwards passed.

Mrd: on Jan 9, by Rev John Davis, Mr R Hamilton Degges to Miss Mary Ann, d/o the late W R Spalding, all of Wash City.

Mrd: on Jan 9, by Rev John Davis, Mr Wm Brown to Miss Sarah Agatha, d/o Mr Ignatius Lucas, all of Wash City.

Died: on Thu, yesterday, Rufus King Harris, aged 21 years, only s/o Jos & Alice Harris, formerly of Oxford, Butler Co, Ohio, late of Wash City. His funeral is today from Mrs Brereton's, F & 7th sts, at 2 p m.

Frederic Clitch, Pa ave, between 9th & 10th sts, informs that his Store is richly supplied for presents.

Hse/o Reps: 1-Ptn of Eliza Pickrell, admx of John Pickrell, dec'd, for the payment of claims against the Shawnee Indians. 2-Ptn of Chas Youngs, of Ohio, for a pension as a soldier of the last war with Great Britain. 3-Ptn of Rev O B Call & others, citizens of Potter Co, Pa, against the annexation of Texas to this Union. 4-Ptn of A

Badolett & 273 other citizens of Lawrence Co, Ill, praying a grant of a portion of the unsold lands in the Palestine, Vincennes, & Shawneetown districts, for the improvement of the navigation of the Wabash river from Terre Haute to its junction with the Ohio river. 5-Ptn of E W Goodwin & 21 others, praying Congrss to enact laws prohibiting ofcrs of the U S from apprehending or detaining slaves. 6-Ptn of Artemas Morton & others, regarding the lighthouse at the mouth of Cattaraugas creek, N Y, for the prosecution of the unfinished works at that place. Also, the ptn of A R Avery & others, for the same. 7-Ptn of Francis Sommerance, an invalid soldier, for a pension. 8-Ptn of J C Guthrie & 74 other citizens, & of Geo Swinger & 26 other citizens, all of Muskingum Co, Ohio, praying for a reduction in the rates of postage.

Meeting of the Whigs of Washington, convened on Jan 9, for the formation of a Clay Club. Dr Wm B Magruder was called to the Chair, & John T Towers appointed to act as Sec. Dr A McD Davis reported the Constitution for the government of a Clay Club, which was adopted. Ofcrs for the Club:

Pres: Jos H Bradley
Vice Pres-5:
| Wm B Magruder | Jos Bryan | Wm D Acken |
| Alex McD Davis | Washington Young | |

Corr Secs:
| Geo Watterston | J L Henshaw | John H Hewitt |

Treas: Robt Farnham
Rec Secs:
| John T Towers | A B Clayton | |

Exec Cmte:
John A Blake	Saml Bacon	Leonard Harbaugh
S Holmes	R S Patterson	Isaac Beers
R C Washington	Jos Borrows	Richd H Stewart
Seth Hyatt	Geo W Harkness	Wm Thompson, 5th st

SAT JAN 13, 1844
Now is the time for bargains: intending to wind up, I will sell out at prime cost, & a great many aticles for less that cost. As I have only a few months to wind up in, having rented my store, it will compel me to sell very low, so those who are in want will be well compensated by calling 8 doors above Brown's Hotel. -Champe B Thornton, Dry Goods store

Circuit Court of Wash Co, D C. Thos A Duley has applied to be discharged from imprisonment under the act for the relief of Insolvent Debtors: hearing on Jan 19. –Wm Brent, clk

Strayed into the enclosure of A Kendall's farm, a small sorrel horse. The owner can have his property by calling at the ofc of A & J E Kendall, on E st, & paying charges.

Hse/o Reps: 1-Ptn of John S Gilbert, asking for delay of all action, & to withhold any appropriation for a dry dock, until the plan can be examined by competent judges. 2-Ptn of Francis Lynch & others, praying a grant of land in Indiana to open the navigation or extend the canal to the mouth of the Wabash. 3-Memorial of Wm S Harpole & 101 others, citizens of Indiana, praying an appropriation of land to complete the central canal to Evansville. 4-Memorial of Geo H Evans, a citizen of New Jersey, praying that a portion of the Oregon Territory be laid out in small farms, to be granted to settlers with a right to use the same, & to will to any one not possessed of other lands. 5-Memorial of P Roche & 48 others, citizens of Indiana, praying an appropriation of lands to improve the Wabash river. 6-Ptn of John Wallace & 49 others, citizens of Muskinghum Co, Ohio, praying for an amendment of the Constitution of the U S. 7-Memorial of Wm S Patterson & 426 others, citizens of South Bend, Ind, praying Congress to make suitable appropriation for continuing the construction of the harbor at Michigan City, Ind. 8-Ptn of Violet Calhoun, of Pike Co, Ind, wid/o John Calhoun, dec'd, a Revolutionary pensioner of the U S, for a pension. 9-Ptn of Levy Johnson, of Hendricks Co, Ind, for a pension. 10-Ptn of Augustus C French & 201 others, citizens of Crawford Co, Ill, on granting a portion of the unsold lands in the Wabash valley for the improvement of the Wabash river. 11-Ptns of Leonard A Doggett, Lewis Gilbert, Eb Johnson, A Townsend, Wm Whitney, & 1,360 others, inhabitants of New Haven, Conn, praying an alteration in the post ofc laws in relation to the franking privilege, & asking a reduction in the rates of letter postage. 12-Ptn of Mrs Frances D Gage & 80 other ladies of McConnelsville, Ohio, praying a revision of the post ofc laws. 13-Ptn of John Test & 185 other citizens, all of Washington Co, Ohio, praying a reduction in the postage rates, & that the franking privilege be abolished. 14-Ptn of Anne W Angus, wid/o Capt Saml Angus, U S Navy, signed by many of the most respectable citizens of the State of N Y, asking that she be placed on the navy pension list.

Farm for sale: 445 acres, about 5 miles northeast of the city of Columbus, Ohio: with a 2 story frame & a 2 story log dwlg on it, a large new frame barn & other outhouses. Apply to the subscriber on the premises, or to Lewis Heyl, Columbus, Ohio.
–C Heyl

$10 reward. On Sat last a sorrel colt with a star on his forehead, threw his rider between Bladensburg & Washington, & has not since been heard of by his owner. The reward will be given for the delivery of said colt, with the saddle & bridle, to Capt Wm Thomas, 13th & F sts. –Thos Y Fletcher

Connecticut papers announce the death of Hon Noyes Barber, who died at his residence in Groton, Conn, on Jan 3, in his 62nd year.

Books at Auction: by order of the Orphan's Court of Wash Co, D C; sale at the salesroom of Wm M Morrison, near Brown's Hotel, on Pa ave, on Jan 16: the large & valuable library of the late Jas Greenleaf dec'd, consisting of standard & well selected works in almost every dept of literature & the useful sciences.
--D A Hall, adm -Wm M Morrison, Auct

Meeting of the friends of Agriculture & Manufacture, held on Jan 10, at the hall of the Hse/o Reps:, Col Taliaferro, of Va, appointed chairman & R E Horner, of N J, & J F Callan, of D C, secs. Hon Wm P Thomasson, of Ky, one of the cmte appointed. Appointed to aid in the Nat'l Fair: Dr Gideon B Smith, of Balt, Dr Jas W Thompson, of Delaware, R E Hornor, of N J, T B Wakeman, of N Y, & Abbott Lawrence, of Boston. Cmte of Correspondence: Hon John S Skinner & H L Ellsworth, of D C, Hon Wm Wilkins, of Pa, Hon Dixon H Lewis, of Ala, & Hon Chas Hudson, of Mass.

The Augusta [Ga] Chronicle states that Capt Edw W Collier, the proprietor of the Richmond Hotel, was murdered in the streets of that city early last Mon morning, by a person named Robt Burns, a runner for the U S Hotel. Burns, overtaking some passengers who were in company with Collier, endeavored to persuade them not to go to the Richmond Hotel, for which he was rebuked by the latter. A scuffle ensued during which Burns stabbed Collier with a dirk or Bowie knife, killing him instantly, & then fled to South Carolina. A reward of $500 is offered by the City Council of Augusta for his apprehension. He is between 35 & 43 years of age, inclining to gray, a little bald, & thick set.

Mrd: on Jan 8, at N Y, at St Paul's Chapel, by the Rt Rev Bishop Onderdonk, Weston R Gales, of Raleigh, N C, to Mary, eldest d/o John J Spies, of N Y.

Mrd: Jan 11, by Rev Jno P Donelan, Geo W Dobbyn to Frances, d/o the late John Davis, all of Wash City.

Mrd: on Jan 10, in Alexandria, by Rev Mr Young, Mr Geo E Shirk, of Wash, to Miss Rebecca Jane Devaughan, of Alexandria.

Died: yesterday, after a long & painful illness, Mr John McCarty, aged about 65 years. His funeral will be from his late residence, on B st south, Capitol Hill, on Sun evening, at 2 o'clock.

David Todd, of Trumbull Co, has been nominated by the Convention of the "Democrats" of Ohio as their candidate for the ofc of Govn'r of that State at the next election.

Whigs of the 21st Congressional District of N Y, composed of the counties of Otsego & Schoharie, appointed Thos Smith, of Cobleskill, as their delegate to the Balt Whig Nat'l Convention. Thos P Danforth was chosen as substitute.

Decatur Braddock, in Jacksonville, East Fla, was killed on Christmas Eve when another of the party twirled his cane so violently around his head, that it struck Braddock, killing him instantly.

MON JAN 15, 1844

From the St Louis republican: Calamitous steamboat disaster on Jan 3: befell the steamboat **Shepherdess**, Capt Howell, within 3 miles of that city, on her way to Cincinnati, The loss of life is estimated at from 30 to 60 souls, but the books of the vessel having been lost it is impossible to ascertain the exact number. The steamer first struck a snag, at Chokia Bend: concussion so severe it must have torn off several of her planks, as in a minute or two the water rose to the lower deck, then up to the hurricane deck. It hit another snag. The steamboat **Henry Bry** & the ferry-boat **Icelander** rescued some of the sufferers. Mr Muir, of Va, & his brother, with their mother & 9 slaves, were on board: 7 of the slaves perished. Levi Craddock, from Davidson Co, Tenn, lost 3 children-himself, wife & 3 children were saved. Mr Green, from the same place, lost his wife & 3 children, & is left with 2 helpless infants upon his hands, the youngest is but 2 months. Mr Snell, for formerly resided withing 2 miles of Louisville, lost a son & dght. Mr Wright, of Mecklenburg Co, Va, was lost & 2 children. His wife was with those saved, but in a very distressing condition. A captain, A Howell, of Covington, Ky, is undoubtedly lost. He leaves a wife & 7 children. His eldest son was with him on board. An English family from Manchester, 10 in number, were all saved. The bodies of 2 children, about 12 years of age, who perished from the cold, have been recovered; as also that of a negro man. Following is a list of the passengers who have reached St Louis: Jane Thomas, Jas Thomas, Jane E Thomas, Sarah Ann Thomas, Wm H Thomas, John Thomas, Edw Thomas, Alfred Thomas, Jos Thomas, Louisa Rachael Thomas, Lawrenceburg, Ind

S R Snell & 2 children, Louisville, Ky
Barney Owens, New Orleans
Solomon Evinger, New Albany, Ind
Henry Wellingcamp, Franklin Co, Mo
David Wayman, Covington, Ky
Wm D Henry, Macoupin Co, Ill
John Mitten, Floyd Co, Ind
Mary Davis & child, Portsmouth, Ohio
J L Beggs, Princeton, Ill
Danl Linsey, Covington, Ky
Wm Lemer, Bartholomew Co, Ind
John Lane, Muskingum Co, Ohio
Horace Minkler, Lawrenceburg, Ind

Hansel Green & child, Nashville, Tenn
John Alward, Harrisburg, Pa
Mr Wright, Mecklenburg Co, Va
Isaac Chriss, Fayette Co, Pa
Stephen Howard, Brown Co, Ohio
C B Fisher, Jerseyville, Ill

Ralph B McCullock, Maysville, Ky
W O Crenshaw, Gtwn, Ky
R Tandy, Hopkinsville, Ky
John Tegan, Alexandria, D C
Geo W Brown, Dayton, Ohio

Stephen P Hart, Louisville, Ky   Page J Bickerill;
Parker Bodwett, Nelson Bodwett, Cincinnati, Ohio
C Canfield, C Meckerson, Hannah Crouse, Mgt Crouse, Portage, Ohio
J S Farrow, A Aldrich, Jas Carroll, pilots, Cincinnati, Ohio

Appointments by the Pres, with the advice & consent of the Senate:
Dabney S Carr, of Md, Minister Resident at Constantinople, vice David Porter, dec'd.
Abraham Rencher, of N C, Charge d'Affiars to Portugal, vice Washington Barrow, resigned.
Benj E Green, Sec of the Legation of the U S to Mexico, vice Brantz Mayer, resigned.
Thos Nelson re-appointed Collector of the Customs for the District of Richmond, Va.
Consuls:
Chas A Leas, of Balt, for Maracaibo, vice S M Cochran, resigned.
A Follins, for Omoa & Truxillo
Geo W Gordon, of Mass, for Rio de Janeiro, vice G W Slacum
Albert M Gilliam, of Va, for San Francisco, in Calf, vice T Carlisle, resigned.
Thos O Larkin, of Mass, for Monterey, in Calf, vice J P Gilliam, dec'd.
Wm S Campbell, of N Y, for Rotterdam, vice John Wambersie
John W Fisher, of Conn, for Guadaloupe, vice F H Swan, dec'd.
Wm H Freeman, of Pa, for Curracoa, vice J H D'Meza.
Stewart Newell, of La, for Sabine, in Texas.
Israel D Andrews, of Mass, for St John's, in New Brunswick, vice Thos Leavitt.
Leonard R Almy, of N Y, for Laguna de Terminos, in Mexican Republic, vice Chas Russell, dec'd.
Pedro de Regil Y Estrada, for Merida & Sisal, in Yucatan, vice C Thompson, resigned.
Hooper C Eaton, of Md, for Lyons, in France, vice N Berry, resigned.
Wm Hogan, of Ga, for Nuevitas, in Cuba, vice Wm H Freeman, resigned.
Geo Morr, for Dresden, vice E F Rivinus, resigned.
Geo F Gerding, of N Y, for Manheim.
Bladen Forrest, of Wash, for Chagres.
Stanhope Prevost, for Lima, vice F L Castelnau.
John Arthur, for Turk's Island, vice John Wilkeson, resigned.
Saml McLean, of Missouri, for Trinidad de Cuba, vice John K Cooke, resigned.
Jos R Croskey, for Cowes, vice Wm Whetten, resigned.
Reg of wills for Alexandria Co, D C:
Bernard Hooe, of Alexandria, vice Alexander Moore, dec'd.
Justices of the peace for Wash Co, D C:
John Cox, John I Stull, Jas Marshall, Edw Mattingly, Lewis Carbery, Thos Carbery.

Adam Horn, convicted during the last term of the Balt Co Court of the murder of his wife, was executed on Fri in the jail-yard at Balt. The American says: "At least 10,000 persons were on the surrounding eminences, & about 1,000 within the yard, as spectators of the event."

Election will take place next Thu, at the Columbia Engine-house, to supply a vacancy in the Board of Common Council, occasioned by the death of Mr Simeon Bassett.

Hse/o Reps: 1-Supplement to an act approved Jun 28, 1838, entitled "An act for the relief of John Hollinsworth, of Blount Co, Indiana:" referred to the Cmte on Public Lands. 2-Cmte of Claims: ptn of Jos Kimball, with a bill for his relief. Same cmte made on adverse report on the ptn of Saml Fuller 3-Cmte on Invalid Pensions: adverse reports on the ptns of Empson Hamilton & Saml W Marshall. Same cmte made an adverse report on the ptn of Lewis H Finney. Adverse also on the ptns of Sarah Talley, wid/o John A Talley; Wm Slocum; Robt E Kelley; Richd Reynolds; & John Bull, jr. 4-Cmte on Invalid Pensions: made a report on the ptn of Jonathan Bean, with a bill for his relief. Same for the ptn of John P Schuyler. 5-Cmte of Claims: adverse report on the ptn of Wm Neilson. 6-Cmte on Private Land Claims: report on the ptn of John McLaughlin, with a bill for his relief. 7-Cmte on Revolutionary Pensions: report on the ptn of Jane McGuire, wid/o Maj Thos McGuire, with a bill for her relief. 8-Ptn of Jos W Briggs & 29 other citizens of Sullivan, Ind, asking a donation of lands to improve the navigation of the Wabash river. Ptn of H L Harmer & 147 other citizens of Ohio, for the same. 9-The ptn & papers of Benj Hewitt, of Troy, N Y, praying for remuneration for certain damages sustained by him: appropriately referred. 10-Ptn of Wanton Howland, of Dartmouth, & 89 others, for the erection of a marine hospital at New Bedford. 11-Ptn of Cyrus Peirce & 141 others, of Nantucket, against the annexation of Texas.

Mrd: on Fri last, in Wash City, by Rev Mr Bulfinch, Erastus Brooks, one of the Editors of the N Y Express, to Mgt D, y/d/o the Hon Chief Justice Cranch, of the U S District Court of D C.

Melancholy suicide. The s/o the Rev Wm Parkinson, of the Baptist Church of Newark, N J, about 28 to 30 years of age, was found on the stoop of the U S Hotel at Newark, on Wed night, in a helpless condition caused by opiate, which he deliberately took himself. He died before a stomach pump could be procured.

Centre Market. Finer beef has seldom been for sale anywhere than we noticed on the stalls of Messrs Saml Little, Crowley, Walker, & other victuallers. Fine mutton raised by Chas Hill & Thos Duckett, of PG Co, were for sale by Messrs Otterback & Speisser & Mr Rhodes. The market-house was in excellent order.

Died: on Sat last, Mary, eldest d/o Jas W & Sydney J Moorhead, of Wash City, aged 9 years, 1 month & 5 days.

TUE JAN 16, 1844
Brick house at auction on Jan 19, on the premises, the brick house on the lot adjoining the house lately erected by Jacob Gideon, on 8th st, in the rear of the Patent Ofc. The house to be removed by Mar 15 next. -Robt W Dyer & Co, aucts

Senate: 1-Ptn from John J McCaughan & others, praying that a patent may issue for certain lands. 2-Ptn from Thos Geo Clinton, in relation to some improvement in the construction of steam-engines. 3-Ptn from D M F Thornton, asking to be allowed a credit in the settlement of his accounts, on account of goods which were destroyed by a hurricane on board the ship **Erie**. 4-On motion of Mr Benton, the papers on file in the Senate in the case of Alex Watson, were referred to the Cmte of Claims. 5-Cmte on Revolutionary Claims: ask to be discharged from the further consideration of the ptn of John Washington, & that it be referred to the Cmte of Claims. Also, from same cmte, asking to be discharged from the futher consideration of the resolutions of the Leg of Ky, in behalf of the heirs of Christopher Miller. Mr Jarnagin said the services were not performed during the Revolution, & did not come within the province of the cmte. It appeared that Mr Miller was employed by Gen Wayne in 1794 to carry a flag to the Indians, that the service was highly important & very perilous, & Mr Miller was promised a very liberal reward if he succeeded. Mr Jarnagin asked that the papers might go to the Cmte of Claims, which was ordered. 6-Cmte on Revolutionary Claims: adverse report on the claim of the heirs of Danl Trueheart, in writing: ordered to be printed. Same cmte: adverse report on the ptn of Mrs Lomax, wid/o Capt W Lindsay, in writing, & ordered to be printed. Same cmte: adverse report, in writing, on the ptn of Chas Morgan, jr, ordered to be printed. 7-Cmte on Post Ofc & Post Roads: adverse report, in writing, upon the ptns of E B & S Ward: ordered to be printed. 8-Cmte on Pensions: a bill making compensation to pension agents. Mr Bates said the bill was prospective in its character, & its provisions as ample as possible, & he asked to be discharged from further consideration of the ptns of Joel M Smith & John Dawson in relation to the subject.

Wm Cost Johnson declines to be a candidate for Congress: my time has been so engrossed for 12 years; & yet I withdraw with no regret: I will not disguise the fact that I have no repugnance to public life. [Letter to W B Clark, Chairman of Wash Co Whig Central Cmte. Dated Washington, Jan 13, 1844.]

Death by Exposure. Mr Moses W Ham, of Farmington, Conn, left the Eagle Hotel, Dover, N H, for his home, with his horse & sleigh, during the storm on Wed. The next morning he was found dead in the road, a short distance above *Gage's hill*, with his horse & sleigh near by.

Agency for Claims in Wash: 6th st, next to corner of F. –Chas Deselding

The dwlg house of Prof Ware, of Cambridge, Mass, was entirely consumed by fire on Tue last. Dr Ware was taken out of the house by a gentleman who was passing in a sleigh, & who gave the first alarm.

Cow lost or strayed: reward of $5 if returned to Dr Washington, on 6th st.

NOTICE: By virtue of 5 writs of fieri facias, issued by B K Morsell, a J P in Wash Co, D C, I have seized & taken in execution 2 bay horses, as the property of Peter Havener, which I will sell for cash on Jan 20, to satisfy judgments due the Mayor & the Corporation. –S Moore, Constable

NOTICE: By virtue of a writ of fieri facias, issued by B K Morsell, a J P in Wash Co, D C, I have seized a bay horse, as the property of Peter Havener, which I will sell for cash on Jan 20, to satisfy a judgment due Wm R Riley. -S Moore, Constable

Hse/o Reps: 1-Resolved, that the ptn of Eliz Fitch & the accompanying papers, asking for the pay of her husband for services in the Revolutionary War, be taken from the files of the House & referred to the Cmte on Revolutionary Claims. 2-Cmte of Claims to inquire into allowing Ephraim Hough, of Surry Co, N C, a sum of money due him for the transportation of the mail, which sum he lost in consequence of the mode in which the Post Ofc Dept directed the payment to be made. 3-Resolved that the memorial & other papers of Janette Taylor & others, heirs of Com Paul Jones, presented to the 24th Congress, 2nd Session, be taken from the files of the House & referred to the Cmte on Revolutionary Claims. 4-Resolved, that the memorial of Robt Greenhow, on the subject of the discovery & title of the Oregon Territory, reported to the Senate, & published in that body, be printed for the use of the House.

Died: on Nov 27 last, at Sault Ste Marie, at the outlet of Lake Superior, Mrs Susan Johnston, wid/o the late John Johnston, of the county of Antrim, Ireland, aged 67. Mrs J was a dght of the celebrated war chief Wabojeeg, the ruling chief of the Chippewa nation during the period of their greatest military efforts, the latter part of the last century. She was instrumental in saving the party of Govn'r Cass from an attack, during his encampment at those falls, in Jun, 1820. Her grandfather, Mongazida, was present on the plains of Abraham, in 1758, among the auxiliaries of Gen Montcalm.

Mrd: on Jan 8, at St Matthew's Church, Washington, by Rev J P Donelan, Edw T Offutt to Miss Ann Williams, both of Gtwn, D C.

Dr Dennis Claude elected, by the Leg of Md, to be Treas of the State, or rather, as his title is, to be Treas of the Western Shore of Md.

Chancery Sale: decree of chancery at Franklin, at Oct term, 1843, in the cause pending between A Pageot & wife, cmplnts, & Jas B Ferguson & others, dfndnts: sale at the courthouse in Nashville, the following valuable lot in Nashville, on which is erected the Nashville Inn, being part of original lots 7 & 8 in said town: beginning on the corner of lot 8, intersection of the public square & Market st; running towards the river to David Vaughan's heirs' brick house, including one half of its wall, should it–the wall–be on the property of the Nashville Inn. –Benj Litton, C & M

We understand that the Hon Jacob W Mill, of the U S Senate, has been called home by the sudden death of his father.

Whig meeting in Bladensburg, Md, on Jan 6, to form a Clay Club: Wallace Kirkwood called to the Chair, & Trueman Belt appointed Sec. Appointed ofcrs of the Club: Chas B Calvert, Pres; Robt Wright, Edmund B Stephen, V Ps; Trueman Belt, Corr Sec; Dionysius Sheriff, Rec Sec; Robt Clarke, Treas; Thos S Ferrall, J T W Dean, & Harrison Waters, Standard Bearers

WED JAN 17, 1844
Hse/o Reps: 1-Cmte of Claims: adverse report upon the ptns of Gideon Walker & J W Crane. 2-Cmte on Private Lands Claims: adverse report upon the ptn of Adam Sterrett. 3-Cmte on Public Lands: adverse report upon the ptn of Geo W Trippe. 4-Cmte on Indian Affairs: made a report on the ptn of Browning & Skinner, purchaser of land from John Mullings, with a bill for the relief of John Mullings. 5-Cmte on Invalid Pension: adverse report on the ptns of Wm Vose & Susan Jackson. 6-Cmte on CLaims: adverse report on the ptn of John J Beck. 7-Cmte on Invalid Pensions: report on the ptn of Jas C Hallock, with a bill for his relief. 8-Cmte on Invalid Pensions: adverse report on the ptn of Elijah C Babbitt. 9-Ptn of Col Jas Bankhead & other ofcrs, for the erection of a chapel on Governor's Island, N Y. Ptn of Theodore Frelinghuysen & others, for the same purpose. 10-Ptn of Chas W Denison, of Boston, for an appropriation for the benefit of a fund of a library to be used by the seamen of the U S Navy. 11-Ptns of Wm B Crews, R H Rich & others, & Jas M Elney & others. [No other information.] 12-Ptn of Martha Bennet, wid/o Rufus Bennet, a Revolutionary soldier. 13-Ptn of W H Hoag, for the payment of a balance due on a contract for constructing a Gov't road. 14-Ptn of Jas Little & 57 other citizens of York township, Morgan Co, Ohio, for a reduction of the per diem compensation & perquisites of Members of Congress, & for such a thorough system of retrenchment as shall bring the Gov't back to its primitive purity. 15-Ptn of W Brown Butler & others, praying a grant of land in Indiana for improving the navigation or extending the canal to the mouth of the Wabash. 16-Ptn for the benefit of Isaac Adkins. 17-Ptn of Hall J Kelly, of Mass, for a grant of land in Oregon. 18-Ptn of Nahum Capen, of Boston, Mass, on the subject of international copyright. 19-Ptn of J M H Allison & 220 citizens of Indiana, asking an appropriation of refuse lands in the Vincennes land district to assist in completing the Wabash & Erie canal.

Ptn of Wm G Ross & 120 citizens of Indiana, upon the same subject. 20-Ptn of Saml Orr & 120 other citizens of Indian & Illinois, asking that Congress would grant to the State of Indiana, the vacant lands in the Vincennes land district for the continuing of the Wabash & Erie canal from Terre Haute to Evansville. 21-Ptn of the heirs of Jos Young, praying for remuneration of losses sustained by their ancestor in the burning of his houses & bldgs by the British forces in the Revolutionary war. 22-Ptn of J H Phelps & others, for the erection of a light house at the mouth of Cattaraugus creek, N Y, & for the prosecution of unfinished works at that place. 23-Ptn of Geo Dean & 76 others, citizens of Indiana, praying for an appropriation of lands to complete the Central canal to Evansville. 24-Ptn of Gen N V Knickerbocker & 512 citizens of Steuben Co, N Y, for a reduction of the rates of postage. 25-Ptn of John Burlison for back pension money. 26-Ptn of Eliss Carpenter, an invalid pensioner of Sherbridge, Mass, praying for the extension of his pension. 27-Ptn of Henry T Harrison & others, citizens of Loudoun Co, Va, for a re-charter of the Bank of Potomac & Farmers' Bank of Alexandria, in D C. Also, ptn of Robt T Luckett & others, citizens of the same county & State, for the same. 28-Ptn of Stephen McCormick, of Va, for the renewal of a patent. 29-Ptn of the children of Apollos Cooper for 7 years' half pay. 30-Ptn of Fred'k Slinkard & 149 others, citizens of Indiana, for land to complete the Wabash & Erie canal to the Ohio river. 31-Ptn of O Blakesly & 29 other citizens of Geauga Co, Ohio, praying a reduction of postage & other amendments in the post ofc law. Same for ptn of E Paine & 172 citizens of the same county. Same for the ptn of Riley Richmond & 31 other citizens of the same county, for the same. Ptn of Simeon H Daniels & 225 citizens of Oberlin, for the same. 32-Additional papers in relation to the claim of Jos Dowey for a pension. 33-Memorial of G W Kinkade & 53 other citizens of Lawrence Co, Ill, for an appropriation of public lands in the Wabash valley for the improvement of the Wabash river. 34-Ptn of John Wilkins & 70 others, citizens of Bangor, Maine, for indemnification for spoliations committed by the French prior to 1800. Ptn of Almon Truitehell & 40 others, citizens of Paris, Oxford Co, Maine, on the same subject. Ptn of the excs of the last will of John Pearson, upon the same subject.

The venerable & distinguished patriot, Gen Jacob Morris, died at his residence, in Butternuts, Otsego Co, N Y, on Jan 10, in his 89th year. He was the 2nd s/o Gen Lewis Morris, one of the signers of the Declaration of Independence, was born at Morrisania on Dec 28, 1755. The commencement of the Revolutionary war found him a clerk in a mercantile house in Phil, which he left to become aid-de-camp to Gen Lee. With him he was present at the battles of *Fort Moultrie* & Monmouth, & excaped capture at Morristown with Gen Lee by being casually absent on a visit to his sick wife at Phil. He was for a short time one of the aids of Gen Arnold, & it is remarkable that this spotted traitor should have had in his military family 2 young men of so much purity & excellence of character as Gen Jacob Morris & Gen Matthew Clarkson. He became a settler on Morris' Patent in 1787, & so entirely unbroken was the wilderness at that time, that, during his attendance on the Legislature in N Y as Assemblyman from Montg Co, for 4 months, his wife saw the

face of no white person except her own children. During the administration of Geo Clinton, he was appointed Clerk of Otsego Co, & held that of until 1801.
–Albany Evening Journal

The Texian papers state that Chas Raymond, Sec of Leg to the U S, is on his way to fulfill his mission.

Columbia [Missouri] Statesman of Dec 29: A day or two since, Robt Kingsberry, about 13 years of age, was killed by his brother, Leonard, while fixing a cap on the lock of his rifle.

Two young men were killed in almost a similar manner near Fayettsville, N C, on Dec 27, riding through the woods in the dark. Fred'k Rollins was dashed against a tree, causing instant death; T Spence was thrown against a limb, which entered deep into his brain.

Salem Gaz mentions the sudden death of Jos Peabody, of that city, & says: Capt Peabody, in the 8 years from 1825 to 1833 paid into the Salem custom-house for duties, under the revenue law, the enormous sum of $1,814,096.22. Some ideas may be formed of the influence of his business upon the trade & activity of Salem. He began life with literally nothing to depend upon but his own exertions.

Hon Thos Russell, the Treas of the State of Mass, was run over by a sleigh at the head of State st last Fri, & very seriously injured. The sleigh, with a 4 horse team, was rapidly turning a corner.

Benoit Lachner, a German, was arrested at N Y on Fri & committed to prison, under a charge of having recently stolen the money trunk from Pomeroy's Express, & some $44,000 of the funds it contained. Lachner was found in his cell quite dead-he had hung himself on Sun. Mrs Lachner, who was also in prison, was directed to be released as soon as the excitement produced by the suicide of her husband had subsided. She is also a German, & has been married since the robbery was committed.

Loss of the steamboat **Shepherdess**, near St Louis: [See Jan 15th newspaper.] Latest on the loss of life, included: the son & dght of Mr Wright, of Va, & 2 other children & a boy; Mr Craddock, of Tenn, lost 3 children; Mr Green, of Tenn, lost his wife & 3 children; a Polander, Casper Levi, was lost; Mr Snell lost a son & dght; Capt Howell & 1 deck hand are lost; Mr Crenshaw, of Ky, lost 3 negroes; Dr Massie, of St Charles, lost 4 negroes; some 5 or 6 other persons are missing. Mr Thomas, of Indiana, lost $5,000 in a trunk. Dr T S Opdyke, of Ohio, lost between $,500 & $1,600 in gold.

Found, on Sat, near the residence of the late Mr Forsyth, a bundle of notes, & bills, which the owner can have by calling at the store of John Sexsmith, Pa ave, between 9th & 10th sts.

Senate: 1-Ptn from Robt Greenhow, a clerk in the State Dept, praying the patronage of Gov't to a book, which he claims as author, in relation to California, Oregon, & the Northwest of America. 2-On motion of Mr Merrick, the papers on file of John H Pennington, in relation to navigating the air, were allowed to be withdrawn. Also, the papers in the case of Thos Quantrill. 3-Cmte on Indian Affiars: bill for the relief of Benj Murphy.

Mrd: Jan 1, Jefferson Barracks, Missouri, by Rev Mr Hedges, Chaplain of the post, Capt Gouverneur Morris, of the 4th U S Infty, to Miss Anna Maria J, d/o Surgeon S G J De Camp, U S Army.

Died: on Jan 16, in Bladensburg, Md, Mr Alex'r Clark, in his 22nd year. His funeral will be on Thu, at 11 o'clock, at his late residence in said village. The members of the I O O F are requested to attend the funeral of their dec'd brother.

Wash Corp: the Cmte of Claims are to report all the facts in the sinking of the schnr **Farmer & Mechanic**, belonging to Capt Pauley, in the Washington canal, with an opinion of the Corp Atty as to how far, if at all, the Corp is liable for the damages sustained.

THU JAN 18, 1844
Fishery for rent: formerly known at *Herd's landing*, adjoining the fishery of Thos Irwin, about 20 miles below Alexandria. –Alex Hamilton, Port Tobacco, Chas Co, Md

The Senate yesterday rejected the Pres' nomination of Isaac Hill, of N H, to be Chief of the Bureau of Provisions & Clothing for the Navy.

Mrd: on Tue, by Rev Wm T Sprole, Mr Wm C Zantzinger to Miss Harriot Ann, d/o Wm Fischer.

Mrd: on Jan 15, at Hagerstown, Md, by Rev J V Rigden, Dr John A Wroe, of Washington, to Miss Martha Jane, d/o Capt David Barr, of Hagerstown.

Mrd: Jan 2, at Wirtland, Fla, by Rev Henry Ellwell, Dr Henry G Wirt, y/s/o the late Wm Wirt, to Louisa Anderson, only d/o the late Alex Browne, of Charleston, S C.

Jas B Holmead & R W Wright have commenced the Auction & Commission business on Pa ave, next to the corner of 4½ st, & offer their services to the public. It is under the name of Holmead & Wright.

Obit-died: on Dec 31, at the residence of Dr Duvall, PG Co, Md, Thos Jones Waters, aged 83 years. He had sustained but slight impairment of his physical & mental vigor.: In his unvarying attachment to the truth of the Christian religion, he found his chief support & comfort.

Mr Emanuel Pierce, the superintendent of the card-room at the Washington factory, about 5 miles from Balt, lost his life on Mon last by getting his clothes entangled in the machinery.

FRI JAN 19, 1844
Richmond, Va, Jan 18. Many of our citizens were engaged during the day in shingling the roof of the Club-house. At sundown, when about to cease work, Mr S F Adie, standing near the center of the roof, announced the order of proceedings for a day, & nearly all present gathered around him. The roof gave way and they were all precipitated a distance of about 25 to 30 feet. No one was killed, but Mr Adie had an arm broken; Mr Robt Maynard, his leg broken; Mr Mays, butcher, arm dislocated; Mr H W Fry, cut in the face; Dr Lemosey, bruised; Mr Ned Allen, much hurt. Mr S H Myers' little son had his arm broken; a s/o Mr Graeme's, arm broken; Mr Walsh's 2 sons much injured. –Compiler [Jan 22 newspaper: injuries-Mr Tyrer's son had his face torn dreadfully by a piece of lumber; Messrs R H Redwood, Reed, [at Meredith's store,] F Childs, Pearson, & Pemberton, [from the country,] & 2 sons of Mr H W Fry, | Mr Jos Robinson's 2 sons, were all much injured. Mr Walsh's son, with both his thighs broken, suffer severely yesterday.]

Senate: 1-Ptn from Pearson Cogswell, late marshall of the U S for the district of N H, praying payment of a judgment rendered in his favor on a suit instituted against him by the U S. 2-Mr Woodbury ask to take the papers of Walter Loomis & Abel Gay from the file, & that they be again referred to the Cmte of Claims. 3-Ptn from Levi S Bartlett, asking indemnity for loss sustained in consequence of a violation of a contract between him & the Gov't. 4-Ptn of Wm Rich, asking compensation for his services as a clerk in the Paymaster Genrl's ofc. 5-Ptn from Josiah Garland, asking confirmation of a certain tract of land. 6-Ptn from Geo E Payne, asking to be allowed the half-pay to which his ancestor's services entitled him. 7-Cmte on Private Land Claims: unfavorable report on the ptn of the widow & heirs of Elihu Hall Bay. 8-Letter from B Silliman, exc of Col Jos Trumbull, in relation to important manuscripts, such as correspondence, & records, of the decisions of the Com'rs under Jay's treaty. These papers had all been transcribed in a fair hand by members of that family; & he asked that they may be purchased & placed in the public archives. 9-Ptn from Little & Brown, of Boston, asking the patronage of Gov't to a stereotype edition of the laws of the U S, which they contemplate publishing.

Franklin Whitney has been chosen one of the delegates from the State of N Y, to represent the Congressional district composed of Chenango & Broome counties.

Died: on Dec 26 last, at her late residence in PG Co, Md, Mrs Susan Wall, in her 73rd year, after a protracted sickness, which she bore with Christian resignation. At an early period of her life she attached herself to the Episcopal Church, & was regular in her attendance so long as her health permitted.

The U S frig **Raritan**, now at the Navy Yard, N Y, will be ready to sail in a short time for the coast of Brazil, to relieve the U S ship **Columbus**, the flag ship of Cmdor Turner. Ofcrs of the **Raritan**: Franics H Gregory, Capt
Lts-5:
Law Pennington	Burritt Sheppard	Maxwell Woodhull
Jas F Miller	Edmund T Shubrick	

Acting Master, John B Randolph　　　Chaplain, John Robb
Surgeon, J M Foltz　　　Lts of Marines, Wm Lang
Purser, A E Watson　　　Prof of Math, Edw C Ward
Assist Surgeon, Thos M Potter
Passed Midshipmen: John K Duer, Robt Townsend
Midshipmen-12:
Paul Shirley	F M Humphries	Milton Haxtun
H K Steven	A F Warley	John H March
E A Hopkins	Chas Dyer, jr	A F Monroe
S P Quackenbush	T C P De Kraft	H C Hunter

Masters' Mates-11:
J T Powers	J H Watmough
Chas Bishop	G D Twiggs
Wm B Hayes	Wm P Humphries
Richd H Simms	B G Lindsay
Edw C Henshaw	___ Meehan
Thos J Botts	
Boatswain, Robt Dixon	Sailmaker, G T Lozier
Gunner, G Newman	Purser's Clk, ___ Aliwinn
Carpenter, Wm M Leighton	Capt's Clk, John S Gregory

News was brought to N Y on Sat, from Malaga & Gibraltar, that about $40,000 worth of property had been recovered from the U S steamer **Missouri** by means of divers in submarine armor. It is feared that all efforts to raise her hull will prove fruitless, as the bows are all blown out from the concussion of the magazine. Preparations are now being made for blowing up the wreck.

Died: on Jan 14, at *Rose Hill*, near Wash City, in his 45th year, Mr John Gengenback, a native of Wurtemberg, Germany, but for the last 10 years a resident of Wash City.

Died: Dec 21, at Cincinnati, Ohio, Col Saml W Davies, aged 67 years, for many years Mayor of that city.

Lt Bartlet, U S Navy, & Mr T C Heakes, of Ohio, are to address the Temperance Meeting at the Medical College this evening at 7 o'clock. Public invited.
–Geo Savage, Pres F V T A S

Hse/o Reps: 1-Ptn & documents of Fred'k Tressler, an old soldier, praying relief. 2-Ptn of Benj & Thos Furman, asking compensation for property lost by their father during the last war. 3-Ptn of Jas Morgan, of N Y C, a Revolutionary soldier, for a pension. 4-Ptn of Jacob Storm, of Indiana, for a pension. 5-Memorial of John J Deming & 132 others, citizens of St Joseph Co, Indiana, complaining of the postage rates. 6-Memorial of John Pilcher & 140 others, citizens of Posey Co, Ind, praying for an appropriation of lands to complete the Central Canal to Evansville. 7-Ptn of A D Livingston & John R Donnell, signed by 260 citizens of York Co, Pa, asking Congress for an appropriation for removing 2 bars at the head of the Chesapeake bay, below the town of Havre de Grace. 8-Ptn of Philip Ridge & 24 other citizens, of Ind, asking a donation of refuse lands to assist in completing the Wabash & Erie Canal to the Ohio river. 9-Ptn of Jemima Finch, wid/o Jonathan Finch, for a pension. 10-Memorial of Capt Henry M Shreve, asking Congress to make an appropriation to purchase for the use of the Gov't his patent-right for snag-boats, & for other purposes, was withdrawn from the file of the Clerk's ofc & referred to the Cmte of Claims.

Furniture at auction: on Jan 19, at the residence of Mr Wm Larkin, on 10th st, between Pa ave & E st: the household & kitchen furniture of the establishment.
-Robt W Dyer & Co, aucts

SAT JAN 20, 1844
Senate: 1-Ptn from Dr Jas Ritchie, a surgeon at the Marine Hospital, in relation to certain deductions made in his accounts. 2-Ptn from Martha A Lawrence & other children of Thos D Conover, asking for a grant of land. 3-Ptn from Robt Towne & others, of Maine, praying indemnification for French spoliations prior to 1800. 4-Ptn from Capt Wm N Ivy, asking an extension of contract for delivering of live oak or timber at Gosport, Va. 5-Mr Bayard ask that the papers on file in the case of Robt Fulton be referred to the Cmte on Naval Affairs. 6-Cmte on Military Affairs, reported a bill for the relief of Mark Simpson.

Orphan's Court of Wash Co, D C. Letters of administraton on the personal estate of Wm Radcliff, late of said county, dec'd. –Matilda Radcliff, admx

Mrd: on Jan 18, at the residence of Gen A Hunter, in Wash City, by Rev T C French, J D Featherstonhaugh to Emily Chapman, eldest d/o S F Chapman.

Hse/o Reps: 1-Cmte of Claims: adverse report on the ptn of Jos M Hernandez. 2-Cmte on the Judiciary: report on the ptn of the legal heirs & reps of Richd Harwell, with a bill to refund a fine imposed upon the late Anthony Harwell to his legal heirs & reps. 3-Cmte on Revolutionary Pensions: made a report upon the ptn of Thompson Hutchinson, with a bill for his relief. Same cmte: report on the ptn of Eliz Jones & other heirs of John Carr, with a bill for their relief. Same cmte: report on the ptn of Thos Harrison, with a bill for his relief. Same cmte: adverse report on the ptn of Wm Butterfield. Same cmte: report on the ptn of Hugh Wallace Wormly, with a bill for his relief. Same cmte: report on the ptn of Enoch McDonald, with a bill for his relief. Same cmte: report on the ptn of Jas Reed, with a bill for his relief. 4-Cmte on Invalid Pensions: adverse report on the ptn of Theodore Gould. 5-Select Cmte on the subject of copyrights, moved that the memorial of Nahum Copen, of Boston, Mass, in relation to international copyright, be printed.

Died: on Jan 19, in Wash City, John J Dermott, Atty at Law, in his 47th year. His funeral will be on Sun, at 2 p m, at the house formerly occupied by him as an ofc on Louisiana ave, near 7th st.

Died: on Jan 18, in his 3rd year, Wm H Harrison, s/o Henry & Sarah Ann Hay, of Wash City. His funeral will be from his father's residence, on 6th, between F & G sts, this evening, at 4 p m.

Died: on Jan 12, at *Locust Hill*, her residence, in Chas Co, Md, after an illness of 3 days, Mrs Ann Delia Stone, w/o Jos Stone, in her 33rd year, leaving a husband & infant dght to lament their irreparable loss.

MON JAN 22, 1844
Proposals will be received for bldg a wharf on the Potomac, near the bridge. For further information call at the corner of 10th & E sts, or at the store near the Bridge. --J S Harvey & Co

For sale: 2 likely mulatto women, one middle aged, an excellent cook, washer, ironer, & a good steamstress; the other young, & a good steamstress & house servant. They are sold on account of the owner not having sufficient employment. Apply to Mr Henry Trunnel, at Gtwn.

From Florida. 1-Letter dated at St Lucia on Jan 5 informs that the large warehouse at *Fort Pierce*, containing all the provisions, farming utensils, etc, of a party of settlers from Ga, who sailed from that port some weeks ago in the schnr **Gen Wm Washington**, has been entirely destroyed. Among the bldgs burned were the residences of Mr Campfield & another gentlemen from Ga, whose name is not stated. *Fort Pierce* was entirely consumed. 2-The Jacksonville Tropical Plant of Jan 13 announces the death of John Locke Doggett, Judge of the County Court of Duval Co, & a member of the Bar of that District.

In this newspaper. A copy of stanzas written on the death of the late R U Hyatt, of Wash, who died in Francisville, La, in Oct last, of yellow fever. The poem is signed J U G, Phil, Jan 11, 1844.

The large flour mill at Marengo, Calhoun Co, Mich, owned by S S Allcott, was entirely consumed by fire on Jan 7th-loss $30,000.

Hse/o Reps: 1-Ptn of the heirs of John Lynd, praying for the confirmation of title to a certain tract of land. 2-Ptn of Wm Russell & 45 other citizens, of Perry Co, Ohio, praying for a reform in the Post Ofc Dept. 3-Ptn of B Olney & 150 other citizens, of New Orleans, praying for a grant of certain lands to aid in the improvement of the navigation of the Wabash river. 4-Ptn of Saml M Asbury, praying to increase his pension; & also asking leave to withdraw from the files of the House his former ptn & proof. 5-Ptn of Barbary Vineyard, of Hendricks Co, Ind, for a pension. 6-Ptn of Wm Savage & other merchants, of Boston, for a restoration of the drawback on spirits distilled from foreign molasses. 7-Ptn of Lemuel Land & 114 other citizens of White Co, Ill, praying a grant of part of the unsold lands in the Wabash valley for the improvement of the Wabash river from Terre Haute to the Ohio river. 8-Ptn of N Whitaker & 30 other citizens of Muskingum Co, Ohio, praying a reduction of the expenses of the Genr'l Gov't.: also praying a reduction of the present rates of postage. 9-Ptn of Chas Williams & others, of Greenfield, Mass, praying a reduction of postage. 10-Ptn of Wm G Shanks & 33 others, citizens of Muskingum Co, Ohio, praying for retrenchment in the expenditures of the Gov't; & praying a reduction of the rates of postage.

Fri last, at Zanesville, Ohio, a young man, Solomon Shoemaker was hanged for the murder of his brother, Elias Shoemaker. An immense crowd was drawn to view the revolting spectacle.

The Hudson River Chronicle records the death by drowning of Mr Nathl Ward, a deaf & dumb man, nephew of Gen Aaron Ward. He was skating on the ice opposite Sparta, when he fell through the ice. The dec'd was about 35 years of age.

Jas J Bartram, locksmith, of Phil, committed sucide on Fri, at a place on which his mother resides, in Kingsessing township, by shooting himself. He was to have been married on Tue next, & had partly furnished a house which belonged to him on Callowhill st. He had complained of being unwell and troubled. It is thought that it was owing to the marriage with the last week of a young lady to whom he had been passionately attached.

Peter Williams, found guilty in N Y of manslaughter in the first degree, for killed a young man named Stanley, in a riot between some firemen in that city, was sentenced on Thu to the State prison at Sing Sing for 21 years & 6 months.

Dr Thos O'Hara Crosswell, of Catskill, N Y, died in that village on Tue. He was appointed postmaster at that place during the administration of Gen Washington, & held the ofc to the day of his death-a period of more than 50 years. He was probably the last postmaster, if not the last ofcr in the U S, appointed by Gen Washington.

Appointments by the Pres:
Geo Floyd, of Va, Sec of the Territory of Wisc, vice A P Field.
Attys of the U S:
John G Deshler, for Iowa, vice Chas Weston
Moses C Good, for the Western District of Va, vice Wm Kinney, resigned.
Wm H Rogers, for Delaware, vice Jas A Bayard, resigned.
Gorham Parks, for Maine, vice John Holmes, dec'd.
Grandison D Royston, for Arkansas, vice A Fowler, resigned.
Marshals of the U S:
Isaac Lefler, for Iowa, vice Thos B Johnson.
Robt Myers, for the District of Apalachicola, in Fla, vice H Hawley, dec'd.
Henry M Rector, for Arkansas, vice Thos W Newton.
Geo M Keim, for the Eastern Dist of Pa, vice Isaac Otis.
Wm H Bassett, for the Western District of La, vice Gervais Fontenot, resigned.
Edw Christian, for the Eastern District of Va, re-appointed.
Jas Points, for the Western District of Va, re-appointed.

Amelia Norman, a young woman, who was tried before the Court of Sessions at N Y last week upon an indictment for an attempt on the life of H S Ballard, has been acquitted.

Mrd: on Thu, by Rev John C Smith, Mr Beverley W Beall to Miss Catharine Plowman.

Mrd: on Thu, by Rev John C Smith, Mr Elias D Gumaer to Miss Mary F Young, all of Wash City.

Died: on Jan 18, in Wash, Charity, 4th d/o the late Wm Newton Croggon, in her 21st year.

Died: on Jan 20, Mary Virginia, only d/o P A & Mary Jane Byrne, aged 11 months & 22 days. Funeral this evening at 3 o'clock.

Died: on Jan 20, Mary Ann, consort of Chas L Coltman, after an illness of 19 days, leaving an affectionate husband & 4 children to lament her loss. Her funeral will be on Tue, at 2 o'clock.

All persons having claims against the estate of Sarah Easton, late of D C, are to present them, legally authenticated; all persons indebted to said estate to make payments to-Caroline Easton, admx

TUE JAN 23, 1844
Senate: 1-Ptn of Julia Ann Lawrence, wid/o Capt Lawrence, of the navy, asking for a renewal of her pension. 2-Ptn of John G Tibbits, asking compensation for work done on the custom house in N Y, which he proposed to refer to the Cmte on Finance. 3-Ptn from the heirs of Nathl Dagget, asking compensation for the services of their ancesteor during the Revolutionary war. 4-Ptn from the son & heirs of the late Admiral Count de Grasse, stating his change of fortune, & asking that Congress will grant him some remuneration in consideration of the services of his illustrious father. 5-Ptn from the wid/o Nathan Blood, asking a pension. 6-Papers in the case of the adm of Wm Grayson were taken from the files & referred to the Cmte on Revolutionary Claims. 7-Papers in the case of Jas Smalley were referred to the Cmte on Military Affairs.

West river land for sale: on Feb 15, the farm on which the late Mrs Rebecca Watkins resided: 150 acres, situated in a neighborhood surpassed by none in Md. It is near the main road from Annapolis to Calvert; about 12 miles from the former place. Improvements are a small dwlg, & a large new tobacco house. For further information apply to Mr S Rogers, on the adjoining farm, or the subscriber in Annapolis. –John Ridout, Agent for Mrs S G Rogers

Trustee's sale: by virtue of a decree of the County Court of Montg Co, Md, Court of Equity, made in the cause of Wm Brent vs Robt Brown: sale on Feb 12, at White's Tavern, a tract of land in said county adjacent to said tavern, being part of *St Joseph's Park*, containing 164 acres, 2 roods & 34 perches. Now held & occupied by said Brown under a purchase from said Brent, & it is sold to satisfy purchase money owing therefore. It is bounded by the lands held by said Brown under several purchases from the reps of Thos Cramphin & from Richd Smith, trustee, & others; & by the lands of Danl Lee, dec'd, & of said Brent. –Clement Cox, trustee

Hse/o Reps: 1-Bill introduced for the relief of Pierre Manard, the legal rep of Antoine Peltier & Jos Placy. 2-Claim of John Anderson for payment for depredations committed by the enemy during the last war. 3-Ptn of Mary B Perry & others, heirs of John Dement. 4-Ptn of Jos L Hamon & 261 citizens of Columbiana Co, Ohio: against the annexation of Texas. Ptn of G W St John & 31 others, citizens of Morgan Co, Ohio, for the same purpose. Ptn of Michl Vincent & 122 others, citizens of Marion Co, Ohio, for the same purpose. Ptn of J W Knowlton & 29 others, citizens of Licking Co, Ohio, for the same purpose. 5-Ptn of Martin Mitchell, of N Y, praying that in case Texas be annexed to the U S the sovereign State of N Y might be annexed to Canada. 6-Ptn of Saml McAlpin & 26 others, citizens of Geauga Co, for an amendment to the post ofc laws.

Mr Jas Meredith, a farmer of Bucks Co, Pa, while engaged a few days since in thrashing, had his right hand caught in the revolving cylinder, and had to have all the fingers on the right hand amputated.

I will sell on easy terms a lot containing 14 acres, about a mile from Alexandria. Apply to me or Reuben Johnston, Alexandria. –John T Mankin

$100 reward for runaway mulatto girl Susanna, about 17 years of age: enticed from the residence of the subscriber, near Millwood, Clarke Co, Va. She was the property of the late John Carter, of #6, near Upperville, & was purchased of his excs last fall. She has acquaintances as far as Washington. –Jos Tuley, Tuleyins, near Millwood, Clarke Co, Va

Mrd: on Jan 16, in Rockville, by Rev L J Gillis, L A Dawson to Miss Mary Eliz Kiger, all of Montg Co, Md.

Died: on Dec 19, in the West Indies, at Trinidad de Cuba, Lt Wm J H Robertson, of the U S Navy. At the time of his death he was the 1st Lt of the brig **Somers**, Lt West commanding. He was not more than 30 years of age. He was a native of Norfolk, Va, a son of the late Purser Robertson.

Died: on Jan 8, at the residence of her son, Col A E Jackson, of Jonesborough, Tenn, Mrs Eliz Jackson, consort of Saml Jackson, dec'd, in her 80th year-a native of the city of Phil, but for the last 40 years an inhabitant of the State of Tenn.

Died: yesterday, Anastatia, d/o the late Michl Coleman, aged 2 years & 4 months. Her funeral is this afternoon, at 2 o'clock, from its mother's residence, Capitol Hill.

The Rev John Boqua, aged 75 years, a venerable Methodist clergyman for half a century, fell dead in one of his fields near Salem, West Jersey, a few minutes after leaving his house, on Jan 9, with a disease of the heart. He was soon discovered by his son-in-law, who sent for Dr Mulford. It was in vain for Rev Boqua was dead.

WED JAN 24, 1844
Senate: 1-Ptn from John Keith, asking a pension. 2-Ptn from John Chew, a surveyor of the port of Havre de Grace, for increase of compensation. 3-Ptn from Hezekiah Hamlet, for a pension. 4-Motion that the papers on file in the case of John Gibson be referred to the Cmte on Naval Affairs. 5-Ptn from Alonnzo B Davis, asking compensation for performing duites of ofcrs of higher grade. 6-Ptn from C W Dennison, asking that a publication of his in relation to the moral & intellectual improvement of seamen may receive the patronage of the Gov't.

Hse/o Reps: 1-Cmte of Claims: adverse report on the ptn of Cornelius Bogard. 2-Bill for the relief of Wm Ellery, owner of the fishing schnrs **Sevo & Ida**, both of Gloucester, Mass, & others. 3-

From England. The ex-King of Holland, Wm Frederick, Count of Nassau, is dead. Madame Catalini is also dead. She was 59 years of age, & has left a fortune of L332,000.

From Mexico. The Chief Minister of Santa Anna, Mr Jos Maria Tornel, who lost his wife a short time ago, has expressed a desire to retire from public affairs & offered his resignation.

Trustee's sale: by virtue of a deed of trust from Francis Hill, et al to me, dated Jan 6, 1843: recorded in Liber B, #3, page 502, of the records of deed for the county of Alexandria, D C: sale in Wash City, on Feb 15, that valuable property in said county, adjoining the Little Falls Bridge across the Potomac, & now in the occupancy of said Hill: 15 acres of land, improved by a large stone mill, ample bldgs for employees about the mill. –Clement Cox, Trustee -Robt W Dyer & Co, aucts At the same time, in virtue of a deed of trust from Geo Hill to the subscriber, dated Jan 20, 1843, all the machinery in said deed. –D A Hall, trustee -Robt W Dyer & Co, aucts

Orphan's Court of Wash Co, D C. Letters testmentary on the personal estate of John Wheat, late of said county, dec'd. -Mary Wheat, excx

Orphan's Court of Wash Co, D C. Letters testmentary on the personal estate of John McCarthy, late of said county, dec'd. –Thos J Barrett, exc

THU JAN 25, 1844
Trustee's sale of house & lot: on Feb 8, on the premises lot #4, in square 487, on G st, between 5th & 6th sts, with the improvements-2 well built 2 story brick houses, renting readily at $120 per annum. –F Datcher, Trustee -Robt W Dyer & Co, aucts

Meeting of the Whigs held, on Jan 23, in Port Tobacco, Chas Co, Md, to nominate delegates to meet a Convention, to be held in Bladensburg on Jan 30, to nominate a suitable Whig to represent the First Congressional District in the U S Congress, on motion the following were nominated:
1st Dist: Jos Young, Thos A Miller, Robt Gray, Dr John F Price, & Richd Posey.
2nd Dist: Geo Brent, Jas Ferguson, Saml Cox, John Ware, & Stouton W Dent.
3rd Dist: John J Jenkins, Allison Roberts, Dr Ferdinand Spalding, Chas Jenkins, & Richd B Gardiner.
4th Dist: John Hughes, Dr B J Gardiner, Edw W Gardiner, Peter Wood, & Dr W F Boarman -Peter W Crain, Chairman -G P Jenkins, Sec

For rent, the 2 story brick dwlg-house on the corner of N Y ave & 12th st, Wash. Has a fine bakery & store-room attached. Apply to F & A H Dodge, Gtwn.

Hse/o Reps: 1-Cmte of Claims, reported the following bills: for the relief of Saml B Folger; relief of Saml B Tucker; relief of the heirs of Wm Augustus Allen; relief of Geo M Jones. A bill to provide for the payment of the passage of Gen Lafayette from France to the U S in the year 1824; accompanied by a report in each case. 3-Ptn of S De Veaux, Peter B Porter, & 45 other citizens of Niagara Falls, for a reduction of postage & revision of the Postage laws. Ptn of B Fairman, & 238 citizens of Orleans Co, N Y, & of S M Burroughs & 154 citizens of Orleans Co, N Y, for the same. 4-Ptn of A Grannis & others of East Haven, Conn, for the erection of a lighthouse on the S W ledge, at the entrance of New Haven harbor. 5-Ptn of Chas Little & Jas Brown, praying Congress to enter into a contract with them for publishing a new edition of the laws of the U S on certain terms & conditions. 6-Ptn of Philip Schnell, a soldier of the Revolution, asking for a pension. 7-Memorial of Martin Collier, of Charlestown, Mass, in relation to the official conduct of Gen Henderson, of the Marine Corps. 8-Ptn of Thos Smith, of Edgar Co, Ill, & 50 others, asking a grant of land in the Wabash valley for the improvement of the Wabash river from Terre Haute to the Ohio river. 9-Ptn of Seymour D Shaw & others, praying for the erection of a lighthouse at the mouth of Cattaraugus creek, N Y, for the prosecution of the unfinished works at that place. Also, the ptns of the following for the same: H Stoddard & others; H Sturns & others; Loren Strong & others; Capt O Connor & others. 10-Ptn of Capt John Martin for a pension. 11-Ptn of Jos Gilmore & 59 other citizens of Indiana, praying for a grant of land to aid in the completion of the Wabash & Erie canal. 12-Ptn of E Short & 40 other citizens of Wash Co, Ohio, praying for an extension of mail route #2,102 from Wash, Guernsey Co, to Lowell, Wash Co, Ohio. 13-Ptn of Robt Miller, Jos Fawcett, & others, asking Congress to pass a law by which the sense of the people of the U S may be taken as to the constitutionality of banks, paper money, etc. 14-Ptn of 91 members of the Leg of Indiana, asking a donation of land to O'Bryant McNamer on account of a bodily disability. 15-Ptn of citizens of Morgan Co, Ind, in favor of granting to Bryce W Miller privilege to dig a mill-race through certain public lands, & for a grant of land for draining the same. 16-Cmte of Claims: on leave given, made a report, with a bill for the relief of Jos M Hernandez. Read twice & committed.

Senate: 1-Ptn from David Myerle, asking indemnity for loss sustained under a contract to supply water-rotted hemp for the use of the Navy. 2-Ptn from J H Caldwell & others, asking to be released as sureties on bonds given by the New Orleans & Nashville Rail Road company to secure the payment of certain duty on iron. 3-Ordered that the papers on file in the case of Francis Cooper be referred to the Cmte on Indian Affairs.

A superb lot of beef, on Sat, Jan 27, at my stall, in Centre Market, for sale. They were raised by Mr Jas Parsons, on the South Branch of Va. –Wm D Bell, Centre Market, #s 61 & 63

Beef, Beef-to the lovers of good living. To the patrons of Wash Centre Market. Fed expressly for market by A A Inakep, of the South Branch of the Rappahannock, Va, & driven with uncommon care. They will be offered at my stalls, #s 54 & 55, on Jan 27, new market. –Wm Linkins

Trustee's sale of house & lot: by virtue of a deed of trust, dated Sep 1, 1840: sale on Feb 26, part of lot 4 in square 567, with a 2 story frame house thereon.
–Henry Naylor, Trustee -Robt W Dyer & Co, aucts

Trustee's sale of real property: by virtue of a deed of trust, dated Oct 17, 1840: sale on Feb 26, of lot 23, as subdivided of lot 5, in square 462, with all the bldgs, advantages, improvements, & appurtenances thereto belonging.
–Henry Naylor, Trustee -Robt W Dyer & Co, aucts

Venison: just received at the Railroad Depot. Apply to the agent of the depot, or to Geo Lambright, next door.

We have just received the 2 first numbers of a new Daily Paper, entitled "The Republic," edited by Duff Green, & issued in N Y C.

Orphan's Court of Wash Co, D C. Letters of administraton on the personal estate of Ferdinand R Hassler, late of Wash Co, dec'd. –E Hassler, Ferdinand E Hassler, adms

FRI JAN 26, 1844
Senate: 1-Ptn from Eliz Maury, wid/o a dec'd naval ofcr, praying a pension. 2-Ptn from Hiram Barney, in behalf of himself & others, asking a resurvey of the Fox & Sacre reservations. 3-Ptn from Jas W Low, praying compensation for his participation in the capture of the British privateers. 4-Ptn from C Edw Lester, Consul at Genoa, on the subject of the purchase of the Durasso library, to be offered for sale at Genoa. 5-Ptn from Mary Ann Maurice, asking a renewal of pension. 6-Ptn from the administrator of John Judge, asking compensation for a machine invented by him for testing the strength of cables. 7-Cmte on Military Affairs: a bill for the relief of Wm De Peyster & Henry N Cruger. 8-Cmte on Revolutionary Claims: an adverse report on the memorials of the heirs of Geo Yates.

Geo C W Werkmeister, a German, about 70 years of age, hung himself in N Y on Fri, in a garret which he occupied in Essex st. He had no relatives or friends in this country.

Wash Corp: 1-Ptn from Nicholas Ferretan: referred to the Cmte of Claims. 2-Mr Lynch presented the credentials of Wm Hicks, member elect from the 4th Ward, vice Simeon Bassett, dec'd. 3-Ptn of Lewis & Elwood, praying remission of a fine: referred to the Cmte of Claims. 4-Ptn of Philip Ennis, praying remission of certain fine: referred to the Cmte of Claims. 5-Ptn of Simon Frazer, concerning the erection of a wharf in front of square 472 & the water-rights & privileges belonging to said square: referred. 6-Cmte of Claims: asked to be discharged from the further consideration of the ptns of Leonard O Cook & of Henry Morris: accordingly discharged.

Wash City Orphan Asylum: ladies chosen Managers for the year 1844:
Mrs Hawley, 1st Directress   Miss Smith, Treas
Mrs Laurie, 2nd Directress   Miss Van Ness, Sec
Board of Managers:
Mrs Brown   Mrs Tucker   Mrs Luce
Mrs Lear   Mrs R S Coxe   Mrs Washington
Mrs Henderson   Mrs Markoe   Mrs Bingham
Mrs R Smith   Mrs Gadsby
Mrs Larned   Mrs Stone

Hse/o Reps: 1-Ptn of Thos Graves, of Russell Co, Ky: referred. 2-Memorial of the adms of Nimrod Farrow & Richd Harris, asking the appointment of a board of arbitrators to settle & adjust a claim of their intestates against the U S. 3-Ptn of Millard Fillmore & others, for a modification of the revenue laws, to allow drawback upon goods re-exported in the original package. 4-Ptn of Chas Rhind, for additional compensation for services in negotiating a treaty with Turkey. 5-Ptn of Alex'r Wilson & 67 others, citizens of Miami Co, praying the establishment of a mail route from Indianapolis to Peru, via Broad Ripple, Farmington, Shieldsville, & Greentown. 6-Memorial of Nathl Blackford & 49 others; also, the memorial of John Saulsbury & 58 others, citizens of White Co, Ill, praying the donation of the refuse lands in the Shawneetown & Palestine land districts for the improvement of the navigation of the Great Wabash river. 6-Cmte of Elections report: Resolved, that Thos W Gilmer is entitled to a seat in this House as one of the Reps from the State of Va.

Near St Johnsville, Montg Co, N Y, a few days ago: Mr Theodore Lasher & his son-in-law, Thos Carman, crossed the Mohawk river in a skiff on Dec 26, &, in expecting to remain some days, they sent the boat back. In the evening, however, they intimated their intention of returning home, & left the house. No more was heard of them until Jan 2, when it was ascertained that they had not returned to their homes as expected. An immediate search was set on foot, & in about 3 hours their bodies were found in the river, across which they had attempted to pass on the ice. They had been in a watery grave 7 days.

Wm T Maddox appointed, by the Exec of Md, Clerk of St Mary's County Court, vice Jos Harris, resigned; & Walter Mitchell, Clerk of Chas Co Court, vice Barnes, dec'd.

It appears that the only cabin passenger who was lost by the late disaster to the steamboat **Shepherdess**, near St Louis, was Mr A R Bickner, of Balt. He was a native of Mass, but for the last 2 years had prosecuted business in German st, Balt. He was about 38 years of age.

From the Northern Light: original purchase of the Island of New York. Curious letter, recording the purchase of the Island of *Manhattan*, 217 years ago, by the Dutch from the Indians, for the sum of 60 guilders, or $24. The tract conveyed contains 13,920 acres . Hooghe Moghende Heeren: Hier is ghister 't scip' Wafen van Amsterdam aengekomen, en is den 23 September uyt Nieu Nederlandt gezylt uyt de rivier Mauritius. Rapporteren dat ons volk daer kloec is en vreedigh leven, hare vrouwen hebben ooc kindered aldaer gabaert; hebben 't eylandt Manhattes van de Wilde gekocht voot de waerde van 60 guilden; is groot 11,000 morgen. Hebben der alle koren half Mey gezeyt en half Augusro gemayd. Daervan veynden de munsterkins van Zomer-Koren, als tarrew, rogge, garst, haver, boucweyt, knarizaet, boontjens en vlas. P Schaghen -Amsterdam, 5 Nov, 1626
Translation.
High and Mighty Lords: Yesterday arrived the ship "The Arms of Amsterdam:" she sailed from the river Mauritius, [Hudson,] in the New Netherlands, on 23 September. They report that our folk there are prosperous and live in peace. Their women have borne children there already. They have purchased from the Indians, for the sum of 60 guilders, the Island Manhattan, which is 11,000 morgen large. They have already sowed grain by the middle of May and reapt by the middle of August: samples of summer crops have come, such as wheat, rye, barley, oats, buckwheat, canary seed, beans, and flax. P Schaghen -Amsterdam, 5 Nov, 1626

Mrd: on Jan 17, in Fredericksburg, by Rev Chas Mann, Wm S Triplett, of Richmond, to Miss Anne O, eldest d/o the Hon Danl Jenifer, of Md.

Mrd: on Dec 10, at the garrison near *Fort Smith*, Arkansas, by Rev D McManus, Lt R E Cochrane, U S Army, to Miss Sally T Beall, 3rd d/o the late Saml T Beall, formerly of Bardstown, Ky.

Died: on Jan 11, in St Louis, Mo, Mrs Caroline R Blair, w/o Montgomery Blair, & d/o Ariss Buckner, of Loudoun Co, Va; leaving 2 children & a large circle of friends to mourn their irreparable loss.

Died: on Dec 14, 1843, at *Fort Sullivan*, Eastport, Maine, Delia N Saunders, aged 10 years & 7 days, dght & only child of Maj H Saunders, U S Army.

Died: on Dec 30, in the city of Havana, Cuba, in his 28th year, after a few days' illness, of yellow fever, Dr Robt Mumford, late of the city of Richmond, Va.

Died: on Jan 13, at Edenton, his residence, in Essex Co, Va, Mr Robt Payne Waring, in his 66th year. To his own house, now deprived of its head, the bereavement is irreparable. Few members of any community can be more missed than he will be by those united to him in the various relations of life.

SAT JAN 27, 1844

Rev Thos S Savage, M D, Protestant Episcopal Missionary to Western Africa, has presented to the Nat'l Institute 45 specimens of superb recently discovered insects from the vicinity of Cape Palmas.

Dr Duck announces he has opened Wavereley Hall for the reception of a select number of persons afflicted with insanity, imbecility, & nervous disorders. He has had extensive experience in the treatment of mental diseases, & conducted a large establishment for insane persons in England. Waverley is about 4 miles from Balt, near the York turnpike road: a farm of 100 acres attached. References: Rev Mr Johns, Rector of Christ Church, Dr Thomas, & Isaac Tyson, jr, of Balt.

The Portland Argus announces the death of the Hon Edw Kavanagh, of Maine, on Sat last, at his residence in Newcastle. Mr Kavanagh was born Apr 27, 1795, & consequently was in his 49th year.

Orphan's Court of Chas Co, Md. Letters of administraton on the personal estate of Thos H Ching, late of said county, dec'd. –John M Latimer, Thos K Ching, adms

Orphan's Court of Chas Co, Md. Letters of administraton on the personal estate of Gerrard H Ching, late of said county, dec'd. –John M Latimer, Thos K Ching, adms

Hse/o Reps: 1-Bill to refund Gen Jackson's fine under consideration, Mr Schenck addressed the Cmte with the following: he was fined for a contempt of court: on Dec 15, 1814, Gen Jackson issued his proclamation declaring martial law. Jan 8 the battle of New Orleans was fought, the enemy repulsed, & victory obtained. On Jan 19, the British camp having been evacuated, & their troops & naval forces withdrawn, Jackson said, "you will not think me too sanguine in the belief that Louisiana is now clear of its enemy;" & on Jan 21, the Gen returned with his triumphant army to New Orleans. On Feb 18 news was received by the way of Jamaica, that a treaty of peace had been concluded by the American & British Com'rs at Ghent. On Mar 3 Mr Louallier, a member of the Louisiana Legislature, published in a New Orleans newspapers of the harsh manner in which certain French subjects of that city had been treated by Gen Jackson. On Mar 5, for this publication, Louallier was arrested by order of Jackson, & thrown into jail. On the evening of that same day, the Judge notified the Gen that a writ had been awarded, & he too was seized & imprisoned, by a party of 60 soldiers, sent under the General's order to his house, where they arrested him. On Mar 6 Gen Jackson received news of the ratification of peace at Washington; & on the same day issued an order for a court martial to convene to try Mr Louallier for his life! On Mar 8 he disbanded the militia. Judge Hall was kept in close confinement until Mar 11, when he was sent 4 miles out of the city under a guard of soldiers, & discharged with indignity. On that day also Louallier was acquitted; but Gen Jackson issued an order disapproving the decision of the court martial, & did not release him until Mar 16. On Mar 22 proceedings were instituted in due form against Gen Jackson for contempt & obstruction of its authority. He was fined. [Coverage continues for 4½ columns in the newspaper.] 2-Ptn of the heirs of Capt Wm Evans: for Revolutionary invalid pension. 3-Papers containing additional evidence in behalf of the claim of the heirs of Maj Tarlton Woodson, for commutation pay, were presented. 4-Ptn of Horace Leet & 100 citizens of Potter Co, Pa, praying a reduction in the rates of postage. 5-Three ptns signed by Amos Judson & 250 citizens of Erie Co, asking an appropriation to continue the public work on the harbor at Erie.

Mrd: at the Narrows, Long Island, N Y, Wm Macomb, U S Navy, to Mary E Stanton, d/o Col Henry Stanton, of the U S Army. [No date-appears recent.]

Mrd: on Dec 28, in the parish of Natchitoches, La, Capt Wm Mayo Fulton, U S Army, to Cornelia C B Patton, grand-dght of the late Col Robt Patton, of Phil.

Mrd: on Jan 16, at *Pleasant Hill*, in Chas Co, Md, by Rev P Courtney, John W Jenkins to Emily A, y/d/o the late Jas Gardiner, all of Chas Co, Md.

Died: at her residence in Port Tobacco, Md, after a long & painful illness, Miss Jane Bruce, in her 48th year. Called at any early age to take upon herself the cares & duties of her parental household, she entered upon this new & untried theatre with an energy that never tired. Upon 4 distinct subsequent occasions, when the desolating hand of death was laid upon the father or the mother, the helpless orphan found in her a soothing friend, a self denying benefactor. [No date-appears recent.]

Died: on Jan 3 or 4, at New Orleans, in her 84th year, Mrs Phoebe Hunter, mother of Lt Hunter, U S Navy.

Died: on Jan 26, suddenly, in Gtwn, in his 59th year, Mr Edw Clark. His funeral is today, at 3 o'clock, from his late residence on High st, Gtwn.

Rockville Academy, Montg Co, Md. The vacancy in the classical dept, occasioned by the demise of the late lamented Principal, has been supplied by the election of Otis C Wright, late of Lowell, Mass, & a graduate of Dartmouth College. Richd J Bowie, Sec-

MON JAN 29, 1844
Mr Andrew Vecklin was killed in N Y on Wed, when he fell from the roof of his house, which he had painted, to the ground, surviving the fall but a few moments

Letter to Francis Markon, jr, Corr Sec of the National Institute from J Dille, dated Newark, Ohio, Jan 2, 1844. Subject: Meterological Phenomena observed by him. In 1810 or 1822, when quite a boy, my father lived near Cleveland. Markon viewed the most splendid exhibitions of the aurora borealis. [Letter is a column in length in the newspaper.] There is another letter to the same, from Prof Francis Lieber, dated Columbia, S C, Dec 29, 1843. Subject: Trustees of the South Carolina College have given him leave for sufficient time to go to Europe: shall leave in March: offers to be of service.

Letter to the Sec of State from Dominico Bartolini, Vice Consul of the U S at Civita Vecchia, dated Cicita Vecchia, Jun 1, 1843. He writes of the arrival in this port on the 20th ult of the U S corvette **Fairfield**, commanded by Capt W C Nicholson. Of antiquities to be presented to the Institute in his name a collection of Etruscan Antiquities:
A Greek vase, of 2,000 years
Greek vase, of same epoch
Greek vase, of the same epoch
Greek cup, of the same epoch
Etruscan Vase, of about 3,000 years
Etruscan Glass, of same epoch, with two.
3-Etruscan vases, funereal, same epoch
Etruscan vase, same epoch, singular form
Etruscan vase, same epoch,
Etruscan Calyx, funeral, same epoch
Etruscan plate, same epoch
Small vase for unguents, Etruscan, same epoch
Egyptian vase of about 4,000 years
Small Etruscan cup of 3,000 years. The objects have been found in places adjacent to the city of Volcia, 32 Roman miles distant from Civita Vecchia.

Handsome furniture at auction: on Feb 6, at the residence of Mr Young, on B st, east of 3rd st, a handsome assortment, all of which has been purchased within the last 6 months, & kept with great care. –Wm Marshall, Auctioneer

NOTICE: by virtue of a distrain for rent, I shall expose to public sale, on Feb 3, in front of the Centre Market-house, in Wash City, the following goods & chattels: a walnut table, one old looking glass, one safe, a stove, a lot of old carpeting, 5 common chairs, a settee, 4 stand casks, 2 decanters & 3 tumblers. Seized & taken as the property of John Reilly, & will be sold to satisfy house-rent due in arrears to John S Devlin. –H R Maryman, Bailiff

Valuable lots for rent: 2 lots on the N E corner of C & 11th sts.
–Saml McKenney, Gtwn

Hse/o Reps: 1-Bill for the relief of John McLaughlin: laid aside. 2-Bill for the relief of the widows & orphans of the ofcrs, seamen, & marine of the U S schnr **Grampus**. 3-Memorial of P B Key, praying the passage of a law to authorize the proper ofcrs to allow compensation for services rendered by the late F S Key, dec'd, to the U S, as counsel in certain cases therein described. 4-Ptn of Josiah Copley, of Armstrong Co, Pa, praying Congress to inquire into the merits of a vessel of war. 5-Ptn of David Fisk & others, praying for the erection of a lighthouse at the mouth of Cattaraugus creek, N Y, & for the prosecution of the unfinished works at that place. 6-Ptn of Jas Stewart, for payment of time while confined as a prisoner in England during the late war. 7-Ptn of S B Ranson & others, of Hunterdon Co, N J, asking for the reduction of the postage rates. 8-Ptn of Geo W Manypeny, of Muskingum Co, Ohio, praying for a law authorizing a patent to be issued to him for certain lands therein claimed. 9–Ptn of Lewis B Loder & others, for a grant of lands in Indiana to aid in the construction of the Wabash & Erie Canal. 10-Ptn of Saml Clark, a soldier of the last war, who was wounded while on duty, for an invalid pension. 11-Ptn of P Cooney & 156 others of Ohio, praying for a reduction of the compensation of members of Congress to $6 per day without perquisites, & for such a system of retrenchment as shall bring the Gov't back to it primitive purity.

Whig Convention in Indiana on Jan 16, at Indianapolis. Following Electoral Ticket was reported:

Henry S Lane	Saml W Parker	Richd W Thompson
J A Brackenridge	Hugh O'Neal	Albert L Holmes
Jas Collins	Jos G Marshall	Horace P Biddle
J A Matson	Geo G Dunn	Lewis G Thompson

Illinois State Register of Jan 19. The Hon Jos Duncan, Ex-Govnr of this State, & formerly Rep in Congress from Ill, died at his residence on Mon last of congestive fever. Sympathy to his family.

A monument has been erected over the spot at *St Augustine* where the remains of the ofcrs & soldiers who fell in the Florida war were deposited on Aug 15, 1842. The monument is an Egyptian obelish, 21 feet high, surmounted by a blazing urn, with appropriate inscriptions on the 4 faces.

The friends of John Van Buren, says the Albany Atlas, will be glad to hear of his safe arrival at the Island of Medeira. The ship **Charles Carroll**, in which he sailed, made the passage from N Y in 19 days. The health of Mrs Van Buren, the restoration of which was the chief inducement to the voyage, was materially improved, & no doubt is now entertained of her entire recovery.

On Jan 19, our esteemed fellow-citizen, the venerable Mr John J Van Voast, entered upon the 104th year of his age. He has acquired decent property, & appears to have had his full share of happiness. –Schenectady Cabinet

The Dubuque Ezpress of Dec 29, says: Mr Butterworth, the mother of one of our most estimable citizens, attended church on Christmas day, leaning upon the arm of our worthy Mayor. This lady is aged about 117 years, & is remarkably active for a person of that age. A few years ago she danced quite briskly at the wedding of her son. She remembers distinctly the battle of Culloden, & of the Pretender escaping & attempting to secrete himself in Ireland.

Wm Perkins, a young man, a native of England, was killed in N Y on Mon last by accidentally falling through the skylight of the bookstore of Messrs Appleton & Co, from the 3rd story down to the first.

Mr Wm Sutton, of Scott Co, a gentleman of excellent character, hung himself about 2 weeks ago. He went up a tree & attached a rope to a limb. No reason can be given for this rash act. –Lexington [Ky] Inq

Mr Fitch Weston, of Salisbury, on Mon last, while conveying a couple of female operatives [factory girls] from the Salisbury Manufacturing Co's factory, his horse, becoming unmanageable, capsized the sleigh, throwing Mr W violently against a stone post, fracturing his skull. A female was also seriously injured, having had her hip dislocated & broken. Mr Weston remained senseless, & expired about 4 hours after the accident. –Boston

On Jan 10, Mr Alfred Doty, of Garrard Co, in attempting to draw a ramrod out of a rifle, an accidental discharge took place and the ball passed through his breast. The young man could not speak, but reached out his hand to take his parting & last farewell of his brother, who was present. –Lexington [Ky] Inq

Appointments by the Pres: 1-Wm F Haile, Collector of Customs for the Dist of Champlain, & Inspector of the Revenue for the port of Plattsburg, N Y. 2-Benj Stiles, Collector at Hardwicke, Ga. 3-Jas Dell, Collector at St Johns, Fla. 4-John Daingerfield, Collector, East River, Va.

Died: on Jan 25, in Alexandria, Mrs H Philippa Ludwell Lee, w/o Cassius F Lee, & d/o the late John Hopkins, of Va. –Alexandria Gaz

Died: on Jan 28, in Wash City, John Fagan, the s/o the late Peter Fagan. Friends & acquaintances of the dec'd & those of David S Phillips are requested to attend his funeral from the residence of David S Phillips, near the Navy Yard gate, Wash, at 2½ o'clock this afternoon.

The St Louis Republican adds to the list of those who lost their lives by the accident on the steamboat **Shepherdess** the names of Rev Elijah Gates, of the Baptist Church, his wife, & servant, of Ky.

TUE JAN 30, 1844
Dr H Fischel, Surgeon Dentist, from Berlin & London, has taken rooms over Mr Johnson's store, Pa ave, between 4½ & 6th sts. Charges moderate.

Senate: 1-Ptn from John H Pennington, asking an appropriation for testing a machine for navigating the air. 2-Ptn from John Martin, an ofcr of the last war, asking an increase of pension. 3-Ptn from John Good, asking indemnity for injury sustained in passing the Cumberland road through his farm. 4-Ptn from Alex'r McIntire & other citizens of Maine, asking a lighthouse at York harbor. 5-Cmte on Revolutionary Claims: adverse report on the ptn of Nathan Ward. Same for Thos D Conover. 6-Cmte of Claims: bill for the relief of Danl G Skinner, of Alabama, with a report, which was ordered to be printed. 7-Cmte on Naval Affairs: bill for the relief of Cmder Jas M McIntosh, with a report, which was ordered to be printed. 8-Cmte on the Post Ofc & Post Roads: bill for the relief of Francis A Harrison. 9-Cmte on Indian Affairs: bill for the relief of Francis A Kerr. 10-Cmte on Pensions: adverse report on the ptn of Simon Kenton.

J Visser, Agent, has just opened a splendid assortment of Ball Goods, Flowers, Jewelry: 5 doors above 9th st on Pa ave.

Public sale: by virtue of an order from Orphans Court of PG Co, Md: sale on Feb 5, all the personal estate of Chas Duvall, of Richard, late of said county, dec'd, consisting of 10 young negroes, mostly men & boys; 12 work oxen, 20 head of other cattle; set of farm horses, saddle horses, one pair fine carriage horses, colts & fillies, sheep, hogs, carriage, buggy, wagon, horse cart, household & kitchen furniture, with all the farming utensils, patent tobacco press, corn, oats, hay, etc.
–G W Duvall, adm with the will annexed

For sale, a negro woman, now in this place: aged about 40 years, excellent cook, washer, ironer, & milk-maid. Apply to the subscriber, who maybe found at Beers' Hotel, Jan 30. –W H Robertson, or of John M Young, at his Coach Establishment, near 13th st.

John S Gallaher has been nominated as the Whig candidate for the Senate of Va, in the Fred'k dist. He was for a long time the editor of the Charlestown Free Press.
–Balt Patriot

Died: yesterday, aged 62, Mrs Jane Bancker Cathcart, relict of the late Jas Leander Cathcart, of Wash City. Her funeral will be from the late residence of the dec'd, on 17th st, at 3 o'clock this afternoon.

Died: on Fri, at his residence in North Chas st, Balt, Md, at the advanced age of 76 years, Dr H H Hayden, long a distinguished Dentist, & a highly respected citizen of Balt

Hse/o Reps: 1-Ptn of Saml Hebard & 93 others, praying a reduction of postage. Ptn of Abel E Fish & 42 others, for the same. Ptn of Asa B Hebard & 27 others, for the same. 2-Ptn of Phebe Hosier, for a pension. 3-Ptn of Sarah Banks, for a pension. 4-Ptn of Geo Winting, of Lancaster Co, Pa, asking to be placed on the pension roll under the act of Jun 7, 1832. 5-Ptn of Sarah Teas. 6-Ptn & papers of Nancy Haggard, of Cumberland Co, Ky. 6-Ptn of Bryant Slone, praying to be placed on the roll of invalid pensions. 7-Ptn of Eliz Raymond, praying for a pension, & for a revision of the existing pension laws. 8-Ptn of Gyrus Russell & other inhabitants of township 33, in range 4, east, in Madison Co, Missouri, asking Congress to authorize a change in the location of the school section in said township. 9-Ptn of Jos Latshaw & 11 others, citizens of Knox Co, Ind, asking a donation of land to improve the navigation of the Wabash river. Ptn of B Graham & 47 others, citizens of Daviess Co; ptn of Edw Moony & 200 citizens of Knox Co; ptn of Jas B Bryant & 96 others, citizens of Martin Co; ptn of Thos Paul & nearly 300 others, citizens of Wheeling, Va; ptn of Zachariah Morgan & 35 other citizens of Green Co, Ind; ptn of Chas Smith & 263 other citizens of Knox Co: all on the same subject. 10-Memorial of Thos F Gordon, soliciting the patronage of Congress for the 3rd edition of a Digest of the Laws of the U S. 11-Ptn of Saml Mullen & 226 other citizens of Vigo Co, Indiana, asking that Congress would grant to Indiana a portion of vacant lands in the Vincennes land district, Ind, & of lands lying in the Shawwneetown & Palestine land district, Ill, for improving the navigation of the Wabash river by removing the obstruction in said river. Ptn of Jas S Freeman & 201 other citizens of Vigo Co, Ind, on the same subject. Ptn of David W Clover & 75 other citizens of Vermillion Co, Ind, on the same subject. 12-Ptn of Loftin Windsor & 28 other citizens of Fairfax Co, Va, asking a recharter of the Farmers' Bank & Bank of Potomac, D C. 13-Ptn of Saml Dutton & others, of Indiana, praying Congress to reduce the price of postage. 14-Ptn of the reps of Gustavus B Horner, a surgeon's mate in the Revolutionary army, for bounty land, or other compensation for his services, & for commutation. 15-Cmte on Revolutionary Pensions to inquire into allowing a pension to Polly Allen, the wid/o Maj Jas Allen, a soldier of the Revolution. 16-Cmte on Revolutionary pensions to inquire into the claims of Amaziah Goodwin to a pension upon papers herewith submitted, with leave to report by bill or otherwise.

WED JAN 31, 1844
Dress-making: Miss Anne Twomey, 12th st S, between C & D sts, next to the corner of Pa ave: strict attention, long experience, & a desire to please.

The fraternity of Free Masons & that of the Independent Order of Odd Fellows, comprehending the various Lodges of this District attached to both fraternities, rendered funeral honors yesterday to the remains of their departed brother, Philip Inch. The procession moved from City Hall to the Congress Burial Ground about 2 o'clock. It was preceded by the marine band, playing a solemn dirge.

Wash Corp: 1-Ptn of Wm McL Cripps & others, for improvement of Mass ave: referred to the Cmte on Improvements. 2-Cmte of Claims: adverse to the ptn of Wm Owens & Hiram Jennings: laid upon the table. 3-Cmte on Canals:asked to be discharged from the ptn of Simeon Frazier.

Senate: 1-Ptn from Elbert Herring, in relation to a very beautiful collection of paintings which he thinks would be useful to the Gov't, & asks that they be received on appraisement in satisfaction of a debt due the U S; & that they be retained & made the base of a collection of a national gallery. 2-Ptn from the heirs of Capt Noble, asking 7 years' half-pay due their ancestor, with interest. 3-Cmte on the Judiciary: bill to refund the fine imposed on Gen Andrew Jackson with amendment: that nothing in this act shall be construed to express or imply any censure of the conduct or character of the Hon Dominick A Hall, by whom the said fine was imposed. 4-Cmte on the Judiciary: bill for the relief of Henry Gardner & others, directors of an association called the New England Mississippi Land Company. 5-Cmte on Revolutionary Claims: unfavorable report in the case of Eliz Lomax. Same cmte: adverse report in the case of the heirs of Danl Trueheart: report recommitted to the cmte for future examination.

Hse/o Reps: 1-Ptn of Peter Von Schmidt in relation to a dry dock. 2-Ptn of Churchill Gibbs. 3-Ptn of Gen Lubrick & others, citizens of Columbia Co, Pa, asking a modification of rates of postage & restriction of the franking privilege. 4-Ptn of Lovel G Mickles, of N Y C, praying an appropriation by Congress, to be expended under the authority of the War Dept, in testing an invention to protect boats navigating the Mississippi & its tributaries from injuries occasioned by snags & sawyers. 5-Ptn of Luther Allen & others, praying for the erection of a lighthouse at the mouth of Cattaraugus creek, N Y, & for the prosecution of the unfinished works at that place. 6-Mrs Caldwell withdrew from the files of the Clerk & presented the ptn of the heirs of Henry King, dec'd, of Ky.

Supreme Court of the U S: Jan 29, 1844. #10-Edmund P Gaines & wife, cmplnts, vs Beverly Chew et al. [This is noted again on Jan 30, 1844.]

Obit-died: on Jan 28, in Wash City, after a short & painful illness, Mrs Rebecca Russell Reding, aged 33 years, consort of the Hon John R Reding, Rep in Congress from N H. Her funeral services will be at her late residence [Mr Stewart's, Capitol Hill,] today, at 2 o'clock, whence her remains will be taken to N H for interment.

Died: on Jan 27, in Gtwn, D C, after a few days' illness, Mr Oran Augustus Hall, of Proidence, R I, leaving a disconsolate widow & 2 children. [The Phil & Eastern papers are requested by the friends of the dec'd to copy the above notice.]

Desirable residence at auction: on Feb 23rd next, on Bridge st, a 3 story brick house, in Smith's Row, on 1st st, adjoining the residence of Dr Warfield. The house is slate roofed, contains 9 chambers, a parlor 18 by 42, with folding doors; a passage 8 feet wide, large & well arranged basement for family purposes, with pantry, closets, etc, in connexion with a spacious & well arranged kitchen, 2 cellars for storage of fuel, dry & warm; a smoke house, stable, & coach house; in short, all the conveniences that might be desired in a family residence. Terms made known at sale.
–Edw S Wright, Auct'r

We understand that the nomination of Jas M Porter, appointed during the recess of Congress, to be Sec for the Dept of War, was yesterday rejected by the Senate.

The Whigs of the 2nd Congressional District of Md have nominated Francis J Brengle as their candidate for Congress. His opponent is John T Mason, late a member of Congress.

Mrd: on Sun, by Rev John C Smith, Mr Jas D Marr to Miss Rebecca Borland, all of Wash City.

The Cumberland Alleghanian of Sat says that Mr David Stinson, a driver belonging to the Good Intent Line of coaches between there & Wheeling, was thrown from his box on Jan 21 & killed on the spot.

Saml Currier was murdered at Norfolk on Mon. He was mate of the schnr **Thomas**, of Boston, now lying at Norfolk, & brother of the captain. He belonged to Newburyport. It appears he was in a fight with 2 sailors in a house of ill fame, & his body thrown into a lumber yard, where it was found. The murderers have been arrested & committed to jail.

THU FEB 1, 1844
Hse/o Reps: 1-Cmte of Claims: adverse reports on the ptns of Wm Thompson & Geo W Dent. Same cmte: bill for the relief of Danl Dean. 2-Cmte of Claims: bill for the relief of Isaac Fessenden. 3-Cmte of Claims: made a report on the ptn of Matilda Drury & other legal reps of Capt Wm S Tillard, late of Md, dec'd. Same cmte, made a report on the ptn of Danl Steenrod, with a bill for his relief. Same cmte, reported bills for the relief of Gervis Foote & Alborne Allen. 4-Cmte on Public Lands: reported an amendatory bill, with title amended to read, "A bill supplemental to an act for the relief of John Hollingsworth, of Blount Co, Ala," approved Jun, 1838, with a report in writing. 5-Cmte on manufactures: adverse report on the ptns of

Aden Bartlett & the heirs of Paul Jones. 6-Cmte on Private Land Claims: adverse report on the ptns of Wm H Cook & Helena Dill. Same cmte: adverse report on the ptn of Jas Greer. 7-Cmte on Revolutionary Pensions: report on the ptn of Jos Bonnell, with a bill for his relief. Same cmte: report on the ptn of Fred'k Hopkins, with a bill for his relief. 8-Cmte on Invalid Pensions: adverse reports on the ptns of Isaac Justice, Catharine H T Johnson, Geo Lynch, Samson Brown, John Burlin, & Dennis Dyot. 9-Cmte on Invalid Pensions: report on the ptn of Jno Farnham, with a bill for his relief. Same cmte: adverse reports on the ptns of Jeremiah Kimball & Theophilus Somerley. Same cmte: adverse reports on the ptns of Darius Hawkins, Palmer Branch, & Chauncey G Store. Same cmte: made a report on the ptn of Arthur R Frogge, with a bill for his relief. Same cmte: referred the ptns of Levi Colmus & Jos Watson, made reports, with bills for their relief. Same cmte: adverse reports on the cases of the heirs of Wilfred Knott, David Bartlett, Jas Butler, Gardner Herring, & John H Goldsby. Same cmte: made a report on the ptn of Simeon Caswell, with a bill for his relief. Same Cmte: adverse report on the cases of Danl Pratt, Eliz Rogers, wid/o Robt Rogers, & Thos Quantrill. 10-Memorial of John A Stephens & others, 481 citizens of Posey Co, Ind, asking a grant of land for the completion of that great national thoroughfare between the Lakes & the Ohio by the improvement of the navigation of the Wabash river. Memorials on the same subject from: Alex'r Devin & 291 citizens of Gibson Co, Ind. Of Wm Kurtz & 28 citizens of Gibson Co, Ind. Of E M Culwek & 30 citizens of Gibson Co, Ind. Of A F Allen & 202 citizens of Orange Co, Ind. Of Saml Hall & 131 citizens of Gibson Co, Ind. Of John R Montgomery & 24 citizens of Gibson Co, Ind. Of Clement Whitney & 36 citizens of Posey Co, Ind. Of H D Allis & 33 citizens of Pundenburg Co, Ind. Of F P Goodsell & 66 citizens of Pundenburg & Warwick Counties, Ind. Of John Burbank & 80 citizens of Pundenburg Co, Ind. Of John Gardner & 48 citizens of Pike & Gibson Counties, Ind. Of Nathan Beach & 26 citizens of Warwick Co, Ind. 11-Ptn of Jas Reilly & 201 others, citizens of Pundenburg Co, Ind, praying for a reduction of postage. 12-Ptn of Walter Vandeusen & others, for reduction of postage. 13-Ptn of M Farrington, for a pension for services in the last war. 14-Ptn of Jacob Dunham, for losses sustained by pirates. 15-Ptn of Thos Fowler, praying for arrears of pension. 16-Ptn of John J Janney & 85 other citizens of Warren Co, Ohio, praying reduction of postage. 17-Ptn of Thos Hunter & Alex'r Caldwell, of Ky, praying to be released from a judgment of the Circuit Court of the U S for the Ky district, for $2,000, against them as bail for Wm Hunter. 18-Ptn of W H Baldwin & 50 other citizens of Ohio, asking entrenchment & reform in the administration of the General Gov't. 19-The ptn & papers of Alex'r Noel, of Adair Co, Ky, were withdrawn from the files of the Clerk's ofc & presented to the House. 20-Withdrawn from the files of the Clerk's ofc: the ptn of Fielding Pratt. 21-Memorial of Oliver Newbury, & 200 ship owners & forwarding merchants of Detroit & ports in Michigan, praying that the general provisions of law applicable to cases on the high seas & in the coasting trade of the U S may be extended over the commerce, shipping, & navigation of the Lakes.

Gurdon Steele, of Boston, died at Trinidad on Jan 2. He was well known in that city as for many years the Cashier of the North Bank. He went to Trinidad for his health, & died in about a fornight after his arrival there. He was a strictly honest, upright, & honorable man. -Atlas

Senate: 1-Ptn from the excs of Saml Ball, praying the payment of a loan office certificate. 2-Ptn of John Hanes was referred to the Cmte on the Judiciary. 2-Mrs Julia Martin had leave to withdraw her papers. 4-Cmte on Military Affairs: asked to be discharged from the further consideration of the memorial of John H Pennington, relating to an appropriation for an experiment upon a flying machine. Also, asked to have the papers in the case of Lt Don Carlos Buell, of the 3rd infty, printed. 5-Cmte on Indian Affairs: reported a bill for the relief of Wm Henson.

The Hon Alex'r Porter, one of the Senators of the U S from Louisiana, died at his plantation in the parish of St Mary, on Jan 13, in his 58th year. He was a native of Ireland, whose father perished on the scaffold, a martyr to the cause in which Emmett & his compatriots laid down their lives. Immediately after this event, the son emigrated to this country, & settled down in Attakapas, La. He was eminently successful in his private affairs, & died wealthy.

From the Pennsylvanian: Count Bradish [Gen Eliovitch] so celebrated in Phil & in other sections of the world, has the skill of humbugging the natives. He is an illustrious swindler.

Stray cow found on Jan 27. Owner to come forward, prove property, pay charges, & take her away. –J D Hinebread, 16th st, North, on Boundary st

The Falmouth Cotton Factory for sale: by resolution adopted at a late meeting of the Stockholders: sale on Mar 20, 1844, in front of the Factory: property is now in full & successful operation; Stockholders cannot manage it themselves.
–J W Ford, Wm Pollock, R C L Moncure

Patapsco Female Institution-Ellicott's Mills, Md: has been brought into successful operation by Mrs A H Lincoln Phelps-Principal. We warmly commend this institution to all who desire to place young ladies in a situation where they will receive a solid education.

Mrd: on Jan 30, by Rev F S Evans, Mr David Weaver to Miss Ellen Wurton.

Mrd: on Jan 16, at *Pleasant Hill*, Chas Co, Md, by Rev P Courtney, John W Jenkins to Emily A, y/d/o the late Jas Gardiner, all of Chas Co.

Died: on Jan 20, in Phil, at the residence of his mother, Chas C P Hough, printer, in his 36th year, formerly a resident of Wash City.

Died: on Jan 20, at Nashville, very suddenly, Maj Henry M Rutledge, the only s/o the Hon Edw Rutledge, one of the signers of the Declaration of Independence, & formerly Govn'r of S C. He was born at Charleston, S C, in Apr, 1775. At age 22, in 1797, he joined at Paris Gen C C Pinckney, in the embassy sent to France, as his private sec; & on his return to the U S, in 1799, he received a commission as Maj in the U S Army, & became also the aid of Gen Pinckney. After several terms in the Legislature of his native State, he removed to Tenn in 1816. –Banner

Died: on Jan 22, at her residence in Leesburg, in her 28th year, Mrs Marion Steward Rhodes, w/o Lt H H Rhodes, of the U S Navy, at present attached to the ship **Constellation**, on a cruise in the Pacific.

Died: at his residence in Westmoreland Co, Va, in his 97th year, Mr Jas Deatty. After faithfully serving his country during the Revolutionary war, he settled himself in the above place, where his long life was a pattern of honesty & strict integrity. He leaves a large circle of friends & relatives. [No date-appears recent.]

Ptn of Wm H Tuck, adm d b n C T A of Levin Boone, filed in a cause pending in PG Co Court, as a court of Equity, for the appointment of a trustee, under the will of Jos Pope, dec'd, on the application of Susan Osborn. The ptn states that, upon the ptn of the said Susan Osborn, such proceedings were had that a sale of the real estate of the said Jos Pope was made & ratified by the court; & that the auditor stated an account of the proceeds by which Eliz Soper, Colemore Pope, Jos Pope, & Saml Marshall are each entitiled to the sum of $346.07, under the will of the dec'd, & that the said sums remain in the hands of the trustee, under the control of the court; that before the commencement of the said proceedings, the said Levin Boone had purchased from the said Eliz, Colmore, Jos & Saml, their interests in the said land of Jos Pope, dec'd, & paid them the purchase money. The petitioner, as administrator of the said Levin Boone, claims to be substituted in their places as to the said fund, & prays that the trustee may be directed to pay the said sums of money to him, with a due proportion of interest; & it appearing to the court that 2 several writs of subpoena have been successively issued, directed to the said Eliz Soper, commanding her to appear & answer the said ptn, which said writs were issued & delivered to the sheriff for service thereof at 20 days preceding the commencement of the terms of the court in which they were respectively returnable, & which have been returned not summoned, it is ordered by PG Co court, sitting as a court of equity, this Jan 9, 1844, that the said petitioner, by causing a copy of this order to be published in some newspaper in D C, give notice to the said Eliz Soper of the substance & object of the said ptn, & warn her to appear in this court on or before the first Mon of Apr next, to answer the premises & show cause why relief may not be granted as prayed.
–Clement Dorsey -Jno B Brooke, Clerk

Died: Jan 28, at his residence, in the vicinity of the Navy Yard, Mr Philip Inch, master painter of the yard, aged 50 years, a naïve of Plymouth, England, but for the last 30 years a resident of Wash City.

Mr Bechnell, of Richmond, Ind, on Jan 13, while crossing the ford at Whitewater on horseback, with his wife behind him, carrying in her arms an infant child, the horse became frightened by a cake of ice drifting against his legs, & precipitated them all into the stream. Mr Bechnell, who could not swim, was carried down the stream some distance, & with considerable difficulty saved himself. Mrs Bechnell & her child were both drowned.

Boarding: Mrs A Cochran, on F, between 13th & 14th sts, has a handsome front Chamber on the 2nd story, in which she will be pleased to accommodate a gentleman, or a gentleman & his lady. Also, 2 or 3 small rooms.

Stray cow came to my farm, near the first toll-gate on the Rockville Turnpike. Owner is to pay charges & take her away. --G Taylor

FRI FEB 2, 1844
Hse/o Reps: 1-Ptn of A Hathaway, for the redemption of a Treas note alleged to have been cancelled, but which exhibits no mark of cancellation. 2-Memorial of B Leas & 101 others, citizens of Huntingdon & Bedford Counties, Pa, praying for a post route from Oblsonia, in Huntingdon Co, to *Fort Lyttleton*, in Bedford Co. 3-Ptn of R Odthoudt, of Brockport, Monroe Co, N Y, claiming an additional pension from the time he left the service in 1813 or 1812, from which time Congress granted him one. 4-Memorial of Gen John McNiel, asking for arrears of pension on account of wounds received in the battle of Bridgewater, Jul 25, 1814, & for injuries received in the U S service at Chicago in Dec, 1822, while in command at that post. 5-Ptn of Robt Dickey, of Harrisburg, Pa, heir of Lt Comm Dickey, for compensation for services rendered during the Revolutionary war. 2-Cmte on Private Lands Claims: bill for the relief of Geo W Allen & Reuben Allen: read twice & committed.

Capt Wm B Shubrick, U S N, has been appointed by the Pres, to be Chief of the Bureau of Provisions & Clothing for the Navy.

Mrd: on Jan 30, by Rev J P Donelan, Mr Edw A Thomas to Miss Eliz J Kreemer, all of Wash City.

Mr J B Perrault, late Cashier of the Citizen's Bank of New Orleans, tried in that city for embezzling $20,729, belonging to the Bank, has been acquitted. Although Perrault had received the money, it had never been in possession of the bank, second, the limit of time which the law allow for prosecuting had expired-some of the transactions charged in the indictment having taken place 2 or 3 years ago.

On Mon last, a little s/o Mr Knox, Morocco dealer, residing in Mulberry near Peal st, Balt, was so dreadfully burnt, from its clothes taking fire, that it died the next day. The accident happened from a pot of varnish taking fire in the room where the child had been left.

Senate: 1-Ptn from Jos Pulcifer, a soldier of the late war, for a pension. 2-Ptn from Robt Perkins, asking compensation for re-capturing a merchant vessel which had been taken by the enemy in 1814. 3-Papers in the case of Rufus Lane to be referred to the Cmte on Pensions. 4-Papers of John Hibbert to be referred to the Cmte on Pensions. 5-Papers of Jos Roby to be referred to the Cmte on Public Lands.

Private boarding: Mrs Stilson, late of Balt, is ready to accommodate a limited number of boarders, at her residence on Missouri ave, between 3rd & 4½ sts.

Circuit Court of Wash Co, D C. Thos Payne has applied to be discharged from imprisonment under the act for the relief of Insolvent Debtors: hearing on the first Mon of Mar next. –Wm Brent, clk

SAT FEB 3, 1844
Annual meeting of the stockholders of the Wash Canal Steam Boat Co, on Mon, 7:30 p m. –Wm Ingle, Chairman

Annual of the stockholders of the steamboat **Phoenix** in Alexandria, Feb 5, at 11 a m. –Stephen Shinn, Treasurer

On Sat at the old Centre Market-house, a lot of very fine Southdews Mutton, grazed & fattened by Col W D Bowie & Dr Benj O Mullikin, of PG Co, Md. The price shall be according to the times. -Otterback & Speiser

Hse/o Reps: 1-Cmte on the Judiciary: bill for the relief of Jos Ramsey: read twice & committed. 2-Message received from the Senate, informing the House of the death of Mr Alex'r Porter, a member of that body. The orphan child was brought to the U S by an uncle at a very tender age. He received in Tenn such an education as could then be obtained at a common country school. In 1809 he emigrated to Louisiana & established himself in the practice of the law. He was intimately acquainted with the Roman, French, & Spanish law. He resigned his judgeship about 1830, & was soon elected to the U S Senate. He died on the 13th ult, at his plantation, after a protracted & painful illness. 3-Ptn of Jos Potter, of Schuylkill Co, Pa, asking compensation for losses sustained in the late war. 4-Ptn of Richd Colton & 35 others citizens of Northfield, Mass, praying for a remission of duties upon the iron imported for the Fitchburg railroad.

Mr Levi Derrick, of Cato, N Y, dropped dead while traveling thence to Skaneateles on Monday night.

Late from Texas. From the correspondence between Gen Thompson & M de Bocanegra it appears that Santa Anna has never had any intentions of relinquishing the claims of the Mexican Gov't to the territory of Texas. The bill for the annexation of Texas to the U S has met with great favor in the Texian Congress. Jas B Miller has been appointed Sec of the Treas, & Thos Wm Ward Com'r of the Genr'l Land Ofc. About 195 emigrants arrived at Galveston, a few days since, from Germany. They are about settling on the Colorado. The Texian Democrat announces the arrival in the country of Gen Mercer, a distinguished citizen of Va. He is concerned in some of the recent contracts for colonization in Texas. He proposes to visit Germany soon.

Heights of Gtwn: for rent, a desirable residence on Congress st, Gtwn, now occupied by Thos B Addison. The house is large & convenient, & a large lot of ground belongs to it. Possession given on Apr 1 next. Apply to the subscriber at the 3rd Auditor's ofc, or at his residence adjoining the premises. –John Harry

The Caddo [Louisiana] Gaz of the 10th ult states that Judge Hansford was most cruelly murdered a few days previous in Harrison Co, Texas, by an old man named Mosely & his son-in-law, whose name is Bullard. The murder originated in a quarrel respecting a lawsuit.

Thos Huff, a mail contractor & carrier between Rockport & Fredonia, Ind, was arrested yesterday at the post ofc in this city, charged with robbing the mail. –Louisville Journal, 27th ult

Mrd: on Feb 1, by Rev Mr Samson, Mr Geo Cudliff to Miss Somerville Underwood, both of Fredericksburg, Va.

Died: on Feb 2, after an illness which she bore with Christian fortitude & resignation, Therese Luxen, aged 55 years. Her funeral is this evening at 3 o'clock, from the residence of her son-in-law, J H Smithson, on 4½ st.

Died: on Jan 21, 1844, in Poolesville, Md, Mrs Sarah Ann E Poole, w/o Dr Thos Poole, in her 36th year. Respected & beloved while living, her memory will be warmly cherished by all who knew her.

New Family Grocery & Variety Store: on Capitol Hill, a few rods southeast of the south Capitol gate. -Wm W Stewart

MON FEB 5, 1844
Annapolis Herald: Walter W W Bowie, of PG Co, Md, has consented to be the Democratic candidate for Congress for the First District of Md.

On Board steamboat **Sydney**, Jan 30, 1844. To Capt J W Rogers: the undersigned, passengers in your boat, cannot take leave of your without a full acknowledgment of your kindness & most judicious conduct, passing the whole distance of some 60 miles throught ice from 9 to 10 inches thick.

J M Mason	J H Palmer	E A Stribling
Thos Towson	C B Lovell	E P Molineaux
Peter Adams	D W Kennedy	L M Prevost, jr
J Hamilton Potter	Jno S Wootton, jr	F Pratt, jr
E W Holmes	A J Abbott	
Jos T Ligon	C W Anderson	

Hse/o Reps: 1-Cmte of the Whole: bill for the relief of John T McLaughlin was read a 3rd time & passed. 2-Bill for the relief of Jane McGuire, wid/o Thos McGuire: to be reported. 3-Bill for the relief of Jos Kemball: to be reported. 4-Bill granting an increase of pension to Isaac Plummer: to be reported. 5-Bill for the relief of Jonathan Bean: to be reported. 6-Bill for the relief of John P Schuyler coming up, & giving rise to some discussion. 7-Ptn of Medad Butler, for a pension for services in the Revolution. 8-Ptn of Wm F Pain & 89 other citizens of Ill, praying a grant of land in the Wabash valley for the improvement of the Wabash river from Terre Haute to the Ohio river. Ptn of Wm Thume & 48 others, citizens of Ill, for the same. 9-Memorial of John Tucker, Pres of the Phil & Reading Railroad Co, & others, Presidents of sundry railroad companies, & individual citizens, urging the restoration of the law which admitted iron for railroads free of duty. 10-Resolutions of the Genr'l Assembly of Georgia, in support of the claims for losses sustained by Jas L Daniel & others by occasion of the late Creek war, & which have been paid by the State.

Mr Edw O'Connor, formerly of N Y, & who had resided in Boston but a short time, committed suicide on Tue from the effects of laudanum taken the previous evening. He left a letter for his wife, to whom he had been married about 4 months, & who left the city on Mon on a visit to her friends in Portland, in which he assigned the depression of his pecuniary circumstances as the reason for the act.

Meeting of the Members of the Bar of the Supreme Court of N C, held at the Courtroom in the Capitol on Jan 25, 1844: Tribute to the memory of the Hon Wm Gaston, late a Judge of the Supreme Court, struck down suddenly by the hand of God in the midst of his judicial labors; dying, as he had lived, in the devoted service of his country. Copy of the proceedings to be transmitted to his family.

Mr Robt Maynard, who sustained a fracture of the ankle joint in the accident of the Club-house, has had to submit to the amputation of his leg at the knee. He bore the operation manfully. It has been some 2 days since it was performed, & he is doing well. –Richmond Compiler

Death of Benj Romaine. Benj Romaine, Revolutionary patriot, departed in his 82nd year. He had been for many years past the custodian of the bones of the martyrs of the Prison Ships deposited in the vault in Jackson st, in Brooklyn, N Y. 13 large coffins filled with the bones of these heroes are lying in the vault, & an empty coffin lined with tin in their midst it is understood Mr Romaine deposited there for his own remains. Now that the old verteran has left us, it is probable that effective measures ill be taken to give the martyrs a becoming monument. –Brooklyn Star [No date-current item.]

On Wed on board the steamboat **Farmer**, running from Market st, Phil, to Camden, there was a leak in some part of the boat, & after the arrival of the boat at the wharf Capt Redrow went below to look for the leak. While thus occupied, & directly under the crank, the boat was started, & the ponderous mass of iron, in descending, came in contact with the back part of the head, crushing the skull in a most frightful manner, & causing instant death. No blame is to be attached to the engineer, as the captain neglected to inform him that he was going below.

Last Wed Chas Bottsford & Geo Gage were arrested at N Y on a warrant from S Rapelje, charged with robbing the U S mail in Apr last.

Household furniture at auction: on Feb 9, at the residence of Miss Harrison, on E st, between 10th & 11th sts, the household & kitchen furniture.
-Robt W Dyer & Co, aucts

Accounts from Florida to Jan 27th, state that Lt Alex'r T Hoffman, of the 2nd regt U S Infty, a native of N Y, died at St Augustine on the preceding Thu.

Between the Deaths & Marriages in the Newark Daily of Feb 1, appears this notice: Unmarried. "At the Jan Term of the Court of Chancery of this State, Thos J Geurin & Jane, his wife, of the county of Morris, were divorced by a decree of said Court."

Died: on Jan 28, Theodore Middleton, of PG Co, Md, in his 85th year. He was a captain in the Revolutionary war, & during his whole life maintained a character for probity & honor unsurpassed.

Died: yesterday, in Wash City, suddenly, in his 64th year, Mr Owen McCue, a native of the county of Donegal, Ireland, but for the last 40 years a citizen of this place, leaving an orphan daughter & many disconsolate friends to deplore his loss. His funeral will take place from his late residence, on 9th st, near F, this afternoon at 3 o'clock, which the members of the Sodalities of the Blessed Virgin & other friends of the dec'd are invited to attend. He attended early mass & received the holy communion in St Matthew's Catholic Church yesterday, at 8 o'clock, & at 9 his soul had wafted "on angel's wings to heaven." He was an affectionate husband, a tender parent, a good citizen, a kind friend, & an honest man. May he rest in peace! -C

TUE FEB 6, 1844
Hse/o Reps: 1-Ptn of John Robinson, praying compensation for losses in the late war with England. 2-Ptn of Henry King, exc, praying the passage of a law for the settlement of the accounts of his testator for services as an ofcr in the Revolutionary war. 3-Ptn of Nelly Hawkins & 63 others, citizens of Indiana & Ky, praying Congress for a grant of the unsold lands in the Vincennes land district to complete the entire line of canal from Lake Erie to the Ohio river at Evansville. Memorial of Wesley Jones & 86 others, citizens of Orange Co, Ind, asking for the same. 4-Ptn of Solomon Price & 33 others, citizens of Ill, praying a grant of public land for the improvement of the Kaskaskia river. 5-Ptn of Dunning McVain for extra compensation as a mail contractor. Same ptn for Peters, Moore & Co. 6-Ptn of F J B Crane & others, in favor of a reduction in the rates of postage. 7-Ptn of Audley Clarke & others, of Newport, R I, praying for indemnity for French spoliations. 8-Ptn of W J H Bayley & others, of Bristol, praying for a reduction of postage & the abolition of the franking privilege. 9-Ptn of Thos Hadley & 45 others, citizens of Brandford, N H, praying for the reduction of postage. Ptn of C C Huchins & 22 others, citizens of Bath, N H, for the same. 10-Request to withdraw from the file of the House the ptn of Alice Usher, of Gloucester, R I.

Senate: 1-Ptn from Peter Amie, a seaman, asking a pension. 2-Ptn from Reuben M Gibbs, a soldier in the last war with Great Britain, asking arrears of pension. 3-Ptn from J P Hutchinson, late consul at Lisbon, asking compensation for diplomatic services during the absence of the Charge d'Affaires. 4-Additional documents presented in the case of John G Tibbetts. 5-Additional documents in relation to the ptn of Miles King, & the assignees of the late Pennsylvania Bank of the U S, were presented. 6-Cmte on Revolutionary Claims: asking to be discharged from the further consideration of the memorial of the son & heir of the Count de Grasse. 7-Cmte on Revolutionary Claims: adverse report on the memorial of the heirs of Danl Trueheart. Same cmte, an adverse report on the case of the heirs of Nathan Daggett; adverse report on the case of Thos D Conover. Same cmte, asking to be discharged from the memorial of W C McCall, & that it be referred to the Cmte on Naval Affairs. 8-Cmte of Claims: adverse report on the memorial of Wm A Weaver, asking further payment as superintending clerk of the census of 1840, which was ordered to be printed. 9-Cmte on Pensions: to inquire into allowing a pension to Lt Sales Hatfield, now of Henry Co, Ill, for his meritorious & gallant services at the head of his company of volunteer riflemen in the sortie at *Fort Erie* on Sep 17, 1814.

Trustee's sale: by virtue of a deed of trust, executed by Chas A Howle, on Mar 28, 1835: sale on Feb 17, of lot 13 in square 453, on I st. –Johnson Hellen, Trustee -Robt W Dyer & Co, aucts

Trustee's sale: by deed of trust executed by Josiah Essex, on Jan 9, 1838: sale on Feb 19, of lot 13 in sq 453, on I st. –Johnson Hellen, Trustee -Robt W Dyer & Co, aucts

Marshal's sale: in virtue of a wit of fieri facias, issued by the Circuit Court of Wash Co, D C: sale on Mar 6 next: all that piece of parcel of ground in Wash City, known as lot 12 in square 321, with all the legal estates & interest of Geo Miller, late of said county, in said lot, with improvements thereon, being a frame house, 1½ stories high in front, & a 2 story brick in the rear. Seized & levied upon as the property of the said Geo Miller, & sold to satisfy judicials 27 to Nov Term, 1843, in favor of John J Lloyd. –Alex'r Hunter, Marshal D C [Sale postponed until May 1 next.]

Died: on Jan 25, at his residence, in Hallowell, Maine, Dr Benj Page, aged 74 years. The medical works of New England were enriched by his observations & experience.

Died: on Feb 4, in Wash City, Mrs Ann Wells, aged 74 years. Her funeral will be from the residence of Mr Thos Connor, her son-in-law, on I st, near the West Market, this morning at 9 o'clock.

Died: on Dec 29 last, at his farm, in Chickasaw Co, Miss, of consumption, Chas O'Neale Bowen, in his 27th year, s/o Capt Geo Bowen, of Waterloo, Laurens District, S C. Though for a long time confined to his room anterior to his death, he bore his afflictions with Christian fortitude & resignation, retaining his senses to the very last.

WED FEB 7, 1844
Hse/o Reps: 1-Ptn of Juliana Shaw for a pension. 2-Ptn of Millard Fillmore & others, praying for an appropriation to widen Buffalo creek. 3-Ptn of Edw J Kelly, praying for compensation for money lost in its transmission through the post ofc. 4-Ptn of Arad Gilbert & 175 others, & also the ptn of Nathan Puffer & 67 others, of Mass, praying Congress to recognize the independence of Hayti. 5-Ptn of Thos Gregg, of Pa, praying an appropriation to test a ball-proof vessel invented by him, & to extend his patent right for the same. 6-Ptn of Eliz Wilson, of Indiana, asking a pension on account of her late husband, accompainied by sundry vouchers & a copy of Butler's History of Ky. 7-Ptn of Abner E Van Ness, of Casa Co, Ind, praying indemnity for losses sustained while engaged in surveying the public lands. 8-Ptn of Jas Pepper for confirmation to a certain entry of land.

Dick Ratcliff, a half-breed, was hung in the Cherokee nation in the early part of last month for the murder of his wife. He was wealthy, & had previously enjoyed a respectable reputation, & had been sheriff of one of the districts. The source of his crime was intemperance.

Circuit Court of Wash Co, D C. Fred'k W Mantz has applied to be discharged from imprisonment under the act for the relief of Insolvent Debtors: hearing on the first Mon in Mar next. –Wm Brent, clk

Senate: 1-Ptn from David Jones & Erastus Bailey, asking the right of pre-emption to certain lands in the Green Bay district. 2-Cmte on Commerce: report on the case of Thos M Latham, referring the papers in the case to the Sec of War. 3-Cmte on Pensions: adverse reports on the ptns of Nicholas Thomas; of the widow of Benj Coit; of the widow of Abraham Guiles; & of Jacob Olingary. 4-Mr Fulton, on leave, introduced a bill for the relief of Ephraim D Dixon. 5-House bill for the relief of Jno McLaughlin was referred to the Cmte on Military Affairs.

Died: on Feb 5, Davis S Simmons, [stonecutter,] in his 24th year. Friends of the family, & the Northern Liberty Fire Co, of which he was a member, are invited to his funeral this day, at 2 o'clock, from his late residence on L st, between 9th & 10th sts.

Port Gibson [Miss] Herald: accident in that county on Jan 16: two boys, a son & a brother of Col M D Shelby, were riding to school mounted on the same horse: a tree fell upon them, instantly killed the s/o Col Shelby, a boy about 7 years of age, & also the horse upon which he rode. The other had one of his ribs broken, & is otherwise very badly injured.

On Sun, 2 little sons of Mr Wm Umberger, innkeeper, Wm & Jacob, 7 & 9 years of age, were drowned in the Susquehanna, opposite Harrisburg, Pa, when the ice broke through while playing on it.

Yesterday, Wm Darnoldson, living about 4 miles from Gtwn, presented himself at the Bank of the Metropolis with a check, purporting to be drawn on said bank by Francis A Dodge, for $89.95. It was evident it was a miserable attempt at fraud & forgery. He was committed to prison for want of bail.

It was reported that Horace Stone, a young man of very dissolute habits, was found lying in the canal near Fowler's Tavern, on Sat night, & there may have been foul play. He was seen to have a fight with Fowler and either tumbled or jumped into the canal, whereby he broke the ice & was drowned. The circumstances should be thoroughly & judicially investigated.

THU FEB 8, 1844
Senate: 1-Additional documents in the case of David Myerlee were presented. 2-Ptn from Ann Maria Baldwin, asking compensation for loss of time & services in attending upon the court in D C as a witness in the case of R W White & Richd White for the burning of the Treasury bldg in 1834. 3-Ptn from the widow & heirs of Albert Pawling, of ofcr of the Revolution, asking to be allowed commutation pay. 4-Ptn from Wm P McMurtrie, asking reimbursement of expenses incurred in his outfit to join the exploring squadron as a member of the scientific corps, which appointment was revoked before the squadron left the U S. 5-Ptn from Lardner Vanuxen, in behalf of the heirs of Jas Vanuxen, asking indemnity for French spoliations prior to 1800. The memorialist asks that measures may be taken to

collect the amount, & copies of such evidence of each claim, as a just people should require for liquidation. 6-Ptn from the wid/o Jonas Sautell, a Revolutionary soldier, for a pension. 7-Ptn from the wid/o Jas Grey, a Revolutionary soldier, for a pension. 8-Ptn from the selectmen of Camden, Maine, asking that a pension may be granted to the widow of Peter Barrow, a Revolutionary soldier. 9-Cmte on Commerce: bill for the relief of Hiram Murch, with a report. 10-Cmte on Military Affairs: unfavorable report on the ptn of Geo Tyler & others. 11-Cmte on Private Land Claims: unfavorable report on the ptn of Philip C S Barbour.

The U S brig **Lawrence** arrived at Pensacola on Jan 25, in 12 days from Santa Martha; ofcrs & crew quite well. The following list of the ofcrs of the vessel has been forwarded to us for publication:

Wm H Gardner, Cmder
Henry J Hartstene & Wm B Beverley, Lts:
T Harman Patterson, Acting Lt
J Fenwick Stenson, Acting Master
Andrew D Crosby, Purser
John O'C Barclay, Assist Surgeon

Jas H Spotts, Passed Midshipman
Francis B Wright, Master's Mate
John McKinley, Acting Boatswain
Geo Marshall, Acting Gunner
Chas B Sterling, Purser's Steward

FRI FEB 9, 1844
Fire & loss of life: in Black Neck, Fairfield township, N J, on Sun last, by which the house of Mr John Robinson, with its contents, was consumed; & 2 children, Danl & Eliz Jane Newton, 15 years & 9 years, perished in the flames.

Wash Corp: 1-Ptn of Saml M Emery, in relation to a theatrical license: referred. 2-Cmte of Claims: to whom was referred the ptn of Richardson Gray, asked to be discharged from its further consideration. From the same cmte: an act for the relief of R Hartwell: read twice.

For rent: a desirable residence called *Oakville*, in the neighborhood of Wash & Alexandria: dwlg house contains 9 rooms, a garret, kitchen, & out-houses in excellent repair. Apply at the ofc of Messrs Swann, on 5th st, opposite the City Hall.

We learn from Boston that Abner Rogers has been acquitted of the willful murder of Mr Lincoln, Warden of the Massachusetts State Prison. The jury returned a verdict of "not guilty, by reason of insanity." Rogers was conveyed to the Insane Hospital at Worcester.

Mrs Phebe Hunter, a member of the Soc of Friends, who died lately at New Orleans, was born 84 years ago in the city of Phil, & was an acquaintance of the great Franklin. She was the mother of Lt Hunter, of the Navy, the inventor of submerged propellers for steamships.

Orphan's Court of Wash Co, D C. Letters of administraton on the personal estate of John J Dermott, late of said county, dec'd. –Rd Dement, adm

Died: on Feb 8, after an illness of 3 days, of the scarlet fever, Henry Allen, s/o Thos D & Merceiner Bell, aged 2 years & 4 months. His funeral is today at 4 o'clock.

Mrd: on Feb 4, by Rev Mr Van Horseigh, Mr Geo Bully to Mrs Caroline Rhodes, formerly Miss Crampton, all of the Navy Yard.

Mrd: on Feb 5, by Rev Wm Matthews, Thos Contee Magruder, of Wash City, to E Olivia, d/o the late Capt Geo Morgan, of St Mary's Co, Md.

Hse/o Reps: 1-Memorial of Harvey Newcomb & 52 others, of Needham, relating to the official desecration of the Sabbath. 2-Memorial of Jabez W Gott, of Rockport, in support of the claim of several citizens of that town, for materials furnished for the Breakwater. 3-Ptn of John H Russell & others, for allowance of fishing bounty. 4-Ptn of Eliz Graves for an increase of pension. 5-Ptn of Elisha Adams, praying for an indemnity from the Govn't for continental paper. 6-Ptn of Susannah Powell. [No other information.] 7-Ptn of Mary Ann Brenner, of Putnam Co, Ind, & of other citizens, asking Congress to give relief to her for the sum of $77.57 she advanced & paid into the Register's ofc at Crawfordsville, Ind, for the purpose of purchasing a certain tract of land therein named. 8-Ptn of Jacob Lebengood, a Revolutionary invalid soldier, praying for a pension. 9-Ptn of Jas Donabay, a soldier of the Revolutionary & Indian wars, praying for a pension. 10-Ptn of Esther Standish, for a pension.

Senate: 1-Ptn from Lewis H Bates & Wm Lacon, asking indemnity for an illegal seizure & detention of their property by the collector of N Y. 2-Mr Jarnagin asked leave to withdraw the papers of Hugh Barton, adm of Andrew Stewart, but the Senate refused leave. 3-Cmte of Claims: bill for the relief of Ephraim D Dixon, without amendment. 4-Cmte on Indian Affairs: bill for the relief of the legal reps of Wm Walker, without amendment, & with a written report, recommending that the bill be indefinitely postponed. 5-Cmte on Public Lands: bill for the relief of Henry Newsman, with amendments, with a report, which was ordered to be printed. 6-Cmte on Pensions: to inquire into allowing to Esther J Burroughs, wid/o Norman Burroughs, a Revolutionary soldier, the benefit of the law of Congress granting half pay & pensions to certain widows of those who served in the Revolutionary war.

SAT FEB 10, 1844
Senate: 1-Cmte of Claims: asking to be discharged from the further consideration of the claim of John Washington. 2-Cmte on Public Lands: two bills for the relief of Jos Campau, with reports in each case; which were ordered to be printed.

On Thu night a fire broke out in the bldgs on the corner of Gay & Lombard sts, Balt, occupied by various Notaries Public, Insurance Agents, etc. The loss is fully covered by insurance. The bldgs were owned by Messrs John Donnell & Sons, whose counting room was in a part of them.

Bargain in Dry Goods: 2nd door west of 7th st, & opposite the Centre Market.
–Wm M Perry

The Hon Henry A Wise, one of the Reps in Congress from Va, has been appointed to be Minister of the U S to the Brazils. His nomination was confirmed by the Senate yesterday.

Sir Hudson Lowe, to whom was entrusted the custody of Napoleon at St Helena, died in London on the 10th ult, of paralysis.

Naval: Michl Cummings, seaman, on board of the U S brig **Lawrence**, was killed [day not mentioned] by the premature & accidental explosion of the cartridge while engaged in ramming a gun, the crew being exercised at the time. His body was blow overboard, & sunk immediately.

Mr Danl S Clark, of New Orleans, met with an accident on Sun week, while out gunning with a party of friends, his fowling piece accidentally discharged, & both his thumbs were blown away. He likewise received some injury in his face.

Cornell, who was indicted for the murder of his wife at Jamestown, N Y, last Feb, had his trial at Mayville last week: resulted in a verdict of guilty. He was sentenced to be hung on Mar 14 next.

The Larnards, charged with the robbery of the Milbury Bank, have been tried in Worcester, Mass, & found guilty.

Hse/o Reps: 1-Ptn of John Gilchrist & 54 others, citizens of Butler Co, Pa, praying for the construction of a national road from the Cumberland road, near the base of Laurel Hill, by the arsenals of Pittsburg & Meadville, to the harbor of Erie. 2-Ptn of Jas Miles & 68 others, citizens of Erie Co, Pa, praying for an appropriation to improve the harbor of Erie. 3-Memorial of Allen Sackrider & 507 others, citizens of Clarke Co, Ill, asking a grant of land from contiguous land districts, to complete the national thoroughfare between the Lakes & the Ohio river, by the improvement of the navigation of the Wabash. The memorial of David Bailey & 76 others, citizens of Edgar Co, Ill, upon the same subject. 4-Ptn of John Anderson; ptn of A E Rhodes & 32 others: all citizens of Fulton, Miami, & Wabash Counties, Ind, praying the establishment of a mail route from Rochester, Fulton Co, via Troy, Gilead, Niconza, Jos Beckner's, to Wabash, in Wabash Co.

Hse/o Reps: [Ptns presented by John Quincy Adams at the 28th Congress, 1st session, with the disposal of them by the House. Continued from the Nat'l Intell of Dec 28, 1843.]

1-Hinshaw, Seth, & citizens of Indiana, against the annexation of Texas. Foreign Affairs.
Same for: Conant, A H, & citizens of Illinois; Crocker, Russel, & inhabitants of Montgomery.
2-Aldrich, Susan, of Mendon, Worcester Co, Mass, Revolutionary widow's pension. Revolutionary Pensions.
3-Houghton, Jacob, inhabitants of Chautauque Co, N Y. Huldah Saxton, widow of Jas Saxton; pension. Revolutionary Pensions.
4-Chapin, Willard, & citizens of Ashtabula Co, amend the Constitution, abolish property representation, or to dissolve. Judiciary.
5-Herbert, Jacob, & legal voters of Austinsburg, Ashtabula Co, Ohio, against the American slave trade. Excluded by the Speaker.
6-Hawley, C E & legal voters of Austinsburg, Ashtabula Co, Ohio, against any rule limiting the right of ptn. Judiciary,
7-Chaffee, Hosea R & citizens of Woodstock, Conn. 1-Abolish slavery & slave trade in D C & Territories. 2-To admit neither Florida nor any new State whose Constitution tolerates slavery. 3-Measures for amending the Constitution to abolish slavery, or to release the people of each State from sustaining it. 4-To form diplomatic & commercial relations with the Republic of Hayti. Excluded by decision of the Speaker, sustained an appeal by the House as within the rule. Same for: Stone, Jasper & citizens of Roxborough, Mass. Same subjects for: Holmes, Nathaniel, & citizens of Provincetown, Mass.
8-Nicholson-Revolutionary Pensions.
9-De Grass, Count-Revolutionary Pensions.
10-Rochambeau, heirs of Marshal Count de-Revolutionary Pensions.
11-Hibbart, Joel B & citizens of Cortland Co, N Y, against the annexation of Texas or any State whose Constitution tolerates slavery. Foreign Affairs.
12-Jackson, Alex'r S, of Newton Middlesex Co, Mass, & 28 others, for an invalid pension. Invalid Pensions.
13-Tappan, Arthur, chairman of a meeting at Brooklyn, against the annexation of Texas. Judiciary.
14-Jewett, Jos & others, in behalf of Keziah Hobart, for a pension. Revolutionary Pensions.
15-Secor, P S & citizens of Illinois, to repeal the 21st rule. Laid on the table.
16-Sperey, Levinus, & citizens of Illinois, demand the repeal of the 21st rule. Laid on the table.
17-Dobbins, Robt B & inhabitants of Illinois, against the annexation of Texas, & ask to be heard by a cmte. Foreign Affairs.
18-De Kalb's heirs. Revolutionary Claims.
19-Green, Thos C & inhabitants of Saratoga, against the annexation of Texas. Judiciary. Same for: Thayer, Eliphaz, & citizens of Braintree, Mass.

20-Rogers, Susan, wid/o Dr Wm Rogers. Revolutionary Pensions.
21-Ames, Julius R & inhabitants of Albany Co, against the annexation of Texas.
22-Sprague, Horatio.
23-Wileman, Mahlon, & citizens of Ohio, measures to obsolve the citizens of Ohio from all participation in support of slavery. Judiciary.
24-Thomas, Jacob, & citizens of Ohio, same prayer. Judiciary.
25-Moore, Wm, & people of Ohio, abolish all laws sanctioning slavery, Excluded by rule.
26-Gray, Smith, & citizens of Walpole, Norfolk Co, Mass, to abolish property representation, or extend it.
27-Wileman, Mahlon, citizens of Ohio, discard movements for the annexation of Texas. Foreign Affairs. Same for: Bishop, David, & citizens of Ohio.
28-Wright, R N & citizens of Boone Co, Ill, remonstrance against the annexation of Texas. Foreign Affairs. Same for: Warren, Jas H, & citizens of Illinois; Losey, Lucretia H, & citizens of Ill; Woodruff, Geo H, & citizens of Illinois.
29-Telfair, Mary M, of Providence, R I, bounty lands & final settlement of certificates. Revolutionary Claims.
30-Brown, Thos H of Alexandria, pension. Invalid Pensions.
31-Frosser, Thos, of Jersey City, N J, to reduce duties on iron. Ways & Means.
32-Ballard, Joshua, & voters of Cortland Co, N Y, to repeal all laws authorizing the sale in D C of persons for jail fees. Judiciary.
33-Williams, Danl, & citizens of Cayuga Co, N Y, to cut off the slave representation. Judiciary.
34-Wallace, John, & citizens of Muskingum Co, Ohio, amendment of the Constitution, representation, & free population. Select cmte on the subject.
35-Hubbard, Wm G, & inhabitants of Illinois, protest against the annexation of Texas. Foreign Affairs. Same for: Reed, Rowland T, & citizens of Indiana; Edgerton Walter, & citizens of Indiana..
36-Young, Ezekiel J, & citizens of Phil, appropriation for a dock. Commerce
37-Teale, Hiram. Claims.
38-Baldwin, Saml, & citizens of Ohio, absolve citizens of Ohio from all participation in support of the continuance of slavery in the U S & Territories. Judiciary.
39-Burdick, Perry, town of Scott, Cortland Co, N Y. Revolutionary Pensions. Barber, Alonzo, D C etc, Cortland & Madison Counties, in aid of Burdick's ptn for a pension.
40-Thurman, Richardson, jr, & inhabitants of Clinton & Essex, N Y, to abolish slavery & the slave trade wherever Congress has jurisdiction. Excluded.
41-Barton, Eliza L, & women of Clinton Co, N Y, to abolish slavery & the slave trade in D C. Excluded. Same subject: Thomas, John, & voters of Cortland Co, N Y.
42-Hoag, Pliny E & men & women of Clinton Co, N Y, to prohibit domestic slave trade. Excluded. Same for: Story, Rachael, & females of same.
43-Jay, John, & citizens of N Y, to prohibit U S ofcrs from aiding to capture fugitive slaves. In hands of Speaker.

44-Edward, Jos, of Salem, Essex Co, Mass, to forbid the employment of slaves in & about the Capitol. Cmte on Public Bldgs & Public Grounds.
45-Bacon, Hannah. Foreign Affairs.
46-Dunbar, Amasa, dghtr of, relief. Revolutionary Pensions.
47-Gibson, A P. Foreign Affairs.
48-Rayall, Mrs Anne. Revolutionary Pensions.
49-Schnell, Jas H. Public Bldgs, etc.
50-Wright, Wm. Judiciary

Circuit Court of Wash Co, D C. Ashton Garret has applied to be discharged from imprisonment under the act for the relief of Insolvent Debtors: hearing on the first Mon in Mar next. –Wm Brent, clk

Public Sale: by virtue of an order from the Orphan's Court of Chas Co, Md: sale on Feb 27, all the personal estate of Thos H Ching, dec'd, consisting of 2 likely negro men, one negro boy, 2 negro women, & one small boy aged about 2 years.
–John M Latimer, Thos K Ching, adms of Thos H Ching, dec'd.

Wm H Keevil, fashionable, practical, & one price Hatter, 74 Balt st, near Holiday st, Balt, Md.

Mrd: on Feb 8, in St John's Church, by Rev Wm Hawley, Alex'r H Evans, [formerly of Va] to Miss Maria Matilda, d/o the late Col Richd Coxe, all of Wash City.

Mrd: on Feb 1, by Rev Dr Mines, at *Hayes*, the residence of Robt P Dunlop, Nathan Lufborough to Mrs Harriet Margaret Thomas, both of Montgomery Co, Md.

Died: yesterday, after an illness of only a few hours, of malignant scarlet fever, Mary Eliz Cambloss, in her 12th year, d/o Geo Cambloss. Her funeral is this afternoon at 4 o'clock.

MON FEB 12, 1844
The Utica Gaz of Sat chronicles the death of Hon Jos Kirkland, one of the pioneers of that city. He has occupied a prominent position in Oneida Co for the last half century; & was the first Mayor of Utica. More than 20 years ago he served one year as a Rep in Congress from his district.

The following legacies have been left by Israel Munson, a worthy citizen of Boston, who died on Fri week, at an advanced age:
Mass Gen Hosp: $20,000   Blind Asylum: $4,000
Harvard College: $15,000   Farm School: $3,000
Yale College: $15,000   Eye & Ear Infirmary: $3,000
Yale Medical School: $5,000   Retreat at Hartford: $5,000

Richd R Cuyler has been appointed by the Pres to be Atty of the U S for the District of Georgia, in the place of Alex'r Drysdale.

Louis Ramson was arrested on Feb 1, at New Orleans, on the charge of picking a gentleman's pocket, in the St Charles Hotel. He was taken to the First Municipality prison & locked up; a short time afterwards it was discovered he had hung himself.

Mr J S Rice, of Hartford, Conn, a few days since, with one of Wesson's cast steel rifles, hit a target at the distance of 208 years seven times successively. So says the Times.

Mr Joshua Dyett, who for some time has been connected with the editorial management of the N Y Citizen, died very suddenly of disease of the heart, at his residence in Carmine st, on Tue morning.

Promotions in the Navy:
Wm B Shubrick, a Capt in the Navy, to be Chief of the Bureau of Provisions & Clothing, vice Chas W Goldsborough, dec'd.
Wm K Latimer, to be a Capt in the Navy from Jul 17, 1843, vice Capt Saml Woodhouse, dec'd.
Abraham S Ten Eick, now a Cmder, to be a Capt in the Navy from Dec 10, 1843, vice vacancy occasioned by the resignation of Capt Wm A Spencer.
John Pope, to be a Cmder in the Navy from Feb 15, 1843, vice Cmder Wm Boerum, dec'd.
Levin M Powell, to be a Cmder in the Navy from Jun 24, 1843, vice Cmder Edw S Johnson, dec'd.
Chas Wilkes, to be a Cmder in the Navy, from Jun 13, 1843, vice Cmder Alex'r J Dallas, dec'd.
Elisha Peak, to be a Cmder in the Navy, from Jul 17, 1843, vice Cmder Wm K Latimer, promoted.
Thos J Manning, now a Lt, to be a Cmder in the Navy from Jul 24, 1843, vice Cmder Alex'r B Pinkham, dec'd.
Wm Pearson, now a Lt, to be a Cmder in the Navy from Dec 10, 1843, vice Cmder A S Ten Eick, promoted.
Jos H Adams, to be a Lt in the Navy from Feb 15, 1843, vice Lt John Pope, promoted.
Wm A Parker, to be a Lt in the Navy from May 16, 1843, vice Lt Jas T Homans, resigned.
Jas D Johnston, to be a Lt in the Navy from Jun 24, 1843, vice Lt Levin M Powell, promoted.
John N Maffit, to be a Lt in the Navy from Jun 25, 1843, vice Lt John B Cutting, dec'd.
Washington Gwathmey, Wm Ronckendorff, Wm B Beverly, & John Hall, to be Lts in the Navy from Jun 28, 1843, from which time they were promoted, in the recess,

to fill vacancies occasioned by the loss of Lts A E Downes, Geo M McCreery, Wm B Swann, & Hunn Gansevoort, on board the schnr **Grampus**.
Francis Lowry, to be a Lt in the Navy from Jun 4, 1843, to fill the vacancy occasioned by the dismission of Lt Edw M Vail.
Wm E Leroy, to be a Lt in the Navy from Jul 13, 1843, vice Lt Chas Wilkes, promoted.
Maxwell Woodhull, to be a Lt in the Navy from Jul 17, 1843, vice Lt Elisha Peck, promoted.
Strong B Thompson, now a Passed Midshipman, to be a Lt in the Navy from Jul 24, 1843, vice Lt Thos J Manning, promoted.
Lafayette Maynard, now a Passed Midshipman, to be a Lt in the Navy from Oct 19, 1843, to fill the vacancy occasioned by the cashiering of Lt A R Taliaferro.
Roger A Stembel, now a Passed Midshipman, to be a Lt in the Navy from Oct 26, 1843, vice Lt Geo J Wyche, dec'd.
Geo Colvocoressis, now a Passed Midshipman, to be a Lt in the Navy from Dec 7, 1843, vice Lt A H Marbury, dec'd.
Washington Reid, now a Passed Midshipman, to be a Lt in the Navy from Dec 10, 1843, vice Lt Wm Pearson, promoted.
Francis S Haggerty, now a Passed Midshipman, to be a Lt in the Navy from Dec 19, 1843, vice Lt Wm H H Robertson, dec'd.
Wm Worthington Russell, to be a 2nd Lt in the Marine Corps from Apr 5, 1843, at which time he was appointed to fill a vacancy occasioned by the resignation of 2nd Lt John J Berrett.

Hse/o Reps: 1-Papers in relation to the case of John P Landernau for the confirmation of a land claim: referred. 2-Ptn of C W Turner, for the refunding of foreign tonnage duties paid on ship **Alexandria**, at New Orleans. 3-Ptn of Peter L Lake, & 43 citizens of Southport, Wisconsin Territory, praying Congress to improve the Fox & Wisconsin rivers.

Public auction of the Cooper Cotton Co, in Dayton, Ohio: on May 13 next. Order of the stockholders. –Alex'r Grimes, Henry Stoddard, Saml McPherson, David Stout, John W Van Cleve, cmte

Died: on Feb 2, at Farmington, Maine, Mrs Louisa A Follansbee, w/o Mr Joshua Follansbee, aged 20, after an illness of only 10 days. Mrs F was well known in this city, having resided for 3 years in the family of her uncle, Dr Sewall. Her last illness was one of great suffering. She requested that her dec'd infant might, after her own death, be placed upon her arm & be interred in the same coffin. A devoted husband & a large circle of attached friends lament her early death.

TUE FEB 13, 1844

Hse/o Reps: 1-Ptn of P Ord, requesting compensation for acting as clerk in the ofc of the Solicitor of the Treas from May 28, 1832, to Jun 1, 1836. 2-Ptn & papers of the heirs of Nathan Faris, dec'd. 3-Ptn & papers of Cyrus C Scott, of Adair Co, Ky.

Grand Piano for sale: made by the most famous makers of Germany, on the model of the famous Evards, in Paris & London. Also, six square pianos, from the manufactory of Rosenkranz, in Dresden, of rosewood & mahogany; English & German action. –G J Conradt, 155 Balt st, Balt, Md

Circuit Court of Wash Co, D C. Francis R May has applied to be discharged from imprisonment under the act for the relief of Insolvent Debtors: hearing on the first Mon in Mar next. –Wm Brent, clk

The Slander on Mr Ogle. From the Bedford [Pa] Inquirer of Feb 9: the Commonwealth against Geo W Bowman, for libel on the late Chas Ogle, tried the preceding week at Somerset before Judge Black, resulted in a verdict of Guilty. The same paper states that Govn'r Porter has subsequently granted a pardon to Bowman.

Mr Edw Dodd, of Brenford, Canada, was thrown out of his wagon, & kicked to death by his horse, a few days since.

Senate: 1-Ptn from John J Russuam, asking the interest on the amount obtained for commutation pay. 2-Ptn from Jas R Howinson, asking that the same compensation that has been allowed to others for services in the exploring expedition may be extended to him. 3-Ptn from Fiedler R Dorset & others, watchmen in the War ofc, asking an increase of compensation. 4-Ptn from Chas L Williamson, asking a reconsideration of his former ptn asking pay for injuries received while serving in the U S Navy.

Death of Judge Magruder. The Hon Richd B Magruder, one of the Associate Judges of the Sixth Judicial District of Md, died suddenly at Balt yesterday, in his 57th year, of an affection of the heart.

Mrd: on Feb 8, in Fredericksburg, at the residence of Mrs Juliett A Neale, by Rev Dr E C McGuire, Lewis M Prevost, jr, of Florida, to Laura Emma, d/o Albert G McCarty, of Richmond Co, Va.

Mrd: on Sabbath afternoon, by Rev John C Smith, Mr Thos E Williams to Miss Joanna M King, all of Wash City.

Died: on Feb 12, in Wash City, Patrick Lynch, a native of the county Meath, Ireland, aged 38 years. His funeral will be from his father's residence, on 7th st, this afternoon at 3 o'clock.

Died: on Jan 9, in St Louis, Mo, Mrs Susan Blunt, formerly of Alexandria, D C, in her 54th year.

Died: in N Y, Miss Jeanette Taylor, aged 68 years, niece of Adm John Paul Jones, one of the most celebrated naval heroes of our Revolutionary struggle. This lady published in Scotland a biography of her distinguished ancestor, & came to this country to present before Congress a claim for moneys due him at the time of his decease. The claim has been unsuccessfully pressed upon that body for several years past. [No date-appears recent.]

Died: on Feb 4, at **Rosemont**, his late residence, near Leesburg, [Va] Capt John Rose. He removed to Loudoun in 1792, &, being commissioned in 1800, he soon became a useful & energetic magistrate. In 1818 he was appointed a School Com'r, & in 1825 chosen Pres of the Board, which ofc he held till 1842, when his increasing infirmities compelled him to resign. As Pres of the Leesburg Turnpike Co for 24 years, as High Sheriff of the county, as exc, adm, Guardian or trustee on various estates, as Pres of the Union Banking Co, as Mayor of Leesburg, as a Trustee of the Methodist Episc Church, & asting as presiding Magistrate of the County Court-in all these relations Capt Rose discharged his duties with zeal & integrity.

WED FEB 14, 1844
Lost, on Mon, between Gadsby's Row & Mrs Visser's, on the Avenue, a small Gold Pencil, with a very dark green stone in the top. The finder will be suitable rewarded by leaving the same at this ofc.

Hse/o Reps: 1-Ptn of Walter Howard & 34 others, citizens of Wyoming Co, N Y, praying for a reduction of postage, & a limitation of the franking privilege. 2-Mr Blackwell: withdrew from the files the memorial of Wm King & Thos Rowland, asking pay for services rendered to the Gov't during the late war. 3-Ptn of Jason Wetherlee & others, of N H, praying that the duties on railroad iron may be remitted. 4-Ptn of Henry Little & Elijah L Hamlin & 725 others, citizens of Bangor & vicinity, Maine, for a reduction of the postage rates. 5-Ptn of Heman Humphrey, Pres of Amherst College, in behalf of the faculty, praying Congress to take measures for the purchase of the Durezzo Library. 6-Ptn of Schuyler Ross & 135 citizens of Buffalo, for appropriation for widening Buffalo creek, & remonstrating against an outer harbor. 7-Ptn of Lyman Warner & 67 other, citizens of Muskingum Co, Ohio, praying for retrenchment in the expenditures of the Genr'l Gov't. 8-Ptn of Chas Gillam & 224 others, citizens of Green Co, Ind, asking donation of land to complete the Wabash & Erie Canel to the Ohio river. 9-Ptn of Jos Fair & 64 others, citizens of Butler Co, Pa, praying for a national road from Cumberland road, by way of the Arsenals of Pittsburg & Meadville, to the harbor of Erie. 10-Memorial of John Burtis & 94 others, citizens of Vandenburg & Posey Counties, Ind, praying Congress for a grant of the unsold lands in the Vincennes land district, to complete the whole line of canal from Lake Erie to the Ohio river, at Evansville. 11-Ptn of Wm Johnson & 50 others, citizens of Daviess Co, Ind, upon the same subject. 12-Ptn of Crafton F Coakerly & 146 others, citizens of Vigo Co, Ind, praying for a reduction in postage rates. 13-Ptn of Chas Lee & Geo W Goldman, citizens of Teneas parish, La, for confirmation as front proprietors of a certain tract of land fronting on the Mississippi river, known as lots 4 thru 8 of township 10, range 11 east, in the district north of Red river, La. 14-Ptn to confirm Eliz Burris, her heirs or assigns, in their title to a tract of land. 15-The claim of Fielding Brown for a pension. 16-Ptn of Robt Clark, of West Baton Rouge, La, for confirmation of the n w qrtr of section #4, township 5, & range 11.

Montgomery Blair has been appointed Judge of the St Louis Court of Common Pleas, in place of Judge Engle, resigned. His acceptance vacates the ofc of Atty of the U S for the District of Missouri, held by Mr Blair.

At Columbus, Ohio, on Fri last, Wm Clark & Hester Foster were publicly executed for the crime of murder. The colored woman seemed much affected, but Clark appeared utterly hardened. The multitude assembled is estimated at from ten to twenty thousand.

Mrd: on Feb 8, at the **Briars**, residence of Dr Robt P Page, Clark Co, Va, by Rev Mr Jones, Passed Midshipman J M Wainwright, U S Navy, to Maria, eldest d/o Dr Page.

Died: on Feb 10, in Phil, Lt John Frelinghuysen Mercer, of the U S Navy, aged 32 years.

Died: on Feb 9, at Newcastle, Dela, aged 35 years, Mrs Mary Jane Rodney, w/o the Hon Geo B Rodney, [Rep in Congress from Delaware,] after a lingering & painful illness of 4 months.

Died: on Nov 15, 1843, much regretted, at her estate near St Louis, Mo, at the advanced age of 80 years, Mrs Bissel, wid/o Gen Bissel, a gallant ofcr of the U S Army.

Died: on Feb 2, in Flemingsburg, Ky, Mrs Mary Anderson, w/o Dr L D Anderson, of that place.

Died: on Tue, at the Union Hotel, Gtwn, D C, Chas Crawford, aged 8 years, 7 months & 9 days, only s/o Chas & Julia Gordon. His funeral is on Wed [this day] at 4 o'clock.

On Tue, at the Ceresville Mills, a burr mill-stone exploded, scattering fragments in every direction. A young man, W Eves, had his leg broken, & was much injured. –Fred Herald

Dahlonega, Ga, Feb 1. On Fri last a difficulty occurred at a grocery store belonging to Jas R Long, about half way between this place & Aurelia, in which Mr Long, Peter Trammell, Jas Helton, & Landawick Dobbs were engaged, & which resulted in the stabbing of the 3 latter by the former, & the death of Dobbs, which ensued the following evening. Trammell & Helton may recover.

American Hotel, Phil: on Chestnut st: built by John J Ridgway, & contains upwards of 100 rooms, many of which are parlors with bedrooms adjoining. Bathing rooms are attached to the Hotel, where warm & cold baths will be in readiness.
–Henry A Charter, C Jas McLellan, Proprietors

Senate: 1-Cmte on Pensions: adverse report on the ptn of Leah Gray, with a report, which was to be printed. 2-Cmte on Revolutionary Claims: adverse report on the memorial of the heirs of Dr Geo Yates, a surgeon in the army of the Revolution, with a report, which was to be printed. 3-Cmte on Naval Affairs: adverse report on the case of Chas E Sherman, with a report, which was to be printed. 4-Cmte on Pensions: adverse report on the ptn of Jno Hibbert.

Orphan's Court of Wash Co, D C. Letters of administraton on the personal estate of Philip Inch, late of said county, dec'd. –Mary Inch, J O'Neale, Adms

Orphan's Court of Wash Co, D C. Letters of administraton on the personal estate of Henry O'Neale, late of Montgomery Co, Md, dec'd. –Susan H Leonard

Orphan's Court of Wash Co, D C. Letters of administration on the personal estate of Sarah Peter, late of Wash Co, dec'd. –Susan H Leonard

Wash Corp: 1-Cmte of Claims: asked to be discharged from the further consideration of the ptn of Nicholas Ferreton: they were discharged accordingly.

THU FEB 15, 1844
Died: on Feb 10, at the Eagle Hotel, in Fredericksburg, Va, in his 72nd year, Mr Carter Beverley, till late & for many years a resident of Culpeper Co, Va. He was reared in affluence & connected with several of the most influential families of Va. A near relative of the Lees, the Carters, & the Randolphs, men who efficiently aided to form our system of gov't. He reared a large family of children, nearly all of whom survive him. –Fredericksburg Herald

Died: on Feb 2, at Mount Vernon arsenal, Alabama, Dr Otis McDonald, s/o the late John G McDonald, of Wash City, in his 27th year. He was the commandant of the post where he died.

Died: on Feb 7, in Boston, Grace, aged 6½ years, d/o Fletcher Webster.

Died: on Feb 13, Geo Robt Thompson, infant s/o Henry & Henrietta Thompson, aged 15 months.

Died: on Feb 13, of croup, Mary A, d/o J B & J I Wingerd, aged 2 years. Her funeral is this afternoon at 2 o'clock, at the residence of Wm Anderson, corner of 12th & G sts.

Obit-from the Benton Banner. Died: on Dec 29 last, at the residence of his sister, Mrs Richardson, near Benton, Miss, of enlargement of the heart, Beverly Robinson Grayson, in his 61st year. He was born at *Belle Air*, near Occoquan, Prince Wm Co, Va, on Sep 3, 1782, & came to this State whilst it was a Territory. He was Clerk of the Territorial Legislature, & afterwards a member of the Legislature from Adams Co. He had been a member of the Methodist Church about 25 years. He has left an aged & infirm wife & a numerous circle of relatives & friends. -M

Senate: 1-Ptn from John A Robbins, asking that an appropriation may be made for testing the superiority of wire over hemp rigging for vessels of war. 2-Ptn from Robt Macguire, a soldier in the last war, asking compensation for clothing taken from him by the Indians, & for pay during the time he was a captive. 3-Ptn from R H McGoon, asing remission of a judgment obtained against him by the U S as a trespasser on the public lands. 4-Cmte on Revolutionary Claims: adverse report on the case of the executor of Saml Ball. 5-Cmte on Pensions: adverse report on the ptn of Geo W Cummings. 6-Ptn for the relief of Mark Simpson was taken up, & recommitted to the Cmte on Military Affairs.

Circuit Court of Wash Co, D C. 1-Francis J Kellenberger has applied to be discharged from imprisonment under the act for the relief of Insolvent Debtors: hearing -first Mon in Mar next. –Wm Brent, clk

The British sloop-of-war **Vestal**, of 26 guns, has arrived at N Y from Portsmouth, Eng, having on board the Rt Hon Richd Packenham, Envoy Extra & Minister Plenipotentiary to the U S from the Court of St James.

Farms at public auction on Mar 18: that valuable tract of land lying on the north side of the road leading from the turnpike gate to Benning's bridge, containing about 200 acres. This property belonged heretofore to Col Bomford & Cmdor Rodgers & Decatur, & can be divided into 2 or 3 farms, viz: the farm formerly belonging to Col Bomford contains about 100 acres & a comfortable farm-house. The ***Rodgers tract*** contains 29 acres, with a comfortable farm-house. The ***Decatur tract*** contains about 68 acres, without improvements. –John T Young -Robt W Dyer & Co, aucts

FRI FEB 16, 1844
Hse/o Reps: 1-Cmte of Claims: made a report on the ptn of the heirs of Robt Fulton, with a bill for their relief. Same cmte: adverse reports on the ptns of Jos E Caro, Israel Thomas, & Edw J Kelly. Same cmte: report on the ptn of Wm H Hoag & others, with a bill for their relief. Same cmte: adverse reports on the ptns of Nicholas Fleanor, John J Beck, & Martha Demmon, heirs of Archibald Campbell, dec'd. Same cmte: report on the ptn of the heirs & legal reps of Jas C Watson, with a bill for their relief. Same cmte: report on the ptn of Chas M Gibson, with a bill for his relief. 2-Cmte on Commerce: report on the ptn of Danl Grant & others, owners of the schnrs **James & Henry**, with a bill for their relief. Same cmte: report on the ptn of Lewis Eldridge, with a bill for his relief. 3-Cmte on Revolutionary Pensions: to inquire into placing on the pension roll, Hetty Focsett, the wid/o of John D Alvey, late paymaster of the army of the Revolution. 4-Non-private ptns from the following on diverse subjects: from Jas Kusman & others, of Lawrence Co, Ill. From Jas N May & others of Richmond Co, Ill. From W L Nicoll & W H Morris & others of Havre-de-Grace, Md. From John D Rose & others of Porter Co, Ind. From Wm M Tatman & others of Jasper Co, Ind. From Richd Shiffen & others of Clarion Co, Pa. From Danl M Adams & others of the counties of Knox, Franklin, & Licking, Ohio. From Thos R Stocking & others, of Buffalo. Ptn of Stephen C Clark & others of Buffalo, N Y. 5-Ptn of Foster Henshaw & Wm A Shepard, for additional allowance to the militia of the Revolution. 6-Ptn of shipmasters & merchants for an appropriation to Robt Hugunin for his chart of Lake Erie, & to enable him to complete the same. 7-Ptn of Catharine Drinker, for a naval pension. 8-Ptn of Wm Speiden, for payment of purser's stores lost in the sloop of war **Peacock**. 9-Remonstrating against any reduction of the duty on salt: John Reed & others of Westmoreland Co, Pa. Garret Curson & others; John B Tarr & others; John Painter & others; Jesse Kilgore & others; E Cowan & others; Alex'r Kilgore & others. 10-Praying an increase of the duty on salt: Danl Hill & others, citizens of Armstrong, Ind, Westmoreland, & Alleghany Counties, Pa. Also, the ptn of the following of similar import: David Jordan & others; Wm H Wray & others; Edw Carleton & others; Wm Painter & others; Wm Marshfield & others; Isaiah Hill & others; & J Noble Nesbitt & others. 11-Memorial of Reuben H Grant, as agent of Jubal B Hancock, protesting against the confirmation of the claim of Alabatcha, a Choctaw Indian woman. 12-Ptn of Fielding S Brown, for a pension for disabilities incurred in the service of the U S. 13-Ptn of Beverly Chew & others, survivors of Beale's rifle company, of Louisiana. 14-Ptn of Peter Laidlow, register of the land ofc at New Orleans, praying to be allowed ofc rent.

New Cabinet appointments: Wm Wilkins, of Pa, was yesterday nominated by the Pres to be Sec for the Dept of War: immediately confimed by the Senate. Thos W Gilmer, of Va, was yesterday nominated by the Pres to be Sec of the Dept of the Navy, & forthwith confirmed by the Senate.

The Hon Esek Cowen, a Justice of the Supreme Court, of N Y, died at his lodgings, in the city of Albany, Sun last, after a severe illness of a week's duration. He was appointed to the bench of the Supreme Court in 1836, having for 8 years previous, discharged the duties of the Fourth Circuit. –Jrnl

Savannah, Feb 8. A passenger who arrived here today, in the steamer **St Matthews**, stated that Dr Church, an old resident of St Mary's, committed suicide on Mon last, by drowning himself. He was a native of one of the Northern States, but had resided in St Mary's about 20 years. His body has been recovered. A note was found in his desk, stating that he intended to commit suicide, but giving no reasons for doing so. Dr C was a single man. -Repub

On Thu week, Mr Chas Lockwood, of Camden, [Canada West,] went with his wife to a friend's, a few miles distant, leaving 6 children at home, the oldest about 13 years of age. During their absence, the house took fire, & all the children perished, save one, the second oldest, who crept into a kind of root-house that communicated with the dwlg. The house was a log one with only one door, near which the fire seems to have begun, & thus the escape of the children was cut off.

Senate: 1-Cmte of Claims: bill for the relief of the heirs of Christopher Miller, with a written report, was ordered to be printed. 2-Cmte on Pensions: adverse report on the claim of Eugene E T Smith.

Biography of John Randolph, of Roanoke, by Mr Sawyer. Sir Thos Randolph was of a collateral branch, who on several embassies served Queen Elizabeth, one of the wisest sovereigns that ever sat on the English Throne. Mr Thos Randolph, the poet, was great-uncle to Sir John. Sir John's father resolved to try his fortune in this part of the world. Sir John's second son, Peyton, was Pres of the first Congress; his third son, John, was the King's Atty Gen for the colony of Va, & his son Edmund held the highest ofcs in the State of Va & of the Federal Gov't. John Randolph, of Roanoke, was the great-grandson of Sir John's elder brother, Richd Randolph, of Curls, in Henrico Co. John Randolph, of Roanoke, was born at Cawson's, in PG Co. Mr Sawyer's account of the Randolph family is all guess work: it must be a source of regret to Mr Randolph's kindred, that the sacred duty should have been attempted by one so little qualified for it. –R R Washington, Feb 15.

Mrd: on Feb 15, in St Peter's Church, by Rev Mr Van Horseigh, Mr Geo W Talburt to Miss Catharine Arthelia Mattingly, 2nd d/o Mr Geo Mattingly, of Wash City.

Died: Feb 12th, in Wash City, Lucy Maria Evans, only d/o Antonio & Mary Grinder, aged 18 months.

Died: Feb 15th, Leon Stanislaus Welhelm Rawice Gawronski, aged 3 months & 20 days, infant son of Leon & Henrietta Gawronski.

Circuit Court of Wash Co, D C. Robt Crump has applied to be discharged from imprisonment under the act for the relief of Insolvent Debtore: hearing on the first Mon in Mar next. —Wm Brent, clk

By virtue of a writ of fieri facias, issued by H Clements, a J P for Wash Co, D C, at suit of John Lee, use of Horatio R Maryman, against the goods & chattels, lands & tenements of Nicholas Kuland, to me directed, I have seized & taken in execution all the right, title, interest, claim, & demand, at law & in equity, of the said Kuland in one 2 story frame dwlg house on 4th st, being on lot 9 in square 792, on Captiol Hill, Wash City, & give notice that on Feb 22, 1844, on the premises, I will offer for sale the said property so seized & taken in execution, at public auction, to the highest bidder for cash. -Henry S Wood, Constable

The stable, belonging to Mr B F Miller, on Stoddart st, Gtwn, was consumed by fire Wed.

Household furniture at auction: on Feb 20, at the residence of Jonathan Guest, on N Y ave, between 13th & 14th sts. -Robt W Dyer & Co, aucts

SAT FEB 17, 1844
Senate: 1-Ptn from J S McFarlane, physician of the naval hospital at New Orleans, asking to be paid a certain sum improperly withheld from him by the accounting ofcrs of the Treasury. 2-Ptn from Susan Brown, of N Y C, wid/o Philip Brown, who was a sailing master at the battle of Lake Champlain, in the Saratoga, in which engagement he greatly distinguished himself-in consideration of which service the Congress of the U S presented him a sword, which the widow says she still possesses & cherishes as a sacred memento. She was granted a pension, which continued down to 1838. She is now in feeble health, & has been obliged to find a home in the widow's asylum of N Y. She asks that the pension be continued to her. 3-Ptn from Evelina E Porter, asking the outfit to which her late husband was entitled as resident Minister at Constantinople; & also asking to be placed on the pension fund, on the same footing with the widows of other ofcrs of her late husband's rank. 4-Ptn from E S Michler & 28 other citizens of Northampton Co, Pa, praying the passage of a law exempting canal boats employed in the coal trade & transporting merchandise from paying coasting license. 5-Cmte on Pensions: adverse report on the claim of Wareham Kingsley, which was ordered to be printed.

Hse/o Reps: 1-Cmte on the Judiciary: report on the ptn of Mary Reeside, of Phil, excx of the late Jas Reeside, dec'd, & it was ordered that the said cmte be discharged from the further consideration of that subject, & that it be referred to a select cmte. Same cmte: made a report on the ptn of Robt G Ward, with a bill for his relief. 2-Cmte on Private Land Claims: report on the ptns of Wolcott A Strong & Pierre S Derbanne, with a bill for their relief. 3-Cmte on Indian Affairs: made a report on the ptn of Milly, an Indian woman of the Creek nation, with a bill granting her a pension. 4-Cmte on Naval Affairs: adverse report on the ptn of Wm Easby. 5-Cmte on Revolutionary Pensions: made a report on the ptn of Sarah Parker, wid/o Jotham Parker, with a bill for her relief. 6-Cmte on Public Lands: adverse reports on the resolution of the Florida Legislature relative to pre-emption grants, & the ptn of Thos R Brashear & Henry Begnette. 7-Cmte on the Post Ofc & Post Roads: adverse report on the ptn of Josiah F Caldwell. 8-Cmte on Revolutionary Pensions: which were referred the papers & documents of Richd Elliott, made a report, with a bill for his relief. 9-Cmte on Invalid Pensions: adverse reports on the ptns of March Farrington, Alphonso Wetmore, Edw Myers, Griffin Kelly, Saml Drew, & Susannah Langreen. Same cmte: adverse report on the ptn of Wm Keller. 10-Cmte on Revolutionary Pensions: report on the ptn of Lois Cronk, alias Cronkite, with a bill for her relief. 11-Cmte on Revolutionary Pensions: made a report on the ptn of Henry Freman, with a bill for his relief. Same cmte: bill for the relief of John Rose. 12-Cmte on Invalid Pensions: adverse report on the ptn of Ezekiel Lincoln. Same cmte: bill for the relief of Simeon Dennin. Same cmte: adverse report on the ptn of Geo Armstrong. Same cmte: adverse report on the cases of Horatio S & Mary Ann Fitch, legal reps of Wm Lyle & Saml Clark. 13-Cmte on Invalid Pensions: bill for the relief of Danl Dunham. Same cmte: adverse report on the ptns of John P Reed, Ira Wright, Holly Gild, Harriet Barney, Geo Reiley, Cornelius A Reeve, Juliana Birchmore, & Stephen F Heminway. 14-Ptn of Mary Bulher for confirmation of land inherited from Adam & John Tinckle, in the parish of East Baton Rouge, La. 15-Memorial & papers of Dr A W Bayard, a citizen of Center Co, Pa, praying for a pension. 16-Memorial of Rev J M Peck, of Ill, a passenger on board the steamer **Shepherdess** at the time of the destruction thereof, giving an account of the obstructions to the safe navigation of the Mississippi river & its tributaries, & calling the attention of Congress to the removal of the same. 17-Ptn of Mary Pike for a pension. 18-Ptn of Thos D Morrison for arrears of pension. 19-Ptn of Henry M Poor & others that Thos D Morrison may receive arrears of pension. 20-Ptn of Jeremiah Noble & Moses Noble, owners of the schnr **Privado**, for a fishing bounty.

Duel in Va, near the Chain Bridge, yesterday, between Mr Julian May & Mr Jos Cochrane, both of Wash City. The parties fought with rifles, & Mr Jos Cochrane was, at the first fire, shot through the head. He was still living at 7 o'clock last night. Mr May was not hurt. [Feb 19th newspaper: Mr Cochrane died yesterday, at Mr Nelson's farm, in Fairfax Co, Va, near the place of combat. See Jos Cochrane-obit: in same newspaper.]

A marble statue, 9 feet high, of Sir Chas Metcalfe, late Govn'r of Jamaica & now Govn'r of Canada, is completed, & to be erected opposite the Senate House, in Spanishtown, Jamaica.

Elihu Burritt, of Worcester, Mass, who understands 52 languages, & is known as the "learned blacksmith," now publishes a journal called the "Christian Citizen."

As the steamboat **New Haven** was off Falkland Island, on her passage from Norwich to N Y, on Tue, Mr A Rogers, of New London, fell overboard & was drowned. He was very sea sick, & while leaning over the side, the boat lurched & losing his balance, he fell overboard.

Capt Lovell, of the brig **Wasp**, arrived at N Y in 50 days from Sierra Leone, informs that the British brig of war **Rapid** captured a Brazilian slaver about 3 weeks before he sailed. The slaver had 250 slaves on board, all of whom were liberated, & the vessel seized as a prize.

Mrd: on Feb 14, in Phil, by Rev Saml Beach Jones, Danl Elmer, Assoc Justice of the Supreme Court of N J, to Mary, d/o the late Maxwell Ewing.

Died: on Jan 22, at his residence in St Louis Co, Missouri, in his 79th year, Geo H Lanham, formerly Sheriff of PG Co, Md, & a resident thereof during his whole life until the last 9 years, when he emigrated to Missouri.

House servants for sale: 2 negro women, brought up to housework, neither over 25 years; & a bright handsome mulatto boy, very much devoted to horses. May be seen at Judge Dorsey's, near Bladensburg, & will not be sold to traders.
–Henry G Gardner, Adm of W H J Dorsey, Chaptico, Md

For sale: superior cigars, just arrived, of the finest quality & flavor.
–W H Winters, #6, east of Gadsby's, sign of Jim Crow.

Household furniture for sale, at auction, by order of the Orphan's Court of Wash Co, D C: sale on Feb 21, at the residence of the late J J Dermott, his furniture, & books.
-Robt W Dyer & Co, aucts

MON FEB 19, 1844
Hse/o Reps: 1-Bill for the relief of Jonathan Bean, under discussion, was finally rejected. 2-Bill for the relief of John P Schuyler, was taken up by the Cmte of Whole. 3-Bill for the relief of Wm Glover was laid aside.

Schnr missing. Letter to Hon H A Wise, dated-Eastville, Feb 12, 1844. Dear Sir: My vessel, the schnr **Exchange**, from Cherrystone, left that harbor on Jan 12 with the person that plastered your house, whose name is Mr Flinn, as I understand. You will much oblige me by writing to his friends, where they may live, & inquiring of them whether or not they have heard from him, as I believe that she is lost. I have never heard from her for more than 4 weeks. My vessel was bound to Balt with a cargo of oats on board. Your friend, Edw W Nottingham. [Feb 22nd newspaper: the **Exchange** arrived safely at the wharf here on Mon; she had been detained by ice; all on board were well. –Balt Sun]

It is stated in the American that Mr Thos Winans, of Balt, together with Mr Jos Harrison, of Phil, have the secured the contract-the largest of the kind ever made in the world, for furnishing locomotives & burden cars for the railroad now constructing in Russia, between St Petersburg & Moscow. The road will be about 400 miles long, the number of locomotives to be built is 162, with tenders for each. The cost will be upwards of four millions of dollars.

The Hon Saml Beardsley, one of the Reps in Congress from Oneida Co, N Y, has been nominated by the Govn'r of N Y, to be a Justice of the State Supreme Court, vice Hon Esek Cowen, dec'd.

Due to the severe indisposition of Capt Ezekiel Jones of the U S Revenue Marine Service, he was compelled, some weeks ago, to go into sick quarters on shore, surrendering his charge, the cutter **Morris**, stationed at Portland, to 1st Lt J B Fulton, her present cmder. Capt Jones is so reduced by his disease, so spectre-like is his present appearance, that his former most intimate acquaintances can now hardly recognize him. Our best wishes to him. –Portland Adv

Wash City taxes: 10% deduction for prompt payment. –W Rothwell, Collector

Mrd: on Feb 8, by Rev Mr Ufford, at Elkington, the residence of Alfred Parker, Dr Geo L Upshur, of Norfolk, to Sarah A Parker, youngest d/o the late Dr Jacob Parker, of Northampton Co, Va.

Died: yesterday, Jos Cochrane, aged 18 years. His funeral will be at his late residence, in 6th st, at 11 o'clock, Feb 19. Friends of the dec'd & of his family are invited to attend.

TUE FEB 20, 1844
Hse/o Reps: 1-Cmte on Private Land Claims: to inquire into making a grant of bounty land to Richd Stokes for his services as a Canadian volunteer during the late war with Great Britain. 2-Ptn of Saml McKeetran, of Wash Co, Pa, relative to the treatment of the crew on board the brig **Somers**: referred to the Cmte on Naval Affairs. 3-Ptn of Geo Harrison, of Ky, a paymaster of the war of 1812, praying relief against a demand of the Gov't for money overpaid by him to the regiment to which he was appointed paymaster. 4-Ptn of David Melville, of Newport, R I, adm on the estate of Benj Fry, dec'd, asking for the payment of a sum of money due from the U S to Fry, as appears by the certificate of the jury in the case of the U S vs Fry.

In Chancery. Geo Kerby, exc of John B Kerby, cmplnt, vs, Barbary Young, admx, & others, heirs-at-law of Ignatius F Young, dfndnt. Claims against the estate to be presented on or before Mar 9 next, at the ofc of the Auditor. –Jos Forrest, Auditor

Senate: 1-Memorial from John F H Claiborne, one of the com'rs for examining claims under the treaty of Dancing Rabbit Creek, representing the gross frauds practiced upon the ignorant Indians by speculators, & asking the intervention of Congress to stop these frauds & to do justice to the Indians. 2-Memorial from Calvin Blythe, Collector of the port of Phil, & Surveyor of said port, representing the dilapidated & unsafe condition of the present custom-house, & asking that a new one may be made, or that the old U S Bank bldg may be purchased for the purpose, which they recommend. 3-Ptn from Eleanor W Houston & Ann S Houston, surviving children of Dr Houston, a surgeon in the Revolutionary war, asking compensation for the services & losses incurred by their father during that period. 4-Ptn from Benj F Ferguson, a soldier in the war with Great Britain, asking a pension. 5-Communication from Jas P Spring & others, asking that the troops stationed at *Fort Gibson* may be removed to old Fort Wayne.

Valuable Loudoun farm for sale: on Mar 26, that well know farm, *Sailor's Rest*, owned by the late Capt John Rose: 6 miles north of Leesburg, Va: contains about 600 acres: with a large well-built frame dwlg-house, 2 stories high, with wings attached, in good order. Another dwlg house on the tract now occupied by Mr Frye. --Thos H Clagett, Adm with the will annexed of John Rose, dec'd.

Two executions: on Feb 9, Jas Williams, convicted of the murder of his wife, & negro George, of the murder of his master, in St Mary's Co, Md, were executed at Leonardtown, in the presence of an immense concourse of persons from the surrounding country.

Public sale of valuable stock: all the perishable property of which Thos Fitzhugh, dec'd, died possessed in Fauquier Co, Va. Property consists of about 200 head of cattle. Sale will taken place on the 3 tracts of land in said county of which the testator died seized: about 7 miles below Warrenton: will commence on Mar 18 next. --Henry Fitzhugh, Berkeley Ward, excs of Thos Fitzhugh, dec'd.

For sale: *Frescati*, late the seat of Judge Barbour, dec'd. About 1,300 acres of land, near Gordonsville, Orange Co, Va. The dwlg house is of brick, large, commodious, & elegant; plastering is done with plaster of Paris: roof is of tin; erected by the foreign workmen who assisted in erecting the bldgs at the Univ of Va. All the bldgs have been erected within the last 22 years. Undisputed title can be conveyed. My son, Mr S Barbour, will show it after the month of Apr. --Frances T Barbour

Burns, who murdered Edw W Collier, a citizen of Augusta, Ga, some weeks since, was arrested on Feb 4, at Memphis, Tenn, by an ofcr from Ga. He was at the time on board the steamboat **Hempstead**, bound for New Orleans, & had registered his name as Jas Owens.

A Nurse wanted. An elderly woman, without family, who can come well recommended, & is able to take charge of 2 little girls of 4 & 6 years of age, may hear of a situation by applying at my ofc, 15th st, near the Treas ofc. –Thos W Pairo

Mrd: on Feb 15, by Rev Mr Hawley, Jas W Brown, of the Treas Dept, to Mrs Susan Ann Stretch, d/o the late Alex'r Scott, all of Wash City.

Died: on Feb 18, at his residence near the Navy Yard, Mr Andrew Forrest, in his 52nd year. His funeral is today at 2 o'clock.

Died: on Feb 16, in Gtwn, after a short illness, Chas French, s/o Maynadier & Virginia Mason, aged 9 years & 3 months.

Died: on Jan 31, at his residence, near Orange Court-house, after a very brief illness, Reynolds Chapman, in his 67th year. For more than 40 years he had filled with ability & fidelity the ofc of Clerk to the Hustings & Superior Courts of the county.

WED FEB 21, 1844
Senate: 1-Ptn from W Harding, asking an increase of his pension. 2-Papers relating the claim of David Robb were presented. 3-Cmte of Claims: bill for the relief of Gideon & Shadracre Bachelder, with a special report: ordered to be printed. 4-Cmte on Indian Affairs: bill for the relief of Jos Bryant, Harrison Young, & Benj Young, with a report: ordered to be printed. 5-Cmte on Pensions: unfavorable report on the ptn of Reuben M Gillis. 6-House bill for the relief of Isaac Plummer: referred to the Cmte on Pensions. 7-Bill for the relief of Jane McGuire, wid/o Thos McGuire: referred to the Cmte on Pensions. 8-Bill for the relief of Geo Davenport was taken up & ordered to be engrossed.

Horrid tragedy occurred at Sandtown, in the upper part of Burlington Co, N J, on Sun last. A young man by the name of Andrew Jarvis cut the throat of his brother Napoleon, while sleeping, so badly that he was not expected to survive. No cause is assigned for the dreadful act.

Hse/o Reps: 1-Ptn of John Parrott or Julia Parrott, for a pension. [Copied as written.] 2-Ptn of John A Gustin & another, securities of Wm F Rodgers, a defaulting postmaster, praying for relief. 3-Ptn of Eliz Randolph, of Mercer Co, Ky, praying a pension. 4-Memorial of John W Hockett, praying payment for labor performed by him on the Cumberland road. 5-Memorial of John W Barr, a soldier in the late war with Great Britain under Gen Andrew Jackson, praying Congress to grant land to all those who served their country in said war. 6-Ptn of Susanna Barker, wid/o Zebadiah Barker, praying a pension on account of the Revolutionary services of her late husband. 7-Ptn of Lyman N Cook, for an increase of pension. 8-Ptn of Jos R Gilman, to be placed on the invalid pension list.

For rent: a 2 story brick house on 18th st, between H & I sts. Inquire next door of Richd Joyce.

The Hon Noah Noble, ex-Govn'r of the State of Indiana, died at his residence near Indianapolis on Feb 8. He was about 50 years of age & was Govn'r of the State for 6 years.

Died: yesterday, after an illness of 24 hours, Mrs Ann Coomes & her infant dght, w/o Saml Coomes, in her 35th year, leaving an affectionate husband & 6 children to mourn their irreparable loss. Her funeral will be from her late residence, near the corner of I & 15th sts, this evening, at 3 o'clock.

Newark Daily Advertiser of Thu: Dr Theo Johnes, of Morristown, [s/o Dr John B Johnes,] while engaged in a post mortem examination on Thu last pricked his finger, & a portion of the blood, was springled upon it. Aware of danger, precautions to prevent the spread of the poison were taken, but without effect, for yesterday he expired at the early age of 25 years.

Louisville [Ky] Journal: The bust of Mr Clay by Mr Allan, s/o the Hon Chilton Allan, of this State, is by far the best effort to give an accurate representation of Mr Clay we have ever seen. It is, in almost every respect, perfect.

The Mormons, alias Latter Day Saints. Mr John E Page, Elder of the Latter Day Saints' Church, will preach in the Franklin engine lecture room on Feb 22 at 7 o'clock. Seats free.

Wash Corp: 1-Bill for relief of Geo T McGlue was passed. 2-Bill for relief of W G W White was referred to the Cmte on Improvements & passed. 3-Ptn from Geo Bean & others: referred to the Cmte on Improvements. 4-Ptn of Saml M Emery, in relation to a theatrical license, to be referred. 5-Cmte of Claims: asked to be discharged from the further consideration of the ptn of David S Waters, for selling dry goods contrary to law; & they were discharged accordingly. 6-Ptn of Michl Nourse & others, praying for flag footways on 13th st, across E & F sts: referred to the Cmte on Improvements. 7-Ptn of Wm Campbell, praying remission of a fine: referred to the Cmte of Claims. 8-Ptn of Wm Bird & others, for a footway across Md ave: referred to the Cmte on Improvements. 9-Cmte of Claims: bill for the relief of Jas Dixon, made a report recommending the indefinite postponement of the bill. 10-Ptn of Wm Thorpe, praying to be released from the payment of certain fines superseded by him for other persons: referred to the Cmte of Claims. 11-Communication from H L Ellsworth to the Mayor, respecting certain improvements on the judiciary square: referred to the Cmte on Improvements. And then the Board adjourned.

Mrd: on Feb 15, by Rev John Davis, Mr John D Bradburn to Miss Eliz Ann, eldest d/o Mr Wm Cammack, all of Wash City.

The latest dates from Vicksburg inform that recently in Clark Co, Miss, Mr G W Gardner left home for the purpose of hunting hogs, leaving in charge of his house his wife & children, & a little brother about 13 years old. On returning, he found his house burned down. It is supposed the family was murdered & the house set on fire.

THU FEB 22, 1844
Very late from Europe: the papers announce the death of Sir Francis Burdett & of his lady; of the reigning Duke of Saxe Coburg, father of Prince Albert; of the Archduchess Maria Caroline, eldest d/o the Austrian Duke Reynier, Viceroy of the Lombardo-Venetian Kingdon; she was in her 23rd year, & was about to be married to the Prince de Carignan, eldest s/o the King of Savoy; of the Marquis of Hastings, s/o the Lord Rawdon of our Revolutionary war.

Naval Intelligence. The U S frig **Raritan** sailed from N Y on Tue for Rio Janeiro. List of her ofcrs: Francis H Gregory, Cmder

Lts
Lawrence Pennington	Edw T Shubrick	Woodhull
Bassit Shephard	Maxwell	

Passed Midshipmen:
John R Duer	Robt Townsend

Midshipmen:
Henry H Stevens	S P Quackenbush	Milton Haxtun
Paul Shirley	Andrew F Monroe	J H March
Edw A Hopkins	Henry C Hunter	
Chas Dyer, jr	J C P De Krafft	

Doing duty as Midshipmen:
Richd H Simms	Edw C Henshaw	Chas W Bishop
Geo D Twiggs	Wm P Humphries	
Beverley G Lindsay	John M Meehan	

Adol Eug Watson, Purser	John B Randolph, Acting Master
Jonathan M Foltz, Surgeon	Thos M Potter, Acting Surgeon
Edw C Ward, Prof of Mathematics	John S Gregory, Capt's Clerk
John Robb, Chaplaim	Mathew W Aylwin, Purser's Clerk
Jas T Powers, Warranted Master's Mate	W B Hays & J H Watmouth, Acting Master's Mates
Robt Dixon, Boatswain	John W Danenhower, Purser's Steward
Gustavus Newman, Gunner	Jas T Jones, Yeoman
Wm M Laighton, Carpenter	Robt D Taylor, 2nd Lt, Marine Ofcr
Geo T Lozier, Sailmaker	

Geo W Gordon, the newly appointed Consul at Rio, & family, were passengers.

New Lumber Yard: on the corner of 14th & Canal sts. –O J Preston

Senate: 1-Cmte on Military Affairs: a bill for the relief of Mark Simpson.

Died: on Tue, at his residence, on 8th st, near the Navy Yard, after a painful & protracted illness, Geo Adams, in his 65th year. The dec'd was a native of Chas Co, Md, but for the last 35 or 40 years a resident of Wash City, where he was well known as an honest, upright man. His remains will be conveyed to the Methodist Episcopal Church this afternoon, at 2 o'clock, when his funeral sermon will be preached by the Rev Jas H Brown.

Obit-died: on Feb 12, 1844, at Washington, Mrs Hetty Jane Keyser Drayton, y/d/o Mrs Saml Keyser, of Balt, after an afflicting illness of nearly 2 months. She was the w/o Henry J Drayton, of Phil, & was led to the altar only last Oct a blooming bride, in company with a beloved sister, who was married at the same time. A few short months & the distressed survivor of her companion in womanhood & marriage followed her "dear Jane" to the dark chambers of death, to mourn over her irreparable loss, & see the bridal wreath of her sister changed to bitter ashes. Sad, sad reverse? But God's will be done, & not poor feeble man's. Her afflicted & aged mother, her sorrowing sisters, & her heart-stricken brothers loved her as the apple of their eye. May God grant her devoted mother the strength to bear up against the dispensation that hath snatched from her her most beloved dght.

Died: yesterday, after a long-continued illness, Mrs Ann White, in her 24th year. Her funeral will be at the residence of Mr Jas C White, Pa ave, at 12th st, this day at 3 o'clock.

Thos Kinnicutt, Speaker of the Massachusetts Hse/o Reps, has resigned his station on account of ill health; Mr Richardson, of Woburn, a Locofoco member, introduced resolutions highly complimentary to the retiring Speaker. [Feb 23rd newspaper: Saml H Wally, jr, elected Speaker of the Hse/o Reps of Mass, vice Mr Kinnicutt, resigned.]

Appointments by the President:
Land Ofcrs-Registers:
Wm T Walmsley, at Natchitoches, La, vice P O Lee, resigned.
Geo R Girault, of Granada, Miss, re-appointed.
Receivers:
Richd B Servant, at Kaskaskia, Ill, vice Saml Crawford
Thos Barrett, at New Orleans, La, vice Greenbury Dorsey, declined the appointment.
Robt H Booth, at Tallahassee, Fla, vice Robt B Semple, resigned.
Robt W Lausing, at Mineral Point, Wisc, vice Saml S Bowne, resigned.
Saml J Bayard, at Fairfield, Iowa, vice Jos C Hawkins.

Orphan's Court of Wash Co, D C. Letters testmentary on the personal estate of Louisa Coombs, late of said county, dec'd. –I C Dawes, Jas Lusby, Excs

Circuit Court of Wash Co, D C. John L Stull has applied to the discharged from imprisonment under the act for the relief of Insolvent Debtors: hearing on the first Mon in Mar next. –Wm Brent, Clk

FRI FEB 23, 1844
Hse/o Reps: 1-Ptn of Chas W Short & 19 other citizens of Lawrence Co, Ind, asking a donation of land to improve the navigation of the Wabash river. 2-Ptn of Peter Peterson & 104 other citizens of Butler Co, Pa, praying for a national macadamized road from Cumberland road, by way of the arsenals of Pittsburg & Meadville, to the harbor of Erie. Ptn of Thos McNair & 61 other citizens of Butler Co, Pa, of similar import. 3-Ptn of Abraham Brinker, of Butler Co, Pa, praying that he may be paid the amount due him for the Revolutionary services of his father. 4-Ptn of Isaac Eckright, of Armstrong Co, Pa, praying an increase of his pension. 5-Ptn of Wm Stubblefield, of Mason Co, Ky, praying that a pension may be granted to him on account of services in the Indian wars from 1791 to 1794.

Feb 22: celebrated in veneration for the founder of this great Republic-the illustrious Father of his Country. The volunteer companies of this city & Gtwn were all out in full uniform, with banners flying & music playing. They marched along Pa ave, early in the day:
The Wash Light Infty, Capt France
The Nat'l Blues, Capt Tucker
The Mechanical Riflemen, Capt McClelland
At meridian Capt Buckingham's company, the Columbia Artillerists, fired a nat'l salute.
Military parade was augmented by the arrival of :
The Union Guards, Capt Harkness
The Potomac Dragoons, Capt Mason
The Morgan Rifle Corps, Capt Duvall

Wash Corp: Act for the relief of Geo T McGlue: that the fine imposed by judgment of Saml Drury for the violation of a law relative to taking sand from the streets & gutters, be & the same is herby remitted: Provided, the said McGlue pay the cost of prosecution.

Pocket book lost on Feb 22, containing about $30. It may have been left in some store: information concerning it to Mr S P Franklin, at Mrs Taylor's Boading-house, or at Messrs Muller & Moore's. Or it may be returned to the owner, G S Griffith, Upholsterer & Paper hanger, 100½ Market st, Balt.

S S Wright & Aaron Dress, 2 citizens of N Y, who participated in the insurrection in Canada several years ago, & were tried & sent to Van Dieman's Land by the British authorities, have returned to their homes by way of London, after an absence of 4 years. They were released, with several others, for general good conduct. They state in a letter in the N Y Tribune, that 54 Americans are still in captivity in Van Dieman's Land.

Gtwn Corp tax sale, for cash, of the following lots & parts of lots in Gtwn, the same having been seized by me in distrain, & will be sold to satisfy taxes due, for the several years annexed thereto.
All that part of lot 35 on south side of Bridge st & running back to the Canal. Assessed in the name of Thos Astley, but is supposed to be owned by [blank,] Assessment: $12,000/1842 & 43/$18.00
Parts of lots 64 & 65 on east side of Jefferson. Assessed to John Connelly's heirs. Assessed $200/1843/$1.50.
An lot in Holmead's addition, not numbered, Monroe & Beall sts. Assessed to Rachael Steel's heirs. Assessed $250/1842 & 43/$2.75
Two undivided 3rd parts of a lot, containing 1½ acres, more or less, in Holmead's addition, with a frame house thereon, formerly attached to the old Paper Mill, bounded on the west by the ground of Thos Woodward, & on the north by Rock Creek. Assessed to Edgar Patterson & Chas Carroll's heirs. Assessed $300/1841 & 42/$4.05.
One undivided third part of the last said lot, in Holmead's addition. Assessed to Andrew Way's heirs. Assessed $150/1841 & 42/ $2.02½.
Lot #23, Beatty & Hawkins' addition. Assessed to Mary Sand's heirs. Assessed $800/1842 & 43/$12.00.
Extreme east parts of lots 201, 199, & 197, Threlkeld's addition, beginning on 7th st. Assessed to Nancy Hill's heirs. Assessed $160/1842 & 43/$2.70.
All the west part of lot 13, beginning on the north line of Bridge st to the west boundary of the property of Nicholas Travers. Assessed to Dryden Tyler's heirs. Assessed $1,200/1842 & 43/$18.00.
-Wm Jewell, Collector of the Corp of Gtwn, Feb 21, 1844.

Late Foreign papers. The last of the Stuarts still lives at Tweedmouth, having completed his 115th year at Christmas, 1843.

Gotleib Willams, jr, about 16, killed a lad named Peter Doescher, in Phil, on Tue, by stabbing him with a butcher knife. They got to quarrelling & blows were exchanged.

The negro Wm Jones alias Squire, committed to jail on Dec 2, 1843, on a charge of being a runaway slave, was yesterday demanded by his master John W Faulconer, of Essex Co, Va, from whom he absconded in Nov last. At an earlier time he was purchased of Mr Jas Durham, of Essex Co, Va, & ran away about 5 days after he was purchased. –Jas Marshall, J P: Wash, Feb 21, 1843

Mrd: on Tue last, by Rev Chas A Davis, Mr Wm Vermillion to Miss Harriet Ward, all of Wash City.

SAT FEB 24, 1844
Teacher wanted at the Hillview school. All letters addressed to the subscriber, post paid, Great Mills, St Mary's Co, Md, will be received by the trustees. –Wm Coad

Bible Socitey of Wash will hold their annual meeting in the First Presbyterian Church, 4½ st on Feb 26 at 7 p m. Hon John M Berrien & Hon Chas Hudson will address the Society. –M H Miller, Sec

Senate: 1-Ptn from J N Peck, one of the survivors of the steamboat **Shepherdess**, lost near St Louis, asking an appropriation, & proposing a plan, for the improvement of the navigation of the Western rivers. 2-Ptn from excs of Uriah Emmons, asking a renewal of patent for a cylindrical planing machine. 3-Ptn from Lydia Rundlett, wid/o a Revolutionary soldier, for a pension. 4-Ptn from Danl Bowen, a Revolutionary soldier, for a pension. 5-Ptn from the legal reps of Rudolph Brenner, for pay to which he was entitled as an ofcr in the Revolutionary army. 6-Ptn from Chas Kohler. 7-Sec of War to examine the drawings & plan of Capt Wm T Colquhon, of Va, for removing sand bars in the navigable rivers of the U S, & report to the Senate the opinion of the Dept on the subject.

Circuit Court of Wash Co, D C. John Frizzel has applied to be discharged from imprisonment under the act for the relief of Insolvent Debtors: hearing on the first Mon in Mar next. –Wm Brent, clk

Hse/o Reps: Bills considered in cmte & were reported to the Hse/o Reps: [All for the RELIEF of-]

Jas C Hallock	Geo M Jones	Isaac Justice
Thompson Hutchinson	Danl Dean	Jos Ramsey
Eliz Jones & others	Isaac Fessenden	Adam L Mills
Thos Harrison	Gervis Foote	Robt G Ward
*Hugh Wallace	Alborne Allen	Geo Wallis
Wormley	Jehu Hollingsworth	Henry Freeman
Enoch McDaniel	Jos Bennel	John Reese
Jas Reid	Fred'k Hopkins	Simeon Denison
Wm Ellery	John Farnham	Richd Elliott
Saml B Folger	Arthur R Grogge	Wm H Hoag & others
Saml B Tuck	Levi Colmus	Levi Eldridge & others
Wm Augustus Atlee	Jos Watson	
Louis Crouk, alias Croukhite		
Sarah Parker, wid/o Jos Parker		

Danl Grant, Sarah Grant, Israel P Stone, & Emily Pinkham, owners of the fishing schnr **James & Henry**, of Cape Porpoise, Maine [*Feb 26 newspaper: Bill for the relief of Hugh Wallace Wormley was not among the private bills which received the sanction of the Cmte of the Whole on Sat last, & were subsequently reported to the House. Please correct our insertion in that report.]

Hse/o Reps: 1-Memorial of Thos Bingham, of Phil, private in the late war, for his monthly pay: referred. 2-Ptn of Lt J A Winslow, of the navy, for remuneration for services: referred.

Biennial Register, or Blue-book, for 1843, containing the name, compensation, etc, of every person holding ofc, or connected with the Gov' t of the U S, including a complete Table of Post Ofcs, just printed under the direction of the Dept of State. Over 1,100 pages: price-$3.50 per copy. -J & G S Gideon, Printers & Bookbinders, 9th st, Wash

MON FEB 26, 1844
Wash City town meeting on Feb 21, 1844: Mayor called to the chair, Joshua L Henshaw appointed sec; Mr Wm Archer, Mr John C Harkness, & Mr J E Dow addressed the meeting. Mr Jas Maher offered a proposition for adoption. Mr John Wilson addressed the chair. Mr Jos H Bradley addressed the meeting. Subject: bill now before Congress to incorporate the citizens of Washington. Following citizens are appointed to act as judges to receive votes & conduct election of ofcrs in the several wards, viz: [-W W Seaton, Chairman]

Geo W Harkness	John C McKelden	John B Ferguson
Saml Stott	S P Franklin	Jas Owner
Matthew Hines	John Boyle	Wm Ashdown
Robt Farnham	W J McCormick	Robt M Combs
Wm H Gunnell	Danl Homans	Lewis Newman
John C Rives	H N Crabb	Francis Riley

St Patrick's Day dinner celebration meeting on Feb 16: Edw Stubbs, called to the chair; Timothy O'Neale appointed sec. Cmtes were appointed:

Arrangements:
Jas Maher	Patrick Sullivan	
Michl O'Brien	Philip Ennis	

On toasts:
Edw Stubbs	John Boyle	Peter Brady

On invitations:
Gregory Ennis	Jas O'Riely	Ambrose Lynch

Managers of Wash:
Thos Jordan	Timothy O'Neale	Francis Reily
Bernard Giveny	Michl Dooly	Dr Philip Smyth
John Ousley	Patrick O'Donaghue	

Managers of Gtwn:
Capt R E Duvall   Saml Rainey   Bernard Brien
Peter O'Donaghue   Timothy O'Donaghue
John Carroll   Jas O'Riely
Managers of Alexandria:
Dr Jas Carson   John Lapher   Matthew Maher
Jas Roach   Edw Sheehan
Managers of the Wash City Benevolent Society:
Thos Wall   David Little   John Trane
P McGarry   S Calnan   Jas McCarthy
Terrence Luby   D Calaghen

It was also agreed that dinner be on the table at 4 o'clock precisely. Tickets $1.50, to be had of any of the managers.

Criminal Court sits today & the undermentioned gentlemen were summoned by the Marshal to serve as grand jurors during the Dec term: [They are expected to be in attendance.]

Thos Carbery   John Mason, jr   John McCobb
John W Maury   Robt White   Jos Smoot
Jacob Gideon   Chas A Burnett   Chas R Belt
Henry McPherson   John Cox   Danl Kurtz
Richd Cutts   Jos Forest   Edw Simms
Lewis Johnson   John Boyle   Geo Thomas
Benj Ogle Tayloe   Roger C Weightman   G C Grammer
Thos Fenwick   Hamilton Lufborough   Wm H Campbell

Circuit Court of Wash Co, D C. Wm P Prather [colored] has applied to be discharged from imprisonment under the act for relief of Insolvent Debtors: hearing on the first Mon in Mar next. –Wm Brent, clk

The nomination of the Hon Saml Beardsley [one of the Reps in Congress from N Y] to be a Justice of the Supreme Court of this State has been confirmed.

Hse/o Reps: 1-Ptn & papers of Col Moses Wright, of Wayne Co, Ky, were presented & referred. 2-Ptn of F Johnson, the heir of Drury Holland, for arrears of pension. 3-Ptn of Wm Hackworth for bounty lands.

Fish! Fish! Fish! The subscribers inform the citizens of St Mary's Co that they have taken the Fishery at Piney Point, & will be prepared to furnish fish to the neighborhood at prices to suit the times. Salt will be sold on the most reasonable terms. –Nocholas L Queen, Geo Sinclair

Died: on Feb 20, in her 72nd year, Mrs Grace Hamilton, consort of Jas Hamilton, of Balt, Md.

The house of Dr Lucien Spencer, of Bethany, Conn, was totally consumed by fire on Tue last, with all its furniture, clothing, etc; & what is most sad to relate, Dr Spencer & 2 of his children perished in the flames. Dr S had succeeded in getting out a part of his family, his wife & 3 of the children, & returned for his 2 remaining children; before he could escape with them the chamber floor fell through & all perished. The fire originated from a pail of ashes in which some live coals remained. The Dr was a graduate of Yale College.

Mrd: on Feb 20, at Wheeling, Va, by Rev Wm Armstrong, Dr John C Campbell, of Brooke Co, to Mrs Amelia Hay Vance, wid/o the late Lt J C Vance, & eldest d/o the late Saml Sprigg, of Wheeling.

Died: on Feb 12, at his residence in Balt Co, Cornelius Howard, in his 90th year of a life distinguished by probity, usefulness, & the unlimited confidence of all who knew him. [See below.]
+
Died: on Feb 21, at her residence on the paternal farm, in Balt Co, in her 85th year, Mrs Violetta West, sister of the dec'd, & eminent in the primitive virtues which marked her generation.

Died: Feb 19, at Pittsburg, Pa, Benj Bakewell, in his 78th year, for many years a distinguished citizen.

Died: on Thu last, at N Y, Alvey Augustus Adee, M D, Surgeon in the U S Navy, aged 41 years.

Died: on Feb 10, at the residence of his friend, Chas Bispham, at Mount Holly, N J, Marmaduke Burrough, M D, in his 46th year. Dr Burrough had passed many years in India, China, the Sandwich Islands, South America & Mexico. He was 4 years U S Consul in the Mexican port of Vera Cruz, & on returning home from that city with a broken constitution, he made a tour of Europe in the hope of re-establishing his health. An insidious disease resumed its ravages & he sank into the grave.

The citizens of New Orleans were shocked on Feb 14, by the announcement of the death of Albert Hoa, a member of the Senate of La from this city. Mr Hoa had been ill a few days only. He was about 38 years of age, a native of the city, & a prominent lawyer. The disease to which Mr Hoa fell a victim was the same which deprived the country of the gifted Hugh S Legare. -Tropic

After Mar 1 the subscriber will be found at his ofc on La ave near 7th st, in the house lately occupied by John J Dermott, where he will attend to all business entrusted to him. –T C Donn, J P

TUE FEB 27, 1844
Senate: 1-Additional documents in the case of the heirs of Dr John Houston, of the Revolutionary war, were presented. 2-Ptn from Ebenezer Swann, asking for a pension. 3-Ptn from Wm H Freeman, complaining of the proceedings of a court martial. 4-Additional documents in the case of John Dillard, for subsisting the Camanche & other Indians. 5-Cmte on Revolutionary Claims: adverse report on the claim of the heirs of Wm Grayson. Also, on the claim of the widow of Albert Pawling. 6-Cmte on Naval Affairs: adverse report on the memorial of Julia L Weed, wid/o Elijah J Weed, for an increase of pension.

Pinckney Hill lost his life in Troup Co, Ga, on Feb 3. He went out on a hunting excursion & a large tree fell on him, trapping his leg. He was found to have severed his leg from the rest of his body, but was found dead a short distance from the tree. He was about 18 years of age.

Furnished house to let by the month or year, the genteelly furnished & well appointed residence of the late Mrs Tudor, on I st, in front of the Pres' House. Apply on the premises to C S Stewart, Exc, or to Richd Smith, Cashier of the Bank of the Metropolis.

$15 reward for strayed or stolen sorrel horse. –John H Smoot, on the Navy Yard hill.

The New Bedford Mercury received intelligence that the Poor House at Quaise, Nantucket, was entirely consumed by fire on Feb 20, & the following perished in the flames:

Paul Jenkins	Wm Hutchins
Thos Hull	Jonathan Cathcart
Phebe Jones	Wm Holmes
Sophia Bube	Adiah Davis

WED FEB 28, 1844
Senate: 1-Ptn from Benj Wyatt, asking indemnity for French spoliations prior to 1800. 2-Cmte on Patents: asking to be discharged from further consideration of the ptn of the heir of Danl Pettibone: referred to the Cmte on the Public Bldgs. 3-Adverse report on the ptn of David C Wilson, late marshal of the district of Delaware, asking an allowance for ofc rent.

Easton [Md] Gaz: the Hon John Leeds Kerr, late U S Senator from Md, died last Wed, after a long & painful illness, in his 65th year. Some time previous Mr Kerr had been assailed by the disease which finally terminated in his death.

A very great sinner. The Cleveland Herald states that the grand jury of Lorain Co have found 16 bills of indictment against H C Taylor, late editor of the Oberlin Evangelist, to most of which, if not all, it is understood he will plead guilty.

On Sat last the flourishing village of Montgomery, Orange Co, N Y, was visited by a conflagration, which destroyed 7 bldgs owned by Mr D W Waring, [formerly the property of Joshua Conger, dec'd,] a double dwlg house the property of Gen Borland, & the dwlg of Mr Abner Bookstaver.

John Riley, the landlord of the Bunch of Grapes Tavern, #10 Front Levee, First Municipality, New Orleans, committed suicide on Feb 12, by drowning himself in the Mississippi. He had a wife & 1 child, & was long regarded as an upright & industrous man. He left a letter. He paid a boy to take him out near the center of the river in a skiff, & when there he jumped into eternity.

Hse/o Reps: 1-Ptn of Mary Harris, wid/o Newsom Harris, praying for a pension. 2-Ptn of Nancy G Van Rensselaer, wid/o Col Henry K Van Rensselaer, which was taken from the files & referred to the Cmte on Revolutionary Pensions. 3-Ptn of Mrs Sarah Hammond, wid/o John Hammond, dec'd, praying that a law may pass allowing to her a pension commensurate with the services of her husband in the Revolutionary war. 4-Certain documents were presented in support of the claim of Thos C Miller, relative to a contract with the U S for working an ore bed near Harper's Ferry, Va.

Mr H Wallis, a Veterinary Surgeon, who has come to reside in Washington, & who has been confined to his room for a month from a severe accident, will be able to attend to his professional business in a few days. He will be heard of at Messrs Walker & Kimmell's ofc.

Balt, Feb 26. Mr R W Pooler, one of the seconds in the late duel near Gtwn, was arrested this morning at Barnum's Hotel, where he had been sojourning, by ofcrs Hays, Zell, & Ridgely, charged, on the oath of John S Lutz, who is also boarding there, with stealing from him the sum of $200-found in the prisoner's drawers. Witnesses were Mr Z Barnum, Mr Lutz, & Patrick Quinn. -Patriot

Madame Catalani, in her letter to a Leipsic journal, denying emphatically the report that she is dead. She adds, that at age 64, she still retains good health, & lives in quiet retirement. This is the 4th time my decease has been announced. I read with satisfaction the many praises with which my fancied decease was accompanied. Her letter is very pleasantly written.

Wash Corp: 1-Cmte of Claims: asked to be discharged from further consideration of the ptn of Wm Markward: ordered to lie on the table. 2-Ptn of Jos Swaggart: ordered to lie on the table.

Criminal Court-Wash. 1-Jeff Robinson, Grafton Harper, & John Bennett were indicted with Jas Ellis, for an assault on various persons & a riot at Gtwn in Aug last. The dfndnts were found guilty. 2-Arthur Bridge, indicted for an assault on Bernard Kelley, & for resisting F P Bostar, a constable, in the discharge of his duty, was found guilty on both indictments, but recommended by the jury to the mercy of the Court. After admonition from Judge Dunlop, he was sentenced to a fine of $5 & costs for the first offence, & $10 & costs for the second offence. 3-Benj Harper, indicted for an assault on Geo Chamberlane, found guilty. 4-Thos Hill, John H Bean, & John O'Neal, tried on 3 separate indictments for assaulting Moses Latham, found not guilty.

Mrd: on Feb 22, by Rev Mr Samson, Mr Jas B Wright to Miss Mary Parker, all of Wash City.

Mrd: on Feb 19, at Columbus, Ga, by Rev Albert Williams, Mr Wm K Moore, formerly of Wash City, to Miss Cornelia C Hays, of Muscogee Co, Ga.

Died: on Feb 25, at his late residence on 2nd st east, near the Catholic Church, Saml W Lewis, in his 62nd year.

THU FEB 29, 1844
Instant death by the bursting of one of the large guns on board the U S ship **Princeton**, of Sec Abel P Upshur, Sec Thos W Gilmer, Cmdor Kennon, & Virgil Maxcy. She was underway yesterday in the river Potomac, 14 or 15 miles below this Wash City. Yesterday was appointed, by the courtesy of Capt Stockton, Cmder of the Princeton, for receiving visiters to his fine ship lying off Alexandria: not less in number than 400, among whom were the Pres of the U S, the Heads of several Depts, & their families. Stockton allowed the gun to be fired again, below *Fort Washington*. Explosion followed. The above 4 were all slain, as was Mr Gardner, of N Y. 17 seamen were wounded, several badly & probably mortally. Capt Stockton was stunned by the explosion; as was Col Benton, of the Senate; Lt Hunt of the **Princeton**; W D Robinson, of Gtwn. The bodies of the killed remained on board the ship last night. They will be brought to the city this morning. [Slain: Sec Upshur-Sec of State. Sec Gilmer, recently placed at the head of the Navy. Cmdor Beverly Kennon, a gallant ofcr. Virgil Maxcy, lately returned from a diplomatic residence at the Hague. Mr David Gardner, of N Y, formerly a Member of the Senate of N Y.] [Mar 4 newspaper: We are glad to hear that Capt Stockton, who, though not seriously wounded, was so much stunned by the explosion as for some days to threaten serious consequences, is gradually recovering.] [See Mar 13, 1844 extraction.]

Hse/o Reps: 1-Bills reported-for the relief of: Harvey Heth; heirs of Hyacinth Lassell; of Stanley White; & of Beziah, an Indian. 3-Ptn & papers of Jas McAvoy, of Hendricks Co, Ind, asking for compensation for work done on the national road. 4-Papers on the application of Levy Johnson, of Hendricks Co, Ind, asking for a pension for wounds received in the last war. 5-Ptns of Philo C Fuller & others, & of O M Willey & others, for the abolition of franking privilege & a reduction of the postage: referred to the Cmte on the Post Ofc & Post Roads. 6-Ptn of Andrew Robeson & others, to import iron for the Fall River Railroad free. 7-Ptn of John J Giles & 191 other citizens of Rockport, Mass, for an appropriation to complete the Sandy Bay breakwater. 8-Memorial of S W Stephens & 93 others, citizens of Indiana, in favor of a grant of lands to complete the central Canal to Evansville. 9-Memorial of Alex'r Burns, jr, & 222 others, citizens of Indiana, in favor of the abolition of the franking privilege & the reduction of the postage.

Another shade of insanity. On Thu, at East Cambridge, Mass, Miss Fanny Weir, of Lowell, was convicted of administering oil of tansey to her sister's illegitimate infant. One ground of defence was, that she had a monomania for the destruction of illegitimate children.

This is a continuance of ptns presented by John Quincy Adams to the Hse/o Reps: at the 28th Congress, 1st session, with the disposal of them by the House. 1-Ptn of Thos G Copeland, & inhabitants of Cortland Co, N Y, amendment of the Constitution, abolish slave representation. Same for Geo G Jesap, & others of Palmyra, Wayne Co, N Y. Same for Jairus Lincoln, & citizens of Hingham, Mass. Same for Isaac Alden, & citizens of East Bridgewater, Mass. Same for Mino Pratt, & citizens of West Roxbury, Mass. 2-Ptn of J M W Geist, & citizens of Lancaster Co, Pa, to reduce postage & abolish franking. 3-Ptn of John C C Hall, & citizens of Md, law for the recovery of fugitive slaves. 4-Ptn of H D Finney, & citizens of Tioga Co, N Y, amendment Constitution, slave representaion. 5-Ptn of Winthrop Wright, & inhabitants of Will Co, Ill, against annexation of Texas. Same for Saml H Woods, & citizens of Indiana. Same for S M Archer, & citizens of Indiana. 6-Ptn of Wm H Freeman, complaining of a sentence of a court martial. 7-Ptn of Eliz Crane, wid/o Peter Crane, Canton Mass, for a pension: referred to the Cmte on Revolutionary Pensions. 8-Ptn of Chas Larrabee, Hartford, Conn, to investigate a paragraph of the message of Pres Jackson of Dec 8, 1829: referred to the Cmte of Invalid Pensions. 9-Ptn of citizens of the State of N Y, for the adoption of measures to procure the release of certain American prisoners in Van Dieman's Land: referred to the Cmte on Foreign Affairs. 10-Ptn of Edw Van Horn, & citizens of Harrison Co, Ohio, in relation to the case of John L Brown, a prisoner in Fairfield district, S C: referred to the Judiciary. 11-Ptn of Mabbett, & 143 other citizens of Erie Co, N Y, praying that representation may be based upon free population. Referred to the select Cmte on Massachusetts Resolutions.

Died: on Mon last, Sophia, infant dght/o Saml & Mary Ann Bacon, aged 6 months & 7 days.

The Editor of the Vermonter has been shown a lock of hair taken from the head of Mrs Mary Barton, of Hinesburgh, Vt, on the day when she was 102 years old. It is black & glossy: the health of the old lady is exceedingly good; she dresses & undresses herself with perfect ease; her appetite is good, & her intellectual faculties remain unimpaired.

Died: on Feb 11, at the residence of his son, in North Woodbury township, Bedford Co, Pa, Henry Kifer, a Revolutionary soldier of 1776, who had attained the astonishing age of 110 years & 6 months.

Yesterday the lady of Mr Joel K Post administered, as she supposed, a spoonful of rhubarb to her dght about 2 years old; it was discovered laudanum had been given. The child died last evening. –New Haven Palladium of Fri.

The body of a young man named Eastman was found in his father's barn, in Topsham, Vt, a few days since. He had a stepmother who hated him, & excited his father to indulge in ill feelings towards him. On the evening previous to his being found he had an altercation with his parents on his going to singing-school, & it is supposed they had murdered him.

Senate: 1-Ptn from John S Bell, Ezekiel Starr, & John R Rogers, in behalf of certain Cherokee Indians, representing the grievances under which they labor, & asking the interposition of the Gov't. 2-Ptn from W P McConnell, asking an appropriation for the construction of a steamship upon a plan invented by him. 3-Cmte on Indian Affairs: bill for the relief of the legal reps of Geo Duvall & other Cherokees. 4-Cmte on Naval Affairs: adverse report on the memorial of Alonzo B Davis. Same cmte: joint resolution in favor of D M F Hunter.

Nicholas Biddle died yesterday morning, at his country residence in Andalusia, on the Delaware, after a sickness marked by excessive pain, born with manly constancy. Mr Biddle was a native of Wash City; he was little more than 58 years old, having been born in 1786. He was a s/o Chas Biddle, distinguished for his attachment to the Whig cause. He is known now for his connection with the U S Bank. –Phil U S Gaz of yesterday morning.

Circuit Court of Wash Co, D C. Wm H Marquis has applied to be discharged from imprisonment under the act for the relief of Insolvent Debtors: hearing on the first Mon of Apr next. –Wm Brent, clk

Mrd: on Feb 22, in Barnsville, Montg Co, Md, by Rev John M Jones, the Rev Jas G Hening, of the Methodist Episcopal Church, to Miss Alice Ann, y/d/o the late John Webster Wilson, of Balt.

Died: on Sunday, at her late residence, *Forrest Hall*, St Mary's Co, Md, Mrs Emily Forrest, relict of the late Gen Jas Forrest. For the last 12 months her health had been gradually declining, under the irritative influence of general rheumatism. Since Sept she had been confinced almost entirely to her bed, unable to change her position without assistance. Her children & friends will long mourn the loss of her society & example. [Feb 28th newspaper: Died: on Feb 18, at *Forest Hall*, St Mary's Co, Md, after a long & painful illness, Mrs Emily Forrest, relict of the late Gen Jas Forrest.]

Died: on Feb 25, at Hoboken, N Y, Mrs Harriet Sands, w/o Cmder Sands, U S Navy, & d/o the late Col John Stevens.

FRI MAR 1, 1844
Gentlemen: Merchant Tayloring & Fashionable Clothing Store, opposite Concert Hall. –C Eckloff

Agency for Claims at Washington- claims upon either of the Depts or Congress. –Chas De Felding, Rm 11 Todd'd Bldg, Pa ve, Wash City.

W B Todd, Fashionable Hatter, sign of the Golden Hat, west of Brown's Hotel: a tasty hat, he will introduce on Fri.

For rent: convenient house on 12th st west, near the late residence of Lewis H Machen. Apply on the premises to Dr Hunter, or to Capt Warder next door, or to: -E Coolidge, G, near 21st st.

Crape-jet & blue black crape: suitable for articles for mourning, at F Pulvermacher's Branch store, Pa ave, between 9th & 10th sts.

Public sale: by virtue of a decree of the Circuit Court of D C for Wash Co, pronounced in a cause wherein Geo Bomford is cmplnt & Chas J Nourse & others are dfndnts, the following valuable property, [late of Jos Nourse,] sale on Apr 2 next. Lots 6 & 7 in square 141, Wash City. Part of lot 6 in square 78. Dwlg houses & other improvements on each of the above lots. Part of lot 10 in square 168. Lots 19 & 20 in square 77. Lots 13 & 14 in square 101. Lot 3 in square east of square 87. Lot 6 in square 48. Lots 6, 7, 9, 10, 11, 12, 16, & 17 in square 67. –W Redin, Trustee -Holmead & Wright, Auctioneers

From official notice: Atty Gen [Hon John Nelson] has been appointed Acting Sec of State, & Cmdor Lewis Warrington to be Acting Sec of the Navy.

The bodies of the lamented Upshur, Gilmer, Maxcy, Kennon, & Gardner were brought to Wash City yesterday, in coffins, from the ship **Princeton**, & were conveyed, with due solemnity, to the Pres' House, & placed in the East room, there to await the funeral ceremonies, to take place on Sat at 11 o'clock. No death has occurred besides those mentioned, except that of a servant of the Pres, a colored man, who was near the gun at the time of its exploding. The Hon David Gardiner, was of Suffolk Co, Long Island.

Mr Robinson, of Va, the 1st Lt of the U S brig **Somers**, died at Trinidad de Cuba on Jan 18. The Somers arrived at Pensacola on the 13th ult.

Mrd: Feb 22, in PG Co, Md, at the Chapel of the Holy Trinity, by the Rector, Rev Mr Mackenheimer, Nicholas H Shipley, of Fred'k Co, to Margaret, d/o the late John Contee, of PG Co, Md.

Coal for sale: on hand at his woodyard, on 10th st, from 60 to 70 tons of gray Ash Coal, which will be delivered low for cash. –Peter Casanave

In Chancery, Circuit Court of Wash Co, D C. Ann Sophia Simpson, by her next friend, Jas A Simpson, et al, vs, Maurice W Hoffman, Catherine Baer, John H Hoffman, Jas H Hoblitzel & Catherine his wife, Thos A Healy & Emily his wife, Zelia Hoffman, John H Harrison, Thos C Harrison, Wm J N Harrison, Maurice H Harrison, Wm C Hoffman, John Reich & Juliana his wife, & all others, legal reps of John Hoffman, late of Fred'k Co, dec'd, et al. The bill charges that said John Hoffman, dec'd, during his life & up to his death, was seised in fee simple of the legal estate in lot 14, of Beatty & Hawkins' Addition to Gtwn, with the appurtenances, & the above named dfndnts comprise his legal reps so far as known, in whom said legal estate now vests by descent from him, & that said legal estate is so held subject to an obligation by agreement & bond of conveyance of said John Hoffman to convey the same for the separate use of said Ann Sophia Simpson & of her children, who are also parties ccomplainants, in several estates set forth in the bill. The objects of the bill are to effect such conveyance, & for general relief. And forasmuch as it is averred & made to appear that the said named dfndnts reside & are out of D C, it is by the Court, this Feb 29, 1844, ordered, that said dfndnts do, on or before the first Mon of Jul next, appear in Court & show cause, if any they have, why the complainants should not have relief as prayed. –Jas S Morsell
-Wm Brent, clk

Honey in the Comb: just received from N Y. –S Holmes, Grocer, 7th st

Orders will be issued in token of respect for the memory of Capt Beverly Kennon, late of the U S Navy, & Chief of the Bureau of Construction.
–John Tyler, Feb 29, 1844

Criminal Court-Wash, Feb 28. 1-John Warwick was found not guilty of assaulting Dr Doniphan with a shoe-knife. 2-John Parker & Jos Jingle were tried for a riot at a camp meeting. The former was found guilty; the latter was found not guilty. 3-Wm Garner was found guilty of stealing an anchor of the value of $3, the property of John McPherson. 4-Jane Hewitt, a slave, was put up on trial in the latter part of the day under an indictment charging her with the heinous & capital offence of attempting to poison Mrs Mary Ann Jeffers, by mixing up white lead in the milk which was put into the chocolate drank by Mrs Jeffers on Oct 24 last. Case was still before the Court & Jury when the Court adjourned.

SAT MAR 2, 1844
Assignee's sale in Bankruptcy: by order of virtue of sundry decrees, passed by the Circuit Court of Wash Co, D C: sitting in Bankruptcy: sale on Mar 11, at the auction room of Wm M Morrison, the pieces & parcels of property & effects hereinafter specified in the cases set forth, to wit: in the matter of John Hoover will be sold a judgment obtained by the said Hoover, on May 7, 1838, vs Job Alberger, of Buffalo, N Y, in the proper court of the said State, for $11,433.64, with all the rights of the official assignee to prosecute & recover the same at the cost of the purchaser from the said Alberger. In the matter of John R Dorsey, a lot of silver plate, in amount sufficient to accommodate a large boarding establishment. In the matter of Wm McGrath, sundry notes & accounts due & assigned by decree in bankruptcy. In the matter of John P Van Tyne, all his interest, right, title in a certain patent, granted & issued on Mar 31, 1837, to Elijah Jaquith, for a truss, for the use of the hernia, being one entire half of the said patent. All of which effects & property will be sold to the highest bidder for cash at the time & place above mentioned. –D A Hall, Assignee - W M Morrison, Auctioneer

Obit-died: at Mount St Mary's College, Emmittsburg, Md, after a painful illness, Robt Randolph Dulaney, 2nd s/o Capt Bladen Dulaney, U S Navy. He had not reached his 13th year. His innocence & goodness rendered him doubly dear to his devoted parents & family. [No date-current item.]

To be at the funeral of those lost on the ship **Princeton**: 1-Wash Light Infty to meet at their Armory this sat at 9 o'clock, in winter uniform, for the purpose of joining the funeral procession. –R France, Capt 2-Nat'l Blues, in full winter uniform. By order of Capt Tucker: Geo Emrick, 1st Sergeant. 3-Mechanical Riflemen: in full winter uniform. By order of Capt McClelland: R E Doyle, O S. 4-Franklin Fire Co to meet at the Engine-house, to attend the funeral. –Wm Durr, Sec

English Papers. Announcement of the demise of Mrs Lytton Bulwer, by which event Sir E L Bulwer succeeds to the ancient mansion & estates of Knebwath, in Herts, to which she was the heiress. -Herald

The remains of Mr Virgil Maxcy were brought from the Pres' mansion to the house of Francis Markoe, jr, his son-in-law, late on Feb 29, from whence, at any early hour the following morning, they were conveyed to the estate of the dec'd, at West River, Md, to be interred in the family vault, in accordance with the wishes of the family.

Death has stricken another victim in the midst of us, in the person of the Hon Henry Frick, one of the Reps from Pa, who breathed his last yesterday, at his lodgings in Wash City. He was in the 50th year of his age, & was in delicate health when he came on to attend Congress. He has left a widow & a number of children, one of whom was with him for several days before his death. His remains are to be taken home for interment at the place of his residence.

Hon Saml Fowler, of Sussex Co, N J, died at his residence at Franklin Furnace on Feb 26, in his 66th year. Dr Fowler was a distinguished member of the medical profession, & had twice represented N J in the Nat'l Legislature.

At the celebration of Washington's birthday in New Hanover, Pa on Thu last, Mr Jacob Decker, of the New Hanover Artillerists, a young man, was killed by the premature discharge of the artillery while loading it. He died in a few minutes.

Orphan's Court of Wash Co, D C. In the case of Eleanor C Simmes, admx of John D Simmes, dec'd. The admx has appointed Mar 22 for final settlement of said deceased's estate. –Ed N Roach, Reg/o wills

Members of the Foreign Diplomatic Corps are invited to attend the funeral of the Hon Abel P Upshur, the Hon Thos W Gilmer, Capt Beverly Kennon, the Hon Virgil Maxcy, & Hon David Gardiner, at 11 o'clock, on Mar 2, at the President's Mansion. Pall-bearers to precede the hearse: The Hon Mr Archer of Va & members of the Cmte on Foreign Relations of the Senate. The Hon C J Ingersoll of Pa, & members of the Cmte on Foreign Affairs of the Hse/o Reps. Family & relatives of the Hon Mr Upshur; of the late Hon Mr Gilmer; of the late Capt Kennon; of the Hon Mr Maxcy; of the late Col Gardiner follow. The Pres of the U S & Cabinet Ministers; Ex-Presidents of the U S; Pres of the Senate & Sec, etc, will then follow.

The following gentlemen will be respected as Assist Marshals, & will be on horseback with appropriate badges:

Wm B Randolph	Thos Blagden
Jos H Bradley	R Barker
Wm D Nutt	Wm B Woodward
J M Cutts	Robt Lawrence
Thos Woodward	Wm A Gordon
F H Davidge	Chas Van Ness
Theodore Kane	Richd McCulloh
Wm B Magruder	C A Alexander

Robt S Chew
Thos Allen
L B Hardin
-Alex'r Hunter, Marshal of D C

J Robbins
R Patterson
Col Stull

Hse/o Reps: 1-Cmte of Claims: bill for the relief of the legal reps of Capt Saml Shannon, dec'd. Bill for the relief of Geo W Clarke, Harris Cook, & John Brainen, 2nd, with a report in each case. Adverse reports in the cases of Cornelius V C Ludlow, John W Custer, Cyrus C Scott, John Webb, dec'd, Ira Carpenter, & Spencer Price. 2-Cmte of Claims, reported joint resolutions of the following titles, to wit: for relief of Saltmarsh & Fuller. Relief of Wm Fuller, with a report in each case. 3-Cmte of Claims: adverse report on the ptn of the exc of Robt Sewall. 4-Cmte on the Public Lands: bill for the relief of Eaton Nance, reported the same without amendment. 5-Cmte of Claims: adverse report on the ptn of Wm N Maver. 6-Cmte on the Public Lands: adverse reports upon the ptns of Geo H Collins & of members of the Legislature of Indians, for a donation of land to O'Brien McNamee. Also, a report on the ptn of Mary Ann Bruner. 7-Cmte on the Judiciary: act for the relief of Edw Kennard, reported without amendment. Same cmte: report on the ptn of Thos Hunter & Alex'r Caldwell, of Ky, with a bill for their relief. Same cmte: report on the ptn of Chas Holt, with a bill for his relief. Same Cmte: adverse reports on the ptns of David Cooke & Benj Heartt. 8-Cmte on Private Land Claims: report on the case of Woodsen Wren, of Mississippi, with a bill for his relief. Adverse report on the case of John P Lauderman. Same cmte: report on the ptn of Jas Pepper, with a bill for his relief. Same cmte, bill for the relief of John Miller. 9-Bill for the relief of Jas Journey. 10-Cmte on Private Lands: to which was referred the bill to authorize the location of the land claims of Antoine Vasquez & others, confirmed by an act of Jul 4, 1836, reported back the same with a report. 11-Cmte on Military Affairs: bill for relief of the heirs of Gen Wm Eaton. 12-Cmte on Naval Affairs: adverse report on the memorial of Lewis Warrington, John B Nicholson, Philip F Voorhees, & John Percival, in behalf of the ofcrs & crew of the ship **Peacock**. Same cmte: adverse report on the ptn of pensioners in the Naval Asylum at Phil. 13-Cmte on Revolutionary Claims: bill for the relief of Eliz Fitch. Same cmte: bill granting a pension to Bethia Healy. Same cmte: bill for the relief of Betsey Clapp. Same cmte: bill for the following: relief of Danl Ingalls; & of Abigail Gibson. Same cmte: relief of Franklin P Ambler, Chas P Ambler, & Eliz Pearce, surviving children of Eliz Rowe, with a report in each case. 14-Cmte on Revolutionary Claims: bill for the relief of Violet Calhoun. 15-Cmte on Revolutionary Pensions: bill for the relief of Susanna Scott, wid/o Wm Scott. 16-Cmte on Invalid Pensions: adverse report on the ptn of Moses Davis. Same cmte: adverse reports on the ptns of Moses Davis, Levi Brown, Jas Donohay, & Danl Woolford. Same cmte: adverse reports on the ptns of Francis Ducoing & Bartlett Holmes. Same cmte: bill for the relief of Saml Butler. Same cmte: adverse report on the ptn of Levi M Roberts. Same cmte: bill for the relief of Elijah Blodget. 17-Cmte on Public Lands: adverse report on the ptn of Michl Sullivant. 18-Cmte on Commerce: bills for the relief of Jos Hidden, owner of the fishing schnr **Mary Frances**; Joshua Knowles, jr & others, owners of the fishing schnr **Garnet**; & Zaccheus Knowles, owner of the fishing schnr **Florilla**.

Orphan's Court of Wash Co, D C. Letters testmentary on the personal estate of Geo Adams, late of said county, dec'd. –Jamima Adams, John Geo Adams, Thos Nelson Adams, excs

Circuit Court of Wash Co, D C. Alfred Gray has applied to be discharged from imprisonment under the act for the relief of Insolvent Debtors: hearing on the first Mon in Apr next. Same for Tarpley Lucas. -Wm Brent, clk

MON MAR 4, 1844
General Convention of the Whigs of Middle Tenn was held at Nashville on the 22nd ult: nomination of Henry Clay for Pres was received with bursts of applause. Speeches were made by Gov Jones, John Bell, Wm B Campbell, Mr Collum, of Smith, E H Ewing, & others. Selected as delegates:

Geo Glascock	Walter Coleman	John J White
John B McCormick	D M Leatherman	Jos Miller
W B Hoffa	A M Rosborough	Geo W Martin
Micah Taul	W P J Burrus	W W Pepper
Thos C Whiteside	Thompson Anderson	E H Foster, jr
J H Jones	Simeon Venable	Gen Richd Cheatham

To be let: the large house on Pa ave, nearly opposite Fuller's & Gallebrun's Hotel, heretofore occupied by the Treas Dept, at present by Mrs Turpin as a boarding house. –Thos Munroe

We learn from Springfield, Mass, that on Mon, as Mrs Pyncheon, a widow lady, & Miss Lucretia Bliss, a lady who resides in her family, were starting in a sleigh on an errand, their horse became frightened and ran down the street with great speed. They were thrown out with great violence and Miss Bliss hit a tree & died in about an hour. Mrs Pyncheon was bruised.

The wounded of the steamer **Princeton**:
Jos Traisol, quarter-gunner, severe contusion of the hip
John Potter, quarter-gunner, contusion of the breast
Wm Taylor, ordinary seaman, wound of the knee-joint & fracture of the legs
Jas M Green, seaman, contused leg
Chas Lewis, capt of the forecastle, wounded face, with face & hands burnt
John L Kissich, gunner's-mate, face wounded & burnt; also, contusion of the thigh
Jas H Dunn, marine, severe contusion of the left side
Chas H Robinson, seaman, contusion about the eyes & forehead
Wm H Canning, seaman, wound & contusion of the leg

The Pres of the U S has respited the execution of David Babe, convicted of piracy, for the term of 30 days from the 8th instant. The letter enclosing the reprieve is dated the 27th ult, & was one of the last official acts of the late Sec of State.

It has been stated in several papers that the steamer **Princeton** was under the command of Lt McLaughlin. This is not the fact. Lt McLaughlin was not attached to the ship, but among the guests on board. Immediately on the occurrence of the accident, he very handsomely volunteered for duty, & was assigned the charge of the wounded & dead by Lt Thomson, who, as the first ofcr, took command of the vessel, Capt Stockton having been wounded. –Alexandria Gaz

The French painter Ingres, the rival of Horace Vernet, has just received $20,000 for decorating with the Four Seasons an apartment in the castle of the Duke De Luynes.

Robinson Gordon, a merchant from Ohio, committed suicide at the Merchant's Hotel, Phil, on Wed. He had been there for a number of days sick. A tendency to mania was apparent on Wed, & he snatched a small knife from the table of his brother, & inflicted deep wounds on his person.

The Elyria [Ohio] Atlas gives the sentence of H C Taylor, a clergyman, & editor of a religious paper in the West, who pleaded guilty to the crime of seduction, & stealing, was sentenced to be imprisoned in the county jail for one year, pay a fine of $200, & the costs of prosecution, & fined $25 on 3 charges of larceny.

New Orleans, Feb 22 1844. Whig Mass Convention: venerable patriot of 76, Gen P Thomas presided, assisted by 17 Vice Presidents, one from each Senatorial district, among whom were ex Govn'r White, Ex-Govn'r Roman, Hon T A Chinn, Gen Morgan, & Hon G S Guion. Hon S S Prentiss, of Miss, addressed the assemblage. Gove Poindexter spoke. Cmte appointed Roman as Pres, & Chinn & Hon T Butler as Vice Presidents. Electors below:

Jacques Toutant	G S Guion	Jacques Dupie
Zenon Cavelier	Lafayette Saunders	Edw Sparrow

Washington's Birthday Celebration at Gtwn College, was observed on Feb 27, [delayed from the usual Feb 22nd] when Mr Wm F Brooke, of Md, read the Farewell Address of the Father of his Country, & an oration was delivered by Mr Edw O Donnell, of N Y.

TUE MAR 5, 1844
Phil Gaz of Mar 2: the funeral of the late Nicholas Biddle took place from the residence of his brother-in-law, Francis Hopkinson. A very long train of private carriages followed the body, which was borne in a hearse, to Christ Church Burial Ground, in Arch st, below Fifth. Interment was made in the family vault. Dr Dorr, Rector of Christ Church, read the service.

Mr Chas Augustus Davis, of N Y C, was on board the U S steamer **Princeton** at the time of the explosion. He says he was standing about 10 feet from where the gun was fired, behind Capt Stockton. He owes his escape to having clambored up on the inner rigging, with a lady, [Mrs Wethered, of Balt,] a few feet above the deck, and the only injury he received was a slight contusion on the upper lip. Wm Strickland, of Phil was also on board. He writes that Capt Stockton had all his hair burnt off. Strickland remembers being prostrated on the deck.

Jane E Hewitt, a slave, indicted for attempting to administer poison to Mrs Ann Jeffers of Wash City, Oct 24 last, was resumed yesterday, and she was found not guilty.

Senate: 1-Ptn from Jas M Breedlove, asking compensation for the use of his steamer employed against the pirates in 1841. 2-Additional documents were presented in the case of H P Lawson, Jno Mullikin, Robt Ford, & others. 3-Ptn from David Baker, asking a renewal of his patent for the invention of a curvilinear saw. 4-Message was received from the Hse/o Reps on the death of Henry Frick, of Pa. Mr Frick was born in Northumberland Co, Pa, in 1795. At an early age he learned the noble art of printing in the city of Phil. Whilst yet in his minority, he united himself to a volunteer company & took up arms in defence of his country during the late war with Great Britain. In 1816 he established a political journal in his native county, which he conducted for more than 20 years, & is still owned & conducted by members of his family. He died on Fri last, after a long & lingering illness. He was an affectionate husband, a kind father, & a sincere friend. The widowed partner of his boson requested that his mortal remains be carried home for interment. His body left on Sat last, accompanied by his son & 2 of his friends from the other House. The Senate do now adjourn.

Hse/o Reps: 1-Ptn of Robt Brady, of Phil, praying Congress to indemnify him for the loss of the schnr **Eagle**, taken from him for the public service in 1813. 2-Memorial of John McManus 63 other citizens of Clarke Co, Ill, asking a grant of lands to complete the national thoroughfare between the Lakes & the Ohio, by the improvement of the Wabash. 3-Memorial of Solomon Malon & other citizens of the Clarke Co, Ill, asking an appropriation on the Cumberland road.

Wanted to hire: a smart colored Girl, to take care of an infant. One with good character may apply at Mrs Manning's, on 13th st, between E & F sts.

Died: on Sat last, in N Y, at age 89 years, Joshua Waddington, one of the oldest & most respected inhabitants of that city. He was a merchant, & had been, from its commencement in 1784 up to last year, a Dir of the Bank of N Y, & punctual in his attendance.

Died: on Feb 23, in Louisville, Ky, Rev Wm Jackson, rector of St Paul's Church in that place, & formerly rector of St Paul's Church in Alexandria, D C, a minister of the exemplary life & character.

Died: on Feb 26, at Rokeby, Fauquier Co, Va, in her 24th year, after a few days' illness, Eliza Carter Randolph, w/o Nathan Loughborough, jr, & d/o the late Thos Turner, of Kinloch.

Died: on Feb 20, at *Rosemont*, his residence in Clark Co, Va, Geo H Norris, in his 70th year, truly respected & deeply regretted by a large circle of friends & acquaintances.

Montg Co, Md. In the matter of Basil B Pleasants, vs Henry Howard, Virginia P Howard, Laura P Howard, Marshall Howard, & Hamilton Howard. On application of Basil B Pleasants, representing that he is interested in taking the testimony of Thos Rigg, of Saml, & Richd Brooke, touching the time Jas B Pleasants, of said county, has boarded with said Basil, & the terms of & allowance for said board, to be used against the said Henry, Virginia, Laura, Marshall, & Hamilton Howard, all of whom are non-residents, & have no agent or atty in the State, except the said Marshall, who resides in Balt, & requesting that notice of the time & place of taking said depositions may be given to them by advertisement or otherwise, it is this day, Feb 29, 1844. Depositions to be taken on Apr 1, 1844. –Jas Cook, Com'r

Circuit Court of Wash Co, D C. Wm Johnson has applied to be discharged from imprisonment under the act for the relief of Insolvent Debtors: hearing on the first Mon of Apr next. –Wm Brent, clk

WED MAR 6, 1844
Trustee's sale of Dry Goods: at the store of Mr C B Thornton, on Pa ave. –Wm Marshal, Auctioneer

Senate: 1-Ptn from Adam Carson, asking a right of pre-emption to a certain tract of land. 2-Ptn from Edmund Roberts & other sureties of Felix H Prain, dec'd, late Indian agent, asking reimbursement of the amount of judgment obtained against them by the U S. 3-Ptn from J Robertson & other assignees of the late Bank of the U S, asking the repayment of a sum of money advanced by that Bank to a contractor of the Gov't, as allowed by the accounting ofcrs in the settlement of his account. 4-Ptn from Robt Ramsay, a seaman, for increase of pension. 5-Ptn from Robt Fossett, a Revolutionary soldier, for a pension. 6-Ptn from a Ledoux & Co & Geo C Hall, asking permission to surrender certain lands entered as public lands, which proved to be subject to claims under Spanish grants, & to locate others in lieu thereof. 7-Cmte on Pensions: bill granting a pension to Geo Whitten. Same cmte: adverse report on the ptn of Jonah Bartow.

Signor Vito Viti will have a sale next week of China & plated ware, figures, vases, lamps, & Girondoles. –Wm Marshall, Auctioneer

Very handsome & superior furniture at private sale: just received from Mr S B Thomas, of Phil. –Wm Marshall's, Auction & Commission store, Pa ave, between 8th & 9th sts.

For rent, a desirable residence on Congress st, Gtwn, now occupied by Thos B Addison. The house is large & convenient. Apply to the subscriber at the Third Auditor's ofc, or at his residence adjoining the premises. –John Harry

Hse/o Reps: 1-Ptn of Isaac Strohm & 135 other citizens of the counties of Greene & Montg, in Ohio, praying for a reduction of postage, & for a limitation of the frankling privilege. Ptn of Geo W Wright & 60 others, citizens of Genesse Co, N Y, praying for the same. Ptn of Laban Hoskins & others, of Cayuga Co, N Y, praying for the same. 2-Ptn of Saml Jones, of Va, for a claim for services during the Revolutionary war. 3-Claim of Catharine Knaggs, of Monroe, Mich, for payment of damages sustained during the last war. 4-Ptn of Thos Boyle & 80 others, citizens of Indiana & other counties, Pa, praying that there may be no reduction of the duty on salt. 5-Ptn of John Scott, of DeWitt Co, Ill, praying compensation for a horse lost in the Revolutionary war.

The earthly remains of Virgil Maxcy, one of the sufferers on board the steamer **Princeton**-which, at the desire of his widow, were taken to his residence at *Tulip Hill*, on West river, by his son-in-law, Capt Hughes, U S A, & John Mercer, [one of his earliest & nearest friends,] were deposited in the family burial-place on Sat, attended by a numerous train of mourning friends & neighbors.

We learn by the arrival of the barque **Elizabeth**, from a whaling voyage, at Fall River, that Capt Winslow & 5 of his crew were lost on the coast of Kamschatka about the middle of Jun last. Those lost in the boat's crew were: Bradford W Winslow, capt; Geo Evans, Danl Reed, Benj Hall, foremast hands, all of Freetown; David Hathaway, boatsteerer, of Fall River. It appears that the capt's boat made fast to a whale; after 2 days the boat was found detached from the whale, bottom up. It is believed that the boat & all on board of her were carried down by the line getting foul, & not having time to extricate it.

Beautiful country seats at public sale: having divided my Farm into 3 portions containing about 60 acres: sale on Apr 15, [finding farming incompatible with my other pursuits.] Farm #1-60 to 70 acres, with a small dwlg. Farm #2-from 50 to 60 acres: with a mansion house, 40 feet by 39, 2 stories high, built of brick & pebble dashed, & covered in with slate; splendid portico with fluted columns. #3-about 60 acres. Taxes on the whole of the property are only $10 a year. Property will be shown by Mr Thomas, my manager, living on the place. –R France

The Hon Ebenezer Seaver died at his residence in Roxbury, Mass, on Fri last, at age 81. He was the Rep in Congress from that district 40 years ago, & continued it for 10 successive years.

Criminal Court-Wash. 1-Eliza Moran found guilty of keeping a disorderly house. 2-John Wise not guilty for an assault upon his wife. 3-Z Hazell found not guilty of keeping a disorderly house.

David Gardiner, who was killed by the accident on the steamer **Princeton**, was a resident of N Y, formerly of Easthampton, L I, near Sag Harbor, & in 1823 was brought forward by the People's Party in opposition to the regular Tammany candidate, Dr Huntington, of the same town, & elected to the Senate of the State by a large majority. He was about 55 years of age, a gentleman of fortune, & has left an interesting family to mourn his loss. Mr Gardiner was a brother of Saml S Gardiner, of Shelter Island, & formerly of N Y. The remains of Mr Gardiner, accompanied by his family, arrived on Mon in Balt from Wash, & were conveyed on in the Phil train for N Y. [Mar 7 newspaper: Visiter on board the **Princeton** said: In such a throng of visitors, moving & pressing about in all directions, it could scarcely be regarded as singular that entire order as to stations of ofcrs & crew should not be completely preserved, even if no accident had occurred-but this was not the fact.]

Meeting in Wash on the subject of establishing a system of public schools. Wm Archer, Chairman.
Cmte to elicite public feeling:

C A Davis	Wm Lloyd	B B French	Saml B Beach
G J Abbott	Saml Bacon	J B North	Thos Thornley
A F Wilcox	J F Callan	S Byington	Jas Crandle
John Wilson	Thos Donoho	S Frazier	
J F Haliday	N C Towle	J C Fitzpatrick	
-A F Wilcox, Sec			

The Legislature of Pa passed an act last week legalizing a marriage contract between Mr R F Brunson & his wife. The parties were uncle & niece, but were not acquainted with the fact until a considerable time after their marriage.

Wash Corp: 1-Ptn from Jos Abbott & others: referred to the Cmte on Improvements. 2-Ptn from John P Van Ness & others: referred to the Cmte on Improvements. 3-Cmte of Claims: referred the ptn of Geo McCauley: decided in the affirmative. 4-Ptn of Eli Davis, praying remission of a fine: referred to the Cmte of Claims. 5-Ptn of John T Clements & others, for improvement of 5th st west: referred to the Cmte on Improvements. 6-Ptn of W W Seaton & others: for a curb & footway on 7th st: referred.

Mrd: on Mar 5, at St John's Church, Wash, by Rev Mr Hawley, Maj A D Steuart, Paymaster U S Army to Mary B Atkinson, d/o the late Thos Bullitt, of Louisville, Ky.

Died: on Mar 2, Grenville C Cooper, Purser of the U S Navy, in his 44th year.

Died: on Mar 2, in his 78th year, Mr Benj Solomon, for the last 47 years a respected & esteemed citizen of Balt.

THU MAR 7, 1844
Hse/o Reps: 1-Ptn & papers of Skelton Felton, of Troy, N Y, praying a remuneration for damages sustained in the last war. 2-Ptn of Benj Parker & others, praying for an amendment of the Constitution so as to make the basis of representation uniform throughout the country. 3-Ptn of Henry Palmer & others, for a change of post route from Monroe to Ypsilanti, Mich. 4-Ptn of Mary W Thompson, asking for a pension. 5-Ptn of Grudon J Leeds & 96 others, citizens of N Y C & vicinity, praying for a repeal of the spirit ration law of the navy, & for some useful substitute therefore. 6-Claim of Henry Parke for balance of payment due him for services as surveyor, heretofore allowed, but not paid. 7-Ptn of the heirs of Capt Richd Lucas, praying the passage of a law granting to them the commutation pay due to their ancestor. 8-Ptn of Eliz James, wid/o Wm James, of Edgar Co, Ill, asking for a pension. 9-Ptn of Eliz Coy, wid/o Christopher Coy, of Lawrence Co, Ill, asking for a pension.

Senate: 1-Ptn from Seth M Leavenworth, asking the payment of a balance due him on a contract for carrying the mail. 2-Ptn from Rhodes Thompson, for a pension. 3-Ptn from the citizens of Cumberland Co, Va, asking that pensions may be granted to the widows & children of the ofcrs & crew of the U S schnr **Grampus**, lost at sea. 4-Ptn from the heirs & legal reps of Thos G Peachy, asking indemnity for property destroyed by the enemy during the Revolutionary war, while in possession of the continental troops. 5-Cmte on Pensions: was discharged from the further consideration of the ptn of Jas Low: it was referred to the Cmte on Naval Affairs. 6-Ptn of Wm McPherson was taken from the files & referred to the Cmte on Naval Affairs. 7-On the ptn of Mrs Susan Twigg: Mr Crittenden had leave to withdraw her papers from the files of the Senate. 8-On the ptn of the heirs of John B Chandonai: Mr White had leave to withdraw their papers. 9-The adverse report in the case of Eunice Pawling, reported from the Cmte on Revolutionary Claims: laid on the table. 10-Cmte on the Judiciary: ptn of David C Wilson, reported. Same for the ptn of Richd H Foote, adm of Wm Grayson. 11-Cmte on Naval Affairs: on the ptn of Julia L Weed: laid on the table. 12-Cmte on Pensions: memorial of Wareham Kingsby: laid on the table. 13-Bills engrossed: relief of Wm De Peyster & Henry M Cruger; & relief of Danl G Skinner, of Ala.

Copies of a Memorial lately addressed by Lt John T McLaughlin, of the Navy, to the Hse/o Reps of the U S, can be found in this newspaper: 2 columns. [Last one is dated Washington, Feb 15, 1844.]

A cow came to the subcriber's house on Mar 1, on *Greenleaf's Point*. Owner is to come forward & prove property, & pay charges & take her away.
–John Peak, *Greenleaf's Point*, 4½ st

Valuable manufacturing property for sale in the town of Milton, N C, belonging to the company. -J Wilson, agent Milton Mfgr Co

The Hon John C Calhoun, of S C, was yesterday nominated to the Senate by the Pres of the U S to fill the ofc of Sec of State: unanimously confirmed. 2-Ex-Govn'r Wilson Shannon, of Ohio, was nominated to be Minister to Mexico. Capt Wm C Bolton, U S Navy, to be Chief of the Bureau of Construction & Repairs of the Navy.

The U S ship **Delaware**, Capt Chas S Macauley, bearing the broad pennant of Cmdor Morris, arrived in Hampton Roads, from the Mediterranean, on Mon-time of leaving not yet known.

Whigs of East Tenn: chosen Electors-Thos A R Nelson; Robt H Hinds; John H Crozier. Assist Electors: Wm G Brownlow; Jas M Toole; Luke Lea. Alternates: Chas H Coffin, Danl L Coffin, & Jas Williams. Wm Heiskell was Pres of the Convention.

The trial of Thos Wilson Dorr for treason was commenced before the Supreme Court of R I at Newport on Feb 29. He demurred to the indictment on the grounds that the Court had not jurisdiction to try him in that county, as the offence, if any, was committed in Providence.

Died: on Mar 3, 1844, Mr Bennanuwill Barney Bowers, in his 45th year.

Fatal occurrence at New Orleans on Feb 24: misunderstanding between Col Danl H Twogood & L C Hornsley, in which Col Twogood was killed. Hornsley was committed to prison. Col Twogood's funeral was the largest ever known in New Orleans.

FRI MAR 8, 1844
Hse/o Reps: 1-Cmte of Claims: bill for the relief of the heirs of John Forsyth. Same cmte: adverse report on the ptn of Conrad Haire. Same cmte: adverse report on the ptn of Lowell G Mickles & F J Southworth. 2-Cmte on Revolutionary Pensions: bill for the relief of Eliz Gresham. 3-Cmte on Revolutionary Pensions: bill for the relief of Sarah Blackemore, wid/o Geo Blackemore, & a bill for the relief of Jas Crawford, with a report in each case. 4-Cmte on Revolutionary Pensions: bill for the relief of

Bartholomew Maguire. Same cmte: adverse reports on the cases of Jas Burr, Chas Young, Alex'r S Jackson, Parmelia Slavin, Wm Henderson, Dennis Doyle, & Wm Newton. 5-Cmte on Invalid Pensions: adverse reports on the ptns of Fielding G Brown & Jacob Libengood. Same cmte: bill for the relief of Lathrop Foster. 6-Cmte of Claims: bill for the relief of Capt Ira Baldwin. 7-Cmte on Invalid Pensions: adverse reports on the ptns of Lewis Gordon & Richd Oathondt. Same cmte: adverse reports on the ptns of Amos Daniels, Thos H Brown, Wm Allens, & Jas Maines. 8-Cmte of Accounts: report on the ptn of Geo Page, for his machine for cutting paper envelopes. 9-Joint Cmte on the Library, to which was referred the ptn of Thos F Gordon, reported a joint resolution for subscription to Gordon's Digest. Same cmte: adverse report in relation to the purchase of *Russell's Planetarium*. 10-Cmte on Revolutionary Pensions: to inquire into the placing of Geo Singly, a Revolutionary soldier, on the pension roll, under the act of Jun, 1832, & that his papers be referred to that cmte. 11-Cmte on Indian Affairs: to be authorized to summon Maj Eaton to testify in relation to the Cherokee claims. 12-Cmte on Military Affairs: was referred a bill to divide the U S into 2 military districts: seeking a communication from Maj Gen Winfield Scott on the merits of said bill. 13-Ptn of Maj Truman Cross, praying compensation for services rendered as acting Quartermaster Gen of the Army. 14-Memorial of Jas Mitchell, asking pay for losses sustained by his father during the Revolutionary war.

Senate: 1-Ptn from Chas D Chesterfield, stating that gross frauds were practiced by several surveyors of public lands in Florida, & asking that Congress will adopt means to prevent them in the future. 2-Ptn from Cyrus Taber, asking that patents may be issued for certain lands purchased from the Pottawatamie Indians. 3-Cmte on Naval Affairs: bill for the relief of Revnell Coates, Walter R Johnson, & Wm B McMurtrie. 4-Introduced: bill for the relief of Gideon Foster. 5-Passed: bill for the relief of Wm De Peyster & Henry M Cruger. Bill for the relief of Danl G Skinner, of Ala: passed.

Md House of Delegates, on Mar 5, the following resolution & preamble, submitted by Mr Johnson, were unanimously adopted by the House: It appears that Cmder Wm J Belt, of PG Co, was dismissed the naval service of the U S, by a court-martial, in 1842, after having received, in defence of his country, many & severe wounds, & been subjected to numerous privations & sufferings; it further appearing to this Genr'l Assembly, by testimony of several ofcrs of the navy, that the said Cmder Belt, up to the period of the accusation against him, deservedly enjoyed the reputation of a faithful, gallant, & accomplished ofcr, & that his dismissal from the service is regretted by them, & that since the sentence, Wm J Belt, has, by his exemplary life, won for himself the esteem, confidence, & affection of his neighbors & friends. Resolved by the Assembly, that the Pres of the U S be requested to reinstate Cmder Wm J Belt to the station he held in the American navy, & from which he was dismissed by a court-martial in the year 1842.

Circuit Court of Wash Co, D C. Wilkerson G Williams has applied to be discharged from imprisonment under the act for the relief of Insolvent Debtors: hearing on the first Mon in Apr next. Same for Thos S Briggs. —Wm Brent, clk

On Tue last, Jos Eaches was re-elected Mayor of the town of Alexandria for the ensuing year.

House for rent: a large frame dwlg on 7th st south of the Tiber, & near the residence of W A Bradley. -Simon Fraser

A card from C H Winder in regard to his connexion with the Lt John T McLaughlin affair. The accounts presented to me by him induced the Sec of the Navy to give me instructions to examine them. The vouchers of Lt McL were printed in pamphlet form. Purser McLaughlin had only to have the approval of Cmder McLaughlin, & his accounts would pass. The expenditures of the expedition was about $500,000. At the outset of this expedition McL was notoriously poor; on his return he exhibited the evidences of such great wealth as to give rise to embarrassing surmises & queries. McL told a gentleman that he had recovered a large amount from the estate of a dec'd gentleman in Balt. The family of Lt McL deny in total this story. His father, a tailor, died heavily in debt. —C H Winder

Circuit Court of Wash Co, D C. Wm B Burger has applied to be discharged from imprisonment under the act for the relief of Insolvent Debtors: hearing on Mar 16. —Wm Brent, clk

On Mar 6 the following Delegates were elected for Wash City:

John D Barclay	Jas F Haliday	Jas H Birch
W B Magruder	Robt Coltman	Saml Burche
Wm Wilson	John France	John Purdy
R M Harrison	Peter Force	Saml Bacon
Chas A Davis	Walter Lenox	Leonard Harbaugh
John C Rives	Jos Bryan	J T Clements
John McClelland	John W Maury	Saml Byington
Wm Lloyd	Jacob Gideon	John L Maddox

Criminal Court-Wash: Mar 6, 1844.
1-Geo Dean, alias McKendree Dean, found guilty for an assault & battery upon Sarah McGee. Also found guilty of assault & battery on Susan Cokely.
2-Mary A Harper, found not guilty of stealing a gold watch, the property of Mrs Johnson.
3-Nathan Gray, found guilty of stealing a cow's hide of value of $1, the property of the Corp of Gtwn.
4-John Bennett, found guilty of a riot at the house of Ignatius King.
5-Philip Miller found not guilty of keeping a disorderly house.

Mar 7, 1844:
6-John Thomas, free negro, found guilty of an assault & battery on Benedict Herbert.
7-Giles Oliver, found guilty of an assault with intent to kill Saml Martin, by snapping a loaded gun at him.
8-Wm Gallaher, found guilty of stealing a piece of wood of the value of $1.50, property of J D Wall.

Mrd: on Wed last, by Rev Mr Harris, of Rock Creek parish, Mr Richd L Ross, of "*Glenn Ross*," Montg Co, Md, to Miss Louisa Taylor, d/o Geo Taylor, of D C.

Mrd: on Mar 5, by Rev Mr Edwards, Mr Jas H Tucker to Miss Harriet A Gingles, all of Wash City.

Died: on Wed, in his 61st year, Mr Robt Dunn, formerly of Phil, & for many years a tallow-chandler in that city, but latterly a resident of Wash. His funeral this afternoon, at 4 o'clock, from his late residence on C st, near 10th, to which the friends of the family are respectfully invited.

Died: on Wed, Michl Holland, aged 30 years, from the parish of Killbritain, Cork Co, Ireland, & for the last 7 years an honest & faithful porter at the Nat'l Hotel in Wash City. His funeral will take place this day at 3 o'clock, from the residence of Mr Martin Murphy, Pa ave, near 4½ st. The members of the Sodality are requested to attend, as also his friends & acquaintances

Died: on Wed last, suddenly, Mrs Eliz Wimsatt, relict of the late Saml Wimsatt. Her funeral will take place this day at 1 o'clock, at St Patrick's Church, F st. Mrs Wimsatt, a respectable & elderly lady, who resided near the Steamboat wharf, fell down in the street on the way from Church last Wed night, & almost immediately expired.

St Patrick's Church: Rev Dr Ryder will continue his discourses on Catholic doctrine on Fri, at 5 p m.

SAT MAR 9, 1844
Alfred York, about 20 years of age, of Portland, Maine, who had recently commenced trading near the New Gloucester line, accidentally shot himself on Fri last. He lived but 2 hours.

Students of Mount St Mary's College, held a meeting on Feb 27, to express their regret for the death of one of their number, Robt Randolph Dulany, s/o Capt Bladen Dulany, of the U S Navy. Signed in behalf of the students:
Geo E Cooper, of Phil, Pa   Theodore Mosher, of Gtwn, D C
Jos Le Bourgeois, of New Orleans, La   Edw G McCormick, of Taunton, Mass
Edgar T Garvin, of Gettysburg, Pa

The Hon Gabriel Duvall died at his seat in PG Co, Md, on Wed. He had survived the autumn of life, & lived far into its winter. He was in the 93rd year of his age. He was a fine old gentleman, & a noble specimen of the race of American descendants of the Huguenots. The first appearance of Judge Duvall in the Genr'l Gov't was in the Hse/o Reps:, which he entered in May, 1794: in Dec, 1802, he was appointed by Pres Jefferson to be Comptroller of the Treasury.

Mr Squire Pierce was killed at the Saunders' print works, at Providence, R I, on Sat last. He was caught by the limbs in the machinery & crushed to death.

Senate: 1-Ptn of Stephen Snow, a soldier in the last war with Great Britain, for a pension. 2-Ptn from G B Sinclair, a lt in the U S Navy, asking compensation for services performed belonging to ofcrs of higher grade. 3-Ptn from A P Brittingham, asking compensation for a vessel improperly seized by the Mexican Gov't in 1836. 4-The papers in the case of J H Bradford were withdrawn from the files & referred to the Cmte on Pensions. 5-Cmte on the Judiciary: bill for the relief of Mary Reeside, excx of Jas Reeside. Same cmte: asked to be discharged from the further consideration of the ptn of Jas Robertson & others, on the ground that it more properly belonged to another cmte. 6-Cmte on Naval Affairs: asked to be discharged from further consideration of the memorial of C W Dennison.

Presidential Electors-Pennsylvania:

Chester Butler	Wm Hiester	Jas Mathers
Townsend Haines	John S Hiester	Andrew J Ogle
Jos G Clarkson	John Killinger	Danl Washabaugh
John Price Wetherill	Alex E Brown	John L Gow
John D Neinsteel	Jonathan J Slocum	Andrew W Loomis
John S Littell	Henry Drinker	Jas M Power
Eleazer T McDowell	Jas Pollock	Wm A Irvine
Benj Frick	Fred'k Watts	Benj Hartshorn
Isaac W Vanleer	Danl M Smyser	

[Simeon Guilford, for Canal Com'r. Wm B Reed & John Strohm, Delegates to the Nat'l Convention.]

The public authorities & citizens of Richmond, Va, including the military companies, paid appropriate funeral honors to the remains of the late Hon Thos W Gilmer on Thu last, on which day they reached that place on their way to his former residence in Va.

The Hon John S Pendleton, of Va, has solicited his recall from the mission to Chili, & may be expected in the U S probably in Aug. He will be welcomed by his political friends with open arms. -Richmond Whig

Nominations of Cabinet ofcrs which have been made since Mar 4, 1841:
State Dept:
Danl Webster, of Mass, resigned
H S Legare, of S C, dec'd
A P Upshur, of Va, dec'd.
J C Calhoun, of S C
Treas Dept:
Thos Ewing, of Ohio, resigned.
Walter Forward, of Pa, resigned
C Cushing, of Mass, rejected
C Cushing, of Mass, rejected
C Cushing, of Mass, rejected
J C Spencer, of N Y
War Dept:
John Bell, of Tenn, resigned
J C Spencer, of N Y, resigned
J M Porter, of Pa, rejected
W Wilkins, of Pa
Navy Dept:
Geo E Badger, of N C, resigned
A P Upshur, of Va, resigned
David Henshaw, of Mass, rejected
T W Gilmer, of Va, dec'd
Post Ofc Dept:
F Granger, of N Y, resigned
C A Wickliffe, of Ky
Attorney Genr'l:
J J Crittenden, of Ky, resigned
H S Legare, of S C, dec'd
John Nelson, of Md

Hse/o Reps: 1-Cmte of Claims: bill for the relief of True Putney & Hugh Riddle. Same cmte: adverse reports on the cases of John Elwyn & Roxanna Evans. Same cmte, reported a bill for the relief of Pacificus Ord. Same cmte: bill for the relief of John Fraser & Geo A Trenholm. 2-Cmte on Public Lands: bill for the relief of Geo Davenport of Rock Island, Ill, same reported without amendment. 3-Cmte on the Judiciary: made a report on the ptn of Langtree & Jenkins, with a bill for their relief. 4-Cmte on Naval Affairs: bill for the relief of Enoch Mildew. 5-Cmte on Invalid Pensions: bill for the relief of Wm R Joynes. Same cmte: bill for the relief of David Akenson. Same cmte: adverse report on the ptn of Wm Scott. Same cmte: bill for the relief of Francis Sommeroner. Same cmte: bill for the relief of A D W Bodley. Same cmte: adverse report on the ptn of John Martin. 6-Bills read a third time & passed: relief of John P Schuyler; of Wm Glover; of Thomson Hutchinson; of Eliz Jones & others. Bill to refund the fine imposed on the late Anthony Haswell, under the sedition law, to his legal heirs & reps. 7-Bill for the relief of Geo W & Reuben Allen was passed. 8-Bill for the relief of John Mullings was passed. 9-Bill for the relief of Jas C Hallock was passed. 10-Ptn of the widow & heirs of John B Chandona, of St Jos Co, Ind, praying compensation in land for services rendered during the last war by said Chandona.

Orphan's Court of Wash Co, D C. Letters of administraton on the personal estate of Andrew Forrest, late of said county, dec'd. –Alex'r Forrest, Adm

Orphan's Court of Wash Co, D C. Letters testmentary on the personal estate of Jas L Cathcart, sen, late of said county, dec'd. –Jas L Cathcart, Exc

Constable's sale: by virtue of 2 writs of fieri facias: sale on Mar 14, at Steamboat Hill, on 11th st, 1 frame house & all the title of Capt Jas Guy to the lot on which it stands. Said lot is #9 in square 355, seized & taken in execution at the suit of Dr W H Gunnell against said Jas Guy. –John Magar, Constable

Convention of Wash City Delegates-present on Mar 8:

J D Barclay	John France	Jas H Birch
Wm Wilson	Peter Force	Saml Burche
R M Harrison	Walter Lenox	John Purdy
C A Davis	Jos Bryan	Saml Bacon
John McClelland	J W Maury	L Harbaugh
Wm Lloyd	Jacob Gideon	

MON MAR 11, 1844
Miss Eliza Ann Cushing, a young girl employed on one of the power presses in a printing ofc in Boston, was severely injured on Wed when her hand was caught between the blanket-roller & the tympan frame. Surgical aid was summoned, & Dr Herman, Dr Winslow Lewis, & Dr J Mason Warren, were in attendance. She was the support of an invalid mother & 2 sisters. The hands in the ofc volunteered nearly $50 towards her relief & comfort.

Fatal duel at Vicksburg, Miss, on Feb 29, between Mr Hammett, editor of the Vicksburg Whig, [& brother of the member of Congress from Mississippi,] & Mr Ryan, editor of the Sentinel. They fought with pistols, & on the 4th fire Mr Ryan fell mortally wounded, being shot directly through the lungs. Mr Hammett was wounded in 2 of the previous fires. Mr Ryan was the successor of Dr Hagan in the editorial chair, who was killed within the last year.

A mortal combat took place on Feb 27, between Mr Saml Wimbish & John Baker, the latter son-in-law of the former, both planters in the parish of West Feliciana, near the mouth of Bayou Tunica, in La. Mr Wimbish was shot in the head by a pistol ball, & expired in a few minutes.

Mrd: on Mar 5, by Rev Mr Sprole, Mr Geo W Lewis, of N Y, to Miss Anna Stewart, eldest d/o Mr Robt Brown, of Wash City.

New Orleans Picayune of Mar 3: disaster on Mar 1, on the Mississippi river, between the steamer **De Soto** & the steamer **Buckeye**: they ran afoul of each other just below Atchafalaya, & with such violence that the latter sank to her hurricane deck in less than 5 minutes. 68 are estimated to have been lost. Mr Hyams, of Alexandria, whose family was with him, lost his dght, Miss Eliz Smith, his wife's sister, & some 15 negroes; Col Richd King lost 2 children; Mr Alex Mackenzie, late of Florida, lost his wife, 7 children, & several negroes; Mr John Blunt, also from Florida, lost his wife, one child, & 7 negroes; a young man, name unknown, lost his 2 sisters; Mr Beard attempted to swim ashore with a little nephew, & both were drowned. A young man named Pollard, of Natchez, was also lost, & a child of Mr White. The **De Soto** was but little injured, & had reached New Orleans with many of the sufferers on board.

Hse/o Reps: 1-Bills passed: relief of Thos Harrison; of Hugh Wallace Wormley; of Enoch McDaniel; of Jas Reid. 2-Bill for the relief of Wm Ellery coming up on the question of engrossment. 3-By Mr Kennedy, of Indiana: Ptn of W A Ruggs & others, praying for a mail-route from Dunstan to Liberty Mills. 4-Ptn of Wm Cotton, an old Revolutionary soldier, for a pension. 5-Ptn of John Ozias, of Preble Co, Ohio, with papers, praying that the price of a certain tract of land, entered & paid for by him, may be refunded with interest, the Gov't having at the time of the purchase no title to the said land. 6-Ptn of Stephen T Covall & 196 citizens of Corning, Steuben Co, N Y, praying the reduction of postage, & for a law abolishing the franking privilege in every form.

Criminal Court-Wash, Mar 9. 1-Wm Garner, convicted of petit larceny, in stealing an anchor, the property of Thos Perkins, fined $5 & 5 days in jail. Also convicted of stealing a pair of andirons, the property of Richd Brook. To be imprisoned 2 years in the penitentiary. 2-Wm Stone & Jas H Winifrey, who pleaded guilty of stealing property of Jas D Dana, to be imprisoned 2 years each in the penitentiary. 3-Giles Oliver, convicted of an assault & battery with intent to kill Saml Martin, to be imprisoned 2 years in the penitentiary. 4-Wm O Brian, convicted of an assault with intent to kill Bernard Brien at Gtwn, to pay a fine of $50, to be imprisoned 6 months in the county jail, to give security in the sum of $500 for his good behavior & to keep the peace for 2 years, & to stand committed until the security be given. The D A prayed a commitment in this case until the fine & costs are paid. 5-Wm Gallagher, convicted of petit larceny, & recommended to the mercy of the Court, was sentenced to pay a fine of $5 & be imprisoned 10 days in the county jail. 6-Nathan Gray, convicted of petit larceny, to pay a fine of $5 & be imprisoned 3 months in the county jail. 7-Eliz Moran, convicted of keeping a disorderly house, to pay a fine of $25, to be imprisoned 10 days in jail, to give security in the sum of $100 for her good behavior, & keep the peace for 1 year, & to stand committed till the security is given. 8-Jeff Robison, Grafton Harper, Jas Ellis, & John Bennett, convicted of a riot at Gtwn, to pay a fine of $25 each, to be imprisoned each 20 days in the county jail, to give security each in the sum of $100 for his good behavior, & to keep the peace for 1 year, & to stand committed until such security be given. The same dfndnts were convicted of assaults growing out of the riots, & sentenced to pay $5 each.

Died: on Mar 9, William H, s/o Dorothy S & Saml Kilman, aged 2 years & 10 months. His funeral will be this evening, at 3 p m, from their residence on 13th st, between C & D sts.

The lady of Gen Canalizo, president ad interim of the Mexican Republic, died in the city of Mexico on Jan 21.

Thos S Donoho & Edw Warner, have this day, Mar 11, 1844, formed a copartnership for the practice of Law in D C & adjoining counties. Office in the east wing of the City Hall, #31.

For rent: 2 story frame house on the corner of East Capitol & 10th sts. Attached to the house is 3 acres of ground. Apply on the premises to: Wm J Baldwin.

TUE MAR 11, 1844
$50 reward will be paid by the subscriber, whose dwlg was forcibly entered on Sun and property stolen: silver spoons, sugar tongs-marked on the handle W B R, & made by Wm A Willaims. Silver mustard spoon; silver salt spoons-marked W B R, & made by B Barton. 1 jet breastpin set in gold, & 1 new fur hat. –W B Richards

Hse/o Reps: 1-Ptn of Walter Monroe, of N Y C, N Y, [a colored man,] praying a pension for services rendered as a soldier in the Revolutionary war. 2-Ptn from Sarah Sergeant, of N Y C, N Y, wid/o Jas Sergeant, dec'd, praying a pension in consideration of the services of her late husband as a soldier in the Revolutionary war. 3-Ptn of Thos Hanegan, of Phil, praying Congress to grant him a pension for military services in 1795 and 1798. 4-Memorial of Saml R C Buckener & 81 others; of Lazarus Ritter & 110 others, of Green Co, Indiana; of John B Herrington & 90 others; all praying a grant of lands in the Vincennes land district, Ind, for completing the Wabash & Erie Canal to the Ohio river. 5-Cmte on Revolutionary Pensions: to inquire into allowing pensions to:

Lavinia Holland
Nancy Reed
Judah French
Eleanor Kington
Catharine Taylor

Nelly White
Saml Williams
Dennis Hopkins
Delilah Johnson
Hugh Warren

Providence Journal: the trial of Thos W Dorr has been fixed for Sep 26, the earliest day at which the engagements of the Supreme Court of Rhode Island would allow the trial to come on.

For lease: the National Hotel, Washington, now kept by Gadsby. Application to Chas B Calvert, Bladensburg, Md, or to R C Weightman, Wash, D C.

Notice: committed to the jail of Fred'k Co, on Feb 29 last, as a runaway, a mulatto man who calls himself Caleb Ogleton; age about 25 years. Owner to come & have him released, or he will be discharged according to law.
--Geo Rice, Sheriff of Fred'k Co, Md

Senate: 1-Memorial from H R Warren & other citizens of Onandaga Co, N Y, asking the reduction of the postage rates. 2-Ptn from Absalom Tipton, for commutation pay on account of the services of Capt Tipton, killed in the Revolutionary war. 3-Ptn from Chas V Johnson & others, praying Congress to take some steps to procure a more regular reception of the Southern mail. 4-Ptn from Saml S Buckingham & other citizens of Pattan, Conn, asking the Senate to reconsider the vote of last year, by which a treaty of navigation & commerce with Texas was rejected. 5-Memorial from R H Eddy & other engineers, inventors, & manufacturers, & others interested in the promotion of the useful arts, suggesting alterations in relation to the law of patents. 6-Ptn from the heirs of Gen Thos Nelson, of Va, asking the commutation pay & interest due to a Surgeon General of the State line of Virginia. 7-Ptn from Geo H Matthews & other citizens of Va, for the relief of the surviving families of the ofcrs & crew of the U S schnr **Grampus**. 8-Cmte on Pensions: discharged from further consideration of the ptn of Eliza Maury, & it was referred to the Cmte on Naval Affairs. 9-Cmte on Pensions: ptn of Robt Ramsey was referred to the Cmte on Naval Affairs. 10-Cmte on Pensions: adverse report on the claim of the heirs of Thos H Peachy. 11-Cmte on Private Land Claims: bill supplementary to an act entitled an act for the relief of Wm Wynn. 12-Cmte on Naval Affairs: adverse report on the memorial of Evelina Porter, wid/o the late Cmdor Porter.

Semi-official reports of the daily transactions in the Supreme Court: the validity of the will of Stephen Girard has been elaborately argued in the Supreme Court at the present term, & decided in favor of the City of Phil, the general legatee of the Testator.

The Young Whigs of Balt assembled in Convention, have delegated the undersigned to solicit, in their name, your attendance at the Convention to be held in Balt-May 2.

S Teackle Wallis	Chas Webb, jr	Chas H Pitts
Levi James	Horatio L Whitridge	Levi Fahnestock
A S Gatchell	J S Nicholas	John B Dallam
R H Brooke	J B Streets	Thos Sewell, jr
John N Millington	Wm S Browning	

New Orleans, on Mar 3: the boiler burst on the steam towboat **Pilot**, Capt Alex'r Gow, at Gretna, above the city. Capt Gow & his son, & Mr Nuckerson, chief engineer, as well as 7 of the hands, were dreadfully scalded, & 2 others jumped overboard & drowned. -Tropic

District Court of the U S for Md district, the Hon Upton S Heath presiding: Geo M Gill appointed sec. Tribute of respect. Z Collins Lee, D A, on Sat last, announced the death of the Hon Gabriel Duvall, who for many years was the Chief Justice of the Circuit Court of the U S for the Md district.

Died: on Mar 8, suddenly, at Brown's Hotel, Mr Lawson J Noell, formerly of Va, but for the last 8 years a resident of Montgomery, Ala. He had been in a low state of health some time. He came to this city, where he has an only brother living. He was beloved & respected by all who knew him.

Died: on Feb 2, 1844, at his residence, St Inigoes, St Mary's Co, Md, Peter Gough, in his 70th year. He was a man of high moral character, & was possessed of a sound discriminating judgment. He was ever ready to assist the widow & the orphan, & his loss will be deeply felt by the community in which he lived. He has left an interesting family & a large circle of friends to deplore his loss.
-Leonardtown Herald

Died: on Mar 3, at his residence near Port Tobacco, Chas Co, Md, Henry A Neale, in his 68th year. Long of an enfeebled & impaired constitution, the dec'd had ever sought a refuge beyond "this vale of tears," &, by his manly virtues & strict attendance to the duties of his church, gained that 'blessed peace" which marked his last end. During his illness, which was short but painful, his comportment was characterized by an unrelenting patience in his sufferings, a perfect resignation to the will of Divine Providence, & an unshaken confidence in the goodness & mercy of Almighty God.

Very handsome furniture at auction: on Mar 12, at the residence of the Hon Danl Webster, on President's Square: various articles of household furniture.
-Robt W Dyer & Co, aucts

WED MAR 13, 1844
Senate: 1-Cmte on Private Land Claims: adverse report on the claim of Julius Culbertson. 2-Cmte on Foreign Relations: bill for the relief of J Pemberton Hutchinson, late Consul of the U S. 3-Cmte of Claims: bill for the relief of Jas Ritchie. 4-Cmte on Naval Affairs: bill for the relief of Wm McPherson. Same cmte: asking to be discharged from the further consideration of the ptn of Peter Amie. Same cmte: asking to be discharged from the futher consideration of the ptn of Jonas Preston.

Report of the Naval Court of Inquiry into the conduct of Capt Robt F Stockton. Court convened on Mar 6. [In 1839, Capt Stockton was in England & his attention was attracted to large masses of wrought iron as a substitute for cast iron.] The Court is of the opinion that not only was every precaution taken which skill, regulated by prudence & animated by the loftiest motives, could devise, to guard against accident, but that Capt Stockton, Lt Hunt, & Mr King, the gunner, who attended to the experiments & trials of these guns, exhibited only a due confidence in what they had witnessed in placing themselves in a position apparently not only more dangerous than any other, but that which might have been deemed the only perilous situation on board the vessel. The Court adjourned sine die. -W C Bolton, Pres -Richd S Coxe, Judge Advocate [See Feb 29, 1844 extraction.]

Thos Wallace, of Petersburg, the Van Buren Elector for that District, has declined the post. Mr Wallace was a friend of Mr Calhoun.

Died: on Mar 2, at *Stratford*, his residence, in Westmoreland Co, Va, Henry D Storke, aged 52 years.

Died: on Mar 9, at N Y, of congestion of the brain, Capt John H Clack. His friends knew him best, held him in great esteem as a man & an ofcr, & stood fast & firmly by him in all the vicissitudes of his fortune.

"The Grumbler," by Miss Ellen Pickering, novel, complete for 25 cents. –F Taylor

For rent: the house recently occupied by the late Sec of State will be rented until Jul 1 next, when the present lease will expire. The carpets & other furniture will be disposed of to the renter or others by private contact, if desired. Apply to Chas H Winder, State Dept. Or to G P Upshur, on the premises, corner F & 21st sts.

THU MAR 14, 1844
Hse/o Reps: 1-Ptn of Mrs Martha Canon, claiming compensation for property lost during the last war. 2-Two several ptns of John McConnell, Chas Powers, & others, citizens of Ohio & Indiana, praying for a mail route from Maumee City to White Pigeon. 3-Ptn of Randolph Lawson, of Cumberland Co, Ky, asking a pension for services in the Revolutionary war. 4-Ptn of John Stone, a soldier of the late war with Great Britain, praying a pension in consequence of wounds received while in the service of his country. 5-Ptn of the legal heirs of the late Andrew English, an ofcr in the war of the Revolution, praying payment for forage furnished the army by order of the commander-in-chief of the army. 6-Ptn of J Putnam & 90 other citizens of Monroe Co, N Y, asking for a fortification at the mouth of the Genesee river. 7-Correction by the newspaper: the resolutions offered on Mon in relation to the bill to divide the U S into 2 military districts was introduced by Mr Milton Brown, & not by Mr A V Brown.

Senate: 1-Ptn from Jas Donoho & other citizens of Westmoreland Co, Pa, asking that a pension may be granted to Wm Parkeson. 2-Ptn from Jas D Cobb, asking to be restored to his rank in the army, of which he complains of being illegally deprived by sentence of court martial. 3-Cmte on Naval Affairs: to whom was referred the memorial of David Myerle: adverse report on the same. 4-Bill for the relief of F A Kern was considered in the Cmte of the Whole, & ordered to be engrossed.

Handsome furniture at auction, on Mar 21, at the residence of the late Capt B Kennon, on H st, between 13th & 14th sts, [De Menou Bldgs,] household & kitchen furniture, all of which is of the best kind & make. Also, one buggy & 1 barouche carriage, & 2 horses, one a very fine carriage horse, the other a very fine ladies' horse. The house is for rent & possession given immediately. Inquire of Robt W Dyer & Co, aucts.

Household furniture at auction, on Mar 18, at the residence of Mr Griffith, on F st, near 7th st, [Gideon's Row,] his household & kitchen furniture. The furniture is nearly new & in good order. -Robt W Dyer & Co, aucts

Household furniture at auction, on Mar 19, at the residence of Mr N B Tinsdall, on south B st, between N J ave & 1st st, & adjoining the residence of Capt Crabb. Also a general assortment of kitchen requisites & cooking stove.
-Robt W Dyer & Co, aucts

Late from the African Coast. On Dec 12, about 70 miles below Cape Palmas, the frig **Macedonian**, Cmdor Perry, sloop **Saratoga**, Cmder Tatnall, & sloop **Decatur**, Cmder Abbott, came to anchor a mile off Bereby. A white flag was raised upon the shore and the next day the ofcrs & crews of the vessels to the number of about 500, fully armed, landed upon the beach. The African King & his interpreter came down, with a number of his people, all armed. The Cmdor continued to press close upon the King his questions concerning the fate of the schnr **Mary Carver** & her crew, who were murdered about 2 years ago. A palaver was held but the whole conversation was very unsatisfactory. The King & his people ran towards the jungle; but a volley from the American sailor instantly killed him, as well as the interpreter & others of the fugitives. The town was burnt to ashes. The women & children had been removed from the town by the natives, evidently prepared for battle. In another town the register of the **Mary Carver**, a private letter of the captain of the vessel, & other papers were found, thus clearly proving that punishment was being inflicted in the right quarter. Just before the Saratoga left Monrovia, information was received of the death of the Rev Mr Sawyer, one of the missionaries stationed about 50 miles below that colony. Midshipman Law, of the frig **Macedonian**, returned to this country in the barque **Bacchus**, along with Lt Ferris, who communicates the above information. [Mar 16 newspaper: Mr Ferris was Purser's Clerk in the ship **Saratoga**.]

Reuben H Walworth, of N Y, at present Chancellor of that State, was yesterday nominated by the Pres as an Associate Justice of the Supreme Court, to supply the vacancy occasioned by the death of Judge Thompson. John Y Mason, of Va, at present District Judge of the U S for the Eastern district of Va, was also nominated to the Senate yesterday for the ofc of Sec of the Navy. [Mar 15 newspaper: John Y Mason was confirmed. Robt Rantoul to be Collector of the port of Boston, was rejected.]

Sale this day: the stock & fixtures of M Moon's gentlemen's furnishing store on Pa ave & 4½ st.

Trustee's sale: on Apr 11 next, on the premises, pursuant to a decree of the Circuit Court of Wash Co, D C, made in the case of Augusta R Theriot vs, the heirs of Peter Passett & others, sale of lot 31 in square A, in Wash City. –Jos H Bradley, Trustee

Marshal's sale, in virtue of a writ of fieri facias from the Clerk's ofc of the Circuit Court of Wash Co, D C: sale on Apr 10 next, before the court house door of said county: all that part of lot 3 in square 343 in Wash City, seized & levied on as the property of Wm W Stewart, & sold to satisfy judicials #118 to Nov term, 1843, in favor of Kerr & McLean. –Alex'r Hunter, Marshall of D C

FRI MAR 15, 1844
In Bethlehem is a large monastery of Franciscan monks, on a commanding height, looking down on the valley. In the magnificent church within the monastery is a chapel under ground, finely ornamented, where 50 massive lamps of silver are suspended & kept constantly burning. Here is pointed out, in the form of a star in marble, the place where He came forth, who was declared the Everlasting Father, & Prince of Peace. –Rae Wilson on Judea

Orphan's Court of Wash Co, D C. May 4 next appointed for settlement in the case of Richd G Briscoe, adm of John Dix, dec'd. –Ed N Roach, Reg/o wills

To let, a large convenient house on Capitol hill, on south B st. Inquire of Rev Mr Tindall, residing in the house, or to the subscriber, on 3rd st, near the Railroad depot. –B Thruston

A Card. John Ermerick invites citizens & strangers to his new Wine & Coffee House, which he has just opened, on 6th st, near Gadsby's Hotel. [J Emerick having retired from his old business of Boot & Shoe manufacturing, hopes his friends & the public will bestow their patronage on his sons, which they so kindly bestowed on him.] -John Emerick

Mr Josaiah McIlyar, postmaster at Guernsey, Ohio, lost his life on Mon week by the accidental discharge of his rifle whilst he was preparing to go on a hunting excursion.

Criminal Court-Wash, Mar 12. 1-John Collins, free negro, was found not guilty of stealing a pocket-book, the property of Geo W Rowles. 2-Arthur Bradley, free negro, found guilty of stealing a sow the value of $9, the property of Alex'r Jackson. 3-Robt Hodge, indicted under the statute of Md of 1751, for enticing a slave, the property of Mr Walter Berry, to run away, was found not guilty. 4-Thos Tanner & Kendree Dean, alias McKendree Dean, were found guilty of stealing 3 pieces of sails, a straw bed, 2 blankets, & a bolster, of the value of $4.50, the property of John Coburn. They were also found guilty of stealing a shirt of the value of $1, the property of Jas Cissell. Dean had been before convicted of grand larceny in the Criminal Court, & was presented by the grand jury in that form, & the indictment was so framed by the D A. [Mar 18 newspaper: On Fri last McKendree Dean attempted to escape, but was pursued by the bailiffs. Mr Wall, the carpenter, threatened to shoot Dean with a pistol, & Dean surrendered.]

Wash Corp: 1-Ptn of Patrick Goings, praying remission of a fine: referred to the Cmte of Claims.

Wood for sale: Geo McDuell, corner of 14th & C sts.

From Day's Historical Collections. Died: on Dec 19, 1830, at his residence in Mifflin township, Cumberland Co, Pa, Wm Denning, in his 94th year. He was an artificer in the army of the Revolution. It was Denning who made the only successful attempt ever made in the world to manufacture a wrought iron cannon, 2 of which he completed at Middlesex, and began another larger one at Mount Holly, but could get no one to assist him who could stand the heat, which is said to have been so great as to melt the lead buttons on his clothes. The unfinished piece lies at either Holly Forge or the Carlisle barracks. A completed one was taken by the British at the battle of Brandywine, & is now in the tower of London. The British Gov't offered a large sum & annuity to the person who would instruct them in the manufacture of that article; but the patriotic blacksmith preferred obscurity & poverty in his own beloved country, to wealth & affluence in that of her oppressors. –Hazard's Reg, vol 7

Superior Pianos: Nunens & Clark's N Y Piano Agency, under Apollo Hall, has 2 of these pianos for sale: one of rose-wood, 6½ octave, the other of mahogany, 6½ octave. Wm Morrow

Col Robt Elliott, for many years, Assistant Postmaster at Albany, died in that city on Mon. His health had been failing for a year past.

Mr Geo Weaver of Phil, has just completed a rope for one of the inclined planes on the Alleghany Portage Railroad, a mile & a half in length & 8 inches in circumference. The largest rope yet manufactured in Phil.

The Hon Amos Gustine, a Rep in the last Congress from Pa, died at his residence in Lost Creek Valley, on Sun week, after an illness of several months.

Rev Walter Colton, chaplain, states that the recent Navy order substituting the gown [for the regulation dress of chaplains] for the blue coat & navy button was issued at the request of the chaplains, & originally suggested by those of them who are not Episcopalians.

Trustee's sale of splendid wharf property in the City of Balt: on Apr 17, the property on Fell's Point, in Balt, known as *Waters' Wharf*, & conveyed by Henry Wilson to Mark Pringle, John Sherlock, & Hezekiah Waters, by deed duly recorded in Balt Co Court, in Liber W S #79, folio 125, with bldgs thereon. Property has a front on Wolfe st of 65½ feet, & on Thames st of upwards of 93 feet. Title is indisputable. –J S Nicholas, Wm H Collins. Court-house Lane, Balt, Trustees.
-Hoffmans & Co, Aucts

Hse/o Reps: 1-Ptn from Benj F Worley, an invalid, asking for a back pension. 2-Ptn of Henry Hurat, adm of John Fichlie, dec'd, one of the securities of A P Hoy, formerly a receiver of public money at Jeffersonville, Ind, praying to be released from the payment of the interest due the Gov't on the defalcation of said Hoy. 3-Additional papers in the claim of Jas McAvery, for compensation for work & labor done on the Nat'l Road.

Serious accident on Mar 9, at Duncan's Island, 16 miles above Harrisburg, which resulted in the instant death of an estimable citizen. After a gunning excursion with a number of others, the gun of Saml Dreyfoos accidentally discharged and its contents lodged in the breast of John Conn, of Lancaster City, who was standing in the darkness and could not be perceived.

Senate: 1-Gaetano Carusi given leave to withdraw his papers. 2-Cmte on Military Affairs: bill for the relief of Mary A E Zantzinger, wid/o Maj Richd A Zantzinger, dec'd. Same cmte: bill for the relief of Catherine E Clitherall, wid/o Dr Geo C Clitherall, late a surgeon in the army of the U S. 3-Bill for the relief of F A Kerr: passed.

A German named Jacob Eller, with his wife & child, perished in N Y C on Fri last by the burning of the house in which they lived.

Died: on Tue, at the residence of Mrs McDaniel, 4½ st, Harriet Maria, d/o the Hon D L Seymour, of N Y, aged 1 year & 18 days.

SAT MAR 16, 1844
Senate: 1-Cmte on the Judiciary: adverse reports on the ptns of John Hawes & P S V Hamot. Same cmte: bill for the relief of John Grant. 2-Cmte on Pensions: adverse report on the claim of Micah French.

Rev Mr Mulledy, Vice Pres of Gtwn College, will preach in St Patrick's Church the Panegyric of the patron Saint of this church tomorrow at 11 a m. Rev J H Morrison, from India, will preach in Bridge St Church, [Mr Berry's,] Gtwn, tomorrow at half past 3 p m. Rev Kincaid, the eminent missionary from Burmah, will preach tomorrow at 11 a m in the First Baptist Church on 10th st. He has been for many years a most successful missionary in the Burman Empire.

Valuable lots in the Northern Liberties for sale: lots 7, 8, & 9 in square 424, fronting on 8th st west & north N st. I would prefer selling the whole together. –A Coyle

Household furniture at auction: by order of the Orphan's Court of Wash Co, D C: sale on Mar 22, at the residence of the late Chas W Goldsborough, 21st & G sts, his household & kitchen furniture. Also, 2 cows, supposed with calf, & a year old bull calf. We shall sell a pew, #55, in St John's Church, subject to a claim of $42 to the Church, & one share of stock in steamboat **Oceola**. -Robt W Dyer & Co, aucts

Notice to the Public. We notify the public, & particularly Alex'r Hunter, Marshal of D C, his deputies, & all others concerned, that the property advertised for sale by the said Marshal on Mar 21, in virtue of the several writs of fieri facies named in the ad, & described as part of lot 5 in square 408 in Wash City, in subdivision thereof as lot B, with improvements, being a 2 story brick bldg, fronting on 9th st, was not the property of Wm Hayman at his death, nor for several years before the same, & that it is the property of one of the subscribers, Eliz Washington, who purchased the same from the other subscriber, Geo W Garner, on Aug 15, 1838, & that the said Garner was in possession of the same, under a written conveyance bond from said Hayman, from the day of sale to him up to the aforesaid time, when he sold the same to the said Eliz Washington, who has possessed it ever since. We further notify that the said Wm Hayman was fully paid for said lot. We also state that we shall institute a suit in chancery, at the coming Court, against the heirs of said Hayman, to execute a good deed to said lot, in conformity to his written obligation of conveyance. We give this notice to prevent any person from buying the same at said sale.
–Geo W Garner, Eliz [her x mark] Washington

Trustee's sale of valuable property: by virtue of a deed of trust from Mathias Jeffers & others to me, dated Jul 25, 1842, recorded in liber W B 96, folios 55 thru 59, & 69, of the land records of Wash Co, D C: sale at auction in front of the premises on Apr 8, all the west part of lot 5, with a 2 story brick dwlg thereon. –John Kurtz, Trustee -Robt W Dyer & Co, aucts

Hse/o Reps: 1-Bills passed: relief of Saml B Folger; of Saml B Tuck; of Wm Augustus Atlee; of Geo M Jones; of Danl Dean; of the owner & crew of the schnr Success. 2-Ptn of Lucretia Foote, for a pension: referred. 3-Bill for the relief of John P Schuyler was passed.

Clover & Timothy seed for sale law by Geo & Thos Parker. [Local ad.]

Appointments by the Pres: Mar 8, 1844.
Amos J Bruce, Indian Agent at St Peters.
Isaac H Bronson, Judge of the U S for the eastern District of Fla, from Mar 14, 1844, when his commission expires.
Seth T Otis, to be Consul at Basle.
Jeremiah A Townsend, of Ill, Consul at Panama.
Saml Stettinius, Justice of the Peace for the county & city of Wash, D C.
Clement T V Coote, Justice of the Peace for Wash Co, D C.
Saml D King, Justice of the Peace for Wash Co, D C.
Collectors of the Customs:
John O Dickey, Coll of the Customs for the District, & Inspector of the Revenue for the port, of Sackett's Harbor, N Y, vice Leonard Dennison, removed.
Peleg Buchard, Coll of the Customs for the District, & Inspector of the Revenue for the Port, of Cape Vincent, N J, vice Judah A Ainsworth, removed.
Jas W Roach, Coll of the Customs for the District, & Inspector of the Revenue for the Port, of St Mary's, Md, vice Wm Coad, removed.
Murphy V Jones, Coll of the Customs for the District, & Inspector of the Revenue for the Port, of Wilmington, N C, vice W C Lord, removed.
Collier H Minge, Coll of the Customs for the District, & Inspector of the Revenue for the Port, of Mobile, Ala, vice Jas Perrine, removed.
Chas S Garrett, Surveyor & Inspector of the Revenue for the Port of Camden, N J, vice Philip J Gray, removed.
Wm B Mowry, Surveyor & Inspector of the Revenue for the Port of Pittsburg, Pa, vice John Willock, removed.
Thos W Hay, Surveyor & Inspector of the Revenue for the Port of Nottingham, Md, vice Dennis M Williams, dec'd.
Lewis Stone, to be Surveyor & Inspector of the Revenue for the Port of Town Creek, Md, vice Wm Floyd, removed.
Aloysius Thompson, to be Surveyor & Inspector of the Revenue for the Port of Llewellensburg, Md, vice Wm J Edelin, removed.
Alfred Palmer, to be Surveyor & Inspector of the Revenue for the Port of Urbanna, Va, vice Augustus Owen, dec'd.
John Bryan, to be Appraiser for the Port of Charleston, S C, vice Jeremiah A Yates, removed.

Postmasters:
Nathl Greene at Boston, Mass, vice Geo W Gordon, resigned.
Wm Hardin at Frankfort, Ky, vice Danl H Harris, removed.
John Roy Anderson at Chillicothe, Ohio, vice Chas Martin, removed.
Thos Blair at Dayton, Ohio, vice Jas Brook, resigned.
Jas W Greenhow at Vincennes, Ind, vice John Scott, resigned.
David P Blair at Columbus, Miss, vice Jos Blair, dec'd.
Chas K Miller at Bangor, Maine.
Isaac Sherman, jr, at Bridgeport, Conn.
Wm Lynn at Cumberland, Md.
Alex Galt at Norfolk, Va.
Nicholas D Coleman at Vicksburg, Miss.
John W Townsend at Mobile, Ala.
Joshua D Coffee at Florida, Ala.
Receivers of Public Money:
Stephen R Rowan, at Shawneetown.
Jas Swann, at Dixon, Ill, vice Danl G Gawsey, removed.
Geo L Ward, at Chicago, Ill, vice Edw H Haddock, removed.
Geo R Smith, at Springfield, Missouri, vice Nicholas R Smith, removed.
Geo Jeffries, at Helena, Ark, vice Ed McNamee, dec'd.
Wm H Whitehurst, at Washington, Miss, vice John Branch, resigned.
David G Bright, at Jeffersonville, Ind, vice Wm G Armstrong, removed.
J Albert Helfenstein, at Milwaukie, Wisc, vice Rufus Parks, removed.
Geo W Cole, at St Augustine, Fla.
Register of the Land Ofc:
John Myers, at Vincennes, Ind, vice Hiram Decker, removed.
Abraham B Morton, at Clinton, Missouri, vice J L Yantis, removed.
John W Rush, at Crawfordsville, Ind, vice Wm T Noel, dec'd.
John Hogan, at Dixon, Ill, vice J Albert Helfenstein.
Rejections in the Senate, Mar 8, 1844:
Crawford W Hall, as U S Atty for the District of East Tenn, vice Geo W Churchhill, removed.
Ebenezer H Stacy, as Coll of the Customs for the District of Gloucester, Mass, vice Geo W Pearce, removed.
Henry Chapin, appointed during the recess of Congress as Postmaster at Springfield, Mass, vice Solomon Warner, removed.
Enoch C Chapman, appointed during the recess of Congress Postmaster at Norwich, Conn, vice S M Downer, removed.
Dana Winslow, appointed during the recess of Congress as Postmaster at Burlington, Vt, vice Henry B Stacy, removed.
Appointments by the Pres, Mar 14, 1844:
John Y Mason, of Va, Sec of the Navy, in place of Thos W Gilmer, dec'd.
Robt J Chester, to be Marshal for the Western District of Tenn, re-appointed.

Saml Rush, of Pa, & Geo S Gaines, of Ala, to be Commissioners under the treaty of Dancing Rabbit Creek, vice John F H Claiborne & Ralph Graves, removed.
Attorneys of the U S:
Jas S Green, District of N J.
Jos A S Acklin, for Northern District of Alabama, re-appointed.
Richd M Gaines, for the Southern District of Mississippi, re-appointed.
Henry W McCorry, for the Western District of Mississippi, re-appointed.
Wm M McPherson, for the Dist of Missouri, in the place of Montgomery Blair, resigned.
Rejections:
John Cain, as Postmaster at Indianapolis, Ind.
Danl C Weston, as Postmaster at Augusta, Maine.
Aaron G Chandler, Collector for the District of Passamaquoddy, Maine.
Robt Rantoul, Collector at Boston.

Orphan's Court of Wash Co, D C. Letters of administraton on the personal estate of Lawrence J Noell, late of the State of Alabama, dec'd. –Wm N W Noell, Adm

Grape Vines: 4,000 roots of the Catawba Grape will be sold on accommodating terms, if immediate application be made. Inquire at the Drug & Seed Store of J F Callan, Washington.

Large stock of groceries at auction: on Mar 25, his entire stock: also a lot of store fixtures. –J Lipscomb, Gtwn -Edw S Wright, auct

MON MAR 18, 1844
Dissolution of Partnership, existing under the firm of Murray, Randolph, & Semmes, is dissolved by the withdrawal of Wm M Randolph. Murray & Semmes will continue the business. –Jno R Murray, Wm M Randolph, Jno H Semmes

For rent: house on 2nd st, north of St Peter's Church, at present occupied by J M Selden, having a large garden, & a pump of good water at the door. Inquire of Mr Jas Owner's, Virginia ave.

F Pulvermacher intends to close his store, on Pa ave, between 9th & 10th sts, & offers the entire stock of Goods for a mere bargain.

The trial of Curtain & Murray, who were indicted on a charge of robbing & an attempt to murder Mr Selby, of Montg Co, have been removed to the Howard District Court.

At Albany last week while shingling a house, the giving way of a scaffold, caused the death of Mr Jas Bailey.

Purchases made for the Gov't on which the General Post Ofc stands, embraces:
Of Wm Kibby, 3 story brick house & lot, south part of lot 13, cost: $6,000.
Of H Hardisty, jr, 3 story brick house, & north part of lot 13, including right to alley: $6,000. Of same, 3 story brick house, & south part of lot 12: $5,000.
Of Jas Adams, exc of Thos Law, dec'd, part of lots 6 & 7, including part of alley, [the other part owned in England]: $5,243.75.
Of John P Van Ness, the south end of lot 9: $1,000. –C A Wickliffe
Several individual proprietors of ground are willing to take the prices formerly named by them, including Mrs Benning's, will be $28,275, viz:
Jas Cadens' lot & 2 story frame house, #8: $7,000.
J P Van Ness' lot & 2 story brick, part of #9: $5,375.
C F Wood's lot & 3 story brick, part of #10: $3,100.
Jacob Gideon's 2 story brick, & parts of $10 & 11: $5,075.
Elbert Emack, part of #11: $3,200.
Mrs Benning's 2 story brick: $4,450.
A power of atty had been executed by the rep in England, before the sale could be perfected.

Criminal Court-Wash, Mar 13, 1844. 1-Jas Mitchell, free negro, not guilty of stealing property of Jos Boulanger. 2-John Brown, free negro, guilty of stealing property of Wm Braddock. Mar 14, 1844: 3-John M Farrar, not guilty for letting houses for lewd purposes. 4-Hanson Dines, free negro, not guilty of assault & battery on H R Maryman. 5-Geo W Wren & Wm H Taylor, not guilty for keeping a Faro Table, & other common gaming tables in Gtwn. Mar 15, 1844: 6-John Foley, guilty of assaulting & beating Cornelius Collinson, a constable of Wash Co. Fined $10. 7-John Lloyd, guilty of assaulting & beating Henry Thomas, a constable of Wash Co. Fined $10. 8-Arthur Bradley, convicted of stealing one sow: 3 years in the penitentiary, to take effect from the rising of the next Circuit Court. 9-John Collins, an old offender, convicted of stealing, to be imprisoned 3 years in the penitentiary. 10-McKendree Dean, convicted of stealing property of John Coburn, 3 years in the penitentiary. For stealing property of Wm Cissell, one year in the penitentiary, to commence at the expiration of his former sentence. 11-Thos Tanner, as accomplice with Dean, of the same offences: 4 months in the county jail & fined $5; second case, for 2 months, & pay $5 fine.

The Counterfeit Note Case: Gideon Brown, of Balt had been arrested & held to bail under the charge of passing counterfeit $10 notes. The Grand Jury ignored the bill, & became satisfied that there was no criminal intent on the part of Mr Brown. Letters were received from the most respectable citizens of Balt, who speak of Mr Brown's integrity in the highest terms.

Mrd: Mar 10, by Rev C A Davis, Mr Henry A Klopper to Miss Ellen E G Tarlton, all of Wash City.

Mrd: on Feb 29, at *Fort Jesup*, La, Jos K Barnes, Assistant Surgeon U S Army, to Mary T, d/o Maj T T Fauntleroy, U S Rifles.

Died: on Fri, in Wash City, Mrs Agnes Lowrey, relict of the late Saml Lowrey, of Balt, in her 75th year. Her funeral will take place this afternoon from the dwlg of Rev John C Smith, on N Y ave. [No death date given.]

Died: on Mar 16, Mrs Maria J Devereux, w/o Wm Devereux, of Wash City, in her 32nd year. Her funeral is at 11 o'clock today.

Died: on Thu last, in Wash City, the Rev Peter J De Vos, aged about 64 years. This pious & holy priest was a native of Flanders, & emigrated to this country about 1817. He has been employed upon the mission in Md, where he will long be rememberd for his untiring zeal.

Died: on Mar 10, in Wash City, John Prescott, s/o Wm & Charlotte D Martin, in his 6th year.

New Orleans, Mar 8, 1844. Sumner Lincoln Fairfield, poet, died in this city suddenly on Wed last, & was yesterday buried. Only a few days ago, the son of Fairfield, the firstling of the poet's heart, fell sick & died, & was buried at Vicksburg. This weighed heavily on poor Fairfield, for the sod on his child's grave was yet moist with his tears when he sank into the arms of death.

Hse/o Reps: 1-Bill for the relief of Danl Dean: passed. 2-Following were passed-relief of: Isaac Fessenden; Gervis Foote, Alborne Allen; Jos Bonnel; Fred'k Hopkins; John Farnham; Arthur R Frogge; Levi Colmus; Simeon Caswell; Isaac Justice; Jos Ramsey; & Wm H Hoag & others. Bill for the benefit of Jos Watson. Bill supplemental to an act approved Jun 28, 1838, for the relief of Jehu Hollingsworth. 3-Ptn of W O Russell, of N Y, for compensation for services & expenses in the arrest of Babe & Mathews, pirates: appropriately referred. Also, of W H Taylor & 106 others, in aid of the aforesaid petition.

Ptn from the proceedings of the Massachusetts Leg on Feb 28: ptn of Alex'r Hamilton, of Worcester, desirous of changing his name to Edward Hamilton. Reasons: present name is inconveniently long, both to write & to speak. A burden to support so renowned a name. Petitioner feels keenly & bitterly that he is obliged to diclose his name to a stranger. No inconvenience to other persons by the change. He is intending to publish some musical compositions of his own. Hopes to rebuke the too prevalent practice of burdening children with high sounding names. Edward is a good name in itself. Referred.

Liberal reward for the return of lost or mislaid Bank of Washington notes: $250. Return them through the Post Ofc of to Mrs Angelica Simpson, at her residence corner of 6th st & La ave.

Stage driver, Sherman P Fowler, on the route between Montomery & Mobile, Ala, was instantly killed on Feb 26, by the upsetting of the stage, which it is supposed struck a stump in the road.

TUE MAR 19, 1844
Miss Mgt G Meade is now prepared to enlarge her Young Ladies' Day School: on 20th st, between G & H sts, Washington. References:

Rev Wm Matthews	Maj Andrews	Hamilton Machlin
Madame Sigoigne, Phil	Rev Jas Ryder, Gtwn	Lt Walsh, U S Navy
	Rev J P Donelan	Wm W Seaton

Maj Jas D Graham, Corps Topographical Engrs

Mr Bossier, of La, is at present detained from his seat in the Hse/o Reps by a severe indisposition.

Died: on Mar 18, in her 35th year, Mrs Mary Ann Burnett, consort of Richd Burnett, & d/o Robt P & Dorcas Wade, of Mong Co, Md. She died of consumption, under which she labored for about 7 months with true Christian patience. Her funeral will be at St Patrick's Church today at 3 o'clock. The members of the Sodality of the B V Mary, of which she was a member, are invited.

Died: on Mar 17, at the Navy Yard, suddenly, Mrs Johanne Fisterer, a native of Germany, aged 63 years, having been a resident of Wash City for 27 years. Her funeral will take place today at 1:30, from her residence on 11th st, near M, in the 6th Ward.

WED MAR 20, 1844
Saint Patrick's Day celebration was held in Wash City with the usual procession, dinner by Mr Lafon, at the Wash Assembly Rooms. Geo W P Custis presided at the festive board, sitting with the Mayor of Washington and Mr John Boyle. The Rev Mr Donelan addressed the company.

Our townsman, Mr P Haas, has just published an excellent portrait of the late Sec of the Navy, Mr Gilmer. It was drawn by that talented artist, M Gibert, from the daguerreotype of Mr Haas.

The nomination of that veteran democrat Henry A Muhlenburg is exerting the happiest effect. -Albany Argus

Senate: 1-Ptn from John Carter, of D C, asking permission to bring a slave, of which he is the owner, from S C into said District. 2-Ptn from Marquis Fulton Johnson, asking the right of pre-emption to a tract of land in the State of La. 3-Ptn from Belah Young, a soldier of the late war, for an increase of pension. 4-Ptn from the widow of Condy Raquet, asking compensation for the diplomatic services of her husband while Consul at Rio de Janeiro. 5-Ptn from the heir of Timothy Parker, asking compensation for the military services of his ancestor. 6-Ptn from Mary Williams, a wid/o a Revolutionary soldier, asking a pension. 7-Papers of Rose Howe were referred to the Cmte on the Public Lands. 8-Mr David Myerle had leave to withdraw his papers. 8-Cmte of Claims: asking to be discharged from the further consideration of the claim of Adam B Stewart. 9-Cmte on Revolutionary Claims: asking to be discharged from the further consideration of the claim of the heirs of David Nobles; of the memorial of the heirs at law of Rudolph Bunner. Same cmte: adverse reports on the claims of the heirs of Richd Dallinar; of the heirs of Maj Thos Nelson; & of the heirs at law of Abraham Tipton. 10-Cmte on Pensions: adverse reports on the ptns of Jos Pulcifer & of John Keith.

Wash Corp: 1-Cmte of Claims: bill for the relief of W G W White: passed. 2-Ptn from G L Thompson, praying the remission of a fine: referred to the Cmte of Claims. 3-Ptn of Richd Dement & others, praying for curbstone & footway on 2nd st west: referred to the Cmte on Improvements. 4-Cmte on Improvements: asked to be discharged from the further consideration of the communication from H L Ellsworth. 5-Cmte of Claims: recommended the rejection of the bill for the relief of Jas Dixon. 6-Cmte of Improvements: was referred the ptn of John McDermott & others, & of John T Clements & others, with a bill for improvement of 5th st west: read twice. Same cmte: ptn of Joel Downer & others, for improvement of 8th st west: read twice. 7-Cmte of Claims: ptn of P H Brown: ought not to be granted, which was adopted. 8-Cmte of Claims: ptn of Danl Paullind: ought not to be granted, which was adopted. 9-Ptn from Jas P Espy, asking the purchase of his invention for ventilating the holds of ships. 10-Cmte on Pensions: adverse report on the ptn of Stephen Snow. 11-Citizens of Norwich, Conn, asking that a pension may be granted to Nancy Parker. 12-Cmte on Pensions: adverse report on the ptn of Hannah Thompson. 13-Cmte on Pensions: bill for the relief of Jane McGuire, with amendment, & recommending that it be indefinitely postponed. 14-Resolved, that the Sec of the Navy be & he hereby is requested to furnish Saml Colt with such facilities & assistance in boats, anchors & men, authorized by the joint resolution of Congress, approved Aug 31, 1842, as may be requisite to enable him to complete his preparations & submarine experiments for testing Colt's Submarine Battery.

As the steamboat **Clipper** was leaving the wharf at Cincinnati on Mon for Pittsburg, a signal gun was discharged on board, the wad of which mortally wounded Mr Evans, of Covington, & injured 4 others, one of them quite seriously.

Providential Dispensations: Omens-Results of 1840. To welcome the arrival of Gen Harrison at Zanesville, Ohio, on an electioneering tour, before the election, the flag of the U S was displayed. While the old man was waiting to address the assembled multitude, a bolt of thunder rent the flag & shivered the pole. Its echoes had hardly died away, when an express arrived informing the Gen of the death of a beloved son. A picture of Pres Harrison was hung with great care in the Congress Library. One evening it fell from its position, the frame dashed in many pieces, & the picture left standing against the wall of the room. The steamer **President** sailed for England with news of Harrison's inauguration, having the eloquent Cookman on board, whose last sermon had been preached in his presence, & the gallant ship has never been heard of since. The brave Macomb, who led the President's funeral escort, was, in less than 90 days, by a stroke of apoplexy, sent to accompany the Chief he had so recented committed to the tomb. Fire seized the residence of Gen Harrison at North Bend, & it was partially consumed; & the tomb, which had been constructed from his last resting place, fell in & crushed a man who was plastering a niche for his coffin.

For rent: large 3 story brick house & store, 10th & Pa ave, in the present occupancy of Michl Combs & Madame May. For terms apply to Michl Sardo, 10th & H sts.

Hse/o Reps: 1-Cmte of Claims: bill for the relief of Jeanette C Huntington, relict & sole excx of Wm D Cheever, dec'd; & a bill for the relief of Harvey Parke, with a report in each case. Same cmte: adverse reports on the ptns of Henry Stoker; the ptn of Mary Amelia Lewis, wid/o Capt Andrew Lewis, dec'd; the ptn of Capt Henry McKavett; & the ptn of Danl Brayman. Same cmte: report on the ptn of Jno P Converse, with a bill for his relief. Same cmte: report on the ptn of C P Sengstack, with a bill for his relief. 2-Cmte on Public Lands: adverse report on the ptn of John Bruce. 3-Cmte on the Judiciary: bill for the relief of David Alpack. 4-Cmte on Revolutionary Claims: bill for the relief of Saml Richards, exc of Wm T Smith, late of Phil. Same cmte: bill for the relief of Henry King. 5-Cmte on Private Land Claims: bill to confirm the claim of Antonio Chenino to a tract of land in Louisiana. 6-Cmte on Military Affairs: adverse report on the memorial of Truman Cross. 7-Cmte on Revolutionary Pensions: bill for the relief of Geo Singley. Same cmte: adverse report on the ptn of Eliz Wilson, wid/o Thos Wilson. Same cmte: bill for the relief of Geo Wenthing; for the relief of Uriah Loomis; for the relief of Amaziah Goodwin. Also, bill for the relief of Wilmot Marsden, of Oneida Co, N Y, wid/o Geo Marsden, dec'd; & a bill for the relief of John Edmarson; accompanied by a report in each case. Same cmte: bill for the relief of Mary Ann Linton; relief of Peter Wilson; relief of Mariah Robinson; relief of Mary B Perry & others; accompanied by reports in each case.

For sale or rent: house recently occupied by the late Mrs Easton, G & 19th sts, back of the Seven Bldgs. For terms inquire on the premises.

A carpenter, John Lane, stated to have belonged to N Y, a passenger in the schnr **State**, Capt Thomas, from Charleston to Phil, jumped overboard in the Gulf Stream, on Feb 29, & was drowned. He was laboring under temporary insanity at the time. He has left a wife & family.

On Thu last the Columbia Cotton Factory, on Herring Run, 3 miles from Balt, was entirely destroyed by fire, with all its machinery & stock on hand. Owned by Mrs Ann Hall, occupied by Amon Green & Co, who owned the machinery.

THU MAR 21, 1844
Senate: 1-Ptn from Wm Fowle & Sons, merchants of Alexandria, D C, asking a revision of the commercial treaties & regulations between the U S & foreign Powers. 2-Ptn from Chas Morgan, in relation to a land claim. 3-Cmte on Private Land Claims: bill for the relief of Wm Fisher. 4-Cmte on Military Affairs: asking to be discharged from the claim of John McLaughlin, & that it be referred to the Cmte on Claims. 5-Resolution to furnish facilities to Mr Saml Colt, to test his marine battery, was taken up & passed.

Wm R Riley has just received a cheap & well-assorted stock of seasonable Dry Good: 8th st, opposite Centre Market.

For rent: desirable residence on 12th st between C & D sts, now occupied by Mrs France. Possession given Apr 1 next. Apply on the premises, or to Mary B Alexander, Pa ave, between 12th & 13th sts.

Martin Luther, one of the Dorrites of R I, who was indicted for acting as moderator of a town-meeting under the spurious Constitution which a portion of the people of R I attempted some 2 years ago to carry into effect, had his trial before the Supreme Court at Bristol last week, & was found guilty. The Court sentenced him to 6 months's imprisonment & a fine of $500, that being the minimun punishment for the offence.

The brig **Emily**, which arrived at N Y on Tue from Charleston, came in contact on Mon off Sandy Hook, during a gale, with the schnr **Virginian**, Capt Bedell, from Norfolk, striking her and cutting her down to the water's edge. The following passengers perished: Wm Fitzgerald, Garrett Venderburg, & H Johnson.

Rev Jacob King, who has for about 50 years been a worthy local minister of the Methodist Episcopal church in Balt, died in that city on Wed, in his 86th year.

Died: on Mar 8, at Greenfield, Mass, Mr Geo Grinnell, aged 93, the oldest inhabitant of that town. He was father of the Hon Geo Grinnell, formerly for several years a Rep in Congress from that district.

Died: on Mar 15, at the residence of her father, in Fauquier Co, Va, in her 31st year, Mrs Mary Catharine Neill, w/o Wm Van Dyke Neill, & d/o Dr Thos Triplett. She has left behind her a husband & 4 children to lament their great loss, while a father, a sister, & a large circle of friends will mourn her death. –Alex Gaz

$10 reward for runaway, John Gibbons, an apprentice to the Paper-making Business, about 17 years of age. I likewise forewarn any person hiring, harboring, or employing said apprentice, as I am determined to put the law in force against them. –Danl Lamborn, Elkridge Landing, Howard District of Anne Arundel Co, Md.

Notice of partnership in the wholesale & retail Grocery business, under the name of Peddecord & Holland: store on Centre Market space, between 8th & 9th sts, next door to the dry goods store of Darius Clagett. –E Peddecord, Jas S Holland [All goods bought of us will be delivered in any part of the city free of charge.]

FRI MAR 22, 1844
When the Constitution of the U S first went into operation, it was decided that the proper style of addressing the President was Geo Washington, President of the U S. Not His Excellency or His Highness.

Senate: 1-Ptn from W P Vaughan, praying an extension of the time for completing his contract. 2-Ptn from John Frasee, asking payment of balance due him for services as architect & superintendent of the custom-house at N Y. 3-Ptn from Thos Allen, former printer to the Senate, asking that he may be paid a balance due him for printing the compendium of the 6th census. 4-Ptn from the excx of Oliver Connell, asking arrears of pension. 5-Ptn from Sarah Dagget, R M Bowen, Mary Reynolds, & Dorothea Harender, for renewal of their pensions. 6-Ptn from the widow of Benj Netherland, for a pension. 7-Cmte of Claims: adverse report on the claim of Thos Fillebrown, jr, accompanied by an elaborate report. 8-Mr Tappan submitted a joint resolution, that the Sec of State be directed to purchase of Hiram Powers, of Ohio, busts in marble of such of the Presidents of the U S as he may have modeled from life, or from authentic materials, at a price not exceeding $500. Read & ordered to a second reading. 9-Bill was introduced for the relief of Wm De Buys, late Postmaster at New Orleans. 10-Adverse report on the memorial of Mrs Evelina Porter came up, when it was laid over for further investigation.

Sig Vito Viti will have his last auction sale on Mar 27, at candlelight, at Todd's Concert Hall, Pa ave. Among the items: Oil Paintings: Madonna, after Carlo Dolce; ditto, after Morigles; Mary Magdalen, Sea Scenery, & Landscapes, by that eminent artist Thos Birch, of Phil. –W Marshall, Auctioneer

On Fri one of the boilers of the steam flouring mill at Green & Broome sts, in N Y, burst. Mr E H S Mumford, the proprietor of the mill, was so severely scalded by the steam that he died on Sunday.

Supreme Court of the U S, Mar 15, 1844. Thos P Alricks, of Md, was admitted an atty & counsellor of this Court. #13: R Porterfield's excs vs Clark et al: from the Circuit Court for Ky: affirming the decree of the Circuit Court in this cause with costs. #35: Austin L Adams et al vs Julia Roberts. In error to the Circuit Court for Alexandria, D C: affirming the judment of the Circuit Court in this cause with costs. #56: Louisville, Cincinnati, & Charleston Railroad Co vs Thos W Lelson: in error to the Circuit Court for Sourth Carolina: affirming the judgement of the Circuit Court with costs & 6% damages. #27: R Grignon et al vs J J Astor et al: in error to the Supreme Crt of Wisconsin: affirming the judgement of the Supreme Crt of Wisc in this cause with costs. #32: John Catts vs Jas Phalen et al: in error to the Circuit Court for Alexandria, D C: affirming the judgement of the Circuit Court in this cause with costs. #38: Sally Ladiga vs Richd M Roland et al: in error to the Supreme Crt of Alabama: reversing the judgment of the said Supreme Crt with costs, & remanding the cause for further proceedings in conformity to the opinion of this Crt, & as to law & justice shall appertain. #34: Simeon Stoddard et al vs Harry W Chambers: in error to the Circuit Court of the U S for Missouri: reversing the judgment of the Circuit Court with costs, & remanding the cause with directions to award a venier facias de novo. #45: Jas Rhodes vs Moses Bell: in error to the Circuit Court for Wash, D C: affirming the judgment of the Circuit Court in this cause with costs. #46: Jane Dade vs Thos Irwin's executor: appeal from the Circuit Court for Alexandria, D C: affirming the decree of the Circuit Court in this cause with costs.

Farm for sale: on Apr 4: 160 acres, adjoining the Anandale Post Ofc, on the Little River turnpike; a house with 8 rooms, kitchen, & loft; cellar, milk-house, shed & loft, over a fine spring; a well, stable, & loft; large cow-house & loft, sheds, granary, hog sty, poultry house, garden, & plenty of timber. Inquire of Thos Love, Fairfax Court-house, J H Bradley, Wash, or S Scott, B st, Capitol Hill, Wash.

Circuit Court of Wash Co, D C. Thos Johns; Fred'k Miniette; Geo Tyler; Conrad Hess; & Johnson Simonds, have applied to be discharged from imprisonment under the act for the relief of Insolvent Debtors: hearing on the first Mon of Apr next. –Wm Brent, clk

On Mar 10 a company of 20 blacks took their departure from St Louis, Mo, for New Orleans, destined for Liberia, in Africa. They were set free by the will of Thos Lindsay, of St Chas Co, on condition of their removal to Liberia. They know how to perform many kinds of labor, & will make useful settlers in Africa.

Mrd: on Mar 19, by Rev Mr Samson, Mr John Kendrick to Miss Frances M Edmunds, both of Wash City.

Died: on Mar 21, Mrs Mgt H Hamilton, consort of Jas H Hamilton, of the Post Ofc Dept. Her funeral is this day at 11 o'clock, from his residence on 10th st.

Letter from an ofcr on board the frig **Potomac**, dated at sea. Feb 9, 1844. On Jan 18, we lost a man overboard: Wm Tefts, from Spring Garden, Phil. He was in the mizen chains heaving the lead, when the ship gave a heavy roll, he slipped & fell. It would have been madness to have lowered a boat with such a sea on. He was much liked by all on board, & his untimely death cast a melancholy gloom over the whole ship's company.

John P Stallings, having seen his name on tickets of invitation to balls, as manager, begs leave to state that it was placed there without his consent. He is a friend to the needy, but he cannot allow light amusements to interfere with the calls of his business.

Orphan's Court of Wash Co, D C. Letters testmentary on the personal estate of Greenville C Cooper, late of the U S Navy, dec'd. –Jane A Cooper, excx Note: All claims to be presented to Geo W Riggs, jr, at the ofc of Corcoran & Riggs.

St Patrick's Day Anniversary, by the Wash Benevolent Society of Wash City, held on Mar 18, 1844, met at their hall on 5th st at 3 o'clock, formed into a procession, & passed round to St Patrick's Church, on F st, attached to which is the institution for the Sisters of Charity. Dinner at 5 o'clock in the Assembly Rooms. Mr A Lafon, caterer; Geo Wash Parke Custis, of Arlington House, a scion of the Washington family, presided, assisted by Messrs John Boyle, Jas Hoban, Edw Stubbs, & Peter Brady. Toasts were given by:

A D Harrell	Francis Reilly	John Maguire
Thos Wall	Wm Dowling	John Ousley
John Richey	Pierce Spratt	Jas McGuire
Michl McDermott	John Foy	Ambrose Lynch
Jas Fitzgerald	Jas Maher	John Lynch
Philip Ennis	J T Ennis	J Hack
John Boyle	John McLeod	Jas W Sheahan
John O'Conner	Hon Felix G McConnell	Thos Jordan
Bernard Kelly		G Ennis
W E Stubbs	Geo B Wallis, of Va	Edw Sheehy
Thos Cordiel, of Phil	Edw Stubbs	Wm P Faherty
Jas McGrath	Terence Lubin	Owen Connolly
Chas F McCarthy	Peter Brady	
	Martin Renehan	

Meeting adjourned at 10 o'clock after several hours of rare entertainment. There were 156 persons at dinner, & a number came in after the cloth was removed.

Hse/o Reps: 1-Ptn of Martin Moody for a pension. 2-Praying a grant of land to extend the Wabash & Erie Canal from Terre Hute to Evansville: Ash C Whaly & 72 others; Abraham Grider & 60 others; Sanders M Ferris & 119 others; Albert Larr,

Wm D Littell, Jonathan Hail, Martin Wines, Reuben Bedwell, Wm Osborn, Thos Butler, Joshua Dobbins, Alex Cleary, Thos Burke, S M Orchard, John Crook, Thos McCella, Jos Blair, H F Garlick, Saml A Smith, Andrew Cristy, F C Dunn, West C Walker, John Goodright, John W Hyneman, & many other citizens, of Indiana. For the same: Chas Scott & 61 others, citizens of Knox Co, Ind. Also, Martha Ann Davis & 240 other ladies of Daviess Co, Ind, for the same object. 3-Ptn of G A Hall, adm with the will annexed of Jas Hampson, dec'd, praying compensation for distributing money for the U S expended on the Cumberland road east of Zanesville, Ohio. 4-Statement of Henry Nicoil, of N Y, & a copy of a fee bill, in relation to costs taxed in the U S Courts in admiralty cases. 5-Ptn of Thos Cordis & 26 others, of Boston, in favor of a grant of land for the completion of the Wabash & Erie Canal. 6-Communication of Lt John S Devlin, with accompanying papers, in relation to the pay of the ofcrs of the U S Marine Corps. 7-Ptn of Peter Yarnell & Saml Mitchell, of Wheeling, Va, asking to be released from a judgment against them & Alex'r Mitchell, their security, rendered in favor of the U S in the District Court for the Western District of Va. 8-Ptn & proof in the case of John Owens, of Pulaski Co, Ky, asking compensation for a horse lost in the U S service. 9-Ptn of E E Pynchou. [No other information.] 10-Ptn of W N Stevens & others, citizens of Plymouth, Mich, for a reduction in the rates of postage. 11-Ptn of Jesse Campbell, of Mason Co, Ky, a soldier in the late war with Great Britain & one of the captives confined in the Dartmouth prison, in England, praying that Congress may pass a law for his relief, he now being poor & an invalid, aged & infirm. 12-Ptn of Jas L Loyd, of Owen Co, Ind, praying an increase of pension as a wounded marine. 13-Ptn of John Jay & other citizens of N Y, for an international copy right law.

SAT MAR 23, 1844
Senate: 1-Ptn from Rebecca Beckham, heir of Robt Lovell, asking arrears of pay & commutation to which her ancestor was entitled. 2-Cmte on Pensions: asking to be discharged from the further consideration of the ptn of the wid/o Peter Borrows, & that she have leave to withdraw her papers. 3-The bill for the relief of John Mullings: passed.

Board of Managers of the Missionary Society of the Meth Episc Church, held at N Y on Wed late. Interesting communications from Rev Jason Lee, the superintendent of the Oregon mission: dates are to Oct 28, & came via Pensacola. Three detachments of emigrants from the Western section of the U S had arrived at the Columbia river. One man in the last detachment had died on the way, & his widow & 4 children arrived at the mission station on the Willamette. Rev Dr Whitman returned to his charge on the Columbia in good health. Mr Brewer is dangerously ill. Rev Mr Perkins had been assaulted by one of the Indians from the interior. The chiefs had assembled in council, assisted by Dr White, the U S agent, & determined that the Indian should be publicly whipped, & he received 25 lashes.

The New Haven Palladium publishes the confession of Lucien Hall, lately convicted of having murdered Mrs Bacon on Sept 24 last, at Middletown, Conn, while her husband & the rest of the family were at church, & for which crime he is now under sentence of death. He went to the house to rob it, but having been discovered & recognized by Mrs Bacon, he felled her to the floor, stabbing her, & thus terminated her life. He then completed the robbery & returned to his house.

Mrd: on Thu last, by Rev F S Evans, Mr Wm Kidd, of Balt Co, Md, to Miss Jane E Skippon, of Wash City.

Mrd: on Feb 22, at *Harpers' Ferry*, Va, by Rev Thos D Hoover, Mr John E P Daingerfield, of Rockingham Co, Va, to Miss Matilda W Brua, of the former place.

Hse/o Reps: 1-Following bills were read a 3rd time & passed. Relief of:
Wolcott Alleyn Strong & Pierre S Derbanne
Elis Gresham, wid/o Geo Gresham
Sarah Parker, wid/o Joham Parker
Lois Croill, alias Cronkhite
Richd Elliott
Henry Freeman
John Rose
Simeon Dennin
Danl Dunham
Robt G Ward

2-Bills laid aside to be reported to the House: relief of:
Hugh Wallace Wormley
Legal reps of Capt Saml Shannon
G W Clarke, Harris Cook, & John Brainer, 2nd
Chas Holt
Woodson Wren
Jas Pepper & others
John Miller
Jas Journey
Eliz Fitch
Bethis Healy
Betsey Clapp
Danl Ingalls
Abigail Gibson
Emanuel Shrofe
Sally McCraw
Elijah Blodget
Jas Crawford
Lathrop Foster
Ira Baldsin
P Ord
True Putney & Wm Riddle
John Frazer & G A Franklin
Geo Davenport, of Ill
Sarah Blackemore, wid/o Geo Blackemore

Also, bill for the benefit of Antoine Vasques et al; granting a pension to Bartholomew Maguire; bill for the benefit of Thos Hunter & Alex'r Caldwell.
3-Bill granting a pension to Milly, an Indian woman, of the Creek nation 4-Ptn of David Myerle with accompanying papers: referred.

Jacob Gates, mate of the ship **Oxford**, who plead guilty to a charge of smuggling, was sentenced in the N Y U S Court on Wed to be imprisoned 30 days, & to pay a fine of $2,000, & to stand further committed till the fine is paid. Gates is the sole stay of a sister & aged mother.

Meeting of the Whigs of St Mary's Co, Md, at the Court House in Leonardtown, on Mar 12, to appoint delegates to the Gubernatorial Convention, to convene at Balt on Apr 30 next. Col Wm Coad called to the chair, & Wm Ford appointed sec. Messrs Jos Dunbar, Jas T Blakistone, Geo G Aschon, Henry Sewall, & John W Bennett, appointed a cmte. John W Bennett, Wm Coad, John M S Causin, & Benedict I Heard, appointed delegates. Richd Thomas recommended as the candidate of our choice of the whole State, for the Executive ofc of the State. Henry Clay is the first, the last, & the only choice as a candidate for the next Presidency. That Robt M Biscoe, Henry Sewall, Robt Ford, & J J Gough, are appointed alternates of the delegates appointed.

Died: on Mar 22, in Gtwn, after a painful & lingering illness, in her 16th year, Sarah Ellen, eldest d/o John H & Ellen J King. Her funeral is on Sun, at 3 o'clock.

Public sale: by virtue of 3 writs of fieri facias at the suit of John Costigan, against the goods & chattels, lands, & tenements of Thos M Fugitt: I have seized & taken in execution all the right, title, interest, & claim of the said Fugitt in & to one horse, one cart, & cart gear, & a lot of seine & rope; sale in front of the Centre Market house, Wash City. –H R Maryman, Constable

Household furniture at auction: on Mar 26, at the residence of Mr Grubb, on F st, near 11th st, his household & kitchen furniture. -Robt W Dyer & Co, aucts

Sale of valuable real estate: on Apr 6, by order of the Orphan's Court of Wash Co, D C, the 2 story brick house & lot fronting on 16th st west, on lot 6, in square 200, lately owned & occupied by Danl H Haskell, dec'd. -Holmead & Wright, auctioneers

Valuable bldg lots at auction: on Apr 1: lots 14 & 15 in sq 127, on 18th st, near Pa ave; lot 10 in sq 142, on G st, between 18th & 19th sts, near the residence of Col Andrews. -Robt W Dyer & Co, aucts

Trustee's sale: under 2 separate deeds of trust executed by Jas Moore, jr, one dated Oct 22, 1834, & the other dated Nov 27, 1837: sale on Apr 23, of part of lot 4, with improvements; a leasehold interest of lot 5 with improvements; & the whole of lot 6, with improvements, in square 381. Also, at the same time & place, lots 10 & 11 in square 529. –John Moore, Henry Naylor, Trustees

MON MAR 25, 1844
Mr Wm P Clark, from Va, was robbed on Thu night, while crossing in the steamboat of the Mail Pilot Line, between Camden & Phil, of $1,100, in Virginia, South & North Carolina bank notes. His inner skirt coat pocket was cut, & the bills pulled out of his pocket-book.

Hse/o Reps: 1-Cmte on the Public Lands: a report upon the ptn of Jas Anderson, of the Territory of Iowa, with a bill for his benefit. 2-Cmte of Claims: adverse reports upon the ptns of Thos Taten, Nancy Egnew, & J T Beyer. Same cmte: act for the relief of Wm De Peyster & Amy N Cruger, & the bill from the Senate-act for the relief of Danl G Skinner, of Ala, reported the said bills severally without amendment. 3-Bill read a 3rd time & passed-relief of:

Adam L Mills	Danl Ingalls
John Miller	Abigail Gibson
Thos Hunter & Alex'r Hunter	Violet Calhoun, wid/o John Calhoun
Chas Holt	Sally McCrain
Woodson Wren, of Miss	Elijah Blodget
Jas Pepper & others	Sarah Blackemore
Jas Journey	Jas Crawford
Eliz Fitch	Lathrop Foster
Bethia Healy, wid/o Geo Healy, dec'd	True Putney & Eliz Maguire
Danl Clapp & Betsey Clapp	
Legal reps of Capt Saml Shannon, dec'd	
G W Clarke, Hanse Cook, & John Brainers, of Conn	

4-Pension to Bartholomew Maguire: passed. 5-Pension to Emanuel Shrofe: passed. Bill for the relief of John Frazer & G A Franklin coming up. 6-Ptn of Robt McIntosh for a pension: referred. 7-Ptn of Saml Stout & 19 other citizens of Indiana, asking an appropriation of land to complete the Wabash & Erie canal.

Died: on Mar 9, at his residence, in Gibson Co, Ind, Mr Geo Holbrook, who, on Oct 7 preceding, completed the 100th year of his age. His 3rd wife, aged 59 years, preceded him to the grave but 4 days.

Furnished rooms for rent: in a new bldg in the immediate vicinity of the War & Navy Depts. Inquire of B Jost, corner of Pa ave & 17th sts.

Genteel furniture at auction, Mar 27, at the residence of the Rev C Butler, on Bealle st, his household & kitchen furniture. --Edw S Wright, auct

We have reason to fear, due to his dangerous illness, that Gen Peter B Porter, a distinguished citizen of this State, has been gathered to his fathers. The next intelligence from the West will probably confirm this melancholy anticipation. --Albany Evening Journal of Mar 20.]

Wash Corp: An Act for the relief of Wm G W White: that the Register pay to White $6.67, being the amount of 2 fines paid by said White.

Cmte of the Nat'l Institute to meet on Mar 26, at the Treas Dept, to take measures for the execution of the duties assigned to them. The following compose the cmte referred to:

Hon John C Spencer	Benj Ogle Tayloe	Geo W Riggs, jr
Hon Jos R Ingersoll	Matthew St Clair Clare	John D Barclay
Hon Robt J Walker	John C Brent	John T Sullivan
Hon Wm C Preston	John P Van Ness	Saml Harrison Smith
Hon Abbott Lawrence	Dr Thos P Jones	Henry L Ellsworth
Hon Wm C Rives	B B French	Walter Lenox
Hon Rufus Choate	John W Maury	Rev O B Brown
Alex Dallas Bach	Wm Gunton	Rev Wm Matthews
W W Seaton	Geo Watterston	Rev R R Gurley
Peter Force	Dr Thos Sewall	Richd S Coxe
Capt Robt F Stockton	Dr John M Thomas	Francis Markoe, jr
Capt Geo W Hughes	Dr J H Causten, jr	Josiah F Polk
Maj Wm Turnbull	Chas Hill	Lt P Kearney
Lt M F Maury	Roger C Weightman	Lt J T McLaughlin
W W Corcoran	Wm A Bradley	Alex'r Hunter
Robt Lawrence	John C Harkness	W T Carroll
John D Wilson	Lt W H Emory	Dr Winne
F H Davidge	Robt S Chew	W Q Force
Dr McClery	J K Townsend	Lt Totten
Silas H Hill	H K Randall	Chas Abert
Dr Magruder	Bayard Smith	J C McGuire
Dr Marcus Buck	McClintock Young	

TUE MAR 26, 1844
Hoffman's Law Institution, established at 117 South Fifth st, Phil, for the reception of Law Students from every part of the Union. –David Hoffman

Senate: 1-Ptns & memorials referred: from the citizens of Muskingum Co, Ohio, asking that Jos Watson, a soldier of the last war, be placed on the pension list. 2-Ptn from Wm G Brown, asking compensation for services as paymaster to a detachment of mounted volunteers. 3-Ptn from Jas Larned, asking the graduation of a square of ground belonging to the Gov't within the corporate limits of Washington. 4-Ptn from Peter Van Schmidt, asking compensation for translating from the Russian language a pamphlet on the culture of hemp, & also asking that facilities may be afforded to test a process to render timber impenetrable by marine insects. 5-Ptn from Geo Renwick, in relation to error in a certain survey of the township of Salem, in Michigan. 6-Ptn of Peter Frost, for a pension. 7-Cmte on Naval Affairs: bill for the relief of Chas W Morgan. 8-Cmte of Claims: adverse report on the ptn of Saml Thompson. Same cmte: adverse report on the claim of Jos H Warring. 9-Cmte on Claims: adverse reports on the following Hse/o Rep bills: relief of Saml B Folger; of Saml B Tuck; of Geo W Jones. 10-Cmte on Public Lands: bill for the relief of John

Milliken & others, with an elaborate report. 11-Cmte on Revolutionary Claims: bill for the relief of John S Russworm, heir at law of Wm Russworm. 12-Cmte on Pensions: House bill for the relief of John Reed. 13-Cmte on Revolutionary Claims: asking to be discharged from the further consideration of the bill for the relief of Benj Netherlands, & also of the bill for the relief of Wm Barber, & that they be referred to the Cmte on Pensions. 14-Cmte of Claims: bill for the relief of Gerris Foote, & for the relief of Wm H Hoag & others, without amendment. 15-Cmte on Commerce: House bill for the relief of Isaac Fessenden.

The public are cautioned against trading for a note drawn by me in favor of C Stanton, of N Y, for $50, dated Feb 8, 1844, at four months, as I will not pay said note. –Wm Blanchard

Orphan's Court of Chas Co, Md. Letters of administration on the personal estate of John Herbert, late of said county, dec'd. –Clarissa Herbert, John H Duley, adms of John Herbert

Hse/o Reps: 1-Cmte on Revolutionary Claims to inquire into allowing to the heirs of the late Col Wm Grayson the commutation pay due to him as an ofcr in the continental army during the war of the Revolution, & who was reduced in pursuance of the resolutions of Congress of the 3rd & 21st of Oct, 1780. 2-Cmte on Revolutionary Pensions to inquire into granting a pension to Mary Crysal, & that the accompanying papers be referred to said cmte. Same cmte: to inquire into allowing a pension to Mrs Nancy Hardel, of Horry district, S C, the widow of a Revolutionary soldier. 3-The papers in the case of John W Custin, referred to the Cmte of Claims, & by that cmte reported upon adversely, be referred to the Cmte on the Judiciary with instructions to inquire whether the evidence of the loss of the horse in this case is not sufficient to establish the fact under the law of Congress of Oct 14, 1837, upon strictly legal principles of evidence. 4-Resolved: that the ptn of papers of Saml Drew be recommitted to the Cmte on Invalid Pensions. 5-Bill for the relief of Jonathan Bean: read twice & committed. 6-Ptn of Isaac Atkinson, asking a grant of land. 7-Ptn of Jos W Ross, of Gallia Co, Ohio, praying for a pension: referred. 8-Ptn of Rufus Kibbie & others, citizens of Michigan, for a new mail route. 9-Ptn of Archibald D Palmer, for confirmation of land titles. 10-Ptn of A A Pickard & 50 others, praying the grant of a certain township of land therein named. 11-Memorial of the heirs of Jacob Vandevoort, for a pension.

N Y, Mar 24. Gen Peter B Porter died at his residence at Niagara, aged 71 years. His history is closely allied with that of the U S for his services during the late war; but it is also with the history of Western N Y, which is under more obligations to him than to any other man she ever claimed as a citizen. [No date-recent.]

Orphan's Court of Chas Co, Md. Letters of administraton on the personal estate of Thos Price, late of said county, dec'd. –Richd Price, Jos Price, Adms

Public sale at auction of a large & valuable real estate in the town of Alexandria: sale on Apr 25, property belonging to the estate of the late Guy Atkinson, formerly a merchant of that city. [There are 6 properties, with specific locations, and improvements, listed.] -Christopher Neale, Francis L Smith, Commissioners. –By Geo White, Alexandria

Valuable estate on James river for sale: virtue of a deed of trust, dated Mar 15, 1844, to secure the payment of $13,000, I will sell on the premises, on May 1, all that tract of land in Surry Co, Va, know as *Bacon's Castle*, with mill & all other improvements, together all the chattel property now thereon. There are 1,640 acres of land, on Chipoak's creek. The house on the plantation is of brick, large & comfortable. Any inquiries to T S O'Sullivan, Bacon's Castle, Surry Co, Va. –Tazewell Taylor

Orphan's Court of Wash Co, D C. Letters of administraton on the personal estate of Wm J H Robertson, late of the U S Navy, dec'd. –Susan D Robertson, Admx

Mexican News. The papers of the 23rd contain the official orders for the funeral of Dona Josefa Davila de Canalizo, [the amiable & generally esteemed consort of the Pres ad interim.] She was to be buried with all the ceremonies which the Mexican law provided for rendering honor to a dec'd Pres. These were enacted upon the occasion of the death of Pres Barragan on Feb 29, 1836.

Mrd: on Mar 13, at Edenton, N C, by Rev Saml J Johnstone, Geo B Dixon, of Mississippi, to Mary B, d/o Gen Duncan McDonald, of the former place.

Died: on Mar 25, near the Navy Yard, in Wash City, after a long & lingering illness, Mrs Catharine, consort of Mr Michl Quigley, in her 60th year. Her funeral is today at 2 o'clock.

WED MAR 27, 1844
Senate: 1-Memorial from Jas Lynch, stating that the manufacturing interests of the country will be greatly benefited by the annexation of Texas to this country, & expressing the hope that Congress will take steps to secure so desirable a result. 2-Ptn from Mgt & Agnes Bigham, asking the repayment of money advanced by their ancestor & compensation for his services. 3-Ptn from Catharine Gale for a pension. 4-Ptn from Patience Brown, wid/o a Revolutionary soldier, for a pension. 5-Ptn from Jas Banker, asking arrears of pension & additional allowance for services in the last war with Great Britain. 6-Ptn from Adin Stanley, for a pension. 7-Cmte on Revolutionary Claims: adverse report on the ptn of the heirs of John Houston. 8-Cmte on the Judiciary: bill for the benefit of Thos Hunter & Alex'r Caldwell. 9-Cmte on Revolutionary Claims: bill for the relief of Wm Rich. 10-Cmte on Patents: bill for the relief of the reps of Uri Emmons. 11-The Senate took up the

adverse report on the memorial of Mrs Emeline Porter, which report was concurred in. 12-Bill for the relief of Jas M McIntosh, a cmder in the U S Navy. 13-Bill for the relief of Wm McPherson.

The Williamsport [Md] Banner of Sat nominates Col Isaac Munroe, the veteran Editor of the Balt Patriot, as a candidate for the ofc of Govn'r of the State of Md.

N Y Mar 22, 1844. The following have been appointed Delegates from the N Y Historical Society to the Apr Convention of the Nat'l Institute, viz:

Hon Albert Gallatin
Wm B Lawrence
Hon Benj F Butler
Hon Gulian C Verplanck
Geo Folson
John W Francis, M D
Gen P M Wetmore
Jos Blunt
Prof John W Draper, M D
Rev T De Witt, D D
Prof E Robinson, D C
Prof C Mason, D D
Hon Luther Bradish
Hon H Fish, M C
H R Schoolcraft

From Geo Folson, Domestic Corr Sec N Y H S To: F Markoe, jr, Corr Sec Nat'l Institute.

Justice Oliver M Lowndes, with his dght, left N Y for Wash on Mar 14. He remained one day in Wash, & on his return to Balt became very ill from a severe cold, & died suddenly on Mar 20, deeply regretted by a large circle of sincere friends.

Utica Gaz: Mrs Harriet Wallace was drowned on Wed, in a cistern attached to the house of her brother, Mr Bowers, in Broadway, where she was living. She was 38 years of age, & had ben married but a few days. Her husband was absent, & circumstances induce the suspicion that her death was intentional.

Gen Geo B Porter died on Mar 20, at Niagara Falls, in the 71st year of his age.

Died: at the residence of her brother, Dr Thos Triplett, in Fauquier Co, Va, Mrs Eliza Alexander, in her 72nd year, a lady of the most respectable connexions, whose life had been distinguished by all the virtues which adorn the female character. [No date-current item.]

A seaman, Wm Parkhill, lately paid off & discharged from the U S ship **Delaware**, was found drowned in the county dock at Norfolk on Sun last. He had taken his passage for N Y in the packet schnr **Ann**, Capt Driscoll, & carefully deposited his money, about $200, with Capt Driscoll. Being intoxicated, he fell into the dock & met his untimely end. He was a native of Belfast, Ire, & had relations in Liverpool, though some of his shipmates say that he has been upwards of 20 years in the U S Navy. He appeared to be about 40 years of age, & of a fine athletic person.

$25 reward for the person who stole silverware on Mar 25. –Ann S Hill, H st, between 14th & 15th sts.

Hse/o Reps: 1-Ptn of Eliz Ragsdale, wid/o Godfrey Ragsdale, & Ann Bryan, wid/o Barrick Bryan, both asking pensions. 2-Memorial of Francis Johnsonn asking pay for horses lost during the last war with Great Britain. 3-Ptn of Lodera Knapp & others, for a continuation of pension.

Balt Annual Conference of the Meth Episc Church adjourned last Mon. The following appointments were made for the Potomac District: Thos B Sargeant, presiding Elder
Alexandria: Alfred Griffith, Wm Evans
Foundry: Henry Tarring
Wesley Chapel: Norval Wilson
Gtwn: Wm Wicks, Stephen Asbury Roszell
Leesburg: Francis McCartney
Fairfax: Jas Watts, Chas E Brown
Loudoun: Jos White, Saml Kepler
Warrenton: Philip Rescorl, Jas Bunting
Stafford: Robt D Nixon, Irvine H Torrance
Fredericksburg: Stephen Saml Roszell
Westmoreland: Jas Bradds, Wm Murphy
King Geo: Thos C Hays
Bladensburg: Thos Wheeler, Wm R White
Lancaster: Alfred A Eskridge, Thos F McClure
Wash City Mission to be supplied.

Incendiarism on Sun last, not far from Mrs Billings' cottage. The carpenter's shop of Mr D Gardiner, near the Treas Bldg, was completely destroyed by fire in the evening. He is a second time a great sufferer. Mrs Billings cottage was consumed by fire in the morning, & was insured for $1,500.

Public sale: on Apr 2, on the premises on 13th st, near Pa ave: 21 cases, large board & stands, large stone & stand, iron chase & side sticks, stool, stoves & pipes, trough, rules, bucket & roller, & 1 sign. Siezed & taken as the property of Wm Coale & A C Dickinson, for rent due in arrears to John McDuell. –Michl Rearden, Bailiff

THU MAR 28, 1844
Alien wife should be naturalized. It was decided by Judge Kent in the N Y Circuit Court, on Sat, that a wife born abroad, & not naturalized, canot inherit property devised to her by a husband.

Senate: 1-Ptn from the legal reps of Thos Earnes, asking to be indemnified for property illegally confiscated, & reimbursed for the expenses incurred. 2-Ptn from Joel A Matheson & Hardin Bigelow, asking indemnity for the illegal seizure & detention of railroad iron by the collectors of the ports of Cincinnati, Cleveland, & St Louis. 3-Cmte on Naval Affairs: adverse report on the memorial of Geo F Sinclair for extra pay. Same cmte: adverse reports on the memorials of Amos Cheek & J R Howison for extra pay. 4-Cmte on Pensions: bill for the relief of Benj F Ferguson. 5-Bill for the relief of John Atchison: engrossed. 6-Bill for the relief of Wm Henson: engrossed.

Hse/o Reps: 1-Ptn of Robt Lang & others, citizens of Georgia, praying for an alteration of the pilot laws, so as to exempt coasting vessels from paying pilot license. 2-Ptn of Thos Lee & Mary Jane Lee, asking an allowance in right of Ann Pearson, dec'd, who was the widow of Lt Thos Pearson, dec'd. 3-Ptn of Wm D Ausment, praying some adequate compensation for services rendered the country. 4-Ptn of G F Wright & other citizens of the Territory of Wisconsin, praying the reduction of postage. 5-Ptn of Simeon Guilford & numerous others, citizens of Lebanon Co, Pa, protesting against any interference with the tariff of 1842. 6-Cmte on Private Land Claims: adverse report on the ptn of Jacob Kerr. Same cmte: bill for the relief of the heirs of Wm A Baker, dec'd. Same cmte: bill for the relief of the heirs of Saml Moore. 7-Cmte on Indian Affairs: adverse report on the memorial of Thos Talbot & others. Same cmte: adverse report on the memorial of Lawrence Taliferro. Same cmte: bill for the relief of John A Bryan. 8-Cmte on the Judiciary: adverse report on the case of John Harper. Same cmte: adverse report on the ptn of David Melville, adm of Benj Fry. Same cmte: bill for the relief of Wm P Duvall; & relief of Richd Snead. Same cmte: bill for the relief of the legal reps of Cozeau, of Montreal, Canada. 9-Cmte on Claims: bill for the relief of the heirs & legal reps of Capt Presley Thornton, dec'd. 10-Cmte on Naval Affairs: adverse report on the ptn of Mary Barry. 11-Cmte on Revolutionary Pensions: bill for the relief of Patrick Masterton.

St Mary's School, Raleigh, N C: Rt Rev L S Ives, D D, Visiter, Rev Albert Smedes, Rector. The 5th session of this school will commence on Jun 1, & continue 5 months.

FRI MAR 29, 1844
Wash Corp, Mar 25, 1844. 1-Ptn from Wm Jasper, praying remission of a fine: referred to the Cmte of Claims. 2-Ptn of Gustavus A Clarke, messenger & watchman in the City Hall, asking for the use of an additional room in the basement story of the bldg: referred to the members from the 3rd ward. 3-Ptn of Wm M Maddox, praying the remission of a fine: referred to the Cmte of Claims. 4-Same cmte: asked to be discharged from the further consideration of the ptn of Saml M Emery: & they were discharged accordingly. 5-Bill for the relief of Capt Danl Paullin: passed. Board adjourned.

In the Rotundo of the Capitol, we observed yesterday a portrait of Mr Webster, by Lawson, much more *like* him than his portraits generally are, & well worth seeing. We saw also in the hands of the inventor, Benj Cushwa, a model of a simple invention, supplying a desideratum in saw-mills, which he calls the Self-adjusting Log brace, of which he has individual, county, or State patents for sale. It enables the sawyer to cut with greatly more accuracy, particularly long timber.

Hse/o Reps: 1-Cmte on Invalid Pensions: introduced a bill for the relief of Thos Pierce. Same cmte: adverse reports on the ptns of Jas Gee, Lyman N Cook, Danl Sprague, & Oliver Herrick. 3-Memorial of John S Gilbert, setting forth the merits of his patent balance floating dock, & asking Congress to examine & report upon the same. 4-Ptn of Edmund Robinson, praying an extension of his pension on account of his disability, arising from wounds received during the war of 1812. 5-Ptn of John S Frick & Geo W Hinkle, numerously signed by citizens of York Co, Pa, praying Congress earnestly that no change shall be made in the tariff law of 1842. 6-Cmte on the Library: to be discharged from the consideration of the ptn of T & J W Johnson, law publishers of Phil, & that it do lie upon the table.

Medical College: Prof Hallowell having resigned the chair of Chemistry in this Institution, on account of the inconvenience of his distant residence, the Trustees have appointed Chas G Page, A M M D, of Wash City, in his place. Dr Page is a graduate of Harvard Univ.

Laws of the U S: passed at the 1st Session of the 28th Congress. 1-Act to refund the fine imposed on Gen Andrew Jackson: fine was imposed at New Orleans, Mar 31, 1815, to be repaid to him, together with the interest, at the rate of 6% per year since then. Approved, Feb 16, 1844. 2-Act for the relief of John Mullings: title to land in the Columbus land district of Miss, heretofore located to satisfy the claim of Alabatcha, the wife of John Mullings, be & the same is hereby confirmed to the said John Mullings, to have & to hold the same right & interest in the same as he would have held had he been returned in Ward's register; & the Pres is directed to cause a patent to be issued to the said John Mullings for described lands. Approved, Mar 26, 1844

Chateau Roux, Feb 5, 1844. Before this letter can reach you, the journals will have announced the deplorable event which has overwhelmed with grief the family of Gen Bertand, my brother, who died in this town on Jan 31. He arrived in Paris from N Y in excellent health, happy in getting back to France, & proud of the brilliant welcome with which he was received in your beloved country. While about to set out for Chateau Rous, he found himself slightly indisposed; but not so seriously as to cause any apprehensions from a journey of 18 hours. Unfortunately, the night proved an intensely cold one, which brought on severe sufferings, &, soon after his arrival, he was snatched from us by the hand of death. –Mons Bertrand Boislarge

Millinery: Miss Louisa Dorsey, 114 Balt st, Balt, Md. [Ad]

Senate: 1-Cmte on the Judiciary: bill for the relief of Asa Andrews. 2-Bills passed: for the relief of John Atchison; & relief of Wm Henson.

Boarding: Miss S C Polk, on Pa ave, between 3rd & 4½ sts, Wash.

$100 reward for runaway negro Wallace Marshall, about 30 years of age. He was purchased several years ago of the estate of Thos Mundell, dec'd, near Piscataway. He has relations in Port Tobacco, Chas Co; also in Balt at Mr Geo H Keerl's. –Thos Clagett, Upr Marlboro, PG Co, Md

The late Hon Nicholas Brown, of Providence, R I, in his last will, bequeathed, on conditions, the sum of $30,000 toward the erection of an asylum for the insane in his State. A meeting of the corporators took place at Providence on Wed last, when Cyrus Butler, subscribed the sum of $40,000 toward the object, on condition that the futher sum of $40,000 shall be raised by subscription among the citizens generally.

Mrd: on Mar 26, by Rev Geo W Samson, Mr Wm S Mullin to Miss Eliz Codrick, all of Wash City.

Died: on Mar 19, at Montgomery, Ala, Mrs Sarah Alicia Trapier, wid/o the late Paul Trapier, of Charleston, S C, & sister of Cmdor Shubrick; a lady excelling in all the graces which adorn this life & give assurance of bliss in the life to come.

Died: on Mar 28, of scarlet fever, Danl Sharp, s/o Edmund F & Eliz M Brown, aged 10 years. His funeral is this morning, at 10 o'clock, from the residence of his father, on I st, near 7th.

Died: on Mar 26, in her 5th year, Edith, y/d/o A H & Mgt Mechlin, of Wash City.

SAT MAR 30, 1844
Senate: Ptn from John S Gilbert, asking that the Sec of Navy may be directed to contract with him for the construction of a dry dock on a plan proposed by him. 2-Ptn from W Kohn, a soldier of the last war, for a pension. 3-Ptn from Laomi Kelton, asking a pension for disability incurred in the discharge of his duty. 4-Cmte on Naval Affairs: bill for the relief of Robt Fulton.

Fire & death in New Orleans on Mar 19, at the corner of Bienville & Royal sts. By the falling of a wall of one of the bldgs, the following were severely wounded: Ralf Depas, Robt Lynch, J C Denman, Geo Fosdick. Mr John Haynes died during the night, & some of the others were in critical condition.

Hse/o Reps: 1-Ptn of Wm Hogshead & 126 others, praying that the company of Capt J B Crozier, volunteers called out by the Govn'r of Tenn in compliance with a requisition of the Pres of the U S in 1836, be allowed pay for their services at the same rate others were paid. 2-Memorials of Danl Agnew & 38 others, John Pugh & 94 others, & Philip Bentel & 100 others, citizens of Beaver Co, Pa, against alteration of the present tariff. 3-Ptn of Mott Wilkinson, of Indiana Co, Pa, a Revolutionary soldier, for an increase of his pension. 4-Cmte of Claims: bill for the relief of Drucilla Giesey, wid/o Valentine Giesey. Same cmte: bill for the relief of Lund Washington. 5-Cmte on Commerce: bill for the relief of the owners & crew of the schnr **Privado**; relief of the acting owner & crew of the fishing schnr **Two Brothers**. Same cmte: bill for the relief of John H Russell & others. Same cmte: bill for the relief of the owner & crew of the schnr **Dove**. 6-Cmte on Invalid Pensions: bill for the benefit of John Perham. 7-Cmte on Revolutionary Pensions: bill for the relief of Alice Upshur. 8-Cmte on Commerce: adverse report on the ptn of Benj Evans. 9-Cmte on Public Lands: bill for the relief of Francis Yoast & John P Rogers. 10-Cmte on the Public Lands: to be discharged from the consideration of the ptn of Wm Sholar & Debulan Parr, for aid in boring for salt: said ptn laid upon the table. 11-Cmte on Indian Affairs: report on the bill for the relief of Harvey Heth. Same cmte: bill for the relief of Philip B Holmes & Wm Pedrick. 12-Cmte on Naval Affairs: adverse report on the ptn of Levi H Parish.

The Hon Ben P Major, State Senator in Missouri, was stabbed a short time since at Warsaw, Mo, by a Mr Cherry, & died of the wound. Cause, a political quarrel.

Died: on Mar 17, Gen Edmund Jones, of Wilkes Co, N C, aged 73 years, a venerable patriot, who had repeatedly served the public, in various capacities, with faithfulness & integrity.

Died: yesterday, Augusta Fuller Black, y/d/o Capt Furman Black. Her funeral is this afternoon, at 4 o'clock, from her father's residence.

Died: on Mar 27, at his residence, **Woodland Plains**, Chas Co, Md, Maj Townly Robey, in his 73rd year. He left an aged widow & a number of children, together with a large family of friends, to lament his loss.

Died: on Mar 27, in Wash City, Mrs Catharine Baxter, in her 68th year, wid/o [blank] Baxter, late of Chas Co, Md.

Died: yesterday, Mr Jas Birth, sen, in his 74th year. For 48 years he had been a resident of Wash City. His funeral from his late residence on 3rd st, at 3 o'clock, on Sunday.

Geo Page, Machinist, Balt, Md: all orders may be favored with on the shortest notice, & at the lowest possible price. Wm Brown, clerk, in Balt.

The devisee of the late Howes Goldsborough, of Havre de Grace, in Md, has authorized me to sell the following valuable & extensive property in Wash City, belonging to the estate of said Goldsborough, & through which the Chesapeake & Ohio Canal passes, viz: lots 1, 2, 4, 5, 6, 7, 17, & 18, in square 8, with bldgs thereon. A large wharf on the channel of the Potomac river, forms a part of this property. For terms of sale apply at my residence on north G st, near the property. --Nathl Frye

Chas Co, Md, Whig Meeting on Mar 20, at the Court-house in Port Tobacco, Chas Co, Md. On motion of Peter W Crain, Maj Theodore Mudd was appointed Pres; Col Hugh Cox & Col John Hughes, V Ps; & Jas McCormick & Geo P Jenkins, Secs. Remarks by John J Jenkins: Gen John G Chapman, suitable person for the next Govn'r of Md. Cmte:

Walter M Miller	Dr John R Ferguson	Henry H Hawkins
Walter Robertson	Alexius Lancaster	Geo Gardiner
Richd B Posey	Richd Gardiner	Peter Wood
Robt Gray	Geo P Jenkins	Dr Walter F Boarman
John R Robertson	Francis Robey	
Peter W Crain	Hezekiah Brawner	

MON APR 1, 1844
Cmdor Edmund Pendleton Kennedy, of the U S Navy, died at Norfolk on Fri last, aged 65 years. He was a native of Md, & entered the Navy in 1805; &, at the time of his death, was in command of the ship of the line **Pennsylvania**, the flag-ship of the Norfolk station. His remains were committed to the tomb with appropriate honors on Sat.

A Court of Inquiry has been ordered at *Fort Leavenworth* to try Capt Cook, U S Army, for his conduct towards Col Snively's party last spring. Capt Cook was sent out to protect the Santa Fe traders, & that on falling in with Capt Snively & the party of Texians under his command, he captured & disarmed the entire force. The Court will consist of Col Kearney, Col Vose, & Maj Wharton.

Local ads: 1-Jos H Daniel, Merchant Tailor, a few doors west of Brown's Hotel, Wash. 2-Palm Leaf Hats just received at Allen's, Pa ave, between 9th & 10th sts. --John Allen 3-Window Glass, of all sized & of superior quality. --R H Miller, Alexandria

Geo V Nellis, aged about 19 years, hung himself in Albany jail last Tue. He was charged with stealing a trunk, & averred his innocence. A relation left him $5,000 a few days ago.

Mrd: on Mar 28, by Rev W B Edwards, Mr Thos J Magruder to Miss Sarah A P Boteler, both of Wash City.

TUE APR 2, 1844
Paper Mill for sale or lease: the Matoaca Manufacturing Co will lease on moderate terms their Mill near Petersburg, Va. –Saml Mordecai, Agent of said company.

Orphan's Court of Chas Co, Md. Letters of administration on the personal estate of Francis Nalley, late of said county, dec'd. –Jas Oliver, adm of F Nalley

Fort Moultrie, S C, Feb 29, 1844. Leave of absence for 30 days, from Mar 1, is granted to 1st Lt B Bragg, 3rd artl; at the expiration of which he will rejoin his company. By order of Brig Gen Armistead: W A Browne, Lt 3rd artl, A A A G

Hse/o Reps: 1-Ptn of Danl Bull & 300 citizens of Wood Co, Ohio, praying for a reduction in the rates of postage. Ptn of J W Allen & 509 citizens of Cuyahoga Co, Ohio, for the same. 2-Memorial of Jos H Raymond & others, heirs of Joshua Raymond, dec'd, praying for a pension. 3-Memorial of Edw Whitney & 298 other citizens of Norwich, Conn, praying that the spirit ration in the navy may be abolished. John B Fletcher & 208 other citizens, of N Y, upon the same subject. Memorial of Fred'k Hemrill & 234 other citizens of N Y, upon the same subject. Memorial of Jas McKie & 401 other citizens of N Y, upon the same subject. Same for Geo Hull & 714 other citizens of the city of Brooklyn, N Y.

Senate: 1-Ptn from the heirs of Jas Bell, in relation to the claim of their ancestor. Mr Tallmadge examined the claim, & had no doubt but that it was a perfectly fair & just one. 2-Ptn from Benj Ballard, asking confirmation to his title to a tract of land in Louisiana. 3-Ptn from Jas Sollers & Albin S Pennock, stating that they had made a contract with the Post Ofc Dept for certain mail bags, which, when finished, had been left on their hands. They ask to be indemnified, or that the Post Ofce Dept take the bags. 4-Ptn from W Miller, a soldier in the last war, for a pension. 5-Ptn from Harrison Wingate, asking the payment of a forfeiture, the information having been given by him to the Gov't. 6-Cmte of Claims-recommending the passage of the following bills: relief of Geo W Clarke, Harris Cook, & John Brainerd 2nd, of Rhode Island. Relief of John Putney & Hugh Riddle. Relief of W R Davis. Relief of the legal reps of Capt Saml Shannon; also, bill for the relief of J C McPharian. Same cmte: adverse report on the ptn of the heirs of Thos Eames, asking payment for cattle ellegally confiscated. 7-Cmte of Claims: adverse report on the memorial of Jas Rundlet. Same cmte: on the ptn of the trustees of Richd Linthicum, asking compensation for materials delivered for the repair of certain light-houses, accompanied by a resolution that it be referred to the dept for certain information. 8-Cmte on Pensions: adverse reports on the ptns of Hezekiah Hamlet, Rufus K Lane, Lydia Baker, the wid/o Jonas Sawtell, Jacob M Follansbee, & Wm Harder; also, on the House bill for the relief of Gideon Foster. Same cmte: asking to be discharged from the further consideration of the ptn of Geo S Gaines. Same cmte: House bill for the relief of Jas C Hallock, without amendment, & recommending its passage.

9-Cmte on Revolutionary Claims: bill for the relief of Fred'k Seigle. Same cmte: adverse report on the bill for the relief of the heirs of Wm Augustus Atlee. 10-Cmte on Pensions: adverse report on the bill for the relief of Jos Watson. Asking to be discharged from the further consideration of House bill for the relief of Eliz Jones & others; & from the ptn of Mary Reynolds. Also, an adverse report on the ptn of Eliz Connell.

Fort Monroe, Va, Mar 28, 1844. Meeting on Mar 28, of the Ofcrs of the Army at *Fort Monroe*, to adopt such measures as might be deemed appropriate, consequent to the decease, on Mar 26, of their late brother ofcr Surgeon Edw Macomb, of the Medical Dept, Col J B Wallach called to the chair, & 1st Lt & Adj J H Miller appointed Sec. Cmte constituted: Lt Col De Russy, Maj Belton, brevet Maj Brown, Capt Huger, & Assistant Surgeon Wells. We sympathise with his afflicted widow for her irreparable loss.

Nashville Union announces the death of Gen Wm Carroll, late Govn'r of Tenn, whose name is familiar to the country besides, in connexion with his military service as commander of a volunteer corps in the war of 1812, & for public services rendered since in various civil capacities.

Circuit Court of Wash Co, D C. Anthony Smidley applied to be discharged from imprisonment under the act for the relief of Insolvent Debtors: hearing on Apr 8. –Wm Brent, clk

Fire destroyed the Boot & shoe store of Mr Hugh Bell, in Centre Market space, near Balt, on Sat. Also consumed were the stores of Mr John N Ovear, hatter; of Mr Simon Frank, dry goods dealer; of Mr S W Merryman, dry goods dealer. Mr Thos Wilson, dry goods dealer, lost considerable by water.

Delhi, N Y, Mar 27. On Sat, 2 girls, cousins, aged about 14 years, drowned near Mr Danl Pine's, in Walton. One, a d/o the late David Robinson, was living at Mr Pine's; the other, a d/o Mr Henry Beers, of Hamden, but living in the neighborhood, on a visit to her cousin. It appears they slid on the ice directly across into an open space. The body of one has been recovered.

The trial of Mr Hornsby, indicted for murder for killing D H Twogood, in Banks' Arcade, New Orleans, was brought to a conclusion on Mar 22, when the jury brought in a verdict of manslaughter. The law fixes the punishment for this crime to be in the penitenitary for not less than 7 nor more than 21 years, in the discretion of the court.

Died: on Mar 23, in the borough of Manheim, Lancaster Co, Pa, Dr Thos W Veazey, a s/o Ex-Govn'r Veazey, of Md, in his 39th year.

Died: on Apr 1, after a short & painful illness, Geo Cookman, infant s/o Chas H & Ann E Lane, aged 19 months & 16 days. His funeral is this afternoon, at 2 o'clock, from his father's residence, on Indiana ave, near 3rd st.

WED APR 3, 1844
Senate: 1-The number of lots conveyed under donations from Congress to charitable & literary institutions were 771, & valued at $70,000: Orphan Asylum, 29 lots, valued at $10,000. For the Sisters of Charity, 70 lots, valued at $10,000. For the Columbian College, 182 lots, valued at $25,000. For Gtwn College, 490 lots, valued at $25,000. 2-The papers in the case of the wid/o Danl McKessie were taken from the files. 3-Papers in the case of the wid/o Miles Goforth were referred to the Cmte on Revolutionary Claims. 4-Cmte on the Judiciary: asking to be discharged from the consideration of the ptn of Richd McGoon, & that it be referred to the Cmte on Public Lands. Same cmte: adverse report on the ptn of Anna Maria Baldwin. Bill introduced authorizing the Sec of the Treas to compromise & settle the accounts with the sureties of John H Owen, late receiver of public moneys at St Stephen's, Ala. 5-Mr King expressed hope that he should be indulged to take up the bill for the relief of Catherine E Clitherall, which had passed the Senate some 2 or 3 times. Same was ordered to be engrossed for a third reading.

Hse/o Reps: 1-The cadets at *West Point* receive $16 per month, while the private soldier of the line got but $7. It appeared that the clothing of the cadets cost $60 a year, that of the soldier $30. The cadet paid $90 for his board, the soldier nothing. 2-Ptn of John R Williams for damages incurred during the last war. 3-Ptn of Coit, Kimberly & Co, & others, for a lighthouse at the mouth of the Cattaraugua creek, Lake Erie, N Y. 4-Ptn of Mrs Mary Hicks, of Jessamine Co, Ky, wid/o Wm Hicks, dec'd, a soldier of the war of the Revolution, praying that her claim may be made to commence Mar 1, 1842. 5-Ptn of Pierre Chouteau & others, praying Congress to inquire into & adjust the claim of the legal reps of Julian Dubuque to a certain tract of land in the Territory of Iowa, granted by the Baron de Caroudelet, Intendant Genr'l of Louisiana, to said Dubuque, on Nov 10, 1796.

Boarding: Mrs J C Turner, at her house on 6th st, between E & F sts, east of the Genr'l Post Ofc.

Masonic: meeting of Columbia Chapter #15 at their Hall, 12th & Pa ave, on Apr 3, at 7 p m. –Wm Greer, sec

Orphan's Court of Wash Co, D C. Letters testmentary on the personal estate of Beverly Kennon, late of the U S Navy, dec'd. –B W Kennon, excx N. B. The house recently occupied by Com Kennon is offered for rent. Apply to H M Morfit.

Genteel furniture at auction: on Apr 3 at 3 p m, at the residence of Mr J Lipscomb, on High st, Gtwn, his entire stock of household furniture. –Edw S Wright, Auct

Wash Corp: 1-Ptn of Anthony Holmead & others for flag footways: referred to the Cmte on Improvements. 2-Cmte of Claims: bill for the relief of Wm M Maddox: passed.

Philadelphia American of yesterday: death of our fellow-townsman, Peter S Duponceau, perhaps the most eminent savant in this country, died on Mon. He was a native of France, &, in the capacity of Aid, accompanied Baron Steuben to this country about the commencement of the Revolutionary struggle. At the close of the war he studied law in Phil, where he has since resided. He was Pres of the American Philosophical Society, the Pa Historical Society, & the Law Academy of Phil. He was in the 85th year of his age.

Capt Abraham S Ten Eick, U S Navy, died at New Brunswick, N J, on Mar 28, in his 58th year. He was a native of N J, & entered the Navy as a Midshipman in 1811.

New Orleans, Mar 14. A duel took place yesterday between Gen Wm Debuys, the State Treasurer, & Mr Richd Richardson. They fought with sharpened foils. Mr Richardson was severely wounded in the shoulder, & Gen Debuys was run through the lower part of his body. Faint hopes were entertained of his recovery. -Tropic

THU APR 4, 1844
Senate: 1-Ptn from Benj R Tinslar, a Surgeon in the Navy, asking compensation for doing duty as an ofcr of a higher grade. 2-Ptn from Danl Whitney, asking confirmation of a title to land. 3-Ptn from Peter Von Schmidt, asking that an experiment may be made of his invention of a pneumatic dry dock. 4-Ptn from C Stewart & other citizens of Arkansas, asking a reduction of the rates of postage. 5-Cmte on Pensions: asking to be discharged from the further consideration of the ptn of Catharine Gale, & that it be referred to the Cmte on Naval Affairs. 6-Cmte of Claims: adverse report on the ptn of John Bruel. 7-Mr Crittenden asked that the bill for the relief of the heirs of Christopher Miller be taken up. The motion having been agreed to, the report on the merits of the bill was read, [which was full of interesting incidents in the life of said Christopher Miller as a spy upon the Indians under Gen Wayne;] & the bill was then ordered to be engrossed for a third reading.

Geo Templeman has for sale at his Bookstore, opposite Fuller's hotel, all the laws, documents, journals, & Registers of debates, & all other books subscribed for or published by order of Congress; also, Niles' Weekly Register, in 65 volumes, from 1811 to Mar, 1844.

Bank & Steamboat stocks at auction, on Apr 12, by order of the Orphan's Court of Wash Co, D C: belonging to the late Jos Johnson. -Robt W Dyer & Co, aucts

For rent, the south part of the house & lot at present occupied by Mr Randolph Coyle, Md ave & 12th st west, containing 5 rooms & a good cellar, & kitchen, stable, with 2 stalls. Inquire of Mr Fitch, north end of said bldg, or of Edw Mattingly, near the Navy Yard, Wash.

Adm's sale of improved & other property, on Apr 12, by order of Orphan's Court of Wash Co, D C, the following property belonging to the estate of the late Capt Jos Johnson: lot 1 in square 664, with 2 story dwlg house. Lot 10 in square 660, near the Eastern Branch, with a small frame dwlg house. Lot 2 in square 662; lot 4 in square 602; lot 10 in square 609; half lot 1 in square 660; part of lot 16 in square 770, on 3rd st, between M & N sts. Also, a lot in square 906, on 7th st, near the Navy Yard, with improvements. –Jas Johnson, H D Gunnell, adms -Robt W Dyer & Co, aucts

Hse/o Reps: 1-Cmte on Military Affairs: adverse report upon the ptn of John Otis. 2-Cmte on Public Lands: which was referred the ptn of John Milstead for the correction of an error made at the Tallahasee land ofc, made a report thereon, with a bill for his relief. Same cmte: bill for the relief of Henry Newington. 3-Cmte on the Public Lands: made a report upon the application of Isaac Barker for an increase of pension, with a bill for his relief.

Died: on Mar 4, in Cuba, in her 26th year, Mrs Mildred C Taylor, consort of Alex'r F Taylor, & only child of Capt Jas Lindsay, of Albemarle Co, Va, leaving an affectionate husband, 3 interesting children, & many relatives & friends to mourn her premature death.

Died: on Thu last, on board the steamboat **Diamond**, after the boat's arrival at Cincinnati, Louis Henderson, aged 12 years, s/o the Hon John Henderson, Senator from Mississippi. His bereaved parents were anxiously awaiting the arrival of their 2 sons to join them in Washington, when the elder was attacked by scarlet fever, & fell victim to that ruthless disease.

Beautiful country seat & lots at public auction: on the premises, on Apr 15. #1-60 acres with dwlg, barn, stables, & apple orchard. #2-50 acres, on which stands the owner's house: choice piece of land. #3-28 acres-peach orchard. I have laid off the land lying on the Rock creek Road, opposite to Col Doughty's, into 5 acre lots. A plat of the entire place can be seen at my ofc, near 4½ st. –R France -Robt W Dyer & Co, aucts

Something New! My invention for raising water from the springs: forcing pump & wheel: just completed one for Capt Wm G Sanders, at his residence near Rock Creek Church, carrying the water a distance of 1,600 feet, raising an elevation of 68 feet, which is now in full operation. Has a certificate from John Glenn, of Balt, for whom he put up a similar pump. –Geo Page, Manufacturer, Balt, Md

The *Ocean House*, Newport, R I, a new & fashionable establishment for Summer visiters, will be completed & ready for the reception of visiters about Jun 1 next. –John G Weaver

Orphan's Court of Wash Co, D C. Letters of administration with the will annexed, on the personal estate of Mgt N Milstead, late of said county, dec'd, be granted to Alex'r McWilliams, a creditor, unless cause to the contrary be shown on or before Apr 30. –Ed N Roach, Reg/o wills

Jefferson College, Pa: the oldest in the West, still retains its pre-eminence as to numbers & usefulness. Present faculty: M M Brown, D C, Pres; Jas Ramsey, D D, Prof of Hebrew; Wm Smith, A M, Prof of Languages; Alex'r B Brown, A M, Prof of Belles Lettres & Latin; Henry Snyder, A M, Prof of Math; Saml R Williams, A M, Prof Physical Science; John Penny, A B, Tutor. College is located in Canonsburg, a small village. –M B

FRI APR 5, 1844
A new mode of lighting churches has been fallen upon in Cincinnati: lighted up last Sun for the first time: affords a soft light, equal to that from 120 common burners, requiring 8 feet of gas per hour. The light is enclosed within 2 thick glasses, firmly held in iron & copper frames. It was invented & made by Mr Jas Cruthett.

The fine old family mansion of the late Col Pickman was sold on Wed last for $9,100 to Nathan W Neal. The house was built rather more than a 100 years ago, we believe, for the grandfather of the late venerable occupant. The paper hanging on the front entry are the same which were placed there when the house was built, & which were imported from England for the purpose. –Salem paper

Vicksburg Sentinel: recent affray at Richmond, La, in which a man named Bradford was killed by John T Mason. Bradford had challenged Mason to a duel, which was refused on account of the advanced age of the challenger. Latter Bradford denounced Mason as a coward. Mason went to his residence & armed himself with a double-barrelled shot gun, came out into the street, where he met Bradford. The latter attempted to draw a pistol, when the former fired both barrels of his gun, which were charged with buckshot, & mortally wounded his antagonist. Bradford died in a few minutes.

The house of P W Eastman, of Newcastle, Canada West, was destroyed by fire on Mar 11, & 3 of his children, of age 5, 7, & 9 years, were burnt to death. Mr & Mrs Eastman were only able to get the 2 children who were on the below floor. All was lost, & Mrs Eastman was burnt.

At New Orleans, on Mar 21, Antonio Martorel, an Italian by birth, committed suicide by stabbing himself with a large butcher's knife. He had lost all his money at gambling the night before.

Mr Danl Malony, carpenter, while at work on Mon on the top of the tower of the new German Catholic Church, in Balt, Park & Saratoga sts, building his way up by laying the stairs, accidentally lost his balance & fell through the space below, striking against the scaffolding in his fall, into the organ gallery, upwards of 50 beneath. He was taken up, & Dr Chatard immediately called to his relief, when he was found to have sustained only a slight sprain in one of his legs, & some scratches about the head & face, apparently from striking against the scaffolding in the fall.

On Mon last, one of the agents of Leech & Co's line, named Jas Wilson, while passing with a train of burden cars a short distance above Parkersburg, on the Columbia railroad, from Phil, was knocked from the top of one of the cars by coming in contact with a bridge, & falling upon the railroad, the train passed over him, nearly severing his legs & one of his arms from his body, & causing his death in 2 minutes afterwards.

Newport [R I] Times: Mrs Ann Cole, w/o Mr Geo W Cole, of this place, while on her way home on Wed last, at the commencement of a thunder storm, from the residence of Mr Wm Stevens, at whose house she had been visiting, accompanied by Mr Stevens, when they reached the corner of Thames & Marlborough sts, she became very much frightened at a sharp & sudden flash of lightning, & was compelled by exhaustion to stop at the house of Mr Harvey Sessions, where she was taken with vomiting blood, & by the time her family could be sent for expired. The physicians who were in attendance think the fright & exertion together caused the bursting of a blood vessel.

Senate: 1-Ptn from Eliza M Cloud, wid/o a naval surgeon, praying a continuation of her pension. 2-Ptn from Sarah Cardoza, wid/o a Revolutionary soldier, for a pension. 3-Bill for the relief of Christopher Miller was read a 3rd time & passed.

Hse/o Reps: 1-Ptn & documents of Mary Tewksbury, asking Congress to grant her compensation for extra naval services of her husband. 2-Ptn of Col C S Kendig, Owen McCabe, & numerous other citizens of Dauphin Co, Pa; also, the ptn of Danl Larer, Jas V Johnson, & others, citizens of Schuylkill Co, Pa, protesting against any interference by Congress with the tariff of 1842. 3-The ptn & documents of Wm Gump were referred to the Cmte on Invalid Pensions. 4-Ptn of the heirs of Sarah & Jas Craig, dec'd, praying an allowance under the provisions of the act of Jul 7, 1838, in consideration of the Revolutionary services of their father.

For rent: commodious 2 story brick house on Prospect st, Gtwn, the late residence of Mrs Pearson. It commands a view of the Potomac, Washington, & the surrounding country. Apply to Dr N W Worthington, [by note,] Gtwn.

Hse/o Reps at the 28th Congress, 1st session, continued. 1-Ptn from Jas Roberts & 85 citizens of Tassalborough, Kennebec Co, Maine, to repeal the gag rule. 2-Ptn from P Nickles & 41 citizens of Loraine Co, Ohio, appropriation for works on Black river: referred to the Cmte on Commerce. 3-Ptn of Alamson Bills, of Indiana Co, Pa, for a pension for militia services: referred to the Cmte on Revolutionary Claims. 4-Ptn of Edmund Quincy Sewall & 84 citizens of Scituate, Mass: observance of the Sabbath. 5-Ptn of J Ancrum, of N C, to emancipate his slaves.

Railroad accident at Madison, Ind, on Mar 28, when the wood car struck the passenger car & dashed it to pieces. Killed were: Thos Bondurant, of Madison, Ia; [Blank] Enoch, of Bloomington, Ia; Gilbert Durling, of Brownsville, Ia; & Eli Branson, of Belmont Co, Ohio. Injured were John Roberts, Miss Craig, Mr Lockhart, & Mr Crane, all of whom had limbs broken.

Died: on Wed last, in Balt, Rachael Ann, consort of Moses G Hindes, in her 22nd year, & eldest d/o Jos Simms.

Died: on Mar 21, in her 65th year, Mrs Mgt H Hamilton, the excellent w/o Mr Jas H Hamilton, of Wash City. She had been for many years a worthy member of the Presbyterian Church, in the communion of which she died. Her sufferings under the distressing malady which terminated her mortal life were long & often excruciating. –J L

Died: on Apr 3, of croup, Caroline P, aged 6 years, d/o Lemuel & Caroline Williams.

Richmond Whig of yesterday mentions the death, on Sat last, of Mr John W Barrett. The dec'd took a very active part at the fire which occurred on Mar 16, on Cross st, where he fell through a trap-door and broke one of his legs, which caused his death.

Horrible tragedy in Pittsburg, Pa, last Mon, by a dissipated person named Chas Diel, who, after murdering his wife & 2 children, & seriously wounding a 3rd child, partially cut his own throat, in which state he was arrested. This deed appears to have been prompted by the demon of intemperance. Diel's own wound is said not to be dangerous, & the 3rd child is expected to recover.

On Mar 14, a young man, Levi Jacksen, while hewing timber near Canandaigua, N Y, accidentally received a stroke from the axe of one of his companions, which caused his death.

On Mar 20, as a canoe was crossing the St Lawrence from Lisbon to the Canada shore with Mr Jacob Wagoner, a Mr Monroe, & Miss Polly Lytle, d/o Mr Jas J Lytle, of Lisbon, when near the shore was struck by a squall & upset. Miss Lytle was drowned: age 22 years.

SAT APR 6, 1844
Delinquent lands in Alleghany Co, Md. Ordered that Normand Bruce, Collector of Taxes for 1843 in said county, advertise the list or statement returned by him, with the number of acres supposed to be in each tract, lot, or parcel of land, & give notice that unless the taxes due on said lands, shall be paid to the Collector, or his agent, Chas Farquharson, in Balt City, on or before Jun 1 next ensuing, the lands will be sold at public acution. –Geo W Devecmon, Clerk to Commissioners of Alleghany Co.
Owners' names: names of tracts & number of lots: year-taxes
Brooke, Matthew E/part of *Cherry Tree Meadow*, 1 tract no name: 282½acs/1843-$11.59
Brooke, Matthew & Allen/*Point Pleasant Valley*: 300 acres /[blank] *Parks & Rights of Man*: 689 acres /1843-$33.72
Buffington, John/Part *Western Connexion*: 1,108 acres /1843-$7.07
Brengle, John/lots 3089 2493 2429 2585 2588 2603 2604 2605 2606: 450 acres /1843-$1.96
Coulter, Henry/lots 183 879 979: 150 acres /1841-42-43-$5.85
Cook, Wm/*Stony Ridge* 388 acres, *Deer Park* 2,000 acres, *Much ado about Nothing* 612 acres /1843-$12.11
Campbell, Wm, heirs/Part *Cherry Tree Meadows* 569 acres, *Pink of Alleghany* 1,384 acres, part *Wild Cherry Tree Meadow* 500 acres, *Mill Seat Improvement* 5 acres, part of lots 1755 & 302 & lots 3023 3225 2022 225 a: total 3,000 acres /1843-$37.70
Chester, Thos/lot 1372: 50 acres /1843-$1.77
Conner, Marmaduke W/lot 1378: 100 acres /1841 thru 1843-$9.22
David, Jos, heirs/*Mount Nebo, Rich Bottom*, lot 265: 226 acres /1843-$4.39
Davis, John, of Balt/Lots 1242 1928 469: 150 acres
Ellicott, Thos & Meredith/Lots 1632 2698 2701 2702 2703 2704 2760 2761 2762 2763 2214 3315 3216 3217 4131 4133 4135 4137: 900 acres /1841 thru 1843-$11.54
Everly, Henry/Lots 1400 1403 1486: 150 acres /1843-$1.96
French, Geo/*Walnut Botton*, part *Castle Hill*, Dunham: 1,176 acres /1843-$29.61
Fitzhugh, Geo/Lot 2499: 50 acres;1843-$1.00
Grammar Fred'k/*White Oak Flat, Walnut Ridge, Little Worth, Grammer's Discovery*, lots 241 844 845 1371 911 215 1106 213 1171 846 847 4152 4158 3121: 4,152 acres /1843-$9.74
Galloway, Thos/Part *Rights of Man*: 189½ acres /1843-$4.82
Jones, Richd J/Lots 183 879 979: 150 acres /1843-$2.78
Johnson, Wm & John/*Polly* & addition to Polly, *Mount Airy*: 621 acres / 1841 thru 1843-$18.07

Johnson, Reverdy/*Eden's Paradise Regained*: 1,000 acres /1843-$12.90
Kennedy, Anthony/Lots 1920 1721 930 1172 168 1809: 300 acres / 1841 thru 1843-$7.46
Leakin, Shepherd C/Lot 1309: 50 acres /1843-.63
Scott, Gustavus, heirs/Now or Never 600 acres, Robey's Delight 421 acres /1843-$6.56
Singleton, John/1-3 *Goodly Lands*: 201 acres /1843-$2.01
Vanmeter, Jacob/*Robey's Adventure*: 169 acres /1843-$3.07
District No 2
Boger, Christian, heirs/Lots 2692 2676 2680 2681 2688: 250 acres /1843-$6.46
Brice, John/*Huron, Grove, Ington, Jepso, Brempton, Aristotle, Drummond*: 1,200 acres /1843-$8.98
Chapman, John G/Lots 2692 2702 2705 2708: 200 acres: 1843-$3.54
Eckles, Richd/Lots 18 19 20 in Selbysport/no acres given/1843-$2.02
Enlow, Josephus/No name given: 50 acres /1843-$1.40
Enlow, John/Sugar Camp: 22½ acres /1843-.93
Fearer, John/*Simpkins' Kindness* 25 acres, Lots 2786 2788 100 acres /1843-$3.35
Friend, John of Jos/*Lapwing, Mill seat*, part of *Gleanings*: 82¾ acres /1843-$3.08
Feach, John/Lots 3245 3247 3250 3225: 200 acres /1843-$3.79
Felger, Geo/Lot 2580: 50 acres /1841 thru 1843-$7.56
Friend, John G/Part of *Gleanings*: 50 acres /1843-$1.02
Griffith, John/4 Lots, numbers not known: 200 acres /1843-$1.65
Grammer, Fred'k/Lots 4152 4158: 100 acres /$2.02
Hall, Benedict/4 Lots, numbers not known: 200 acres /1843-$2.02
Hatherington, Jas?*Black Oak Ridge, Narrow Escape*, Lot 2710: 166 acres /1843-$3.08
Heller, John/Lot 2710: 50 acres /1843-$1.65
Logsdon, Edw/Lots 2875 2877: 100 acres /1843-$2.02
Longley, Lewis/*Ex Post Facto*: 55 acres /1843-$2.17
Mealey, Wm, heirs/Lots 2621 3246 324 3251: 200 acres /1841 thru 1843-$13.18
Murdock, Geo, heirs/*Orm's Mistake* 230 acres, *Orm's Trouble* 180½ acres, *Orm's Mill Seat* 161 acres /1843-$6.63
Magruder, Wm/Lot 3225: 50 acres /1843-.83
Marberry, Capt/*Squirrel Range*: 187½ acres /1843-$3.35
Marberry, John/Lots 2960 2962 2949 2945: 200 acres /1843-$3.79
Potts, Richd & Geo M/*Orm's Mistake, Orm's Mill Seat, & Orm's Trouble*: 550 acres /1843-$14.04
Raymond, Danl/Part of *Eden Spring* 111 acres, *Betty* 7 acres, *Long Boat* 28¼ acres /1843-$4.09
Umble, Danl/Part Lots 2929 2930 2931: 50 acres /1843-$2.02
Vanbibber, Andrew A & Hester/Lots 3455 3456 3458: 300 acres /1843-$2.78
District No 3
Armstead, John B/Part *Internal Improvements*: 1,616 acres /1843-$9.48
Davis, Benj/1 Lot 50 acres, *Mill Seat* 7 acres /1843-.69

Edwards, Alice/Lots 2744 2745 2766 2675 2674 2671: 300 acres /1841 thru 1843-$13.61
Parker, Jas/Lots 2387 2982 2989 2990: 200 acres /1841 thru 1843-$12.46
Gaither, Henry C/Lots 2136 2137 2138 2139: 200 acres /1843-$2.54
Gaither, Geo/Montgomery: 130½ acres /1843-$2.48
Hoskins, Henry/Lots 2318 2319 2298 2299: 200 acres /1841 thru 1843-$13.90
Hammond, John S/Part *Roanoke*: 200 acres /1843-$5.31
Hardin, Abraham/*Pleasant Ridge*: 147¾ acres /1843-$4.11
Halkerson, Robt/Lots 2060 2061 2066 2067: 200 acres /1841 thru 1843-$14.67
Jewell, Wm/*Jewelry, Test*: 911½ acres /1843-$4.22
Kennedy, Thos, heirs/11 Lots: 550 acres /1841 thru 1843-$10.89
Kelly, Wm/Lots 1348 3132: 100 acres /1843-$2.02
Mason, Thos, heirs/Lots 2072 2076 2077 2079: 200 acres /1843-$2.78
Marberry, Jos, heirs/Lots 2073 2074 2076 2077: 200 acres /1843-$2.78
Morgan, Ch & W Brewer/*Improvements*: 1,000 acres /1843-$6.46
Michael, David/Part *Jno Michael, jr lands*: 100 acres /1843-$4.08
Miller, Peter/*Grasshopper*: 118¼ acres /1843-$2.29
Nourse, Chas J & G Templeman/*Ardon Corrected*: 150 acres /1843-$10.00
Pres & Dirs U S Bank/Bank Property: 1,622½ acres, [Bank lot, Bank Territory]/1843-$57.25
Ramsey, Nathl, heirs/Lots 2127 2146 2144 2147: 200 acres /1843-$2.02
Reese, Thos/Lots 2001 2002 2002 2004: 200 acres /1841 thru 1843-$12.46
Raymond, Danl/Part *Bear Camp*: 500 acres /1843-$4.55
Theobold, Thos S/*War of Independence*: 255 acres /1843-$3.40
Vanbibber, Andrew A/Land, number acres not known/1843-$8.96
Woods, Garrett, heirs/Lots 2148 2149 2150 2151: 200 acres /1843-$2.02
Willett, Chas S/Lots 1882 3114: 100 acres /1843-$2.02
Young, Wm/Part *Mount Aetna*: 359 acres /1843-$6.21

District No 4
Beatty, Thos, heirs/*Flowery Mead*; 528 acres /1843-$4.76
Burke, Garrett/Lots 3206 3207 3211 3212: 200 acres /1841 thru 1843-$11.71
Fowler, Benj/*Fowler's Lot* 1,298 acres /1843-$7.97
Green, Duff/*Burnt Mill Seat* 100 acres, *Limestone* 50 acres, Lots 1 2 3 4 9 19 49: 300 acres, *Leatherwood Bottom* 29½ acres, *Bt Yard* 12 acres, *Shepherd's Park* 21 acres /*Pretty Prospect* 430½ acres, *Poland's Sugar Camp* 86½ acres, Half of *Ray's Discovery* 12 acres, Part of Lot 313 7 acres, *Coal in Store* 15 acres, *Factories*, *Pig Iron*, 1,082 2/3 acres /1843-$95.76
Howard, John E, jr/One ninth of *Betty's Plains*: 900 acres /1843-$23.52
Jackson, Saml H/*Timothy Level*: 237¾ acres /1843-$10.49
Jenkins, Benj: *Reverton*: 66½ acres /1843-.75
Sigler, Jacob, heirs/*Defiance* 44 acres, *Jacob's Kindness to Jacob* 55¾ acres /1843-$8.09
Union Company/Coal & Iron Banks 5631 acres, *Gen Duff Green's iron & ore lands* 5128¼ acres, *Hoye's coal*, iron, & lime discovery 2752 acres, The *Rose Bud* 28¾

acres, Part *Flowery Meads* 414 acres, *Coromandel* 158 acres, *Hoye's Fortune* 47 acres, *Dan's Mountain* 139½ acres, *Inba & Lyphase* 50 acres, *Stupe* 3½ acres, *Flamborough* 116½ acres, *Millstone Point*, 363 2/3 acres, A *Rustic Hat* 50½ acres, Lot No 20-50 acres, *What you Will* 10 acres /1843-$242.00

District No 5
Cowperwait, Jas & Thos Dumlap & H Cope/A tract, no name 200 acres, *Soldier's lot* 50 acres, A tract, no name 2,933½ acres /1843-$26.70
Foster, John/Part 3996 3999 lots 14 & 15: 80 acres /1843-$2.02
Green, Duff/Lots 3993 3995 3997 3999 4000: 250 acres /1843-$21.60
Howell, Chas & Co/Part of 3 tracts of land belonging to R Logsdon's heirs: 50½ acres /1843-$4.33
Peter, Geo W/*Mark Amended*: 4,131 acres /1843-$70.80

District No 6
Beatty, Jas/The *Request* 156¾ acres, *Lost Glove* 56¾ acres /1841 thru 1843 $19.69
Conner, Peter, heirs/2 lots in Cresaptown, 32, 33: 55 acres /1843-$2.02
Coe, Jonathan, heirs/*Hill & Dale* extended 53 ½ acres, *Willow Bank* 9½ acres /1843-$1.20
McCracken, Jas P/House & lot in Cresaptown/no acres given/1841 thru 1843-$9.95
Maxcy, Virgil, & others/*Quarto* 126 acres, *Trio* 116½ acres, *Rabbits Walk* 100 acres /1843-$8.80
Newman, Andrew/*Iron Mine*: 9 acres /1843-$1.28
Purgett, Henry, heirs/House & lot in Cresaptown/no acres given/1843-$1.28
Potts, Wm/*Friendship*: 15½ acres /1843-$2.05

Cumberland Town
Newman, Andrew/Lot No 61, 62, *Mill seat* & Addition 70½ acres, Part *Hoffman's Delight* 11¼ acres /1843-$3.38
Howard, J B, heirs/1 lot on Blocher st, land adjoining: 14 acres /1841 thru 1843-$17.20
Hepeline, Joh, heirs/Lot No 2 in Skipton, part *Seven Springs*: 46 acres /1843-$2.30
Hettick, Chas F/*Miller's Chance* 20½ acres, *Wilson's Risk*: 57¼ acres /1843-$1.73
Oglebay, Christian, heirs/Lot in *Skipton*, lot above Skipton/no acres given/1843-$2.78

District No 8
Causine, N P & Ann Turner/*Flora's Goodwill* 115 acres, *Mill Seat* 171 acres, *Black Oak Ridge* 71¼ acres, *Sideling Hill Improved* 17 acres, *Welcome Here* again 87½ acres /1843-$10.28
Evans, John, heirs/*Evans' Purchase* 150 acres /1841 thru 1843-$12.73
Gregory, Saml J/Part *Sweepstates* 300 acres /1843-$17.86
Goodrich, Lawrence/*Dry Hill* 22 acres, *Fox Chase* 29 acres, *What you please* 12 acres /1841 thru 1843-$13.58
Hook, Jas/*Piney Plains* 987½ acres /1843-$25.52
Orme, Rich J/*Lovely* 119½ acres /1841 thru 1843-$11.75
Vowell, Ebenezer, heirs/*Two Yankees* 70½ acres, Part *Partnership* 68 acres, *Beef & Chickens* 25 acres /1843-$2.68

Vansant, Chas, heirs/*Mount Misery* 25 acres, *King's Sorrow* 8 acres /1843-$1.58
Warfield, Chas H/Part *Far Enough* 130 acres / 1843-$8.42
District No 9
Martin, Chas/*Collins' Adventure* 296 acres /1843-$8.25
District No 10
Armstead, John B/*Sportman's Field* 280 acres /1843-$2.60
Chapman, Henry H/Part *William & Mary* 225 acres /1843-$2.21
Johnson, Car & Chas/*Covent Garden* 1840 acres /1841 thru 1843-$27.58
Kreightbaum, Conrad/Part *Addition* 95 acres /1843-$2.31
Koontz, Jacob/Lots 1406 1861 196 4056 1331 1470 1825 1870 969 1732 273 2094 2095 2779 2780: 750 acres /1841 thru 1843-$8.87
McLaughlin, Marietta/Lots 2033 2504 1790 149 1610 210 84 1639 101 1202 104 1054 1398 1030 878 2010: 800 acres /1843-$5.31
Nelson, Robt & Richd H Beattee/Lots 2495 2296 2297: 150 acres /1843-$2.21
Oliver, Chas/*Lock Isle* 6245½ acres, *Faub Park* 607 acres, *Emancipation* 7137 acres, *Common Sense* 1,279 acres, *Park & the Rights of Man* 9,816¾ acres, *White Oak Point* 286 acres, *Land Flowing with Milk & Honey* 2,745 acres, *Good Hope* 389 acres, *The Royal Charter* 2,000 acres, *Chance* 880 acres, *The Range* 200 acres, *Stewart's Delight* 201¼ acres, *Netherland* 549½ acres, *Kingness* 2,072, *Thomas & Ann* 200 acres, *Henche's Discovery* 1,001 acres, *Deep Creek Farm* 851 acres, *Paradise* 737½ acres, *Cascade* 365¾ acres, *Point Addition* 322¾ acres, *All the Chances* 705¼ acres, *Two-third Republic* 8,373 acres, *Pink of Alleghany* 3,519 acres, *Carmel* 341 acres, lots No 868 2561 2562 2563 2564 2565 1110 1703 3882 3883 3884 3885 3886 2355 2356 2357 2358 2611 2612 2613 2614: 1050 acres; Credit on the above lands $62.50, for damage by a road/1843-$477.64
Paca, John P/*Buck's Bones* 500 acres /1843-$3.35
Richey, John/*Constitution Vale* 301 acres, *Rich Glades* 306 acres, *Addition to Hunting Ground* 533½ acres, *Elk Lick* 201 acres, *Potato Garden* 206 acres, Lots 1357 1391 1493 1304: 200 acres /1843-$10.37
Richie, John P/Lots 1348 1606 1422 1126 1124 4156 2735 2723: 100 acres /1843-$2.02
Wealsh, John/Lots 1574 1575/1843-$2.02
Warring, Marcus S/Lots 358 1013: 100 acres /1843-$2.02
Walter, Henry/House & lot in Hoyesburg/no acres given/1843-$2.02

Senate: 1-Cmte of Claims: adverse report on the ptn of Geo Harrison.

Since the death of Gov Veazy, of Md, which occurred about 12 months ago, the most lamentable mortality has visited the members of his family. On Mar 6, Thos B Veazey, the brother of the late Govn'r, & on Mar 7, Mary L Veazey & Sarah Lusby, his dght & niece, were all suddenly stricken with death. On Mar 23, at Lancaster, Pa, Dr Thos W Veazey, a s/o the late Govn'r, died in the 39th year of his age. Mrs Veazey, the grief-stricken widow, has outlived, in sorrow, nearly all her earthly ties.
-Ledger

Cmdor Wm Compton Bolton appointed by the Sec of the Navy to the command, as Port Capt, of all the forces afloat at the Norfolk station, which command was recently made vacant by the death of Cmdor Kennedy.

Died: on Apr 2, at the residence of his brother, in Prince Wm Co, Va, Wm J Bronaugh, jr, s/o Wm J Bronaugh, of Wash City, in his 24th year. This most estimable young man came to his death by the accidental discharge of a fowling piece.

Died: on Mar 29, in Orange Co, Va, Miss Lucy M Taliaferro, in her 21st year; & on Mar 31, Jas Barbour Taliaferro, in his 19th year. Both the dec'd were children of the late Mrs L M Taliaferro, of King Geo Co, & grandchildren of the late Govn'r Barbour.

Died: on Apr 4, at his residence, Bel-Air, in PG Co, Md, Benj Ogle, in his 70th year. Born the same year with the lamented Harrison, he has been cut off, like him, by the same fatal disease, after a few days' illness, & upon the anniversary of his death. Having had the advantages of education in England, with an unusually retentive memory, his mind was stored with information & anecdote that he was every ready to impart, which made him the delight of society, both of the old & the young. With a taste for field sports, he prosecuted them with ardor almost to the last year of his life. For nearly 50 years he resided upon his patrimonial estate. He died without reproach. He was an affectionate & devoted husband & parent, a kind & indulgent master, a sincere friend, a true patriot, & an unassuming Christian.

Appointments by the Pres with the advice & consent of the Senate:
Jas C Palmer, to be Surgeon in the Navy from Oct 27, 1841.
Jas D Wasson, to be Postmaster at Albany, N Y.
Thos J Marvin, to be Postmaster at Saratoga Springs, N Y.
Jas Belknap, to be Postmaster at Newburgh, N Y.
Saml Henderson, to be Postmaster at Indianoplis, Ind.
Manuel Simon Cuculla, to be Collector of the Customs for the District of Mississippi, in La, in place of Greenbury Dorsey, rejected by the Senate.
Wm O'Hara Robinson, to be U S Atty for the Western District of Pa, vice Cornelius Darragh, resigned.
Thos C Lyon, to be U S Atty for the Easter District of Tenn, vice Crawford W Hall, rejected by the Senate.

Notice to lovers of good Mouton: I shall have, on Sat next, at my stall in the old Centre Market, a superb lot of Mutton, grazed & fattened by Judge John Scott, of Fauquier Co, Va. –Philip Otterback

Millville Mills: under & by authority of a decree of the Circuit Superior Crt of Law & Chancery for Jefferson Co, Va, pronounced on Oct 17, 1843, between Catharine Scholfield, plntf, & Danl Snyder & others, dfndnts, the com'rs will on Apr 26, before the court-house, offer for sale the valuable property known as *Millville Mills*, on the Shenandoah river in said county. 95 acres of land with a 2 story brick dwlg house & other out houses & bldgs. –Robt Y Conrad, Wm C Worthington, Com'rs

Circuit Court of Wash Co, D C. Jos Martin, jr, has applied to be discharged from imprisonment under the act for the relief of Insolvent Debtors: hearing on Apr 29. –Wm Brent, clk

MON APR 8, 1844
Third Baptist Church: the congregation under the pastoral care of the Rev Mr Samson, who have assembled of late for public worship in the Aldermen's Chamber, met yesterday for the first time in the basement story of their new edifice on E st, between 6th & 7th sts. Mr Mann is the architect & carpenter.

Perserverance Fire Co: election of ofcrs on Thu, which resulted as follows:
Caleb Buckingham, Pres   Silas H Hill, Treas
Geo S Gideon, V Pres   Alex H Clements, Capt of Enginemen
V Harbaugh, Sec   Thos Lewis, Capt of Hosemen

The body of a man was found on Sat last, as one of the Alexandria & Wash steamboats was plying in the Potomac. His clothing showed him to be of genteel dress. He was about 35 to 40 years of age, about 5 feet 9 inches, stout, well made, with black hair & whiskers. A hat & coat was found on the bank of the Potomac. In the coat pocket was a card printed on one side "Eagle Hotel, Balt," on the other side, written with ink, "I W Willson, Carbondale, Luzerne Co, Pa, & above the writing, in pencil, in the same hand-writing, 'This is my true name." We are led to believe that the unfortunate gentleman committed suicide. Orders were given for the decent interment of the body.

Letters were received in Wash City on Sat, announcing the death of the Hon Heman Allen Moore, one of the Reps in Congress from the State of Ohio. He left this city a week or 2 ago, in consequence of ill-health, for his residence at Columbus. He lived to reach his home, where he died on Apr 3.

The colored citizens of Wayne Co, N Y, have sent in a ptn to the Legislature praying that the services of the black citizens of that State, while in a state of slavery, up to 1827, may be paid, amounting to twenty five millions of dollars! It was laid on the table.

Orphan's Court of Wash Co, D C. Letters of administraton on the personal estate of Fred'k Stevens, late of the U S Navy, dec'd. –Th Holdup Stevens, Adm

In Chancery: Circuit Court of Wash Co, D C: J B H Smith, vs, Jas Marshall, & Jas K Marshall, Edw Marshall & others, heirs at law of John Marshall, of Va. The bill of cmplnt states that part of lots 1, 2, 12, & 13 in square 219, in Wash City, as the said lots are designated upon the public plot of Wash City; that Jas Marshall, one of the dfndnts, is also seized in fee in one undivided third part of said lots; & the heirs at law of said John Marshall are seized in fee in the remaining their undivided part of said lots; that it is for the interest of all the said parties that the lots should be equally divided between them, & that the same are capable of such division. The bill prays that such division be made, & states that all the parties reside out of the jurisdiction of this Court. It is therefore ordered by the Court that the cmplnt give notice to said absent dfndnts of this order, warning the dfndnts to be & appear in said Court in person or by solicitor, & show cause why a decree should not be passed as prayed, & answer the said bill; otherwise that the same be taken pro confesso against the said dfndnts, & each of them, & a decree made accordingly. By order of the Court.
Test: W Brent, clk

Hse/o Reps: 1-Ptn of the heirs of Capt Thos Martin, dec'd, asking commutation pay: referred. 2-Ptn in favor of the estate of the late Jas S Thatcher, purser of the U S Navy: referred. 3-Ptn of Geo Ogden, J H Thornberger, M Tiernan, J B Guthrie, & 59 others, of the city of Pittsburg, favorable to the construction of a ship canal around the Sault St Marie, or outlet of Lake Superior.

From Mexico: Two of the Mier prisoners [Maj T W Murray & Mr Donald Smith] reached New Orleans last week in the schnr **John Barr**, from Vera Cruz, whence she sailed on the 24th. They owe their liberation, it is said, to the intercession of Gen Thompson, & it is further stated, that the remaining prisoners, or a majority of them, will be liberated at an early day.

Texian prisoners in Mexico. Maj Murray, one of the Mier prisoners recently released through the efforts of Mr Bankhead, we learn that all the Texians who have been confined during the past year in Santiago, with the exception of 6, are now at the castle of San Juan de Ulos, near Vera Cruz, & at work. Three were left at Santiago-Capt Pearson, H H Van Vechten & Ezekiel Smith-all of them, either from age or sickness, unable to travel. Three more-Alex Mathews, Jeremiah Leon, & T B Malby, were left at the hospital at Puebla sick. Capt Baker, now at San Juan de Ulos, is not compelled to labor. The unfortunate Antonio Navarro, who was on the first Santa Fe expedition, & the only one of that party not released, is also at the castle of San Juan. Maj Murray speaks in the warmest terms of the kind treatment he received from Col F Bareta, the commandant of Santiago, & of the attentions of the prefect of San Jual del Rio & Dr Jordan while he was sick. Duncan C Ogden & Israel Canfield, [the latter released at the request of the Ex-Pres Adams,] sailed from Vera Cruz for Pensacola in the U S brig *Somers*. Peyton A Southall, with dispatches from our Gov't, arrived at Vera Cruz in the *Somers*, & left on Sun last for the capital. Gen Thompson was a Jalapa, on his way down, when the schnr *John Barr* sailed.

Harrisburg, Pa: the Hon Almo H Read passed through that place on Apr 4, in extreme ill-health, on his way home, being able to travel only by easy stages of a few hours a day.

Rockville [Md] Journal states that a few days since a young man, Garrison Iglehart, while blasting rocks near that place, was dreadfully lacerated by the premature explosion of the blast. He will probably lose both his eyes, while his face & arms are frightfully burned by the powder.

Senate: 1-Ptn from Richd A Galpin, asking that an examination may be made of a plan prepared by him for the construction of a dry-dock, the merit of which entirely dispenses with the costly process of piling. 2-Ptn from G Griffin, asking compensation for a schnr taken by the British during the last war while in the employment of the Gov't. 3-Ptn from a gentleman styling himself Tobias Harper Mitchell, imploring Congress never, on any consideration, to admit Texas into the Union. 4-Presented: documents in relation to the case of Col Wm Scott.

Battles between the British in India & the Natives during the month of Feb, 1844, in Gwalior. The enemy were the first to commence hostilities, by firing on the baggage party under Col Sleeman, of the 26th, & then on a reconnoitering party sent out on the 28th. Sir H Gough attacked the Mahrattas in their position of Mahrajpool, while our left wing, under Maj Gen Grey, did so a Punniar, & gained a complete victory over them. Our loss has been very severe: 141 killed & 866 wounded; the enemy amounts to between 4,000 & 5,000 killed & wounded. Our ofcrs who have fallen in these actions, or have since died of their wounds: Gen Churchill, Col Sanders, Maj Crommelin, Capts Stewart, Magrath, & Cobban, Lts Newton & Leaths, & Ensign Pray. The fort at Gwalior surrendered to us.

Great Whig Meeting in Boston on Wed last: Sargeant S Prentiss, of Miss, delivered a speech, which for aptness & fluency of language, happy & graceful delivery, & sound political doctrine, we have rarae heard equalled. --Atlas.

Hartford Courant: Geo Goodwin, who was connected with this establishment as editor & publisher for about 60 years, & now in his 88th year, was one of the first to deposite his vote yesterday.

A young man calling himself sometimes Jas McMan, & sometimes Jas Blackwell, was arrested last Tue at Buffalo, N Y, & committed to prison for obtaining money under false pretences.

Mrd: on Apr 2, in N Y, by Rev Dr Erskine Mason, Hon Solomon Foot, a member of Congress from Rutland, Vt, to Mrs Mary Ann Dana, of Clarendon, Vt.

Died: on Fri last, at Phil, after a short illness, in his 58th year, Prof John Sanderson, of the Phil High School. His Biography of the Signers of the Declaration of Independence evinced ability of no common order, & it has passed through innumerable editions. The American in Paris appeared to find the true bent of his genius. —Pennsylvanian

Died: on Apr 6, after a protracted illness, Wm M Walling, in his 37th year. His funeral will be this afternoon, at 3 p m, from his late residence, corner of 13th & D sts.

Died: on Mar 27, near Fredericksburg, Va, Mortimer M, s/o Mortimer & Eliz M Bainbridge, aged 13 months & 12 days.

TUE APR 9, 1844
Dissolution of the partnership between Wm A Griffith & Michl O'Brien in the stone cutting business, is this day mutually dissolved. Settlement of accounts at the old shop, 9th & E sts, with Wm A Griffith, who will continue the Marble & Freestone business at the old stand.

Senate & Hse/o Reps: Announcing the death of the Hon Heman Allen Moore, of Ohio: was a native of the town of Plainfield, Vt. His parents were respectable, but poor. He was self-educated. About 6 years ago he removed to Ohio, & settled with his family in Columbus. He had chosen law for his profession, but, being poor, he obtained employment as a schoolmaster for present support. Gen Moore had not been many weeks attending Congress until he was compelled by disease to devote his whole care to his own preservation. On Apr 3 he expired. He died at age 34 years. Condolences to his widow: to her the loss is irreparable. She is now the protector of her 3 helpless children. [Dec 27th newspaper: following the error of some other paper, we lately announced the death of Hon Heman Allen, of Vt, late Minister to Chili, & formerly a Rep in Congress. That gentleman, we now learn from good authority, is alive & well, residing at *Highgate*. The gentleman whose death must be regretted by every one, was the Hon Heman Allen, of Burlington, Vt, who also had served as a Rep in Congress at different times for several years with enviable repute.]

Whig Meeting in Montgomery Co, Md, on Mar 23, to consider the forming of a District Clay Club, at which Allen Davis acted as Chairman & Roger B Thomas as Sec. Clay Club formed & the following gentlemen were elected ofcrs: Allen Bowie Davis, Pres; Wm Brown & Otho Magruder, V Ps; Elisha R Griffith, Treas; Roger B Thomas, Corr Sec; Caleb B Moore, Recording Sec. Wm Lingan Gaither, State Senator from Montg, & State Elector for Pres & V P, responded with forcible & eloquent remarks. Jas B Ricaud & Wm L Gaither were elected Electors for the State at large.

Commission for the Armistice between Mexico & Texas: assembled in Sabinas, Feb 15, 1844: Brig Gen Antoine Maria Jauregui, Col Manuel Maria Landeras, Messrs Geo W Hockley & Saml M Williams, the 2 first appointed by the Genr'l-in-Chief of the 1st Brig, Don Adrian Woll, to treat with the latter as commissioners by the Dept of Texas for the armistice.

Mrd: on Sabbath evening, by Rev John C Smith, Mr Chas W Arnold to Miss Eliz Ann Talburt.

Died: on Apr 3, at Aldie, Va, Edmund Tyler, Postmaster; for many years a respected merchant of that place, leaving a wife, 5 children, & numerous relatives to mourn their loss.

Died: on Apr 4, at the University of Virginia, of consumption, Harriet W, eldest d/o Prof Edw H Courtenay, in her 12th year.

Having employed a private teacher in my own family for the education of my own children, I will take in addition 6 boys, from 12 to 14 years, as boarders. The gentleman employed is a graduate of Amherst College, Mass. My residence is in the upper part of Loudoun Co, Va. –John A Carter

Miss Jane E Biscoe, due to the great increase in her business, has taken the upper part of the house on Centre Market space, over the store of Messrs Peddecord & Holland, & next door to the store of Darius Clagett. She has a large & splendid assortment of Millinery, all of which will be exhibited on Apr 11, in the spacious room of her house, fronting on Pa ave.

Circuit Court of Wash Co, D C. Phineas B Bell has applied to be discharged from imprisonment under the act for the relief of Insolvent Debtors: hearing on Apr 29. –Wm Brent, clk

The subscriber has on hand a new suit of U S Naval uniform the property of a gentleman no longer connected with the service, which he will dispose of on very reasonable terms. –Saml Fowler, Pa ave, between 3rd & 4½ sts.

WED APR 10, 1844
For sale or rent, the house recently occupied by the late Mrs Easton, at the corner of I & 19th sts, back of the Seven Bldgs. For terms inquire on the premises.

The Hon Wm R King, Senator of the U S from Alabama, was yesterday nominated by the Pres to the Senate to be Envoy Extra & Minister Pleni to France, & was confirmed. The nomination of Govn'r Shannon, of Ohio, to be Envoy Extra & Minister Pleni to Mexico, to succeed Gen Thompson, was confirmed yesterday by the Senate.

Senate: 1-Ptn from the heirs of Jas Maglennan, praying for compensation for a horse lost during the late war. 2-Ptn from David Beardsley, asking compensation for his heirs as agent for removing Cherokee Indians. 3-Ptn from Jas D Mason & others, asking permission to register a vessel of foreign construction, purchased by them & refitted. 4-Ptn from Martin Phillips, for a pension. 4-Cmte on Pensions: adverse reports on the following House bills: relief of Henry Freeman; of Simeon Casewell; of John Farnham; of Thompson Hutchinson; of John P Schuyler; of Maj Thos Harrison, & of Richd Elliott. Same cmte: adverse reports on the following memorials: of Normand Burroughs, Danl Bowen, wid/o Nathl Rundlet, Ebenezer Swann, Timothy Parker, Nancy Parker, John Becraft, Jas Banker, & John Martin. Also, from the same cmte, favorable reports on the following House bills: relief of Isaac Justice; of Sarah Blakemore; of Wm Glover; of Abigail Gibson; of Bartholomew McGuire.

Hse/o Reps: 1-Resolved, That the Doorkeeper of the Hse/o Reps contract with Robt Grant for lighting the Hall of the Hse/o Reps with oxhydrogen lime light, or Drummond light, & that the sum of $1,000 be appropriated from the contingent fund of the House for that purpose. The resolution was a second time rejected. 2-Cmte of Claims: bill for the relief of Philip Swartzwauver. Also, an act for the benefit of the heirs of Christopher Miller, reported the same without amendment. Same cmte: adverse report upon the case of Chas S Matthews & Jas Hall, in behalf of themselves & the reps of Chas Wood, dec'd. Same cmte: adverse report upon the case of Bennett M Dell; & the ptn of John Monroe; & upon the case of Solomonn Fitch & others. 3-Cmte on Commerce: report upon the case of Barnabas Baker, jr, & others, owners of the schnr **Union**, of Dennis, Mass, with a bill for their relief.
4-Ptn of Philip Lehi, for an increase of his pension. 5-Ptn of the heirs of Philip R Rice, dec'd, late of Bracken Co, Ky, praying compensation for a vessel lost in the service of the U S in the war of the Revolution. 6-Memorial of John Adams, Jos Atkins, jr, & 135 others, of Provincetown, Mass, praying against the repeal of the fishing bounty & the reduction of the duty on salt. 7-Ptn of Michl Whiteford, of Harford Co, Md, asking remuneration for services rendered during the late war with Great Britain. 8-Ptn of Rich Brown, sen, & David White, of Missouri, asking the privilege of changing certain entries on public lands made by them through error.

Considerable progress has been made in the construction of the Magnetic Telegraph, the invention of Prof S F B Morse: the line of conductors is constructed as far on from Wash as to a point on the line of the railroad opposite to the residence of C B Calvert, [6 miles,] & the work is progressing at the rate of a mile a day. A trial of it was made yesterday, as the cars passed Mr Calvert's, by communication the fact of their passage to the point at which the line begins in Wash; & an answer, acknowledging the receipt of the intelligence, was received back in two or three seconds.

Charleston Courier: Rt Rev Dr Reynold, Roman Catholic Bishop of Charleston, arrived in the Wilmington boat yesterday, & took possession of his See.

On Mar 28, Titus Hale arrived at Balt from St Louis, Mo, of which latter place he was a resident merchant. He had been married to his second wife only about 19 days prior to his arrival there, & was on his way to N Y to purchase goods, his lady with him on a visit to friends in Burlington, N J. On his way he wounded himself in the middle joint of his finger when carving at the table on board the steamboat. It was so slight that he paid not attention to it. It became painful, became swollen, & became very infected. On Sun he became delirious and died on Tue. -American

Inquest was held at the City Hospital, N Y, Thu, on the body of Thos Calahan, who died on Wed of injuries received in N J while cutting down a tree. Jumping out of the way of the tree, he stumbled over a stump & fell, dislocating his spine, which caused his death.

On Wed, as the cars were leaving Burlington for Trenton, Chas Naylor, about 11, s/o Mr Allen Naylor, of Burlington, fell upon the rails & the train passed over both of his legs. The boy died while the operation to amputate his limbs was going on.

Mrd: on Apr 8, by Rev Mr Gassaway, of Gtwn, Mr Thos H Osburn, of PG Co, Md, to Miss Eliza A, d/o S E Scott, of Wash.

Mrd: on Apr 9, by Rev John C Smith, Mr Thos E France to Miss Annabella Brockett, all of Wash City.

Mrd: on Apr 9, by Rev H Myers, Mr Edmund Brooke to Miss Eugenia Queen, both of the District.

Died: on Apr 8, Jas B McLeran Deitz, s/o Wm H & E C Deitz, in his 8th year. His funeral will be from his father's residence, N Y ave, between 12th & 13th sts, this day at 3 p m.

The barque **Pearl**, Blackenship, of Sippican, was totally lost on Aug 10 last: Wm Johnson was drowned in the forecastle. Abraham Penny, Philip Penny, Philip Allen, John McGinnis, John Frederick, & Richd Parks were lost in attempting to save a boat. The captain & the remainder of the crew remained on the wreck for 3 days, when they were taken off by the ship **Champion**, of Edgartown, & the captain was transferred to the ship **Nassau**, of New Bedford.

Mules for sale. Can be examined at my stable on the corner of Indiana ave, on 2nd st north, in the rear of the railroad depot. Inquire of the subscriber on the premises or at the Auditor's Ofc of the Post Ofc between 9 a m & 3 p m. –C Monroe

Capt Ball, of the barque **Emma**, who arrived at this port on Thu from the Indian Ocean, reports the loss of Capt Edwin J Ames & Mr Gilbert Beebe, of the ship **Clematis**, of New London, killed by a whale. While in the act of fastening the whale, the monster struck with its flukes into the boat. Capt Ames received the blow on his left side, & Mr Beebe on the right side of the head, both of whom were killed almost instantly. Another seaman was considerably injured.
—New Bedford Mercury

Obit-died: Wm J Bronaugh, jr, near Haymarket, Prince William Co, Va. On Apr 2, in company with his brother, he was attracted by the distress of a neighbor in his unsuccessful efforts to extricate his wagon from a situation involving its safety, with his characteristic kindness, he hastened immediately to his relief. Seeing it safe he returned for his fowling piece, [double barreled;] which he had laid on the hill side, a few yards from the wagon; thoughtlessly seizing it by the barrel just below the mouth, he drew it towards him; scarcely had he advancecd one step when it fired, [the cock being retracted by the brambles on the hillside,] the contents entering his right side below the last rib, taking an upward direction into the liver. He consoled his neighbor & spoke of his family most feelingly; of his mother particularly, of her anguish when the intelligence should reach her of his death. He lived 7 hours from the time of the accident. He was a Christian in heart from early boyhood. -M

Circuit Court of Wash Co, D C. Richd H Gordon has applied to be discharged from imprisonment under the act for the relief of Insolvent Debtors: hearing on the first day of May next. —Wm Brent, clk

THU APR 11, 1844
Alex McCormick & Dionysius Sheriff, Attorneys at Law, Bladensburg, Md.
[Local ad]

Public sale: deed of trust from John T Young, dated Feb 28, 1842, made for the benefit of Col Bomford, & by his direction, & with Mr Young's consent, will expose to sale on the premises, part of the *Long Meadows*, bounded on the south by the Eastern Branch, on the west by lands of Mrs Decatur, on the north by lands of the heirs of E B Caldwell & Jos Gales, & on the east by lands of the heirs of John Dobbyn, containing 96 acres, more or less, with improvements thereon.
—W Redin, Trustee

For sale: a Rockaway wagon, for 1 horse, of the latest style, made by one of the best coachmakers in Phil. It has a small seat for children, which can be removed at pleasure; leather curtains, lined, with side & back lights, very complete in every respect, price $150. Inquire of R Rainey, hack-driver, Bridge st, Gtwn.

New Boarding House: Miss Mary A B Cummin [late of Maryland] on Pa ave, #3, 5 doors west of the Capitol. Meals furnished without lodging if desired.

Classical & Mathematical School, near West Point, N Y: Z J D Kinsley, a graduate of the U S Military Academy, & for many years Instructor of Artillery there, residing on his farm, contiguous to West Point, will receive into his family & instruct a limited number of pupils in the usual branches of a thorough English education, &, if desired, in so much of the classics as to prepare them to enter college. For board, tuition, lodging, lights, washing, & fuel, per term, for pupils under 10 years of age: $100. Pupils over 10 & under 16 years: $125. Pupils entering under 10 & remaining 4 years in the schook, for the whole period, per term: $100. Books, stationery, & clothing can be furnished on reasonable terms, at the expense of the pupil.
References:
Rev P P Irving, N Y
Rev C Mason, N Y Univ
Capt John B Stanhope, Cuba
Gen Jos M Hernandez, St Augustine
Gen R C Weightman, Wash
Col Jas Bankhead, U S Army
Col R E DeRussy, U S Engineers
Col S Thayer, Boston
Gen Rufus King, Albany
Gov Wm H Seward, Auburn
Jas B Schoonhoven, Troy
Rev L P W Balch, N Y
Rev N Sayre Harris, N Y
Pres Lindsley, Nashville, Tenn
Matthew St Clair Clarke, Wash
Maj Chas Davies, U S Army, West Point
Col Jos G Totten, U S Chief Engineer
Prof B Silliman, Yale College
J L Kingsley, Yale College
C A Goodrich, of Yale College
Prof Horace Webster, of Geneva College
D Prentice, of Geneva College
The undersigned have been personally acquainted with Mr Kinsley for many years, do with confidence recommend him to parents & other guardians of youth:
D H Mahan, Prof of Engineering
A E Church, Prof of Mathematics
M P Parks, Chaplain & Prof of Ethics
Wm H C Bartlett, Prof Nat & Exp Philosophy
J W Bailey, Prof Chem Min & Geology
Pocket money must be depositied with the Principal, & the amount must not exceed 25 cents per week, except on 4th Jul, Christmas, & New Year's day, when, with the consent of the parent or guardian, the amount may be from 25 cents to one dollar.

Hse/o Reps: 1-Cmte on Public Lands: bill for the relief of Solomon Sturgess, assignee of Humphrey Richcreek. 2-Cmte on Private Land Claims: adverse report on the ptn of Aaron Hubbell. Same cmte: bill for the relief of Abelard Guthrie. Same cmte: made a report on the ptn of Thaddeu Spalding, exc of the estate of John Hart, dec'd, with a bill for the relief of the heirs of John Hart. 3-Cmte on Indian Affairs: bill for the relief of Isaac S Ketchum; & a bill for the relief of Isaac S Ketchum, late special agent. Same cmte: made a report on the claims of Henry S Commager against divers Indians of the Ottawa tribe, with a bill for his relief. 4-Cmte on Military Affairs: bill for the relief of Josephine Nourse, wid/o Benj Franklin Nourse, late an assistant surgeon in the U S Army. 5-Cmte on Naval Affairs: referred the ptn of W L Hudson, cmder, & other ofcrs of the ship **Peacock**, which was wrecked at the mouth of the Columbia river, made a report thereon, & moved to be discharged from its further consideration.

Mrs Fulton proposes opening a School for Young Ladies on Apr 15, at her residence on Missouri ave, between 4½ & 6th sts. References:
Hon W S Fulton
Hon H Dodge
Hon Wm A Harris
Hon Saml Simons
Col Wm Brent
Jas Hoban
John F Callan

Law of the U S passed at the 1st Session of the 28th Congress: An Act for the relief of Geo Davenport, of Rock Island, Ill: he is hereby, authorized to enter the fractional qrtr section of land upon which he resides, on Rock Island, Ill, it being the s e fractional qrtr of section 25, in township 18 north, range 2 west of the 4th principal meridian, upon his paying to the receiver of public moneys of the U S land ofc at Dixon the minimum price of $1.25 per acre for the same, upon which a final certificate & patent shall issue, as in other cases. Approved, Apr 2, 1844

Senate: 1-Ptn from Chas S Lee, asking the right of pre-emption to certain back lands in the State of Louisiana. 2-Ptn from the heirs of Christopher Taylor, asking to be allowed commutation pay. 3-Cmte on Naval Affairs: asking to be discharged from the further consideration of the ptn of Eliza M Cloud. Same cmte: adverse report on the claim of Jas W Breedlove.

Orphan's Court of Wash Co, D C. Letters of administraton on the personal estate of Ann Gardiner, late of Wash Co, dec'd. –J B H Smith, adm

FRI APR 12, 1844
Mr Jonas Shivers, of Davidson Co, Tenn, was accidentally killed on Sun week by being thrown from his horse. He was a native of N C, & at the time of his death was in his 75th year.

Mr Jas Percy Brown, of Mississippi, recently a Rep in the Legislature of that State for Bolivar Co, but who has made Nashville his summer residence for several years past, committed suicide on Apr 3.

Chas G Ferris was yesterday nominated to the Senate as Collector of the Customs for the port of N Y, vice Edw Curtis.

Augustus W Bradford was unanimously appointed Elector of Pres & V P of the U S for the 4th Congressional District of Md, & Chas H Pitts unanimously elected the delegate to represent the said district in the Nat'l Whig Convention.

The wife of Henry Toner [dyer at Louviers, Delaware,] gave birth last week to 2 fine boys, who have been christened Clay & Clayton. The father is a good Whig. –State Journal

Hse/o Reps: 1-Memorial of Thos Towns, asking pay for property taken from him during the Revolutionary war by a press-master of the U S army. 2-Ptn of Hammond & Dexter for balance due for building light houses in Louisiana. 3-Ptn of J B Hancock for confirmation of certain lands located by virtue of an act of Congress in his behalf. 4-Mr Tibbats withdrew the ptn & papers filed in behalf of the wid/o Andrew Lewis, dec'd, late an ofcr of the U S army, praying to be reimbursed the cost & charges of a suit instituted against him for responsibility incurred by him in his official capacity.

Fatal accident at Burtonsville, Montgomery Co, N Y, on Fri last: the Schoharie creek is crossed there by a rope ferry. The scow tipped & 3 persons on board drowned: Messrs Wm Ketcham & John W Gage, of Duanesburgh, & Mr Jas Lander, of Fla. Mr Ketcham was one of the oldest & most respectable inhabitants of the town. He leaves 18 children to mourn his loss.

Wash Corp: 1-Cmte of Claims: asked to be discharged from the further consideration of the ptn of Wm Jasper. 2-Ptn of Wm Lord & others, for curb-stone & paving: referred to the Cmte on Improvements. 3-The Board, on motion, took up for consideration the bill for the relief of Jas Dixon: bill was rejected.

Mobile Herald: Gen Chas Fenton Mercer, formerly of Va, & more recently of Fla, has entered into contracts with the Gov't of Texas by which he obtains from that Republic a grant of 2 tracts of land, one embracing 16,400 & the other 8,000 square miles. The grants are made on condition that the lands be settled.

Died: on Thu, in his 73rd year, Mr Jacob Carter, for many years a resident of Gtwn, D C, & for the last 15 years a resident of Wash. His funeral is this afternoon, from the residence of Wm G W White, on 4½ st, near City Hall, at half past 4 o'clock.

Died: on Mar 27, at New Orleans, of consumption, Geo Hargrove French, printer, aged 27 years, a native of Balt.

Died: on Apr 9, in Wash City, Chas Sheppard, aged 11 years, only child of Mrs Ann Sheppard, late of N Y.

Meeting of citizens residing on Pa ave was held on Wed last, to adopt measures for relieving themselves from the present excessive annoyance & injury, arising from the clouds of dust, which constantly, during the dry season, fill the air, & render a residence on the ave almost insufferable. The following citizens were appointed to raise funds to defray the expense of scraping the ave, & having it regularly sprinkled, to superintend the work-Messrs:

Purdy	Geo Parker	Fischer
Gilbert	Phillips	Sessford
S Masi	Clagett	J France
P W Browning	Washington	Haslup
Maury	Franklin	Weedon
Pepper	J Sexsmith	J C Rives
Kibby	Dyer	E Owen
Todd	Kinchey	Lamb

Appointments by the Pres:
Cmdor Chas Morris, to be Chief of the Bureau of Construction, Equipment, & Repairs.
W Crump, of Va, to be Charge d'Affaires to Chili.
John Tyler, jr, Sec to sign Land Patents.
Hiram Paulding, to be a Capt in the U S Navy.
Wm L Howard, to be a Cmder in the Navy.
Theodore Barrett & J K Madison Mullany, to be Lts in the Navy.
Theodore Kane, to be a Justice of the Peace for the District of Columbia.

SAT APR 13, 1844
Senate: 1-Ptn from Albert Williams & Eliza A Williams, of Oswego Co, N Y, asking a reduction of the rates of postage & to abolish the franking privilege. 2-Cmte of Claims: adverse report on the ptn of Wm G Brown.

In the matter of the ptn of Catherine Finney, mother, & next friend of Francis Finney, son & infant child of Danl Finney, late of Chas Co, dec'd, orderd by the Chas Co Court, sitting as a Court of Equity, this Mar 27, that the report of sales made this 26th day of this month by Wm D Cobey & Francis E Dunnington, trustees, be ratified & confirmed, unless cause to the contrary be shown on or before the 3rd Mon in Jun next. –C Dorsey. The report states that the amount of sales of the interest sold under the said decree to be $930. –Walter Mitchell, clerk

Hse/o Reps: 1-Cmte on Invalid Pensions: reported an amendatory bill for the relief of Jonathan Bean. Same cmte: bill for the relief of Robt Monroe. Same cmte: to be discharged from the further consideration of the ptn of Mgt Evans: laid on the table. Same cmte: to be discharged from the consideration of the ptns of Thos Hanegan, Jesse Cline, & Jos H Gilman: laid on the table. 2-Cmte on raods & Canals: discharged rom the consideration of the case of Henry M Shreve: referred to the Cmte on Patents. Same cmte: discharged from the consideration of the memorial of Joshua W Kirk in relation to a guard for steamboats: laid on the table. 3-Cmte on Patents: adverse report on the ptn of Stephen McCormick. 4-Cmte on Invalid Pensions: bill for the relief of Asa Davis. Same cmte: report on the ptn of Danl W Church, with a bill for the relief of John Sweeney.

For rent: superior 2 story brick house on Capitol hill, a little north of St Peter's Church. Inquire of Mr Jas Owner, Virginia ave.

Valuable land for sale: a tract of land in Jefferson Co, Va, being part of the *Shannon Hill Farm*, adjoining the lands of Mr W W Lane & Mr Geo Risler, containing about 115 acres . Apply to Richd Williams, who lives near the land. Communications to the subscriber, in Wash City, will be promptly attended to. —A B Fairfax

Perry's Gymnastic Academy, Nat'l Hall, C st, opposite the Exchange Hotel. Mr Perry informs the citizens of Wash of his intention of opening an Academy for Athletic Exercises: mode of teaching has been proved from much experience; call at the Exchange Hotel.

Orphan's Court of Wash Co, D C. In the case of the excx of John Wells,jr, dec'd. With the approbation of the Court, May 7 next has been appointed for the final settlement of the estate. —Ed N Roach, Reg/o Wills

Hse/o Reps: 1-Ptn of John H McCaughen & sundry other citizens of Harrison Co, Miss, praying a grant of certain lands in said county, in lieu of certain 16th sections, which are valueless or otherwise appropriated. 2-Ptn of Wm C Seaman, of Biloxi, Miss, praying indemnity for the loss of the schnr **Pauline**, seized, condemned, & sold under an alleged forfeiture of her coasting license. 3-Bill for the relief of John Fraser & G A Trenk: passed. 4-Bill for the relief of Danl Grant, Sarah Grant, Israel P Stone, & Emily Pinkham, owners of the fishing schnr **James & Henry**, of Cape Porpoise, Maine: passed. 5-Bill for the relief of Levi Eldridge & others: passed. 5-Memorial of Lyman Robinson & 76 citizens of Wattsburg, Pa, against any alteration of the tariff of 1842.

Circuit Court of Wash Co, D C. Thos W Ridgaway has applied to be discharged from imprisonment under the act for the relief of Insolvent Debtors: hearing on Apr 20 next. —Wm Brent, clk

Chas Co Court of Equity, Mar Term, 1844. Francis J Brummett & others, vs, Alex'r Shepherd, Saml S Barnard, & Robt Clark. In 1842, Josephus Brummett, of said county, contracted with the dfndnts for the purchase of 2 tracts of land called *Martin's Freehold* & *Tortoise Shell*, in said county, on the Potomac river, to which there is a fishing shore attached; in Jan 1842, the dfndnts executed to said Brummett a bond, in a penalty of $6,000, to give, on or before the end of 6 months thereafter, to the said Brummett a good & sufficient deed for the above lands, except 30 acres attached to the said shore, & running simultaneously with the river to the extent of the said shore, for which the dfndnts bind themselves by their aforementioned bond to give to said Brummett a lease for 99 years, renewable forever; that the fishing shore was reserved by said dfndnts; that a portion of the purchase money was paid by said Brummett in his lifetime, & that by the cmplnts, his only children & heirs at law, the residue of the purchase money has been paid; that notice may be given to Saml S Barnard & Alex'r Shepherd, who are out of the State, & that a subpoena may issue to Robt Clark, of PG Co, Md, to come in & answer to the bill of complaint of the complainants, & show cause, if any, why they will not give a deed for the above lands, having been often requested so to do, & according to the tenor of the above bond, which the bill of cmplnt recites; & that the said Josephus Brummett died intestate; & whethere the contract was not entered into as stated, & whether the money has not been paid, & whether they have executed a deed according to the contract. Hearing on the third Mon of Jun next. –Clement Dorsey
-Walter Mitchell, clk

Chas Co Court as a Court of Equity, Mar Term, 1844. Allison Roberts, vs, Eliz M Acton, Theodore M Acton, Richd C Acton, & Eliz M Acton. Ptn was filed by Hillary Langly, in 1837, for the sale or division of the real estate of W Stuart, of said county, dec'd, & a commission issued to 5 sensible & discreet men of Chas Co, to wit, John Gardiner, Theodore Mudd, Jas M Murry, Henry L Mudd, & Underwood Langly, to divide or sell the real estate of Wm Stuart, & the com'rs did divide, according to law, a portion of the said estate among the reps of Wm Stuart, & after giving legal notice, did sell to the highest bidder a part of the said real estate, called *Betsey's Delight*, containing 160 acres, lying in Chas Co, Md, & that one Matthew Acton became the purchaser, as appears by the bond given for the purchase money, which bond is exhibited & made a part of the bill, & that the complnt became security for the payment of the purchase money, & that Matthew Acton has since died, leaving 3 of the dfndnts his heirs at law, to wit, Eliz M Acton, Theodore M Acton, & Richd Acton, & the 4th dfndnt, his widow; & that no part of the purchase money has been paid; & to the intent that the purchase money may be paid to the legal reps of said Wm Stuart, & that the cmplnt may be released from his liabilities for the purchase money as security on said bond, the bill prays a decree that the said lands should be sold, the personal estate having been exhausted by Eliz M Acton, as excx of the said Matthew Acton; & that supoena may issue to the dfndnts to appear in said Court: hearing on the 3rd Mon of Jun next. –C Dorsey -Walter Mitchell, clk

Mrd: on Apr 11, by Rev G W Samson, Mr Saml C Wroe, of Wash City, to Miss Vanduden Dodson, of PG Co, Md.

Died: on Apr 12, Mrs Eliz Holroyd, aged 55 years, a native of Yorkshire, Eng, but for the last 24 years a resident of Wash City. Her funeral will be on Sun, at half past 2 o'clock, from the residence of her son-in-law, Mr Saml Marks, near the Protestant Church, Navy Yard.

Died: on Mar 28, at the residence of Maj Wm H Chase, near Barrancas, Pensacola, Col Geo Chase, a native of Mass, & formerly an ofcr in the U S Army.

Wilmarth Heath was on Sat convicted at Briston, R I, of acting as moderator of a town meeting held under the Dorrite Constitution; & Nathan C Smith was convicted of attending the same meeting. Sentences postponed.

MON APR 15, 1844
Notice: The public are cautioned against paying to W H Ward any debts due to the firm of W H Ward & Co & from dealing with him in regard to any of the property of the said firm, as he has no authority to receive the said debts or to dispose of said property. –Antone Mangett

On Thu last Mr Thos Baldwin, accompanied by the under sheriff of PG Co, removed from our county jail, on the requisition of the Govn'r of Md, Jas Redding, who stands charged with receiving stolen money from Wm Meeker, alias Clarke, as a bribe to let the said Meeker escape, near Beltsville, the latter being in Redding's custody & charged with felony. Redding's trial is expect to come on today at Upper Marlborough.

Hse/o Reps: 1-Ptn of Benj G Perkins, of Jefferson, Coos Co, N H, for a pension: referred.

We learn from the newspapers that R K Cralle has been appointed by Mr Secretary Calhoun to be Chief Clerk in the Dept of State.

Lilly, the puglist, pleaded guilty to the killing of McCoy in a fighting match, & was sentenced to pay a fine of $500.

Fatal duel in New Orleans on Apr 5, between Mr John De Buys, a s/o Gen Wm De Buys, & Mr Victor Castein. The weapons were double barreled guns, loaded with ball, & at the first fire Mr De Buys shot his antagonist dead. Mr Castein was a young man of fine promise, & could not have been more that 22 years of age. -Herlad

Cmdor Dallas reached Honolulu on Sep 12, in the ship **Erie**, & hoisted his pennant on board the ship **Cyane**. He was in search of Cmdor Jones, who had sailed thence on Aug 21 in the frig **United States** for the Society Island, at which place, report says, he only meant to touch, & then proceed to Bombay, where he intended to haul the old frigate up in dry dock for repairs, as she was in a bad condition.

We understand that Danl Ullmann, of N Y, has purchased the Phillipsburg Estate, lying in Centre, Clearfield, & Cambria Counties, N Y. The property contains upwards of 70,000 acres. –Phil U S Gaz

Genteel furniture at auction on Apr 18, at the residence of the late Mrs McPherson, on 10th st, between F & G sts: household & kitchen furniture.
-Robt W Dyer & Co, aucts

Mrd: on Apr 9, at N Y, by Rev John Murray Forbes, Wm Farley Gray, of Va, to Magdalena, only d/o the late Henry Gahn, Consul from Sweden.

Died: on Thu last, at N Y, after a short illness, Jacob Walton, Rear Admiral of the Red H B M Navy, in his 77th year.

Died: on Apr 13, at the residence of her grandfather, Alex'r Maron, in Wash City, Frances Mahon, d/o Henry Buehler, of Harrsburg, Pa, aged 1 year, 10 months & 13 days.

TUE APR 16, 1844
Senate: 1-Copy of the letter from the Hon W R King to the Hon Willie P Mangum, Pres of the Senate, resigning as Senator of the U S: member more than a quarter of a century; entering upon a new theatre of public service. 2-Ptn from Moss Meeker, asking the passage of a law giving the right of appeal from the decisions of the com'rs respecting claims to town lots in Galena, Ill. 3-Ptn from Byron W Darling & others, praying an allowance of fishing bounty. 4-Cmte on Pensions: House bill for the relief of Levi Colmer, without amendment. Same cmte: unfavorable reports on the following House bills: relief of Enoch M Daniel; of Arthur R Frogge; of Danl Dunhan; of Isaac Plummer. Same cmte: adverse reports on the ptn of Sarah Daggett, & the ptn of Theodosia Netherland. 5-Cmte on Revolutionary Claims: bill for the relief of the legal reps of Jas Bell, dec'd. Same cmte: adverse reports on the ptn of Mgt & Agnes Bigham, heirs at law of Thos Armor; also, upon the ptn of the heirs of Christopher Taylor, a surgeon's mate in the Revolution; also, on the ptn of Rebecca Beckham, d/o Robt Lovell, of the Revolution. 6-Cmte on Pensions: adverse report on the ptn of Wm Miller, a soldier in the war with Great Britain. 7-Cmte on Indian Affairs: bill for the relief of David Robb, accompanied by a report. 8-Resolved: that the Cmte on Pensions be instructed to inquire into granting to the heirs of Rebecca Morehouse, wid/o David Morehouse, a soldier of the Revolution, the pension which was due the said Rebecca at the time of her decease.

Mr Jos Jones, who was shot during the riotous proceedings at St Louis on Apr 1, has since died of his wound. The murderer is not yet known.

Died: on Apr 8, in Wash City, Henry P W Handy, s/o Saml Handy, formerly of the Treas Dept, aged 29. Thrice within the brief space of little more than a year has the hand of death smitten this family. May the Comforter be with its aged head, & may he not sorrow as one without hope!

Died: on Mar 30, at Moulton, Ala, in his 71st year, Dr Edw Stoughton Gantt, formerly of Va.

Hse/o Reps: 1-Ptn of Robt Furlong for a pension; also, ptn of Susan Brum for a pension: both referred. 2-Ptn of Wm Bromaghin for a pension: referred. 3-Ptn of Mrs Catharine Gale, of Lincoln Co, Ky: referred. 4-Ptn & papers of Israel Cryder, of Huntingdon Co, Pa, praying for remuneration for provisions furnished by his father to the Govn't during the Revolutionary war.

$100 reward for runaway negro William, about 22 years of age. He was raised in or near Fredericktown, Md. He stated that his mother was free & lived in Balt. -Jas French, Warrenton, Fauquier Co, Va

Wanted, by a man & his wife, who have no children, a situation in the city or country, the country would be preferred-the man as laborer & the woman as housekeeper. Apply at Mr Rutherford's, corner of 13th & D sts, Wash.

WED APR 17, 1844
Senate: 1-Ptn from Chas M Keller, of Wash, D C, to be allowed to take out a patent for an invention discovered by him, & which he is precluded from doing by his connexion with the ofc, being Examiner of Patents. 2-Ptn from Jas Richardson & others, of Dedham, Mass, asking that Congress will not pass any international copyright law. 3-Cmte on Pensions: House bill for the relief of Sally McCraw, & recommended its indefinite postponement. 4-Cmte of Claims: bill for the relief of Pierre Menard, Josiah J Betts, Jacob Feaman, & Edw Roberts, of Illinois.

Hse/o Reps: 1-Ptn of Jos Walker & others, for a confirmation of certain land titles. 2-Ptn of B T Wade & 60 other citizens of Ashtabula Co, Ohio, against any reduction of the tariff.

Dr J L Martin, formerly Principal Clerk in the Dept of State, has been appointed by the Pres of the U S, with the advice & consent of the Senate, to be Sec of Legation to France.

The remains of the Hon Alex'r Porter having been conveyed to Nashville, Tenn, they were committed to the tomb in the cemetery near that city on Apr 7, where they now rest in peace beside the body of his wife who died some 25 years ago.

At Richmond, on Fri, Mr Goodman, drayman, was killed by a blow to the temple. One of the shafts hit Mr Goodman, & killed him instantly.

Mrd: on Apr 15, by Rev Mr Sprole, Wm Ferguson to Eliz Doig, all of this place.

Mrd: on Apr 14, in Wash City, by Rev Mr Van Horseigh, Mr Abraham Brown, of PG Co, Md, to Miss Eliz Hodges, of Montgomery Co.

Mrd: on Apr 9, at *Spring Hill*, Somerset Co, Md, by Rev Saml G Callahan, Mitchell W Travers, of Gtwn, D C, to Miss Eliza Ellen, d/o Edw Fowler, of the former place.

Extract from a letter of apology to Mr John Reilly, engineer, of this city, who has resided here for the last 4 years. I most sincerely regret the ill-advised course I pursued, by which I have injured a man above all suspicion, & wounded most deeply the feelings of his family & friends. –Henry A Clarke

THU APR 18, 1844
Wm H Nalley informs his friends & the public that he has opened a Bookbindery on Pa ave, next door to Beers' Temperance Hotel. He may always be found ready to execute all orders left with him.

Notice to Gunners & others: $2 per dozen will be given for the eggs of the Wood or Summer Duck, or for living young summer ducks a more liberal price will be given. Apply at the hall of the Nat'l Institute to R J Pollard.

Senate: 1-Ptn from Wm J Moody, a soldier of the last war with Great Britain, asking an increase of his pension. 2-Ptn from David Eggleston & Thos Hawkins, asking reimbursement of money paid by them for certain public lands. 3-Adverse report on the ptn of Geo Harrison was reconsidered, & again committed to the Cmte of Claims. 4-Cmte of Finance: asking to be discharged from further consideration of the ptn of Joel A Matteson & Hardin Bigelow, & that they have leave to withdraw their papers. Same cmte: adverse report on the ptn of Wm D Ross. 5-Cmte on D C: unfavorable report on the ptn of Wm Easby. 6-Cmte on the Public Lands: made a report on the case of Noah Miller, which was ordered to be printed. 7-Cmte of Claims: unfavorable report on the ptn of Lyon & Howard. Same cmte: House bill for the relief of Wm C Easton, without amendment, & recommending its passage. 8-Cmte on Pensions: unfavorable reports on the ptns of Chas Williams & Wm Geller. 9-Cmte on Private Land Claims: bill for the relief of Jas Anderson, of Iowa Territory.

Washington Branch Railroad: ofc of Transportation B & O R R, Balt. W S Woodside, Superintendent

Hse/o Reps: 1-Cmte on the Judiciary: made a report upon the ptn of Miles W Dickey, with a bill for his relief. 2-Resolved, That the Pres of the U S be requested to inform this House why the sum of $4,000, appropriated at the last session of Congress to Jeremiah Smith, jr, has not been paid to him, & what action will be necessary on the part of Congress to enable the said Smith to draw his money. 3-Cmte on Commerce: adverse report on the ptn of Jas McIntyre. 4-Ptn of Jeremiah Wright, of Livingston Co, N Y, praying Congress to grant him a pension from the time of his discharge, in the summer of 1815, in the last war, until Nov, 1828, when he was placed on the pension roll. 5-Memorial of John R St John, alleging that he has discovered a principle by which the variation of the magnetic needle from the due north at all times & places, under any circumstances may be readily & accurately ascertained; & also has invented a machine for accurately measuring the distance a vessel sails in a given time; & praying Congress to make an appropriation for purchasing the same for national use.

The subscriber wishes to employ a competent married gentleman to educate his children. Address, postage paid, *Montevideo*, near Darnestown, Montg Co, Md. –John P C Peter

For rent: the neat cottage residence on south C, near 12th st & Md ave. The neighborhood is pleasant, & the walk convenient to the Post Ofcs. Inquire on the premises of Edmund Brooke.

Wanted, a Wet nurse, who can take entire charge of an infant. A healthy married woman, who can furnish testimonials of character, is desired. Apply on 8th st, between E & F sts, or to Messrs Robt W Dyer & Co, aucts. –John F Boone

Valuable Potomac land at Public Sale: on Jun 17, on the premises, that farm called *Pope's creek*, now in the occupancy of J W Hungerford. It is in Westmoreland Co, Va, near the mouth of Pope's creek, & contains 1,869 acres of land. Improvements consist of a frame dwlg, qrtrs, stabling, necessary for the use of farm of its size. Reference is made to W R Mason, of King George Court House, Va. Possession will be given on Jan 1 next. –W T Somerville, Balt, Md

The late English papers announce the death of the Rt Hon Sir Henry Vaughan Halford, Bart. This celebrated physician was medical attendant to 4 English sovereigns in succession. His name was orginally Vaughan, & he was brother to Sir Chas R Vaughan, formerly British Minister to the U S, to Mr Barron Vaughan, & to Sir John Vaughan, Dean of Chester.

Died: on Apr 13, at his residence, in Sussex Co, N J, Job S Halsted, who had attained the good old age of three score & ten. He was an honored member of the bar of N J for near half a century. He was ever beloved & honored for the distinguishing virtues of the patriot & the Christian. –Newark Adv

Died: on Apr 17, Samuel, infant s/o Thos & Mary C Young, aged 1 year, 8 months & 17 days. His funeral will be on Fri at 10 o'clock.

For rent: handsome & commodious house on 12th st, between F & G sts. Apply to J M Krafft s, corner of F & G sts. N B: The present occupant of the house would dispose of a portion of the furniture, adapted to the house, on accommodating terms.

Dissolution of the partnership between Marion S Williams & John Kalklaser, by mutual consent. John Kalklaser will settle the business of the firm.
-M S Williams & J Kalklaser

Piney Point oysters for sale. Apply to Thompson Tyler, Exchange Hotel.

FRI APR 18, 1844
Wash Corp: 1-Ptn from John Y Bryant, Pres of the Northern Liberties Fire Co: referred. 2-Ptn from Simon Fraser: referred to the Cmte on Improvements. 3-Cmte of Claims: reported without amendment the bill from the Board of Common Council for the relief of Capt Danl Paullin: ordered to lie on the table. 4-Ptn of Adam Delany: referred to the Cmte of Claims. 5-Cmte of Claims: asked to be discharged from the futher consideration of the ptn of G L Thompson: ordered to lie on the table. 6-Ptn of Isaac Beers, praying remission of a fine: referred to the Cmte of Claims.

Hse/o Reps: 1-Mr Adams rose & said he had been requested to present, on behalf of a distinguished citizen of Md, now no more, the camp chest of Gen Washington, used by him during the Revolutionary war. Camp chest was presented through the last will of Wm Sidney Winder, a distinguished citizen of Md: along with a letter from John Wethered; Wm Sidney Winder's will; his letter unsigned, with that of Mary S Winder; Henry Maynadier to Govn'r Winder; Henry Maynadier to W S Winder. The acceptance, at the last session of Congress, of the Sword of our nation's great heroic Revolutionary commander & chief by Saml T Washington, of Kanawha Co, Va, was probably the inducement to the late Mr Winder to devolve upon presenting this additional relic. Letter: West Point, Aug 16, 1779. Dear Doctor: I have asked Mrs Cochran & Mrs Livingston to dine with me tomorrow, but ought I not to apprize them of their fare? As I hate deception, even where the imagination only is concerned, I will. It is needless to premise that my table is large enough to hold the ladies, of this they had ocular proof yesterday. To say how it is usually covered is rather more essential, & this shall be the purport of my letter. Since our arrival in this happy spot we have had a ham [sometimes a shoulder] of bacon to grace the head of the table, a piece of roast beef adorns the foot, & a small dish of greens or beans [almost imperceptible] decorates the centre. When the cook has a mind to cut a figure, [and this, I presume, he will attempt to do tomorrow,] we have two beefsteak pies, or dishes of crabs, in addition, one on each side the center dish, dividing the space & reducing the distance between dish & dish to about six feet, which, without them, would be near twelve apart. Of late, he had the surprising luck to discover that apples make pies, & it's a question if, amidst the violence of his efforts, we do not get one of apple instead of having both of beef. If the ladies can put up with such entertainment, & will submit to partake of it on plates, once tin, but now iron, [not become so by the labor of scouring,] I shall be happy to see them. I am, dear Doctor, your most obedient servant, Go Washington. [To Dr Cochran, New Windsor.] 1a-This camp chest was inherited from his father, Govn'r Winder, a contemporary & fellow ofcr of the Father of his Country in our Revolutionary struggle, & the descendant of a family which emigrated to this country 2 centuries ago, & which has ever held in this land of their choice the most respectable standing. It was presented to Govn'r Winder by Col Maynadier, of Annapolis, himself an ofcr of the Revolution, who received it from the executors of Gen Washington. It was Govn'r Winder who, on Jul 4, 1815, laid the corner-stone of that beautiful monument erected to the memory of Washington in Balt city, & which constitutes its chief ornament. For several years it had been the purpose of the late Mr Winder to consign this relic to the care of Congress, but such was his attachment to it that the hour of parting with it never arrived, & it is, unhappily, to the hand of death that we are indebted for it now. 2-Ptn of John Halloway, asking to be placed on the invalid pension list. 3-Ptn of Melinda Martin, of Colesville, N Y, praying that the law making it an offence to write on the margin of a newspaper sent through the mail may be repealed. 4-Ptn of Enos Manning, of Piqua, Ohio, asking a pre-emption right to 320 acres of land. 5-Ptn of Simon Ruffner for an increase of pension. 6-Ptn of Mrs Eliz Brunot, wid/o & relict of Dr Felix Brunot, a surgeon in the army of the Revolution, asking for a pension. 7-Memorial of a cmte of citizens of Euphrata, Lancaster Co, Pa, respectfully setting forth that in the fall of 1777, immediately after the battle of Brandywine, about 50 sick & wounded soldiers were brought from the American army to Euphrata, & placed in bldgs fitted up as hospitals for their reception by the Society of Seventh Day Baptists of the village; that during the following winter about 200 of them died, & were buried on the summit of a hill called **Mount Zion**, in the vicinity, which is about 100 feet high; that this hill is now overgrown, & these memorialists pray your honorable bodies to grant them a small appropriation to assist them in finishing a suitable monument which the citizens have now begun, to the memory of the dead.

Household furniture at auction, on Apr 22, at the residence of Mr Graeff, at the corner of 15th st & Pa ave, his household & kitchen furniture.
-Robt W Dyer & Co, aucts

The Black River Journal announces the almost simultaneous deaths of the Hon Egbert Ten Eyck & the Hon Micah Sterling, esteemed citizens of Watertown, N Y. Mr Sterling was first attacked with scarlet fever, which, causing inflammation upon the lungs, terminated fatally. Though a native of Conn, he had resided for more than 30 years in Jefferson Co. He was about 63 years of age. Judge Ten Eyck, too, was much respected at home & abroad. Yesterday, soon after dinner, without any previous attack of illness, he suddenly expired. They were both among the earliest settlers of our county & village, & were of the original stock of lawyers which contributed to make our bar one of the most able in the State, from the earliest organization of the county.

Valuable bldg lots at private sale. Lot 14 in square 127, fronts on 18th st. Lot 10 in square 142, fronts on G st, & is a very desirable location for 2 handsome houses, being between the houses occupied by Mr Parrot & Mr Theodore Kain, & in the rear of the new bldg of Lt Gilli, which fronts on F st. -Robt W Dyer & Co, aucts

Suicide on Mar 27 last, a young man named E L Budd, formerly clerk to Dibble & Bostwick, of N Y. He retired to bed at his hotel, Dunning's, on Sunday night. On Mon he was found dead by shooting himself with a pistol.

SAT APR 20, 1844
Senate: 1-Ptn from Mary Sergeant, asking to be allowed the 7 years' half pay due her father. 2-Cmte on the Post Ofc & Post Roads: bill for the relief of Wm De Buys, late postmaster at New Orleans.

Orphan's Court of Wash Co, D C. That letters of adm on the personal estate of Henry Ingle, dec'd, be granted to Peter Callan, unless cause to the contrary be shown on or before Tue, May 14 next. -Ed N Roach, Reg/o Wills

Rockville [Md] Journal of Wed last announces the death of Brice Selby, Clerk of Montgomery Co Court, in his 70th year of his age.

Geo P Scarburg has been appointed by the Executive of the State of Virginia to be a Judge of the General Court of Va, in place of Thos H Bayly, resigned.

New Orleans, Apr 10. U S Circuit Court: a true bill was found yesterday by the Grand Jury, & not until yesterday, against Robt E Klady, pilot of the steamer **Buckeye**, for manslaughter; some 50 or 60 persons, it is alleged in the indictment, having lost their lives, who were on board when it collided with the steamer **De Soto** in consequence of misconduct, negligence, & inattention to his duty. It is the first time a party has been criminally sued for any similar catastrophe. Klady has given bonds for his appearnce in the sum of $5,000. -Picayune

Tom Chew, a slave, convicted in the County Crt of PG Co, Md, of causing the death of a slave of W B Hill, by kicking him the abdomen, has been sentenced to be banished into some foreign country, out of the U S, & be sold as a slave for life. Geo Payne, for stealing a mare belonging to Allen P Bowie, has been sent to the penitentiary for 10 years, & Wm Snowden, free colored, for 7 years, for entering the store of Mr S Phillips & stealing $46.

Columbia [Missouri] Statesman of Apr 5 says: on Sat last, about 9 miles n w of this place, a young man, Jefferson Blankenship, hung himself to a tree. He was about 16 years old. Cause is unknown.

Yesterday, as Mr Britain M Brown, of the firm of Bayles & Brown, sparmakers, N Y, was superintending the hoisting out of a vessel's mast, by the breaking of the guy rope, the handle of the windlass flew suddenly round & struck Mr Brown on the head, causing his instant death.

New Orleans papers: duel fought on Apr 10, near the city, between Cmdor Riebaud, late of the Mexican navy, & Gen Santmanat, late Govn'r of Tobasco, the weapons pistols, distance 10 paces. At the third fire Riebaud received the ball of his adversary in the upper chest, inflicting a severe & dangerous wound.

Valuable land for sale in D C. Undersigned are authorized to dispose at public sale about 150 acres, adjoining the farms of Capt Wm G Sanders & Mr Alex'r Shepperd, about 1 mile from Rock Creek Church. Apply to Geo A Digges & Chas Digges, residing near Bladensburg, Md.

Hse/o Reps: 1-Cmte of the Whole was discharged from the consideration of the joint resolution for the relief of W P Zantzinger. Resolution was passed.

On Sat next, Mr Colt will make a Submarine Explosion, to clear away the sunken wreck of the ship **Styx**," on which he made his late experiments. An alarm gun will be fired from the Navy Yard previous to the explosion. [Apr 22nd newspaper: explosion was successful.]

Desirable improved farm for sale: having determined to reduce farming operations, will offer on May 20, a farm in PG Co, Md, containing a 153 acres: with a new 2 story dwlg, barn, corn house, & fruit trees. Apply to Messrs Johnson & Callan, Washington, or Jos Smoot, Gtwn. Or apply to the subscriber, Wallace Kirkwood, living on the adjoining farm.

Mrd: on Apr 8, in Phil, Lt Wm Eustis, U S Dragoons, to Eliz, d/o the late Triton Grelaud.

Mrd: on Apr 17, at Warrenton, Va, by Rev Geo Lemmon, Alex'r S Campbell, of Fauquier Co, to Mary Tyler, only d/o the late Robt R Horner.

Died: on Apr 15, in Boston, Chas Bulfinch, aged 81. He was educated at Harvard Univ; traveled in Europe, where he gratified a strong taste for architectural studies; returned & engaged in commercial pursuits. He was appointed in 1817, by Pres Monroe, to the ofc of Architect of the Capitol of the U S, & directed the completion of the wings & the erection of the central bldg of that edifice. In 1830 he returned to Boston & spent his life in calm preparation for the future world. He was a kind friend, husband, father, & a devoted Christian.

Died: at his residence, at South Reading, the Hon Thaddeus Spaulding, a member of the Exec Council of Mass, a worthy man & an excellent citizen.
[No date-current item.]

Died: on Apr 11, in Charlottesville, in his 68th year, Col John Fry, for many years a resident at the Warm Springs, Va.

Died: on Apr 9, at Fayetteville, N C, the venerable D Anderson, a truly pious man, a native of Scotland, but for 60 years a citizen of Fayetteville. He was in his 78th year.

Rev Dr Ryder will continue his exposition of the Catholice doctrine of the Eucharist tomorrow, at 4 p m, at St Patrick's Church.

Wash City squares & lots for sale. –Saml D King, agent, F st, between 13th & 14th sts, Wash.

MON APR 22, 1844
Circuit Court: action in which Emily Blue, a colored woman, sues John & Mary Williams & Wm S Colquhoun, to obtain her freedom, on the ground of an illegal transportation from Va to D C, under the act of Assembly of Md of 1783, forbidding the removal of slaves from one State to another under certain restrictions. Court will resume this morning. [Washington-local affair.] [Apr 26 newspaper: jury returned a verdict for the defendants.]

Hse/o Reps: 1-Cmte on Invalid Pensions: bill for the relief of Wm McCauley. Same cmte: adverse reports on the ptns of Wm Turney, Leonard Swallow, & Saml Lusk. 2-Cmte of Claims: bill for the relief of Josiah Dillon, late Assist Qrtrmaster Gen of the army. 3-Cmte on Commerce: bill for John Sands. 4-Cmte on Naval Affairs: bill for the relief of Wm McPherson, without amendment. 5-Ptn of Wm Depew, relative to the duty on Canary wines, & praying a reduction thereof.

Gen Waddy Thompson, late Minister of the U S to Mexico, arrived at New Orleans on Apr 12, in the U S brig **Bainbridge**, Cmder Mattison, which sailed from Vera Cruz, Mexico, on Apr 1. Gen Thompson obtained the liberation of the remainder of the Texian prisoners taken in Sept, 1842, at San Antonio de Bexar. 31 of the 35 prisoners liberated came on in the **Bainbridge**, the remainder preferring to continue for the present in Mexico. Those released on the occasion of Gen Thompson's farewell, viz:

Wm Bugg	A J Leslie
Jas H Brown	Jas L Truehat
Edw Brown	G A Voss
T B Beck	John Young
L Colquhoun	Nathl W Faisan
David J Davis	Melvin Harrell
Augustus Elly	Edw Mantom
Simeon Glenn	A H Morrell
Nathl Harbert	Jas C Robinson
Thos Hancock	Jos Shard
Francis McKay	John L Lehman
S L Noble	Chauncey Johnson
R S Neighbors	John Lee
C W Peterson	*J C Morgan
John Perry	*Jno Smith
M L B Raper	*H A Alesbury
Geo Shaeffer	*Isaac Allen
Saml Stone	

[*Remained in Mexico.]

Mr Michl Schrack, a young man, of Upper Providence, was killed when training a colt on Fri last. He was thrown down & dragged until mangled terribly. He died instantly. –Norristown [Pa] Herald

Lt Monroe, who killed Col Fawcett in a duel in England lately, has been compelled to fly his country, & has been struck from the rolls. In a letter to a friend he writes: I have been forced to fly from my country, my profession, & my beloved wife, children, father, mother & relations. The Gov't must endeavor to prevent the inevitable disgrace which falls on an ofcr for refusing a challenge, if it desires to put down dueling in the army.

Died: on Apr 21, after an illness of 12 hours, of scarlet fever, Pheba Emma, y/d/o J Bartram & Phebe North, aged 4 years & 5 months. Her funeral will be from the residence of her father, New Jersey ave, Capitol Hill, this afternoon, at 11 o'clock. [Note: Pheba & Phebe as copied.]

The trial of John Gordon & Wm Gordon for the murder of Mr Amasa Sprague, of R I, concluded on Wed. Evidence was wholly circumstantial. Verdict of the jury was guilty as to John, & not guilty as to Wm.

Trustee's sale: by deed of trust from Michl Stone & wife to me, dated Jul 21, 1842, & recorded in Liber W B #95, folios 346 etc, of the land records of Wash Co, I offer on May 13, part of the tract called *Alliance*, containing 34 acres, in said county, adjacent to Gtwn, & bounded by the lands of John Cox, trustee, E Rhodes, Henry Kengla, & others. The land is improved by a 2 story frame dwlg & other bldgs. –John Kurtz, trustee -E S Wright, auctioneer

Trustee's sale: by deed of trust to me, dated Aug 29, 1842, recorded in Liber B S #XI, folios 254 etc, of the land records of Montg Co, Md: sale on May 13, of land containing 77+ acres, being part of a tract called *Friendship*, lying in said county, near D C, & bounded by the lands of Mrs Brooke, & Messrs Thompson, Shoemaker, & others. –Clement Cox, trustee -E S Wright, auctioneer

12½ cents reward will be given for the apprehension of Jas Conner & Geo Fastnaugh, indented apprentices to the Gardening business-Conner to John Douglass, sen, the latter to John Douglass, jr. Half the above reward will be given for the apprehension of either, or the whole for both. –J Douglass, sen & J Douglass, jr

TUE APR 23, 1844
Profitable investment of money may be made at the postponed sale of Pomonkey. On Jun 3 I will dispose my estate, called *Pomonkey*, on the banks of the Potomac river, in Chas Co, Md. Farm contains about 700 acres: dwlg house is large & spacious with all necessary out-bldgs. The health of the farm is equal to any river situation in the U S. In support of this I can refer to Dr R S Briscoe, Pomonkey post ofc, Chas Co, Md, who is a practicing physician in the neighborhood, & has tended the family there for many years, & never knew of a case of bilious fever there. The property has been possessed by my family for more than 70 years as a residence, & is now offered for sale owing to my inability to give it my personal attention, from my professional occupation. The Large Shad & Herring Fishery is under a lease to Messrs Hollis & Brotherton until the spring of 1846 & is in the neighborhood of *Craney Island*, more than an acre of land, average rent of $1,500 per year. The 3 fisheries on the same side of the river, average a rent of $1,100 per year. I will sell a number of mules, sheep, oxen, & other horned cattle; farming utensils, household furniture, & corn fodder. The steamboat *Augusta*, Capt Rogers, will land passengers who desire to visit the premises. Inquire of Col Wm L Brent, in Wash, or to the subscriber. –Robt J Brent, Balt, Md

For sale: a farm of 150 acres, more or less, in PG Co, Md, 6 miles from the city: with a good dwlg & necessary out houses. Also, for rent a 2 story frame house, to a good tenant. –T C Donn, Justice of the Peace, Louisiana ave, near 7th.

Bloomingdale at private sale: 4 miles west of Rockville, adjoining the country residence of the Hon Geo C Washington, containing 250 acres. Improvements consist of a dwlg containing 9 rooms, with a kitchen, smoke-house, dairy, granary, stables, & large frame barn, which needs repair. Apply to Mr Wm Clements, residing on the premises, or to the subscriber in Gtwn. –B Clements

Senate: 1-Cmte on Pensions: adverse report on the bill for the relief of Eliz Gresham. Also, on the bill for the relief of Wm Moody, & asking to be discharged from the further consideration of the ptn of Geo Ripp, & that it be referred to the Cmte on Naval Affairs. 2-Bill introduced granting a pension to Jas Duffy.

House & lot for sale: 2 story brick bldg, on Md ave, near the house formerly occupied by Col Johnson. –M Jeffers, Missouri ave

Wash Co, D C. I certify that Ignatius Howe brought before me, as an estray, a gray gelding. –Jas Marshall, J P. Owner to come forward, prove property, pay charges, & take him away. -Ignatius Howe, near the Navy Yard bridge.

To the public-the subscriber, one of the boys of 1814, an old resident of the District, who crossed the river & went to Benedict, & was taken prisoner by the British & brought as a prisoner to Wash City when the Capitol was burnt, & made his escape & has ever since that period resided here, now offers his services as a Collector & Constable. All business, bills, & judgments, for me, can be left at my box at the magistrate's ofc of T C Donn, La ave. –Thos Donaldson

Estray cow came to my premises. Owner to come forward, prove property, pay charges, & take her away. –John F Boyle, near the Observatory.

$100 reward for runaway negro John, about 24 years of age. –J D Starke, living near Allen's Fresh, Chas Co, Md.

The Hon Henry Baldwin, one of the Assoc Justices of the Supreme Court of the U S, died at the Merchants' Hotel, in Phil, on Sunday last. The malady was paralysis, of which he had a severe attack on Mon of last week, under which he gradually sank. He was about 65 years of age, & was, we believe, a resident of Pittsburg.

Mrd: on Apr 18, in Springfield, Mass, Capt Wm H Swift, of the Corps of Topographical Engineers, to Hannah W, d/o John Howard.

Govn'r Shannon has resigned the ofc of Govn'r of the State of Ohio, in consequence of being confirmed by the Senate as Minister to Mexico. Thos W Bartley, Speaker of the Senate, now becomes Govn'r. He is the s/o the Whig candidate for the ofc of Govn'r, being himself opposed in politics to his worthy father.

Public Notice. The subscriber notifies that for reasons considered conclusive by all who know them, the permission heretofore frequently accorded to neighbors & citizens to deposite in his vault on Mausoleum square the remains of their deceased, cannot be continued; & it is therefore hoped & expected that no further applications for that purpose may be made. -John P Van Ness

Port Tobacco Times. This is the name of a new paper just issued at Port Tobacco, Md, by Elijah Wells, jr, & G W Hodges. No doubt it will meet with liberal support from the citizens of Chas Co.

Wm P Ross, a Cherokee, has issued a prospectus to publish a weekly newspaper at Tahlequa, in the Cherokee nation, to be called the *Cherokee Advocate*, the price to be $2 per year.

WED APR 24, 1844
Senate: 1-Ptn from W E Robinson, native of Ireland, but a naturalized citizen of the U S, now residing at New Haven, Conn, praying the passage of such laws as will protect naturalized citizens against claims of other countries to their perpetual allegiance.

Wanted at the Penitentiary of D C: from 10 to 20 tons good sound Brush of the Broom corn, for which the highest market price will be given. Apply to John B Dade, Warden.

A private family near the Patent Ofc has desirable chambers unoccupied, & would be pleased to let them, with or without breakfast & tea. Inquire at this ofc, or of R P Anderson or Jesse E Dow at the Capitol.

A concert was lately given in New Orleans by Madame Cinti Damoreau & Mr Artot, in aid of the French Society of Benevolence & Orphans, the net receipts of which amounted to $1,425.90

Pensacola, Apr 13, 1844. Naval: vessels of war now lying in this harbor:
The U S frig **Potomac**, bearing the broad pennant of Cmdor David Conner-off the navy yard.
The U S ship **Vincennes**, Capt Buchanan-off the city.
The U S brig **Somers**, Lt Com'dt Brent-off the navy yard.
The U S steamer **Poinsett**, Lt Com'dt Semmes-off the navy yard.
The French corvette **La Brillante**, Cmdor Regnaud-off the city.
The French brig of war **Griffon**, Commandant Gasquett-off the city.
The Revenue Cutter **Woodbury**, Capt Foster-off the city.

J P McKean informs that his Ice Cream parlors are now open to receive company, & he will be happy at all times to serve them to the best of his ability. –J P McKean

Hse/o Reps: A personal re-encounter took place between Mr White of Ky, & Mr Rathbun, of N Y. The Reporter heard nothing, though he witnessed the several violent gesticulations that preceded it. Members were leaping on tables, endeavoring to get into the center of what now began to assume the appearance of a general melee. Note by the Reporter: a pistol was discharged by a citizen from Ky, Wm S Moore, & the ball penetrated the thigh of one of the ofcrs of the Capitol, John L Wirt, wounding him seriously, but it is believed not dangerously. Mr Davis, of Ky, stated that the man who had fired the pistol was a respectable man, the s/o a Revolutionary ofcr of the Va line, who had been here prosecuting a claim for his father's half pay. Resolved: That Wm S Moore, now in the custody of the Sgt at Arms, be imprisoned until the close of the present session of Congress. He attempted to kill a member of this body, thereby badly wounding a police ofcr.

R K Watts was elected by the Board of Aldermen & Board of Common Council of Wash City a police magistrate of the 2nd ward, in place of Jesse E Dow, resigned.

Late from England. 1-Bernadotte, King of Sweden, is dead, who was, with the exception of Marshal Soult, the last of the early & successful soldiers of Napoleon. 2-Letters from Copenhagen announce the death of Thorwaldsen, the celebrated sculptor.

Mrd: on Apr 9, at Sugar Grove, Ky, by Rev W Smith, Tomlin M Banks, M D, of Cincinnati, to Miss Clarissa L Harrison, granddaughter of the late Gen Wm Henry Harrison.

Died: on Apr 20, of dropsy, in his 45th year, Jos Ratcliff, late of Montg Co, Md.

Henry D Miller, Register of Wills of Cecil Co, Md, died at Elkton, on Wed last.

THU APR 25, 1844
The copartnership of W H Ward & Co of the Washington Foundry, is this day dissolved by mutual consent, & Messrs M Mason & John Skirvin have been appointed arbitrators to settle all business of the said firm. –W H Ward, Antone Mangett [John H Goddard appointed to collect for the firm.]

Senate: 1-Ptn from Thos Herrick, praying compensation for carrying the mail. 2-Ptn from Sarah Shepherd for the renewal of her pension. 3-Ptn from the heirs of John Stiles, asking indemnity. 4-Cmte on Naval Affairs: asking to be discharged from the further consideration of the ptn of Geo Ripp, asking the renewal of M F Green's pension.

To the Editor. I observe that some of the N J & Balt papers, in announcing the death of Mr Thos Oakley Anderson, of Newton, N J, formerly a lt in the navy, state that he was the last survivor of the ofcrs who assisted Decatur in the destruction of the frig **Philadelphia**, in the harbor of Tripoli, which, having fallen into the hands of the enemy, had been manned with 300 Turks, & bore the flag of the hostile Power. There is an error in this, which justice to a distinguished ofcr still living requires should be corrected. Cmdor Chas Morris, then a very young midshipman, & now Chief of the Bureau of Construction, Equipment, & Repairs, was also one of that gallant little band, & is now the only surviving ofcr of those who achieved that most daring & unexampled exploit. The pilot, Catalani, who laid the Intrepid & her boarders alongside of the frig, is also still alive, & resides near the navy yard at this place. Wash, Apr 24, 1844. -A
+

Died: on Apr 14, at Newton, Sussex Co, N J, Thos Oakley Anderson, formerly a Lt in the U S Navy. At an early age he entered the Navy as a Midshipman & shared in the romantic & dangerous enterprises projected & executed on the Mediterranean during the war with Tripoli, by such daring spirits as Decatur, Lawrence, McDonough, Bainbridge, Stewart, Somers, & Thorn. He distinguished himself by his bravery in the crowning enterprise of that short but eventful war-we mean the destruction of the frig **Philadelphia**, in the harbor of Tripoli. Cmdor Preble matured a plan for destroying her while she lay at anchor, & entrusted the execution of the perilous enterprise to Lt Stephen Decatur. The date was Feb 16, 1804. Without the loss of a man, he had annihilated the infidel crew of 300 Turks, & wrapped the huge frig in one vast sheet of consuming flame. Ofcrs engaged in this unparalled exploit, were: Lts Decatur, Lawrence, Bainbridge, & Thorn; Dr Heerman, surgeon; S Catalano, pilot; & Midshipmen McDonough, Anderson, Izard, Morris, Laws, Davis, & Rowe. Mr Anderson was promoted to a Lt shortly after the close of the Tripolitan war, which commission he subsequently resigned, & returned to his native village, where he has for more than 30 years resided among us. He died at the age of nearly 61 years. –Newton Register

$10 reward for runaway negro man named Basil Dorsey, about 36.
–Henry N Young, living in Wash.

Mrd: on Apr 24, by Rev Mr Bean, Thos J Stelle, of Wash, to Anna Maria, 2nd d/o the late Francis Hopkinson, of Phil.

Died: on Apr 18, in Wash City, after a lingering illness of 5 months, Peter Kurtz, in his 54th year, leaving a wife & 3 children to mourn his irreparable loss.

Died: yesterday, Mr J H Howell, after a lingering disease of the consumption, which he bore with Christian patience & fortitude. His funeral is on Fri at 2 o'clock, from the residence of Mr Payne, on G st, near the corner of 11th st. Members of Columbia Lodge, #10, & sister lodges are invited to attend the above.

Bereavement in the family of Mr A C Squier, of this town. In less than one month they have lost 5 children, all but one with scarlatina. On the 19th ult Esther, an infant, died; on the 6th inst Elihu, aged 5 years; on the 7th Julia, aged 3; on the 12th Clark, aged 7; & on the 14th Louisa, aged 9. Not a solitary bud has been left on the parent stem. –Columbia [S C] Carolinian

The Kaskaskia [Ill] Republican: John Stufflebeau, aged 109 years died in that vicinity. He was born on the banks of the Hudson river, 12 miles from Albany, N Y, Feb 15, 1735. His eyesight was unimpaired. His 3rd wife is still living, at age 82 years, & was able to attend the remains of her dec'd husband to the grave. [No date-current item.]

For sale: a small farm of 130 acres 1 miles from Bladensburg, & will be shown by the subscriber, living in Bladensburg. –Wm T Brown.

For rent: 2 story brick house on Pa ave, next door west of the residence of Cmdor Warrington. Apply at the next house west.

FRI APR 26, 1844
Wash Corp: 1-Cmte of Claims: bill for the relief of Adam Dulany: passed. 2-Ptn from Ann Whitmore: referred to the Cmte of Claims. 3-Ptn from John C Rumnell & others: referred to the Cmte on Improvements. 4-Ptn of Wm B Wilson, praying payment for work done on 7th st west & Mass ave: referred to the Cmte on Improvements. 5-Cmte of Claims: act for the relief of Eliz Purrell, reported without amendment. Same cmte was referred the ptns of Geo T McGlue, of Eli Davis, & of Patrick Goings, & asked to be discharged from the further consideration of the same.

Senate: 1-Message was received from the Hse/o Reps announcing the death of the Hon Pierre E Bossier, a Rep from the state of Louisiana; who died last night, after a long & lingering illness, which had been borne with calmness & fortitude that became the Christian. The Senate will attend the funeral tomorrow at 12 o'clock meridian. He died at his lodgings last night in Wash City. He was a native of La, of French descent, his family being among the earliest settlers of the colony.

Circuit Court-Wash: Tue. Trial in which Emily Blue, a colored woman, sued John & Mary Williams & Wm S Colquhoun to obtain her freedom. The jury returned a verdict for the dfndnts.

A gentleman from Westmoreland named Mertland, drowned himself yesterday by jumping into the Alleghany river from the upper bridge. –Pittsburg Chronicle

Insolvent debtors applying to be discharged from imprisonment: Chas Kiernan & Wm D Bell. –Wm Brent, clk

For sale, valuable lands in Prince Wm & Fairfax Counties, Va. In Pr Wm Co, one tract of land on *Little Bull Run*, containing about 600 acres, believed to be now occupied by C C Marstelle. A tract of 127 acres, believed occupied by Howson Pinn, in the neighborhood of Bethlehem Meeting house. One other tract nearby containing about 240 acres, believed occupied by Walter Woodyard. One other tract called *Bradley*, containing about 1,376 acres, believed to be occupied by Alex Howison. One tract adjoining *Bradley*, containing 10 acres, occupied by Alex Howison. One tract containing about 80 acres, adjoining *Hazel Plain*, the former residence of Bernard Hooe, dec'd, & believed now occupied by Jas Robinson. In Fairfax Co: tract of land on Cub Run, containing about 658 acres, believed to be now occupied by Warren Croson. One other tract called *Wood Lawn* containing about 358 acres, believed to be occupied by Garrett Freeman. One other tract containing about 477 acres, believed to be occupied by Jas Fewell. Mr Thos B Gaines, who resides near to Haymarket, Pr Wm Co, will show the lands. –Bernard Hooe, John Powell, Com'rs of sale. After the above sale, I will offer a tract of land in Pr Wm Co, containing about 1,100 acres; about 35 miles from Alexandria. –Bernard Hooe

Decease of another member of Congress. Hon Mr Bossier, of Louisiana, died on Wed, & his funeral will take place today.

Hon Irby Hudson, of Eatonton, Geogia, for many years Speaker of the House of Reps of Ga, died at his residence in that town on Apr 13.

An expedition under the superintendence of the Jesuits of the St Louis Univ will leave St Louis for the Rocky Mountains about the last of the present month. Those wishing to take a trip to the mountains, for health or pleasure, are invited to join it.

Geo Melcher, jr, the late Cashier of the Commercial Bank of Portsmouth, N H, has been prosecuted by the Bank. Some time since it was discovered that the books of the Bank had been mutilated; & it appearing that $20,000 has been purloined.

Mrd: on Apr 23, by Rev Mr Van Horseigh, Mr Wm McCarthey to Miss Catherine Johnson, both of Wash City.

Mrd: on Apr 22, by Rev French S Evans, Mr Henry Beall to Miss Matilda Ann, d/o Thos J Belt, all of Wash City.

For rent: 2 comfortable dwlgs. Apply to Sam McKenney, or to Mr Osborn, next door east of the post ofc, Bridge st, Gtwn.

SAT APR 27, 1844
To let, well finished house containing 8 rooms. Apply to Robt Keyworth.

Beautiful Shoes & Boots for sale. —Walter Clarke & Son

$100 reward for runaway negro man Dony Barney, age 23. He was purchased by me from the estate of Thos C Reeves, near Bryantown, Chas Co, Md. He has a father & other relations in that neighborhood. —Benedict Gough, Chaptico, Md

The funeral of the Hon Mr Bossier took place in the Catholic Church, in the faith of which he lived. The sermon was delivered by Rev Mr Ryder.

Mrd: on Apr 15, in Fred'k Co, Md, by Rev Thos D Hoover, Mr Abraham Barnhart to Miss Amanda Hurdle, both of Fred'k Md.

Mrd: on Apr 22, by Rev Thos D Hoover, at Harper's Ferry, Va, Mr Wm McLaughlin to Miss Mahaley Blue, all of Jefferson Co, Va.

Mrd: on Apr 25, in Alexandria, D C, at Mr Edw Smith's, by Rev Benj A Young, Chas H Ross, of Balt, Md, to Clarissa A, d/o the late Gen Jesse Green, of Concord, Delaware.

Died: on Fri last, at his residence in Gettysburg, Pa, the Hon Geo Barnitz, aged 74.

Died: at *Blantyre*, the residence of her mother, in Fauquier Co, Va, of consumption, Janet Henderson, d/o the late Richd H & Orra M Henderson, in her 15th year. [No death date-current item.]

Died: on Mar 27, in Fred'k, Md, in her 42nd year, Ellen L, w/o Thos Turner, formerly of Gtwn, D C.

Carroll Co Court, Apr Term, 1844. Caleb Price vs Mortico Merryman, Philip Gore, & Saml Myers. On Apr 4, 1844, Michl Hoffman, the purchaser at the sale made by John Krantz, constable of Carroll Co, under the writ of fieri facias issued by Jacob Kerlinger, give notice to Philip Gore, who now resided in the Territory of Iowa, that he is to appear in this court, either in person or by solicitor, on or before Jul 1 next, to show cause, if any, why the said sale shall not be ratified & confirmed.
—Thos B Dorsey, T H Wilkinson, Nicholas Brew. —Jacob Shower, clk

Insolvent debtor, Thos N Davis, has applied to be discharged from imprisonment.
-Wm Brent, clk

MON APR 29, 1844
Thos Marsh, indicted for the murder of Phebe Cheddick, at Newark, N J, was submitted to the jury on Fri, & they came into the court with a verdict of not guilty.

Boilers in the Pa Rolling Mill, at Pittsburg, exploded on Tue last, & Thos Updegraff, engineer, on duty at the time, was severely scalded & died in a few hours.

House of Reps:: 1-Claim of Hiram Burnham, of Saline, Mich, for services. 2-Claim of Capt Francis Ceohe, of Detroit, for damages done by the Indians during the last war. 3-Ptn of Elisha Morrell, administrator of Jos Icard, dec'd, for the payment of Icard's proportion of money awarded to the owner of the ship **Carlos**, withheld to satisfy a claim of the U S against John S Roulet, another joinr owner of said ship.

Rev Mr Carey, whose admission into the Protestant Episcopal Church occasioned so much excitement in N Y during the last year, died recently on the passage to the Havana, whither he was going in pursuit of health. He was a young man of extraordinary attainments in his profession, & of rare ability.

Died: on Thu last, suddenly at Uniontown, Pa, L W Stockton, Pres of the Nat'l Road Stage Co.

Died: on Apr 11, at Havana, Dayton Williamson, late Cmder in the U S Navy. He visited the Island of Cuba for the benefit of health, & appeared while in Havana to convalesce rapidly. He left Havana for Guinea, about 45 miles in the interior, & grew rapidly worse. He was attacked with hemorrhage of the lungs, which was succeeded by an effusion of water, & he died.

Died: on Mar 30, at Key West, Fla, Lt Benj C Edes, of 6th Regt U S Infty. He had just returned from Havana, where he had been for the improvement of his health.

Died: on Apr 24, after an illness of 4 days, of scarlet fever, Alice, only d/o Chas S & Lavinia Wallace, aged 2 years & 5 months.

On Jan 21, at New Hartford, some young people went on the Farmington river, Conn, for a short sail, & the boat upset. Caroline Harris, age 19, was drowned.

Stray cow came to the subscriber's farm, near Benning's bridge, on the Eastern Branch, last Sun. Owner is to come forward, prove property, pay charges, & take her away. –Henry Miller

Improved property for sale: farme house with spacious lot, on I st, in Wash City. Apply to D A Hall, Pa ave, over W B Todd's Hat store.

New Family Grocery Store: recently occupied by Messrs Boteler, Donn & Co, south side of Pa ave. –Wm M Randolph

To let: house on Pa ave, between 3rd & 4½ sts. Also, a 2 story brick house on G st, between 12th & 13th sts. Apply to Geo Mattingly.

Delegates to the Whig Young Men's Convention of Ratification on Tue at Concert Hall. List of Delegates appointed by the Clay Club of Wash:

Wm D Acken	L C Brown	J H B Beck
Jas Adie	A Baldwin	B Burns, jr
Jos Abott	J A Bender	E L Birch
Thos Ambler	C W Boteler	Joy Benjamin
Saml t Ashby	C W Boteler, jr	P Ball
W Adams	Wm Bates	Jos B Bryan
Jos Anthony	Thos Boyle	Robt Bassett
G Anderson	J R Bailey	Fred Bates
Richd Adams	Cornelius Boyle	A B Claxton
A R Allen	John C Brent	Geo Collard
J Alexander	H J Brent	John Cullum
Jas Allen	Saml Bacon	Patrick Crowley
Jos H Bradley	P F Bacon	John F Coyle
Henry Bradley	Chas Bell	Andrew Coyle, jr
C Bestor	J A Bender, jr	J H Chezum
J A Blake	Isaac Beers	Jas Clephane
W S Burch	Jos W Beck	Chris Cammack
Jos Bryan	Jas Bowen	Jas T Crossfield
W B Burger	Benj F Bailey	Judson S Clagett
R R Burr	Thos Bernard	Darius Clagett
R W Burr	W A Bradley	John B Clagett
T S Burr	C Buckingham	Geo Cochran
Saml Burche	E F Buckingham	Henry Carter
R W Burche	Levi C Bootes	W M Clarke
S F Burche	John T Ball	G C Collins
WW Birth	Wm Bird	Peter Callan
L S Beck	P B Bell	J M Carlisle
Marshall Brown	A Butler	H L Cross
Richd Butt	Wm Blanchard	H Cruttenden
Wm Banter	V Blanchard	Geo Crandall
Saml Butt	J Beardsley	Wm Clarke
Wm Burroughs	Jas Becker	John Clarke
Dr Jos Borrows	Tillotson Brown	Jas Charles
Wm F Bayly	Jas H Birch	N Callan, jr
Edw W Brown	E W Brevett	W Cooper, jr
R W Bates	Wash Berry, jr	Danl Campbell
John Bates	Chas Bishop	A H Clements
P H Brooks	Thos Blagden	J T Catlett
John Bowen	Thos W Burch	J B Chezum
Gustavus Bell	Jos A Burch	L B Cooper
P W Browning	J P Boss	W S Cleary

Wm Colquhoun	Wm Easby	D A Gardiner
Robt Clarke	J W Eckloff	W F Gardiner
R H Combs	Josiah Essex	Wm Grimes
Elijah Craven	Ch Eckloff	John Grimes
Henry A Clarke	F Edmonston	R L Glover
D B Clarke	C C Eckloff	J B Harrison
Robt Cruit	Wm P Eliot	J H Hewitt
Dr F Dawes	Frad Eckloff	Isaac Hall
Wm T Dove	J B Eaton	B Hall
T S Donoho	Rezin Estep	W Hellen
J O P Degges	Jas Ellis	S Holmes
W H Degges	Chas Edmonston	G W Harkness
R H Degges	M G Emery	S Hyatt
Dr A McD Davis	Evan Evans	J L Henshaw
R W Dyer	S C Espy	J C Harkness
E C Dyer	N Edmonston	N Hammond
Jacob Durff	Wm R Franklin	T W Howard
C Denham	R Farnham	J Z Hartt
Z W Denham	John Fill	J W Henderson
Saml Duvall	J B Ford	Jas F Haliday
Saml Devaughn	Robt B Fowler	Jos Harbaugh
Jos Downing	R France	L Harbaugh
Terrence Drury	Jos Fallansbee	D A Hall
Wm Downing	S P Franklin	R M Harrison
F W Dawes	J W Ferguson	G W Hinton
Saml Douglass	Geo W Fales	Thos F Harkness
M Delany	W R Fales	Wm E Howard
Willard Drake	T C Farquhar	Wm Hoover
Wm G Deale	Danl Fister	Wm Harriss
W J Douglass	H S M Farnam	Danl Harkness
H Dallman	Henry J Fossett	V Harbaugh
John Dufief	A Fuller, jr	John Hand
J Y David	R Fitzhugh	Nelson Henning
J Deeble	P Finnegan	Geo Humes
John M Donn	E H Fuller	B Henning
Oliver Donn	Z D Gilman	A Holmead
Marc Dubant	W H Gunnell	Saml Hoover
J M Dorsett	B T Greenfield	Edw Hall
H M Dallinger	J H Gibbs	Thos Havenner
Joel Downer	R Griffith	E G Handy
Wm Durr	C Goddard	Jas S Harvey
Wm Dennison	J R Grimes	A S Harvey
J T Dennison	J T Given	Henry Hay
P M Deritt	G S Gideon	Jas Hepburn

John Hoover	Basil Lee	H Nailor
John Hodgson	A Lazenby	Chirs O'Neale
Jas S Hall	J E Lewis	Wm Orme
T Hurdle	Saml Lewis	Thos Owens
Gustavus Hill	D Moore	S J Ober
J Hollige	F McCarthy	R Patten
Wm Harford	W McCarthy	Wm T Porter
R M Hanson	H H McPherson	G H Plant
Dr R F Huntt	Jas Mankin	R S Patterson
Wm Hodge	Z L McElfresh	S Parker
Geo Hartman	J B Morgan	A Perry
P Havenner	T P Morgan	W M Perry
S Havenner	W J McCormick	Geo W Palmer
Jas Hollingshead	C McNamee	Jos Pilling
J B Holmead	N L Milburn	John Plant
S W Handy	John W Martin	M T Parker
John Holmead	Wm B Magruder	Denton Potter
E T Ingraham	G C Morgan	A B Proctor
Fred Iddins	Geo Moore	Geo W Phillips-
H Janney	C D McPherson	[Cap Hill]
C L Jones	John McClelland	Jas B Phillips
C H James	Dr J F May	Jos Pleasants
Wm Johnson	Henry May	W H Perkins
P H King	Hugh McCormick	J M Pierce
F A Klopfer	Chas Miller	John Purdy
R S Kinsley	J C McKelden	John Peabody
W A Kennedy	B F Middleton	A Provest
Jas King	John E Morse	Dr J R Piper
Jos Klunk	W E Morcoe	T A Provest
Chas Klunk	R M Milburn	John M Porter
J H Kirkwood	A McCormick	Geo Patten
Wm B Kibbey	J U Moulder	Geo W Palmer
V King	D McLelland	F B Posten
A Kirkwood	J F Maher	F Pistorius
Edw Klopfer	A McWilliams	Jas V Patten
F King	Jas Marshall	M Riordan
Danl Kealey	Edw McKenny	B W Reed
Walter Lenox	F Mattingly	R J Roach
W Linkins	John Moore	J G Robinson
F B Lord	Col McLeod	Fayette Ringgold
Jas Leach	Jas I Martin	Eph Richmond
J A Linton	W H Moore	W M Randolph
Thos Lewis	Jas Nokes	E Rodbird
Wm Lord	Geo S Noyes	G A W Randall

Jos A Ratcliffe	F Spicer	David Vann
John Reitz	S Shelton	W H Upperman
Wm H Stewart	M H Stevens	R C Wrightman
Thos Sessford	John T Towers	T H Weightman
Thos Stanley	Enoch Tucker	Jas Williams
John A Smith	Edw Turner	J H T Werner
L Stegagnini	Lemuel Towers	C H Wiltberger
H W Sweeting	Wm B Todd	R C Washington
Jas Skirving	Andrew Tate	G Watterston
Edw Simms	Henry Taylor	Saml W Walker
Wm Samuels	Wm Towers	Wm A Williams
W W Stewart	Jos Thompson	Wm Wise
Wm B Sasscer	B O Tayloe	Milton M Ward
Geo W Stewart	Wm Thompson	C P Wannall
Jos Smoot	Jas M Towers	J Wilson
Jos Stanley	Jos B Tate	W Henry Winter
R H Stewart	R Tonge	J T Walker
T F Semmes	T Tonge	W Wilson
Geo Savage	Wm Thompson-carpenter	C Woodward
Saml Stott		C F Wood
H C Stewart	John Thompson	R Wright
B O Shekells	Wm Tabler	R Wallach
Chas H Sherman	Jacob Tabler	T M Wright
Gerard Stith	Frank Taylor	Wm Wallis
And Sessford	J Tonge	Wm Waters
Jos Semmes	Wm Thorn	Jas L White
Dr J Smoot	T L Thurston	J A Wise
Henry Smoot	S W Tucker	Saml Wroe
Chas Smoot	John H Thorn	J Williams
Luther Smoot	Elias Travers	A Williams
Walter Stuart	John Thompson	A Wallingsford
John M Stuart	G E W Thompson	M Worden
John V Shields	Thos Tench	Edw Warner
Geo Smith	Mathew Thomas	W Whitney
R E Simms	Wm Thompson-cabinet maker	Jos Williamson
J H Simms		John West
Alexius Simms	B Verdan	Thos Young
G Stettinius	L Vivans	

TUE APR 30, 1844
Five stray cows came to the subscriber's farm, on the Wash & Rockville turnpike road, about 4 miles from Wash City. Owner is to come forward, prove property, pay charges, & take them away. –Henry Ould

Senate: 1-Ptn from Deborah Mason, for renewal of her pension. 2-Ptn from Nancy Smith, wid/o a soldier, praying for a pension. 3-Ptn from Robt Milles, asking an examination of a plan devised by him for faciliting trigonometrical surveys. 4-Cmte of Claims recommended the passage of: act for the relief of Saml B Folger; of Saml B Tuck; & of Geo M Jones.

Orphans Court of Wash Co, D C. Letters testamentary on the personal estate of John H Howell, late of said county, dec'd. —A P Skinner, Gabriel Moran, excs

Died: on Apr 29, John Hughes, a native of the county of Momohan, Ireland, & for the last 25 years a resident of Wash City, aged 67 years. His funeral is today at 4 o'clock, from his son's residence, corner of G & 2nd sts north.

Died: on Apr 29, of pulmonary consumption, Mrs Maria Smith, w/o Wm Smith, aged 36 years. Her funeral will take place this afternoon at 3 o'clock, from her late residence on 9th st.

Insolvent debtor, Gaylord Meachan, has applied to be discharged from imprisonment. —Wm Brent, clk

WED MAY 1, 1844
Senate: 1-Ptn from John Cocke, asking to be allowed, in the settlement of his accounts as a com'r for treating with the Cherokee Indians, money advanced by him. 2-Cmte of Claims: adverse report on the House bill for the relief of Alborne Allen, of Mass. Same cmte: bill for the relief of Geo Harrison & his securities: read a second time. 3-Postponed the orders to take up the bill for the relief of David Robb, of Ohio. 4-Bill for the relief of W R Davis: ordered to be engrossed. 5-Bills considered in the Cmte of the Whole & ordered to be engrossed: bill for the relief of Hiram March; of Ephraim D Dickson; of Henry Newman; of Jos Campau; of Geo Duval & other Cherokees. Bill authorizing a patent to be issued to Jos Campau, for a certain tract of land in the State of Michigan.

Messrs Flinn & Kaine, editors of the Pittsburg Aurora, have been fined $50 & $75, & sentenced to 3 months' imprisonment each, for calling, in their paper, Judge Grier an ass.

Miss Laforest, d/o Mrs Laforest, the actress, is seriously ill at her mother's residence in Phil, of severe shock which her nerves received several days since, from undergoing what is termed a shock of animal magnetism.

Maryland: appointments by the Gov'r of Md: John A Carter, to be Clerk of Montg Co Court, vice Brice Selby, dec'd. Wm A Gilpin, to be Register of Wills for Cecil Co, vice Henry D Miller, dec'd.

Pensacola, Apr 20. A naval general court martial will convene at the Navy Yard on May 22, for the trial of Lts John W West & R C Cogdell.

On Mon last Rev Mr Colton, at Fayetteville, N C, was lacerated when a bottle filled with some combustible matter exploded. On the same evening, Mr Jas Campbell, of Fayetteville, was thrown from a restive horse & killed. He was about 50 years of age, & has left a wife & 4 children. –Observer

House of Reps: 1-Ptn of Thos Williams, of De Kalb Co, Ala; also, of John Duncan, of Jackson Co, Ala; also, of Obadiah M Binge, of De Kalb Co, Ala, for Revolutionary pensions. 2-Ptn of Mrs Knight, widow & executrix of Simeon Knight, dec'd, asking the settlement of the accounts of her husband as late quartermaster general.

Insolvent debtor, Philip Miller, has applied to be discharged from imprisonment. -Wm Brent, clk

Died: on Apr 30, Noble Felice, s/o martin & Angelina R King, aged 3 years. His funeral is this afternoon, at 4 o'clock.

Wash Library Co elected a Board of Dirs for the ensuing year on Apr 1:
Peter Force, Pres
Z W Denham, Treas
J F Haliday, Sec

Directors:
John Sessford
Robt P Anderson
Jas C McGuire
John F Harkness

THU MAY 2, 1844
Senate: 1-Ptn from the heirs of Geo White of the Revolutionary army, asking to be allowed commutation to which their ancestors were entitled. 2-Bills passed: relief of Henry Newman; of Ephraim D Dickson; of Hiram March; of Jos Campau; of Wm R Davis; of Geo Duval & other Cherokees. Bill authorizing a patent to be issued to Jos Camapu, for a certain tract of land in Michigan.

Execution of Rosanna Kean. This wretched girl was executed at Bridgeton, Cumberland Co, N J, last Fri, for poisoning the family of Mr Seeley last autumn.

In Chancery: Circuit Court of Wash Co, D C, Mar Term, 1844. Geo Peter, vs David Peter's heirs at law. Geo W Peter, the trustee in the above cause, reported the re-sale by him of *Mill Seat*, containing 27 acres, 2 roods, & 18 perches, which the late John Laird had previously purchased of the late Thos Peter, the former trustee, & for whose default the same was ordered by the Court to be re-sold, Richd Butt became the purchaser for $1,122.66. –W Brent, clk

House of Reps: 1-Ptn of Anna Yerrington, of Salem, Conn, praying for a pension.

Died: on Apr 27, Marian Lenthall, infant d/o Elexius Simms.

Md Whig Gubernational Convention: Delegates to the Convention:
Alleghany Co: John Hoye, Leonard Shircliff, Ed McCarty, Jas H Hoblitzell, Henry Bruce.
Wash Co: John Miller, T E Buchanan, Elias Davis, J D Romain, Horace Risley
Fred'k Co: L P Balch, Griffin Taylor, Robt Annan, Dr J Baer, Francis Brengle, Richd Coale
Carroll Co: Joshua C Gist, M G Cockey, W Shepard, John Wadlow, Jonas Deal
Anne Arundel Co: Thos S Alexander, R Sellman, C S W Dorsey, A Randall, B E Gantt, C R Stewart
Chas Co: Walter M Miller, P W Crain, John Hughes, J J Jenkins
Montg Co: Ephraim Gaither, Phil Biays, R J Bowie, John Poole, Dr T Pool
Balt City: Peter Fenby, N L Wood, A W Bradford, Asa Needham, B C Ross, C H Pitts
Balt Co: W W Keyser, W Tagart, Jas Turner, Josiah Marsh, F A Gatch, E G Kilbourne
Queen Ann's Co: John Brown, J B Spencer, Mathias George, Dr Saml Harper
Dorchester Co: Jas Thompson, Jos R Eccleston, J R Keene, J R Martin, H L McNamara
Somerset Co: Edw Long, J B Rider, John Turner, Danl Ballard, Jas Brittingham, J R Handy
Worcester Co: Teagle Townsend, Zadock P Henry, Dr W R Selby, Edw Lambdin, Dr J S Martin
Caroline Co: Abraham Jump, John Nichols, Jacob C Wilson, Wm Hardcastle
Cecil Co: Jas L Craig, J H Jamar, John Janney, Lewis S Todd John B Yarnall
Kent Co: Jas B Ricaud, Geo Vickers, Wm Maffitt, W S Constable
Talbot Co: T R Lockerman, John Harrington, Geo T Tilghman, G Dudley
PG Co: R L Jenkins, Jas Harper, Saml Arnold, Truman Belt, G W Duvall
St Mary's Co: John W Bennett, W Coad, J M Causin, B I Heard
Harford Co: H W Archer, Dr J Montgomery, G W Bradford, W B Bond, F T Amos
Calvert Co: G W Weems, T J Helen, J G Mackall, A R Sollers

Old Capitol Boarding House: corner of Capitol square: table supplied with the best the market affords. Terms reasonable. -H V Hill

Extensive sale of greenhouse & ornamental flowering shrubs at auction, on Sat next, at the greenhouse of Mr Wm Buist. –R W Dyer & Co, aucts

FRI MAY 3, 1844
Farmland for sale: about 200 acres, part of the *Glenn Ross Farm* in Montg Co, Md. Inquire of R L Ross, *Glenn Ross*, or Geo Taylor, Genr'l Land Ofc.

Chancery sale: by decree of the Circuit Court of Wash Co, D C, in the matter of John King, cmplnt, against Jas Marshall, adm, & the heirs at law of Geo Webster, dec'd, dfndnts: sale on Jun 6, of *Chichester*, lying on the east side of Anacostia river, beginning at the n w corner of Nathl Brady's lot, purchased out of the same tract: surveyed & plotted by Davis on Nov 24, 1828, & all the interest & estate of Geo Webster at the time of his decease, which has descended to his heirs at law in & to the same. –Richd Wallach, trustee

Boarding: Mrs Cecilia Smith, 5 Louisiana Ave, & 7th st.

Wash Corp: 1-Cmte of Claims: asking to be discharged from the further consideration of the ptn of M P Mohun: discharged accordingly. 2-Ptn of R J Morsell & others, praying for a gravel footway near Vt ave & L st: referred to the Cmte on Improvements. 3-Ptn of P Kinchy & others, for the improvement of G st, from 14th to 15th sts: referred to the Cmte on Improvements. 4-Ptn of A Carothers & others, praying the curbstone to be set in fromt of square 320 on 11th st, between F & G sts: referred to the Cmte in Improvements. 5-Cmte of Claims: ptn of Wm Campbell, reported a bill for his relief: passed. Same cmte: asking to be discharged from the further consideration of the ptn of A Shaw. Same cmte: asking to be discharged from the further consideration of the ptn of Geo T McGlue, on Apr 22, was taken up & agreed to. 6-Ptn of Jas Cox, for remission of a fine: referred to the Cmte of Claims.

House of Reps: 1-Cmte on Revolutionary Claims: bill for the relief of Mary M Talfair. Same cmte: adverse report on the ptn of Archibald D Palmer. Same cmte: bill for the relief of Francis Christien & widow Baptiste Berard. 2-Cmte on Indian Affairs: Act for the relief of F A Kerr, with amendment. 3-Cmte on Military Affairs: Act for the relief of Caroline E Clitherall, wid/o Dr Geo C Clitherall, late a surgeon in the U S Army: recommended that it do not pass. 4-Cmte on Naval Affairs: Act for the relief of Jas M McIntosh, a cmder in the U S Navy: recommended that said bill do not pass. 5-Cmte on Naval Affairs: adverse report on the claim of Thos W Jordan. 6-Cmte on Foreign Affairs: ptn for the release of all American prisoners at *Van Dieman's Land*, was unanimously adopted. Resolved, that the Pres of the U S be requested to interpose his good ofcs with the British Gov't for the release of Benj Mott, of Alburg, Vt, Saml Newcome, of Cheteauguav, N Y, & all otherAmerican prisoners at *Van Dieman's Land*. 7-Cmte on Revolutionary Pensions: bill for the relief of Susannah Warner. Same cmte: bill for the relief of Marcey Olds, wid/o John Stewart. 8-Cmte on Public Lands: bill for the relief of Stanly White, without amendment.

Abraham Bishop, a venerable citizen of New Haven, died on Sun. He was a graduate of Yale College in 1778, in which also graduated Joel Barlow, the poet, Minister of France; Josiah Meigs, Pres of the Georgia Univ; Chief Justice Zephaniah Swift, Senator Uriah Tracy, Noah Webster, & Gov Oliver Wolcott. Mr Bishop was a descendant of one of the small band who broke the silence of the wilderness with the woodman's axe, to prepare for the settlement of the town of New Haven; & we believe that all his ancestors lived upon the spot where he died, a venerable mansion on the corner of Elm & State st.

Mobile, Apr 24. Chas Steele, jr, who was waylaid & beaten some 2 months since, died on Mon last at his father's residence on the Spring Hill road, having never recovered from his wounds. -Advertiser

Died: yesterday, after a lingering & painful illness, Mr Horatio Hagan, a native of Ireland, but for many years a respectable resident of Wash City. His funeral will take place at St Peter's Church this afternoon at half past 3 o'clock.

For rent: the house occupied by Mr Jas Owner, on Va ave, a short distance from Mr Danl Carroll's; or the house nearly opposite Mr Watterston's. Both are supplied with good water. Inquire at the house on Va ave.

A free colored man, Chas Adams, was killed on Mon, at Balt, by the explosion of a soda fountain in the Mineral Water establishment of Mr Randall, under Barnum's Hotel. He died a few minutes after the explosion from severe lacerations on the neck & throat.

SAT MAY 4, 1844
Saml J Burr has been appointed by the Pres, & confirmed by the Senate, to be Sec of the Territory of Iowa.

Among the passengers in the packet ship **Siddons**, which sailed from N Y on Mon for Liverpool, was Col Saml Moore.

Senate: 1-Ptn from Ephraim Whitaker, for a pension. 2-Ptn from John Stone, for a pension. 3-Cmte of Claims: bills for the relief of Ephraim D Dickson; & of Wm R Davis, reported the same without amendment.

Valuable farm for sale: in compliance with a decree of the Circuit Court of Alexandria Co, D C: sale on May 15 next, of the farm on which Thos Thompson now resides, lying near Ball's x roads, [it being the land mentioned in said decree,] belonging to the heirs of the late John A Somers. Contains 186 acres with a good farm house. –John Dulin, Com'r Also, at the same time & place, will be sold under a decree of said Court, a tract of land near the above, late the property of Matilda Mason, dec'd, containing 150 acres

Organization & proceeding of the convention at Canton: Rev Mr Bascom, of Ky opened with a prayer. Mr T Yates Walsh, on behalf of the Cmte of Two Delegates from each State in the Union, then proposed the following ofcrs to preside at the Convention: Pres: Jno M Clayton, of Dela Vice-Presidents:

E P Burbank, of Maine	Dr Doyle, of Louisiana
Geo T Davis, of Mass	P L Edwards, of Mo
W W Boardman, of Conn	John Preston, jr, of Ark
Portus Baxter, of Vt	Wm Rollston, of Ala
Jas N Reynolds, of N Y	R C Weightman, of D C
H W Archer, of Md	Wm S Patton, of R I
John Berley, of N H	J W Miller, of N H
Edw Stanly, of N C	T M T McKennan, of Pa
Geo S Bryson, of S C	Jas Lyons, of Va
Wm Belt, of Ohio	Wm C Smedes, of Miss
Francis F Chambers, of Ky	Gen C Jones, of Tenn
John J Hardin, of Ill	Thos Butler King, of Ga
A S Williams, of Mich	

Secretaries:

Jos Baker, of Maine	Robt A Dobbin, of Md
Geo Dawson, of N Y	Edw D Freeman, of N C
D C Wickliffe, of Ky	J H Strong, of Ark

Balt, May 1, 1844: The ofc of announcing the result of the Convention has been assigned to us: John McPherson Berrien, J Burnet, Erastus Root, Abbott Lawrence, Wm S Archer.

For sale or rent: 4 story stone Warehouse of the subscriber, on G st & Potomac, below Gtwn: building is about 100 x 50 feet. One of the best wharfs on the river belongs to the property. –T W Pairo

Circuit Court of Wash Co, D C-in Chancery. Rose Ann McGuire, vs Thos C Miller, et al. The cmplnt's bill charges that on May 24, 1836, the dfndnt Miller bought from Geo Peter, surviving exc & trustee of the will of David Peter, dec'd, square 149 & lot 14 in square 13 in Wash City, & for part of the purchase money gave his bonds with Wm Hayman as surety, each for $51.21, on interest from said date, the legal title being retained by said Peter as a further security; that said bonds remain unpaid & judgments have been had thereon, on the common law side of this court, against said Hayman, with costs, amounting to $25.04 or thereabouts, which judgments are incumbrances on real estate held by said Hayman at the date thereof, & which he has subsequently conveyed to, or for the security of, the cmplnt & others. One object of said bill is to enforce the equitable lien of said Geo Peter, for the benefit & relief of cmplnt, by a resale of the property so sold to said Miller, to satisfy said judgment. It appears that Thos C Miller resides & is out of D C, & he is to appear in court & answer said bill, on or before Sep 5 next. –Jas S Morsell -Wm Brent, Clk -C Cox, for cmplnt.

$100 reward for runaways, Tom-about 40 –45, & his wife Judy, 19 years of age. Jacquelin A Marshall, Robt Douthats, living at *Leed's Manor*, Fauquire Co, Va

MON MAY 6, 1844
Death of Fred'k S Agate, an artist of amiable character & fine talents. His pictures of the Dead Child, Metamora, Ugolino, & the Old Oaken Bucket, all possess a remarkable degree that purity of feeling so characteristic of his own mind. He was born at Sparta, Winchester Co, N Y, in 1807; at 13 he was under the tuition of that veteran teacher John R Smith, & then became a pupil of S F B Morse, Pres of the Nat'l Academy of Design. In 1834 he sailed for Europe & studied for some time in Italy, since then he has been a resident of this city, & at his death was an Academician & Curator of the Nat'l Academy of Design. –N Y Evening Post

David McDaniel was found guilty in the U S Circuit Court of St Louis, for participation in the robbery & murder of Charvis, the Santa Fe trader. This is the third prisoner convicted in this case. It was submitted to the jury on Apr 25.

Danl Kelly, residing in Buckingham, Pa, came to his death on Fri while engaged quarrying limestone, when a keg of powder accidentally exploded.

House of Reps: 1-Ptn of Shelton Felton, of Troy, N Y, praying for a pension: also praying for compensation for losses sustained in the last war. 2-Ptn of Zachariah Lawrence, of Ohio, praying for compensation for the capture of the British ship **Venture** in 1813. 3-Ptn of Wm Pitman, a soldier of the last war, asking for a pension.

Died: Thu last, at Alexandria, after a long & painful illness, Mr Augustine Newton, aged 56 years, leaving a bereaved widow & 6 children. His was a man of few words, distinguished amid his compeers for purity & charity of thought, word & deed.

Died: on May 3, in his 53rd year, after a long & protracted illness, Mr Jos Warren, at his late residence, about 4½ miles from Wash City, to which place he recently moved. He was an old & respectable citizen, & for many years was the chief messenger in the Dept of State.

Executor's sale of real estate: on May 13, on square 449, near the Poor house, for & on account of the estate of the late Fred'k Hall, of Wash City, dec'd, viz:
In square 69, lot 4   In square 411, lot 2, west half
In square 370, lot 2   In square 539, lot 2
In square 424, lot 2   In square 484, lot 3
In square 449, lots 1 thru 5, 15 thru 24
The title to these lots is believed to be perfect. –Danl W Hall, David A Hall, excs

Insolvent debtor, John J Wilkins, [negro] has applied to be discharged from imprisonment. –Wm Brent, clk

Balt, May 3. Arrival of the U S steamer **Union**, yesterday. List of her ofcrs:
Lt Commanding, H H Bell
1st Lt, Roger Perry
Acting Master, A D Harrell
Chief Engineer, Wm P Williamson
Purser, Chas Murray
Passed Assist Surgeon, Jas M Minor
Passed Midshipmen: M B Woolsey, Chas Deas
Capt's Clerk, J W Marshall
1st Assist Engineers, Levi Griffin, Wm Taggert
2nd Assist Engineers: Wm D Young, Jno M Middleton

Boarding: Mrs J C Turner, 6th st, between E & F sts. Terms accommodating.

$5 reward for return of strayed large red cow. –Adam C Brown, living near Bladensburg.

TUE MAY 7, 1844
Newark Daily Advertiser: Theodore Frelinghuysen is descended from the Rev Theodorus J Frelinghuysen, who emigrated to this country from Holland in 1720, & settled in Somerset Co. He is said to have been a great blessing to the Reformed Dutch Church of America. He left 5 sons, ministers, & 2 dghts, who married ministers. One of his sons, the Rev John Frelinghuysen, was pastor of the Church of the Millstone, [as his father was,] & died in 1754. A monument still remains to his memory in the graveyard at Somerville. His son Gen Fred'k Frelinghuysen, [the father of the present Chancellor] was born in 1753, & only 22 when sent by N J to the Continental Congress, which place he resigned in 1777. He was elected to the U S Senate in 1793, & resigned in 1796. He was appointed Maj Gen of Pa & N J, & rendered important military services to his country. He ranked among the purest citizens of his State, & died in 1804. He left 3 sons, of whom Theodore [the candidate for the Vice Presidency] only survives. He was born at Millstone, Somerset Co, N J, in 1787, & is 57 years of age. He graduated at Princeton College in 1804, the Hon Saml L Southard, Thos H Crawford, Geo Chambers, Jos R Ingersoll, & Pres Lindsley, of Nashville Univ, were among his classmates. He studied law with the late Richd Stockton, & admitted to practice in 1808. In 1839 he was selected Chancellor over the Univ of N Y C, which station he now occupies.

Died: on Apr 26, in Albany, Hon Rufus Palen, of Fallsburg, Sullivan Co, N Y, aged 37 years. He was a member of the 26th Congress from Ulster & Sullivan, & was universally beloved & respected for his unobtrusive worth, & his kindness.

Information wanted of Mrs Sarah P More & Ann E A Thomas who came into this county early in last Apr, from Wash City vicinity in search of relatives, thought to be residing here, & on Apr 9, at Hickory, separated, & have not since heard of each other. Mrs Thomas is at present at the residence of Mr John Wolf, sr, in Canton township, & would be deeply grateful for any information in regard to the whereabouts of her sister. –Wash [Pa] Reporter

Phil Chronicle: railroad collision on Sat 4 miles below Havre de Grace: the Phil & Balt trains collided. A brakeman, Jas Russell, belonging to Wilmington, Dela, & a fireman, Jas Merritt, of Balt, wer killed. Mr Chas Hill, of Balt, one of the conductors, had a leg broken & subsequently amputated. Several distinguished citizens were in the Balt train, Hon Danl Webster & Mr Graham, of N Y C. [May 8th newspaper: among the injured: Mr Crosby, of Columbus, Ohio, leg bruised; J F Welsh, of Ill, head cut; G W Reeves, Sumerville, Tenn, legs, head & side bruised; Mr Durald, U S Navy, shoulder & legs bruised; P Brown, West Phil, legs & side bruised; S Schenck, Auburn, N Y, legs cut; J W Lutz, Circleville, Ohio, one leg badly crushed; Mr Whitaker, of Northeast, Md, thigh bruised.]

Senate: 1-Ptn from Jos Smith, praying Congress to allow him to raise a company of armed volunteers, for protection of emigrants to the unsettled territories of the U S. 2-Ptn of Jas G Bell, asking the right of pre-emption to a certain tract of land in Louisiana. 3-Cmte of Pensions: adverse reports on the ptns of Sarah Cordoza, of John Stone, & of Martha Philips.

Died: on May 6, Mary Isabella, infant d/o John & Martha Wilson, aged 18 months & 16 days. Her funeral is on Tue, at 3½ o'clock, from the residence of her father, corner of N Y ave & 11th st.

Notice. Left his father's house on May 6, Jas W Stringfellow, who is about 14 years of age. Any information concerning him will be gratefully acknowledged by his afflicted parents.

WED MAY 8, 1844
Wash Corp: 1-Cmte of Claims: asking to be discharged from the further consideration of the ptn of Travis Evans: discharged accordingly. 2-Cmte on Improvements: asking to be discharged from the further consideration of the ptn of Mary Ann Ragan: discharged accordingly. 3-Relief of Wm Campbell: referred to the Cmte of Claims. 4-Bill for the relief of Capt Danl Paullin: laid on the table. 5-Cmte of Claims: bill for the relief of Wm M Maddox, reported the same without amendment. Same cmte: bill for the relief of Adam Dulany: indefinite postponement. Same cmte: bill for the relief of Wm Thorpe, was read. Same cmte: ptns of Saml Hoover & others, of Isaac Beers, of Patrick Robbins, & of Jas Cox: asking to be discharged from the further consideration of the ptns of the same: accordingly discharged.

Circuit Court of Wash Co, D C: Bernard McKenna vs Chas B Fisk. The jury returned a verdict for the dfndnt on Sat. The plntf brought an action of trespass against the dfndnt for the alleged destruction of the plntf's shanty & breaking up his business, on the occasion of the great disturbance on the line of the canal some years ago, when the military were called out to restore order, & when so many acts of violence were perpetrated by the insurgents.

House of Reps: 1-Ptns of John Cripps & David Johnston for pensions. 2-Ptn of Jos Parks, for an increase of pension. 3-Ptn of Richd Bland Randolph, of Va, praying for a pension on account of services rendered as an ofcr of the U S navy in the war of the Revolution. 4-Ptn of the widow Hannah Dubois, praying for a pension for services rendered by her dec'd husband in the late war.

Dreadful riot at Phil at Kensington on Mon. While the Native Americans of the 3rd Ward held a public meeting, a party of Irish took possession of their flag & destroyed it. Geo Shifler was almost instantly killed, a ball having passed through his head. J W Wright, a young man, was taken up dead, a ball having pierced his left breast. Nathan Ramsey, a blind-maker, received a shot through the breast bone, & was mortally wounded. Jas Cox was dangerously wounded in the groin. Chas Vanstavoren was dangerously wounded. Adam Boozer was shot in the arm; Patrick Fisher was shot in the forehead, not dangerously wounded.

Warren Roebock, well known among the sporting circles of Balt, committed suicide on Mon. He was standing in Light st, near Balt, talking with some friends. He then walked a few steps to a door stoop & shot himself with a pistol. He died in about 15 minutes. Coroner's inquest was held by Jacob D Hair. –American

A passenger by the name of Wherry died very suddenly in the public stage on Apr 24 while crossing a bridge at Louisville, Ky.

Phil, May 6. Mr W T Donaldson, mast maker, on Sat, in the yard attached to his dwlg, next to Coffin & Landell's factory, on Penn st, Kensington, a sudden flaw of wind struck the south side of the wall being erected, & precipitated the mass of bricks directly upon him, inflicting so severe an injury that he died yesterday. –U S Gaz

Mail robber arrested: Thos H Freeman, formerly postmaster at Carrolton, Mo, & who effected his escape while in custody of the Marshal last Nov, charged with having robbed the mail, has been recently arrested at London, Upper Canada, & escorted to Missouri for trial

J McDaniel, David McDaniel, & Jos Brown were sentenced on Sat week in St Louis to be hung on Jun 14 next. The sentence of Thos Towson was deferred. These persons have been convicted of the murder of Charvis on the Santa Fe road.

During Mr Kendall's sojourn in the City of Mexico, Mr Edgerton, an English painter, & a female who lived with him, were cruelly murdered. The assassins have been arrested & were executed on Apr 23 on the spot where the murder was committed. Several of the accessories were condemned to periods of imprisonment.

Mrd: on May 2, by Rev Mr Stringfellow, Richd Dement to Mrs Jane H Compton, both of Wash City.

Norfolk Beacon: accident on board the brig **Henry**, of North Yarmouth, H K Means, master, lying at Hampton Roads at the time, the 2nd ofcr, Jos Dedrick, of Prospect, Maine, & one of the crew, a colored man named Charles, belonging to N Y, were drowned. The man fell from the yard, & in endeavoring to save him the boat was lowered, & it blowing a strong gale she swamped, & the Dedrick drowned.

Judge Murray, of the Court of Muscogee Co, Ala, committed suicide about a fortnight ago, by blowing out his brains with a pistol. The judge was engaged to a young lady, but her father refused his consent to the union.

For sale: farm at Beltville, PG Co, Md: public auction on Jun 1, at Holtzman's Tavern, Beltsville: all that tract of land containing 263 acres . The cultivation of the farm has been too much neglected for several years past, owing to my constant absence from it. P S: I have in Wash an excellent Steam Engine of about 3 horse power, nearly new, which I will sell at private sale. Inquire for this of G W Venable, 12th & Pa ave. –Thos Allen

Cottage farm for sale: wishing to devote exclusively to the Piano business, I offer for sale this desirable estate, in Fairfax Co, north of the Little River Turnpike Road: contains 150 acres: well finished frame dwlg house, & outbldgs. Richd Davis-may be found at his Piano store, Alexandria, daily from 9 to 5; other times on the premises.

Circuit Court of Wash Co, D C-Mar Term, 1844. In the matter of the estate of Abner Cloud, dec'd. The Com'rs appointed to make divison of part of the estate of Cloud among his heirs-at-law, having made return of their proceedings, & that they had made division & partition of part of said real estate among Susan P Cloud, Lewis Carbery, Helen & Eliz Carbery, & Naomi Boone, the heirs at law of said Abner Cloud, according to the plat annexed to the return of said Com'rs, & that they had allotted to Lewis Carbery lot 1, part of said real estate divided, to said Helen & Eliz Carbery lot 2, & to said Susan P Cloud Lot 3, & to said Naomi Boone, lot 4. -Wm Brent, clk

THU MAY 9, 1844
Senate: 1-Cmte on Finance: House bill for the relief of John Fraser & Geo A Trenholm, with an amendment. 2-Cmte on Military Affairs: adverse report on the memorial of Peter A Carns: ordered to be printed. 3-Cmte on Finance: asking to be discharged from the further consideration of the ptn of John Fraser & Co, praying that the sum of money might be refunded, & also from the memorial relating to drawback on domestic spirits. 4-Bill for the relief of the legal reps of Joshua Kendy, of Ala, for losses sustained in 1813, in consquence of his house having been occupied as a fort by the troops of the U S.

Wood Park for sale: my beautiful estate in Va, formerly owned by Purser Thornton. It contains 722 acres; 12 miles north of *Montpelier*, the seat of Mrs Madison; 30 miles from *Monticello*, the former residence of Mr Jefferson. Having purchased this estate to gratify the wishes of my family, & particularly those of my eldest son, who was instructed by a scientific English farmer, our efforts & money have been freely expended for nearly 4 years in its rapid improvement; hence it has not hitherto proved lucrative. My price is $30,000 for the whole property, including the furnished house, pictures, library, & the growing crops. Apply to me personally, Marcus Bull, jr, on the premises, or by mail at Orange Courthouse, Va, or in either of the above modes to the subscriber at 84 Broadway, N Y, or at the City Hotel, Hartford. I refer to Messrs Buckland Bull, of Hartford; J S Huber & T D Nancrede, Phil; John Scott & Son, Fredericksburg; R Mayo & Talliaferro, of Richmond, all of whom have visited the property. –Marcus Bull, Hartford, Conn

Dwlg house for rent: the subscriber being about to remove to the country, offers the house he now occupies, at 6th & F st north. The key may be had next door. –E J Middleton, at the City Hall.

More rioting at Phil on Mon: the man who is said to have fired the first musket was John Taggart. Chas Rhinedollar, ship carpenter, shot dead; Geo Young, of South st, Southwark, s/o Mr Young, distiller, was wounded supposedly mortal; Augustus Peale, dentist, was shot in the left arm; Peter Albright, ex-constable of the Northern Liberties, was wounded in the hand; Chas Stibel, rope maker, was shot in the neck, & through the lungs & heart; Henry Hesselbaugh, tavern keeper, an elderly man, was shot in the hand; Jas Whittaker, was shot mortally in the hip; Chas Orte was shot in the head, but not killed; Willis H Blaney, late high constable, was shot in the heel-badly wounded; Louis Grevel, of Southwark, was shot in the forehead, scattering his brains; Wright Artis, shipwright, shot though the thigh; John Lusher, shot through the left breast, thought to be mortal; Wm E Hillman shot through left shoulder; A Abbott Lawrence, of Boston, a spectator, was struck by a ball over the breast; John Shrieves, a painter, was shot in the head; Jas Rice, in one of the Irish houses, was shot in the heart; John S Fagan, Irish Protestant, shot in the shoulder; Matthew Hammett, shipwright, 50 years old, was shot in the head & killed.

Mrd: on Tue last, by Rev J P Donelan, Mr John Larcomb, jr, to Miss Catharine Smith Parker, d/o the late Southey Parker, all of Wash City.

Died: on May 8, after a long & painful illness, of consumption, Mrs Eliza Lawrence, w/o Jos Cuvillier. Her funeral is this afternoon, at 3 o'clock, from her residence, near the Navy Yard.

FRI MAY 10, 1844
Senate: 1-Ptn from Sarah Bishop, wid/o Calvin Bishop, late postmaster at Tuscumbia Co, Ala, asking compensation for losses sustained by her husband in consequence of a change of his duties by the Postmaster Genr'l. 2-Ptn from Robt Poindexter, asking a pension for military services. 3-The Shawnee Indians had leave to withdraw their ptn & papers. 4-Cmte on Naval Affairs: asking to be discharged from the further consideration of the ptn of Mrs Julia L Weed. 5-Cmte on the Post Ofcs & Post Roads: favorable reports on the bill from the House for the relief of Adam L Mills.

House of Reps: 1-Announcement of the death of Mr Henry R Brinkerhoff, member elect from Ohio. Gen Brinkerhoff was born of humble but honest parents, in Adams Co, Pa, from whence, in early boyhood, he emigrated, with his father's family, to Cayuga Co, N Y, then a trackless wilderness. On the breaking out of the war with Great Britain, he repaired to the frontier, in command of a company of volunteers of the N Y militia, & at the battle of Queenstown Heights distinguished himself as a brave & patriotic soldier. For many years he was major genr'l of the N Y State Militia. He was twice a member of the N Y Legislature. In 1837 he removed to Huron Co, Ohio. He was attacked with the disease which finally terminated his existence at his residence in Huron Co, on Apr 30th last, at age 56 years. His widow & orphan mourn his loss.

Valuable land for sale on Jun 4: a tract of 146 acres, on Oxen Run, adjoining lands of Mr Washington Berry, in D C. Inquire of Holmead & Wright.

A verdict of $2,000 damages has been rendered against Moses Y Beach, editor of the N Y Sun, for libellous article affecting the character of Mr Benj H Day, published in the Sun nearly a year ago.

Obit-died: on Apr 28, at Amherst, Mass, Rev Isaac Orr, aged 51 years. He was the inventor of the Air-tight Stove, & for some years an able Reporter for this paper. Mr Orr was a native of N H; 1818 graduate at Yale College; was a teacher in the Asylum for the deaf & dumb in Hartford, Conn; studied for the Christian Ministry, but owing to feeble health, performed but a brief time.

Mrd: on May 8, by Rev Norval Wilson, Jacob Marks to Lucretia Lusby, all of Wash City.

Mrd: on May 16, by Rev Mr Dickey, Mr Saml A Coyle, of Hoguestown, Cumberland Co, to Miss Eliza Linn, of Landisburg.

$100 reward for the following servants: Travers, a dark mulatto man, from 38 to 40 years old; & a negro boy, Warren, about 17. The above reward will be given if they are taken & secured so that we can get them. –G W Carlyle Whiting, John A Carter, near Upperville, Fauquier Co, Va.

SAT MAY 11, 1844
Letters received by the last steamer confirm the death of Rev R O Dwight, of the Madura mission. We hear also that the same disease, spasmodic cholera, have taken the life of Mrs Cherry, & of Mrs North. Mrs Dwight & Mr Muzzey were brought very low, but were spared. We also received word of the death of Rev Mr Graves, of the Bombay mission. This event has been expected for some time.

House of Reps: 1-Ptn of Catharine Jackson, praying for a pension by the reason of the services of her late husband, John Jackson, in the Revolutionary war. 2-Ptn of Geo Fisher, Martin Kendig, & 114 others, citizens of Dauphin Co, Pa, protesting against any change in the tariff of 1842.

Public sale of valuable improved lands above Gtwn, near Tenallytown. By deed of trust executed by the late Jos Nourse, to the subscriber, Walter Smith, dated Feb 11, 1811, & of another deed of trust executed by him to the subscriber, Richd Smith, dated Sep 30, 1825, & of the decree of the Circuit Court of Wash Co, D C, pronounced in a cause wherein Geo Bomford is cmplnt & Chas J Nourse & others are dfndts, appointing the subscriber Wm Redin, trustee, will be offered for public auction at the auction rooms of E S Wright, in Gtwn, on May 13 next, the following land, late the residences of the late Jos Nourse, & of Chas J Nourse, namely:
Part of a tract called *Friendship*, continging 8¾ acres .
Another of the same containing 7¾ acres .
Another of the same containing 70½ acres
Part of a tract called *Pretty Prospect*, containing 82¾ acres
Part of a tract called *Mount Airy*, containing 45½ acres
Part of a tract called *Gizor* containing 46 acres 1 r & 10 p
Part of a tract called *Resurvey* or *Lucky Discovery*, containing 31 acres 2 roods & 21 perches. Also, part of a tract called *Pretty Prospect*, containing 3 acres . On one tract is a 2 story stone dwlg house & all necessary out-bldgs.
-Walter Smith, Richd Smith, W Redin, trustees
[Oct 29th newspaper: Caution. For all such parts of the above described property as are now in my occupation I hold a lease, which expires in Apr, 1846, at that time & not earlier possession may be had. –Chas J Nourse]

Senate: 1-Cmte of Claims: bill for the relief of John H McIntosh. 2-Cmte on Patents: joint resolution to authorize the issuing of a patent to Geo M Keller. 3-Bill for the relief of Christopher W Morgan.

Insolvent debtor, Henry L Turner, has applied to be discharged from imprisonment. -Wm Brent, clk

Appointments by the Pres-all re-appointed: 1-Edw McCrady, to be U S Atty for South Carolina. 2-J F Cox, Henry Naylor, Joshua Pierce, Chas R Belt, Lewis Carbery, John Cox, & Robt White, to be members of the Levy Court in Wash Co, D C. 3-Thos Sewall, Thos Donoho, & Wm Minor, to be Inspectors of the Penitentiary, D C.

Mrd: on May 9, by Rev Mr Muller, Mr Jas Wimer, of Lancaster, Pa, to Miss Eliz J Collison, of Wash City.

Died: yesterday, in Wash City, James A, eldest s/o Alex'r & Mary Rutherford, aged 4 years & 10 months. His funeral is this evening, at half past 4 o'clock.

Thos W Door has been convicted before the Supreme Court of the State of R I, sitting at Newport, of the crime of treason against the State. Thereupon Mr Dorr moved an arrest of judgment, founded on a bill of exceptions.

Rochester, N Y, May 7. Railroad accident yesterday, as the cars were going around a curve they met suddenly with a horse & buggy containing 3 boys, 2 of them sons of Porter Carson, & the other a s/o Mr Cleveland. One boy was seriously injured & it was necessary to amputate one of his legs immediately. He is not expected to recover.

House of Reps: 1-Cmte on the Post Ofc & Post Roads: bill for the relief of Dunning R McNair.

MON MAY 13, 1844
Alfred A Smith, late Comptroller of the Finances of N Y C, died on Thu last, having suffered severely from a pulmonary disease for 4 months past.

At St Kitts, in Mar last, Lt Lithbridge, of the 85th light infty, walked from the barracks to Basseterre, 12 miles, & back. A match was made between him & a cpl. The cpl did it in 6 hours & 23 minutes, the lt in 4 house & 23 minutes, under a tropical son. On Apr 1 both cpl & lt were carried to their graves.
[No name given for the cpl.]

Mrd: on Apr 22, at Nashville, Tenn, by Rev Dr Edgar, C C Norvell, Editor of the Nashville Whig, to Ann Janette, d/o Capt Jas Gordon, of Nashville.

A Julien, Pa ave, between 17th & 18th sts, announces that the apartments recently occupied by Hon Isaac Van Zandt being vacant, he would be happy to accommodate a small family or a mess of gentlemen. He is prepared to furnish dinners & parties in the French style, on reasonable terms.

Died: on May 4, at Newport, Ky, Mrs Mary Aurelia Lewis, aged 39 years, relict of the late Capt Andrew Lewis, U S A, & d/o the late Danl Mayo, of Newport.

Died: on Thu, Mr Edw H Billings, a delegate from Vt to the Whig Ratification Convention lately held in Balt. He was taken ill shortly after his arrival there, & died on Thu. His mortal remains were deposited in the Mausoleum at *Green Mount Cemetery*, where they will remain until demanded by his relatives. He was a lawyer, & a resident of Woodstock.

Died: on Fri, in his hotel, Barnum's City Hotel of Balt, David Barnum, proprietor. He was sick only a few days, though he had been for some time in feeble health, the immediate cause of his death was pleurisy. He was in his 75th year. He was a kind husband, an indulgent father, & was one of the oldest hotel keepers in this country. –American

For rent: convenient frame house & vacant lot, N Y ave & 12th st. Apply to Mr Buist, opposite the premises, or to the subscriber, living on 12th st. –Lambert Tree

THU MAY 14, 1844
Senate: 1-Ptn from C R Hill, asking the right of pre-emption to certain tracts of land. 2-Documents in relation to the claims of Geo West were presented. 3-Cmte on Pensions: bill for the relief of Lois Croul with amendments; & House bill for the relief of Danl Ingolla without amendment, & recommending that the latter be indefinitely postponed. 4-Unfavorable reports on the ptn of Laomi Kelton. 5-Cmte on Pensions: unfavorable report on the ptn of Robt Poindexter.

Trustee's sale: by deed of trust executed by Henrietta Syrock, dated Jun 21, 1841, & recorded in Liber W B 89, folio 101 thru 103, of the land records for Wash Co: auction on May 29, of lot 12 in square 388; & part of square 353, with the houses, bldgs & improvements, belonging or appertaining. –Holmead & Wright, aucts

Committed to the jail of Balt Co by John Farmer, a J P, on Apr 28, 1844, Chas Johnson, charged with being a runaway, but says he was free born, & raised in Leesburg, Va. He is about 30 years old. Had in his possession a pass, supposed to be forged, signed Chas G Eaxridge. The owner, if any, is to come forward, prove property, pay charges, & take him away; otherwise he will be discharged according to law. –Danl Steever, Warden

A monument to Jos Lovell, M D, late Surgeon Gen of the U S Army, has been placed this past winter in the *Congressional burying ground* near Wash City. The Medical Ofcrs of the Army have caused it to be erected. The structure was designed & executed by Mr Robt E Launitz, of N Y, in the Grecian style, of finest Italian marble, weighing about 10 tons, & reaching a height of 15½ feet. Cmte on behalf of the Medical Staff:

T G Mower, Surgeon U S Army
S G I De Camp, Surgeon U S Army
C S Tripler, Surgeon U S Army
W V Wheaton, Surgeon U S Army

Robt C Wood, Surgeon U S Army
H L Heiskell, Surgeon U S Army
J P Russell, Asst Surgeon U S Army
Benj King, Asst Surgeon U S Army

The following are the inscriptions on the Monument:

On the front of the monument:

>   Joseph Lovell,
>   Late Surgeon General
>   of
>   The Army of the United States.
>   Born in Boston, Massachusetts,
>   December 22d, 1788;
>   Died in the city of Washington,
>   October 17th, 1836.

On the right face of the monument:

>   In April, 1812,
>   On the eve
>   Of Hostilites with Great Britain,
>   He entered
>   The military service of his country
>   as Surgeon
>   and served with distinction
>   throughout the war.
>   After six years' arduous duty
>   in Camp and in the Field,
>   He was called,
>   on the reorganization
>   of
>   The General Staff of the Army,
>   from the station
>   of Hospital Surgeon
>
>   The Head of the Med'l Departm't,
>   which
>   till the close of his life,
>   He directed, improved, & adored.

On the left face of the monument:
>In September, 1817,
>He was united in wedlock,
>>with
>
>Margaret Eliza Mansfield,
>The devoted & cherished
>Partner of his life,
>who rests beside him
>under this tomb.
>Exemplary members of the church,
>In all their domestic relations
>>they lived
>
>Patterns of excellence,
>>and dying,
>
>Bequeathed to their posterity
>a rich inheritance
>In their bright example.

On the rear of the monument:
>As a testimonial
>>of
>
>His private virtues
>>and
>
>Public services
>The officers of the Medical Staff
>>have caused
>
>This monument to be erected,
>>December, 1843

"Virtus, repulsae, nescia sordidae,
Intaminatis, fulget honoribus."

Household & kitchen furniture at auction: on May 15, at the residence of Mr Wm Smith, on 9th st, near N Y ave.

House of Reps: 1-Ptn of the heirs & legal reps of J R Granger, for confirmation of title to 800 arpens of land on Bayou Plaquemine Boule, in Opelousas, Co, La. 2-Ptn of John Gilleylen, of Monroe Co, Miss, praying to be refunded a sum of money paid for a certain tract of land in Miss, which was not subject to entry, & for which he can obtain no patent. 3-Ptn of Wm Morrison, Geo Tomb, & Jas Wilson, praying for the renewal of a patent for an improvement in a machine for clearing & deepening rivers, called the Floating Excavator.

Trustee's sale of Dry Goods at auction: Champe B Thornton, having determined to close his business on May 17: store is 8 doors above Brown's Hotel.
-Holmead & Wright, aucts

Died: on Apr 22, at Vicksburg, Miss, in his 83rd year, Maj Burwell Vick, an old & much esteemed resident of that place. He was a native of Southampton, Co, & was born in 1761. During the Revolutioanry war he served his country in several campaigns as a volunteer, was engaged in the battle of Stono, below Charleston, & at the capture of Cornwallis. In his 21st year he emigrated to N C, in which State he resided until 1807, when he removed to the Territory of Miss, where he had since resided as a planter,

Died: on May 13, in Gtwn, Miss Emily Magruder, aged 34 years, after an illness of 3 days, of scarlet fever. Her funeral is this day, at 1 o'clock, from the residence of her father, Mr Geo B Magruder, on 3rd st.

For sale or rent: 2 story brick dwlg house on Mass ave, between 11th & 12th sts. Apply at the residence of Mr Richd Elliott, N Y ave, between 12th & 13th sts.

WED MAY 15, 1844
Rev Wm C Crooker died at Monrovia, Liberia, Feb 26, 1844. He was of the Baptist African Mission. Mr C arrived from Boston in the ship **Palestine**, on Feb 24. His death was caused by the rupture of a blood vessel, by which he lost between one & two gallons of blood.

Senate: 1-Cmte on Private Land Claims: bill for the relief of John Miller: to be printed. 2-Cmte on Commerce: asking to be discharged from the further consideration of the memorial of Robt Mills, requesting an examination of a plan devised by him for facilitating trigonometrical surveys. 3-Cmte on Military Affairs: adverse report on the ptn of Robt McGuire.

Sale of valuable property: as contained in the last will & testament of J H Howell, dec'd, said will being of probate in the Orphans Court of Wash Co, D C. For sale, on Jun 4, a lot of ground in square 383, on south B st; together with the 2 two-story frame bldgs thereon. –A P Skinner, Gabriel Moran, excs. Wm Marshall, auct

Association of American Geologists & Naturalists. List of the members who have thus far been present: May 14, 1844

Prof John Locks, Cincinnati
B Silliman, jr, New Haven
Prof Oliver P Hubbard, Hanover, N H
Dr Douglass Houghton, Univ of Mich
Prof Henry D Rogers, Phil
Prof Edw Hitchcock, Amherst, Mass
Prof Wm W Mather, Athens, Ohio
Jas D Dana
Prof Walter R Johnson

Prof Wm B Rogers, Univ of Va
Prof Robt E Rogers, Univ of Va
Dr H King
L Wilder, Hoosic Falls, N Y
Z Allen, Providence, R I
Prof S S Haldeman, Marietta, Pa
J P Couthoy, N Y
Isaac Lee, Phil
Wm C Redfield, N Y C

Chas H Olmsted, East Hartford, Conn
Isaac Hays
Prof Jas Hall, Albany
Alfred Langdon Elwyn, M D, Phil
Lardner Vanuxem, Bristol, Pa
Prof E Mitchell, Chapel Hill, N C
John Bacon, jr, M D, Boston
M Tuomey, Petersburg, Va
J Lawrence Smith, M D, Charleston, S C
Peter Edwin Henderson, F R S, Civil Engineer, York, England

J W Mighels, Portland, Maine
Edwards Hall, N Y C
Capt Chas Wilkes, Wash
Hon Nathan Appleton, Boston, Mass
Lt J W Bailey, West Point
Amos Binney, M D, Boston
John L Hayes, Portsmouth, N H

More on Frelinghuysen: Rev Theodore Jas Frelinghuysen was a distinguished Minister of the Reformed Dutch Church, who came from Holland in 1720, died in 1754, leaving 5 sons, all educated for the ministry, & 2 dghts who were married to ministers. Rev John Frelinghuysen succeeded his father as paster of the church at Raritan, N J. Rev Theodorus Frelinghuysen, another of the sons, preached at Albany, N Y, & became a distinguished as a preacher. The other 3 sons died soon after entering upon their ministry. Fred'k Frelinghuysen, s/o the Rev John Frelinhuysen, was born on Apr 13, 1753, graduated at Princeton in 1776, & in the war of the Revolution was conspicuous among the good & the brave. In 1775, at age 22, he was sent to N J to the Continental Congress; a post which he resigned in 1777, in order to continue in the field as capt of a volunteer corps of artl, whose services had been tendered to Congress. As colonel in the militia of his native Somerset Co, he was in the battles of Trenton, Monmouth, & others. He rapidly rose to maj gen of the troops of N J, & enjoyed the respect & confidence of Washington. He died on the anniversary of his birth in 1804, aged 51 years. Gen Frelinghuysen left 3 sons, John, Fred'k, & Theodore, of whom only the last named survives, & he is now Chancellor of the Univ of N Y, & the Whig candidate for Vice Pres of the U S.

A citizen, named Madeiras, of Mohawk, Ohio, died on Mon seized with lock-jaw, from a prick on his finger under the nail with a steel pin.

I will sell at private sale a small farm of land containing between 70 & 80 acres, within 3½ miles of Wash. This farm lies between the farms of Chas H Wiltherger & Capt Sanders, about ¼ mile from Rock Creek Church. –Thos Murphy

Household & kitchen furniture at auction: on May 17, at the residence over the store of Mr Fowler, merchant tailor, on Pa ave, between 3rd & 4½ sts.
-R W Dyer & Co, aucts

Orphans Court of Wash Co, D C. Letters of administration on the personal estate of Henry Ingle, late of said county, dec'd. –Peter Callan, adm

Orphans Court of Wash Co, D C. Letters testamentary on the personal estate of Patrick H O'Rielly, late of said county, dec'd. –E P Scott, exc

THU MAY 16, 1844
House of Reps: 1-Memorial of John J Dickson, asking pay for property destroyed by the Tennessee volunteers under Gen Wool, in 1836. 2-Ptn of Eliz Taylor, wid/o Maj Wm Taylor.

The Buffaloes which have been exhibiting for a few days in Wash City, will be turned loose on the Washington Course on Sat, when the citizens will have an opportunity of beholding with what astonishing tact the Mexican Arraro will throw his lasso, mounted on his steed, trained by himself. He has been upwards of 30 years catching wild horses & buffaloes. Admittance to proprietors' stand 25 cents. –Wm G Wilkins

By writ of fieri facias, I shall expose to public sale, on May 23, sundry goods & chattels of John Hodgkin, to be sold to satisfy a judgment due to Benj F Middleton & Benj Beall. –R R Burr, constable

For sale, a tract of land in Montg Co, Md, containing 248 acres: near Colesville, & adjoins the lands of Elias Perry. Apply to M Mason in Gtwn.

Senate: 1-Ptn from Wm Archer, praying compensation for services in preparing designs & estimates for the construction of a bridge across the Potomac river as authorized by an act of Congress. 2-Bill for the relief of W D Cheever. 3-Bill for the relief of Henry Gardner & others, directors of an association called the New England & Mississippi Land Co, was taken up. 4-Bill for the relief of the legal reps of Wm Walker, laid on the table. 5-Bill for the relief of C E Sherman, laid on the table. 6-Joint resolution authorizing an allowance to Purser D M F Thornton in the settlement of his accounts. 7-To be engrossed: bill for the relief of Gideon Batchelder & others; relief of Jos Bryan, Harrison Young, & Benj Young; relief of Reynall Coates, Walter R Johnson, & Wm B McMurtrie; & relief of Peter Von Schmidt; & a pension to Geo Whitten.

House of Reps: 1-Cmte on Invalid Pensions: favorable report on the application of the widow Hannah Duboise, & reported a bill for her relief. 2-Cmte on Claims: bill for the relief of Geo Harrison & his sureties, reported without amendment. 3-Cmte on Commerce: bill for the relief of Amos Proctor. 4-Bill for the relief of Hiram Murch, reported without amendment. 5-Cmte on the Judiciary: bill for the relief of John Atchison, reported without amendment. 6-Cmte on Naval Affairs: made a report on the ptn of Sarah P Mather, with a bill to test the utility of the Submarine Telescope. 7-Cmte on Indian Affairs: bill for the relief of Wm Hendon, without amendment. 8-Cmte on Patents: adverse report on the ptn of Wm Beach.

Valuable Loudoun Farm for sale: on Jun 10, that well know farm, *Sailor's Rest*, owned by the late Capt John Rose; situated 6 miles north of Leesburg; contains about 600 acres: improvements are a large well built frame dwlg house, 2 stories high, with wings attached, in good order. Also, a blacksmith shop, & comfortable dwlg for a Smith's family, & another comfortable dwlg house on the tract now occupied by Mr Frye. Immediate possession. –Thos H Clagett, adm, with the will annexed of Jno Rose, dec'd.

Mrd: on Tue last, by Rev Mr Wilson, Mr Talburt M Grant, of Portsmouth, Va, to Miss Mary Eliz Piggott, of Wash City.

Died: on May 13, after a lingering illness, Mrs Eleanor Doughty, in her 74th year. Her funeral will take place from *Mount Hermon*, the country residence of her husband, Col Wm Doughty, this day, at 4 o'clock.

Virginia, to Wit: at a Circuit Superior Court of Law & Chancery held for Prince Edw Co, at the Courthouse, Apr 27, 1844. The Commonwealth of Va, who sue for the benefit of the Literary fund, plntf, against John Clark, administrator of John Julian, dec'd, John Foster, & Saml T Clark, dfndnts. This suit is to recover of the said administrator the residue, after the payment of funeral charges, debt's & expenses, of the goods & chattels of said John Julian, dec'd, a native of France, & who died intestate in Prince Edw Co, Va, leaving neither wife or child, & without relations known to this Court. The Court doth order that all persons claiming an interest in the estate aforesaid, as distributes of the said John Julian, dec'd, do appear here on the first day of the next Term of this Court & make themselves party dfndnts.
–B J Worsham, clk

FRI MAY 17, 1844
Senate: 1-Bills passed: settlement of Purser D M F Thornton's accounts; relief of Gideon Batchelder & others; relief of Jos Bryan, Harrison Young, & Benj Young; relief of Reynall Coates, Walter R Johnson, & Wm B McMurtrie; relief of Peter Von Schmidt; relief of Henry Gardner & others; & pension to Geo Whitten.

Giesler, for the murder of Alex'r Smith & wife, at Huntington, Long Island, has been sentenced to be hung on Jun 7 next, between the hours of 12 & 2 o'clock.

Pleasant rooms for rent on 3rd st, near the Depot. –W W Birth, 3rd & Pa ave

Buffalo, N Y, May 13: Lake disasters. The schnr N **Biddle** & the schnr **Shamrock**, were capsized in the gust which passed over the lake on Sat last. One hand lost on the **Shamrock**. In Saturday's paper the schnr **Freedom** capsized & John Wright [14] & John Herrick, of Lexington, & Oliver Taylor, of Algonac, were lost.

Mrd: on May 9, at Rockville church, by Rev Mr Gassaway, Capt Jos Smoot, of the U S Navy, to Miss Ann Eliz Darne, d/o Wm Darne, of Montg Co, Md.

Died: on May 15, Mr John Gadsby, long known as a respectable & useful citizen of this place. His funeral will take place on Fri at 4 o'clock from his late residence, President's square.

Died: last Mon, at Hartford, Conn, in his 88th year, Mr Geo Goodwin, long & extensively known as the former publisher of the Connecticut Courant.

Died: on Thu, of consumption, Sarah Ann, d/o John Ellis, in her 29th year. Her funeral will take place from her father's residence, F & 9th sts, at 2 o'clock, today.

Died: on May 12, Wm Aloysius, s/o Christopher & Eliz Gill, aged 11 years, 2 months & 23 days.

Died: on May 11, James, aged 14 years, & George, aged 17 years, both of them sons of Mr Guy Graham, of Wash City. These interesting boys were in the enjoyment of full health on Tue last, & on the succeeding Sunday were deposited in one grave.

Died: on Sun last, at the residence of her late dght, Mrs Slacum, in Alexandria, D C, Mrs Julia Matilda Howard, at the advanced age of nearly 104 years. This venerable lady was born on Jun 12, 1740, & had she lived but a month longer would have completed her 104th year. She preserved until within a year or two past all her faculties of mind & body to a degree of remarkable vigor. She was probably the oldest inhabitant of D C. She has left a numerous & wide-spread circle of descendants. She enjoyed seeing & conversing with her children of the 5th generation; & has been called on to mourn the early death of others who came into this uncertain life more than a century after her.

House of Reps: 1-Cmte on Commerce: bill for the relief of Jos Curwen, surviving partner of Willing & Curwen. 2-Cmte on Post Ofc & Post Roads: joint resolution for the relief of Sellers & Pennock. Same cmte: joint resolution for the benefit of Saltmarsh & Fuller, with amendment; & joint resolution for the benefit of Wm Fuller, without amendment.

SAT MAY 18, 1844
House of Reps: 1-Resolved, that the ptn & papers of J W Nye, assignee of Peter Bargy, jr, & Hugh Stewart, now on file, asking further remuneration for losses sustained in macadamizing a large portion of Pa ave in 1832, be referred to a select cmte, to report to the House by bill or otherwise.

For rent: 2 story brick house on 7th st, first door above the Nat'l Intell ofc.
–Mrs R Cheshire, 4½ st, near the City Hall

Trustee's sale of land in Alleghany Co, Md: by decree passed by the high Court of Chancery of Md, in a cause in said Court depending, wherein Geo W Peter is cmplnt, & Duff Green & the Union Co are the dfndnts: sale on Jun 8, at the tavern of Wm P Searight, in Cumberland, at public auction, the tract of land called *The Mark Amended*, in said county, which was patented to the said Geo W Peter, & contains 2,344 acres. This land lies in the Frostburg coal district. –S M Semmes, trustee

The subscriber wishes to employ a married gentleman to educate his children. Direct, postage paid, to Montevideo, near Darnestown, Montg Co, Md.
–John P C Peter

Notice: Geo J Abbot will attend to any business on my account, after my leaving the city. –S G Bulfinch

MON MAY 20, 1844
City Ordinance-Wash. Act for the relief of Wm Campbell: that the fine imposed for a violation relative to stove pipes passing through bldgs, is remitted, provided he pay the cost of prosecution. Approved: May 17, 1844.

Robbery on Fri night at the barber shop of Mr Moffat, E & 7th sts, & stolen therefrom were all the razors & shaving apparatus, a coat, & other articles.

Senate: 1-Bills passed: relief of Isaac Justice, of Tenn; relief of Sarah Blackmore; & a bill granting a pension to Bartholomew Maguire. Relief of Wm Glover & for the relief of Abigail Gibson were amended, & the bills were read a 3rd time. 2-Bills indefinitely postponed: relief of John P Schuyler; relief of John Farnham; relief of Simeon Caswell; relief of Henry Freeman; & bill granting a pension to Richd Elliott.

We are informed that Rev Edw Waylen, of Phil, has received the unanimous invitation of the Vestry of Rockville Episcopal Church to the Rectorship thereof.

Fatal accident, on Tue, after the arrival of the train from Wash, as the cars were coming out of the depot at Pratt st, Thos Muldoon, aged about 12 years, was instantly killed by being crushed between one of the cars & the post at the gateway. –Balt Sun

A few days ago, in the absence of Hon S S Prentiss from Vicksburg, an offensive publication in relation to him was made by Mr T E Robbins of that place. Mr Downs', a law student in Mr Prentiss' ofc, challenged Robbins. They fought with yagers, & Downs fell, severely if not mortally wounded. A dispute arose between the seconds of the parties. In a street fight, Mr Macklin, the second of Downs, was cut with a Bowie-knife, & we hear he is dead. –Louisville Journal

On May 6, a young gentleman of St Louis, Wm B Goodfellow, a student of medicine in the ofc of Dr White, & s/o Mr John Goodfellow, attempted to swim a creek with his horse, & was drowned.

Appointments by the Pres:
Archibald W Hyde, to the Collector of the Customs for the district of Vt, & Inspector of the Revenue for the port of Alburg, Vt, vice Wm P Briggs, removed.
Geo H McWhorter, to be Collector of the Customs for the district, & Inspector of the Revenue for the port of Oswego, N Y, vice Thos H Bond, removed.
Thos Gatewood, to be Naval Ofcr for the district of Norfolk & Portsmouth, in Va.
Michl Kennedy, to be U S Consul for Cayene, French Guiana.
Josiah Raymond, to be U S Consul for Manzanillo, in the island of Cuba.
Robt P de Silver, of Pa, to be U S Consul for Port Louis, in the Isle of France.
Thos W Waldron, to be U S Consul for Hong Kong, China.
Paul S Forbes, to be U S Consul for Canton, vice P W Snow, dec'd.
Thos G Peachy, to be U S Consul for Amoy, in China
Richd S Belt, to be U S Consul for Matamoras, Mexico, vice Danl W Smith, resigned.
F M Auboyneau, to be U S Consul for La Rochelle, France.
Henry J Brent, to be U S Consul for Ravenna, Italy.
Warder Creson, to be U S Consul for Jerusalem, in Palestine.

Mrd: on May 2, in Boston, Lt H L Eustis, U S Engineer Corps, to Sarah Augusta, d/o J T Eckley.

Mrd: on May 7, in Phil, Lt Edwin J De Haven, U S Navy, to Mary, d/o John C Da Costa.

Died: on Sat last, Chas F Bihler, long a respectable citizen of Wash. His funeral is this afternoon, at half past 3 o'clock, from his late residence, F & 14th sts.

Died: on May 4, at Newport, Ky, Mrs Mary Aurelia Lewis, aged 39 years, relict of the late Capt Andrew Lewis, U S Army, & d/o the late Danl Mayo, of Newport.

Died: on May 16, in Portsmouth, Va, Mr Thos H Moran, aged 30 years.

TUE MAY 21, 1844
To the Public! The subscriber has invented a new mode for opening lock gates for passing boats, which possesses great advantage over the old plan, & having obtained a patent for his improvement, he is now prepared to sell his rights for any portion of the U S, either for canal or river navigation. –Henry McCarty, Pittsburg, May 11, 1841.

$100 reward for runaway negro man Geo Jenifer, about 36 years old. He took with him his fiddle. –John L Johnson, near Bryantown, Md

Died: on May 18, after a protracted & painful illness, Mrs Bridget Caton, aged 70 years.

Died: on May 5, at the house of his brother, in Columbus, Ga, John L Moore, in his 31st year, 2nd s/o Jas Moore, printer of Wash City.

Died: on May 11, at Avondale, Wash Co, Md, Mary Barnes Winter, consort of Rev John Winter, & eldest d/o the late John Thomson Mason, aged 44 years.

Singular coincidence. While Mr Clay was passing through Cumberland, Alleghany Co, Md, on Tue last, Washington Evans, of that place, brought up & introduced to him his 2 sons, one aged 14 years, named Henry Clay, & the other, 12 years old, named Theodore Frelinghuysen.

Oxford Academy, Granville Co, N C. There will be a vacancy in the ofc of Principal in the Female Dept of this Institution at the end of the present session, by the resignation of the Teacher under whose care it has been conducted for several years. Letters of application for a successor, must be post paid. –Jeremy Hilliard, sec

Teacher wanted: the trustees of Primary School District 7, Anne Arundel Co, Md, wish to employ a Classical Teacher immediately. Liberal salary will be given. Address the undersigned, Bristol, Anne Arundel Co, Md. –Plummer S Drury, Edw McCeney, Jas Higgins, trustees

The subscriber, wishing to retire from his profession as a teacher of young gentlemen, offers for rent his establishment, built for the purpose, & handsomely furnished. Address, postage paid, Wm Hamilton, Balt, Md.

Orphans Court of Wash Co, D C. Letters of administration on the personal estate of Mgt Freeman, lae of said county, dec'd. –Saml Agnew

WED MAY 22, 1844
Senate: 1-Communication from Saml Colt, in relation to his submarine battery & remuneration for his services in testing its merits by a series of experiments under a joint resolution of Congress. 2-Ptn from the heirs of Robt M Hardy, praying for a settlement of their claim for property destroyed during the insurrention in Florida previous to the grant of the territory to the U S. 3-Ptn from Joshua Shaw, who claims to be the inventor of the percussion lock in 1822, which is now adopted throughout the world; stating that the lock has been in use by the U S for a long time; &, as the inventor met with much loss of time & money in testing the use of his invention, he asks to be allowed what Congress may deem a fair consideration for its

use by the army & navy. 4-Ptn from David Conner & others, citizens of the U S, praying the annexation of Texas. 5-Cmte on Pensions: unfavorable report on the House bill for the relief of John Rose. Same cmte: favorable reports on the following House bills: relief of Simeon Deunnin; & relief of Lathrop Foster. Same cmte: asking to be discharged from the further consideration of the House bill for the relief of Hugh Wallace Wormley, & that it be referred to the Cmte on Naval Affairs. 6-Ptn of Wm Brown. 6-Cmte on Pensions: resolution explanatory of the act for the relief of Mary Williams, wid/o the late Jacob Williams. Same cmte: House bill for the relief of Violet Calhoun, wid/o John Calhoun, without amendment. 7-Bills passed: bill for the relief of Pierre Menard, Josiah T Betts, Jacob Feaman, & Edmund Roberts, of the State of Ill, sureties of Felix St Vrain, late Indian agent, dec'd. Act for the relief of Abigail Gibson. 8-To be engrossed for a 3rd reading: bill for the relief of Louis Croule; relief of the heirs of Wm Fisher; & relief of the heirs of Benj B Ferguson. 9-Bills from the House, read a 3rd time, & passed: bills of the relief of Jas C Hallock; relief of Jas Reid; relief of Jos Bonnell; relief of Levi Colmus; relief of John Miller; relief of Violet Calhoun. 10-An act to explain an act of Congress passed Mar 3, 1843, for the relief of Eliz Gresham, wid/o Geo Gresham. 11-Bills indefinitely postponed: increase of pension to Isaac Plummer. Bill for the relief of Enoch M Daniel; relief of Danl Durham; relief of Danl Ingalls; relief of Sally McCraw; increase of pension to Gideon Foster; bill for the benefit of Arthur R Frogge. 12-Ptn of the widow of W White, for a pension, presented. 13-Cmte on Pensions: adverse report on the ptn of Fanny Massey. Same cmte: adverse report on the ptn of Bela Young. 14: The Senate then proceeded to consider the report made in the case of Mrs Julia L Weed, which was debated & postponed until tomorrow.

On Thu last, as some young men were shooting in the Neck, Eccles, aged 16, was accidentally shot in the breast by one of his companions. He expired at a late hour the same night. –Phil Inquirer

A sword fish was taken a few days since in Chimney creek, near Tybee, by Mr Jos Ross, of Savannah, measuring 15 feet from the tail-fin to the end of the sword, 4 feet in diameter, & about 8 feet in circumference.

Mr Brainard, of Westmoreland, N Y, in trying to get a book his son accidentally dropped into the well, the hook caught a bag, which contained 22 pounds of arsenic. His barn & contents were burned 2 or 3 weeks ago, supposed by an incendiary.

Mr Jas Kerley, of Dexter, NY, was instantly killed there on Sat last, by being caught on the shaft of a grindstone driven by water. His bones were crushed to fragments.

Levi Fort, who was convicted of a riot in attempting to break the line of the military, at 5th & Prune st, with the Weccacoe Hose, was sentenced on Sat to 10 days in jail & fined $1.00

Lt John Dutton died on Sat, from inflammation of the lungs, contracted while on duty as a military ofcr in suppressing the Kensington riots. He was Lt of the first company of State Fencibles, under the command of Col Page. He has left a large circle of warm friends to mourn his loss.

On Sat the Recorder committed Saml Paul, in default of $5,000 bail, for a further hearing on the charge of having been arrested in the late riot at Kensington. —Ledger

A little boy, the child of Washington Hurt, near the Broad Ford, in Smythe Co, Va, aged 2 years last Feb, wandered from home on Apr 27, & was not found for 5 days. When found, the child knew its parents & exhibited no signs of fear.
—Wytheville Republican

In the matter of the ptn of John Weems, next friend of Francis W Weems, Eliz S Hawkins, & Eliz Ann Weems, infants, vs, Walter H Weems, Jas I Weems, & Lock Weems. Object of this bill is to procure a decree for a sale of a certain tract of land in Chas Co, Md. The bill states that a certain Mary Smoot & Eleanor Smoot were possessed in their lifetime, as tenants in common, a tract of land in said county, containing about 200 acres; that the said Eleanor died in 1836, leaving by her last will & testament her one-half interest in the said land to her sister Mary for life, remainder over to be divided in 6 equal parts, among Walter W Weems, Jas I Weems, Lock Weems, Eliz Ann Weems, infant d/o Josias Henry & Sarah Ann Hawkins, & John Weems & Francis W Weems, sons of John N Weems, late of Chas Co, dec'd. The bill also states the the said Mary died in 1843, leaving by her last will & testament her one-half interest in said land to Sarah Ann Hawkins for life, remainder over to be equally divided among her children. The bill further states that Walter H Weems, Jas I Weems, & Lock Weems, reside out of the State of Md. They are to appear in person or by solicitor, on or before the 3rd Mon of Jun next.
-C Dorsey -Walter Mitchell, Clerk of Chas Co Court.

Died: on Tue, Guy Graham, aged 21 years. By this dispensation his afflicted parents mourn the death of the 3rd son within the space of 9 days. His funeral will be from the residence of his father, on 21st st, near the gate of Kalorama, today at 9 a m.

Stray cow came to the subscriber's. Owner is to come & take her away, which he can do by paying for this advertisement. —Wm Holmead

THU MAY 23, 1844
Lives lost: a schnr, which left Balt on Wed last for one of the lower counties, was capsized on the next day off the mouth of the Patuxent in a heavy squall of wind, & 7 out of the 9 on board were lost: Miss Flowers, the captain's sister; Mrs Cent, a widow lady; a little girl about 7 years old named Rockwell; Mrs Triggel & child; & a white boy & a black man, deck hand. The capt & one other person were saved.

Senate: 1-Memorial from Moses Springer & others, citizens of Maine, asking indemnity for French spoliations prior to 1800. 2-Cmte on Naval Affairs: asking to be discharged from the further consideration of the ptn of John H Roebling, asking an appropriation to test the efficacy of wire rope for the standing rigging of vessels. Also, ptn of Peter Von Schmidt for pneumatic dry-dock, & ptn to make experiments for the preservation of timber. Also, ptn from Richd Gilpin for examination of a plan for constructing a dry-dock. 3-Bills passed: relief of the heirs of Wm Fisher; & relief of Benj B Ferguson.

Annual pay of British & American ofcrs

	British pay	American pay
Admiral of the Fleet	$10,512	
Admiral	$8,760	
Vice Admiral	$7,008	
Rear Admiral	$5,256	
Capt, 2nd rate	$3,350	$3,500
Capt, 4th rate	$2,393	$3,500
Cmders	$1,447	$2,500
Lts, 7 years	$961	$1,500
Lts	$874	$1,500
Mates	$312	$750
Midshipmen	$149.76	$400
Gaugers, average	$490	$680
Seamen, ration not included	$8.90 p mo	$12 p m

The pay of an English ofcr was given by the month of 4 weeks, making 13 months in the year, 12% should be added to the calculation made of an English Captain's pay. [May 24th newspaper: the above reflects corrections in the annual pay.]

Mr Geo Van Ness, one of the Mier prisoners lately confined in Mexico, arrived at N Y from Vera Cruz on Sun last.

House of Reps: 1-Ptn of Geo Leadrum, of Louisiana, praying that his tract of land be confirmed & his improvements paid for. 2-Ptn of Thos Janner, for bounty land & extra pay, for services in the U S army in the late war with Great Britian. 3-Memorial of the heirs of Capt John Mountjoy, dec'd, of the State of Ky, praying the the commutation for five year's full pay of a captain be paid to them, with lawful interest thereon. 4-Ptns of Mary Fellows, Hanna Ward, Mary Danforth, Lucy Dame, Betsey Cheney, Mehiable Wrine, Rebecca Hobart, Patty Holt, Sarah C Weeks, Mary French, Tamson French, Mary Carter, Eliz Stickney, Nancy Abbott, Huldah Evans, Mary Elliott, Eleanor Gleason, Eliz Moore, Merriam Hoyt, Mgt Milles, Judith Tilton, Naomi Campbell, Eunice Morrill, Ruth Fop, Eliz Calley, Susanna Drowt, & Mary Greenleaf, for a further allowance of 2 years pension to commence on Mar 4, 1841.

Household & kitchen furniture at auction: on May 28, at the house lately occupied by the Mexican Minister, Gen Almonte, on F st, between 12th & 13th sts. -R W Dyer & Co, aucts

Household & kitchen furniture at auction: on Jan 29, at the residence of Mr J P McKean, on Pa ave, between 4½ & 6th sts. -R W Dyer & Co, aucts

Horses for sale at the stables of the Farmer's Hotel, 8th & D sts. Apply to Owen Conolly, proprietor.

The subscriber has a large supply of Tin Ware, comprising every article usually called for by house keepers, at his establishment on Pa ave, between 3rd & 4½ sts. -F Y Naylor

For sale: the house [with store] & lot on 12th st, between G & H sts, in the occupancy of Mr John Phillips, & now under rent at $204. Inquire on the premises.

For sale or rent: 2 story brick dwlg house on Mass ave, between 11th & 12th sts, near Franklin row. Apply at the residence of Mr Richd Elliott, on N Y ave, between 12th & 13th sts.

FRI MAY 24, 1844
Senate: 1-Ptn from John Ericson, asking compensation for his services in planning & superintending the construction of the machinery of the steamer **Princeton**. Mr E states that the Navy Dept having denied his claim for services, which took up his time & exhausted his resources, he has no course left but resorting to the Reps of the American people. 2-Cmte on Naval Affairs: asking to be discharged from the further consideration of the ptns of A B Quimby, relating to steam-chimneys in steam-boilers. Also, from the ptn of Wm P McConnell, asking an appropriation to build a steamship. Also, from the ptn of Thos G Clinton, asking an examination of his improvement in steam-engines.

Death of Abner Rogers, jr. This wretched man, & State prison convict, who killed Mr Lincoln, late Warden of the Mass prison, on Fri, in Worcester hospital, where he was recently sent by the Supreme Court, suddenly sprang & leaped through the window, breaking sash & glass, & falling some 15 feet upon an arch. He was taken up senseless, living until Sun morning, when he expired.

Fatal accident on the Lowell railroad, on Mon, near Woburn, by some defect or displacement of a switch, the engine & tender were thrown from the track. Killed, the engineer, Caldwell, of East Cambridge, a capable young man of good character, & a s/o the Mr Caldwell who lost his life a few years ago by being run over by a train of cars. The fireman, McNamara, was dangerously & severely scalded by the discharge of water & steam upon him while so confined that he could not escape.

Wash Corp: 1-Bill for the relief of Wm Thorpe: referred to the Cmte of Claims. 2-Ptn of G A W Randall & others, praying improvement of 12th st west, between Pa ave & the canal: referred to the Cmte on Improvements. 3-Ptn of Robt Tweedy & others, praying the improvement of I st, from 4th to 6th sts: referred to the Cmte on Improvements. 4-Ptn of D Clagett & others, praying that a law may be passed to prohibit the occupancy of the sidewalks on Pa ave for sales by auctioneers: referred to the Cmte on Police. 5-Bill for the relief of Thos Lewis & the bill making an appropriation for the completion of the road from 7th st to the Catholic burial ground were passed. 6-Bill for the relief of Wm M Maddox: rejected. 7-Bill for the relief of Ann Whitmore: referred to the Cmte of Claims. 8-Cmte on Improvements: asking to be discharged from the further consideration of the ptn of Jno C Rumnell & others: discharged accordingly. 9-Cmte of Claims: asking to be discharged from the further consideration of the ptns of David Garret, of Edw Hawkins, of Thos Welsh, of J W McGee, & of H Johnson: discharged accordingly. 10-Nomination by the Mayor of John T Van Reswick as an assessor, in place of Thos Blagden, declined-was read & laid on the table. 11-Commissioners elected to hold an election on the first Mon of Jun next, for Mayor & one member of the Board of Aldermen from each Ward, for a term of 2 years. Duly elected:

Saml Drury	John C Harkness	John B Ferguson
Robt W Bates	G C Grammer	Jas Owner, sr
Saml Stott	John C McKelden	Jas Johnson
John McClelland	John T Frost	Jas Marshall
Lewis Johnson	Danl Homans	Wm Ellis
Willard Drake	Wm J McCormick	Noble Young

Orphans Court of Chas Co, Md. Letters of administration on the personal estate of Geo Dement, late of Chas Co, dec'd. –Julianna E Dement, Chas F Dement, adms will annexed of Geo Dement.

Insolvent debtor, Wm Jas Douglass, has applied to be discharged from imprisonment. –Wm Brent, clk

House of Reps: 1-Ptn of Jas Ferris, of Casey Co, Ky, asking an allowance for services in the Revolutionary war, & as an Indian spy.

Railroad accident on May 15, on the Palmer & Machias Port Railroad, when the engine tender & 2 lumber cars ran off the track. The engineer, Mr Butler, has his hip dislocated, the fireman, Michl Corrett, was badly if not dangerously hurt.

Sudden death; a young man, Wm Watson, residing in Calvert Co, Md, lost his life last week by being thrown from his horse whilst riding a race for the amusement of himself & another young man with whom the dec'd was in company.

The following named Midshipmen in the Navy have been examined by a Board of Ofcrs, convened for the purpose at the Naval Asylum near Phil, & found qualified for promotion. They are arranged in the order of merit fixed by the Board:

1-Saml Marcy	20-Saml Edwards
2-John P Bankhead	21-Thos L Dance
3-Jas Foster	22-Chas W Place
4-Geo W Clark	23-Alphonse Barbot
5-Geo B Bissell	24-Wm H Jamesson
6-J W A Nicholson	25-Albert N Smith
7-Thos G Corbin	26-Wm H Hudson
8-Gustavus V Fox	27-Chas T Crocker
9-John Mathews	28-John C Febiger
10-John C Beaumont	29-D R Lambert
11-Chas M Fauntleroy	30-Fred'k W Colby
13-Wm B Fitzgerald	31-Henry S Newcomb
14-Miles K Warrington	32-John S Maury
15-Henry K Davenport	33-Pierce Crosby
16-N B Harrison	34-Richd T Renshaw
17-Edw F Tattnall	35-Chas W Hays
18-S E Woodworth	36-Johnston B Creighton
19-Jas H Moore	

Mrd: on May 21, by Rev J P Donelan, Thos Reid to Miss Sophia R Peckham.

Died: on May 16, at her residence, in Fauquier Co, Va, Mrs Polly Whiting, w/o Thos Whiting, aged about 70 years.

Died: on May 17, at his residence, in New Brunswick, N J, after a long & painful illness, Geo P Molleson, Atty Gen of the State of N J, aged about 37 years. The Church of Christ, of which he was also an early & exemplary member, has sustained a loss. In his death his family have suffered an irreparable loss. In early life, Mr Molleson was a promising graduate of Nassau Hall, studied law with Geo Wood, & was admitted to the bar about 1827.

SAT MAY 25, 1844
Jacob Van Alstyne, the last Revolutionary soldier in Montg Co, N Y, died at Fonda on May 11, in his 96th year.

On Fri week Danl Deas, alias Graham, was executed in Edgefield, S C, for the murder of his stepfather, Wm Barefoot. After ascending the scaffold he addressed a large crowd of people, confessing the murder & the justice of his doom.

Mrd: on May 23, by Rev Joel C Bacon, Pres of Columbian College, Mr Wm C Simms, of Balt, to Virginia Alice, d/o the late Benj B Myers, of Wash.

Mrd: on May 13, at N Y, at St Peter's Church, by Rev John Power, Edw C West, of Madison Co, Ill, to Julia, y/d/o the late Matthew Carroll, of that city.

Mrd: on May 16, at N Y, at St George's Chapel, by Rev Jas Milner, Wm Francis Dominick, of Chicago, Ill, to Lydia, 3rd d/o Elisha Wells.

Died: on May 17, in Balt, Wm Gaston, infant s/o Raphael Semmes, aged 5 months & 10 days.

Senate: 1-Ptn from John P Watson, asking the removal of obstructions in the Bayou Lafourche & Bayou Blue: referred. 2-To be engrossed: bill for the relief of J Pemberton Hutchinson, late U S Consul at Lisbon. Also, bill for the relief of Jas Ritchie. 3-Act for the relief of Adam L Mills: read a 3rd time.

House of Reps: 1-Cmte of Claims: bill for the relief of Jos Nock; bill for the relief of John Adams & John Adams, jr. Same cmte: adverse reports on the ptns of Wm McCabe, John Robinson, Jas B Estes, the heirs of Benj Furman, dec'd, & Elijah S Bell. Same cmte: adverse report on the ptn of Hammond & Dexter. Same cmte: adverse reports on the ptns of Geo Steele & Teacle Savage, administrators of Bolitha Laws. 2-Cmte on Commerce; bill for the relief of Horvey & Slagg. 3-Cmte on Public Lands: bill from the Senate for the relief of Jos Campau, reported the same without amendment. 4-Cmte on the Revolutioary Claims: bill for the relief of the reps of Maj Gen Baron De Kalb, dec'd. Same cmte: bill for the relief of Chas W Morgan, without amendment. Same cmte: report on the ptn of Jas A Stevens, with a bill directing the employment of said Stevens to perform certain experiments therein mentioned. 5-Cmte on Military Affairs: bill for the relief of Mrs Mary W Thompson. 6-Cmte on Patents: adverse reports on the ptn of Isaiah Burson, & the ptn of Wm Morrison, Geo Tomb, & Jas Wilson. 7-Ptn of Truman Enos & others, praying that a pension may be granted to Seth Morton, of Oneida Co, N Y. 8-Ptn of Maj Beall & other ofcrs of the U S Army, & of 45 citizens, for a post route to be established from *Fort Towson* to *Fort Washita*, Choctaw nation. 9-Memorial of Andoniram Chandler T B Wakeman & others, on the subject of the Patent Ofc Fund, & remonstrating against its misapplication to the erection of a new bldg.

Orphans Court of Wash Co, D C. Letters of administration on the personal estate of Chas F Bihler, late of said county, dec'd. –Rosalie Bihler, admx

Valuable farm for sale: the subscriber having removed, for professional considerations, to King Geo Court-house, Va, offers for sale his farm called *Moorlands*: in said county: consists of 558 acres: dwlg house is small but comfortable. H M Tennent, in the neighborhood, will show the farm; or myself, at King Geo Court-house, Va. –Thos L Hunter, King Geo Co, Va

Trustee's sale: by deed of trust, executed to me by Dr W S McPherson, of Fred'k Co, Md, for certain purposes therein mentioned, the undersigned Trustee will sell at public sale, on Jun 11 next, on the premises, all that tract of land called ***Prospect Hall***, on which said Wm S McPherson now resides, about 1 mile from Fred'k City, containing 475 acres, with a well finished brick dwlg house, about 70 by 40 feet, & numerous out-bldgs. Also, I will sell all the stock & farming utensils on said farm. Also, I will sell at private sale all the servants of said Wm S McPherson, consisting of about 37 negroes. Also, on the next day, will be sold at the City Hotel, in Fred'k, that valuable dwlg house & lot, fronting on Church st, in Fred'k City, formerly owned by John Nelson, a most desireable residence, & now in good repair. Also, a vacant lot on South st, & part of a vacant lot adjoining. –J Dixon Roman, trustee

Insolvent debtor, Francis Fenwick has applied to be discharged from imprisonment. -Wm Brent, clk

On application by ptn in writing, to me the subscriber, Chief Judge of the Orphans' Court of Chas Co, [it being in the recess of the County Court of said county,] from Robt B Burrows, praying for the benefit of the act of Assembly, passed at Nov session 1805, & the several supplements thereto, a schedule of his property & a list of his creditors on oath as far as ascertained being annexed to his ptn; & that Robt B Burrows having satisfied me, by competent testimony, that he has resided in the State of Md 2 years immediately preceding the time of his application: it is ordered by me that the Robt B Burrows be hereby discharged, provided a copy of this order be inserted in some newspaper published in D C once a wekk for 3 months prior to the 3rd Mon of Aug next, notifying the creditors of said Robt B Burrows to be & appear in Chas Co Court on the said time, for the purpose of recommending a trustee for their benefit, & to show cause, if any they have, why the said Robt B Burrows shall not have the benefit of the said act of Assembly, & the several supplements thereto, as prayed. –Richd Barnes -Walter Mitchel, clk Feb 7, 1844.

Strayed or stolen, on Capitol Hill, on Tue last, a Sorrel Horse. Liberal reward for return of said horse to Conrad Hartman, Capitol Hill.

MON MAY 27, 1844
Affray last Thu in Fuller's Hotel, between Mr Henry J Drayton, & Mr Chas H Winder, in which the latter received a severe wound in the head by the application of a heavy cane in the hands of Mr Drayton. It will probably lead to an investigation at the next Criminal Court, from the particulars of the assault.

Senate: 1-Bill for the relief of Jas Ritchie: passed. 2-Bill for the relief of J Pemberton Hutchinson, late U S Consul at Lisbon: passed. 3-Bill for the relief of Wm Wynn: to be engrossed.

Hon Elias Howell died at his residence in Licking Co, Ohio, of apoplexy, on Thu last. He represented the district composed of Licking & Muskingum Counties in Congress in 1834, & held other public stations. -Newark Gaz

Wash City Ordinance: Act to compensate Wm B Wilson for spreading earth on Mass ave, between 6th & 7th sts: to be paid $40. Approved: May 22, 1844.

House of Reps: 1-Memorial from Gen Joe Smith, Comder-in-Chief of the Latter Day Saints, modestly dictating to Congress the provisions of a bill authorizing him to raise an army of 100,000 volunteers to take Oregon, annex Texas, & spread the wings of the American eagle over all territories adjacent to the U S & elsewhere; & rendering it highly penal in anywise to resist or molest him in so benevolent a design. Yeas 79, nays 86. So the House refused to go into cmte. 2-Cmte of the Whole reported the following bills to the House: relief of:

Edw Kennard	Patrick Masterson
Saml Butler	Sherman Pierce
Langrey & Jenkins	Drusilla Giesey
E Hiddon	Harvey Heth
Wm R Joyne	Alice Usher
D Akison	John Milsted
Francis Sommeraner	Henry Newingham
A D W Bodly	Isaac Baker
Benj Murphy	John Perham
Harvey Peake	P Schwartztrawber
J P Converse	Danl W Church
C P Sengstack	John H Russell, et al
David Allspach	Heirs of P Thornton
Geo Singley	Heirs of Christopher Miller
Geo Wentling	Francis Cazea, of Montreal
Uriah Loomis	Susannah, wid/o Wm Scott
Amaziah Goodwin	Francis Yoast & J P Rogers
John Edmonson	P G Holmes & W Pedrick
Mary A Linton	Abel Guthrie
Peter Wilson	Henry S Commager
Maria Ostraunder	Jonthan Bean
Mary B Perry, et al	Robt Munroe
Ferguson & Reid	Asa Davis
Wm De Peyster & another	Wm McPherson
Danl G Skinner	Josiah Dillon
W P Duvall	John Sands
Richd Snead	Wm McCauley
W J Baker	Mrs M M Telfair
Saml Moore	Susannah Warner
J A Bryan	Marcay Olds

E D Dickson
Wm R Davis
F A Kerr
Mgt Dougherty
Hiram Murch
John Atchison
Wm Henson
Jos Chapman
Chas W Morgan
Sellers & Rennock
Saltmarsh & Fuller
Wm Fuller
Heirs of John Hart
Peters, Moore & Co
Arsenath Orvis, wid/o G Orvis
Widow Hannah Duboise
Isaac S Ketchum
Isaac S Ketchum, late special Indian agent
Wilmot Marsden, wid/o Geo Marsden
Manlius V Thompson, sole exc of Miles W Dickey
Ann Hunter, wid/o Robt Hunter
Nancy Wilson, wid/o Capt Wm Wilson
Francois Chretian & widow Baptiste Berard
Solomon Sturges, assignee of Humphrey Richcreek
F P Ambler, C P Ambler, & Eliz Pearce, heirs of Eliz Rowe
Owner & crew of the schnr **Mary Francis**
Owners & crew of the schnr **Garnett**
Owner & crew of the schnr **Florilla**
Owners & crew of the schnr **Privado**
Owner & crew of the schnr **Two Brothers**
Owners & crew of the schnr **Dove**
Barnabas Baker & others, owners of schnr **Union**, of Dennis, in Mass
Claim of Antonio Cherino to a tract of land in Louisiana
Incorporate *Gtwn College*, in D C

Hurricane in the village of Charlestown, in Kanawha Co, Va, visited last Mon night: the ropewalk of Mr Downward was completely prostrated; the adjoining house, a 2 story brick, occupied by Mr Jos Caldwell & family was completely wrecked to the floor of the 2nd story, the roof being carried more than 100 yards. Two little girls, who were in bed in one of the chambers, were blown some distance with the bed & timbers. One had her should broken & much bruised, & the other's face was much bruised.

Leesburg & Winchester Stage: will leave for the future the old ofc kept by Peck, opposite Brown's Hotel, Wash. Leaves Wash, D C, every Tue, Thu, & Sat, at 3 a m. Leaves Winchester, Va, every Mon, Wed, & Fri, at 3 a m. To the patrons of the Seminary at Bellmont, Va, under the management of Miss Mercer, we will pay every attention to their packages, & will deliver & call for passengers to the school. –Faidley & Johnson, Proprietors at Leesburg, Va. Jos Peck, Agent

Died: on Sat last, at his residence on the borders of this city, Jos H Hand, Chief Clerk in the Patent Ofc.

Board will assemble at West Point for the inspection of the Institution on Jun 10th, & will be composed of the following:
Maj Gen Winfield Scott
Brevet Brig Gen W J Worth, of the Infty
Col T Cross, Quartermaster' Dept
Col J B Crane, of the Artl
Lt Col J Kearney, Corps of Topog Engineers
Maj R L Baker, Ordnance Dept
Bvt Maj L Thomas, Adj General's Dept
Capt Robt E Lee, Corps of Engineers
Capt J Sanders, Corps of Engineers
Capt G G Waggaman, Commissary's Dept
-Wm Wilkins, Sec of War

The U S surveying brig **Washington** got underway from the Navy Yard, N Y, & anchored off the Battery on Fri preparatory to service. Ofcrs of the Washington: Thos R Gedney, Cmder; Lts, Jos C Walsh, Chas Steedman, Alonzo B Davis, John Hall, Roger N Stembel, Francis Haggerty; Acting Master, S Chase Barney.

TUE MAY 28, 1844
Senate: 1-Ptn from Thos L Adams, praying the discontinuance of the spirit ration in the navy. 2-Bill for the relief of the heirs of Robt Fulton: postponed.

House of Reps: 1-Ptn of Ruth Ranson for a land warrant, in lieu of a former one lost. 2-Ptn of Jas McGown & of Simon H Hadman, for pensions.

Wanted, by a man & his wife, who have no children, a situation in the country or city-the country would be preferred, the man as laborer & the woman as housekeeper. Apply at Mr D Nailor's, 13½ & D sts, Wash.

By writ of fieri facias, issued by Saml Stettinius, J P, at the suit of Patrick McKenna, against the good & chattels, lands & tenements, of John Hill, I have seized one gray horse, which I will offer at public auction, on Jun 4. –H R Maryman, constable

Mrs R Smith, removed her Boarding House to one of Mr J Gideon's new & handsome bldgs at F & 7th sts, & has a few vacant rooms in most complete order. Her terms are very moderate, varying from $3 to $4.50 per week.

The case of the U S vs Maj Andrew Talcott, was closed yesterday. The Gov't claimed a balance of $16,000 from Maj T, while his accounts showed a balance of upwards of $7,000 due to him, allowing the $16,000. The jury returned a verdict in favor of Maj Talcott, assessing the amount due him at $3,152.87. -N Y Courier

Insolvent debtor, Michl McCarty, has applied to be discharged from imprisonment.
–Wm Brent, clk

Appointments by the Pres, with the advice & consent of the Senate:
Saml K Haring, to be Collector of the Customs for the District, & Inspector of the Revenue for the Port of Michilimackinac, Mich.
Thos R Hampton, Edw W Clark, & Thos Donoho, to be a Justices of the Peace in Wash Co, D C.
Geo C Washington, & John T Mason, to be Cherokee Com'rs.
Thos H Harvey, to be Superintendent of Indian Affairs for the District of St Louis.

Freebooters have been committing depredations around the Catskill Mountains, N Y. Sat last, a reward of $50 was offered by the Sheriff for the body of Alfred Corwin, leader of the band. Two young men, Merritt & Hall found him in a thicket, when he presented his large horse pistol at Hall, but the pistol did not go off, the powder having been wet, & Merritt leveled his rifle & shot the daring outlaw through the head, killing him instantly. Corwin's band dispersed, but some will be arrested.

Mr Geo Miller, of Barree township, Pa, was returning home on horseback from a military parade, being intoxicated, he was seen asleep by some boys, who to do him a kindness, attempted to stop his horse, when the animal suddenly jumped aside & threw his rider, who fell on a stump, greatly injuring his breast. He was taken to an adjacent house & then removed to his own home. He lingered until the next evening, when he died.

Died: in Mar last, on board the frig **Columbia**, at sea, on his voyage from Rio de Janeiro to the Mediterranean cruising station, Capt Edw R Shubrick, a gallant & highly esteemed ofcr of the U S Navy. He died of chronic affection of the liver. The command of the ship devolved on her 1st Lt, John R Goldsborough.

Died: on Thu last, at Plymouth, Mass, the venerable Dr Jas Thatcher, aged 90 years. He was born at Barnstable, & entered the Revoltionary army at Cambridge at the commencement of the war as a surgeon's mate under the late Dr Warren, of Boston. He was soon promoted to be a surgeon, & in that capacity served during the war. He was present at many of the principal battles of the Revolution, & terminated his services at Yorktown. He was an eye-witness of the execution of Andre, & has fully described the scene in his Military Journal. At the close of the war he settled in this town as a surgeon, where he had since resided. –Old Colony Memorial

Assault near the War Dept yesterday, by a gang of desperadoes, Justice Drury had his head cut, & they drew a knife upon Justice H C Williams, while these magistrates were endeavoring, in the execution of their duty, to arrest the offenders. Rioters secured: John E Moody, Geo A Moody, & Jas F Moody.

Democratic Nat'l Convention at Balt, May 27, 1844. Jas Carroll, of Balt, was nominated as their candidate for Govn'r. Following ofcrs were chosen: Hendrick B Wright, of Pa, President of the Convention.

Vice Presidents:

R J Ingersoll, of Conn	Linn Boyd, of Ky
Saml Young, of N Y	Wm H Fulton, of Ark
Jos Edsell, of N J	Stephen Emory, of Maine
J L Dawson, of Pa	Ehenry Hubbard, of N H
Wm Frick, of Md	Henry H Childs, of Mass
Jas N Sutton, of Dela	Luther B Hunt, of Vt
Wm H Roane, of Va	Olney Ballou, of R I
R M Saunders, of N C	Nicholas Schumacker, of Ohio
B J Shield, of Ala	Ephraim A Brown, of Ind
John W Howard, of Ga	Jas Snow, of Ill
Powhatan Ellis, of Miss	J Coffman, of Mo
Thos L Williams, of La	Robt S Gilson, of Mich
Gave Johnson, of Tenn	

Secretaries:

Wm F Ritchie, of Va	Geo A Vroom, of N J
Thos A Mitchell, of N Y	Chas A Bradford, of Miss

WED MAY 29, 1844
Local Affairs: we recommend to our readers the Patent Condensing Coffee Boiler invented by Mr D Rowland. It makes coffee strong, rich, & well-flavored.

Wash Corp: 1-Bill for the relief of Thos Lewis: passed. 2-Bill for the relief of Wm Thorpe: indefinitely postponed. 3-Ptn of H G Ritter, praying the remission of a fine: laid on the table. 4-Ptn of Saml Kirby & others, for the improvement of 8th st west from D to E sts north: referred to the Cmte on Improvements. 5-Ptn of B Thruston & others, for the improvement of Mass ave from 3rd to 6th sts: referrd to the Cmte on Improvements. 6-Ptn of Wm Johnson, praying the remission of a fine: laid on the table. 7-Cmte on Police: asking to be discharged from the further consideration of the ptn of D Clagett & others: laid on the table.

Senate: 1-Cmte on Private Land Claims: House bill for the relief of Jas Pepper & others, without amendment. 2-Ptn from Alice Pew, wid/o W Pew, a soldier of the Revolution, asking to be allowed arrears of pension. 3-Ptn from Sarah Searls, wid/o a Revolutionary soldier, for a pension. 4-Cmte on Naval Affairs: bill granting a pension to Jas Duffey, without amendment. Same cmte: House bill for the relief of Hugh Wallace Wormly, without amendment, & recommending that it be indefinitely postponed.

Orphans Court of Wash Co, D C. Letters of administration on the personal estate of Abraham H Quincy, jr, late of Wash Co, dec'd. –Thos H Quincy, adm

House of Reps: 1-Cmte on Naval Affairs: ptn of Benj Church, with a bill to provide the payment of certain pensions paid out of the privateer pension fund. 2-Cmte on Invalid Pensions: bill for the relief of Saml Neely. 3-Cmte on Naval Affairs: act for the relief of Peter Von Schmidt, reported the same without amendment.

Correspondence between B C Wilcocks, of Phil, & Mrs Susan Decatur: Fuller's Hotel, Wash, Apr 26, 1844. Madam: You will, I am sure, pardon an intrusion which is induced principally by an exalted respect for the memory of your gallant & lamented husband. A large space of ground, containing about 75 acres, has been lately appropriated to the purpose of a Cemetery in the immediate neighborhood of the city of Phil. The proprietors are desirous of receiving under their care as a sacred deposite the remains of Cmdor Decatur, & of erecting over them a monument not unworthy of his fame. It is in the neighborhood of his native city, in part of what is called *Woodlands Estate*. Interments have not yet been made there. Should you accede to the request which I have the honor to make that the removal may be made to the place which have designated, measures will be taken to carry the object into effect. –B C Wilcocks, Pres of the Board of Mgrs of the Woodlands Cemetery Co. Gtwn, D C, Apr 29, 1844. Dear Sir: I have had the honor of receiving your highly gratifying communication of the 26th; I have no language which can express the intense feeling of gratitude with which it has inspired me. Some years previous to his awful & deplorable fate, I heard him say that if he were permitted to choose the place of his interment, it would be near the tomb of his parents at the Church of St Peter, Phil; I have reserved the place alluded to. His remains are now deposited in the private vault of a friend at Washington to wait the period of my death, when they will be removed to Phil. And I pray you to believe me always most gratefully & respectfully yours. –Susan Decatur

Cow lost: $5 reward for her recovery. Dr B Washington, 6th st

For rent: well finished brick house next door to the Rev Dr Laurie's, Pa ave. Apply on the premises, or at Mr Anderson's Boot & Shoe Factory, next door.

For rent: 2 brick dwlg-houses on F st, between 18th & 19th sts. Apply at the residence of Wm Wilson on 20th st.

For rent: 2 new two story brick houses, with attics & back bldgs. The keys are at Mr Wannal's Store, 9th & I sts, where the above houses are located. For further particulars, apply to Wm D Acken, on Md ave, near 4½ st.

Orphans Court of Wash Co, D C. Letters testamentary on the personal estate of John Gadsby, late of said county, dec'd. –Provey Gadsby, Jas Eakin, Alex'r McIntire, excs [Applications to be made to Alex'r McIntire on business of the estate, & all accounts duly proved & passed by the Orphans' Court presented to him.]

Mrd: on May 23, at the residence of Wm Bosher, by Rev R H Bagby, Chas H Smoot, of Wash, to Miss Mary J Bosher, of King Wm Co, Va.

THU MAY 30, 1844
House Servant for sale: a boy 17 years old, a first rate dining room servant. For terms apply to Morgan Johnson, Postmaster of the House of Reps, or to F H Whiting, Alexandria.

Naval. The U S ship-of-the-line **Columbus**, the U S ship **John Adams**, both from Rio Janeiro, & the U S schnr **Vanderbilt**, & the U S schnr **Gallatin**, both from Phil, arrived at N Y on Mon. The Hon Wm Hunter, late U S Minister at the Court of Brazil, comes passenger in the **John Adams** from Rio de Janeiro. The U S ship **Boston**, Cmder Pendergrast, was at Montevideo. The U S frig **Congress**, Capt Voorhees, sailed from Rio on Mar 16 for the river.

Ofcrs of the **Columbus** from Rio Janeiro, Apr 15:
Benj Cooper, Capt; F Chatard, 1st Lt; A H Kitty, 2nd Lt; T Y Page, 3rd Lt; Wm H Taylor, 4th Lt; B F Sands, 5th Lt; D B Kedgely, 6th Lt; L Maynard, 7th Lt; H Cadwalader, 8th Lt; F K Murray, Acting 1st Master; L McDougal, Acting 2nd Master; B F Bache, Surgeon; Y N Todd, Purser; A N Breevort, Capt of Marines; E L West, Lt of Marines; P G Clarke, Chaplain; J McDuffie, Prof of Mathematics; V L Godon, Passed Assist Surgeon; Y Hastings, Assist Surgeon; R T Maxwell, Passed Assist Surgeon; S Belin, Capt's Clerk; H Spaulding, Purser's Clerk; Midshipmen: H K Stevens, A J Dallas, R P Mason, & Paul Chirley.

Ofcrs of the **John Adams**, from Rio Janeiro, Mar 25:
Thos A Conover, Cmder; Henry Moor, Lt; Oliver Lad, Lt; E M Yard, Lt S Stoddard, Lt; H C Flagg, Lt; H W Greene, Purser; M B Chase, Chaplain; Isaac Brickerhoff, Surgeon; Edw J Nicholas, Acting Master; Wm Flye, Prof of Mathematics; C Francis, Capt's Clerk; Midshipmen: J V McCallum, W V Gillis, Saml Magaw, Robt Stuart, F A Roe, Edw A Selden, J S Tillaston, & J B Yates; Peter G Smith, Acting Boatswain; Wm R Obear, Acting Gunner; Peter Dutcher, Acting Sailmaker; Edw Barnicoat, Acting Carpenter; John D Nason, Master's Mate.

Mrd: on May 14, at Harper's Ferry, Va, by Rev Thos D Hoover, Mr Jas H Burton, formerly of Wash, to Miss Cornelia F Mauzy, of Harper's Ferry.

Mrd: on May 26, at Alexandria, by Rev Mr Danforth, Hon Abraham McClellan, of Sullivan Co, Tenn, to Mrs Mary Houston, of Alexandria.

Died: on May 25, in Gtwn, after a lingering & painful illness, Mrs Ann Maria Hogmire, consort of Conrad Hogmire, in her 45th year of her age.

Died: on May 19, at his residence, near Port Tobacco, Chas W Semmes, ex-Sheriff of Chas Co, after a lingering & painful illness.

Died: on May 23, at the residence of his father, Hon Arnold Naudain, Wilmington, Dela, Jas S Naudain, M D, of Middletown, Dela, in his 33rd year. Society has lost an eminent physician, cut down in the prime of life, & in the midst of his usefulness.

Capitol Hill Boarding House: Mrs Mary A B Cummin [late of Md] has taken a house in Dr May's row, N J ave, about 1 square south of the Capitol.

$130 reward for negro boy Henry Thomas, aged 19 or 20 years. Also, at the same time, on Mon last, a negro man Joshua Isaacks, frequently called Tom Walker, aged 26 years. –John W Brown, White House, Balt & Wash T Road

FRI MAY 31, 1844
Juvenile rowdies arrested: gang of lads calling themselves Gumballs, attempting to create a riot: Wm Baker, Saml Spalding, Jas Norbeck, & Hunt Parker.

Laws of the U S passed at the 1st Session of the 28th Congress.
1-Act for the relief of Isaac Justice, of Tenn: to be placed on the roll of invalid pensions, & is entitled to receive $12.75 per month, during his natural life, from Jan 1, 1838.
2-Act for the relief of Sarah Blackemore, wid/o Geo Blackemore, late a Revolutionary pensioner, of Lincoln Co, Tenn, to be placed on the pension roll, under the act of Jul 17, 1838, entitled An act granting half pay & pensions to certain widows, at the rate of $46.22 per annum, from Mar 4, 1836, to Mar 4, 1841; & also, from Mar 4, 1843, to Mar 4, 1844. Furthermore: Sarah Blackemore shall be entitled to the full benefit of the laws & resolves which shall herefter be passed continuing in force the said act of Jul 7, 1838, & the several acts & resolves amendatory thereof.
3-Act for the relief of Levi Colmus: to pay to him, from & after the passage of this act, $4 per month, for & during his natural life.
4-Act for the relief of Jos Bonnell: to place his name on the pension roll: & to be paid a pension, for 18 months service as a private soldier in the Revolutioanry war, under the act of Jun 7, 1832.
5-Act for the relief of Jas Ried, of Ill: to place his name on the invalid pension roll, & to pay him $8 per month, from & after Feb 4, 1842.
6-Act for the relief of Jas C Hallock, of Dutchess Co, N Y: to place his name on the pension list of invalid pensioners of the U S; & that he be entitled to receive a pension of $8 per month from Jan 1, 1836, & to continue during his natural life.
7-Act for the relief of the legal reps of Capt Saml Shannon, dec'd, late an assist quartrmaster in the U S service: to credit his accounts with the allowances made under the audit of the Sec of War, in his report to Congress, dated Mar 13, 1843; & to pay to the legal reps of Capt Saml Shannon the sum of $634.93, being the blance declared to be due in the report.

8-Act for the relief of Violet Calhoun, wid/o John Calhoun, late a capt in the army of the Revolution: to place her name on the roll of Revolutionary pensioners of the U S; & that she be allowed annually the full pay of capt, commencing on Jul 7, 1838.
9-Act for the relief of John Miller, of Williams Co, Ohio: he is to be issued a patent for the west half of the n w quarter of section 22, in township 5 north, range 1 east, containing 80 acres, without any further payment of money therefore by said Miller.
10-Act granting a pension to Bartholomew Maguire: the sum of $6 per month, from Apr 1, 1825, being the time he made application for a pension, to Dec 12, 1842, the time at which his present pension commenced.
11-Act to explain an act of Congress, passed on Mar 3, 1843, entitled An act for the relief of Eliz Gresham, wid/o Geo Gresham: The Sec of War is to allow to Eliz Gresham, in common with all other widows who have been pensioned under & received the benefit of the act of Jul 7, 1838, the additional pension for 1 year, which, by the act of Mar 3, 1843, is made payable to such widows as have received the benefit of the said act of Jul 7, 1838; the amount so to be paid, for the additional year, to be the same which was allowed to her annually for 5 years, in pursuance of the aforesaid act of which this act is explanatory.

Yesterday, Col Jas K Polk was announced the nominee of the Balt Convention for President.

Just published & for sale by the Booksellers of Wash City, Mysteries of Washington City, by a citizen of Ohio. Contents include interviews with the Pres; Maj Wm B Lewis; Govn'r Woodbury; friends of Mrs Hamilton; biographical sketch of Levi Woodbury; Chas A Clinton; Dr Hosack; Mrs Lentner's on Amity st, where Col Trumbull lived & died; Albert Gallatin & his lady on Beckman st; & Judge Upshur, personal acquaintance with him.

Valuable real estate at public sale: by order of Montg Co Court, the subscribers will offer a public sale, on the premises, on Jun 20, the Farm on which Thos Getzendanner resided at the time of his death. It lies on the main road leading from Gtwn to the mouth of Monocacy; contains 466 acres; dwgl house, kitchen, & all other necessary outbldgs, a dairy, & a blacksmith. Refer to E T Getzendanner, residing on the premises, for further description. –Burgess Willett, Wm H Offutt, John Gassaway, W H Chappell, Com'rs.

Public sale of real estate: by order of Montg Co Court: sale on Jun 21, on the premises, the farm on which Mr Andrew Offutt resided at the time of his death: contains 408 acres: located on the main road leading to the mouth of Monocacy, 2 miles above Darnestown: large brick dwlg house, & necessary out-bldgs. On the same day, will be sold as above, a house & lot in Dawsonville, a good stand for a store. Inquire of the subscribers, or of Messrs John & J W Offutt.
–Wm Darne, Richd Goff, W O Chappell, Comr's

Public sale of real estate: by order of Montg Co Court: on Jun 19, the farm of which Thos W Offutt resided at the time of his death: land lies on the Potomac river, about 2 miles below Great Falls, & contains 150 acres, a fair proportion of which is in wood. The Chesapeake & Ohio Canal passes through it. Improvements are a frame dwlg-house, meat house, corn house, & stables. This farm will be sold entire, or in lots to suit purchasers. –Burgess Willett, Saml M Beall, Julius West, Com'rs

$400 reward for runaway negro men, Hanson, about 21, & Stephen, about 37 years old. –Thos Berry, living at Oxen Hill, PG Co, Md.

Senate: 1-Cmte on Naval Affairs: adverse report on the ptn of the administrator of John Judge. Same cmte: bill for the relief of Wm Brown.

A letter from Greenville, S C, dated 24th, states that Judge Earle died suddenly of a stroke of paralysis in the village on the morning of that day.

Wm Hoff, found guilty of robbing U S mail, has been sentenced in the U S Circuit Court at N Y to 5 years' imprisonment.

The Hon Francois Xavier Martin, Presiding Judge of the Supreme Court of Louisiana, departed from New Orleans on May 21 for Havre, on his way to Paris, for the purpose of undergoing a surgical operation for the removal of a cataract, which for some time past has considerably affected his sight. The Judge is upwards of 80 years of age, & still preserves his rare mental faculties.

Damages for slander. In the District Court of Phil on Fri last, the jury in the case of Sarah Gregory, against Peter C Dollman, rendered a verdict in favor of the plntf for $5,000. The plntf was a respectable young lady from Berks Co, who came to this city some time ago to learn a trade. On her return home, the dfndnt circulated some very indelicate & injurious reports concerning her, which were proved to be false. The parties are all of German descent, & in moderate circumstances only. The testimony of the witnesses was given in German, & interpreted to the jury.

House of Reps: 1-Ptn of John McLaughlin, Augustus Troxel, Thos Murrans, & other citizens of Harrisburg, Pa, praying Congress to admit Texas as a Territory of the U S. 2-Ptn of Mgt M Chew, of Harford Co, Md, praying for a pension for services rendered by her late husband during the Revolutionary war.

SAT JUN 1, 1844
For sale: 3 likely negro women, 27, 25, & 23, of good character; also, 6 children, all slaves for life. These servants are sold to carry out the purposes of a certain deed of trust executed to the subscriber on the 3rd, & recorded in the Clerk's ofc at Montg Co, on the 15th ult, & not for any fault. Terms at sale. –S T Stonestreet, trustee

Senate: 1- Ptn from Dr Ninian Pinkney, of the navy, in relation to his rank in the navy. 2-Ptn from Benj St Vrain, asking remuneration for provisions furnished the U S troops under a contract, when they went to protect the Santa Fe traders. 3-Ptn from may Ann Morrice, for a pension. 4-Ptn from Lucy A Roberts, for a pension. 5-Bill for the relief of Benj Adams & Co & others: passed. 6-Bill granting a pension to Jas Duffy: passed.

House of Reps: 1-Ptn of Jas H Clark, a purser in the U S navy, praying relief upon sundry items, arising from suspensions, disallowances, & unsettled claims originating in the adjustment of his public accounts. 2-Ptn of Jos F Jennings & others, of Wayne, Maine, for the establishment of a post route & a post ofc at North Wayne.

The undersigned have this day taken into partnership B J Semmes, jr. The business in the future will be conducted under the firm of Semmes, Murray, & Semmes. -Semmes & Murray

Accident took place at the village of Bath, near Kingston, U C, on May 10, when several children, with 2 young women, went out on the bay in a small skiff, which upset. Drowned were Charlotte Priest, d/o Mr Edgar D Priest, aged about 13; Caroline Lewis, d/o widow Lewis, aged 15; & a child of John Webster's about 2 years of age.

Cow lost: reward of $5 for her recovery. J Bartram North, N J ave, 2 squares south of the Capitol

Having engaged a graduate of Amherst College, Mass, as tutor to my own children, I will take in addition 6 boys, from 12 to 14, as boarders. My residence is in the upper part of Loudoun Co, Va, & the neighborhood is remarkably healthy. Direct communications to Upperville, Fauquier Co, Va. -John A Carter.

Washington Academy for sale: located in the upper part of Westmoreland Co, Va; incorporated, but belongs to private individuals, & is alienable by them. Consists of a tract of 40 acres, & a 2 story brick house thereon. Occupied for an Academy for 8 or 10 years. –G W Lewis, Agent for Trustees & Stockholders. Post Ofc, Oak Grove, Westmoreland, Va.

Longwood for sale or rent: situated in Westmoreland Co, Va, on the Potomac river, adjoining the estate on which Gen Washington was born; contains 1,800 acres of land; an old millseat when may be rendered very valuable at a small cost. The dwlg house has been recently destroyed by fire, but there are 2 brick ofcs remaining in the yard capable of being made very comfortable for a family. Horses & cattle may be purchased with the farm. Apply to be either in person or by letter, post paid, to the subscriber, living near Hampstead post ofc, King Geo Co, Va. –R H Stuart

Cynthia Roberts, of Hartford, Conn, & husband, were sentenced to 30 days imprisonment & $7 fine, for the cruel treatment to a bound child, 7 or 8 years old. The ends of her fingers were cruelly pinched with a pair of pincers, taking off the nails as a punishment, also her toes. Her body, from head to foot, was covered with marks as large as the finger.

The 7 year old s/o Mr H Harrington, of East Boston, was, on Sun last, by some means precipitated down a well 70 feet in depth; & strange to say, when rescued was found to be but little injured.

A son of Henry C Corbit, of Phil, was drowned on Sat, while bathing in the Brandywine, near Wistar's Bridge, with the scholars of the Prospect Hill School. The dec'd, who bore his father's name, was about 14 years of age.

Mrd: on Thu, by Rev John C Smith, Mr Saml Butt to Miss Anna Rebecca, eldest d/o B L Bogan, all of Wash City.

Died: on Sunday last, at the Monastery in Gtwn, Sister Clotilda, [formerly Miss Mary O'Reilly,] in her 20th year. Thus another soul has been transferred to heaven, & another name added to the catalogue of saints.

Died: on May 24, at *What-Cheer*, her late residence in Providence, R I, Mrs Sarah Fenner, w/o Jas Fenner, the Govn'r of the State of R I.

Died: on May 14, at her residence, in Pulaski, Tenn, Mrs Sarah W Brown, consort of Hon Aaron V Brown.

Died: May 31, at *Woodbourne*, near Rock Creek Church, after a short inflammatory illness, Wm G Sanders, jr, only s/o Capt Wm G Sanders, aged 26 years.

Died: on May 17, at his residence, in Powhatan Co, Maj John Clarke, in his 79th year. In very early youth, he served his country during the war of the Revolution, first as a volunteer & then in the regular army. He became eminently distinguished for genius, especially in mechanics, which he signally displayed in the construction of the works of the Va Armory, that cannot even yet be forgotten, & which attracted universal attention, & made him an object of admiration to all men. He numbered among his warm personal friends many of the most eminent men of merit in the country. –Richmond Enquirer

MON JUN 3, 1844
Balt, May 31. R W Pooler, the second of Mr May, in the late duel at Wash, in which young Cochrane was killed, has been tried in Harford Co, & acquitted. -Patriot

The N Y Sun records a disaster that occurred in the village of Willaimsbrug, on Fri last, while a number of children were amusing themselves in an excavation made for bldg purposes, in North Second st, the overhanging earth caved in & buried 7 of them, & one survived. Mr Lewis Jones, carpenter, lost 3 children; Mr Paul, druggist, lost one dght aged 9; Mr Darlington lost a dght aged 4 or 5; & Mr Sheme, a laborer, lost a dght aged 14.

Senate: 1-Cmte on Military Affairs: bill for the relief of Benj St Vrain & Co. 2-Cmte on Public Bldgs: adverse report on the memorial of Jas Wilson. 3-Bill for the relief of Wm Bronson, & the bill for the relief of Benj Adams & Co & others: were passed.

Louisa, a girl about 12 years old, d/o Mr Luther Purrinton, of Coleraine, Mass, met her death on May 19. She had gone to a school house, & while in the house saw some flowers under the back window & climed out, but in climbing back through the window the sash fell down upon her neck & held her fast. She was found & life was extinct. –Greenfield [Mass] Courier

Died: on May 23, in Glenville, Schenectady Co, N Y, Mr John Jacobus Van Voast, at the advanced age of 103 years, 4 months & 4 days.

Orphans Court of Wash Co, D C. Letters testamentary on the personal estate of Jas Birth, late of said county, dec'd. –Wm W Birth, adm

House of Reps: 1-Following bills were passed-relief of:

Saml Butler	Saml Moore
E Hiddon	Patrick Masterson
D Akison	Drusilla Giesey
Francis Sommeraner	Lund Washington
A D W Bodly	Alice Usher
Harvey Parke	John Milsted
J P Converse	Henry Newingham
C P Sengstack	Isaac Baker
David Allspach	John Perham
Geo Singley	P Schwartztrawber
Geo Wentling	Henry S Commager
Uriah Loomis	Robt Munroe
John Edmonson	Asa Davis
Peter Wilson	Jos Dillon
Maria Ostrander	Wm McCauley
Mary B Perry et al	John Sands
Ferguson & Reid	Marclay Olds
W P Duvall	Mgt Dougherty
Richd Snead	Amos Proctor
W J Baker	Edw Kennard

Wm R Joines
Sherman Pierce
Abelard Guthrie
Danl W Church
Saltmarsh & Fuller
Wm Fuller
Sellers & Pennock
Langtry & Jenkins
Nancy Wilson, wid/o Capt Wm Wilson
Ann Hunter, wid/o Robt Hunter
Owner & crew of the schnr **Mary Francis**
Owners & crew of the schnr **Garnett**
Owner & crew of the schnr **Florilla**
Owners & crew of the schnr **Privado**
Owner & crew of the schnr **Two Brothers**
Owners & crew of the schnr **Dove**
Isaac S Ketchum
Isaac S Ketchum, late special Indian agent
Francois Chretien & widow Baptiste Berard
Manlius V Thompson, sole exc of Miles W Dickey
F P Ambler, C P Ambler, & Eliz Pearce, heirs of Eliz Rowe
Wilmot S Marsden, of Oneida Co, N Y, wid/o Geo Marsden, dec'd.
Solomon Sturges, assignee of Humphrey Richcreek
Barnabas Baker & others, owners of schnr **Union**, of Dennis, in Mass
Claim of Antonio Cherino to a tract of land in Louisiana
Bill to incorporate **Gtwn College**, in D C

John H Russell et al
Widow Hannah Duboise
Heirs of Mrs M M Telfair
Heirs of John Hart
Susannah, wid/o Wm Scott
Francis Yoast & J P Rogers
Arsenath Orvis, wid/o G Orvis
Ann Hunter, wid/o Robt Hunter

Wash Corp: 1-Act for the relief of Thos Lewis: to be paid $10.10, being the balance due him for completing certain flag footways in the First Ward, authorized by an act approved Sep 23, 1841. 2-Act for the improvement of the Western Burying Ground: that $150 be appropriated for repairing & white washing the fence, & for cleaning & putting the ground in order, under the direction of the com'rs of that burying ground. 3-Act for the completion of the road from 7th st to the Catholic Burial Ground: sum of $140 for completion of the road.

TUE JUN 4, 1844
Virginia Hot Springs: It has been the practice for some years past for invalids who requied the aid of nurses to come to the Hot Springs without an attendant of any sort, thereby involving the proprietor in much trouble & expense, for which he never has been remunerated. In the future every visiter who may require his meals in his room, or the aid of servants to take him to & from the baths or public dining room, will be required to furnish his own attendants, or to pay an equitable extra charge for the same. –Th Goode

Senate: 1-Ptn from Rowland Bennett, asking permission to enter at the Marietta ofc a certain tract of land. 2-Cmte on Private Land Claims; bill to confirm the title of a tract of land in the Territory of Iowa to the legal heirs & assignees of Julia Dubuque. 3-Cmte on Pensions: adverse reports on the following cases: claim of Geo West; ptns of Alice Pews, of Jane Moore, & Sarah Seals: ordered to be printed. Same cmte: House bill for the relief of Mark Simpson, without amendment, recommending its passage. Same cmte: House bill granting a pension to Saml Shrofer, without amendment, recommending its passage. Same cmte: asking to be discharged from the further consideration of the ptn of Mary Ann Maurice, & that it be referred to the Cmte on Naval Affairs. Same cmte: unfavorable reports on the ptns of Peter Ingles, Adam Stanley, & Peter Frost. 4-Cmte on Public Lands: House bill for the relief of Eaton Naull, without amendment, & recommending its passage. 5-Bill for the relief of Wm Elliot, of Fulton Co, Ill, was ordered to be engrossed. 6-Bill for the relief of Mary Reeside, excx of the last will & testament of Jas Reeside, dec'd: laid on the table for the present.

Positive sale of the Milton manufacturing Co, on Jul 11th, 1844, on the premises, in the town of Milton, N C. –W R Hill, Special Agent, Milton, N C

Valuable land at auction: by deed of trust, recorded in Liber W B 106, folios 144 to 150, of the land records of Wash Co, D C: public auction, on Jun 26, of a tract of land containing about 90 acres, being part of the tract called *Giesborough Manor*, & adjoining the lands of Dr C B Hamilton & Wash Berry. –Jas C Barry, trustee -R W Dyer & Co, aucts

$25 reward for runaway female slave Levina, about 30 years old. She took her son, about 2½, named Madison. –Francis A Dickins, *Ossian Hall*, Fairfax Co, Va.

$100 reward for runaway negro man George, 23 or 24 years old.
–Henry H Hawkins, near Bryantown, Chas Co, Md

Died: yesterday, near the Navy Yard in Wash City, Mr Cornelius Henning, in his 38th year. His funeral will take place this afternoon, at 2 o'clock, & will be attended by Eastern Lodge, [I O O F] who invite the members of the Order generally who are in good standing to join them in this last sad testimonial of respect to their dec'd brother. The ofcrs & members of Masonic Lodges are requested to unite with Naval Lodge in paying the last tribute of respect to their dec'd brother; as are also the ofcrs & members of the Columbia Royal Arch Chapter.

On Jun 6 the entire effects of the Billiard Saloon, at Gay & Balt sts, 2nd story, will be sold. –Wm N Dutch & Co, auctioneers, Lombard & Chas St, Balt, Md.

WED JUN 5, 1844
Coach-making, Thos Young, Pa ave, between 3rd & 4½ sts.

Household & kitchen furniture at auction: on Jun 12, at the residence of the Hon H S Fox, late Minister Pleni from Great Britain, on K st, near Pa ave: also two 4 wheeled Carriages, an English Landaulet Chariot, & a German Britzka Barouche.
-R W Dyer & Co, aucts

Household & kitchen furniture at auction: on Jun 7, over the store of Mrs Elexius Simms, F & 13th sts. -R W Dyer & Co, aucts

Negroes wanted: for the New Orleans market, & will give the highest market price in cash for likely young negroes. –Thos Williams

Wilful murder & suicide. A Frenchman, Jules Lesueurs, early on Sat, shot his wife & committed suicide by shooting himself through the body. The deed was committed in the French boarding-house of August Esmoil, in Dock st, Phil. The act was premeditated due to a refusal on the part of the wife to continue to live with the husband.

Senate: 1-Cmte on Public Bldgs: asking to be discharged from the further consideration of the ptn of the heir of Danl Pettibone, asking compensation for use of his rarifying air stove by the U S in the Capitol. 2-Cmte on Pensions: adverse reports on House bills for the relief of Fred'k Hopkins, & the relief of Jane McGuire, wid/o Thos McGuire. 3-Cmte on Indian Affairs: bill for the relief of Joshua Kennedy, of Ala, with an amendment.

Criminal Court-Wash: Grand Jurors-Tue: Peter Force, Foreman

John W Maury	Geo W Riggs	R C Weightman
Geo Watterston	Andrew Coyle	Benj O Tayloe
Washington Berry	Wm B Thompson	Hamilton Luforough
Joshua Pierce	Lewis Carbery	Thos Corcoran
John P Ingle	Wm Grindage	John Kurtz
B K Morsell	Wm Gunton	Thos Blagden
John F Cox	Jos Forrest	
Edw M Linthicum	John Boyle	

Louis Watkins & Edw L Birch, were yesterday admitted as attys of the Court-Wash.

Died: on Jun 1, Wm Albert, infant s/o Wm Henry & A M Upperman, aged 8 months.

Died: on Jun 1, Catharine M Kearny, d/o John Warren, of N Y, aged 12 years.

Died: on Jun 1, at *Poplar Grove*, Queen Anne's Co, Md, the residence of his father, the late Gen Emory, Robt Emory, aged 27 years.

Mayor's ofc-Wash, Jun 4, 1844. Duly elected on Jun 3, 1844:

Alderman:

Wm B Magruder	Walter Lenox	Saml Byington
Wm Orme	Jos W Beck	Thos Thornly

Common Councilmen:

Wm Wilson	John T Towers	Joel W Jones
Chas A Davis	Saml Bacon	John McCauley
Richd M Harrison	Saml Burche	John E Neale
Lewis Johnson	Wm Hicks	Geo H Fulmer
Jas F Haliday	John Johnson	John R Queen
Saml D King	Jas B Philips	Jas Cull

From the Balt American of yesterday: note addressed to R W Pooler by the Jury before whom he was recently tried in Harford Co Court. –Reverdy Johnson Balt, Jun 1, 1844. Sir: We, the undersigned, Jurors impannelled to try your case, had not doubt of your innocence, & would have acquitted you without any instructions from the Court. Signed:

Thos Hope	Michl E Pue	John M Rutlidge
R W Billingalie	Geo Mecham	John Heaton
Chas D Bouldin	Thos Carman	Wm M Eddy
Chas Worthington	Wm Steel	Jas S Robinson

–May 20, 1844

For sale: 2 story dwlg house, at present occupied by the subscriber, on 8th st, opposite the Marine Barracks. –P M Pearson

For rent: new & commodious dwgl on F st, near 7th, adjoining the residence of Mrs Lindenberger. Possession may be had immediately.

I certify that John Downs, of Wash Co, brought before me as strays, trespassing on his property, a brindled cow; also, a young liver colored cow. –W Thompson Owner will come forward, prove property, & take them away.
–John Downs, living on Greenleaf's Point, near the Arsenal.

Insolvent debtor, L F Whitney, has applied to be discharged from imprisonment. –Wm Brent, clk

$5 reward for runaway mulatto boy Archy, about 16 years old. The reward will be paid on application at Harkness' bldgs, N Y ave, between 9th & 10th sts. –S H Cutts

THU JUN 6, 1844
Laws of the U S passed at the 1st Session of the 28th Congress.
1-Act for the relief of Wm Glover, of the town of Brutus, Cayuga Co, N Y: to place his name on the roll of invalid pensioners, & pay to him $8 per month, from Oct 1, 1842, when his evidence was completed, during his natural life.
2-Act for the relief of Adam L Mills: to be paid the additional amount which may be found due him under a contract for carrying the mail from Vandalia, Ill, to St Louis, Mo, dated Oct 17, 1837, at the rate of pay for the highest grade of service mentioned in said contract, from Jul 18, 1838, to the full period for which said Mills carried the mail, under said contract, in four horse post coaches.
3-Act for the relief of Louis Croull, alias Cronkhite, wid/o John Croull, alias Cronkhite, late a cpl in the N Y line of the army of the Revolution: to place her name on the pension roll, under the act of Jul 7, 1838, granting half pay & pensions to certain widows, & also under the act of Mar 3, 1843, entitled An act granting a pension to the widows of certain Revolutionary soldiers, at the rate of $88 per annum. And that said Lois shall be entitled to the full benefit of all laws &
4-Act for the relief of Abigail Gibson, wid/o Geo Gibson, late a Revolutionary pensioner, of Todd Co, Ky, to place her name on the pension roll, at the rate of $26.66 per annum, from Mar 4, 1836, to Mar 4, 1841; &, also, from Mar 4, 1843, to Mar 4, 1844. Also, that said Abilgail Gibson shall be entitled to the full benefit of all laws & resolves which shall hereafter be passed continuing in force the act of Jun 7, 1838, & the several acts & resolves amendatory thereof.
5-Act for the relief of Benj B Ferguson, of Pa, to place his name on the roll of invalid pensioners, at the rate of $5.50 per month; said pension to commence on Jan 1, 1838, & to continue during his natural life.
6-Act for the relief of Mary Williams, wid/o the late Jacob Williams, dec'd: the pension to which said Jacob Williams would have been entitled had he been living on Jun 7, 1832, be deemed, & the same is hereby declared to be, a pension for 2 years' service, & that the Sec of War interpret said act accordingly.

Senate: 1-Cmte on Naval Affairs: House bill to test the utility of the submarine telescope, & the joint resolution authorizing Capt Jas Lowe to assign a certain section of land, without amendment, & recommending their passage. 2-Cmte on Commerce: asking to be discharged from the further consideration of the House bill for the relief of Amos Proctor, & that it be referred to the Cmte on the Judiciary. 3-Cmte on Public Lands: House bills for the relief of Henry Newingham & for the relief of John McColgan, without amendment, & recommending their passage. 4-Bill introduced for the relief of Geo Mayfield: referred to the Cmte on Private Land Claims.

Notice: was committed to the jail of Fred'k Co on May 31, as a runaway, a black man who calls himself Hanson, about 20 years old. The owner, if any, is to come & have him released, or he will be discharged according to law.
–Geo Rich, Sheriff of Fred'k Co, Md.

Middle District Court of Florida, Leon Superior Court-Chancery. Between H G Guyon, et al, cmplnts, & the Southern Life Ins & Trust Co, & Geo Field, et al, dfndnts. On bill for injunction, to set aside assignments, for Receivers, & to apply assets of Company to payment of its debts. All persons claiming to be creditors of said Company, are to present their claims or demands to Jos Branch, Lawrence Branch, & Chas G English, the Receivers appointed by the Court in said cases. Postage must be paid on all letters or they will not be taken from the post ofc. Messrs Bryan & Maitland, of N Y, Benj H Brewster, of Phil, of Bernard Adams & Co, of Boston, will receive any of the said paper for transmission to the Receivers, & forward them free of expense, if placed with them prior to Sep 1, 1844.
-R T Birchett, Clerk, Tallahassee

Notice: was committed to the jail of Fred'k Co on May 31, as a runaway, a black man who calls himself Stephen, about 50 years old. The owner, if any, is to come & have him released, or he will be discharged according to law. --Geo Rich, Sheriff of Fred'k Co, Md.

Wm Beckford, the author of Vathek, died on May 2, at his house in Lanscowne Crescent, Bath. Mr Beckford was in his 84th year, & with Rogers & Wordsworth, at the time of his death, the oldest of the eminent living authors of Great Britain.

John Farkin, convicted at Phil a few days since of murder in the second degree, in stabbing Jas Lemon, into whose house he had gone to repair a clock, was sentenced on Sat to 12 years' solitary confinement in the penitentiary.

Mrd: on May 28, by Rev G W McPhail, P Thornton Lomax to Milly H, d/o J Spotswood Wellford, all of Fred'k, Va.

Mrd: on Jun 4, by Rev Wm Matthews, Dr Patrick H Hamilton, of Md, to Miss Christiana H, d/o the late Saml Hamilton, of Wash City.

Mrd: on Jun 2, in Gtwn, by Rev Mr Roszel, Mr Edwin H King to Miss Albina E Williams, both of Wash.

Died: on May 19, at his residence, at *Charlotte Hall*, St Mary's Co, Md, Mr John Kilgour, aged 68 years.

Eliz Hall & Emma Reed, convicted of assault with intent to kill Susan Creamer, were yesterday sentenced each to 2 years in the penitentiary, to take effect from Jun 15. [Jun 17th newspaper: executive clemency: on Sat last pardoned by the President, & ordered to be discharged from the county jail on Aug 4 next, when they will have been one year in close confinement.]

For sale, a rockway wagon & single harness, each perfectly new, of the latest fashion & highest finish, from one of the best workshops in Phil. –Robt Rainey, Hackman, Bridge st, Gtwn

Dissolution of partnership of the firm of Owen, Evans & Co, mutually dissolved on Jun 1 by withdrawal of John S Owen. Business will hereafter be conducted by Edw Owen, Evan Evans, & Saml W Owen, under firm of Owen, Evans & Co. -Edw Owen, Evan Evans, John S Owen [Just received per steamer **Caledonia**, a rich assortment of gold & silver Epaulets, laces & embroideries. Pa ave, near Fuller's Hotel.]

FRI JUN 7, 1844
Senate: 1-Cmte on Commerce: House bill for the relief of John Sands, with amendments. 2-Cmte on Indian Affairs: bill for the relief of Geo S Gaines, without amendment, & recommending that it be indefinitely postponed. 3-Cmte on the Post Ofc & Post Roads: joint resolution in favor of David Shaw & Mark Simpson.

House of Reps: 1-Ptn of Eliz Cook & 31 others, asking pay for a wagon & team lost by her husband in 1815, while in the service of the U S. 2-Ptn of Ephraim Crabtree & 220 others, for a light house on Green Porcupine Island, at the entrance of Frenchman's Bay, in the State of Maine. 3-Ptn of Humphrey Marshall & 102 others, citizens of the city of Louisville, Ky, & its vicinity, praying the re-annexation of Texas to the Union.

Criminal Court, Wash, Wed. 1-Geo W Earhart, indicted for gambling, was acquitted. 2-Thu: Edw Rhodes, Jos Collins, & John Cole, indicted for being concerned in a riot at Gtwn, were found not guilty. 3-Ann Lucker, indicted for keeping ahouse of ill fame: found guilty. Sentenced to 20 days in the county jail, fined $50, & to give security for her good behavior in the sum of $200, & to stand imprisoned until the security be given.

From Hamilton, N C, dated May 23, 1844, to the editor of the Fayetteville Observer: In haste I write of a murder committed in Wilkes Co, on the body of Maj Peyton, His body was found on May 21, shot through & entirely lifeless. Jas Underwood has been taken up & committed to jail on suspicion. Maj Peyton was a young man of family, & has represented the county in the Legislature.

The New Orleans Courier states that on May 26, Mr Michl Bordelon, brother of Hon Louis Bordelon, the Whig candidate for Congress in the 4th District, fell from the deck of the steamer **Gen Morgan**, & was drowned.

Mrd: on May 30, 1844, at *Beinvenue*, Fauquier Co, Va, by Rev S A Roszel, the Rev Benj F Brooke, of the Balt Annual Conference, to Miss Eliz Glasscock, d/o Enoch Glasscock.

Chas Boyd, who robbed the mail between Augusta, Georgia, & Calhoun's Mills, S C, last March, & then absconded, has been arrested.

M S Cucullu, Collector of the port of New Orleans, died on May 26, at Pass Christian, to which place he had been removed in the hope of the restoration of his health. He was prostrated in the prime of his usefulness.

Four young ladies, dghts of Mr Horner, living near Lebanon, Ohio, were instantly killed by lightning on Thu last. Mr Horner was severely stunned, & his wife was seriously injured.

SAT JUN 8, 1844
House of Reps: 1-Ptn of the wid/o Cmdor Bainbridge, in favor of the re-enactment of the navy pension law.

Potomac Pavilion, Piney Point, will be opened for the reception of visiters on Jun 15, under the superintendence of Mr Thompson Tyler, of the Exchange Hotel. Music under the direction of Mr Knopp, has been provided.

For rent: 2 story dwlg house, on N J ave. Apply to Mrs Wheatley, who will show the premises, or Mr King, near the Navy Yard.

For rent: convenient dwlg-house, one square from the Patent Ofc. Inquire of Mr John Caton, at his grocery store, 5th & G sts.

Household & kitchen furniture at auction: on Jun 11, at the large boarding house of Mrs Ellis, on Pa ave, between 4½ & 6th sts, [formerly Miss Kennedy's.]
-R W Dyer & Co, aucts

Orphans Court of Wash Co, D C. Letters of administration on the personal estate of Thos T Trippelette, of the State of Georgia, dec'd, be granted to Edw Mattingly, a creditor, unless cause to the contrary be shown on or before Jun 28.
–Ed N Roach, Reg/o wills

Insolvent debtor, Richd S Evans, asking to be discharged from imprisonment.
-Wm Brent, clk

Partnership existing between the subscribers has this day been dissolved by mutual consent, the said King having withdrawn & transferred to Hall all his interest in the establishment, lately kept as a Tavern & Eating-house. -Patrick H King, Jas S Hall

Rare chance offered for sale: the subscribers, being about to retire from business, will sell at private sale the entire furniture & fixtures of the Wash Billard Saloon, located on Pa ave & 4½ st. –H J & J Fossett

Mrd: on Jun 6, in Wash City, by Rev Mr French, Lt Delosier Davidson, U S Army, to Clementina M, y/d/o Hon T Hartley Crawford, Com'r of Indian Affairs.

Mrd: on Jun 6, by Rev John C Smith, M Kelly, of N H, to Mary W Walker, of Wash City.

Died: yesterday, Mrs Margaret Bayard, the w/o Saml Harrison Smith, of Wash City. Her funeral is at 1 o'clock on Sunday.

Died: on Jan 5, in Gtwn, Jane Marian, 2nd d/o Matthew & Eliz Helen McLeod, aged 6 years, 4 months & 14 days.

Died: on May 31, at the residence of Mr S H Hawkins, Chas Co, Md, Mr Jas B C Latimer, merchant, Allen's Fresh, Md, at age 40 years.

I am authorized to sell the farm of 72 acres of land, 2 miles from the Eastern Branch Bridge, within D C, with a modern built 2 story frame house, in good order, on the premises, with about 15 acres fenced in. –Louis Baker, Wash

MON JUN 10, 1844
Thos Woodward, coroner, held an inquest last Fri over the body of an Irishman, John Latore, whose body was found that morning floating in the Potomac. He was last seen in Gtwn, on Tue, in a state of intoxication.

Senate: 1-Ptn from Elia Ann Houston & Betsey Smith, praying that their pensions may be extended from 1841 to 1842. 2-Cmte on Indian Affairs: House bill for the relief of Harvey Heth, without amendment. 3-Cmte on the Judiciary: House bills without amendment: relief of Richd Sneed; of Manlius V Thompson, sole exc of Miles W Dickey, dec'd; of David Allspach; & of Amos Prostor. Same cmte: asking to be discharged from the further consideration of the ptn of the heirs at law of Robt McHardy. Also, asking to be discharged from the further consideration of House bill for the relief of Langtree & Hawkins, & that it be referred to the Cmte of Claims.

Miss Drummond informs that she has commenced a School at her residence in the West End, on I st, adjoining the Friends' Meeting house, & is prepared to give instruction in all the branches of Education.

Capt Geisinger has been ordered by the Navy Dept to the Mediterranean, to take command of the U S frig **Columbia**, in place of Capt Shubrick, dec'd. He will sail from Balt early next week, to enter upon the duties assigned him. -Patriot

House of Reps: 1-Cmte of Claims: act for the relief of Gideon Batchelder & others, reported the same without amendment. Same cmte: adverse reports upon the ptns of the heirs of Isaac Snow, Chas Hall, Thos Thompson, Fred'k W Smith, Francis Johnson, Henry Pierson, Shelton Felton, O W Bailey, & Thos Crown. Same cmte: asking to be discharged from the further consideration of the ptn of Peter Von Schmidt, relative to a dry dock. Same cmte: asking to be discharged from the further consideration of the ptn of Geo Kinder, Jubilee Posey, & Joel Whitesides, & that it be referred to the Cmte on Public Lands. Same cmte: made a report on the ptn of Thos Bingham, with a bill for his relief. Same cmte, reported the following: bill for the relief of the estate of Antonio Pacheco, dec'd; & a bill for the relief of Bennet M Dell. 2-Select Cmte: case of J W Nye, assignee of Hugh Stewart, & of Bargy & Van Alatine, made a report thereon, with a bill for his relief. 3-Cmte of Claims: report on the case of Orange H Dibble, with a joint resolution providing for the adjustment & settlement of a claim of Dibble for losses sustained on Potomac bridge contract. Same cmte: adverse report on the ptn of Harry Richardson. 4-Cmte on the Public Lands: bill from the Senate for the relief of Henry Newman, reported the same without amendment. Same cmte: bill for the relief of Hyacinth Lassell, reported the same without amendment: passed. Same cmte: bill for the relief of Besiah, an Indian, made an adverse report thereon. 5-Cmte on the Post Ofc & Post Roads: adverse reports on the ptns of Jas H Jenkins, Nathl Kuykendall, & John S Brooks. 6-Cmte on the Judiciary: bill for the relief of Elisha Morrell, administrator of Jos Icard, dec'd. Same cmte: adverse report on the ptn of Maria S Nourse. 7-Cmte on Revolutionary Claims: bill for the relief of the heirs of Wm Grayson, a colonel in the army of the Revolution. 8-Cmte on Public Land Claims: bill for the relief of the heirs of Adino Goodenow. 9-Cmte on Indian Affairs: bill for the relief of David Robb, reported without amendment. Same cmte: bill for the relief of Jos Bryan, Harrison Young, & Benj Young: passed. 10-Cmte on Naval Affairs: act granting a pension to Jas Duffey, an act concerning furloughs in the naval service, & an act for the relief of Wm Brown: reported the same without amendment. 11-Cmte on Naval Affairs: bill for the relief of Reynall Coates, Walter R Johnson, & Wm P McMurtrie: reported the same without amendment. 12-Cme on Revolutionary Pensions: bill for the relief of the heirs of Seth Chapin. Same cmte: bill for the relief of Eliz Brunet, wid/o Felix Brunet. Same cmte: bill for the relief of Isabella Baldridge, wid/o Capt John Baldridge, dec'd. Same cmte: bill granting a pension to Geo Whittier: reported without amendment. 13-Select Cmte: memorial of Henry M Shreve, in relation to snag boats: bill for his relief. 14-Cmte on Invalid Pensions: bill for the relief of Jos M Rhea.

Insolvent Debtor, John Evans, asking to be discharged from imprisonment.
-Wm Brent, clk

Edw King, of Phil, has been nominated by the Pres of the U S to the Senate to be a Judge of the Supreme Court to fill the vacancy occasioned by the decease of Judge Baldwin.

Valuable real estate at auction: by deed of trust from the heirs at law & devisees of David Peter, dec'd: public auction on Jul 10: part of the estate of which David Peter died seized: lot 25 in Peter's square, Gtwn, D C, fronts on west side of Congress. Lot 17, in same square, fronts on east side of High st. Also, a lot of ground near the little falls of the Potomac river, called *Billingsgate*, valuable for its fishing stands. Also, a tract containing 24½ acres, part of a larger tract called *Mount Pleasant*, lying in Wash Co, D C, near the farm of Mr Little.

Chesapeake & Ohio Canal Co: on Tue, Jas M Coale, of Fred'k was unanimously re-elected Pres of the company, & Frisby Tilghman & J O Wharton, of Wash Co; Wm Price, of Alleghany; Wm Darne, of Montg Co; Danl Burkpyrt, of Va; & J P Ingle, of D C, were elected directors.

Information has reached Wash City of the death of Hon Almon H Read, the Rep of the 12th Congressional district of Pa. He died at his residence in Montrose, Susquehanna Co, having been compelled by declining health to leave this city several weeks since. -Spectator [Jun 11th newspaper: Mr Read was 53 years of age: born at Shelburne, Vt; he was 3 years at the Univ at Burlington, & subsequently a student at Wmstown College, in Mass. In 1814 he settled at Montrose, Pa; in 1827 he was elected a member of the Pa Legislature, & served 5 years in the House of Reps; he was chosen a member of the Senate, where he remained 4 years. He was an affectionate husband & a kind & tender parent. He left no wife to sorrow over his grave, the partner of his bosom having preceded him to the tomb but a few short months. H has left an interesting family, to whom the bereavement must be peculiarly poignant.]

The Salem Register announced the death of the last of the Washington's Life Guards, in the person of Capt Jesse Smith, who died at his residence in Salem on Tue, aged 88. He was in the battle of Bunker Hill, & was draughted into Washington's Guards. He was present in the battles of Brandywine, Trenton, Germantown, & Monmouth. He received his discharge in 1779 from Col Washington. Peace to his manes!

Mr Jas Birch, driver of the city team, came very near losing his life yesterday, when he fell to the ground & the wheel of the cart passed directly over his abdomen. He was not dangerously injured. –Portland Advertiser

Mr Ebenezer Addams, a highly respectable citizen of N Y, aged 35 years, who had been spending a few weeks at Milton, Ulster Co, lost his life by swallowing corrosive sublimate, on May 29. He was told it was cider. –N Y True Sun

Abijah & Jeremiah Learned, brothers, convicted of breaking into the vault of the Milburn [Mass] Bank & robbing it of $17,500, have been sentenced: Abijah to 2 day's solitary confinemant & 10 years in the penitentiary. Jeremiah to 2 days solitary confinement, & 5 years in the penitentiary. Jas Learned, another brother, convicted of participation in the robbery, has been granted a new trial.

Died: on Jun 6, in Wash City, Wm Nevins, in his 3rd year, of scarlet fever, 2nd s/o Moses & Anna M E Hyde, of Balt.

Died: on Jun 8, in Gtwn, D C, suddenly, Mrs Mary Gordon Belt, aged 55 years, relict of the late Jas Belt, of Balt.

Mechanical Riflemen to meet at the Company's Armory this evening, at 8 o'clock. –W F Connell, Sec

Wash Light Infty to meet at the armory this evening at 8 o'clock. –Jos B Tate, Sec

Cincinnati Advertiser chronicles the death of Dr Stephen Wood, of Miami township. He died on Jun 11 in his 83rd year. He was the last survivor of the band of pioneers who were associated with John Clever Symmes in the settlement of North Bend, in 1789, & at the period of his death had resided longer in the State than any individual in Hamilton Co, & probably the whole State of Ohio; at any rate, he was the last of the original pioneers to Cincinnati & its vicinity. It was Dr Wood, in his functions as magistrate, who married the late Pres Harrison to the d/o Mr Symmes in 1792; & it is a remarkable fact that on Apr 1, 1841, almost 50 years after that event, these 3 were all surviving, & in the enjoyment of vigorous health.

By virtue of an order from Peter M Pearson to distrain for ground rent due & in arrear by Geo Lee, I shall offer at public sale, on the premises, one 2 story frame dwlg house & the plank fencing, on lot 10 in square 843, fronting on south B st, between 5th & 6th sts, Wash City, to satisfy the amount of $44 ground rent due & in arrears to the said Peter M Pearson. –H R Maryman, Bailiff

TUE JUN 11, 1844
Postmorten was held upon the body of Theodore Jellison, of this town, who died on Tue. About 15 months ago the dec'd swallowed a bone while eating a dish of soup. He was attacked with a severe cough & pains in the chest, which continued until death. Upon examination, a rough fragment of beef bone was found in the right lung. –Calais Journal

Insolvent debtor, Edw McGowan, asking to be discharged from imprisonment. -Wm Brent, clk

Valuable land near Wash City, containing 146 acres, will be for sale at auction on Jun 18. This land is on Oxen Run, & adjoins the land of Washington Berry, in D C, equal distance between the Navy Yard bridge & Alexandria ferry. –Holmead & Wright, auctioneers

Sale of square 138 & 139, & 15 lots in square 76, the property of the late John Gadsby. The title is indisputable. Sale to take place on & near the 1st named square, binding on N st north, between Conn ave & 19th st west. Terms at sale. –Holmead & Wright, auctioneers

Montg Co, Md. In the matter of Basil B Pleasants, vs Henry Howard, Virginia P Howard, Laura P Howard, Marshall P Howard, & Hamilton P Howard. On the application of Basil B Pleasants, representing that he is interested in taking the depositions of Thos Riggs, of Saml, & Richd Brooke, touching the time Jas B Pleasants, of said county, has boarded with said Basil B Pleasants, & the terms of & allowance for said board, to be used against the said Henry, Virginia, Laura, Marshall, & Hamilton Howard, all of whom are non-residents, & have not agent or atty in this State, & requesting that notice of the time & place of taking said depositions may be given to them by advertisement or otherwise, it is this, Jun 3, 1844, by the undersigned, com'r to take testimony in civil cases for Montg Co, order, that the said B Pleasants notify the said parties above named, that he will take depositions on Jul 6, 1844, before the undersigned, at his ofc in Rockville, Montg Co, at 12, when & where they may attend if they think fit. –John Cook, Com'r

Died: on Jun 2, suddenly, in Fauquier Co, Va, Mrs Nancy Crain, the w/o Maj Jas Crain, in her 60th year. She was the idol of her husband & adored by her children.

WED JUN 12, 1844

N Y papers of Mon: report the death of Thos S Clarkson, who died on Sat last, in his 82nd year, a highly respectable citizen.

Jonathan Jones, about 18 years, was drowned in Chester river, Md, about 1 mile below Millington, on Sun week. The younger brother, being in the act of drowning, the elder in attempting to throw him an oar accidentally fell in. The younger escaped by means of the oar.

Mr Wm McKee, from Salem, Wash Co, arrived at Albany on Fri from N Y, & stopped at the City Hotel. He hung his carpet bag in the hall, behind the bar, & within 15 minutes, it was gone with the $10,000 that was in it. [Jun 14th newspaper: John Daily, [or Dally,] was arrested in company with a girl named Eliz Hanson, for stealing the carpet bag of Mr McKee. They were both committed to the Tombs.]

Richd W Redfield, late Cashier of the Commerical Bank, was called yesterday in the Court of Sessions, but he failed to appear. His bail of $10,000 was declared to be forfeited. Redford was indicted for embezzling upwards of $50,000. –N Y Com Adv

Bridge for sale. I offer at private sale my bridge crossing the Eastern Branch of the Potomac river, called the Anacostia bridge. For terms apply to Mrs Ann Benning, 7th st, between E & F sts, near Post Ofc Dept.

Died: on Jun 10, at their residence, the only child & infant son of Danl & Helen Rowland, of Wash City, aged 4 months & 17 days.

Isaac Long, a citizen of Anderson District, S C, died on May 23, from the bite of a spider. He lived only 4 days after being bitten.

Capt Abisha Jenkins, who resided on his farm near Bristol, Pa, while entering the latter place with his team of mules, was run over by them, & so badly crushed that he shortly afterwards died. The dec'd for many years was a steamboat captain on the river Delaware.

In the U S Circuit Court, Indiana, Judge McLean presiding, Nathl Wilson was found guilty of robbing the mail, of which he was the carrier, between Brookville & Cambridge, about a year ago. He was sentenced to hard labor in the penitentiary for 12 years. He had always previously sustained a reputable character.

Senate: 1-Ptn from Walter S Alexander, of the town of Alexandria, asking a change of venue in a suit now pending in Alexandria. 2-Ptn from D M Evans, for an arrear of pension. 2-House bill for the relief of Henry S Commager, without amendment. 3-Cmte on Indian Affairs: asking to be discharged from the further consideration of the claim of Harman Grigg & Josiah Higgins, for property stolen by the Osage Indians in 1813. 4-Cmte of Claims: asking to be discharged from the further consideration of the memorial of John Frazee, for a balance claimed as due for services as architect on the N Y custom house. 5-Cmte on Pensions: favorable reports on the following House bill-for the relief of: Marcy Olds; & of Danl W Church. Same cmte: adverse reports on the ptns of Ann Huston & of Eliz Smith, for arrears of pension. Same cmte: adverse reports on the following bills, with a written report in each case: granting a pension to Susannah Scott. Relief of Isaac Barker; of Saml Butler, of Va; of Mary B Perry & others; of Franklin P Ambler, Chas P Ambler, & Eliz Pearce, surviving children of Eliz Rowe. 6-Cmte on pensions: favorable reports on the following House bills: granting a pension to Bethea Healey, wid/o Geo Healey; relief of Alice Ushur; & relief of Asa Davis. Same cmte: House bill for the relief of Francis Summeraner, without amendment, & recommending that it be indefinitely postponed. Adverse reports on the ptn of the wid/o Nathan Blood, & on the ptn of Nancy Smith, wid/o Chas Smith. 7-Cmte on Pensions: House bill for the relief of Danl Clapp & Betsy Clapp, recommending that it be indefinitely postponed. 8-Cmte on the Judiciary: House bill for the relief of Wm B Duvall, without amendment, & recommending its passage. 9-Cmte on Pensions: adverse reports on the following House bills-relief of: Susannah Warner; of Sherman Pierce; of Uriah Loomis; of A D W Bradley; & of Robt Monroe. 10-Cmte of Claims: House bills, without amendment, & recommending their passage-relief of: C P Sengstack; of Josiah Dillon, late Assist Quartermaster Gen; & of Mgt Dogherty. 11-Cmte on the Post Ofc & Post Roads: asking to be discharged from the further consideration of the ptn of Sarah S Bishop, wid/o Colin Bishop, late postmaster at Tuscumbia, Ala. Also, the ptns of Thos Herrick, asking compensation for carrying the mail. Same cmte: House bill for the relief of Wm Fuller, without amendment, & recommending that it be laid on the table. House bill for the relief of Saltmarsh & Fuller, & recommending that it be indefinitely postponed.

Strayed or stolen: about May 28, two milch cows. Liberal reward for information that may lead to their discovery. Thompson Tyler, Exchange Hotel

Strayed, from the premises of Capt Boyce, Heights of Gtwn, on Jan 3, a red roan Pony. Liberal reward for for return of the Pony.

For rent: house now occupied by S Murray, on C, between 4½ & 6th sts. Inquire of H Lindsly.

Criminal Court-Wash, Mon. 1-Wm S Wright has been confined in the jail upwards of 6 months under the charge of obtaining money under false pretences. He was tried under 2 indictments: obtaining $250 from Edw Dyer, under false pretences; the other charging him with obtaining $20 from John P Van Ness, also under a false pretence. The jury found the prisoner guilty in both cases.

THU JUN 13, 1844
Senate: 1-Cmte on Private Land Claims: adverse report on the ptn of the heirs of Erastus Brown. 2-Cmte on Indian affairs: favorable reports on the House bills: relief of the heirs of Hyacinth Lafille; of Isaac F Ketchum; of I F Ketchum. 3-Cmte of Claims: bill for the relief of Lucinda Geesy, wid/o Valentine Geesy, with an amendment: passed. 4-Cmte on Private Land Claims: bill for the relief of the heirs of Ebenezer Moore. 5-Bill for the relief of Walter S Alexander, of the town of Alexandria.

$200 reward for runaway negro Fred'k Hall, about 47 or 48 years old. Also, negro Danl Paine, about 26 or 27 years old. The first slave left home in company with another slave belonging to Mr H Brawner, of the same neighborhood. The above slaves are the property of the estate of the late Geo Dement, dec'd, of Chas Co, Md. -Chas F Dement, adm

Mrd: on Jun 6, at Urbanna, Middlesex Co, Va, by Rev Mr Northam, Mr Adoniram Judson Huntington, [of Braintree, Vt,] tutor in the Columbian College, D C, to Miss Eliz G, 2nd d/o Dr Christian, of the former place.

FRI JUN 14, 1844
Senate: 1-Cmte on Pensions: House bills, without amendment, & recommending that they be indefinitely postponed-relief of: Onis Arsenith; of Patrick Masterson, & of Wm S McCauley. Same cmte: asking to be discharged from the further consideration of the ptn of the wid/o Jno Roberts for a pension. 2-Cmte on Revolutionary Claims: bill for the relief of Geo Wontling, & recommending that it be indefinitely postponed. Also, House bill for the relief of David Akenson, of which ther were no papers, & no testimony submitted. 3-Cmte on Commerce-favorable reports on the following House bill: relief of the owners & crew of the schnr **Mary Francis**; & of the owners & crew of the schnr **Privado**. Same cmte: adverse reports on the House bills-for the relief of: Wm Ellery; of the owners & crew of the schnr **Success**; of Danl Grant, Seth Grant, Israel P Stone, & others, owners of the fishing schnr **James & Henry**, of Maine. Also, favorable reports on-relief of: Levi Elridge; of Joshua Knowles & others, owners of the fishing schnr **Gannet**; of the owners & crew of the fishing schnr **Florilla**; of the owners & crew of the fishing schnr **Two Brothers**; of John H Russell & others; & of the owners & crew of the schnr **Dove**; of Barbary Barker & others, owners of the schnr **Union**. 4-Cmte on Pensions: asking to be discharged from the further consideration of the ptn of Asael Spalding, for compensation as pension agent, on the ground of a general bill having been reported. 5-Cmte on Pensions: bill for the relief of John Keith. Same cmte: adverse report in the case of Lt S Chatfield. 6-Cmte on Naval Affairs: joint resolution from the House to authorize the accounting ofcrs of the Treasury to audit & settle the accounts of Wm P Zantzinger, without amendment, & recommending its passage.

One of the oldest & most distinguished inhabitants of the State of N Y, Jas Wadsworth, died at his residence in Genesee, on Fri last, in his 77th year. He had been ill for some time, so aht his death was not unexpected by his friends. Mr W was among the earliest settlers in the western part of N Y, at that time a wilderness, & by his industry & thrift, succeeded in amassing a large fortune. Mr Wadsworth's brother having died a bachelor, left his whole property to the survivor, by which he became, it is estimated, the wealthiest man in the State, next to Mr Astor.

Richd C Gwatkins, who killed Pitman at the White Sulphur Springs in 1838, was acquitted at the late term of the Superior Court of Rockingham. The jury retired but 15 minutes, & on announcing the verdict, there was loud applause.
–Lynchburg Republican

The Senate has confirmed that John C Spencer, jr, to be Purser in the Navy.
-Albany Evening Journal

The Franklin [Vt] Messenger says that on Mon of last week, it was discovered that Simon Locke, an insane person, & his son, Silas, living in the eastern part of the town, were missing, & on searching a pond near by their bodies were found. It is supposed that the father had determined on destroying his life, & the son in attempting to prevent it lost his own.

Orphans Court of Wash Co, D C. In the case of Henry H Dent, administrator, with the will annexed, of the estate of Eliz Brown, late of said county, dec'd. The said administrator having rendered his account, & being ready to distribute certain assets in his hands, & the next of kin & heirs of the dec'd having filed in Court their application that the whole of said estate remaining after the payment of certain legacies by them admitted should be distributed among said heirs according to law, & objection having been made by said heirs to any distribution being made to the society of Md & Va for the education of pious young men for the ministry of the Prot Episc Church, whose seminary is located in Fairfax Co, Va, or to such persons & for such men as the professors of said seminary for the time being may designate, or to the trustees of managers of the Foreign & Domestic Missionary Society of the Prot Episc Church of the U S, whose sessions are held, or were held at the date of said will, in N Y C, for the purposes mentioned in said last will & testament; it is now ordered by the Court, that unless cause be shown to the contrary on or before the 2nd Tue of Jul next, the said estate will then be distributed as claimed by said heirs. --Nathl Pope Causin -Ed N Roach, Reg/o wills

Mrd: on Jun 13, in Wash City, by Rev Mr Wilson, J A Clarkson to Miss Mary A E, only d/o Caleb Tyree, dec'd, all of Richmond, Va.

Died: Jan 12th, Eugene, infant s/o Wm McL Cripps, aged 5½ months.

Died: Jun 10th, Adeline, infant d/o Jas & Martha Riordan, aged 4 months & 12 days.

For rent: 2 story frame house on N Y ave, between 12th & 13th sts. Mr Dietz the present occupant will show the house. Possession may be had on Aug 8 next. Apply to A Shephard.

For rent: large 3 story brick house at present occupied by John S Skinner, Assist Postmaster Genr'l, on the s w corner of F & 12th sts. Possession given on Jul 1. Inquire of Dr Jos M Munding.

Geisler, the German, who murdered the old Mr & Mrs Smith, at Hunterdon, Long Island, underwent the dread sentence of the law, at Riverhead, last Fri, in an enclosure adjoining the prison.

By virtue of an order from Wm Ward to distrain for rent due & in arrears by J W Nye, I shall offer at public sale, on Mo ave, near 4½ st, on Jun 20th, sundry articles of furniture, crockery, & bedding: taken by virtue of said distrain to satisfy the amount of $44.49 due to said Wm Ward. –P Finegan, Constable

Criminal Court-Wash, Wed. The case of Rose Dairy, charged with poisoning John Hellen & Mrs Hellen, terminated on Wed with a special verdict of not guilty, being of the opinion that she was insane when she committed the act. They also found her to be a dangerous person, not proper to go at large, & a pauper.

SAT JUN 15, 1844
Senate: 1-Ptn from Thos Basnett, of Ill, asking encouragement for certain discoveries made in relation to storms & wind. 2-Cmte on D C: adverse reports on the memorials of Wm Archer, of Saml Walker, & of Francis Y Beatty. 3-Cmte on Private Land Claims; House bill for the relief of Walcott A Strong, with amendments. Also, House bill for the relief of Francis Christian & Madame Baptiste Berard. 4-Cmte of Claims: asking to be discharged from the further consideration of the ptn of the assignees of the Bank of the U S. Also, House bill for the relief of Wm Wren, of Miss.

House of Reps: 1-Cmte of Claims: bill for the relief of Jas Ritchie: without amendment. Same cmte: bill for the relief of the legal reps of Alex'r Mitchell; a bill for the relief of Zachariah Lawrence, of Ohio; & a bill for the relief of Edw A Lambert, with a report in each case. Same cmte: bill for the relief of R S Hunter. 2-Cmte on the Judiciary: bill for the relief of Benj S Roberts. 3-Cmte on Revolutionary Claims: bill for the relief of Jas L Campbell. 4-Cmte on Private Land Claims: bill from the Senate authorizing a patent to be issued to Jos Campau for a certain tract of land in Mich, reported the same without amendment: passed. 5-Cmte on Indian Affairs: act for the relief of the legal reps of Geo Duval & other Cherokees, & an act supplementary to an act to regulate trade & intercourse with the Indian tribes, & to preserve peace on the frontiers, reported the same without amendment, & recommended that said bills do not pass.

Orphans Court of Wash Co, D C. In the case of Henry Trunnell, adm of Horatio Trunnell, dec'd. The administrator & Court have appointed the first Tue in Jul next for the settlement of the estate. –Edw N Roach, Reg/o wills

MON JUN 17, 1844
Inquest held on the body of Nancy Collins, who was found dead near Gtwn. She was a woman of intemperate habits & was intoxicated at the time of her death.

Anti-duelling Society at Vicksburg: meeting on May 29. Col Henry W Vick was elected Pres, & N D Coleman & W S Bodley, Vice Presidents.

Criminal Court-Wash, Fri. 1-Wm Clarke alias Meeker, indicted for robbing Mr Fulton, at Tyler's Exchange Hotel, in Mar last, of forty half eagles, [$200,] resulted in the conviction of the prisoner, who is a genteel looking & well-dressed young man, about 24 years of age. Mr Martin N Burn, of Balt was a witness. Clarke had admitted to Burn that he had robbed Mr Fulton. 2-U S vs Geo A Moody, indicted for an assault with intent to kill Saml Drury, a justice of the peace. Moody was engaged in a riot with John & Jas Moody, & a person named Harper, & others, & struck Drury with a severe blow on the head. Verdict: guilty.

New goods, in addition to his former stock of Groceries. –S Holmes, 7th st

Mr Geo Lyons, watchmaker & jeweler, residing on East Bay, next to the French Coffeehouse, Charleston, S C, was found on Wed lying on his bed with his throat cut & a large stab in his thigh, murdered the previous night for the sake of plunder.

At the Court of Common Pleas & Genr'l Sessions of the Peace for Cayuga Co last week, Levi Walker, an atty & counselor of the Court, was convicted for extortion in the receipt of illegal fees, fined $200, & his name stricken from the roll of attys & counselors of said Court.

Serious apprehensions are felt for the safety of the Bremen ship **Johannis**, which has now been out 87 days from Bremen, bound to Balt, having a large number of passengers on board. From the length of time, it is presumed that she is lost.

Two men named Shumenberg & Minor were convicted in the Court of Oyer & Terminer held in Elmira, N Y, last week, on separate charges of forgery on the Chemung Canal Bank, & sent to the State's prison for 5 years each.

Hugh M Tompkins had been arrested at Westfield, Chatauque Co, & taken to Buffalo, under the charge of robbing the mail between Buffalo & Erie, in Jan last.

Appointments by the Pres, with the advice & consent of the Senate:
Tilghman A Howard, of Indiana, Charge d'Affaires to Texas.
R Wickliffe, jr, to be Charge d'Affaires to Sardinia, vice Ambrose Baber, recalled.
Francis J Grund, Consul for Antwerp.
Jos W Beck & Hampton C Williams, Justices of the Peace in Wash Co, D C.
Uriah P Levy, to be a Capt in the Navy, from
Mar 29, 1844.
Chas Boarman, to be Capt in the Navy, from Mar 29, 1844.
French Forrest, now a Cmder, to be a Capt in the Navy, vice Edw R Shubrick, dec'd.
Wm A Piercy, to be a Cmder in the Navy, from Mar 29, 1844.
Richd A Jones, to be a Cmder in the Navy, from Mar 29, 1844.
Jas A Doyle, to be a Lt in the Navy, from Mar 29, 1844.
Mathias C Marin, to be a Lt in the Navy, from Mar 29, 1844.

Arthur P Upshur, to be a Purser in the Navy.
Thos Brownell, now a Master, to be a Lt in the Navy, vice Lt Jas K Bowie, dec'd.
Thos R Ware, to be a Purser in the Navy, vice Purser Jas S Thatcher, lost in the ship **Grampus**.
John C Spencer, jr, to be a Purser in the Navy, vice Purser Fred'k Stevens, dec'd.
Geo F Cutter, to be a Purser in the Navy, vice Wm P Zantzinger, dismissed.
Wm H Kennon, to be a Purser in the Navy, vice G C Cooper, dec'd.
Joel W Newton, to be a Capt in the Navy.
John L Burtt, to be an Assist Surgeon in the Navy.
John F Bartow, to be an Assist Surgeon in the Navy.
Jasper Hall Livingston, to be Sec of Legation to Spain, vice A Hamilton, jr, resigned.
Wm Brent, jr, to be Charge d'Affaires to Buenos Ayres, vice H W Watterson, rejected.
J F Cooper, to be Superintendent of the Branch Mint at Dahlonega, Ga, vice Paul Rossignal, removed.
Thos H Hope, to be U S Marshal for the District of Ill, vice Wm Prentiss, removed.

Custom-house Ofcrs:
Collector of Customs:
John Anderson, for the District of Portland & Falmouth, Maine, vice Nathan Cummings, removed.
Bion Bradbury, for the District of Passamaquoddy, Maine, vice Anson G Chandler, rejected by the Senate.
Gerard Carpenter, for the District of New London, Conn, vice Chas F Lester, rejected by the Senate.
Wm Ennis, for the District of Newport, R I, vice Edw Wilbur, rejected by the Senate.
Lemuel Williams, for Boston & Charleston, Mass, vice Henry Crocker, rejected.
Liman B Langworthy, to be Collector of the Customs for the District of Genesee, & Inspector of the Revenue for the port of Rochester, N Y, vice Jos Strong, rejected by the Senate.
Saml S Downs, to be Collector of the Customs for the District & Inspector of the Revenue for the port of Little Egg Harbor, N J, vice Stephen Willetts, rejected by the Senate.
Danl Clark, jr, to be Surveyor & Inspector at Lafayette, La.
Nehemiah Brown, to be Surveyor & Inspector of Salem, Mass, vice G W Mullett, rejected.
J K Handy, to be Naval Ofcr of Balt, vice Thos E Tilden, rejected.
Penfield B Goodsell, to be Surveyor & Inspector for Hartford, vice John C Burke, rejected.

Land Ofcrs: Register of the Land Ofc:
Alanson Saltmarsh, for the district of Cahawba, Ala.
Duncan B Graham, for the District of Montgomery, Ala.
John S House, for the District of Augusta, Miss.
Wade H Greening, for the District of Sparta, Ala.
Wm S Edsall, at *Fort Wayne*, Ind, vice Wm Polk, dec'd.

Receiver of Public Moneys:
Danl Asby, for the District of Clinton, Mo.
Green P Womack, for the District of Baton Rouge, La.
John W Argyle, for the District of Tallahassee, Fla.
Michal Hinsdell, at Kalamazoo, Mich, vice Henry Gilbert, rejected by the Senate.
Collector of the Customs: Geo Brent, for the District of Alexandria, D C
U S Marshal: Jos B Browne, for the Southern District of Florida
Jas Logan, to be Agent for the Creek Indians, vice Jas L Dawson, removed.
Postmasters: reappointed:
Marcus B Winchester, at Memphis, Tenn
Thos G Scott, at Raleigh, N C
Geo Schley, at Savannah, Ga
Woodson Wren, at Natchez, Miss
John McRae, at Fayetteville, N C
Alfred Huger, at Charleston, S C
Mary Dickson, at Lancaster, Pa
Danl Bryan, at Alexandria, D C
Neil Blue, at Montgomery, Ala
Robt Armstrong, at Nashville, Tenn
Henry W Tilley, at Gtwn, D C
Edw J Mallet, at Providence, R I
Jas Peacock, at Harrisburg, Pa
Abraham Coryell, at Easton, Pa, vice Peter Winter, rejected.
Confirmations by the Senate, by resolution dated Jun 5, 1844.
Jos B Wright, to be promoted Surgeon of the Army, from Mar 26, 1844, vice Surgeon Macomb, dec'd.
Geo Buist, as Assist Surgeon in the Army, in the place of Wright, promoted.
3rd Artl:
2nd Lt Geo H Thomas, to be 1st Lt Apr 30, 1844, vice Ketchum, resigned.
Brevet 2nd Lt John Hillhouse, of 4th Artl, to be 2nd Lt Apr 30, 1844, vice Thomas, promoted.
1st Infty:
2nd Lt Garrett Barry, to be 1st Lt Jan 31, 1844, vice Coxe, resigned.
2nd Lt Geo W Wallace, to be 1st Lt Mar 1, 1844, vice Muse, resigned.
Brevet 2nd Lt Chas D Jordan, of 8th Infty, to be 2nd Lt, vice Muse, resigned.
Brevet 2nd Lt Eugene E McLean, of 2nd Infty, to be 2nd Lt Mar 1, 1844, vice Wallace, promoted.
2nd Infty:
Brevet 2nd Lt Jas W Schureman, of the 7th Infty, to be 2nd Lt Jan 25, 1844, vice Hoffman, dec'd.
3rd Infty:
1st Lt Geo P Field, to be Capt Feb 29, 1844, vice Wheeler, resigned.
2nd Lt Bushrod R Johnson, to be 1st Lt Feb 29, 1844, vice Field, promoted.

Brevet 2nd Lt Andrew J Williamson, of 4th Infty, to be 2nd Lt Feb 29, 1844, vice Johnson, promoted.

6th Infty:
2nd Lt Lewis A Armistead, to be 1st Lt Mar 30, 1844, vice Edes, resigned.
Brevet 2nd Lt Chas T Baker, of the 3rd Infty, to be 2nd Lt Mar 30, 1844, vice Armistead, promoted.

7th Infty:
2nd Lt Chas Hanson, to be 1st Lt Mar 16, 1844, vice Baker, cashiered.
Brevet 2nd Lt Lafayette McLaws, of 6th Infty, to be 2nd Lt Mar 16, 1844, vice Hanson, promoted.

Rejections: nominations made by the Pres of the U S which have been rejected by the Senate:
Anson G Chandler, as Collector of Customs in the District of Passammaquoddy, Maine.
Harvey Chapin, as Postmaster at Springfield, Mass.
Enoch C Chapman, as Postmaster at Norwich, Conn.
John Cain, as Postmaster at Indianapolis, Ind.
Greenbury Dorsey, as Collector of Customs in the District of Mississippi, La.
Geo H Profit, as Envoy to Brazil.
Robt Rantoul, jr, as Collector of Boston.
W G Snethen, as Solicitor of the Land Ofc.
John C Spencer, as Associate Judge of the Supreme Court.
E H Stacy, as Colector of the Customs for the District of Gloucester, Mass.
David Henshaw, as the Sec of the Navy.
Crawford W Hall, as U S Atty for District of East Tenn.
Isaac Hill, as Chief of Clothing Bureau.
Wm S Murphy, as Charge d'Affaires to the Republic of Texas.
Jas M Porter, as Sec of War.
Danl C Weston, as Deputy Postmaster at Augusta, Maine.
David Winslow, as Postmaster at Burlington, Vt.
Stphen Willitts, as Collector & Inspector of Little Egg Harbor, N Y.
Modecai Myers, as Collector of the Customs for the District of Savannah, Ga.
Geo Brown, as Surveyor & Inspector of the Revenue for the port of Pawcatuck, R I.
H W Watterson, as Charge d'Affaires to the Republic of Buenos Ayres.
Alex'r Powell, as Consul to Altona, Italy.
Weston F Birch, nominated to the U S Marshal for the District of Missouri.
Gregory Dillon, as Appraiser for the port of N Y.
John McKibbon, as Appraiser for the port of N Y.
Peter Winter, as Deputy Postmaster, at Easton, Pa.
Robt Thompson, as Register of the Land Ofc at Upper Sandusky, Ohio.
Fred'k Hall, Receiver of Public Moneys, at Ionia Mich, vice Saml Dexter, resigned.
Thos E Tilden, as Naval Ofcr, District of Balt.
Geo W Mullett, as Surveyor & Inspector of the Revenue for the District of Salem & Beverly, Mass.

Geo Dennett, as Collector of the Customs for the District of Portsmouth, N H.
Freeman C Chapman, as Postmaster at Norwich, Conn, vice Enoch C Chapman, rejected by the Senate.
Elijah Aschley, as Postmaster at Springfield, Mass, vice Harvey Chapin, rejected by the Senate.
Henry Crocker, as Collector of the Customs for the District of Boston & Charlestown, Mass, vice Robt Rantoul, jr, rejected by the Senate.
Luther Hamilton, as Chaplain in the Navy, vice John Lathrop, dec'd, who was appointed during the recess.
Wm Shaler, as Navy Agent, at N Y, vice Robt C Wetmore, removed.
David Hayden, a Collector of New Orleans.
Addison Winter, as Collector, Gloucester, Mass, vice Eben E Stacy, rejected. [2nd rejection.]
Ethan A Clary, as Postmaster at Springfield, Mass, vice E Ashley, rejected. [3rd rejection.]
Henry Comegar, as Collector of Miami & Inspector of Maumee, Ohio, vice H C Stowell, rejected. [2nd rejection.]
Chas G Ferris, as Collector of N Y, vice Edw Curtis, removed.

Mr Edw T Hassler, aged 31 years, a native of England, s/o the late Mr Hassler, the distinguished Mathematician & Coast Surveyor, shot himself in the head with a pistol on Thu, at N Y, at the American Hotel. The brother of the dec'd, hearing of his death, came there & identified his brother. In the pocket of the dec'd was found $126, principally in gold, & in a belt around his body $500 & $50 Treasury notes.

Obit-died: on Jun 9th I performed the melancholy duty of attending, with the mourning relatives, the funeral of my much-loved friend Mrs Mgt Bayard Smith, consort of Mr Saml Harrison Smith, to their vault at Rock Creek Church, where her remains were deposited by the side of her two [once lovely] dghts, who departed this life some years since. Mrs Smith, as wife, mother, relation, & friend, was as faultless as human nature would allow. To her husband, children, & grand-children, her loss is irreparable. –A

Thunder storm on Sun at Russell's Mills, Dartmouth, Mass: a young man named Head was killed by the electric fluid.

Mrd: on Jun 13, at Portsmouth, Va, by Rev J H W____, Mr Chas Calvert, jr, of Wash City, to Miss Ann Turrington, of the former place.

Died: on Jun 16, at the residence of Mrs M P Slye, Mary Cecilia Johns, eldest d/o Mr Thos Jones. Her remains will be removed to Broad Creek Church for interment on Jun 18.

Died: yesterday, after a short & painful illness, Mrs Eliz Clendine Parrott, w/o Wm Stuart Parrott, late Consul of the U S for the city of Mexico. Her remains will be taken to Balt for interment tomorrow morning; the preparatory religious ceremonies, according to the Catholic ritual, will be performed this afternoon at 5 o'clock at her late residence on G st.

Died: on Jun 14, in Wash City, Mrs Ann T Gustine, consort of the late Dr Joel T Gustine, late of Gtwn, D C.

Died: on Jun 7, in Wash City, Mr Francis Oscar Hannon, in his 30th year.

Died: in the borough of Washington, Pa, on Monday last, in his 43rd year, the Hon Isaac Leet, formerly the Rep of that district in Congress. He was repeatedly selected as a candidate for Congress, & once elected. In the tender & endearing relations of husband & father, Mr Leet was affectionate & devoted.

Orphans Court of Wash Co, D C. Letters testamentary on the personal estate of Jos W Hand, late of said county, dec'd.

TUE JUN 18, 1844
Laws of the U S passed at the 1st Session of the 28th Congress:
1-Act for the relief of Edw Kennard: to be paid $50 being one moiety of the penalty collected of the said Kennard, by the collector of the port of New Orleans, in 1842, for a breach of the revenue laws, that the said penalty was incurred without willful negligence, & without any design to violate the law. 2-Act for the relief of Danl G Skinner, of Ala: Sec or War to audit & adjust the account of Skinner, for supplies of ammunition & subsistence, alleged to have been taken by military authority in May, 1836, for the necessary use & support of the Alabama militia, then in the service of the U S. Skinner to be paid any balance found due him. 3-Act for the relief of Jos Bryan, Harrison Young, & Benj Young: that their claim & title to the north half of section 19, in township 21, in range 24, in Tallapoosa land district, in Alabama, purchased by them jointly of Benj Chambers, the head of the Creek Indian family, who was entitled to the same under the provisions of the treaty between the U S & the Creek tribe of Indians, concluded on May 24, 1832, be & the same is hereby confirmed. 4-Act to incorporate *Gtwn College*, in D C: a college for the instruction of youth in the liberal arts & sciences, the name, style, & title of which shall be "the President & Directors of Gtwn College." That Jas Ryder, Thos Lilly, Saml Barber, Jas Curley, & Anthony Rey, be, & they are hereby declared to be, a body politic & corporate, with perpetual succession in deed or in law, to all intents & purposes whatsoever, by the name, style, & title as "the President & Directors of Gtwn College," by which name & title they & their successors shall be competent, at law & in equity, to take to themselves & their successors, for the use of said college, etc. That no misnomer of the said corporation shall defeat or annul any donation, gift,

grant, devise, or bequest, to or from the said corporation. That the said corporation shall adopt a common seal.

Acts passed at the 1st Session of the 28th Congress: 1-Acts for the relief of:

Edw Kennard	Abelard Guthrie
Benj B Ferguson	Marcay Olds
Benj Murphy	Lund Washington
F A Kerr	Amos Proctor
John Atchison	Eaton Nance
Wm Henson	Saml B Tuck
Ephraim D Dickson	Saml B Folger
Hiram Murch	Geo M Foote
Jos Campau	Isaac Fessenden
Wm McPherson	John Edmonson
Wm Glover	Wm H Hoag & others
Wm R Davis	Geo Wallis
Chas W Morgan	Henry S Commager
John Mullings	David Allspach
Jas C Hallock	Mary Ann Linton
Jas Reid	Robt Monroe
Jos Bennell	Asa David
Levi Colmus	Danl W Church
Isaac Justice	Chas Holt
Adam L Mills	Harvey Heth
John Miller	Lathrop Foster
Abigail Gibson	Jas Pepper & others
Sarah Blackmore	Alice Usher
Henry Newingham	C P Sengstack
Mgt Dougherty	Mary M Telfair
John Perham	John Sands
Wm P Duval	Pierre S Derbanne
Richd Sneed	Ferguson & Reed

Geo Davenport, of Rock Island, in Ill
Danl G Skiller, of Ala
Walter S Alexander & others
Geo W Allen & Reuben Allen
Woodson Wren, of Miss
Heirs of Hyacinth Lasselle
Heirs of Ebenezer Moore
Lois Cronk, alias Cronkhite
Geo Harrison & his sureties
Heirs of Christopher Miller
Geo Davenport, of Rock Island, Ill
Jos Bryan, Harrison Young, & Benj Young

Legal reps of Capt Saml Shannon, dec'd
Legal reps of John Baker, dec'd
John Frazer & Geo A Trenholm
Isaac S Ketchum
Isaac S Ketchum, late special Indian agent
Ann Hunter, wid/o Robt Hunter
Francois Christian & widow Baptiste Berard
Solomon Sturges, assignee of Humphrey Richcreek
Owners & crew of the schnr **Privado**
Legal reps of Francis Cazeau, late merchant at Montreal
Owner & crew of the schnr **Mary Francis**
Manlius V Thompson, sole exc of Miles W Dickey, dec'd.
Josiah Dillon, late Assist Quartermaster Gen of the Army
Violet Calhoun, wid/o John Calhoun
Geo W Clarke, Harris Cook, & John Brainard, second, of Rhode Island
2-Benefit of:
Thos Hunter & Alex'r Caldwell   Jas Anderson, of the Territory of Iowa
Simeon Dennin
3-Pension to:
Bartholomew Maguire   Emanuel Shrofe
Mill, an Indian woman of the Creek nation
4-Patent to be issued to Jos Campau for a certain tract of land in Michigan
5-Joint resolution authorizing Capt Jas Lowe to assign a certain section of land.
6-Act for the relief of Mary Williams, wid/o the late Jacob Williams, dec'd.

Green Hill for sale: my engagements rendering it desirable to me to quit farming operations, I will dispose of my *Green Hill* estate, lying in Montg Co, Md, containing 800 acres, 17 miles from Wash & Gtwn: improvements consist of a commodious dwlg house, having 9 rooms, 5 on the lower & 4 on the upper, & all necessary out-bldgs. Apply to Saml T Stonestreet, at Rockville, Md, or to the subscriber, Gtwn. --G C Washington

Appointments by the Pres, with the advice & consent of the Senate:
Geo M Bibb, of Ky, to be Sec of the Treasury
Jas D Hallyburton, of Va, to be Judge of the Eastern District of Va.
John Branch, of N C, to be Govn'r of the Territory of Florida, from Aug 11, 1844, vice R K Call, whose commission will then have expired.
Nathl P Tallmadge, of N Y, to be Govn'r of the Territory of Wisconsin, from Sep 13 next, vice J G Doty, whose commission will then expire.
Collector of Customs:
Addison Gilbert, for the District of Gloucester, Mass, vice Addison Winter, whose nomination was rejected by the Senate.
Thos Barrett, for the District of Mississippi, La, vice David Hayden, whose nomination was rejected by the Senate.

Solomon Andrews, for the District & Inspector of Revenue for the Port of Perth Amboy, N J, vice Francis P Brinley, who was rejected by the Senate.
Jas H Forsyth, for the District & Inspector of the Revenue for the Port of Maumee, Ohio, vice Henry Comegar, who was rejected by the Senate.
Edw Hardin, for the District of Savannah, Ga.

Appointments:
Vanburgh Livingston, to be Appraiser in the Customs for the Port of N Y, vice Gregroy Dillon, who was rejected by the Senate.
Jacob Falman, to be Register of the Land Ofc at Kaskaskia, Ill, vice Miles Hotchkiss, whose commission had expired.
Thos Fitsgerald, to be Receiver of Public Lands for the District of Ionia, Mich, vice Fred'k Hall, who was rejected by the Senate.
Abner Root, to be Register of the Land Ofc at Upper Sanduskey, Ohio, vice Robt Thompson, who was rejected by the Senate.
Danl T Witler, to be reappointed Receiver of Public Moneys at Wash, Ark, from Jul 10, 1844, when his present commission will expire.
Matthew Leiper, to be reappointed Receiver of Public Moneys at Fayetteville, Ark, from Jun 10, 1844, when his present commission will expire.
Saml W Higgins, to be Receiver of Public Moneys at Detroit, Mich, vice Jonathan Kearsly, who was rejected by the Senate.
Amos H Bullen, to be Deputy Postmaster at Northampton, Mass, vice Henry Shepherd, who was rejected by the Senate.
John Dey, to be Deputy Postmaster at Newark, N J, vice Jacob K Mead, who was rejected by the Senate.
Wm Noble, to be Deputy Postmaster at Burlington, Vt, vice David Winslow, who was rejected by the Senate.
Galen Ame, to be Deputy Postmaster at Springfield, Mass, vice Ethan C Clary, who was rejected by the Senate.
Asaph R Nichols, to be Deputy Postmaster at Augusta, Maine, vice Danl T Pike, who was rejected by the Senate.
Rev Geo Washington Swan, to be Chaplain in the Navy, vice John Robb, who was rejected by the Senate.

2nd Regt of Artl:
2nd Lt W A Nichols, to be 1st Lt, from Jun 1, 1844, vice Pitkin, resigned.
Brevet 2nd Lt David Gibson, of the 3rd Artl, to be 2nd Lt, from Jun 1, 1844, vice Nichols promoted.

Rejections by the Senate, Jun 15, 1844.
1-Jas S Green, of N J, as Sec of the Treasury. 2-John B Christian, of Va, as Judge of the Eastern District of Va. 3-R R Collier, of Va, as Judge of the Eastern District of Va. 4-John Robb, as Chaplain in the Navy. 5-Benj F Pendleton, as Deputy Postmaster at Norwich, Conn. 6-Jonathan Kearsly, as Receiver of Public Moneys for the District of Detroit, Mich. 7-Nelson Brown, as Surveyor & Inspector of the Revenue for Port of Pawcatuck, R I. 8-Abraham K Mead, as Appraiser in the Customs, for the Port of N Y.

Trial of John M Breedlove, at New Orleans: found guilty of stealing Treasury notes from the Custom-house of that city.

House to let: a 2 story brick house on N J ave, next door to Mr Underwood. Inquire of Elexius Simms, 13th & F sts, or to G B Iardella' Drug Store, Capitol Hill.

Notice. Ran away from the subscriber, a colored bound boy named Danl Homans, aged about 19 years. Whoever will bring the said boy to me in Wash City shall be liberally rewarded with one cent & no thanks. –Basil Lancaster

For sale an extensive & beautiful residence in Alexandria. The owner, Mr Armfield, being about to remove to the South. Delightful establishment for a resident Minister. –Wm D Nutt

$100 reward for runaway negro Fred'k Hall, about 48 years old. Supposed to be with Mr Brawner's man Henson. –Chas F Dement, adm of Geo Dement, dec'd

New Haven Herald of Sat. Obit-demise of 3 of the most prominent citizens of our State-Mr Timothy Dwight, Mr Ithiel Town, & Mr Nathl Terry. Their deaths were almost simultaneous, occurring within a few hours of each other. Mr Dwight was a s/o the late Pres Dwight, of Yale College, & has long been one of our most valuable & respected citizen. Mr Town is the well known architect of many of our public structures, & also of the custom-house in N Y C, which city has been his principal residence for several years. Mr Terry had been on a visit to his son in this city, & but a few days since was walking our streets in his usual health. He has filled many eminent stations in public life, & was highly respected as a citizen & a civilian. [No death dates-current item.]

St Louis, Jun 8. About 6 or 8 weeks ago, the only d/o Mr Edw Ford, of St Louis, & we believe his only child, was taken from, or induced to leave, her father's house. He felt that Mr Low, the auctioneer, had been the man who had planned & executed his dght's ruin. Low refused to give him any information. The father learned on Thu that Low had been to New Orleans, & returned with his dght as far as St Genevieve. After some insulting language, Ford discharged a pistol, the ball striking Mr Low above the right eye. He is not expected to live. Mr Ford was arrested & gave bail of $5,000. -Reporter

Mrd: on May 25, at Church Hill, Ala, by Rev Wm Johnson, the Rev Mr Knapp, of Montg, Ala, to Mrs Ellen Lee Bedford, d/o the late Ludwell Lee, of Va.

WED JUN 19, 1844
Jas Williams' Cabinet & Chair Warerooms: Pa ave, west of 4½ st. Old furniture taken in exchange for new. Old furniture & chairs repaired & repainted.

We learn from Capt Pheatt that Capt Pickering, late master of the schnr **Illinois**, cut his throat & bled to death at St Catharine's within a day or two. It seems the dec'd built a new vessel at Oswego, & in attempting to pass through the Welland Canal, for a western port, became stuck fast, being too wide for the locks, & there remains. Capt Pickering leaves a young wife & 4 children. –Buffalo Com Adv

Christopher McLure, a member of the Natchez bar, was lately sentenced to 4 days' imprisonment & fined $200 for an assault upon Col Lewis Sanders, another member of the bar, within the precincts of the court-house; the provocation being harsh insulting words used against McLure by Sanders in an argument before the Court.

The steamboat **Cleveland** collapsed the flues of her boilers on Fri in passing Trap, & 3 men were badly scalded: among them the engineer, Mr Chas McGinnis, & the cook, whose lives are despaired of.

Appointments by the Pres, by & with the advice & consent of the Senate:
Jeremiah Towle, to be Naval Ofcr for the District of N Y, vice Thos Lord, removed.
Silas Sisson, to be Surveyor & Inspector of the Revenue for Pawcatuck, R I.
Benj Bythwood, to be reappointed Collector of the Customs for the District & Inspector of the Revenue for the Port of Beaufort, N C.
Gershom Mott, to be reappointed Collector of the Customs for the District & Inspector of the Revenue for the Port of Burlington, N J.
Nathl Jackson, to be reappointed Surveyor & Inspector for the Port of Newburyport, Mass.
Amos Palmer, to be Appraiser in the Customs for the Port of N Y, vice Abraham K Meade, who was rejected by the Senate.
Jeremiah Townsend, to be Postmaster at Norwich, Conn, vice F C Chapman, who was rejected by the Senate.
Jas Lawrenson, & E W Smallwood, to be Justices of the Peace, for Wash Co, D C.
Alfred C Holt, to be Assist Surgeon in the Navy.
Thos J Leib, now a Lt, to be a Cmder in the Navy.
Thos O Selfridge, now a Lt, to be a Cmder in the Navy.
Thos M Mix, now a Passed Midshipman, to be a Lt in the Navy.
Francis E Baker, now a Passed Midshipman, to be a Lt in the Navy.

John P Bush, late editor of the Utica [N Y] Observer, died in Boston on Thu of pulmonary consumption. He had been but 10 weeks from the West Indies.

Died: on Jun 18, in Wash City, of consumption, after a long & painful illness, Mrs Mgt Klopfer, consort of Benj D Klopfer, aged 21 years, 8 months & 14 days. Her funeral is today at 4 o'clock, from her late residence, F st, between 10th & 11th.

Isaac Page has been sentenced by Judge Merrick, at Worcester, Mass, to the State prison for 7 years, for burning a bldg in Fitchburg, in Dec last, with intent to defraud a Worcester insurance company. Brigham Knapp, convicted of arson at the Sept term of the Common Pleas, was sentenced to the State prison for life. He was intoxicated at the time of the deed.

Orphans Court of Wash Co, D C. Letters of administration on the personal estate of Cornelius Henning, late of said county, dec'd.

THU JUN 20, 1844
Mrs C B Butler requests that all persons who are indebted to her will call & settle their bills without further delay.

Mrs Klopfer, Tailoress: residence on C st, opposite Tyler's Hotel, Wash.

Protestant Episcopal Church of the Epiphany: pews in this Church will be sold at auction on Jun 24, at the Church, on G st. Plans may be seen at the Store of Mr C H James, at the Church, & at the Bookstores of Messrs Farnham & Morrison, Pa ave. By order of the Vestry: G Rodman, Treas C E

Appointments by the Pres, by & with the advice & consent of the Senate:
Caleb Cushing, of Mass, to be Com'r to China.
Thos G Clemson, to be Charge d'Affaires to Belgium, vice Henry W Hilliard, who asked leave to return from Aug 1 next.
David Martin, to be U S Consul to Trinidad de Cuba, vice John T Cook, resigned.
Wm C Anderson, of Missouri, to be U S Marshal for the District of Missouri, vice W F Birch, rejected.
John Woodbury, as Surveyor of the Port of Gloucester, Mass, vice Danl White, rejected.
John J Plume, to be Postmaster at Newark, N J, vice John Dey, rejected.
Baring, Brothers & Co, to be temporary Navy Agents at London, England.
Edw McCall & Co, to be temporary Navy Agents at Lima.
Wm P Furnies & Co, to be temporary Navy Agents at St Thomas, West Indies.
Rejections: Jun 15th to 17th.
John Dey, a Postmaster at Newark, N J
Benj F Pendlemon, as Postmaster at Norwich, Conn

Mrd: on May 20, at St Croix, West Indies, by Rev M B Johnson, Thos W Dickins, of Wash, to Miss Alice R J Finlay, 3rd d/o Jas Finley, of the former place.

Died: on Jun 17, at Alexandria, David G Prettyman, in his 55th year, after a lingering & painful illness.

Obit-died: on May 26 last, suddenly, Jos Winborn Hand, aged 52 years; native of Madison, Conn: his mother was the d/o Col Meigs, a distinguished ofcr of the American Revolution, & sister of the late Return J Meigs, former Govn'r of Ohio & Postmaster Gen of the U S. He graduated at Yale College in 1813, as one of the best scholars of his class. He studied law in the ofc of Elias B Caldwell, & was admitted to the Bar in this city. After being connected with the Post Ofc Dept for more than 20 years, he was transferred to the Patent Ofc as Chief Clerk, where he remained 8 years until the period of his death. He was a devoted husband, a kind father, & a faithful friend. He was an Elder in the Presbyterian Church.

Orphans Court of Wash Co, D C. Letters of administration on the personal estate of Geo Miller, late of Wash Co, dec'd. –Henry Miller, adm

FRI JUN 21, 1844
Laws of the U S passed at the 1st Session of the 28th Congress:
1-For compensation of the Pres of the U S, $25,000.
2-For outfit to David Porter, late Minister resident to Turkey, to be paid to his legal reps, $6,000.
3-For compensation to Luigi Persico for services rendered & expenses incurred in bringing the group of statues made by him to this country & placing it on the pedestal, by the direction of the Sec of the Treasury, $4,000.

Thu last, a boat belonging to the receiving ship **Ohio**, lying in Boston harbor, was run down & stove by brig **Georgiana** of Thomaston, Maine. Wm A Strong, from Ohio, one of the 5 apprentices in the boat, received very severe injury. He was taken on board, but died soon after.

On May 18, Jas Slater & Philip Fox were drowned in Lake Erie, when their canoe upset, when one of them speared a large sturgeon.

Thos O Page was arrested at Fort Wayne, Ind, on Mon last, on the charge of bigamy. He married Miss Tedman, of Wayne Co, N Y, on Jun 25, 1843. About 3 months afterward he formed an acquaintance with Miss Nettleton, of Alden, Erie Co, who possessed some considerable money, & married her also. He brought her to this city, & put up at the Phoenix Hotel, informing her that a steamer would leave the next morning, on board which he had engaged their passage. He then left her that night, carrying away every thing that his second wife possessed. Page was arrested, convicted, & sentenced to Auburn for 5 years. –Buffalo Gaz

Mrd: on Thu, by Rev John C Smith, Mr John Massie to Miss Caroline Warren; & at the same time, by the same, Mr Augustus Costen to Miss Lucinda Warren, all of Wash City.

Died: on Jun 19, after a very painful illness, Walter Jones, s/o Dr Thos Miller, in his 6th year of his age. His funeral is at 11 o'clock this day.

Criminal Court-Wash, Tue & Wed: 1-Saml Arnold found guilty of stealing 2 books, property of H V Hill. 2-John Bush found guilty of enticing & aiding slaves to escape. 3-Thos Stewart found guilty of stealing wearing apparel, the property of Andrew Hoover. 4-Alfred Beatty was indicted for assaulting & cruelly beating, & thereby causing the death of Matilda Ward. The jury returned with a verdict of not guilty as indicted; but they found the prisoner guilty of assault & battery. 5-Richd Clarke alias Wm Meeker, guilty of robbing Garrett Fulton: sentenced to 3 years in the penitentiary. 6-Geo Costin, convicted of an assault with intent to kill Selby Redin: sentenced to 2 years in the penitentiary. 7-Wm S Wright, convicted of defrauding Gen John P Van Ness of $20: sentenced to 2 years in the penitentiary; for defrauding E Dyer, of $200, was sentenced to 2 years in the penitentiary, to take effect from the expiration of the former imprisonment. 8-John Brown, free negro, guilty of stealing sundry articles, property of Wm Braddock, to be imprisoned 2 years in the penitentiary, from May 25, 1848, on which day his former imprisonment expires for another offence of grand larceny. 9-Thos Stewart, convicted of petit larceny, to pay $5 fine, & 3 months in the county jail. 10-Geo A Moody, a very young man, convicted of assault with intent to kill Saml Drury, a j p, to be imprisoned 2 years in the penitentiary. 11-John E Moody & Jas F Moody, convicted of riot, each to pay a fine of $50 & 4 months in the county jail. 12-John Langdon, convicted of riot, to pay a fine of $50, & 3 months in the county jail. 13-Saml Arnold, convicted of petit larceny, to be imprisoned 2 months in the county jail & pay a fine of $5. 14-Robt Fitzhugh, convicted of an assault & battery on Jos Peck: fined $20. 15-John A Beall, convicted of an assault & battery on David Vann: fined $30. 16-Jas Frere, convicted of an assault & battery on Chas Lucas: fined $20. John Thomas, convicted of attempting to rescue Betsy Brown from the penitentiary, to be imprisoned one month in the county jail, & fined $10. 17-Jeff Butler, convicted of assault & battery on Wm Bell, to be imprisoned in the county jail 15 days, & fined $10. 18-Chas Gates, convicted of assault & battery on the slave of Thos Blagden, by stabbing the slave, to pay a fine of $30. 19-Lewis Goldsmith, convicted of an assault & battery on Mary Ann Hall, fined $20, to give security in $100 to keep the peace, & be of good behavior for one year. 20-Andrew Porter, convicted of assault & battery on Wm Markwood, fined $20.

Michl Douty, of Pottsville, Pa, was crushed to death, when some men were launching a boat in Messrs Packer's boat-yard, by the cars on which the boat rested.
–Phil Ledger

Ceremonies of laying the corner-stone at St Paul's Lutheran Church, corner of H & 11th sts. Ex-President J W Adams & Gen J P Van Ness, friend & patron of the Church, were among the distinguished guests. Rev Septimus Tuston, Chaplain to the Senate & assist Pastor of the F st Presbyterian Church addressed the Throne of Grace in an impressive prayer. Rev Dr J G Morris, of Balt, addressed the multitude. Rev Dr Benj Kurtz, of Balt, enumerated the articles & documents deposited in the cornerstone: parchment stating John Tyler being Pres; W P Magnum, Pres of the Senate; J W Jones, Speaker of the House of Reps, & W W Seaton, Mayor of Wash City. Ofcrs of St Paul's Church: Rev A A Muller, D D, pastor, Church Council: Andrew Noerr, Cornelius Andrae, John C Roemmele, Nicholas Funk, & Albert Heitmuller; John Sessford, Sec. Ofcr of the Gen Synod of the Evangelical Luthern Church in the U S: Rev John G Morris D D, of Balt, Pres; Rev Chas A Smith, Sec; Dr D Gilbert, Treasurer. Ofcrs of Md Synod for 1844: Rev Ezra Keller, Pres; Rev S Sentman, Sec; Rev J P Cline, Treasurer; J G Bruff, Scripsit. Among the articles enclosed were: a silver plate beaing the inscription: Martin Luther, the benefactor of the Christian world, born 10th Nov, 1483, at Eislehen, in Upper Saxony, died at the same place on 18th Feb, A D 1546, aged 63 years. B O Hare, engraver. On the marble slab which covered the recess of the corner-stone: "J P Van Ness consecrates this site to the worship of God the Father, the Son, and the Holy Ghost, 18th Jun, A D 1844."

SAT JUN 22, 1844
A Favier presents to the citizens of Wash & vicinity a new place, between 17th & 18th sts, north of the residence of the late Gen Macomb, called the Wash Spring Garden: mineral waters, ice cream, lemonade, & other refreshments.

Obit-died: Jun 10, Mrs Mary Ann Carroll, of St Mary's Co, Md, relict of the late Capt M B Carroll, of the U S Navy. She has left a son, an only child, & an infant grandson to mourn her death.

Orphans Court of Wash Co, D C. Letters of administration on the personal estate of Catharine Webster, late of said county, dec'd, be granted to Geo M Dove, a creditor, unless cause to the contrary be shown on or before Jul 12 next.
-Ed N Roach, Reg/o wills

If Carl Fred'k Wedel, of Kaltenhaus, Liegnitz, Kingdom of Prussia, will inform the U S Legation at Berlin of his residence, he will be placed in possession of a legacy left him by his brother John Gotlieb Wedel. Editors generally might serve some worthy family in this country by copying the above.

Trustee's sale of valuable estate: the subscriber, as trustee, under decree of PG Co Court, sitting as Court of Equity, will expose to public sale on Jul 30 next, between 900 & 1,000 acres or land, in said county, near the village of Nottingham, it being part of the real estate of which the late John A Turton died seised. Improvements are 4 large & well constructed tobacco houses, & a supply of wood, fencing, & other timber. Also, a lot of woodland, containing about 20 acres, attached to the above.
-Wm H Turton, Trustee

MON JUN 24, 1844
The political abolitionists held a meeting on the large canal bridge at Lockport on Jun 16, & while Alvin Stewart was addressing the people, the railing gave way & a young man named Wolcott, about 20, & a boy named Meredith, were drowned.

The Treasury note case: the trial of Marshall C Halliday & Jas B Watson terminated at New Orleans on Jun 11, in the U S District Court, & a verdict of guilty as charged in the indictment was rendered. The prisoners were charged with forging. There are 4 other indictment still pending against the prisoners.

Mrs. Orinda Sterling, of Millport, N Y, while sitting on the stern of a canal boat in the lock at Lodi, was precipitated into the canal with a child in her arms [18 months old] & before relief could be afforded they were both drowned.

New Haven Courier: Lucien Hall, the murderer of Mrs Bacon, was executed at Middletown, Conn, on Thu last, agreeably to his sentence.

Trustee's sale of Havana cigars, chewing tobacco & snuff, perfumeries, & fancy goods: by deed of trust from Jas M Dawsett & Jas P McKean to the subscribers, dated Aug 11, 1843, to secure the payment of certain debts due to Lewis Johnson, as recorded in Liber W B 103, folios 158 thru 162, one of the land records of Wash Co, D C. To be sold at the store of said Jas M Dawsett, on Pa ave, between 4½ & 6th sts. –Geo M Davis, Wm Orme, trustees

Local News: it is the duty of the police constables to prevent persons from bathing & swimming in the *Wash Canal* in the day time, & within the view of persons residing in the houses & streets contiguous to the canal, Tiber creek, & the Potomac river.

TUE JUN 25, 1844
Valuable tract of land & a large water power for sale. The undersigned, by virtue of the power & authority vested in him by the last will & testament of Jas S Springer, dec'd, now offers at private sale all that tract of land, near Elkton, Md, containing 270 acres . Improvements consist of a 2 story stone dwlg-house & other out houses in tolerable repair. –John G Groome, exc of Jas S Springer, dec'd, Elkton, Md

Mrd: on Thu last, in Wash City, by Rev Wm Hawley, Col David M Bull, of Towands, Pa, to Miss Martha Jane, d/o Wm M McCauley, of Wash City.

Mrd; on Jun 5, at Layton Stone, in Fauquier, by Rev John Cole, Geo Hamilton, of Culpeper, to Miss Lavinia Y, d/o John B Downman.

Died: on Jun 4, at *Oatland*, Montg Co, Md, from erysipelas, after 4 days illness, Mr Washington Bowie, in his 40th year. This event will excite a deep sympathy with his brothers & sisters in their truly irreparable loss.

Died: on Jun 23, in Wash City, Lewis, infant s/o T R Peale, of Phil, aged 11 months.

Died: on Jun 24, John W Brown, only s/o Robt W & Caroline Brown, aged 1 year, 2 months & 10 days. His funeral is this evening, at 4 o'clock, at the residence, on 10th st, between E & F sts.

$10 reward for strayed or stolen sorrel Colt. Reward if delivered to M__ Hancock, in Wash City. –Wm Thomas

WED JUN 26, 1844
Laws of the U S passed at the 1st session of the 28th Congress.
1-Act authorizing a patent to be issued to Jos Camapu, assignee of the children & heirs of Taw-cum-e-go-qua, [an Indian woman,] a patent for section 1, of the Indian reservation at the Grand Traverse of Flint river, in Mich, which section was reserved to her by the treaty concluded with the Chippewa Indians at Saginaw, Mich, on Sep 24, 1819. That before said patent shal be issued Campau shall file, in the ofc of the Com'r of the Gen Land Ofc, proof that he has purchased said land of the children & heirs of said Taw-cum-e-go-qua, & that he paid therefore, at the time when said purchase was made, a fair & equitable consideration.
2-Act for the relief of the legal reps of Valentine Geesey, dec'd, late of Pa: to pay the reps $260.50, being the amount of debt recovered of the estate of said Valentine by a contractor for work done on the nat'l road, while under his superintendence.
3-Act for the relief of Henry Newingham: to issued to him, in the right of Wm Marshall, who was a private soldier in Armand's legion of the continental establishment in the Revolutionary army, a warrant for the bounty land to which Marshall would be entitled, as such soldier; & the Sec of the Treasury to grant scrip for said warrant in the manner & on the conditions prescribed for the grant of scrip for bounty land; the said Marshall having intermarried with the mother of said Newingham, & died without lineal heirs; & having in his lifetime been supported by Newingham, &, in consideration thereof, before his death, delivered to him his original certificates of discharge from the army, & declared his intention that the said Newingham should have the benefit of said bounty land: provided, that nothing in this act shall be so construed as to prejudice the claim of any heirs [if any] of said Marshall.
4-Act for the relief of Walter S Alexander & others. That upon good & sufficient cause being shown by either party that a fair & impartial trial cannot be had in Alexandria, D C, in the trial of a certain issue of densavit vel non, sent to be tried at the bar of the Circuit Court of D C, for Alexandria, by a jury, as in such cases provided by order of the Orphans' Court of said county, in which Walter S Alexander & others are caveaton & plntfs, & Geo Wise is the expounder of the last will & testament of Geo Dent Alexander, dec'd, & dfndnt with others in said issue, the said Circuit Court of D C, for Alexandria Co, shall at its discretion order the said issue to be tried before the Circuit Court for Wash Co, D C, at the next session of

said court, to the same effect that the said issue is required by any law heretofore in force to be tried in Alexandria Co; & it shall be the duty of the clerk of the court to transmit to the clerk the record & all the proceedings in said case, now in said court of Alexandria Co, & all original & other papers filed in the suit.

5-Act for the relief of John Edmonson, of Fulton Co, Ill, to be placed upon the roll of Revolutionary pensioners, & be paid at the rate prescribed in the act of Jun 7, 1832, for two years' service as private in the Revolutionary war; & that his pension commence according to the provisions of said act.

6-Act for the relief of the legal reps of Francis Cazeau, late merchant at Montreal. The sum of $27,352.32 be paid to the reps of Cazeau, or to their legal atty or other person lawfully entitled to receive the same; it being one-fourth of the sum appropriated under an act of Congress approved Mar 3, 1817, with interest from May, 1818.

7-Act for the relief of Geo W Allen & Reuben Allen. That the reversionary interest of the U S in & to the reservation to John B Shadernah, by & under the second article of the treaty with the Pottawatomie Indians of Oct 26, 1832, be & the same is hereby relinquished to Geo W & Reuben Allen, as grantees, have purchased of the said reservee, by authentic & regular deed, his right in & to said reservation; provided that no sale or conveyance of said reservation by said reservee shall be deemed regular, now shall this act have effect until the Pres of the U S shall have approved such conveyanc, & endorsed his approval thereon.

8-Act for the relief of Geo M Jones: he or his heirs, to be paid $320.89, being the balance due him on his account of blacksmith work done & materials furnished to Jonathan Prescott, as agent of the U S, for ths use of the dredging machine while at work in removing the bar at Nantucket harbor, in 1832.

9-Act for the relief of Isaac Fessenden: to be paid $50, being the amount of a fine imposed upon him at Pensacola for leaving the port of Franklin, La, in the schnr **Pearl**, without clearing from the custom-house; afterwards remitted by the Sec of the Treaury, but not in time to prevent its going into the U S Treasury.

10-Act for the relief of Gervis Foote, of the State of N Y: Foote or his heirs to be paid $1,150, being the amount agreed to be paid to him by the agent of the U S, under his contract for delivery of a certain quantity of stone on the bank of Lake Erie, at Barcelona, in 1838 & 1839.

11-Act for the relief of Saml B Folger: to be paid to Folger, or his heirs, $536.74, being the amount of his account of blacksmith work done & materials furnished to Lt Jonathan Prescott, for the use of the public works at Nantucket harbor, then under his charge as an ofcr in the engineer service of the U S, during 1831, 1832, & 1833.

12-Act for the relief of Saml B Tuck: Tuck or his heirs, to be paid a just & reasonable price for thirty & nineteen thirty-sixths chaldrons of Virginia coal, delivered to Lt Jonathan Prescott, as agent of the U S at Nantucket harbor, in 1832; provided the whole amount shall not exceed $412.12.

13-Act for the relief of Woodson Wren, of Mississippi: that he be confirmed in the following tracts & parcels of land, to wit: fractional section 25 , township 7, range 9 west, including the site of the old French fort, & containing about 123 acres; also, apportion of fractional section 24, in township 7, range 9 west, being lot 6, containing 80 acres, situated on the east side of the Bay of Biloxi, in Jackson, Miss, claimed by virtue of a deed from Littlepage Robertson, & reported for confirmation by the register & receiver of the land ofc at Jackson court-house, Miss, dated Jul 12, 1833. The Com'r of the Gen Land Ofc, upon passage of this act, shall issued a patent for the same, which patent shall operate only as relinquishment on the part of the U S of all right & title to said land.

14-Act for the relief of Eaton Naner: it appears that on Jul 2, 1821, a patent issued from the Gen Land Ofc of the U S, where the same was duly recorded, to Eaton Naner, for a tract of land containing 160 acres, being the s e quarter of section 34, of twoship 10 north, in range 8 west, in the tract appropriated by certain acts of Congress for military bounties, in the Territory of Arkansas, which patent was duly countersigned by Josiah Meigs, Com'r of the Gen Land Ofc, but, by accident, was not signed by the Pres of the U S. Said patent shall be deemed & held to be perfect & valid to all intents & purposes.

15-Act for the relief of the owner & crew of the schnr **Mary Francis**: the Collector of the Customs for Marblehead, Mass, to pay to Jos Hidden, late owner of the schnr, & to all persons composing her late crew, or thier heirs, such allowance, to be distributed according to law, as they would have been entitled to receive had the schnr completed her fishing term & returned into port.

16-Act for the relief of Wm H Hoag & others: to pay to Hoag, or his assigns, $442.40; to Geo Taylor or his assigns $272.29; to N P Drake or his assigns $132.75; to David Stiles or his assigns $148.50; to Wm Nesbit or his assigns $325.28; to Cornelius Millspaugh or his assigns $328.80; & to J S Sturgess or his assigns $170.20; in the aggregate of $1,820.22, being the amount of 5% per month forfeited by each of the above named persons, & retained by the U S agent, under their respective contracts to make certain portions of the La Plaisanc_ Bay road in Michigan, in 1833.

17-Act for the relief of Geo Wallis: to be paid $3,000, it being for the destruction of the cattle of Wallis by the Sac, Fox, & Iowa tribes of Indians; that said sum of money be paid out of the annuities payable to said tribes, in equal proportions; that is to say, $1,500 out of the annuities due the Sacre & Foxes of Missouri river, & $1,500 out of the annuities due the Iowas.

18-Act for the relief of Robt Monroe, of Westmoreland Co, Pa: to be placed on the roll of invalid pensioners, & to pay him $4 per month, during his natural life from & after Apr 1, 1844.

19-Act for the relief of Alice Usher, of Providence, R I: to be placed on the pension roll; & that she be paid, for 5 years, commencing on Mar 4, 1836, the same rate of pension allowed by the act of Jul 7, 1832, to a drummer for 12 months' service, & also the same rate of pension allowed by the same act to a drum-major for 6 months' service.

20-Act for the relief of John Ferguson, jr, & Wm Reid, of New Orleans: to allow & credit, on any judgment obtained by the U S on any bonds given to Ferguson & Reid, as principals, upon the importation of 58 bales of cotton from Texas into the port of

New Orleans in Mar & Apr, 1842, the amount of any certificate of debenture issued upon the exportation of said cotton, to J G Stouse, of New Orleans, which have been endorsed or assigned to said Ferguson & Reid, & have not been otherwise cancelled or paid upon the surrender & discharge of the same & upon due proof that the cotton was landed at the port in France for which it was cleared; & if all such judgments have been fully paid & discharged, the said Secretary is hereby authorized & required to pay to Ferguson & Reid, that amount of said certificates, upon the surrender of the same & the proof required as aforesaid.

21-Act for the relief of John Frazer & Geo A Trenholm, of Charleston, S C: to be refunded whatever sum may have been collected of them for the importation of 116 pieces of cotton bagging from the port of New Orleans into the port of Charleston, in the brig **Powhatan**, in Dec, 1842, which pieces were not released from forfeiture by the Sec of the Treasury it appearing that the cause for which the same were forfeited was not any misconduct or neglect of the said Frazer & Trenholm.

22-Act for the relief of Isaac S Ketchum: the Sec of War be directed to retain out of the annuities due the Ottawa, Chippewa, & Pottawatamie Indians, $557.72, & pay the same to Ketchum, the amount due him from said Indians for money laid out in bringing on a deputation of chiefs to Wash City; which expense was to be incurred & paid by said Indians, as agreed upon in council held in Dec, 1840.

23-Act for the relief of Isaac S Ketchum, late special Indian agent: the Sec of Treasury to pay to Ketchum $383.01, the balance due him for provisions purchased & delivered by him, as special agent for the Gov't, to the Ottawa, Chippewa, & Pottawatamie Indians.

24-Act for the relief of Wm De Peyster & Henry N Cruger: to pay to them the value of their slave Romeo, who was sent from *Fort Delhi* to Arkansas, with the Seminole Indians, under the authority of the ofcrs of the U S.

A numerous procession of the Independent Order of Odd Fellows, in full regalia, attended, on Sat last, to the grave, the remains of their late esteemed brother, Wm Truman, of Central Lodge, #1.

A very rich mine of gold has lately been discovered on the lands of John Newland, in Orange Co, N C.

THU JUN 27, 1844
Boston papers of Sat. Died: Mr Saml Sprague, the aged father of Mr Chas Sprague, of that city. Mr Sprague was well known & beloved by a large portion of the citizens of Boston, & in a long life had so sustained all his relations as to make many friends. [No date-current item.]

Julia H Strong, aged 11, d/o Levi Strong, of Bolton, Conn, died when the window at school fell on her. She hung until she was dead before her situation was discovered.

Information recently received that Her Britannic Majesty has extended pardon [subject to the usual condition of good behavior while resident there] to the Americans now in *Van Dieman's Land*, whose names are:

Chauncey Sheldon	Carret Hicks	David A Heustis
Jos Thompson	John Cronkhite	Leonard Delano
Alvin B Sweet	Elow Fellows	Lewis W Willer
Nathan Whiting	David House	Robt Marsh
Jacob Paddock	Saml Snow	Moses A Dutcher
John G Swanberg	Emanuel Garrison	–Madisonian

For sale: 1,000 acres of woodland on the Choptank river, in the lower part of Caroline Co, Eastern Shore, Md. Will be offered at public auction in Easton, Talbot Co, Md, on Jul 25. –Theodore Lockerman, Easton, Md, or N Goldsborough, Md.

Wishing to remove South, I offer for sale the farm on which I reside, **White Hall**, in King Geo Co, Va, containing between 300 & 400 acres . The bldgs are brick dwlg, barn, stables, carriage-house, corn-house, ice-house, & all necessary out-houses. Address me, at Hampstead, or to Mr W R Mason, King Geo Court-house. –Wm Berryman

FRI JUN 28, 1844
For rent: the 3 story brick house on Capitol Hill, now occupied by the subscribe. If preferred, the furniture will be rented with the above house. –Eliza Timms

The partnership under the name of King & Scott, in Gtwn, D C, is this day dissolved by mutual consent. The business will be continued at the old stand, Market space & Cherry st, by Edw P Scott. –Z M P King, E F Scott, Gtwn

Thurston, confined in jail at Charleston on a charge of forgery, committed suicide on Tue last by taking the whole of a dose of medicine which had been prescribed by a physician in small quantities. He left a letter stating his determination to end his life in that way.

Letters from on board the schnr **Shark**, in Panama Bay, May 2, mention that Cmdor Dallas was attacked with paralysis on Apr 25, on board the ship **Savannah**, at Callao. The attack was a severe one, & his recovery is doubtful.

Jos Carter was convicted on Mon at Belvidere, N J, of the murder of the Castner family. Hummer, the hired man of Carter, has had a true bill found against him as a participator, & several others have been arrested as presumed accomplices.

The Supreme Court of R I, sitting at Newport, on Tue sentenced Thos W Dorr to imprisonment for life in the State Prison, for treason against the sovereign power of the Commonwealth. –Providence Journal

Chas Boyd was lately tried before the U S District Court at Savannah on 3 counts: one for stealing the mail, the second for injuring & destroying the mail, & the third for deserting the mail. He was acquitted on one & two; on deserting the mail, Judge Nicholl sentenced him to pay a fine of $500 & costs.

Rencounter at Duncannon Iron Works on Mon week: Miles Evans was killed by Wm Musgrove. They were both employed at the foundry, & the fatal dispute grew out of which was the better workman of the two. --Harrisburg Intell

Laws of the U S passed at the 1st session of the 28th Congress.
1-The following, all of the parish of Pisquemines, La, or their legal reps, are authorized to enter at the land ofc in the southeastern land district in La, within 6 months after the passage of this act, section 17 & lots 1 & 2 in section 18, in township 23, of range 33 east, in said district, upon payment to the receiver of the said land ofc of $1.25 per acre; provided that at the time of the entry they shall file in the land ofc a survey & plat of the land entered, signed by them or their legal reps, specifying thereon the extent of their several claims by occupancy; & that when the said entry shall be made the same shall enure to the benefit of such persons severally, in the proportions & according to the quantities specified on said plat; & provided that his act shall not invalidate any rights which any other person, not herein named, may be entitled to under any law heretofore passed. --J W Jones, Spkr of the House of Reps: Willie P Mangum, Pres pro tempore of the Senate. Named in the act:

Andrew Anderson	John Holland	Wm T Smith
Jas T Allen	David Johnston	Christopher Scheltz
Geo Beason	Henry Johnson	Wm Stevens
John Baily	Jas J Jarvis	Jas Scott
John R Brown	Geo Linton	John Seiler
Edw Bourguin	Cyrus Lamontt	Jas Tyson
Jacob Baker	Cyrus Morgan	Wm D Tolbortt
Wm Brownson	Jas W Morgan	Wm Taylor
Robt Cooper	John Miller	Thos J Vanderslice
Edw Clarke	Hans Myers	Jas B Williams
Tos Cross	Erasmus Newman	Hiram B Webster
Wm C Davis	John Parker	Jas Kelly
Edw G Davis	John Perrin	Wm Denford
Ephraim Eldridge	Asa Payson	Edw Hansbury
Wm Ellis	Peter Robinson	Jos E Dunham
Dennis Finn	Jas B Read	Chas Linguiar
Nathl J France	Francisco Reepe	Gilbert Leonards
John Fowler	David Shepherd	Jos Lamuade
Robt Holliday	Jos Shepherd	

2-Act for the relief of Ephraim D Dickson: to be paid $152. for shoeing 76 horses in Capt E D Dickson's company of volunteer mounted gun-men, in Gen Coffee's brigade of Tenn volunteers, in Sep, 1814, at $2 per horse.

3-Act of the relief of Wm Henson: to pay to him $180 for 90 days' service enrolling Cherokee Indians for emigration; also, $540 for rations by him furnished for the same Indians, averaged at 45 days, making in all the sum of $720.

4-Act fo the relief of the owners & crew of the schnr **Privado**: the Collector of the district of Portsmouth, N H, is to pay to the above: for the fishing season of 1839, to be distributed according to law, the same sum of money thay would have been entitled to as bounty or allowance if she had not foundered on her second fare, in Jun, 1839, but had complied with all the requirements of law to secure said bounty; said vessel having sailed from Portsmouth on Jun 17, 1839.

5-Act for the relief of Abelard Guthrie: that the entry made by Guthrie, at the land ofc in Ohio, on May 21, 1839, of a tract of land known & distinguished on the plan of the surveys of the U S public lands as the east half & the n w quarter of secion 13, in township 3, south of range 5 east, be hereby confirmed; & that the Pres of the U S is authorized to cause to be issued on said entry a patent for the same to the said Guthrie, his heirs & assigns, as in other case where a legal entry had been made.

6-Act for the relief of True Putney & Hugh Riddle, of the city of Balt, Md: to be paid $1,672.61, being the amount of extra work & material not embraced by their contract to do the stone-work of the U S warehouse in said city in 1835, but furnished for said bldg by direction of the architect & superintendent thereof.

7-Act for the relief of Geo W Clarke, Harris Cook, & John Brainerd, second, of Connectiuct: the sum of $316.67 be paid to them, being the amount forfeited by them under a contract to deliver a certain quantity of stone at *Fort Adams*, R I, on Oct 2, 1831.

8-Act for the relief of Geo Harrison & his sureties: Harrison, a regimental paymaster of Ky militia during the late war with Great Britian, be & he is hereby exonerated & acquitted of & from the sum of $393.26, part of the balance reported & claimed as due from him & his sureties to the U S, upon his accounts as such paymaster, together with the interest accrued on said sum; & that the surety of said Harrison, as such paymaster, be & are hereby acquitted of & from all responsibility or liability for or on account of such suretyship, & from all judgments or demands of the U S on that account.

9-Act for the relief of Chas W Morgan, of the U S Navy: he is to be paid $4,200, for extraordinary expenses incurred by him while he commanded the U S squadron in the Mediterranean, in 1841, 1842, & 1843, in conducting the negotiation with the Minister Pleni of the Emperor of Morocco, in relation to the indignity offered to the U S Consul, Thos N Carr; in entertaining the Queen of Prussia & her suite; & in relation to the reception & entertainment of the Prince of Syracuse & the Prince of Lucca; including, also, losses on stores laid in at Toulon for a cruise,which were abandoned & sold upon being suddenly recalled by the Navy Dept; the said allowance being made in full compensation for all extraordinary espenses incurred by the said Capt Chas W Morgan during his command of the Mediterranean squadron.

10-Act for the relief of Lathrop Foster: his name to be placed on the roll of invalid pensioners, at the rate of one-half the pay of a private, from Jan 1, 1840.

11-Act for the relief of Harvey Heth, of Cass Co, Ill: to be paid the sum of $400, out of the annuity which shall be due to the Wabash band of Pottawatomie Indians; the $400 being the value of a field of corn used & destroyed by the Indians, of the property of said Heth, in 1836.

12-Act for the relief of Danl W Church: name to be placed on the invalid pension roll: to be paid a pension at the rate of $12.75 each month from & after Mar 4, 1844, in the manner & at the times other invalid pensions are payable.

13-Act for the relief of Manlius V Thompson, sole exc of Milus W Dickey, dec'd: the sum of $1,125 to be paid to in full satisfaction of a contract made by the said Dickey with the Post Ofc Dept, for transporting the mail from Maysville to Lexington, in Ky, terminating on Jun 30, 1838.

13-Act for the relief of Josiah Dillon, late assist quartermaster in the army: to be paid $138.50, being the balance found to be due Dillon, on vouchers suspended for the want of form in the settlement of his accounts.

14-Act for the relief of Mary Ann Linton, wid/o Wm S Linton, who was lately a pensioner of the U S under the act of 1832, on the pension roll of the act of 1838, & Mar 3, 1843, & to allow her the same amount of pension as was annually allowed to her husband while living; the same to be paid as other pensions have been paid. Mary Ann Linton shall be entitled to the full benefit of all laws & resolves which shall hereafter be paid.

15-Act for the relief of David Allspach, surety of Michl Allspach, late collector of the excise duty in 2 official bonds, be, & he is hereby released from all his liabilities as such surety, on paying any costs that may have accrued by reason of the prosecution of any suit against him on account of his liability. That nothing in this act contained shall be held to discharge the estate of Michl Allspach from the payment of any balance that may be due the U S on account of said bonds.

16-Act for the relief of the heirs of Ebenezer Moore, of the State of N Y, a Canadian volunteer: to be issued to his heirs, a warrant for 160 acres of bounty land, under the act passed Mar 5, 1816, & the act passed Mar 3, 1817.

17-Act for the relief of Henry S Commager: to be paid $206.31, out of any money due or that may hereafter become due the Ottowa tribe of Indians from the U S, by existing treaties, on account of an order drawn by 8 of the chiefs, headmen, & warriors of the said tribe, dated Maumee city, Ohio, Aug 14, 1837, requesting the said sum of money herein directed.

The U S brig **Truxton**, Lt Henry Bruce commanding, left Phil on Tue for the Coast of Africa.

A Convention for the surrender of criminals between the U S of A & his Majesty the King of the French, was concluded & signed by their Plenipotentiaries, at Wash, on Nov 9 last. Signed A P Upshur, A Pageot

The N Y correspondent of the U S Gaz, writing under the date of Wed, says: His Excellency John Tyler, Pres of the U S, was married this morning to the beautiful Miss Gardner, d/o the late David Gardner, who was killed at the time of the explosion on board of the steamer **Princeton**.

Died: on Jun 26, at Annapolis, Md, Hon John Stephen, one of the Judges of the Court of Appeals of the State of Md. He was a member of the Executive Council, & several times represented the city of Annapolis in the Legislature, having resided there until 1824, when he was appointed Judge of the Judicial District, & removed to the village of Bladensburg, PG Co, where he has resided ever since.

Notice: meeting of the Stockholders of the Patriotic Bank of Wash will be held this day at 12 o'clock. –W J McDonald, Sec of the meeting

India Rubber Manufacture, 25 Maiden La, N Y [successor to the Roxbury India Rubber Co] has many styles of goods adapted to the climate of every section of the country. –Horace H Day

Parasols & Sunshades: H C Spalding & Co, 2nd door west from 8th st.

SAT JUN 29, 1844
Virginia-In Chancery. At a Circuit Superior Court of Law & Chancery, held in Fauquier Co, on May 17, 184. Henry Fitzhugh, as exc of Thos Fitzhugh, dec'd, & in his own right, & Henrietta S Fitzhugh wife of said Henry Fitzhugh, plntfs, against Mordecai C Fitzhugh, Giles Fitzhugh, Austin Fitzhugh, Lucy B Fitzhugh, Thos E White & Sophia his wife, Lawrence Fitzhugh, Rufus K Polk & Ellen his wife, Rudolph Fitzhugh, Logan Fitzhugh, ___ Macon & Mary his wife, Rebecca Fitzhugh, Ann Fitzhugh, Wm Payne, Virginia Payne, Lucy F Payne, Mary M Payne, Chas Payne, Wm Fitzhugh, Andrew Fitzhugh, David Fitzhugh, Maria Fitzhugh, Caroline B Withers, Chas Battaile & Nancy his wife, Meade Fitzhugh, Saml Gordon, jr & Patsey Julia his wife, Theodorick Bland, Isaac Winston & Lucy his wife, John Thornton & Mildred his wife, John B Dade, Wm A Bowen & Ellen his wife, Ann Maria Fitzhugh, Geo T Fitzhugh, Seffrein N Vass & Susan his wife, Henry Fitzhugh, Lucy Laura Fitzhugh, Rosalie Fitzhugh, Thos Fitzhugh, Eliz W Fitzhugh, Rosalie Fitzhugh, Thos Fitzhugh, Eliz W Fitzhugh, Ann D Baylor, Thos E Hunton, Jas W Foster & Lucchia his wife, Geo F Thornton, John G Thornton, Wm H Thornton, Edw C Thornton, Addison F Thornton, ___ Berry & Mary Jane his wife, ___Tutt & Ann E his wife, Jacintha ForE Royston, John H Royston, Geo F Royston, Edw C Royston, Wm Royston, Sally F Royston, Wm Royston & Mary A D his wife, Edmund Molley & Elvira J his wife, Eliz D Fitzhugh, Frances Fitzhugh, Thos

Fitzhugh, Warren Fitzhugh, Edw Fitzhugh, Dudley Fitzhugh, Sarah B Edmonds, Maria Catlett, Peter Dudley & Sarah D his wife, Wm F Gordon, Lucy A H Gordon, Edw H Fitzhugh & Maria F his wife, Eliz C Gordon, Eliz Gordon, Maria Gordon, Thos G Gordon, Wm F Thornton, Saml G Thornton, Griffin Thornton, ___ Hall & Susan F his wife, Thos G Battaile, Mary W Battaile, Chas Jesse & Harriet his wife, Robt Turner & Eliz his wife, Thos L Fitzhugh, Francis C Fitzhugh, Jas M Fitzhugh & Mary F his wife, Drury B Fitzhugh, Alverda C Stuart, Louisa C Hooe, Jas Newman & Sally B his wife, Ann Ray Dade, Henry F Dade, Louisa E Dade, Lucy Fitzhugh, John Conway & Mary his wife, Edmund P Barbour & Harriet J his wife, Wm G Stuart, & ___ & Lucy his wife, late Lucy Stuart, dfndnts. The plntfs, by leave of the Court, this day filed a supplemental bill making Richd H Field & Lewis B Williams, trustees of Edmund P Barbour, dfndnts: & the said trustees filed their answer thereto, to which the plntfs, by counsel, replied generally. And the plntfs, by leave of the Court, also filed an amended & supplemental bill making Berkely Ward, an exc of Thos Fitzhugh, dec'd, & in his own right, & Harriet Ward, w/o said Berkeley Ward, dfndnts. The original bill in this case states that Thos Fitzhugh, late of Fauquier Co, dec'd, being seized & possessed of a very large estate, real & personal in Fauquier Co, & in Culpeper Co, duly made & published his last will & testament in writing, dated May 29, 1842, & thereby devised to Henry Fitzhugh, Berkeley Ward, & Thos T Withers, certain slaves, & the sum of $3,000 upon certain trusts in said will mentioned; & of his said will appointed said Henry Fitzhugh, Berkeley Ward, & Thos T Withers executors: that the said testator departed this life on or about the __ day of Nov, 1843, without altering or revoking his said will: & thereupon the said Henry Fitzhugh & Berkeley Ward proved the said will in the County Court of Fauquier, & took upon themselves the burden of the execution thereof & possessed themselves of all the said testator's personal effects: that the said personal effects consisted of large sum of money in bonds, & a great many valuable slaves, & some perishable property: that the said testator & Henry Fitzhugh, Wm Fitzhugh, Geo Fitzhugh, Nicholas Fitzhugh, Battaile Fitzhugh, Giles Fitzhugh, Sarah Fitzhugh, Susan Fitzhugh, & Mary Fitzhugh, were children of Henry Fitzhugh of Bedford; that the said testator died unmarried, & without lawful issue of his body, & the large real & personal estate of which he died seised & possessed, which is undisposed of by his will, by the statute of descents & distributions of Virginia descend & passes to such of his said brothers & sisters of the said testator as survived him, & the children of such as died before him, all of whom are made dfndnts; but states that Cole Fitzhugh, one of the sons of the testator's brother Wm Fitzhugh, who died in his life time, died out of the Commonwealth of Va, leaving issue who are wholly unknown, & who at the death of said testator were entitled to their father's share in the said testator's estate, the same being one ninth part thereof; that the real estate of which the said testator died seized, consister of 3 large tracts of land, containing about 1,000 acres each, in Fauquier Co, & one other tract of about 1,000 acres in Culpeper Co; that besides the children of the said Cole Fitzhugh, the same of the person who intermarried with Lucy Stuart, one of the children of David Stuart, who was one of the 4 children of Mary Fitzhugh, one of the sisters of the testator, who intermarried with Gibbon Stuart, dec'd, is the wholly unknown; that the said Lucy Stuart is entitled to one-third of one-fourth of one eleventh part of said testator's estate; that in respect to many of the share of the said estate, the subdivisions will be so minute as to render impracticable an allotment of the slaves or partition of the land amongst those intererested therein, & that sales thereof will be required to be made. And the said bill prays that the parties enumerated, who are known, may be made dfndnts in the said bill, & that those who are unknown may also be made dfndnts when they become known; that it may be ascertained by the decree of the Court who are entitled to the said estate, & in what proportions respectively; that the said Henry Fitzhugh & Berkeley Ward, submitting to account as executors; that there may be allotment of the slaves & partition of the real estate, or sale thereof, & distribution of the proceeds of sales according to the rights of the several parties, & for further relief. It is ordered that all parties interested in the said bill do appear at the next term of this Court, to be held on Tue after the first Mon in Oct next, make themselves parties dfndnts thereto, file their answer, & assert their rights & claims. -Wm F Phillips, clerk

Orphans Court of Wash Co, D C. Letters of administration on the personal estate of Thos T Triplett, late of the State of Georgia, dec'd. -Edw Mattingly, adm

Chas Co Court of Equity, Mar Term, 1844. Allison Roberts vs Eliz M Acton & others. The bill in this case states that a petition was filed by H May, in 1837, for the sale of division of the real estate of Wm Stuart, of said county, dec'd, & thereupon a commission issued to 5 sensible, descreet men of Chas Co, to wit, John Gardiner, Theodore Mudd, Jas M Murray, Henry L Mudd, Underwood Langly, to divide or sell the real estate of the said Wm Stuart; & that the commission did divide, according to law, a portion of the said estate among the reps of Wm Stuart, & after giving legal notice did sell to the highest bidder a part of the said real estate called *Betsey's Delight*, containing 160 acres, being & lying in Chas Co, Md, & that one Mathew Acton became the purchaser, as appears by the bond given for the purchase money, which bond is exhibited & made a part of the bill, & that the cmplnt became security for the payment of the purchase money, & that Mathew Acton has since died, leaving 3 of the dndnts, to wit, Eliz M Acton, Theodore M Acton, & Richd Acton, & the fourth dfndnt his widow, & that no part of the purchase money has been paid; & to the intent that the purchase money may be paid to the legal reps of said Wm Stuart, & that the cmplnt may be released from the liability for the purchase money as security on said bond, the bill prays a decree that the said lands should be sold, the personal estate having been exhausted by Eliz M Acton, as exc of the said Mathew Acton, & that the dfndnts appear before Chas Co Court & shew cause, if any they have, why said lands should not be sold as prayed. Dfndnts to appear in person, or by solicitor, on or before the 3rd Mon of Aug next. -C Dorsey
-Walter Mitchell, clerk

Dr Otto, one of the oldest & most respectable physicians of Phil, died on Wed in Phil. He had made arrangements to move into the country, & was spending a few days with his son-in-law, Garrick Mallory, at whose house he was taken sick & died.

Notice: I hereby forewarn all persons from harboring or trusting my wife Martha on my account, as she has left my bed & board without just cause or provocation.
-Jesse Morgan, his X mark. Colored.

Mrd: on Jun 26, in N Y, at the Church of the Ascension, by Rt Rev Benj T Onderdonk, Bishop of the Eastern Diocese of N Y, John Tyler, Pres of the U S, to Julia Gardiner, eldest d/o the late David Gardiner.

Loudoun land for sale: the subscriber offers 1, 420 acres, at present divided into parcels: a farm tenenated by Jas Hummer, about 147 acres; a farm tenanted by S & H Jenkins, about 728 acres; a farm tenanted by Wm Miskell, about 317 acres; & an untenanted farm, about 228 acres . They will be for sale, privately, on application to the agent, Benj Bridges, residing in the vicinity, until the 2nd Mon in Aug next, if unsold, they will be offered at public auction. -Wm B Shittenden, Richmond, Va

MON JUL 1, 1844
Earthenware, china, & glassware: Thos Pursell, on Pa ave, opposite Brown's Hotel.

Law of the U S passed at the 1st session of the 28th Congress.
1-Joint resolution authorizing Capt Jas Lowe to assign a certain section of land: Lowe, of Westmoreland Co, Va, be authorized, & he is hereby authorized & empowered to transfer or assign over a warrant for one section of land granted by act of Congress, approved Mar 1, 1843, to Jas Lowe "as a testimonial to him of the consideration in which Congress hold his gallantry & peril in the rescue of an American brig, her crew & passengers from the hands of pirates," & that the assignee of said Lowe be permitted to enter the said section of land as fully & effectually as could be done by the said Jas Lowe in person
2-Act for the relief of Thos Hunter & Alex'r Caldwell: they are hereby released from the judgment rendered against them by the circuit court of the U S for the Ky district, for $2,000 & the costs, except as to the costs; the said judgment being the same rendered against them upon the recognizance of bail by them entered into before Thos B Monroe, Judge of the U S for Ky on Apr 30, 1842, conditioned for the appearance of Wm H Hunter before the said court, at the capitol, in Frankfort, on May 1, 1842, to answer to a charge of felony against the U S.
3-Act for the benefit of John Perham, of Maine: to place his name on the roll of invalid pensioners, at the rate of $72 per annum; said pension to commence on Jan 1, 1837, & to continue during his natural life.
4-Act for the relief of Margaret Dougherty: that the sum of $20.85 be paid to Mgt Dougherty, wid/o & rep/o Owen Dougherty, dec'd; it being the amount due to the said Owen Dougherty under the provisions of an act entitled: An act providing for

the distribution of $100,000 among the captors of the Algerine vessels captured & restored to the Dey of Algirers: approved Apr 27, 1816.

5-Act for the relief of Jas Pepper & others: that entry made at the land ofc at Washita, La, by Jas Pepper & others, of section 52, in township 16, of range 14 east, on May 30, 1836, by certificate number 3,426, be & the same is hereby confirmed; & the Com'r of the Gen Land Ofc is authorized to issue a patent therefore.

6-Act for the relief of Ann Hunter, wid/o Robt Hunter: to place her name on the pension roll, & that she be entitled to receive the same amount which the said Robt Hunter received, agreeable to the provisions of the acts of Jul 7, 1838, & Mar 3, 1843, granting pensions to widows of soldiers of the Revolutionary war.

7-Act for the relief of the legal reps of John Baker, dec'd: that the entry of 507 acres of land, made at the land ofc at St Stephen's, in Ala, by the legal reps of John Baker, on Jul 9, 1839, be & the same is confirmed; & the said legal reps shall be entitled to a patent therefore, as in other cases.

8-Act for the relief of Marcay Olds, of Chenango Co, N Y: to place to place her name on the pension roll, for the services of her first husband, John Stuart, during the Revolutionary war. And that she shall be entitled to the full benefit of all laws & resolves which shall hereafter be passed continuing in force the act of Jul 7, 1838, & the several acts & resolves amendatory thereof.

9-Act for the relief of Lund Washington: that he be paid $200, being the amount due for the services of his minor son, Wm T Washington, as clerk in the War Dept during the first quarter of 1818.

10-Act for the relief of Wm P Duval: the proper accounting ofcrs are directed to settle, under the direction of the Sec of War, the account of Duval, for his services & the disbursements made by him & the expenses incurred as superintendent of Indian affairs in the Territory of Florida, & that he be paid such sum of money as shall be found, on such settlement, to be due to him.

11-Act for the benefit of Jas Anderson, of the Territory of Iowa: he is permitted to enter, at the minimum price of the public land, the fractional 16th section in township 69 north, range 2 west, containing 218 acres & 45 one hundredths, in the district of lands subject to entry at Burlington, in the Territory of Iowa. That the authority having charge of the said school land is authorized to select & report to the register & receiver of the district in which the land is situated, other unappropriated lands of the U S subject to private entry in the said Territory, of similar quantity to that which shall have been entered by said Anderson, for the use of schools for the inhabitants of said township.

12-Act for the relief of Simeon Dennin: to place his name on the invalid pension rolls, & that he be paid at the rate of $4 per month, during his natural life, commencing from & after the passage of this act.

13-Act for the relief of Solomon Sturges, assignee of Humphrey Richcreek: he is authorized to enter one half quarter section of land, of any of the public lands in Ohio subject to sale by private entry, in lieu of the west half of the n w quarter of section 8, in township 5, of range 7, which was entered & paid for with military land scrip at the Zanesville land ofc in Ohio by Humphrey Richcreek, & transferred by him on

Apr 25, 1832, the day on which said entry was made, to the said Solomon Sturges: provided, that Sturges relinquish to the U S all his claim to the land entered.

14-Act for the relief of Pierre S Derbanne, of the parish of Narchitoches, La: he or his legal rep, shall be authorized to make entry & purchase at $1.25 per ac, of lots 2 & 3, being the n w fractional quarter of section 15, of township 9 north, range 6 west, of the n w land district in Louisiana, or so much thereof as does not conflict with the claim of Jean Pierre Valade, agreeably to a diagram approved by the surveyor general of Louisiana, to include his improvements as nearly as practical: provided the lots shall not have been sold by the U S prior to the passage of this act.

15-Act for the relief of Asa Davis: to place his name on the invalid pension roll; at the rate of $6 per month, from & after Mar 4, 1842.

16-Act for the relief of Wm R Davis, of Indiana: to pay him $75, for repairing & cleaning arms & accoutrements used in the regt commanded by Col Geo W Ewing, at the Pottawatomie Indian payment in Sept, 1836, & for furnishing powder, lead, paper, twince, casting balls, & making 1,000 cartridges for said expedition.

17-Act for the relief of the heirs of Hyacinth Lasselle: in 1840 Lasselle was authorized to locate 560 acres of land, at any land ofc in Indiana, at any time prior to Mar 4, 1843, by paying the minimun price fixed for such lands, for 18 acres & fortysix hundredths of an acre, part & parcel of said tract of 560 acres; & whereas, also, Lasselle has dec'd without perfecting the location of the said land. It shall be lawful for the heirs of Laselle to locate the said tract of land, at any time prior to Mar 4, 1846, at any land ofc in Indiana.

18-Act for the relief of Francois Christen & widow Baptiste Berard: That the claims by right of ancient settlement, of Madame Baptiste Berard, wid/o Baptiste Berard, dec'd, & Francois Christien, respectively, on the east side of the bayou Teche-the Berard claim for 11 arpens front by 40 deep, & the other for 12 arpens front by 40 deep-be & the same are hereby confirmed to the aforesaid claimants, recpectively, or their legal reps, to embrace the original improvements of the claimants, & on the return to the Gen Land Ofc of plats of survey, approved by the Surveyor Gen of La, for the aforesaid claims, patents shall issue; that this act, & the patents that may issue, shall only be held to be a relinquishment of the title of the U S, & in no manner affect the rights of the third person, or preclude a judicial decision in favor of any other title, if such exist, to the same tracts.

19-Act granting a pension to Milly, an Indian woman of the Creek nation, & d/o the Prophet Francis: to receive a pension at $96 per annum, payable semi-annually during her natural life, as a testimonial of the gratitude & bounty of the U S for the humanity displayed by her in the war of 1817 & 1818, in saving the life of an American citizen, who was a rpisoner in the hands of her people, & about to be put to death by them; the pension to commence on Sep 4, 1843. The Sec of War is directed to procure & transmit to Milly, a medal with appropriate devices impressed thereon, of the value of not exceeding $20, as an additional testimonial of the gratitude of the U S.

20-Act granting a pension to Bethia Healy, of N Y C, wid/o Geo Healy, dec'd: to place her name on the Revolutionary pension roll at the rate of of 6 months' service, rendered by her late husband in the Revolutionary war as a soldier.
21-Act granting a pension to Emanuel Shrofe, of Brown Co, Ohio: to be placed on the invalid pensioners roll, at $4 per month, to continue during his natural life, to commence on Sep 23, 1843.
22-Act for the relief of F A Kerr, of Arkansas: to pay him $515; it being for actual expenses incurred while engaged in enrolling & issuing rations to indigent Osage Indians from Aug 1, 1838, to Sep 30, 1839.
23-Act for the benefit of the heirs of Christopher Miller. That Isaiah Miller, Mary W Walls, Eliz P Moreland, Gilley C Bethel, Christopher Wayne Miller, Kitty Ann Thomas, Mgt A Showers, Christopher Wayne Thomas, Isaac Hardin Thomas, & Chas Henry Thomas, all of Ky, & heirs at law of Christopher Miller, dec'd, late of Ky, are to enter, without charge or payment, on any vacant or unappropriated lands of the U S now subject by law to private entry, one quarter section of land, each of the first 7 named heirs separately, & the 3 last named heirs one quarter section jointly; & that a patent shall issue therefore, according to the provisions of the general law.
24-Act for the relief of Hiram Murch: to be paid $50, the same being one moiety of the penalty collected of Murch, by the collector of Appalachicola, in 1837, for a breach of the revenue law, & paid into the Treasury, it having been made to appear that the said penalty was incurred without any intention on the part of the petitioner of violating the law.
25-Act for the relief of Benj Murphy, of Arkansas: to be paid the reasonable value of the corn, the cattle, & hogs, the property of Benj, which were taken by the Cherokee Indians west of the river Mississippi, & appropriated to their own use, in Dec, 1828; that Benjamin shall produce satisfactory evidence that his property was taken by said Indians, & the value of such property so taken. The amount so paid shall be retained out of the annuity of the said Cherokee tribe of Indians.
26-Act for the relief of Wm McPherson: his name to be placed on the roll of invalid pensioners, & paid a pension at the rate of $8 per month, during his natural life, to commence on Jan 1, 1843.
27-Act for the relief of John Atchison: the Sec of the Treasury is to cause satisfaction to be entered on a judgment obtained by the U S against John Atchison, in the U S court for the district of Ill, it appearing that the sum agreed to be received by the proper dept in satisfaction of the same has been paid by the said John Atchison.
28-Act for the relief of Jos Campau: it shall be the duty of the Register of the land ofc at Detroit, Mich, on being fully satisfied of the justice of the claim of Campau to a certain tract of land on the border of Lake St Clair, in Mich, designated on the plat of private land claims, surveyed under the authority of the U S by Aaron Greely, as lot 736, containing about 75 acres: to grant to said Campau a patent certificate for said tract, upon which a patent may be issued, under the act of Mar 3, 1807
29-Act for the relief of Mary M Telfair. That warrants for the bounty lands due to Tobias Briggs & Isaac Curtis, privates in the Rhode Island line, for Revolutionary

services, shall be made out by the proper ofcrs, & delivered to Mrs Mary M Telfair, the only heir & legal rep of Israel Pearce, dec'd, who appears to have purchased the right to said bounty lands of the said Briggs & Curtis. Provided, that Mrs Telfair shall execute her own bond to the U S, with good & sufficient security, in such sum as the Sec of War shal require, to indemnify the said U S against the claim of any other person or persons to said lands. That the Sec of the Treasury cause to be paid to Mrs Telfair any moneys which may be due to Scipio Brown, a private in the Rhode Island line of the Revolutionary army, upon the certificae issued to him for his Revolutionary services, which certificate is alleged to have been purchased by & assigned to said Israel Pearce, the father of said Mrs Telfair.

30-Act for the relief of Chas Holt, of N Y C: to be paid $200, with interest at 6%, to be computed from Jul 18, 1800, it being the amount of a fine imposed upon said Holt by the Circuit Court of Connecticut, under the alien & sedition law.

31-Act for relief of Maj Thos Harrison: to be paid $15 per month from Jun 15, 1815, being the time that he was placed on the pension roll, to Mar 4, 1836, the time at which his present rate of pension commenced.

32-Act for the relief of John Sands, of Fredericksburg, Va, [master mariner,] to be paid $200, being the one moiety of 2 fines remitted by the Sec of the Treasury on Nov 27, 1840, & which fines were paid by Smith before the remission of the same could take effect.

33-Act for the relief of Amos Proctor: accounting ofcrs of the Treasury to adjust & settle the claim of Proctor, of one half of one moiety of the appraised value of the goods seized & libeled upon his information & released from forfeiture by the act of Apr 27, 1816, as set forth in his claim; & the same be paid to him or to his legal reps.

34-Resolution authorizing the accounting ofcrs of the Treasury to audit & settle the accounts of Wm P Zantzinger: & to allow him the value of such stores as were thrown overboard from the U S ship **Hornet**; to be ascertained by deducting from what shall appear to have been at that time the usual amount taken on board a sloop of war going upon a cruise like that of the **Hornet**, the quantitiy of which the ofcrs may be of opinion was probably issued or expended between the period of the vessel's sailing from N Y & at the time at which the chase occurred.

Household & kitchen furniture at auction: on Jul 3, at the residence of Hon J C Spencer, on Pres' square. -R W Dyer & Co, aucts

Mr Chas McGuire, the engineer who was so badly scalded by the explosion on board the steamboat **Cleveland** near Pittsburg, died on Thu last.

The U S frig **Hudson** was sold at the navy yard, N Y, on Thu, by auction, for $6,700, to Messrs J D & A W Westake. It is about 14 years since she was in commission.

On Sat Saml Scott, a county constable, was arrest by John Waters, a police ofcr, & taken before Judge Morsell, charged with a breach of the peace, & assault & battery on a man named Tyler, on 7th st. Both had been drinking.

$2 reward for stray cow, if returned within the week, to the subscriber, on the southwest corner of 5th & H sts. –N Wilson

Yesterday, in an affray on 8th st, John Brown, a blacksmith, was dreadfully cut in the head by a man Thos McGuire, who struck Brown with a hayfork several times, inflicting severe wounds.

Mrd: on Jun 20, by Rev P O O'Hannagin, Mr Chas J Wise to Miss Eliz Symington, both of the District of Columbia.

Mrd: in Southampton Co, Va, by Rev Mr Thornton, Mr Jas Lassiter, of Murfreesboro, N C, to Miss Adeline, y/d/o Edwin Hart, of Southampton. [No date-current item.]

Cmdor Barron, the senior ofcr of the navy, is about removing his residence from Phil to Norfolk, where he has purchased a handsome property, & where he formerly resided.

Loss of the canal packet-boat **Kentucky**, about 3 miles west of Logansport, Ind, by which 3 persons lost their lives, viz: Thos Emerson, of Logansport, W Griffin, of **Fort Wayne**, & an Irishman, name unknown.

Joshua G Bogue, of Rensselaerville, N Y, on Jun 24, with a number of the students of the academy, attempted to swim with one of the boys on his back & was drowned.

Drowned. 1-A young law student, a graduate of Wm's College, Henry Kellogg was drowned while bathing in the Connecticut river at Westminster, Vt, on Jun 18. 2- Nathan B Pratt & Henry R Barnes, young men, were drowned at Vergennes, Vt, while bathing. They were employed in the woolen factory at that place. 3-Mr Thos Barnes was drowned by the upsetting of a small boat, in which he was sailing, at Quincy, Mass, a few days since.

A day or two since, as a steamboat was ascending the Ohio, near Louisville, the body of a boy, 4 or 5 years old, was seen floating down the river. A gentleman, named Fagan, residing in Birmingham, who was a passenger on board, remarked that the clothes looked very much like those of a son of his he had left at home. On arriving at his residence, he was startled by the information that his son was missing for several days, & supposed to be lost. Mr Fagan at once conjectured that the body he had seen in the water was that of his son, & started to recover it, which he succeeded in doing, & had it brought back to the city & interred. –St Louis Reveille

TUE JUL 2, 1844
Frankfort, Ky. Mr B H Bryant was accidentally drowned in the Ky river last week. Few men in our community possessed an equal share of esteem. He was connected with some of the best & most numerous families of the county, & was himself a most amiable & exemplary gentleman. –Commonwealth

The steamer **Palestine**, Capt Hough, from Pittsburg, arrived at St Louis on Jun 21. The ofcr stated that on Wed, when near the mouth of the Ohio, smoke was discovered to issue from the hold of the boat, through the deck: alarm was raised; passengers crowded into the yawl which suspended by ropes to the stern of the boat; one of the ropes was cut & all 14 in the boat were precipitated into the river, & all but 2 met a watery grave. Names of the missing so far as they could be learned: Chas Harrington, of Pittsburg; Mr Snodgrass, Mr Findley, Smith Moore, of Platte Co, Mo; Geo W Stevens, Wm Hopson, Mrs Levina Horn, of Haskell Co, Ky; Jos Neal, cook, colored man, & 3 firemen.

On Jun 25, the steamboat **General Vance** left Detroit with a full load of passengers & freight for Toledo. She stopped at Windsor, on the Canada side, to take in passengers, & immediately her boiler burst, tearing the boat asunder, & causing her to sink in a few minutes. Persons known to have lost their lives: Mr Saml D Woodworth, the capt of the boat; the eldest s/o Mr Benj Woodworth, the late well known proprietor of the Steamboat Hotel; Geo Sweeney, of Chatham; Robt Motherwill, engineer; & Maj A C Truax, of Truago, an old & most respectable citizen of Detroit. Mr Gaylord, the engineer of the Vance, was severely but not dangerously injured. Some 30 or 40 passengers were on board.

Burlington [Vt] Gaz of Jun 25. Explosion of Smith's Powder Magazine by a parcel of boys at play, who concluded to have some sport. They ignited some loose powder & it exploded. When the smoke cleared away, 3 of the boys, sons of Nathan J Smith, David Lane, & Variah Brown, ages 6 to 10 years, were dreadfull burnt & disfigured as scarcely to be recognized by their parents. Two have since died.

Maj Gen Scott had his pocket picked of $130 when coming down the North river on Fri, when on board the steamer **Troy**. 4 men have been arrested for being concerned in the robbery.

Dr Norborne A Galt fell from his buggy on Mon. He died yesterday, without having exhibited any signs of consciousness after the accident. He was one of Nature's noblemen, & has left a void in society not easily filled. –Louisville Journal

Nashville Whig: an affray at Gallatin on Jun 17, between Chas Lewis, of Sumner, & Isaac Goodall, a member of the House of Reps from Smith Co, in which Goodall was killed by Lewis who made his escape.

Notice: by an arrangement with the proprietors of *Piney Point* the charge to or from that place to the District in the steamer **Columbia** will be until Sep 15 next only $2, meals included. –Wm Gunton, Pres

Salem Female Academy: Rev John C Jacobson, Principal for the last 10 years will take charge of a Seminary for young gentlemen at the North, & Rev Chas A Bleek, late of N Y, has accepted the appointment as Principal. –Wm H Vanvleek, Theodore Shultz, John C Jacobson, Trustees

Md farm for sale: the subscriber is authorized to sell a farm belonging to the heirs of the late Jos E Janieson, of Chas Co, Md: contain about 300 acres: lies on the road leading from Pomonkey warehouse to Port Tobacco, the county seat, & is within 5 miles of the latter place. Improvements are nearly new. –Hezekiah Brawner

Wash Co, D C: on Jul 1, 1844, personally appeared before me, the subscriber, a Justice of the Peace, in & for said county & District aforesaid, Geo Tyler, & made an oath that on Jun 29, a difficulty took place between him & Mr Saml Scott, constable, in which a considerable scuffle ensued, & that, after due reflection, he believes that Mr Scott did nothing more than any other man would have done under the same circumstances, &, further, that he wishes to remove any unfavorable impression that may be against Mr Scott in consequence of such altercation. –Thos C Donn, Justice of the Peace

M Gilbert has removed from 13th & F to E & 13th, where he will open a French & American Restaurant in the best style. The bar room will be ready on Jul 3.

A d/o Mr Braly, proprietor of The Franklin House in Cincinnati, fell from the balustrade in the rear of the house on Sat & fractured her skull & died in a few hours.

Died: yesterday, after a lingering & protracted illness, Mw Wm S Walker, in his 47th year. His funeral is this afternoon at 4 o'clock, from his late residence on 3rd st east, near Blagden's wharf.

Died: on Sep 9, 1843, at the residence of Dr Geo S Tolson, in PG Co, Md, Mr Thos Hill Jones, late of Black Hall Island, in his 76th year.

For rent: a 2 story frame house, with a basement, on East Capitol st, Capitol Hill, Inquire of Isaac Bassett, at the Capitol or on the premises.

Jos Alfred, of New Orleans, fell down the stairs & was killed by the fall in endeavoring to ascend to his bedchamber while intoxicated.

A cabin passenger, Thos Bumbard, fell overboard from the vessel **West Wind**, on the Ohio, on Jun 22, & was drowned.

The Living Age magazine has lately been established at Boston, under the superintendence of Mr E Littell, many years the editor of the Museum of Foreign Literature & Science, at Phil.

WED JUL 3, 1844
President Tyler returned with his fair bride to the capital on the evening of last Thu. On Saturday the Bride received company, & the rooms were thronged. The Bride, when Miss Gardner, had, with her fair sister, who is now her guest, spent parts of 2 winters with us, & delighted all who had the pleasure of her acquaintance.

Jas Hoy, jr, appointed by the Pres to be Postmaster for the city of Phil, superseding John C Montgomery, removed upon what grounds is known only to the appointing power.

The candle works of Mr Henryl L Kendall took fire on Wed, & communicated to the distillery & salaeratus works of Darius Sessions, all of which were entirely destroyed. Mr Kendall's loss is about $10,000, which was insured. Mr Session's loss is about $5,000, & not insured.

Lt Roberts, a veteran ofcr, Admiralty Mail Agent of the steamship **Acadia,** died on Thu, at the Massachusetts Genr'l Hospital, from the effects of a fit of apoplexy with which he was attacked on the day of the arrival of the Acadia at Halifax. He was in his 70th year, having been for over half a century attached to the British Navy, & participated in several battles. He has held the ofc of Lt since Nov, 1810. He has a wife in Liverpool, but no family.

Mrd: on Jul 2, at the residence of Mr Louis Beeler, Wash, by Rev Mr Wilson, Mr Elijah Murray, of St Louis, Mo, to Miss Eliz Brown, of Wash.

Mrd: on Jul 1, by Rev H Tarring, Mr Mathias Houx to Miss Sarah Eliz Sheid, all of D C.

Died: on Jul 2, in Wash City, Louisa Anna Maria, w/o John F Boone, in her 31st year. He funeral is this afternoon at 5 o'clock.

Cincinnati Gaz of Jun 27: announces the death of Micajah Williams. He died Jun 26, while yet in the very pride of manhood. He was a native of N C, but removed while a youth to Ohio.

The Corner Stone of the Ryland Chapel, Md ave & 10th st, will be laid on Jul 4. Rev Wm Ryland & Rev Norval Wilson will deliver the addresses.

For sale: the large 3 story brick house at present occupied by Mrs Owner as a boarding house, near the north gate of the Capitol. Also, the 3 story brick house occupied by the subscriber fronting the south side of the Capitol square. -Robt Brown

Thos M Milburn will measure brickwork at the shortest notice with accuracy. Drop a note at the furniture store between 9th & 10th sts, south side of Pa ave.

For sale: tract of land containing between 70 & 80 acres: lies between the farms of Chas H Wiltberger & Capt Sanders, near the Rock Creek Church. –Thos Murphy

Household & kitchen furniture at auction: on Jul 3, at the residence of Hon H C Spencer, on Pres square. -R W Dyer & Co, aucts

Handsome Whig Pyramid of Pound Cake, made by Mr Saml Grubb, confectioner, for the ladies table at the Bladensburg Whig festival, will be exhibited at his store on 7th st, between D & E sts.

THU JUL 4, 1844
Yesterday we saw an iron weathercock, which was put up as long ago as 1690 by Wm Penn, Saml Carpenter, & Caleb Pussy, on the flouring mill located on Chester creek, Delaware Co, Pa. It is quite a curiosity, from its old fashioned appearance, & possesses interest on account of the associations connected with it. –Phil Inquirer

Col Wm L Stone, of the N Y Commerical Advertiser, has recovered damages to the amount of $1,200 for a libelous article written by Mr Levi D Slamm, editor of the N Y Plebeian. The damages were laid at $10,000.

The body of Mr B Canfield, who resided near Houston, Texas, was found on Jun 6, in one of the bayous near his residence, where he had gone to fish the previous day. It was discovered that he had been shot in & face & neck with 14 buckshot.

Mrd: on Jul 2, near Knoxville, Fred'k Co, Md, by Rev Thos D Hoover, Mr Wm Crim to Mary Ann Roden.

Mrd: on Jun 11, by Rev Thos D Hoover, at Harper's Ferry, Va, Mr Elisha Lock, of Jefferson Co, to Sarah Ann Yost, of Rockville, Montg Co, Md.

York Springs was opened on Jun 15, under the superintendence of Arnold Gardner, who will do every thing in his power to make these Springs worthy of their patronage.

For rent: a 2 story house on C st, between 4½ & 6th sts. Inquire of Mrs John Gadsby, Pres' Square.

For rent: 2 story brick house on Louisiana ave, between 6th & 7th sts. Inquire of E Hunt.

Dissolution of partnership under the firm of Zales & Glover, by mutual consent. -Wm H Fales, P L Glover

SAT JUL 6, 1844
Fresh turnip seeds: John Douglas, Florist & Seedsman, opposite the State Dept.

$1,000 reward for the apprehension of 4 negroes: 1-Tom-Thos Edwards, about 30. 2-John Watson, about 30. 3-Jordan Williamson-about 30. John & Jordan are left handed. 4-Hampton Bailey, about 22. John's mother absconded some years ago, with several children & her husband, a mulatto man, [belonging to Capt Rose, a resident of Loudoun Co, Va,] calling himself Wm Weims; they have since been heard of in N Y. -Stevens T Mason, near Leesburg, Loudoun Co, Va.

Sale of 1,225 acres of land. In Chancery, Fauquier Co Court, May 31, 1844. Robt W Latham, administrator of Wm H Carter, Fitzhugh Carter, Gustavus A Carter, infants, & John B Carter, Robt Carter, Thos T Carter, Landon Carter, Eliza F Carter, & Harriet Chilton, & Douglas Chilton, infant children of Harriet W Chilton, dec'd, & Josiah Tidball & John A Carter, excs of John Carter, dec'd, & trustees of Landon Carter, dfndnts. The plntf filed his bill, & answers of the dfndnts were filed also, & this cause came on to be heard by consent on said bill & answer, & the examinations of witnesses, & was argued by counsel: on consideration whereof the court doth adjudge, order, & decree, that Saml Chilton & John C Murray, who are appointed com'rs for the purpose, proceed upon 30 days' previous & public notice, to sell to the highest bidder the lands in the bill & proceedings mentioned, with 1/4th of the purchase money to be paid down, & the residue on credits of 1, 2, & 3 years, the deferred payments to be secured by bonds, with good personal security; the title to be retained till the whole purchase is paid up. –A J Marshall, clk
+
Pursuant to the foregoing decree the undersigned com'rs will proceed, on Aug 10, 1844, at the *Dudley Springs*, Prince Wm, to sell the lands in said decree mentioned upon the terms therein provided for. Said land lies about 27 miles from Alexandria, in the Couties of Fairfax, Prince Wm, & Loudoun, contains about 1,225 acres, & adjoins the lands of Messrs P Norville, Alfred Ball, Landon Carter, & the land of Fitzhugh Carter. –Saml Chilton, John C Murray, Com'rs

Citizens of the Commonwealth of Pa: we petition that amendments of the naturalization laws of the U S be made that 21 year's residence in this country [after they shall have declared their intentions to become citizens] be made the indispensable requisite to the admission of foreigners into the inestimable rights of native Americans.

A De Kalb Tarr	E N Grossman	Stephen Porter
Wm L Fairchild	Geo Patchett	M J Swink
Wm W S Miles	Jas S Bonsall	G W Stevenson
Henry B Kennede	Henry J Hiles	G W Ackey
Isaac W Robinson	Geo McMullin	Jas Nicholson
E W Elli	W B Hamilton	Chas Wharton
J C Van Dyke	A C Mikener	Chester Lasell
W D Barnes	F H Campbell	Theodore C Lewis
T Winter	B E Hackett	E S Moulder
Blair M Toland	Chas C Herbert	Jos J Duncan
John Beorncasle	Thos J Jeffries	A C Duncan
Aaron Pancoast	Jos F Hackett	A H Wants
H H K Elliott	Oscar F Harris	Edw Hugsham
Elihu D Tarr	Geo Crosby	R P King
Wm D Muphy	Geo B Smith	Urban Lynch
Thos Ballintine	John W Leebavenan	Geo Toland
Henry Hiles, jr	David W Gihon	Saml S Kelly
Geo McMullin	John T German	John Tillotson
Jos K Newman	John Payne	Edw Gaskill
Chas D Cox	Wm F Hamm	Benj Gaskill
J G Jenkins	Peter Wagner	John H Simmons
Peter Skew Smith	Isaiah Bryan	Philip L Dubosq
Jos S Tenney	Geo W Prentice	T H Palmer
John Flinn	N H Woods	Chas H Masson
Edgar E Petit	T J Herring	John S Lister
Edwin T Chase	John Simpson	J S Brewster
Ambrose Walker	Chas F Brunson	Jas G Gibson
Saml Gilpey	Wm R Moore	B M Shaw
Saml McFate	Saml Robinson	E M David
John U Anna	John M Jones	C J Jacre
John Michl Gummey	Francis Smith, jr	Henry G Esban
Jos L Shaffer	John Roberts	Wm J Carter
R North Jordan	Rufus W Griswold	W S Schaeffer
Thos Bird	Am Hopkins	John Davies
Chas Strine	Thos F Adams	F Rennell
Th Millete	Marmaduke Moore	J H Taibor
John Caldwell	S D Bird	Henry S Taver
Nathan Moore	Geo W Adriance	Jas McCormick
D Neall, jr	J R Colen	Henry B Brooks
W M Robinson	Jas B Smith	Geo M De Grost
J A Robinson	John Robbins	Wm Hallett
Edw J Mierden	Jos Oat	C Sherman
Jas M Roney	Austin Siddons	J R Sherman
Wm Harris	John H Gihon	W D Graham

R G Beryon	Richd T Williams	John H Gihon, jr
R Street	Elisha Parker	Stephen Porter
Thos A Wood	T W Peterson	M J Swingrison
E M Muiler	Wm Sloansker	Davkd Colton
Jas R Arns	J L S Taylor	Alex Elmer
C B Barrett	M Millington	L T Salaignao
Abraham Dothard	W B Zieber	Chas H Elmes
Henry Lott	John R McCurdy	Howard S Elmes
Jas C Catlin	W H Riley	Jos S Williams
Nelson S Johnson	John Clark	John C Copper
Chas Pfeil	Jos M Campbell	Wm Cooper
Peter B Long	G B Zieber	Chas P Thomson
Geo A Brady	Wm H Kern	S H Fisher
Jos Quinn	L C Levin	
Geo Taylor	Jas L Richards	

Jun 15, Referred to the Cmte on the Judiciary.

Wm Pinkney, Surveyor of the port of Balt, has been removed, & Thos Lloyd appointed in his stead.

The steamer **Acadia**, Judkins, left Boston on Wed for Halifax & England, with 74 passengers & a large mail. Among the passengers was Count Napoleon Bertrand, who has been for the last year a visiter to this country.

Died: on Jun 20, in Lincolnton, N C, on his way from the Springs, which he had visited for the benefit of his health, Gen Paul Barringer, of Cabarrus Co, N C, aged 66 years, for a long period of his life distinguished as a prominent, useful, & patriotic citizen of N C, & for many years a member in both branches of her Legislature. He has left a large ciricle of relatives & friends to mourn their loss & revere his memory.

Died: on Jul 5, Theodore Harbaugh, in his 34th year. His funeral is this morning, at 10 o'clock, from his father's house on 7th st.

By virtue of an order from Wm Ward to distrain for rent due & in arrears by J W Nye, I shall offer at public auction, on Jul 6, sundry articles, property of J W Nye, to satisfy the amount of $44.49 due to said Wm Ward. –P Finnegan, Constable

MON JUL 8, 1844
Hollidaysburg, Pa, Jul 3. Killed by lightning, on Thu last, on the farm of Mr Martin Gates, on Spruce creek, in this county. The dec'd were making hay when a storm came up, & they repaired to a tree standing in the field. Killed was a s/o Mr Martin Gates, named Robt; another was Mr Chas McMurtrie, a clerk for Mr Gates; & another, a Mr Jordan, a forgeman, or farmer. -Register

Polly Bodine, who is charged with the murder of the wife & child of her brother, Capt Geo Houseman, was some 2 weeks ago put on trial before the court of Oyer & Terminer sitting at Port Richmond, Staten Island. The jury was unable to agree & was discharged. The prisoner was remanded for a new trial.

Quincy Herald of the 28th: Joe & Hiram Smith, & a number of other Mormon leaders, were in jail at Carthage, confined on certain offences against the laws of the State. The Carthage Grays, a volunteer company, were placed as a guard around the jail. On the 27th, an attempt was made by the Mormons on the outside to rescue the prisoners. A Mormon youth, about 19, began the affray by shooting the sentinel at the door, wounding him severely. The Mormons on the inside, including the Smiths, presented pistols through the windows & doors of the jail, & fired upon the guard without, wounding, it is supposed mortally, 4 of the old citizens of Hancock. The lives of Jos Smith & his brother Hiram, & Richds, Jos Smith's secretary, were quickly taken. Mormons immediately left for Nauvoo to carry the news of the death of the Prophet.

Col H Capron, of PG Co, Md, raised this year one acre of ground, manured by guano, 41 bushels of wheat, which has already been cut & taken to market.

Cyrus B Ackley, about 30 years of age, called upon a clergyman at Rochester, N Y, several days since, with a young woman & several witnesses, to be married. He was married to the young woman. In 3 or 4 days intelligence reached the city that Ackley had a wife & 2 children in Canandaigua. It is supposed that this is not his first crime.

Robt C Wetmore, the able & popular Naval Agent at the port of N Y, on Tue rec'd official information of his removal, & the appointment of Jas H Suydam in his place.

A man named Wood drowned on Thu, when he fell overboard from a boat, while intoxicated. He pushed off in his boat from the shore opposite, into the Eastern Branch.

Mr D W Middleton, of Wash City, while riding a large & spirited horse along Pa ave on Jul 4, was thrown from the saddle. The concussion was so violent as to deprive Mr Middleton for some time of his senses. He is now recovering, & out of danger.

Mrd: on Jul 2, by Rev Dr Wyatt, Cmder Jas P Wilson, U S Navy, to Emily, d/o the late Judge Magruder.

Mrd: on Jul 2, at Phil, by Rev Albert Barnes, Robt Colgate, of N Y, to Mary Eliz, d/o Romulus Riggs, of Phil.

Died : on Jul 6, in Wash City, Nicholas Callan, sr, a native of Dundalk Co, south of Ireland, but for the last 40 years a citizen of Wash.

Died: on Jul 27, in Lancaster, Pa, at the residence of his brother, Col Reah Frazer, Lt Wm Frazer, of the 3rd Regt of U S Artl, in his 29th year, of consumption.

Died: on Jun 11, in Boston, at the residence of his nephew Francis Boyd, Danl Boyd, formerly of Wash City, aged 35 years.

Two men, Timothy McNamara & John Bennet were lately found dead in a mineral hole, at McCue's digging near Galena, Ill. A fire was made of charcoal & occasioned their death in a short time.

An old man, Chas Morrelly, was arrested at St Louis, at the instance of Bishop Kenrick, for collecting money under pretence of being the accredited agent of the order of St Augustine, Mount St Bernard, in France, & exhibiting forged papers in the matter.

For sale: Columbian Academy on 9th st, between G & H sts. The bldg will accommodate 200 scholars. Adjoining the Academy is a handsome cottage, large enough to accommodate a considerable family. –John McLeod
-R W Dyer & Co, aucts

TUE JUL 9, 1844
Hornsby, found guilty at New Orleans some time since of the murder of Twogood, was on Jun 28, sentenced to 5 years' imprisonment in the penitentiary.

The examination of Edw Ford, for the killing of Nathan W Low, was concluded at St Louis on Jun 26. Mr Ford was held to bail in the sum of $10,000, to appear bfore the next term of the Criminal Court. The bail was given, & the prisoner discharged. The case is not regarded as one of murder in the first degree, which is not a bailable offence.

Runaway black man Jacob Jackson, about 60, was committed to the jail of Fred'k Co, on Jun 29. He says he is free, & last from Elkridge, Md. The owner, if any, is to come & have him released, or he will otherwise be discharged according to law.
–Geo Rice, Sheriff of Fred'k Co, Md

Orphans Court of Wash Co, D C. In the case of Geo Ann Patterson, admx of Danl T Patterson, dec'd: the admx & Court have appointed Jul 30 for a second distribution..
-Ed N Roach, Reg/o wills

Intending to remove from Wash City, I offer for sale, a comfortable & well finished frame house, on part of lot 2 in square 196. –Wm Markward

Circuit Court of Wash Co, D C-in Equity. Wm Noyes, cmplnt, vs Zadock Hempstone et al, dfndnts. The bill of cmplnt sets forth that Wm & John Jones, being seized in fee simple of a tract of land in Montg Co, Md, lying on Muddy Branch, & supposed to contain 250 acres, died on Feb 3, 1837, by their bond of that date, bargain, sell, & promise to convey to the said Zadock Hempstone, his heirs & assigns, the said tract of land, for the sum of $1,100; that Hempstone did make, execute, & deliver his bond to Wm & John Jones for the purchase money, payable on Nov 10, 1837, with Christian Hempstone & David English, jr, as his sureties; that on Jun 19, 1837, Hempstone, by an instrument of writing under his hand & seal, reciting that the said David English, jr, had become one of his sureties in the bond aforesaid, did set over & assign to the said David English, jr, all his right, title, claim, & interest in & to the recited contract & bond of conveyance of the said Wm & John Jones, to save the said David English, jr, harmless from any loss or injury whatever as surety for him, the said Zadock, as aforesaid, & to secure him against any liabilities on his account, & delivered the said written contract or bond of conveyance to the said David. The bill further states that Hempstone becoming afterwards insolvent, on Mar 6, 1839, filed his petition before Hon Wm Cranch, Chief Judge of D C, for the benefit of the insolvent law; & the proceedings were had on the said petition that the Zadock Hempstone, by his deed bearing date Mar 15, 1839, did convey all his estate, real, personal, & mixed to Gilbert Giberson, in trust for the payment of his said Zadock's debts; & was, by an order of said Judge, discharged from custody, & fully admitted to the benefit of the laws of insolvent debtors in force in D C. Gilbert afterwards relinquished the said trust, & the cmplnt was, by an order of the Judge, appointed trustee in his place, & qualified as such, & that Gilbert, by his deed dated May 28, 1840 transferred & conveyed to the cmplnt all the estates & credits acquired by him as aforesaid, for the benefit of the creditors of the said Zadock Hempstone. The bill further charges that the whole of the said purchase money for the land so purchased by the said Zadock Hempstone, has been fully paid, & that David English, jr, indemnified in the premesis; & that the claimant, by virtue of the premises, aforesaid, is entitled to have the bond surrendered by David English, & the land conveyed to him by Wm & John Jones, for the benefit of the creditors of Zadock Hempstone. It appears that Zadock Hempstone is not an inhabitant of D C, & that he lives in Montg Co. He is to appear on before the 4th Mon in Nov next, & answer the several matters set forth in the bill of cmplnt.
–Jas S Morsell -Wm Brent, clk

Killed or wounded in the recent riots in Phil:
John Cook, an oysterman, about 30, was killed on the spot.
Elijah Justus, shot through the heart with a ball.
Wm Crozier, residing in Plum st, half his face shot off–died immediately.
Capt Teal, an old patriot, age 50, ball entered his neck, a ball in the stomach.
Jos McDanial, shot through the heart, ball passing out the opposite side.
Theodore Slack, residing in Queen st, wounded in the leg.
Dr Appleton, wounded in the leg & arm.

Thos Street, an old man, wounded in the knees.
Mr Baggs, wounded in the leg, resiging in John st above Front.
Henry Jones, residing in Christian about 3rd, wounded in the right shoulder.
Capt K K Scott, cmder of the Cadwallader Grays, was shot, it is feared mortally, in the spine.
Col Pleasontor, slightly wounded.
Thos Falkner, shot, but not seriously wounded.
Jos Silby, Southwark, mortally wounded.
Capt Lyle's wife, residing in Catharine st, wounded in the arm.
Mr Guy, residing above Southwark. Wounded in both legs

WED JUL 10, 1844
Foreign miscellany: on the 5th an estate of 12,470 acres, situated in Md, U S, was put up for sale by auction in London, & there was not a single bidder.

Orphans Court of Wash Co, D C. Letters of administration, with the will annexed, on the personal estate of Margaret N Milstead, late of Wash Co, dec'd.
–Geo W Thompson, with the will annexed

Mrd: on Tue, in Gtwn, by Rev R T Berry, Mr Chas D De Ford, of Balt, to Miss Maria Vernon, 2nd d/o Capt Wm Noyes, of the former place.

Died: on Jun 24, in Burlington, Iowa, B F Wood, merchant of that place. He was sailing a boat 150 years from the landing, when a gust of wind rendered the boat unmanageable. He tried to pull her round & fell overboard.

Died: Jun 25, at Evansville, Ind, in his 76th year, Maj Jervis Cutler. He was the 2nd s/o the Rev Manasseh Cutler, who for 52 years was pastor of the Congregationalist Church of Hamilton, Mass, the negotiator in 1787 with the Congress of the Old confederation of the famous purchase of a million & a half of acres for the Ohio Company, by means of which was affect the first settlement of that now great State, & from 1800 to 1804 the Rep in Congress from the Lynn district, Mass.

Stockbridge [Mass] Weekly Visiter: died-at his residence in Stockbridge, on Jun 17, Luke Ashburner, in his 72nd year, after a lingering illness of several months. He was born in India, at Tellichery, on the Malabar coast, in 1773, of an affluent & respectable English family, & sent among the English residence in India, at an early age to be educated in England. After wards he returned to India & settled in Bombay, where, having inherited a large landed property, he devoted himself to it improvement. He remained until 1817, when the ill health of Mrs Ashburner & considerations for the welfare of his children induced him to leave it. He emigrated with his family in 1823 & has been a resident of Stockbridge ever since.

Obit-died: on Sat, Jun 8, Nicholas Callan, Sen, in his 78th year, a native of the city of Dundalk, county of Louth, Ireland, but for the past 40 years a resident of Wash.

THU JUL 11, 1844
Accidents on Jul 4th: 1-Josiah Battell, 18, killed when powder exploded, while firing guns at N Y. 2-Mr Hutchinson, one of the citizens of Putnam, N Y, had an arm blown off near the elbow & was otherwise injured, by the premature discharge of a cannon. On Jul 3, while reloading the cannon belonging to the Citizens' Corps, it went off & injured 2 young men belonging to the company: Jas L Beardsley, a student of medicine, & Hugh Roberts, a plane maker, each had an arm blown off.

At Silver Creek on the 4th C Crowell, a chairmaker, had an arm blown off by the premature discharge of a piece of ordnance, which caused his death in about 3 hours. He leaves a wife & child. –Buffalo Advertiser

The elegant country seat, on Harford ave, containing 27½ acres, improved with a handsome mansion house & other bldgs, formerly owned by the late Col Tennant & recently by David Barnum, dec'd, was sold today at the Exchange of Weaver, Cannon & Co, auctioneers, for $12,000, Mr W McClellan, purchaser. It is in a fine state of cultivation & free of all incumbrance. -Patriot

The 20th annual session of the Alexandria Boarding School will terminate near the close of the present month, & will resume on Sep 9. –Caleb S Hallowell & Brother, Alexandria, D C. Reference may be made to the following gentlemen, all of whom have sons or wards now in the institution:

Capt J H Aulick, U S Navy
Hon Alex'r Barrow, Louisiana
Judge Catron, U S Supreme Court
Henry Kinzer, Lancaster Co, Pa
Hon David Levy, Fla

Francis Nixon, Perquimons Co, N C
Col D Saffarrans, Tenn
Gen Montfort Wells, Red river, La
J K Townsend, Sec Nat'l Institute, Wash

Appointments by the Pres:
John Chambers to be Govn'r of the Territory of Iowa, from Jul 15, when his present commission will expire.
J Humphrey to be U S Marshal for the District of Michigan.
Chas Graebe, of N Y, to be U S Consul for the Kingdom of Hanover & the Grand Duchy of Hesse Darmstadt.
Moreau Forrest, to be U S Marshal for the District of Md.
Isaac L Todd, to be Assayer of the Branch Mint at Dahlonega, Ga.
Henderson Willingham, to be U S Marshal for the district of Ga.

Pleasant & healthy quarters for boarders: on E st, between 7th & 8th sts, at present occupied by Mrs McCardle. Apply to Mrs McCardle.

The whole amount of the charitable fund received for the relief of the widows, children, etc, of the ofcrs, seamen, & marines who were lost in the schnr **Grampus**, was $7,141.03. A partial distribution has been made, upon the assumption that each person so lost left a relative entitled to a dividend. –A O Dayton, Wash, Jul 10

Obit-died: on Jun 28, at his residence, in Chas Co, Md, after a most painful & lingering illness, Dr Francis Neale, in his 47th year. As a husband, a father, & master, he had no superior. A devoted wife & children have been left behind him to shed the tears of bitter anguish over their irreparable loss.

Died: on Jul 3, at *Mount Airy*, Richmond Co, Benj Ogle Taylor, jr, in his 19th year, s/o Wm H Tayloe. He never gave his parents pain but when he died.
–Fredericksburg Herald

Died: yesterday, in Wash City, in his 7th year, Geo Tippett, s/o Mr Washington Lewis. His funeral is this morning, at 9 o'clock.

Died: on Wed, Mary Ellen, in her 4th year, only d/o Saml & Ellen Cropley.

Died: on Jul 2, in Wash City, Catherine Ann, y/d/o John S & Catherine A James, aged 1 year, 8 months & 19 days.

The partnership subsisting under the name of Kelly & McDonald is this day hereby dissolved. Persons indebted to said firm are to make payement to the subscriber.
-Jas T Kelly, Wash

Mr Macon B Allen, of Portsmouth, [& formerly of Boston,] a colored gentleman, whose application for admission to the bar in Apr last, under the new act, was, as we stated in our paper at the time, refused on the ground that he was not a citizen of Maine in the contemplation of said act, subsequently applied under the old law to be admitted by examination. The cmte recommended him to the Court, & he was admitted in the District Court. –Portland [Me] Adv

Mr Wm Jas Tilley, of Middletown, R I, met with an injury which resulted in his death last week, from falling off his horse while he was on horseback engaged in raking hay.

Trustee's sale of a valuable lot on Pa ave: pursuant to a decree of the Circuit Court of Wash Co, D C, made in the case of Augusta R Theriot vs the heirs of Peter Passet & others: at public auction, lot 31, in square A, in Wash City: fronts on Pa ave, between Young & McDermott's. –Jos H Bradley, Trustee -Holmead & Wright, auctioneers

Rachael Nunnamaker, about 17 years of age, residing about 11 miles from Cincinnati, died on Sat week with hydrophobia. She was bitten several weeks ago by a dog which was not supposed to be rabid at the time.

FRI JUL 12, 1844
It now appears that the Pres has not pardoned David McDaniel & Thos Towson. They have been respited until Jun 27, 1845, during which time they will be kept in confinement in the St Louis jail. John McDaniel, the captain of the party, & Jos Brown, will be executed [the Republican says,] on Jul 12, unless the Pres should grant them a further reprieve, founded on reps recently sent by a special messenger to Wash.

Casualties in N Y. 1-On Sun, Philip McCardle, with his 3 children, were returning home from church in a wagon, when the vehicle accidentally upset, throwing them all out, & killing one of his dghts, aged 4 years. 2-Wm Freeman, a native of the District of Columbia, aged 21 years, died at the hospital on Sunday from injuries received on the head on Jul 3, by fainting & falling on the pavement.

The Hon J S Dexter died at his residence in Cumberland, R I, on Jun 20, in his 91st year. He was a descendant of one of the oldest families in the State, & was born in Cumberland A D 1754. At the commencement of the Revolutionary war in 1775 he was near completion of his legal studies, with Mr afterwards Gen Varnum, of East Greenwich. He was at that time a member of the Kentish guards, a corps memorable for having furnished no less than 6 field ofcrs & 30 subordinates to the Continental army. He relinquished his studies, & with rank of lt, joined the army at Dorchester 2 days before the battle of Bunker Hill. He served throughout the war, & was frequently a guest at the table of Washington. In 1785 he retired with the rank of major. He commenced the practive of law in providence, but was soon appointed Supervisor of Revenue for Rhode Island by Washington, who with Hamilton, then Sec of State, frequently consulted him on the selection of proper persons to fill the Federal ofcs of the State. At the commencement of the war of 1812 he was offered by Pres Madison the post of adj general of the army, with the rank of brig general. His increasing age compelled him to decline the ofc. In 1830 he retired from Providence to his residence in Cumberland. –Providence Journal

On Sunday last, as Mr Geo Snyder, of Milcreek, Erie Co, Pa, with his wife & dght, a young lady, was proceeding to church in Eagle village, in a buggy, the horse took fright & ran fast overturning the buggy. Mr Snyder was thrown & killed; Mrs S was dangerously injured; the young lady jumped out & was slightly injured.

The d/o Rev Dr Noyes was killed at his residence in Cambridge on Sat. The child fell from the window of the 2nd story upon the brick pavement. She was 4 years of age. Her death has overwhelmed the parents.

Mrd: on Jul 10, by Rev E P Phelps, Mr Stephen G Gould to Miss Ann Maria Griggs, all of Wash City.

Died: on Jun 29, at his residence, in Lindsleytown, Steuben Co, N Y, Capt Wm Lindsley, in his 56th year, leaving a large family & many friends to lament his loss. He was grandson of the late Col Lindsley, of the N J line of the army of the Revolution, & brother to a B & E Lindsley, of Wash City.

New Cabinet Establishment: after an absence of 6 years, carries on the business of a Cabinet maker & Undertaker. Workshops are at his old stand, D st, between 9th & 10th sts. –Jas K Plant

Lost: a Black Hair Bracelet, slightly sprinkled with grey. Suitable reward by leaving it at Mrs Ulrick's, opposite the State Dept.

Dissolution of the partnership under the firm of Brevitt & Jillard, sen, by mutual consent. –John Jillard, sen, E W Brevitt. John Jillard has associated himself in copartnership with his son Geo E Jillard, & will continue the business at the old stand, Pa ave, between 12th & 13th st: general assortment of Paints, Oils, Window-glass, & Artist's materials. –John Jillard, Geo E Jillard

Wash Corp: 1-Ptn of A C Kidwell: referred to the Cmte on Improvements. 2-Cmte of Claims: adverse reports on the ptns of Josiah Dixon & of H G Ritter.

Notice: I hereby forewarn all persons from trusting my wife Barbara Keller [she having left my house & board] on my account, as I will pay no debts contracted by her. –Michl Keller

SAT JUL 13, 1844
The remains of DeWitt Clinton have been privately removed by his friends from Albany to N Y, & now deposited in *Greenwood Cemetery*.

Death of zealous missionary. Dr Grant died at Mosul, of typhus fever, on Apr 24 last. He was the first foreigner & American who ever visited the Mountain Nestorians, a very remarkable people, whose reception of the gospel & whose recent sufferings & slaughter by persecution have rendered them objects of great interest to all Christendom.

For rent, & possession immediately, the pleasant dwlg house on 14th & N Y ave, late in the occupancy of Francis H Davidge. Apply to Benj Holmes, next door, or to Jas Larned, 13th st.

Mrd: on Jul 4, at Topsham, Maine, by Rev Danl Sewall, Wm Flye, Prof of Mathematics-U S Navy, to Miss Mary E Perkins, d/o Maj N Perkins, of Topsham.

Phil, Jul 12. Mr Lewis C Levin was yesterday brought before Recorder Vaux, arrested by Jas Young, High Constable, on a charge of being the editor of the Daily Sun, & publishing the same, therein excited to riot & treason. He was held to bail at $3,000. Also, $1,000 to keep the peace. Mr Saml R Cramer, was bound over in $500 to be of good behavior of 3 calendar months. Col John G Watmough, Surveyor of the Port, was charged with conduct & language calculated to excite to riot: held in his own recognizance of $1,000 to be of good behavior for 3 calendar months. Mr Wm P Hanna: charged with using language to incite to riot: held to bail in $1,500 to answer. A man named Wm Runyon, from Easton, was arrested last evening while attempting to break through the military lines thrown out before the Girard Bank. The Mayor held him to answer at Court in the sum of $500. U S Gaz

MON JUL 15, 1844
On Jul 5, at New Orleans, Judge McCaleb sentenced John A Breedlove, Jas Watson, & Marshal Halliday to 10 years imprisonment in the Penitentiary. Halliday was also sentenced to pay a fine of $25,000. They were guilty of having circulated cancelled U S Treasury Bonds.

Col Saml W Oakey, Locofoco Inspector at the late election, in the 3rd Ward, 2nd Municipality, was arrested yesterday by Capt Winters, in virtue of several warrants, issued upon affidavits of his having maliciously & fraudulently disfranchised a number of legal voters. He was admitted to bail in sum of $1,000, to appear before Recorder Baldwin on Fri next. –New Orleans Bee, Jul 4

D W Adams was lately tried at Raymond, Hinds Co, Miss, for killing Dr Hagan, of Vicksburg, & acquitted. The jury was out but 7 minutes.

Phil: cmte to receive subscriptions for the relief of the widows & families of such of the gallant soldiers as were killed or wounded during the recent riots:

Wm Rawle	Mathew L Bevan	Howell Hopkins
H J Williams	Thos Biddle	Wm H Fry
A S Roberts	F W Hubbell	T W L Freeman
A E Borie	Robt M Lewis	Dr Chas Willing
Sidney G Fisher	Cahs Riche	Chas Macalester
Saml Hart	John M Barclay	C Henry Fisher
Capt Stephen Baldwin	Thos H White	Andrew Miller

Cmte to apprize the Govn'r of the object of the meeting:

C G Childs	J A Phillips	P Pemberton Morris
H J Williams	E Spencer Miller	Clement Biddle, jr
R T Conrad	R R McMurtie	Chas J Biddle
W H Winder	Jas W Paul	B C Tilghamn

The Salem [Mass] celebration by the Whigs was attended by the following Whigs of 1776-1840-44:

Gen Gideon Foster, Danvers, aged 95
Saml Bowden, Marblehead, aged 94
John Howard, Salem, aged 89
Danl Ross, Ipswich, aged 87
Jas Fisher, Salem, aged 85
Thos Cloutman, Marblehead, aged 83
Saml Horton, Danvers, aged 83
Ebenezer Tappan, Manchester, aged 83

In 1840 there were 32 Revolutionary veterans were with us, & now nearly all are dead. Then we had 9 from Salem, & 6 of them have since gone to their reward.

St Johnsbury [Vt] Caledonian: on Jul 4 a premature explosion took place & John W Frazier, of Lyndon, & Isaac Harriman, of Burke, were badly injured. Frazier, 17, had his left arm amputated near the shoulder & 3 fingers taken from his right hand. Harriman, 19, had his hand amputated at the wrist.

Col Le Roy Pope, the founder of Huntsville, Ala, & originally the owner of its site, died there on Jun 14, in his 80th year.

Died: on Jul 10, at Elizabethtown, N J, Isaac H Williamson, in his 76th year. Govn'r Williamson was appointed Govn'r of the State of N J about 1817, & annually re-elected till 1829. He made the Court of Chancery of N J an honor to his native State & an example to others. –N Y American

THU JUL 16, 1844
The case of the U S vs Geo E Pomeroy, for an alleged violation of the Post Ofc Laws, in carrying letters over the railroad route in 1843, has just been tried at Utica, N Y, & decided in favor of the dfndnt. This furnishes another decision in favor of the private right to carry letters.

David P Caldwell has been appointed, by the Govn'r & Council of the State of N C, to be a Judge of the Superior Court, vice Hon Fred Nash.

Jos Smith is said to have left in the hands of his wife a document appointed his successor, which she was directed to open on the 3rd day after his death.

Maj Smith, of the St Louis Legion, was badly injured on Jul 4 by a fall from his horse. He was dragged some distance, but the injury is not dangerous.

U S Circuit Court: John Rider, late postmaster at Bowling Green, Jefferson Co, Ohio, was on trial last week on charges of having stolen & embezzled a letter containing money from his ofc. The jury, absent a few minutes, returned a verdict of not guilty. –Cincinnati Gaz

Mrd: on Jul 11, by Rev Mr Tarring, Mr Lawrence Murphy to Miss Jane E Wells, all of Wash City.

Mrd: on Jul 15, by Rev Mr Tarring, Jonah D Hoover to Angelica P Hoover, d/o Andrew Hoover, all of Wash City.

Died: on Wed, in Raleigh, N C, of apoplexy, after an illness of only a few hours, Thos L West, aged 53 years. He left a wife & a large family of children to mourn his sudden & unexpected end.

Died: on Jul 1, in Raleigh, N C, of paralysis, at an advanced age, John Severeux, sen.

Died: in PG Co, Md, whither her affectionate parents had taken her for health, Emma, y/c/o Hough & Jane Lochrey, aged 9 months. Her funeral will take place from the residence of her parents, on East Capitol st, this afternoon at 4 o'clock.

Jas Cox, for 40 years cashier of the Bank of Balt, died a few days ago at the advanced aged of 75 years. By his will, besides leaving a large amount to his family connexions, he leaves & to the Balt Orphan Asylum, $2,000; American Bible Society, $1,000; Board of Foreign Missions, Presbyterian, $1,000; Md Sunday School Union, $500; & Presbyterian Board of Education, $500.

More arrests for the riots in Phil:
Eaton Harwood, ringleader in bringing up the gun in front of the church on Sun to enforce the demands of the mob. Harwood has been arrested & committed to Court, in default of $13,000 bail, on the charges of riot, murder, & high treason-$3,000 surety on the first charge & $5,000 on each of the other 2 charges.
Wm H Springer, of Southwark, a member of the Grand Jury, was arrested on the oath of Wm H Everly, who, in conversation with him on Mon, heard him say that they would have fixed the military if they had not been withdrawn-that they would have fired brimstone at them.
Washington Conard is charged with knocking down Capt Hill, of the City Guards, was arrested on Sat, & committed by the Recorder in default of $2,000 bail, to answer the chare of riot & murder.
Jas Reese was committed on a charge of using inflammatory language in the presence of the military at their quarters at Green & old York rd.
Wm R Rogers, charged with using highly insulting languarge towards a sentinel in front of the Girard Bank. He was held to bail.
Geo & Edw Simpson, brothers, were arrested on Sun for using inflammatory language & inciting to riot in Dock st, They were committed in default of $5,00 each to answer to court.

General Orders, #33. Headquarters of the Army, Adj Gen's Ofc, Wash, Jul 8, 1844. Promotions & appointments in the U S Army, made by the Pres. & by & with the advice & consent of the Senate, since Jan 1, 1844.

I-Promotions:

2nd Regt of Artl:
2nd Lt Wm A Nichols, to 1st Lt, Jun 1, 1844, vice Pitkin, resigned.
Brevet 2nd Lt David Gibson, of the 3rd Artl, to be 2nd Lt, Jun 1, 1844, vice Nichols, promoted.

3rd Regt of Artl:
Brevet 1st Lt Geo H Thomas, to be 1st Lt, Apr 30, 1844, vice Ketchum, resigned.
2nd Lt Horace B Field, to be 1st Lt, Jun 27, 1844, vice Frazer, dec'd.
Brevet 2nd Lt John Hillhouse, of the 4th Artl, to be 2nd Lt, Apr 30, 1844, vice Thomas, promoted.
Brevet 2nd Lt Chas L Kilburn, to be 2nd Lt, Jun 27, 1844, vice Field, promoted.

1st Regt of Infty:
2nd Lt Garret Barry, to be 1st Lt, Jan 31, 1844, vice Coxe, resigned.
2nd Lt Geo W Wallace, to be 1st Lt, Mar 1, 1844, vice Muse, resigned.
Brevet 2nd Lt Chas D Jordan, of the 8th Infty, to be 2nd Lt, Jan 31, 1844, vice Barry, promoted.
Brevet 2nd Lt Eugene E McLean, of the 2nd Infty, to be 2nd Lt, Mar 1, 1844, vice Wallace, promoted.

2nd Regt of Infty:
Brevet 2nd Lt Jas W Schureman, of the 7th Infty, to be 2nd Lt, Jan 25, 1844, vice Hoffman, dec'd.

3rd Regt of Infty:
1st Lt Geo P Field, to be Capt, Feb 29, 1844, vice Wheeler, resigned.
2nd Lt Bushrod R Johnson, to be 1st Lt, Feb 29, 1844, vice Field, promoted.
Brevet 2nd Lt Andrew J Williamson, of the 4th Infty, to be 2nd Lt, Feb 29, 1844, vice Johnson, promoted.

6th Regt of Infty:
2nd Lt Lewis A Armistead, to be 1st Lt, Mar 30, 1844, vice Edes, dec'd.
Brevet 2nd Lt Chas T Baker, of the 3rd Infty, to be 2nd Lt, Mar 30, 1844, vice Armistead, promoted.

7th Regt of Infty:
2nd Lt Chas Hanson, to be 1st Lt, Mar 16, 1844, vice Baker, cashiered.
Brevet 2nd Lt Lafayette McLaws, of the 6th Infty, to be 2nd Lt, Mar 16, 1844, vice Hanson, promoted.

Brevets:
Lt Col Bennet Riley, of the 2nd Regt of Infty, to be Col by Brevet, "for long, meritorious, & gallant services, to take rank as such from the 2d day of Jun, 1840, the day on which was fought the battle of Chokachatts, in Florida, in which he particularly distinguished himself by his bravery & good conduct."
Capt John J Abercrombie, of the 1st Regt of Infty, to be Major by Brevet, "for gallant & meritorious services in Florida, to rank as such from the 25th Dec, 1837, the day

on which was fought the battle of Okeechobee, on which occasion, he acted, in the language of his Cmder, Brevet Brig Gen Taylor, with the greatest gallantry & coolness."

II-Appointments:
Medical Dept:
Assist Surgeon Jos J B Wright, to be Surgeon, Mar 26, 1844, vice Macomb, dec'd.
Geo Buist, of S C [late Assist Surgeon] to be Assist Surgeon, Jun 5, 1844.
Ordnance Dept:
Richd J R Bee, of Ga, to be Military Storekeeper, Apr 4, 1844.
Transfers:
Capt John C Casey, of the 2nd Artl, to the 3rd Infty, to take place on the Army Register next below Capt Van Horne.
Capt Henry Swartwout, of the 3rd Infty, to the 2nd Artl, to take place on the Army Register next below Capt Grayson.
2nd Lt Cyrus Hall, of the 8th Infty, to the 1st Infty, to take place on the Army Register next below Lt Denman.
2nd Lt Chas D Jordan, of the 1st Infty, to the 8th Infty, to take place on the Army Register next below Lt Clark.
III-The following Cadets, graduates of the Military Academy, are attached to the Army as supernumerary ofcrs with the Brevet of 2nd Lt, in conformity with the law, & the direction of the Pres, to take rank from Jul 1, 1844:
Brevet 2nd Lts attached to the Corps of Topographical Engineers.
1-Cadet Wm G Peck, of Conn
Brevet 2nd Lts attached to the Dragoon Arm:
2-Cadet Jos H Whittlesey, of N Y: Co D, 2nd Drags
7-Cadet Alfred Pleasanton, of D C: Co B, 1st Drags
9-Cadet Augustus Cook, of Ky: Co K, 2nd Drags.
10-Cadet John Y Bicknell, of Tenn: Co L, 2nd Drags
Brevet 2nd Lts attached to the Artl Arm:
3-Cadet Saml Gill, of Ky: Co B, 4th Artl
4-Cadet Danl M Frost, of N Y: Co K, 1st Artl
5-Cadet Asher R Eddy, of R I: Co K, 1st Artl
6-Cadet Francis J Thomas, of Md: Co C, 3rd Artl
8-Cadet Thos J Curd, of Ky: Co C, 1st Artl
Brevet 2nd Lts attached to the Infty Arm:
11-Cadet Simon B Buckner, of Ky: Co B, 4th Inf
12-Cadet John Trevit, of Ohio: Co H, 2nd Inf
14-Cadet Erastus B Strong, of Ark: Co B, 7th Inf
15-Cadet Wm T Burwell, of Va: Co C, 6th Infty
16-Cadet Wm Read, of Dela: Co D, 6th Inf
17-Cadet Jas S Woods, of Pa: Co A, 4th Inf
18-Cadet Winfield S Hancock, of Pa: Co K, 6th Inf
19-Cadet Jas M Henry, D C: Co K, 7th Inf
20-Cadet Alex Hays, of Pa: Co K, 4th Inf

21-Cadet Geo Wainwright, of Mass: Co F, 8th Inf
22-Cadet Henry B Schroader, of Md: Co B, 3rd Inf
23-Cadet Jos Smith, of N H: Co G, 5th Inf
24-Cadet John C Bibb, of Ky: Co D, 3rd Inf
25-Cadet Geo W Hawkins, of N C: Co D, 1st Inf

IV-Casualties:
Resignations [6]
Capt Otis Wheeler, 3rd Infty, Feb 29, 1844
1st Lt Jas M Ketchum, 3rd Artl, Apr 30, 1844
1st Lt Samel E Muse, 1st Infty, Mar 1, 1844
1st Lt Ferdinand Coxe, 1st Infty, Jan 31, 1844
1st Lt Lucius Pitkin, 2nd Artl, Jun 1, 1844
Brevet 2nd Lt Smith Stansbury, Ordnance Dept, May 31, 1844.

Deaths [4]
1st Lt Wm Frazer, 3rd Artl, at Lancaster, Pa, Jun 27, 1844
1st Lt B C Edes, 6th Infty, at Key West, Fla, Mar 30, 1844
2nd Lt A T Hoffman, 2nd Infty, St Augustine, Fla, Jan 25, 1844
Surgeon Edw Macomb, at *Fort Monroe*, Va, Mar 26, 1844

VII-Corrections, made by & with the advice of the Senate.
Capt Fredk Searle, of the Quartermaster's Dept, to be Maj by brevet, "for gallantry & good conduct on several occasions in the war against the Florida Indians, to date from Nov 25, 1839."
The above is a substitute for the announcement made in General Orders #56 of 1842.
By command of Maj Gen Scott: R Jones, Adj Gen
Memorandum: the name of Arnold E Jones, a 1st Lt in the 2nd Regt of Artl, having been changed by the Legislature of the State of Md to Arnold Elzey, he will hereafter be known as recognized in the army accordingly.

The undersigned will sell at Milwaukie, Territory of Wisconsin, on Aug 15 next, at public sale, a large number of valuable lots, eligibly situated in that city. The harbor is now improving under the foster care of the Gov't; the country is rapidly settling all around. –John M McCarty, of Leesburg, Loudoun Co, Va.

Female Institute, Columbia, Tenn: wish to secure by Sep 1, the services of a lady as Teacher of Drawing. Address, post paid: F G Smith, Rector, Columbia, Tenn.

Farm land for sale: about 160 acres, part of the *Glenn Ross* Farm in Montg Co, 7 miles from Wash City. Inquire of R _ Ross, Glenn Ross, or of Geo Taylor, Gen Land Ofc.

Wash Co, D C: I certify that Wm Luckett, of said county, brought before me as an estray a white buffalo milch Cow. –Nathl Brady Owner is to come forward, prove property, pay charges, & take her away. Wm Luckett, near the old Sugar-house, Eastern Branch.

WED JUL 17, 1844
Lost: 2 checks of Gerry L Page, on the Bank of the Metropolis. The public are cautioned against receiving them, payment has been stopped. –Chas J Nourse

Wanted, a colored woman servant, as cook & washer, in a small family; a slave from the country would be preferred, or any other well recommended. Apply to Mrs Fischer, corner of 12th & Pa ave.

For sale: house& lots near the Navy Yard. Inquire of Wm Easby, 1st Ward, Wash.

Death, by drowning, of Mr John W Collier, of Columbia, Mo, is mentioned in the Statesman. Mr C & 3 others were on their way to Nashville, Mo, to assist in removing the effects of the deluged inhabitants, when they lost their way amidst the wilderness of waters. His companions were saved by the citizens of Nashville.

A G A Martin, a mechanic, who arrived in N Y from Heyde, Holstrin, Denmark, a fortnight since, & took lodgings at 42 Dey st, was found murdered on Sat, in the neighborhood of Hoboken. An acquaintance of the dec'd, a German, has been arrested on very strong circumstances of suspicion.

Whig nominations for Reps in the next Congress from the State of Georgia:
Thos Butler King, of Glynn   H V M Miller, of Floyd
Wm H Crawford, of Sumter   Washington Poe, of Bibb
Jon W Underwood, of Habersham   A H Stephens, of Taliaferro
John J Floyd, of Newton   Robt Toombs, of Wilkes

A fine healthy child of Mr Haslup, who lives near the steamboat wharf, came to its death. The child, only 7 months old, was left in the care of a colored girl, who fell asleep, &, overlaying the poor sufferer, it died of suffocation.

The Amherst Cabinet contains the event of the blowing up of a powder mill at Danby, Vt, causing the death of 3 boys. Mr Smith was the first on the scene; he caught up the first boy he came to, whom he did not recognize, when the little sufferer said, I am your boy, Pa. He died in a few hours after.

Improved portable tobacco-press: Price $300. Adapted to packing hay or baling cotton as it is for presses & hogsheading tobacco. –Geo Page, Manufacturer, West Balt st, Balt, Md.

THU JUL 18, 1844
The sons of Maj Joel Snow & widow Martha Knowle, of Eastham, Mass, had their faces severely burned by an explosion of powder on Jul 4.

Thos W Door is employed in the State Prison at Rhode Island, wherein for flagrant & manifold treason he has been sentenced to abide for life, in the painting of fans. He refused to sign a petition for his release, or to take the oath of allegiance to the established & rightful Gov't of the State. --Journal of Commerce

The Whigs of Montg Co, Md, have nominated the following as candidates for the next House of Delegates:
Alex'r Kilgour, of Rockville district
Wm B Howard, of Medley's district
Geo C Patterson, of Clarksburg district
Saml D Waters, of Berry's district

Capt Cyrus Allen, of Harwich, Mass, was seriously injured on Jul 4 by the discharge of a 6 pound cannon, while in the act of loading. Mr Isaac Jones had inserted the cartridge, into the muzzle of the gun, to half the length of his arm, when Capt A undertook to ram it home. Capt's Allen's face & shoulder, & one eye entirely, were destroyed.

Meeting of the Democrats of the District of Kensington, Pa, was held at the hotel of Widow Brighthart, on Jun 18, 1844. John R Sharp, Chairman, Jos Cook & H Brady, Vice Presidents, Thos Peters & Edw Taylor, Secs. Theodore Philips reported a series of resolutions: nominating Jas K Polk, of Tenn, for the Presidency.
Mr Thos Loring, Editor of Raleigh Independent, in favor of Clay & Frelinghuysen.
Mr Ashford Mankin, of Columbiana Co, Ohio, in favor of Clay & Frelinghusen.
Henry O'Reilly, formerly Editor of the Albany Argus, an organ of the Locofoco party of N Y, has requested his name be withdrawn as one of the cmte on resolutions at the meeting in the capitol. He is opposed to the annexation of Texas.
John Henderson, sec of the Locofoco meeting in St Louis, Mo, has repudiated the party now & forever. He cannot swallow annexation of Texas.
Moses P Jewett, formerly a resident of Burlington, Vt, now a distinguished citizen of Cicinnati, writes to Horace Loomis, of Burlington: We shall give Clay 20,000 majority in Ohio-rely on it.
Col Hugh Lindsay, of Berks, Pa, & his associates are making speeches & exposing the corruptions of Locofocoism in a masterly manner.
Hon Ross Wilkins, U S District Judge for Michigan, has abandoned the Locofoco party on the Texas question & joined the Liberty party.
Hon Levi Beardsley, respected citizen of Franklin Co, Ohio, to support Henry Clay.
Mr Wm Lee, of Chillicothe, Ohio, has come out for Clay & Frelinghuysen.
Wm Hines, of Howard Co, Mo, renounces further fellowship with the Locofoco party. As does Ashford Mankin, of Elkrun township, Columbiana Co, Ohio.
Wm P Linvill, of South Solon, Madison Co, Ohio, will go for Clay & Frelinghuysen.

Harvard Univ: the first term of the Law School will open on Aug 10, 1844. The active labors of instruction are shared equally between Mr Justice Story & Prof Greenleaf, who has the immediate superintendence of the Law School

Nunda, N Y, Jul 10. A party of young ladies & gentlemen, from Mount Morris & this village, made an excursion as a picnic party to the tunnel & falls in Portage. While descending the hill near Badger's bridge, one of the carriages upset, & Miss Mary Buck, d/o Prof Buck of this village, was killed. She was a teacher in the Baptitst Institute in this place, & was about 22 years of age.

Mrd: on Jul 16, by Rev Noval Wilson, Mr Jacob Tabler to Miss Eugenia B King, both of Wash City.

Died: on Jul 10, at Springfield, PG Co, Md, after a long & painful illness, which she bore with Christian resignation, Mrs Mary Ann E Brooke, consort of Robt W Brooke, aged 25 years.

Obit-died: on Jul 10, at the residence of her mother, Mrs Grace C Tyler, in Upper Marlborough, PG Co, Md, Miss Jane H Tyler, in her 35th year, d/o Maj Trueman Tyler, late of said county, dec'd. As a dght, she was affectionate & kind; as a sister, ardent & devoted; as a friend, faithful & steadfast. -T

An affray took place in Clinton, Miss, between D B Lewis & Mr Thorn, which resulted in the death of Lewis by a pistol shot. Thorn was acquitted upon trial. The Tuscaloosa [Ala] Monitor of Jul 3: affray in that city on Jun 29, between Wm H Grimes & Wm A Verrell, which resulted in the death of Verrel. Grimes surrendered himself & was discharged.

FRI JUL 19, 1844
Col Pleasanton, of Phil, is still in Balt, under the care of Surgeon Gibson. The wound of which he is suffering was produced by a musket ball, which penetrated his pantaloons pocket, drawers, & both shirts, & was found next his skin flattened. It would have inevitably fatal had it not sturck a purse of half dollars in its course, every one of which made its mark. –Balt American

The Balt American states the Mr Henry J Rodgers, of that city, the inventor of the American Telegraph, has been appointed by Prof Morse, with the concurrence of the Sec of the U S Treasury, Assist Superintendent of the line of Electro Magnetic Telegraphs between Wash & Balt.

Mr T Deloro, of Alton, Ill, was drowned in the cellar beneath his store on Jul 7. It is supposed that the fell through a trap door & was stunned by the fall.

Wash Corp: 1-Ptn of Jas Fraser, sen: referred to the Cmte on Improvements. 2-Ptn fom Wm Easby for the improvements of certain streets: referred to the Cmte on Improvements. 3-Cmte of Claims: bill for the relief of O B Clark: passed. 4-Ptn from Ulysses Ward: referred to the Cmte of Claims. 5-Indefinitely postponed: Ptn of David Little & others; ptn of Henry Walker & others; ptn of John Gadsby & others; ptn of Mrs Delia Tudor & Mrs Delia Tudor Tucker. Also, of Edw Simms for the erection of a wharf.

Mrd: on Jul 18, by Rev Mr Sprole, S Sammons, of N Y C, to Miss Hannah Maria, eldest d/o Josiah F Caldwell, of Wash City.

For sale, on reasonable terms: a 10 pin-alley, with the balls & pins belinging thereto; all of which are in good order. Inquire of Mr Downer, E & 13th sts, or of Mr Gilbert, on the premises.

Farm for sale, & house for rent: nearly 50 acres, about 2 miles from the Capitol, price $6,000 for sale. Also a house in the Northern Liberties for rent, $125 per year. -Edmund F Brown, Agent

SAT JUL 20, 1844
Wanted: a healthy woman, without a child, as wet nurse. Apply at Capt F Black's, 3rd st.

Foreign news: 1-Mr Thos Hudson, a popular comic writer & singer, died in London on Jun 19. 2-The Dowager Lady Glenlyon died on Jun 21 at Dunkeld. 3-Mr Geoffrey Saint Hilaire, whose reputation stood so high in the scientific world, had just expired at age 72, after a long illness.

Cannon Foundry: the Columbian Foundry at the seat of Gov't for sale. At my advanced age, having determined to retire from active pursuits, I offer for sale the well known & long established Cannon Foundry, on the Potomac river, adjoining the town of Gtwn, D C. Apply for terms to the Proprietor, or to Maynadier Mason, Columbian Foundry, Gtwn, D C, or to John Mason, jr, Wash. –J Mason

For rent: small brick bldg on 11th st, near Pa ave. Apply to the tenant in occupancy, or to the subscriber, L st, near Franklin Row. –S A Elliot

For sale or rent: 3 story house on Indiana ave. Inquire on the premises of the proprietor. –A C Wood

For rent: new brick house on N Y ave, between 10th & 11th sts. Apply to Mr J B Morgan, who occupies the adjoining house, or to E Pickrell & Co, Water st, Gtwn.

Wheel-Wrighting & Coach Making: 21st st, near the West Market, lately occupied by Mr Benzett. The subscriber is prepared to make to order Carts, Wagons, Carryalls, & Furniture Cars. –Chas R Jones

Obit-died: on Jun 8, at his residence *Belle Air*, Yazoo Co, Miss, Wm L Chew, jr, M D, of congestive fever, in his 35th year, leaving a disconsolate & broken-hearted wife, & many near & dear friends. But a few months before he carried to the silent grave his lovely dght & only child Rebecca Freeland, with scarlet fever, at which time she had almost attained maturity. This stroke was nearly too much for frail humanity to endure; & there had been but a partial recovery from this great loss when the latter bereavement removed the last earthly hope of a doting wife & mother. They were both members of the Methodist Episcopal Church.

Died: on Jul 15, in Montgo Co, Md, Mr Jacob Rohrer, after a lingering illness of 6 months, aged 62 years.

Orphans Court of Wash Co, D C. Letters of administration on the personal estate of Geo Miller, late of said county, dec'd. –Henry Miller, adm

MON JUL 22, 1844
Phil: a rioter, Elijah Jester, who died in the hospital a day or two since, received his death wound from the rioters with whom he was acting. He stated this on his death bed.

Jos Brown & John McDaniel, who were to have been executed at St Louis, on Jul 12, for the murder of Charvis, the Santa Fe trader, have been again respited to Aug 16.

Mr Jesse M White, a native of Winchester, Va, was accidentally drowned at Swift Creek, near Petersburg, Va, on Jul 15.

Hornsby, convicted of manslaughter for killing Twogood in New Orleans, is allowed a new trial on the grounds that the jury had been allowed to separate & mingle with the community after the trial had commenced, & before the verdict was formed.

Balt Sun: accident at Centreville, Anne Arundel Co, Md, on Fri last, resulted in the death of a highly esteemed young man, Danl Newman, s/o Mr Danl Newman, lumber merchant of that place. The dec'd went into the store of Messrs Arthur Emory & Co, & in taking up a loaded pistol, it discharged the contents of which went into the young man's chest. He expired in about 15 minutes.

All hopes appear to have been given up for the safety of the Bremen ship **Johannes**, bound for Balt. She left Bremen on Mar 22, under the command of Capt Dierkes, with 156 passengers & a crew of 14, & has never since been heard from. The crew belonged to Bremen & its vicinity. -Sun

Pittsburg American: On Fri last, at Livermore, Westmoreland Co, in that State, Miss Ann Jaynes, the d/o Mr Timothy Jaynes, of that vicinity, & sister of Mr Alex'r Jaynes, of Pittsburg, had the day before visited a sick friend, about 4 miles distant, & left to return homes. Her horse reached home, & the young lady was found floating on the canal by the ofcrs of one of Leech & Co's boats, & taken to Livermore, where she was recognized, but life was gone.

Died: on Jul 21, after a short illness, Brevet Capt W K Hanson, U S Army. His funeral will be from the residence of his father, Isaac K Hanson, today at 4 o'clock.

Died: on Jul 21, in his 94th year, after a protracted & severe illness, Cornelius Wells. His funeral will take place this evening from his late residence on Md ave, between 13th & 14th sts.

Died: on Jul 12, at Petersburg, Va, Dr Robt B Banister, Assist Surgeon U S Navy, in his 31st year.

Farm for sale. The subscriber will sell at public sale, on Aug 20, a tract of land containing 226 acres. The farm is 12 miles from Gtwn. –Jos Soper, trustee

Meeting of the Franklin Fire Co on Jul 24. By order, Wm Duer, Sec

St Mary's College, Balt, Md: on Jul 15, Orations were delivered by the candidates for the honors of the Colleg:

Gilbert De Beeles Fetterman, of Pittsburg	Felix Jenkins, of Balt
	Edw Patterson, of Balt
Geo M Robinson, of Boston	John H D Waters, of Balt
Bolivar D Daniels, of Balt	Matthew Bennet, of Balt
Jos H Maddox, of St Mary's	

Degree of A B was conferred on the above men & on Francis X King, of York, Pa.

The degree of A M was conferred on

Thos Wheelan, of Balt	Peter Baudeuy Garesche, of Dela
Lambert A Whiteley, of Balt	Wm Tracy, of Balt
Oscar Miles, of St Mary's Co	T Geo Riordan, of Ireland

Honorary Certificates were awarded to Venceslas Tache, of Quebec, & John Dunnock, of Dorchester Co, Md.

An address was delivered by Thos C Rokhill, of Phil

Distribution of Premiums to:

John Waters, of Balt	Jos H Maddox, of St Mary's
Felix Jenkins, of Balt	Francis Waters, of Balt
Gilbert Fetterman, of Pittsburg	Bernard Reed, of Balt
Matthew Bennett, of Balt	Oden Bowie, of PG Co
Bolivar Danels, of Balt	Geo F Maddox, of St Mary's Co

Louis Desobry, of La
Robt Sutton, of Balt
Jos E Coad, of St Mary's Co
Francis Frick
John Garesche, of Dela
Francis Boyle, of Balt
Talbott Denmead
Arthur Rich
Thos W Coyle, of Balt
E Marmillion, New Orleans
Ramon Herreta, of Chili
Jacob Walter, of Balt
Wm Easter, of Balt
Chas Shroeder, of Balt
David Hays, of Balt
Leo Knott, of Balt
Joachim Antumes, of Mobile
Saml Chile
Chas O Donavan
Wm G Coe
Lestan Prudhomme
Phineas Sanders, of Balt
Thos Kemp
Chas Kemp
John Neale
Wm J Slater, of Balt
John O Donavan
Valsain Marmillion
Wm Kelley
Augustine Emory
Robt Sutton
Fred'k Maddox
Bernard Reed
Edw Goodwin
Thos Coyle, of Md
John Gallaway, of Md
Geo Campbell, of St Mary's
Francis Hall, of PG Co
Henry Rossignol, of Ga
Jos Keenan, of Balt
John Howard
John Ricaud
John McLosky
Wm de Figaniere

Jos Knox
Phineas B Sanders
Wm J C Du Hamel
Hugh McDonald
Saml Child
Edw Munchs
John B Cloutier
Jos Peterson
Amede Petit, of New Orleans
Wm Getty
F X Kelley
Denis McKew
Joachim Antunez, of Mobile
Wm Hart, of New Orleans
Robt Floyd, of Md
J Gallaway
Chas Pochon
E B Marmillion
Eugene Waggaman, of New Orleans
Talbott Denmead
E Cloutier
Fred'k Renshaw, of Caraccas
J Antunez
K Wysham
A Bizouard
E Toledana, of New Orleans
R Fernandez, of Cuba
F Laroque, of Balt
Geo Robinson, of Boston
Vinceslas Tache, of Canada
Raphael Neale
Thos Lanahan
Jas McLosky, of Mobile
T Lanahan
Clement Hill
C Lacroix
W Travers
W Kelly, of Balt
John Foley, of Balt
John S Broadbent, of Balt
Jos Peterson, of Balt
Ernest Toledano, of New Orleans
T Kemp, of Balt
Raymon Gomez

Pedro Gomez
Edw Wysham, of Balt
Jas Hickley, of Balt

Kemp Wysham, of Balt
Solomon Hunter, of Balt

Local News: the dwlg house of Mr Chas Munroe, 2nd st & Indiana ave, was forcibly entered, & the lower part of it ransacked. The robbers had to decamp with but a few silver articles.

To let, Aug 1, a comfortable 2 story brick house, on G, between 11th & 12th sts, now occupied by Mr Reilly. Inquire of G Lambright, near the railroad.

Desirable residence at private sale: *Head of Frazier*, on the Potomac river, nearly opposite Alexandria, being the late residence of John B Kirby, dec'd. The lot contains 5 acres . –Geo Semmes

TUE JUL 23, 1844
Michel Chevalier, of Pars, has just tramsnitted to the Nat'l Institute a copy of a work he has just written upon the question of a Canal across the Isthmus of Panama. In a late letter addressed to the Institute by Robt Monroe Harrison, U S Consul at Kingston, Jamaico, he mentions a Mons I J Hellert, a French engineer, who passed through this place on his way to superintend the canal that is in contemplation to be cut through the Isthmus of Panama.

The Whigs of Montg Co, Md at their Convention hald on Jul 13, nominated Geo Clarke Patterson, Wm B Howard, Saml D Waters, & Alex'r Kilgour, as candidates to represent that county in the next Legislature. They cannot be beaten.

Balt Co: the Whig Convention which assembled at Reisterstown on Sat nominated John Philpot, Wm Kimmell, Jas Mahool, D P Boyd, & W E Coale, as candidates for the House of Delegates.

Chas Co: Whig meeting in Port Tobacco last week, was addressed by Gen John G Chapman & Hon J M S Causin. Gen J G Chapman, Col John Hughes, & John D Freeman, were nominated for the House of Degelates.

The venerable Mark Richards, formerly Lt Govn't of the State of Vt, & member of Congress from Vt, writes: I am now confined to my room, & have been to my bed, & am not able to direct any business. I may get out again, but as the 15th was my birthday 84 years ago, my years must be nearly numbered. I have a great desire to live to the time my friend Henry Clay may be seated in the White House by the voice of the American people. –Boston Atlas

Jamaico Times of Jun 22: by accounts from Panama up to Jun 8, we regret to learn that Cmdor Dallas, of the American Navy, was lying dangerously ill at Callao, & little hopes entertained for his recovery.

Maj L H Osgood, an ofcr of the army of the last war, who served through the whole war, has been removed from the ofc of Measurer in the custom-house of the port of Boston. Jas Holbrook, Editor of a Tyler Locofoco paper in Hartford, Conn, has been appointed to the ofc. –Boston Atlas

From Texas. A desperate action was recently fought near the Pinto Trace-a point nearly equidistant from Bexar, Gonzales, & Austin-in which Col Hays, with only 14 men, defeated a body of Camanche & Waco Indians numbering about 75. The Indians were using spears & arrows, & the Texans their yagers & repeating pistols, whose certain aim emptied many a saddle. 23 of the Indians were counted dead upon the field, & as many more are known to have been wounded; many of them mortally. Of Col Hays' men, Peter Fox was shot through the head & died on the spot; R A Gillespie & Saml Walker [the latter a native of Md formerly of Wash City] were dangerously wounded with lances. Mr Walker supposed to be mortally. He was one of the Mier prisoners who escaped last year from Tacubays, near Mexico.

Hagerstown News: a young man, Franklin Allsberger, of Alleghany Co, on a visit to Graceham, Fred'k Co, lost his life on Tue last. He had gone to a neighboring stream to bathe, & when diving, his head came in contact with a rock, by which he was instantly deprived of life.

Notice: was committed to the jail of Fred'k Co, Md, on Jul 18, as a runaway, a black man, Henry Pearson, about 30 years old. Says he belongs to Resin Coxan, Fairfax Court-house, Va. The owner, if any, is to come & have him released, otherwise he will be discharged according to law. –Geo Rice, Sheriff of Fred'k Co, Md

Nassau Hall, Princeton, N J: the next year of study in the College of N J will commence on Aug 8. The faculty are:
Rev Jas Carnahan, D D, Pres
Rev John Maclean, D C, V P & Prof of Greek Language & Lit
Rev Albert B Dod, A M, Prof of Math
Jos Henry, L L D, Prof of Nat'l Philosophy
Rev Jas W Alexander, D D, Prof of Belles Lettres & Latin
John Torrey, M D, Prof of Chemistry & Nat'l History
Stephen Alexander, A M, Prof of Astronomy & Adj Prof of Math
Evert M Topping, A M, Adj Prof of Greek & Latin Languages
A Cardon de Sandrans, Teacher of Modern Languages
Tutors: John W Sterling, A M; Levi H Christian, A M; Geo M Giger, A M; A Alexander Hodge, A M. -Princeton, N J m Jul 5, 1844

Mr Caleb Nodding had both arms blown off & one eye blown out by the bursting of a brass cannon during the celebration of Jul 4 at Baring, Me, & Mr Sprague was badly injured by the same accident.

Hon Edw Stanly was severely though not dangerously hurt by the running away of his horse Wed, near Pungo creek, on his way to Leachville & head of Pungo, to fill appointments for meeting the people. —Wash [N C] Whig, Jul 12

W Crockford, famous for his gambling operations, died recently in London, worth $1,750,000. He was once a fishmonger. He gives the whole of his immense property: "to my dear wife & her heirs, relying on her doing what is right."

On Sat last, at the barracks at Carlisle, Pa, Saml Sanno, a s/o Maj Michl Sanno, was accidently killed by the discharge of a fowling piece.

Accident at Boston on Thu: a 9 year old s/o Mr David Pulsifer [now absent with the Grays on their excursion to Balt] & another lad named Ford, went on the East Boston Ferry-boat wharf for fishing, & their legs hanging over, were struck by the railing of the ferry-boat, crushing one of Pulsifer's legs, so that amputation will probably be necessary. There is great fear that his life will be endangered. Ford was unhurt.

Univ of Va: the chair in the school of Modern Languages of this Institution having become vacant by the resignation of Prof Chas Kraitsir, meeting will be held on Sep 10 to fill the vacancy. —Willis H Woodley, Proctor

Thos M Aspinwall, of N Y, committed suicide at Brooklyn on Thu by taking laudanum. He was about 50 years of age, a man of wealth, & had retired several years ago, with a large & interesting family. He was subject to occasional slight mental derangement. He was a regular communicant at St Thos' church, & beloved & respected by all who knew him.

Mrd: on Jul 4, at Edenton, N C, by Rev Saml I Johnson, Alex'r Dixon, of Warrenton, Va, to Corissande E McDonald, d/o Gen Duncan McDonald, of the former place.

Died: on Jul 22, Tully R Wise, First Auditor of the Treasury, in his 48th year. His funeral is from the late residence of the dec'd, on G st, at 4 p m this day.

Died: on Jul 19, of pulmonary consumption, at the *Woodyard*, the residence of his parents, Lt Richd Henry West, of the 1st Regt Dragoons, U S Army-to the unutterable grief of his family & the deep regret of many affectionate friends.

Died: on Tue last, in Raleigh, N C, Mary, infant d/o Hon Kenneth Rayner.

Moses Wright, aged 25, residing in the s w part of Nashua, N H, committed suicide on Sun last by hanging himself on a tree in the woods. He was engaged to be married, & the certificate of publishment had been issued, but the mother of the young lady, not liking him on account of his intemperate habits, had forbidden him from the house.

J G Proud, jr, returns his sincere thanks to the members of the Anacostia, Columbia, & other fire companies, & to those citizens who exerted themselves so actively in endeavors to save his steam brick press from destruction by fire on Sun last.

$50 reward for the burglar or burglars who robbed the dwlg of Mr John B Coddington, on B st, near 3rd st, on Mon, stealing silver & money.

Cornelius Wells died on Sun, at his residence, near the Long Bridge, in his 94th year. He was one of "our ragged troops" in the battle at Trenton, on Christmas day in '76, & the next day in the battle at Princeton, where he received a wound from a bayonet, which affected him to the end of his life. He was in the frig **Confederacy** when it was taken, & was sent to a British prison-ship in N Y, from which he was released in the autumn of 1781. He continued in service to the end of the war, & received an honorable discharge. He was poor & illiterate, but a true patriot & an honest man. His wife, who is poor, with 2 children too young to support themselves, cannot obtain a pension, & it is hoped that the sympathies of those in power will be extended to the widow & orphans of him who bravely fought at Trenton, & bled at Princeton. -K

WED JUL 24, 1844
Violent tornado passed through Chambersburg, Pa, on Fri afternoon, accompanied with heavy hail. Culbertson's paper mill was prostrated. Dr Culbertson, the proprietor, was caught between the joist, & remained in extreme agony for half an hour or more.

Edw Perkins, a gambler, killed John White, another gambler, at Memphis, on Jul 9. He shot him with a pistol. The dec'd was a native of Madison Co, Tenn. Perkins was committed to jail.

John Rutzell was killed on the Balt & Ohio Railroad on Sun, at Sideling Hill creek, in Morgan Co, Va. He was lying on the road intoxicated, & was caught in the cow catcher attached to the locomotive, & instantly deprived of life.

A silk factory has been started in Richmond, Indiana, within a year, by I E Jones, worked by water power.

Mrd: on Jul 15, at Phil, Robt L Martin, formerly of Alexandria, D C, to Adelaide West, d/o Saml Nevins, of the former place.

Died: on Jul 19, at his residence, near Wash City, Mr Mauduit Young, aged 62, after a long & painful illness of more than 2 years' duration.

Died: on Jul 15, in Montg Co, Md, Mr Jacob Bohrer, after a lingering illness of 6 months, aged 63.

Wash Corp: 1-Ptn of Simeon Matlock & others for setting the curbstone & paving the footway on west side of squares 425, 426, 427, & 429: referred to the Cmte on Improvements. 2-Ptn of Thos J Earhart, appealing from a judgment rendered against him by J D Clark: referred to the Cmte of Claims. 3-Ptn of Wm P Shedd, praying the remission of a fine: referred to the Cmte of Claims. 4-Cmte of Claims: asking to be discharged from the further consideration of the ptn of Wm Johnson: agreed to. 5-Bill for the relief of Wm B Wilson: passed. 6-Ptn from Elias Abrams & from Bernard Giveny for the remission of fines: referred to the Cmte of Claims.

For sale or rent: 3 story brick house, with a large yard walled in: on Missouri ave, near 4½ st. –Wm War.

Store fixtures & furniture at auction: on Jul 26, in the store lately occupied by Mr Elias Abrams, on Pa ave. –Lewis & Hunt, auctioneers

THU JUL 25, 1844
Appointments by the Pres: Benning Mann, to be U S Marshal for D C.
Levi S Humphrey, to be U S Marshal for the District of Michigan.
Saml H Hempstead, to be U S Atty for the District of Arkansas, in the place of G D Royston, resigned.

Md Nominations:
Carroll Co: the Whigs of Carroll Co, assembled at Westminster on Sat last, & nominated Wm Roberts for the State Senate, & Jas Raymond, John P Thompson, & Jos Ebaugh & Micah Rogers as their candidated for the next House of Delegates.
Calvert Co: The Whig ticket in this county for the House of Delegates is: Jas S Morsell, Richd Harne, & Thos J Hellen.

The Whigs of Tenn call for a grand Mass Convention to assemble in Nashville on Aug 21, & the following eminent speakers have been invited to be present: Hon J J Crittenden, Wm C Rives, Wm C Preston, B Watkins Leigh, S S Prentiss, John M Clayton, Thos Corwin, Ben Hardin, J McPherson Berrien, Thos Metcalfe, Arthur F Hopkins, Waddy Thompson, John M Botts, Balie Peyton, J J Hardin, Randall Hunt, Thos Ewing, & A H Stephens.

Col S W Oakey, one of the inspectors of elections at New Orleans, recently arrested for alleged frauds upon electors, has, after examination, been held to bail in $11,000 [$1,000 on each charge] to answer in the Criminal Court.

Hon Saml Fessenden, of Portland, Maine, late Whig member of Congress, has renounced the support of Clay, in the New England papers, over his own signature. -Globe

Godfrey McRae, aged about 35 or 40, & Caroline Smead, aged 7 years, were drowned in N Y Bay on Fri, by the upsetting of a small sailboat.

Gen Sentmanat's Expedition. The late Mexican papers furnish some new details relative to this ill-advised expedition. Gen Sentmanat was shot on Jun 14 at noon, on the public square of Jalapa, with 13 of his companions, who first landed with him & were captured by the troops of the Govn'r Genr'l. The others, to the number of 77, were not able to land, & consequently were arrested on board the vessel which conveyed them. They are in great part Spanish sub-ofcrs, of the Carlist party, enrolled by Sentmanat during his last sojourn in New Orleans.

During the visit of the U S sloop of war **Saratoga** to the island of St Thomas, off the coast of Africa, May 24, the coxswain in charge of the capt's gig, straining too hard upon the tiller, broke it & fell overboard. While swimming to the ship, he suddenly disappeared, & thereupon the fins & tail of a huge shark emerged from the water, & nothing but a crimson stain of blood & a hat floating, were seen. [Coxswain not named.]

The Presbyterian Church near Liberty, Sullivan Co, N Y, was struck by lightning during Divine service on Sun week, & Mr Henry Burr & Mr Young were seriously injured, with but little chance of their recovery.

Wm McGuffin, of Wash, Pa, aged 18, was thrown from a horse on Jul 15, & instantly killed. He was running his horse at the time with another young man.

Danl T Adams was convicted at New Orleans, on Jul 15, of manslaughter, in having caused the death of an apprentice of his last May, by inflicting a kick on the left side of the boy's head.

Meeting of the ofcrs of the Army stationed at *Fort Moultrie*, S C, on the death of 1st Lt Wm Frazer, of the 3rd Artl, Capt M Burke, 3rd Artl, being called to the chair, & Lt J F Reynolds, 3rd Artl, appointed secretary. Lt Wm Frazer died at the residence of his brother in Lancaster, Pa, on Jun 27, 1844. –M Burke, Capt 3rd Artl, Pres

Died: yesterday, Mrs Jane C Clagett, wid/o the late Zachariah Clagett, formerly of Gtwn, D C, aged 85 years. Her funeral is this afternoon at 4 o'clock from the residence of Mrs Brawner, Pa ave, near the railroad depot.

Died: on Jul 11, at Parkersburg, Va, in her 38th year, Mrs Ellen H, w/o Dr Williamson, of that place. The dec'd has left the consolation to her husband, 3 interesting children, & a numerous circle of relatives & friends, that she died an exemplary member of the Methodist Church, in full assurance of a blessed immortality beyond the grave. –M A W

Medical College of Louisiana: Session 1844-45 to commence on Nov 18, & close on the 3rd Sat in Mar, 1845. –A H Cenas, Dean

Meeting of the Topographical Society this evening, at half past 7 o'clock, at Buckingham's room. By order of the Pres: Jno Lee Smith, Rec Sec'y

Shamrock Hill for sale: this farm is 2 miles north of the Capitol, & is directly approached by N Y ave & North Capitol st extended, & contains upwards of 85 acres. The dwlg house & barn are large: commands a beautiful prospect of the river Potomac, & Wash City. Apply to John Boyle, Wash City, of Junius J Boyle, Navy Yard, Wash.

FRI JUL 26, 1844
H G S Key, of St Mary's Co, has been appointed by Gov Thomas, Chief Judge of the First Judicial District of Md, in place of Judge Stephen, dec'd.

Mr Israel M Parsons, of Springfield, Mass, committed suicide on Sat last by hanging himself while under the influence of insanity. He was 42 years old, & has left a wife & 4 children.

The Cincinnati Gaz says the early settlers are fast passing away. Jos Williams, late Elmore Williams, died on his farm, aged 84, on Jul 14. He laid the first brick in Cincinnati. For the last 36 years he has resided on his farm in Mill Creek, where he died, as he had lived, at peace with God & with man.

St Augustine News of Jul 13: Lt Blake has received orders to commence the survey of a railroad route across Florida, from Jacksonville to Cross Keys.

Mr Chas H Bartlett, a very promising young man, a printer, employed in the ofc of the Hudson Republican, was found dead a day or two since near the town, having been killed no doubt by the accidental discharge of a gun which was found in his hand, the charge of which had lodged in his head.

Died: on Jul 24, Wm Lansdale, infant s/o Dr Thomas.

Died: yesterday, Mary Anna Gold, aged 11 months, only surviving child of Danl & Mary A Gold. Her funeral will take place Jul 26, at 9 o'clock.

Obit-died: on Monday last I attended the remains of a dec'd friend to their final resting place. Capt Wells served in both the army & navy of the Revolution-was at Trent & at Princeton, where, in addition to a bayonet wound, he received a ball in the hip, which he carried to the grave. He was also wounded in the head by a sabre cut, while boarding the British ship **Roebuck**, in her engagement with the frig **Confederacy**, having been the second man on the deck of the boarded ship. His declining years were made comparatively easy by the receipt of a pension from his country, which, in addition to a moderate salary he derived from a situation he had held for several years, sufficed to satisfy his wants, & minister in some degree to the comforts of his old age. –H [See Jul 23rd newspaper: died: Cornelius Wells.]

Bricks for sale: in addition to what he is constantly making, 400,000 bricks of superior quality. Apply to Bates & Brother's Soap & Candle Factory, G st, or to the subscriber who can be found at the brick yard, n e of the Alms house. –John Bates

Gtwn College, D C: Annual commencement was held on Jul 25, 1844.
Degree of A M was conferred on Lt Wm Lynch, U S N.
Degree of A B was conferred on the following students:

Edw C Donnelly, of N Y	Geo Marshall, of Tenn
Eugene Cummiskey, of Pa	Wm P Brooke, of Md
Francis H Dykers, of N Y	Franics M Gunnell, of D C
Wm E Bird, of Ga	

Following students were rewarded with silver medals & premiums, or were honorable mentioned: [Including the above named.]

Peter C Howle, of D C	Eusebius L Jones, of D C
Jos L Brent, of D C	Edmund H Cummin, of D C
Waldemar de Bodisco, of Russia	Jas Donnegan
John E Wilson, of Md	Henry Wilkinson
Jas A Iglehart, of Md	Nicholas Snowden, of Md
Nicholas S Knighton, of Md	Polycarp Fortier, of La
Robt E Doyle, of N Y	Henry J Forstall, of La
Eliel S Wilson, of Md	Chas De Blanc, of La
Richd Rochford, of Ireland	Edw R Smith, of N Y
John H Botts, of Md	Wm W Watson, of Miss
Patrick F Drain, of D C	Jos R Gross, of D C
John Nevins, of D C	C Vivian Brent, of D C
Richd H Clarke, of D C	Thos Hance, of Md
Chas L Denby, of Va	Saml Rainey, of D C
Thos A Carrico, of Md	John L Jenkins, of Pa
Henry D Power, of D C	Gregory I Ennis, of D C

Master Pierre de la Croix
Victor Forstall, of La
Octave Metoyer, of La
John F McCarthy, of D C
Edw Pearce, of D C
Jas H Donnegan, of Ala
Octave Andry, of La
Robt Diggs, of Md
Bernard G Caulfield, of D C
Chas H Pendergrast, of Md
Andrew J Spalding, of Md
John L Jenkins, of Pa
John F Clements, of D C
J Vanbrugh Livingston, of N Y
Patrick Morgan, of N Y
Edw Drouet, of La
Arthur M Snowden, of Md
Ignatius Langley, of Md
Julius Tete, of La
Henry des Rivieres, of Canada
Francis Porche, of La
Wm S Parkhill, of D C
Andrew J Pageot, of France
Jas L Beatty, of Md
Thos H Dawson, of D C
Eugene Forstall, of La
Henry Castellanos, of La
Adrien Lepretre, of La
Chas Guttslich, of D C
Prosper Landry, of La
Pierre de las Croix, of La
Chas Deblanc, of La
Bennett R Abell, of Md
Francis Fitnam, of D C
John Duncan, of Ala
Stanley Vance, of La
Ignatius C Roche, of Md
Roderick Masson, of Canada
Severin Porche, of La
Jos Cassin, of D C
J Francis Boucher, of D C
Edouard Drouet, of La

The oration, On Dueling, by Wm Pinkney Brooke, of Upper Marlborough, Md, was remarkable for its good sentiments, its chaste composition, & correct delivery.

Six cents reward for runaway apprentice boy, Luther Chamberlain, aged about 20 years. All persons are forbid employing or harboring him, otherwise the law will be enforced against them. The above reward, with the addition of a handful of shavings, will be given to any person who will deliver said boy to the subscriber. –Robt Allen, Carpenter, 8th & I sts.

Stray cow came to my premises. Owner is to come forward, prove property, pay charges, & take her away. –Patrick Twomey, 13½ st

SAT JUL 27, 1744
Rev Mr Harvey, a Baptist clergyman, 109 years of age, is still living at Frankfort, N Y, & is engaged every Sabbath in his profession. He made the opening prayer at Utica on the last celebration of our Nat'l anniversary with most impressive effect.

Robt Lyons, one of the rioters who was shot at Phil, died on Wed evening.

Capt Scott, of the Cadwalader Grays, has so far recovered from his wounds, as to be able to walk in his room. His medical attendants have deemed it unadvisable to extract the ball.

List of the State & County *prisons* erected by Mr Haviland, of Phil, on the plan known as the Pennsylvanian, shoring the progress of that system.
1790 the first cells were erected on this system in the Phil Town Jail, by the Phil Prison Society.
1821 the Phil or 1st Pa Penitentitay for 900 convicts was commenced; prisoners first admitted in 1829.
1833 the Pittsburg Penitentiary was reconstructed for 236 prisoners.
1833 Alleghany Co, Pa, erected a County Prison of 40 cells at Alleghany.
1834 the State of N J adopted our system, & erected their Trenton Penitentiary for 300 convicts.
1834 R I adopted the system & erected the Providence Penitentiary of 100 cells.
1835 the Halls of Justice of N Y were erected for 188 untried prisoners on our system.
1836 Essex Co, N J, erected a County Prison of 40 cells at Newark.
1838 the State of Arkansas adopted the system, & commenced a Penitentiary of 300 cells.
1842 Dauphin Co, Pa, erected a County Prison of 40 cells at Harrisburg.

Obit-died: on Jul 21, at Oak Ridge, his residence in Caroline Co, Wilson Allan, in his 71st year. He was a native of New Kent Co. He commenced his career life in the city of Richmond, where he acted for some years as Clerk of the Genr'l Court of Va. In 1807 he married the only d/o Col John Hoomes, of the Bowling Green; after which he became a resident of Caroline Co. He was a firm believer in the Christian religion. He has left a wife & 6 children to lament his loss.

Lt Junius Boyle, of the U S Navy, & now 1st Lt of the Washington Navy Yard, is about to leave for Port Mahon, in the Mediterranean, as Naval Storekeeper, under the act of Congress passed at the late session dismissing the present civil incumbents & authorizing the appointment of ofcrs of the navy.

Paris [Mo] Mercury: an innocent man hung by a mob. Some years since, Mr Jas Barnes, s/o Aquilla Barnes, of Mo, was hung by a mob in Arkansas, because he was suspected of having murdered the "Wright" family in one of the counties of Arkansas. Barnes to the very last asserted his innocence, but the mob hanged him. It now appears from statements in the Van Buren [Ark] Intell, that the real murderers have been found, & are in confinement at Fayetteville, Ark. There are 3 of them, by the names of Starr & Reese. The Barnes family, 26 years ago, lived at Old Franklin, Howard Co, Mo. The father, grandfather, & uncles were men of high standing, & exemplary members of the church of Jesus Christ.

$100 reward for runaway dark mulatto Joshua, aged about 20 years
-John L Fant, Warrenton, Va

On Jul 11, Dr B L Franklin, aged about 26, was instantly killed at a mining establishment in Cherokee Co, Ga, by the machinery employed in the works

Ely Hoye, 18, resident of Cumberland, Md, was drowned on Sat while bathing in the Potomac.

Wash City Reporter: we record the death of 2 of our citizens, Mr Conway Lipscomb & Mr Thos Jefferson Fletcher, who lost their lives last Thu by drowning in the Potomac, not far from the Long Bridge. The dec'd, with C Kemble & P Bowen went fishing in the Potomac at Arlington. It seems that 3 of the party, Messrs Lipscomb, Fletcher & Bowen, made up a match to swim to the channel & back. Mr Lipscomb, possibly seized with a cramp, called out for help, & Mr Fletcher swam to his aid. Mr L so clutched him, that they both sank together. The poor sufferers have left wives & children to mourn their loss.

Died: on Jul 22, near Wash City, in his 55th year, Dr Geo A Carroll. His memory will be long cherished for those peculiar traits of character which most endear us to our fellow man.

Died: on Jul 14, in her 75th year, Mrs Sarah Bedinger, the wid/o Danl Bedinger, late of Jefferson Co, Va, dec'd.

Died: on Jul 17, at Harper's Ferry, at the residence of Mr John Nickolls, Mr Geo Dearing, in his 83rd year. Mr D was formerly a resident of Culpeper Co, Va.

Died: on Jul 20, Emily Francis, eldest d/o Robt & Lucretia Doyle, aged 3 years & 11 months.

Household & kitchen furniture at auction: on Aug 1, at the residence of Mr Robt Brown, on South Capitol st. --R W Dyer & Co, aucts

The subscriber, having been for several years successfully engaged in growing & reeling silk, would like, for the better health of his wife, & in view of an enlarged business, to remove his establishment to Loudoun or Fairfax Co, Va, or D C. I am 50 miles from Boston: wish from 150 to 400 acres to buy or exchange for the farm of 90 acres which he now occupies. –J R Barbour, Oxford, Mass

MON JUL 29, 1844
Capital Trial at Halifax: the pirtical crew of the English ship **Saladin**, were recently arrested & imprisoned at Halifax, & put on trial on Jul 18. Four of them were put on trial. On the next day the prisoners all plead guilty to the charge of the murder of Capt McKenzie. Two were tried for the murder of Capt Fielding. The jury brought in a verdict of not guilty. A similar verdict was returned after the trial of the same men for the murder of Fielding's son.

Academy of the Visitation, B V M, Gtwn, D C. Annual distribution of premiums, took place on Jul 24. Premiums distributed to:

Mary E Howle, of Wash
Mary Catherine White, of Wash
Ellen Spencer, of Phil
Mgt Brady, D C
Loretta Pickrell, of Gtwn
Virginia Dodge, of Gtwn
Eliz Hobbie, of Wash, D C
Emily Noyes, of Gtwn
Ann Howie, of Wash
Cornelia Matthews, of Lynchburg, Va
Amanda Pierce, of Newport, R I
Catharine Masi, of Wash
Eliza Bogue, of Gtwn
Eliz Cox, of Gtwn
Sophronia Pickrell, of Gtw
Inidana Meade, of Pittsburg, Va
Catharine Conly, of Wash
Mary King, of Gtwn
Mary Russel, of Phil, Pa
Mary Jane Reedy, of Charleston, S C
Ann Templeman, of Gtwn
Mgt Leonard, of Gtwn
Mary Nevins, of Gtwn
Helen Standford, of Gtwn
Matilda Semmes, of PG Co
Caroline Dent, of Belair, Ga
Sallie Gibson, of Carlilse, Pa
Dora Hernandez, St Augustine, E Fla
Cecelia Plowden, of Chaptico, St Mary's Co
Eliz Fletcher, of Lynchburg
Emma Keyworth, of Wash
Anna Templeman, of Wash
Martha Branch, of Petersburg, Va
Maria Huntt, of Wash, D C
Eliza Bogue, of Wash, D C
Mary J Russell, of Wash, D C
Mary King, of Wash, D C
Caroline Arney, of Gtwn
Maria Barry, of Gtwn
Caroline Deslonde, of New Orleans
Catharine Turnbull, of Wash, D C
Caroline Stewart, of Charleston, S C
Mary Young, of PG Co
Martha Wheatley, of Gtwn
Mary Slevin, of Phil
Edmonia Edelen, of PG Co
Maria Goldsborough, of Gtwn
Matilda Grammer, of Wash
Fanny Hobbie, of Wash
Catharine Lynch, of Cheraw, S C
Juliana Jenkins, of Balt
Julianan Cox, of N Y
Mgt Donoghue, of Gtwn
Eliz Roche, of St Mary's Co
Fanny Huntt, of Wash
Eliza Voorhees, of Wash
Joanna Middleton, Chas Co
Martha Ann Stone, of Macon, Ga
Caroline Keyworth, of Wash
George Anna White, of Wash
Martha May, of Gtwn
Mary McNerhany, of Wash, D C
Mgt Walker, of Wash
Anna Cummings, of Wash, D C
Henrietta Keller, of Wash, D C
Sarah Donoghue, of Gtwn
Mary Green, of Gtwn
Eliz Boarman, of Gtwn
Augusta Bohrer, of Gtwn
Catharine Templeman, of Gtwn
Mary Hobbie, of Wash, D C
Mary Lufborough, of Gtwn
Eliza Voorhees, of Wash
Miriam Knox, of Montg, Ga
Josephine Clarke, of St Mary's Co
Maria Bohrer, of Gtwn
Ann Scott, of Wash
Helen Gallagher, of Wash
Augusta Scott, of Wash
Sienna Gwynne, of PG Co
Harriet Bennet, of Balt

Agnes Masi, of Wash
Mary Ann Matthews, Lynchburg, Va
Mary Payne, of Gtwn
Sabina Semmes, of Gtwn
Virginia Love, of Gtwn
Fanny Knight, of Gtwn
Virginia Knight, of Gtwn
Anne Donoghue, of Gtwn
Eliz Offerd, of Gtwn
Mary Cutts, of *Fort Jesup*, La
Julia Young, of PG Co
Emily Fitzgerald, of Wash, D C
Amelia Stoops, of Gtwn
Josephine Clements, of Gtwn
Teresa Donelan, of Wash, D C
Maaria Poor, of Balt
Virginia Love, of Balt
C Lindsey, of Gtwn
Helen McLeod, of Gtwn
America Schekell, of Gtwn
Catharine May, of Gtwn
Cora Semmes, of Gtwn, D C
Virginia Brooks, of Gtwn
Maria Poor, of Balt
Julianna Jenkins, of Balt
Mary Turnbull, of Wash, D C
Eliz Fletcher, of Lynchburg, Va
Maria Barry, of Gtwn
Ellen Mary Cox, of Gtwn
Joanna Middleton, of Chas Co
Anna Kelly, of Phil
Virginia Gunnell, of Wash
Mary Ann Matthews, Lynchburg, Va
Henrietta Keller, of Wash
Mary Magee, of Charleston, S C
Sarah Donoghue, of Gtwn
Martha Ann Stone, of Macon, Ga
Mary O'Connor, of Pittsburg, Pa
Joanna Middleton, of Pittsburg, Pa
Josephine Clarke, of St Mary's Co

Saml White, of Licking Co, a candidate for the vacancy in Congress in the Columbia district, died at Delaware, Ohio, on Jul 20, where he had been lying sick since Jul 1.

By virtue of a deed of trust, dated Mar 26, 1844, public sale on Aug 5, of all the household & kitchen furniture of G W Humphries, in the house occupied by him, Pa ave & 3rd st. –D Rowland, trustee -R W Dyer & Co, aucts

House painting & glazing: orders may be left at his residence, C st, between 6th & 7th sts. –M T Parker

For rent, the house & lot at present occupied by Wm Sollers, Md ave & 12th st, square 299. Inquire of Mrs H Fitch, north end of said bldg, or to Edw Mattingly, near the Navy Yard, Wash.

1,500 acres of land for sale: private sale of land belonging to the estate of Alex'r Henderson, of Dumfries: on the waters of Pocatalico river, & principally on Flat Fork, in Jackson Co. Title is indisputable. Apply to Fenton M Henderson, at Parkersburg, Wood Co, Va, who will show the land. –Orra M Henderson, admx de bonis non with the will annexed of Alex'r Henderson, of Dumfries.

Orphans Court of Wash Co, D C. Letters of administration de bonis non on the personal estate of John Van Riswick, late of said county, dec'd.
–John Van Riswick, adm de bonis non

Explosion on Wed, on the Germantown Railroad above Nicetown, killed Henry Dourd, who was blown 10 feet into the air.

The dwlg house of Alanson Cooke, at Montreal, took fire on Jul 17, & a young dght of Mr Cooke & 2 servant girls, Melie Beaura & Louisa Robillard, were burned to death.

A printer, A M Harris, was drowned while bathing at Buffalo on Tue evening.

The N Y papers announce the death of Gabriel Furman, an old respected citizen, in his 89th year.

Henry Gould, aged 20 years, s/o J P Gould, of Albany, was drowned while bathing at that place on Saturday last.

Lafourche Gaz of Jul 6. Celeste Anastasie Lepine, d/o Mr Evariste Lepine, was drowned in Bayou Lafourche week before last by the upsetting of a skiff, in which she was attempting to cross the Bayou.

Geo W Thompson, the murderer of Catharine Hamlin, was executed at Lower Sandusky on Jul 12.

City Ordinances-Wash. 1-Act for the relief of Wm B Wilson: to pay to him $189.30, being the amount due on his contract for grading & gravelling 7th st west.

TUE JUL 30, 1844
Valuable estate at private sale. The subscriber will sell at private sale the farm on which he now resides, 1½ miles of Fred'k City, Md, it being the farm purchased by the subscriber of Edw B McPherson, known as the *Reynolds' farm*: contains 300 acres, 1 rood & 36 perches. There is a spacious brick dwlg house of modern style & finish, & all necessary out-bldgs. Adjoins the farm of Peter Sower. –John Noonan

Bloomsbury for sale, the residence of the late Mr Lansdale, at Have de Grace, Md: contains 506 acres: on the Chesapeake Bay shore for more than half a mile: house commands a beautiful view of the entire cultivated part of the place, of the Susquehanna river, Chesapeake Bay, & town. Inquire of Dr Lansdale, on the premises; to Benj G Mitchell, 50 south 4th st, Phil; to M C Ewing, Alexandria, D C; or to the undersigned. By order of the Orphans' Court. John H Price, trustee, Darlington, Harford Co, Md.

Constable's sale: by virtue of 2 writs of fieri facias, at the suit of Christopher O'Neal, against Galord Meachum. Public sale of sundry furniture & articles, property of Galord Meachum, on Aug 5. –David Little, Constable

Constable's sale: by virtue of 3 writs of fieri facias, at the suits of C W Boteler, John M Donn, & C W Boteler, jr, trading under the firm of Boteler, Donn & Co, use of Geo Mattingley: public sale of the west half of lot 2 in square 320, with improvements thereon, or the interest in said property of Mrs E B Scott, Mrs S A Brown, [late Mrs S A Stretch,] & J Brown, seized & taken in execution. Sale on Aug 26 next. –David Little, Constable

Mr Seaborn Hill, long a trader in the Creek nation of Indians, was killed near the Creek agency in Arkansas on Jul 8, in an affray with Capt J L Dawson, late Creek agent. Capt Dawson has delivered himself to the authorities of that State.

Mr Goldsborough Robinson, a merchant of Louisville, Ky, who just left Belt in the cars for Phil on Sat, protruded his head from a window, & was brought in contact with a partition of the bridge, & severely injured. He was conveyed back to the city for medical aid.

At Balt, on Sat, Mrs Cover lost her life when she fell upon the road, in attempting to get on the back part of a small wagon, when the horse ran away.

Household & kitchen furniture at auction: on Aug 2, at the residence of B H Waring, opposite the residence of Mr J L Edwards, F st, between 19th & 20th sts. –W Marshall, auct [The house is for rent immediately. Inquire of M Shanks, 18th st.]

Died: on Jul 29, Mrs Eliz Grover, consort of Mr Chas Grover, in her 24th year. Her funeral is at St Matthew's Church this afternoon at 4 o'clock. The members of the Ladies Sodality, of which the dec'd was a member, are requested at attend her funeral.

Died: yesterday, after a lingering & painful illness, Mrs Sarah Magee, w/o Patrick Magee, aged 53 years. Her funeral is this morning at 11 o'clock, from the residence of her husband on 21st st west.

For rent: 2 story frame dwlg house on I st north, near 7th st. Apply to A Waggoner, next door to the premises.

Beautiful residence for sale or exchange. I will see the house & grounds on which I now reside, or exchange them for a well improved farm in Va or Md, contiguous to the waters of the Potomac river. The house is large & constructed in the best manner. It is considered one of the handsomest residences in Wash. Terms liberal. -Saml Burche

WED JUL 31, 1844
Some time since Chas Bottsford was arrested in N Y C on a charge of having altered the numbers & passing a quantity of Treasury notes, taken from a Mr Campbell, who was killed in Arkansas. He was taken to Little Rock, tried & found guilty, & immediately sentenced to 15 years' imprisonment in the penitentiary.

Lt Henry Cadwalader, of the U S Navy, died at the residence of his mother in Phil on Sat, of bilious fever, under which he had been laboring for about a week. He was 27 years old, & a son of the late Maj Gen Cadwalader.

Obit-died: on Mar 12, Edw Rutledge Shubrick, the 5th son of the late Col Thos Shubrick, of S C. He entered the naval service of his country, into which 2 elder brothers had preceded him, on Jan 16, 1809: served during the whole of the war with England with Cmdor Rodgers. He was promoted on Feb 9, 1837: in command of the station at Charleston, S C, & on May 18, 1842, called to the command of the frig **Columbia**. He left a dear circle, a fond wife, & sweet children. The climate of Brazil aggravated a disease of the liver, which he had had some time, & soon after leaving Rio he became seriously ill. He died Mar 12th, without a sigh or groan.
+
U S frig **Columbia**, at sea, Mar 15, 1844. Ofcrs of the **Columbia** pay tribute to the memory of their late lamented Capt, Edw R Shubrick. –J R Goldsborough, Lt Com'g U S frig **Columbia**, chairman. S R Addison, Assist Surgeon, sec.

J F Green, Lt	Saml Larkin, Lt
Chas C Barton, Lt	Theo B Barrett, Lt
H L Chipman, Lt	Ed F Beale, Lt
P Kavasales, Chaplain	Sol Sharp, Surgeon
John A Bates, Purser	J Zeilin, 1st Lt Marines
M Yarnall, Prof of Math	C H Stevens
W K Bridge, Act'g Master	Horace N Crabb, Mid
Jos T Bartlett, Mid	Arch A Peterson
Arthur H Otis, Mid	John T Walker, Mid
J J Thornton, Mid	T B Shubrick, Mid
J V N Philip, Mid	John Gale, Mid
D A McDermot, Mid	N H Van Zandt, Mid
Fras G Dallas, Mid	Alfred Bailey, Mid
G H Hare, Mid	J H Nones, Mid
S J Bliss, Mid & Aid	Saml Allen, Gunner
R R Hall, Boatswain	J Ferguson, Sailmaker
C Bordman, Carpenter	W R Chisole, Mast's Mate
J M Ballard, Master's Mate	

Died: on Jul 29, Henry Slicer, infant son of A H & M A Young, aged 5 months.

$100 reward for runaway negro man John Digges, about 23 years of age. He has relations living in Wash & Gtwn, formerly belonging to the Hepburn family. -Mary Weems, Good Luck Post Ofc, PG Co, Md.

Mr Caldwell, of Ky, about 22 years of age, a passenger on board the steamer **Rhode Island**, from Stonington to N Y, leaped overboard on Sat & was lost. He had been for some time past in the Mass Insane Hospital.

Most shocking accident at Pottsville, Pa, on Jul 20. Patrick Devaney, while tending a coal-breaker, fell into it & was killed almost immediately.

On Sat, at Phil, Joshua, about 12 years, s/o Mr Jacob K Search, in Christian st, near 5th st, drowned while bathing at Christian st wharf; & about the same hour Edw Garey, 12 years of age, also drowned while bathing at Almond st wharf.

On Sat, Casper, s/o John Albert, who resides in Mary st, between Front & 2nd, was run over by a railroad car in Dock st, in Phil. He had both of his feet & his left hand crushed. He was conveyed to the hospital

On Thu last, in Milford, R I, a frightened horse ran away with a wagon in which were Mrs Bristoll, Mrs E Clark, & Miss N Clark, the d/o the latter. Mrs Bristoll was thrown from the wagon & has since died. Mrs Clark was injured, but should recover. The dght leaped from the wagon & was but little injured.

THU AUG 1, 1844
Christian Fordyce, a printer employed on the Wmsburg Democrat, was drowned on Sun while bathing at the foot of South Second st, in that village. He was from Newcastle-upon-Tyne, in the north of England, & had been in this country about 15 months.

A $100 bill was mistakenly given to a Polish Jew, Slowman Berrick, residing at the Western Hotel, Beach st, Boston, in payment for a small box of pens purchased of him by the clerk of a mercantile house in Boston. The clerk discovered a deficit in his cash account of $99. At length the money was considered lost. About 15 days afterwards, Berrick returned the identical bill paid him, having just discovered the error. –Boston Courier

Albany Evening Journal: there is no man now living in the State of N Y who rendered more valuable service, endured more privations & hardships, or shed more precious blood, in the Revolutionary war, than the venerable Maj Moses Van Campen, of Livingston Co. In Western N Y, where he has always lived, no man is more beloved or venerated. He has always been a Republican: supported Jefferson, Madison, & Monroe, & though not approving of all they did, went for Jackson & Van Buren. He is opposed to the immediate annexation of Texas.

For rent: possession at any time: 2 story brick house on N Y ave, between 9th & 10th sts. Apply to Jos Bryan.

In consideration of the advanced stage of the season I have determined to sell my entire stock of French Lawns & Balzarines at prime cost. –Geo W Adams

Mr Goldsborough Robinson, who was so severely injured at Canton, near Balt, a few days ago, is in a fair way of recovery.

Mrd: on Jul 24, in Andover, Mass, by Rev Luther Sheldon, of Easton, Mass, Mr Luther H Sheldon, Pastor elect of the Orthodox Congregational Church in Townsend, Mass, to Miss Sarah H, d/o the late Timothy Flagg, of Andover.

Mrd: on Jul 17, by Rev P Slaughter, Mr Dandridge C Williams, of Green Co, Ala, to Miss Christina Robertson, y/d/o Wm Robertson, of Petersburg, Va.

Mrd: on Jul 30, at the residence of Thos Carrico, Chas Co, Md, by Rev Mr Courtney, Mr Benj F Moxley, of Gtwn, D C, to Miss Emily Ann Carrico.

Died: on Jul 31, at his residence near Wash City, Tench Ringgold. His funeral will take be from the residence of his son-in-law, Dr Thomas, this afternoon at 4 o'clock.

Died: on Jul 24, at *Millford*, his residence, near Centreville, Fairfax Co, Va, Jas Lane Triplett, in his 74th year.

Died: on Jul 20, at her residence, *Walnut Grove*, Chas Co, Md, Miss Mary Eliza Edelen, eldest d/o the late Horatio Edelen, in her 24th year. Her memory will be cherished by that happy little family over which she presided with all the affection of a sister united with the solicitude & judgment of the matron. Her orphan sisters may indulge the hope that her pure spirit, as a guardian angel, will hover over them with its wings of love.

Died: on Tue, at Alexandria, Miss Narcissa Moore, d/o the late Alex'r Moore.

Prices reduced on Summer Hats. –E G Handy, between Gadsby's & Brown's Hotels

Was committed to the jail of Balt Co by David H McDonald, a justice of the peace, on Jul 11, Peter Frazier, charged with being a runaway, but says he was free born, & raised by Jos Ennalls, near Cambridge, Dorchester Co, Md. He is about 18 years old. Owner, if any, is to come forward, prove property, pay charges, & take him away, otherwise he will be discharged according to law. –Danl Steeves, Warden, Balt

For rent: 3 story brick house on First st, Gtwn. –N B Vinson, Gtwn

FRI AUG 2, 1844
Correspondence of the Journal of Comerce, St Louis, Mo, Jul 9, 1844. Shawnee Manual Labor School, Shawnee Nation, **Fort Leavenworth** Agency, Jun 4, 1844. The school is under the care of Rev Mr Barker, of the Baptist Missionary Society. The school at present is small.

Lot 2 in square 56 will be for sale at the Auction Room of R W Dyer & Co: all the interest of the late Dr Henry Huntt, in Wash City, in said lot. –Richd Smith, John A Smith, excs of Henry Huntt. -R W Dyer & Co, aucts

Hiram Harding, Capt of the brig **Pearl**, of Boston, lying at Phil, observed 2 boys who were bathing in the Delaware, out of their depth, struggling for life. He leaped from the deck of the vessel, & with great exertion saved both of them.

Rittenhouse Academy: Annual Exhibition of the pupils under the tuition of Messrs Chas H & Jos P Nourse, was held yesterday at Concert Hall, Pa ave. The following young gentlemen acquitted themselves with great credit in the delivery of their addresses:

Chas T Gardner	John M Hanson	Henry P Howard
Geo C Woodward	Thos Underwood	A G Carothers
Geo M Oyster	Chas A Holmes	
Johnson Hellen	Theo F Anderson	

Two old offenders caught. Jas McKean & Richd Morgan, were on Wed committed by Justice Goddard, under the charge of stealing a quantity of copper & iron from the Wash Brewery, near the Navy Yard.

A little boy, Lawrence L McLauren, was shot in the store of Messrs Avery & Hartwell, on Mon. A pistol had been connected by a string to a drawer in the counting-room desk, so that it would discharge by the drawer being opened. The little boy, who is brother-in-law to Mr Hartwell, went to the desk & opened the drawer, when the discharge took place. Eight shot entered his thigh, groin, & lower abdomen, but none are thought to be dangerous, unless the warm weather causes inflammation. –Jackson [Miss] Southron of Jul 15

The venerable Thos Parr, L L D, formerly Prof of Languages in S C College, died at Winnsborough, S C, on Jul 16, in his 80th year.

Mrd: yesterday, by Rev Mr Bean, Capt Jas Edelin, U S Marine Corps, to Miss Nancy Carr, d/o the late Overton Carr.

On Jul 16, Danl Newman, aged 16 years, s/o Danl Newman, of Centreville, Md, was on his way to the Academy, & stopped at the store of A Emory & Co, where he picked up a horse pistol. The gun went off, & the whole charge entered his body near the pit of the stomach, causing his death.

Mr Bennett Brownel, an aged & respectable citizen of Kortright, N Y, was killed on Fri last by being thrown from an unruly colt.

Catherine Hannold underwent an examination on Mon before Alderman Hoffner, of Moyamensing, Phil, on the charge of causing the death of an infant child of Albert G Bird by the mal application of laudanum to a burn, which the infant had received. The accused in the meantime was admitted to bail in the sum of $1,500.

SAT AUG 3, 1844
Meeting of the Alumni of Harvard College at Cambridge on Aug 27, oration by Hon Judge White, of Salem. –Patrick Grant, Chief Marshal

Cmder H H Cocke, of the U S East India squadron, came passenger in the ship **Phenix**, arrived at Sag Harbor Jul 28. His return is on account of ill health.

The Phil papers announce the death of Zachariah Poulson, in his 83rd year, one of the oldest & most respectable citizens of Phil. He was for a great number of years the proprietor of Poulson's Daily Advertiser, [originally Dunlap & Claypoole's paper,] which was a few years since merged in the North American.

Curious Divorce Case. Mrs Mehitabel Marsh, w/o Peter Marsh, jr, who, supposing her husband to be dead, married again, was indicted & found guilty of polygamy under the revised statutes, but was pardoned previous to the sentence. She applied for a divorce from her husband, which on Sat was granted by our Supreme Court, with alimony. –Boston Journal

A cedar shingle was put on the barn of Ensign Abel Bliss, of Wilbraham, in May, 1740, & taken off by his grandson, John Bliss, Jul 9, 1844-making it 104 years old, & yet but little rotted.

Mrd: on Jul 24, at Wynnstay, by Rev Mr Martin, Mr John Bankhead Lewis to Miss Eliz S Briggs, both of Westmoreland Co, Va. [Ky & Miss papers please copy.]

Died: on Jul 28, in Allegheny City, Pa, after 3 months of extreme suffering, Mrs Eliz Rebecca Lowry, in her 30th year, consort of Jos S Lowry & d/o Edw Holland, of this place. She was a devoted wife, a kind mother, a dutiful child, & a sincere friend.

Public sale of about 50 acres on the Marlborough road, adjoining the land of Mr F Magruder. Sale on Sep 2, 1844. –Horatio Newman

Trustee's sale of a valuable house & lot on C st: pursuant to a decree of the Circuit Court of Wash Co, D C, made in the cause wherein David E Twiggs, is cmplnt, & Henry D Hunter, John W Hunter, Alex'r Hunter & others, heirs at law of John W Hunter, dec'd, & Richd Wallach, adm of said dec'd, are dfndnts. The subscriber will sell at public auction on Sep 10, all that piece or parcel of ground in Wash City, being a part of lot 4 in square 533, with all improvements: a large & comfortable brick house & other necessary out houses. It is under lease to Edw Simmes, who now occupies the house until 1846. –Henry May, trustee -R W Dyer & Co, aucts

Orphans Court of Wash Co, D C. Letters of administration on the personal estate of Catherine Webster, late of said county, dec'd. –G M Dove, adm

MON AUG 5, 1844
On Tue last, the 4 year old d/o Mr Wm H Turner, living on the Appleton Corp, accidentally fell from a 3rd story window, a distance of 23 feet, & was found to be without material injury. –Lowell Advertiser

The 14 year old s/o Geo Hall, 25 Bowery, N Y, fell from the box of an omnibus on Tue, & the wheel passed over his neck, producing instant death.

Halifax papers: Jones, Hazelon, Johnston, & Anderson, four of the piratical crew of the English barque **Saladin**, who were recently convicted of murdering their captain & some of their messmates, were executed on Tue. Carr & Galloway, who had been acquitted on 2 indictments, have been remanded for trial on the third.

Card. Dr C Boyle has taken an ofc for the practice of his profession on Pa ave, first door east of Beers' American Hotel.

Feather beds & mattresses for sale. –Wm McL Cripps, 11 st, cabinet, chair, & sofa warehouse.

Dr Maynard has returned to town & resumed the practice of his profession.

For rent: convenient 2 story frame house on 6th st, between G & H sts. Apply to Francis Mohun.

Fire at Gtwn, on Thu, in an old frame bldg on High st, occupied by Mr Jos Boteler as a carpenter's shop. The loss to Mr Boteler, who is ill able to bear it, is estimated at $300. The bldg, some unfinished work & all the carpenter's tools were destroyed.

Danl Chase, a free colored man, was yesterday committed to jail, charged with severely wounding a colored boy about 10 years of age with a brick. Whether the wound will cause the lad's death remains to be uncertain.

In Otis, on Jul 12, Mr Aaron Salisbury was instantly killed by lightning, leaving a large family in needy circumstances.

Great Longevity. The Key West "Light of the Reef," of Jul 13, contains the following: "Died, on the Key, a few days since, a free negro woman named Tina Lewis, who had arrived at the astonishing age of 117 years. She had resided on this coast for the last 30 years, & was formerly a slave in one of the British West India Islands. Her faculties remained unimpaired to the day of her death."

We are glad to perceive that the city authorities are taking measures to abate the disgusting nuisance of smoking in the streets. Nine persons were fined each $2 & costs last week for violating the law which prohibits people from making walking chimneys of themselves in public; & 11 complaints were entered at the Police Court on Mon for the same offence. –Boston Traveller

Nat'l Blues meeting at the Armory this evening at half past 8 o'clock. By order; Michl J Sheahan, sec

$4 reward for a letter in German dropped between the Western Market & Gtwn, passing across the fields to the Observatory, to the lower bridge. Apply to Messrs Farquhar & Morgan, near the 7 Bldgs.

Nurse wanted. A middle aged white woman of good habits & kindly disposition wanted immediately. Apply at Mrs Galvin's, on C, between 3rd & $4½$ sts,

TUE AUG 6, 1844
$50 reward for lost Wallet Pocket-book, containing about $400; also promissory note drawn jointly by John R Wharton & Benj Rucker for $400 payable to the subscriber one day after, dated Nov 18, 1833. –Robt S Wharton, 13th & F sts

Valuable Shad Fishery for rent: the subscriber offers the Fishery in Pomonkey Neck, Chas Co, Md, well known as *Col Fenwick's bar*, or the *Bar Landing*: lies in the reach between the White House & Craney Island. Apply to Edmund J Plowden, near Chaptico, St Mary's Co, Md.

Hon John Holleman, formerly member of Congress from the Norfolk district of Va, & Speaker of the last House of Delegates of Va, died at his residence in Smithfield on Thu last.

Portsmouth Military & Scientific Academy: Teachers wanted-a Principal & Assist to take charge of this Institution. Apply, by post, to John Hodges, Pres of the Board, Portsmouth, Va.

Deplorable accident at Phil on Thu. Two young men, who were relatives, one named Hugh Mooney, were playing with a gun at the door of a house in 4th st, when Mooney jestingly observed to the other, "Don't shoot me, Jimmy." At that instant the trigger was thoughtlessly pulled, & a load was discharged into the head of Mooney, which killed him on the spot.

Executor's sale. Will be sold at the late residence of Chas Chinn, dec'd, near Middleburg, on Sep 31, 1844, all the property which was not divised in the will of said Chas Chinn, dec'd, consisting of several negroes, horses, cattle, hogs, sheep, & 500 to 600 bushels wheat, rye, oats, & corn; farming utensils, & household & kitchen furniture. –John G Chinn, exc, of Chas Chinn, dec'd

Foreign Item: the marriage of Lord Chas Wellesley, s/o the Duke of Wellington, & the Hon Miss Pierrepont, took place on Jul 9th at St George's Church, Hanover square. The newly married couple afterwards left town for Strathfieldsaye.

Mrd: on Jul 23 last, at Neamathla, near Tallahassee, Fla, by Rev Mr Yeager, Thos H Hagner to Catharine Jane, 2nd d/o John G Gamble.

Died: on Sat last, after a few hours' illness, in Wash City, Jane N, w/o Saml S Whiting, & y/d/o the late Guy Atkinson, of Alexandria, D C.

Died: on Aug 4, at the Wash Arsenal, Diaud Kearny, infant d/o Maj Symington.

WED AUG 7, 1844
The hopes which were entertained for the recovery of Mr Goldsborough Robinson, of Ky, who was injured in the railroad cars near Balt a few days ago, have been dissipated by his death, which took place on Mon.

Mrd: on Aug 6, at Gtwn, by Rev Mr Flanagan, Mr Bladen Forrest, of Wash, to Miss Mary Helen Keith, d/o Jas Keith, of the former place.

Died: on Aug 4, of bilious fever, John Higgins, bricklayer & plasterer, a native of Ireland, in his 58th year. The dec'd was favorably known to many ot the citizens of Carlisle, Pa, among whom he formerly resided.

Dissolution of the partnership by mutual consent. –C Alexander, T Barnard
The business will hereafter be conducted by Columbus Alexander at the old stand opposite the west front of the Navy Dept.

Desirable tract of land at auction: about 40 acres, near the Anacostia Bridge, owned by Mr Jas G Coombe. -R W Dyer & Co, aucts

Household & kitchen furniture at auction: on Aug 9, at the residence of the late Tully R Wise, G & 22nd sts, by order of the Orphans Court of Wash Co, D C. –R W Dyer & Co, aucts

We learn that the child wounded by Danl Chase, & for which he was committed to prison last Sun, is in the way of recovery. This we state on the authority of the attending physician, Dr Eliot.

THU AUG 8, 1844
Olney Boarding School for Girls is now in successful operation in Montg Co, Md, 2 miles from Brookville. Inquire of Dr C Farquhar, Sandy Spring Post Ofc, Montg Co, Md. –C Farquhar, Mary W Farquhar [Refer to Benj Hallowell, whose residence is immediately contiguous to the school, who will deliver some familiar lectures to the scholars during spring & fall, on Chemistry, Nat'l Philosophy, & Astronomy. Dr Chas Farquhar, who has opened a Boarding School for Girls at Olney, Md, was associated with me in teaching Fair Hill Boarding School in Md, West town Boarding School in Pa, & as joint partner in the commencement of the Alexandria Boarding school; we have pursued our studies together for about 10 years. His sister, too, who is associated with him, is an able & experienced teacher.
–Benj Hallowell, Rockland, Md]

For rent: fine large 3 story brick house lately occupied by Robt Brown, on South A st, fronting the Capitol square. Apply to Mr Isaac H Wailes, at the Capitol. The key will be found at Mrs Owner's, opposite the north gate of the Capitol. –Robt Brown

For sale: that beautiful place, the residence of the late Jos W Hand, on the turnpike running from 7th st. The house is new. –Jno A Smith

Valuable property at public auction: on Aug 13, on the premises, the house & lot on 12th st, between G & H, now occupied by Mr John Phillips, under rent of $204. –R W Dyer & Co, aucts

On Fri last Mr Augustus C Fenno, of Bangor, Maine, was accidentally shot dead by his intimate & personal friend, Mr Wm Neal. They were out with another person firing at a mark. One of the party fired while Mr Neal took aim, & as soon as the first fired Mr Fenno ran towards the mark, Mr Neal at the same time firing. The ball passed directly through his neck. He fell in the presence of his wife, who was at her house directly on the opposite bank of the stream.

Capt Jos David observed a rainbow on Jul 25, 1844, at about 1 o'clock at night, off *Sharp's Island*, Chesapeake Bay. [Lunar rainbows are like those produced by the sun.] -Clipper

Rev Mr Dyer, of the Episcopal Church, was accidentally drowned at the Chasm of the Ausable, near Keeseville, N Y, on Aug 1. He went with a small party to see the falls. A young lady became dizzy & fell, but was seized by a man in the party. Mr Dyer, in an attempt to save the lady, lost his balance, fell into the rapid current, & was immediately swept out of sight.

Obit-died: on Aug 2, at *Downingville*, his late residence, in Caroline Co, Va, Rufus Downing, in his 61st year. He was a native of the State of Connecticut, from whence he emigrated to Va about 37 years ago. He resided for 2 or 3 years in the family of John Pendleton, late Clerk of the Superior & County Courts of Caroline. During our last war with Great Britain he was called into service from this county, acting as Cornet in the troop of cavalry then commanded by Capt Armstead Hoomes. After his return he intermarried with a d/o Capt Wm Sale, one of our wealthiest farmers, from which time he has engaged in the pursuit of agriculture. He amassed quite a large fortune. He has left a wife & 4 children, who will most sensibly fell their loss. Bowling Green, Aug 6, 1844

Mrd: on Jul 12, at Trinity Church, Newport, R I, by Rev Mr Watson, J G Martin, Lt 1st Artl, to Marianne Baker, d/o the late Geo Read, jr, of Newcastle, Delaware.

Died: on Aug 2, at his residence, in Eastville, Northampton Co, Va, Nathl J Winder, in his 50th year.

Sale of store fixtures, at the store formerly occupied by Mr McKean: a confectionary establishment. –Holmead & Wright, auctioneers

Mr John Emerich has at his house on 6th st, just above Gadsby's Hotel, 2 finely furnished rooms, which he would desire to be occupied by unmarried gentlemen, with or without board.

For rent: a family with no children, would rent 2 rooms of their dwlg to persons similarly situated, or to a single gentleman. Apply to Mr Lucas, at the Navy Dept.

Six & a quarter cents reward: for runaway indentured apprentice, John Wilson Rawlings. The reward will be paid for his recovery. –Chas Schussler

FRI AUG 9, 1844
The Nantucket Inquirer details a sad misfortune which happened on Sat to 2 dghts of Capt Geo Rule, one aged 14 & the other 12. They both were attacked by a big dog & are in critical condition.

Farm for sale: 500 acres, about 19 miles out of Balt, on the Reistertown road. Apply to Chas S Wallach, Atty at Law.

At Elizabethtown last evening, Mrs Jemima Chandler, an aged widow lady of some 70 years, was seized with apoplexy at the residence of her son-in-law, Mr Saml Whitehead, of whose family she was a member, & expired almost instantly. Her dght, Mrs Whitehead, shocked by the spectacle, complained of a headache, & fell dead in an instant. They leave a large circle of bereaved children & friends. –Newark Daily Adv of Sat.

Bay State Democrat: Hon Amasa Stetson, of Dorchester, Mass, died at his residence on Fri. He died in his 75th year, leaving a widow to mourn his loss, but no children.

Mrd: on Aug 7, in Wash City, by Rev Mr Moore, Mr Theodore Barnard to Miss Matilda R Berry, all of Wash City.

Died: on Aug 8, after a protracted illness, Miss Penelope Barnes Alexander. Her funeral is from the residence of her relation Mrs Swann, on 5th st, this day, at 11 a m.

Turtle Soup, at the Post Ofc House, 7th & E sts, this morning at 11 o'clock. Three extra fine Green Turtles having just been received. -P A DeSaules

Household & kitchen furniture at auction: on Aug 21, at the hotel now kept by Mr J Boulanger, on Pa ave south side, between 4½ & 6th sts. -R W Dyer & Co, aucts

Foreign Intell: John Gliddon, U S Consul at Alexandria, Egypt, died at Malta on Jul 3. He breathed his last at the residence of Wm Eynaud, in Malta. The suffering invalid visited the baths of Lucca, in Italy, but with no effect. A large procession, headed by W W Andrews, U C Consul at Malta, followed his remains to the burying ground at Florian. This intelligence will be received with deep anguish by his son Geo R Gliddon, now in Phil, necessarily absent from his lamented parent, but attached to him with a filial affection. –Boston Transcript

SAT AUG 10, 1844
Phil Ledger: a monument is about to be constructed in Phil, to be erected at Laurel Hill over the remains of Cmdor Isaac Hull. It will be of marble, & placed on a granite base, modeled after the plan of the tomb of Scipio at Rome.

N Y papers: John O Sargent, formerly of the Courier & Enquirer, & Epes Sargent, Brothers, & both gentlemen of fine talents, are connected with the editorial dept of the N Y Republic.

Garallan Farm for sale: for sale the Garallan estate in Loudoun Co, Va, a part of that tract of land upon the Potomac river well known as *Douglas' Bottoms*: contains 417 acres: 6 miles of Point of Rocks: dwlg house is now occupied by the tenant & family, & but lately erected. –Robt W Gray, Asher W Gray, excs of Jno Gray, dec'd

$5 reward for return of strayed Cows. –John Foy, D st, between 9th & 10th sts

Thos Reid will reopen his School House on Aug 19: located on 7th st, between L & M sts.

Mrd: on Jul 30, at St Paul's Church, Sharpsburg, Md, by Rev Mr Balch, Rector of St Bartholomew's, N Y, Rev Freeman Clarkson, Rector of St Anna's Church, Fishkill Landing, N Y, to Catharine, eldest d/o L P W Balch, of Md.

Mrd: on Aug 4, at St Matthew's Church, by Rev H Myers, Mr Jos M Peirce to Miss Eliz Jones.

Mrd: on Aug 6, by Rev H Myers, Mr Michl Kelly to Miss Bridget Fitzgerald.

Mrd: on Aug 8, by Rev H Myers, Mr Richd Grafton Elliot to Miss Mary Eliz Clements.

Died: on Thu, in Gtwn, Mrs Mary M Bohrer, at the advanced age of 97 years. She was the mother of Dr B S Bohrer, & distinguished throughout the community in which she lived for some 3/4th of a century, for her piety & Christian virtues.

Died: on Wed last, in Wash City, after a few days illness, Geo S Wharton, of Phil, in his 32nd year. His remains were conveyed to Phil, accompanied by his mother & brother, who had arrived here only in time to receive his last breath & close his eyes.

Died: on Aug 6, in N Y, after a short & severe illness, aged 64 years, Cornelia Paerson, wid/o the late Stephen Van Rensselaer, of Albany.

Died: on Aug 6, afer a few hours' illness, Andrew, y/s/o Wm & Emily Dalton, aged 1 year & 4 months.

MON AUG 12, 1844
On Sat last Edw P Clark, aged 10 years & 5 months, s/o the late Mr Pres Clark, was with several young boys bathing at Little river, where it enters the Connecticut river, & got beyond his depth & immediately sunk, & was not seen to rise again.

Mr Edw T Shurts, age 27, of Clinton township, Hunterdon Co, N J, met a most dreadful death on Fri last by accidentally falling into a burning limekiln.

Waterville, N Y: on Aug 2 John Gilbert, age 21 years, went out on the factory pond in a small boat for pleasure, rocked it over, & fell into the water. He drowned.

Died: on May 12, at sea, Jos Cassin Henry, in his 24th year, & y/s/o Capt H Henry, commanding U S ship **Plymouth**, now in the Mediterranean. Mr Henry was interred on May 18 at Port Mahon.

Died: Aug 11, at *Rose Cottage*, the residence of his grandfather, Francis B, s/o Francis Y & Anne E Naylor, aged 18 months & 17 days. His funeral is this morning at 10 o'clock.

Washington Reporter: Robt Nesbit, age 27, of Canton township, in that county, received a wound on Jul 17 which caused his death on Jul 27. He moved back from a bumble-bee's nest, upon the point of a scythe-blade, severing the main artery.

1-A child of Mr H Jonffroy, resident in Boston, fell out a window on Sat, & was instantly killed by the violence with which it struck the ground. 2-A child about 2 years old, s/o Mr Groves, fell from the 3rd story windown of a house in Wilmington, Dela, on Fri, & died the next day.

Valuable land will be offered at public auction, on Oct 1, the Farm on which Morduit Young, lately resided. It contains about 300 acres; land is east of the Capitol. Inquire of Fielder Magruder, near Bladensburg; or Jas C Hollady, next Nottingham.

House & lot in Carroll's Row at auction: on Sep 25, part of lot 12 in square 729, on the corner of A south & 1st st east. –B C Weightman, surviving, trustee –R W Dyer & Co, aucts

Orphans Court of Wash Co, D C. On the application of Jacob Bigelow for letters of administration on the personal estate of Francis Cazeau, dec'd, who resided at one time in the Province of Lower Canada, & afterwards, it is said, in France, where he died: it is by this Court, ordered that letters of administration be granted to Jacob Bigelow as prayed. –Nathl Pope Causin -Ed N Roach, Reg/o wills

TUE AUG 13, 1844
We, the undersigned cmte, acting in behalf of the passengers on board the steamer **Phenix**, most cordially unite in tendering to Capt Jas Guy our most sincere & heartfelt thanks of his kind & gentlemanly treatment during our excursion of pleasure down the Potomac on Aug 9. –John Brown, Lewis Beeler, & A K Arnold

Hannah More Female Academy: will be opened in Sep next, under the superintendence of Mrs Lyon, who relinquished a school in Paris, Ky, to enter upon a larger field of labor & usefulness. Trustees: Rt Rev Bishop Whittingham, Balt; Washington Van Bibber, Westminster; Franklin Anderson, Reistertown; Rev Chas C Austin, Sec of the Board, Owing's Mills, Balt Co.

Pensacola, Aug 3, 1844. The French brig of war **Mercure** arrived here on Sun last from a cruise in the Gulf. The following vessels are now lying in this bay, viz:
French corvette **La Brillants**, Cmdor Regnard
French brig of war **Mercure**.
U S ship **Vandalia**, Cmder John S Chauncey
U S brig **Lawrence**, Cmder Gardner
U S steamer **Union**, Lt H H Bell
U S steamer **Gen Taylor**, Lt E Farrand
On Mon last was celebrated in our harbor the anniversary of the revolution les trios jours.

Tavern Stand on High st at public auction: Trustee's sale of real estate in Gtwn: in pursuant of a decree of the Circuit Court of Wash Co, D C. Large 3 story tavern on Beall st, lying west of the large stable belonging to the tavern premises of the late Geo Holzman, dec'd. –John Marbury, trustee -Edw S Wright, auctioneer

$700 reward for the following slaves who ranaway, on Aug 4, from the subscriber, living in Chas Co, Md, near Pomonkey Post Ofc: Lewis Brawner, about 35. Saml Pa_ne, about 25. Chas Mastin, about 30. Henry Chapman, about 24. Also, Grandison, about 13 years of age. Vincent, about 20, & his brother Wm, about 15 or 16. One other, Joe, about 20. –Chas F Dement, exc of Geo Dement, dec'd

Hon Henry A Muhlenberg, candidate for the Democratic party in Pa for ofc of Govn'r, died of apoplexy at his residence in Reading on Sun. He had served in Congress & as Minister to Austria, & was a distinguished member of his party in Pa. [Aug 16th newspaper: Mr Muhlenberg was born at Lancaster in 1782, & was 62 years of age. His father died at the age of 62.]

Died: on Aug 8, at N Y, J G Coster, in his 82nd year.

Died: on Aug 12, in Wash City, Harry Luzenberg, infant s/o Worthington G & Virginia Snethen.

Information wanted of Thos Champion, a resident of Phil for some time, & late of Haddonfield, N J, who left his residence on Jun 9 last, to get some medicine, & has not since been heard of. He is about 39 years of age, stoutly built, of light complexion, with brown hair & eyes, & is by trade a smith machinist. Any information addressed to Rachel Champion, c/o Mr J M Moore, 470 south Front st, Phil, will be thankfully received. –U S Gaz

WED AUG 14, 1844
St Louis Republican of Aug 2: announces the death of D C M Parsons, one of the candidates for Congress upon the Genr'l Ticket nominated by the Locofocos-[again in defiance of the law.] [No date-current item.]

The w/o Mr Jas Cooper, formerly of N Y, was killed by lightning at Bunker Hill, Ill, on Jul 31st.

On Mon last a carpenter's shop & stable belonging to Mr D W Oyster, of Gtwn, was willfully burnt down. A negro servant of Mr Oyster has been arrested under suspicion of committing this offence.

Three men, Henry Fox, Jonathan Nixon, & John Rickett, were buried in Miln & Spencer's mines at Pottsville, on Fri, 300 feet below the surface. They were found in about 300 feet of water. [Aug 28 newspaper: the bodies of Henry Fox, Jonathan Nixon, & John Rickets, were recoved on Sat last.]

It is said that a fortune of $3,000,000 has been left by J G Coster, who died on Thu. He was known almost throughout the civilized world as one of the oldest, most enterprising, & most successful merchants N Y ever possessed. He was born in Germany, but had been a resident of N Y C over half a century. –N Y Republic

The Literary Remains of the late Willis Gaylord Clark, edited by his twin-brother, Lewis Gaylord Clark, of the Knickerbocker Magazine, have just been published, by the publishers, Messrs Burgess, Stringer & Co.

A negro man found on the farm of Mr Allen last week a live terrapin, with the initials "E W" 1794, engraved on his belly. From the its appearance he must have been the same size at the above date that he is now. –Lexington [Ky] Observer

Died: on Aug 10, after a short but severe illness, Franklin Beall, y/s/o the late Benj B Myers, of Wash, aged 11 years.

Died: on Aug 10, in Wash City, Georgianna, infant d/o Jerome Richd & Jane Wroe.

Groceries, hardware, crockery, & household & kitchen furniture at auction: on Aug 16, by deed of trust from G W Hinton, duly executed: at the store of G W Hinton, corner of 4½ st & Md ave. -Robt W Dyer, trustee -R W Dyer & Co, aucts

Norman S Fox, 19, a clerk in the auction store of Jos Sampson & Co, died last evening in N Y C with lockjaw. Last Tues he went to bathe in Rabineau's bath, at the Battery, & in diving struck his nose against the bottom. The blow was severe, but the pain passed away. Rigidity of the jaws increased on Wed & he died in convulsions, retaining his consciousness to the last. –N Y Evening Post

On Aug 2, Colin Brooke, aged 7 years & 7 days, only child of Nicholas & Mary Ann Brooke, of Montg Co, Md, was thrown from an ox cart, by it being upset. The cart fell upon his head, fracturing it dreadfully that he lived only about 30 minutes.

Two young ladies drowned, on Wed last, dghts of Mr Jonah Holly, living in the eastern part of this town, & another young lady, went to Cornesus Lake to bathe. The sisters went into the water & suddenly stepped into a bank nearly 30 feet deep. Their names were Sarah, 22, & Frances, 18. –Genesco Republican

A lad about 15 years of age, Hoskins, while climbing over a fence in pursuit of game, nears Simsburg, Conn, on Thu, was instantly killed by the accidental discharge of his gun, the contents of which were lodged in his side.

Three boys drowned at Hartford on Fri last while bathing in the Connecticut river. They were, Thos Jefferson, aged 10 years, Fred'k S, aged 9 years, sons of T S Parker, & Alfred, age 10 years, s/o S Rogers.

Orphans Court of Wash Co, D C. Letters of administration on the personal estate of Jane C Clagett, late of said county, dec'd. –Rd Dement, adm

Orphans Court of Wash Co, D C. Letters of administration on the personal estate of John Higgins, late of said county, dec'd. –Sarah Higgins, excx

For sale: desirable farm, within 5 miles of the Centre market, in PG Co, Md, one mile beyond Rock Creek Church: comfortable dwlg house & other necessary bldgs. Inquire on the premises of Fielder Magruder.

Capitol Hill Female Seminary: Miss McCormick & Miss Whitwell will be open for scholars on the first Mon in Sep next: in the house recently occupied by the late Comptroller, Maj J N Barker, corner of N J ave & south B st. References:

Rev H H Bean	Jas Adams	John Underwood
John P Ingle	Capt J L C Hardy	John S Meehan

Wash Corp: 1-Cmte on Claims: asking to be discharged from the further consideration of the ptn of Pompey Tenney: agreed to. 2-Resolved, that Isaac Beers have leave to take copies of certain papers now in the possession of this Board, in reference to a fine against him.

Marshal's sale: in virtue of 3 writs of fieri facias, on Sep 10: lots T & U, in subdivision of lots N thru U, of the original lots numbered 1, 2, 3, 4, & 10 & 11, in square 452, in Wash City. Lots T & U front on Mass ave, on which there is a new 3 story dwlg house. Seized & levied upon as the property of Jas B Phillips, & sold to satisfy judicials 53 to Mar term, 1844, in favor of Warren Waugh; also judicials 190 & 191 to Mar term, 1844, in favor of the Bank of Metropolis & against said Jas B Phillips. –Alex'r Hunter, Marshal District of Columbia

Notice: the co-partnership existing under the firm of Jas B Holmead & Richd Wright is this day dissolved. The auction & commission business will still be carried on at the old stand, 4½ & Pa ave by the subscriber. –Jas B Holmead

THU AUG 15, 1844
On Fri a sailboat was capsized in Boston harbor, & a colored man, John Roberts, was drowned. His companion, Asa Jackson, was saved by a boat from the vessel **Gen Lincoln**, which was passing at the time.

Mrd: on Aug 13, by Rev Henry Myers, Mr John McMahon to Miss Bridget McCue, both of Wash City.

Phil: the steamboat **Portsmouth**, Capt Jas Devoe, on Tue, for Cape May, exploded one of her boilers, & Mr Thos Massey, of Wilmington, & Edw Stevens-2nd engineer, of the boat, died afterwards. [Aug 16th newspaper: Mr Massey, was an elderly man, & a passenger. Mr Stevens in his agony sprang into the river, from which he was taken by some persons in a small boat. Isaac Ames, 1st engineer & Gilbert Jackson, the colored cook, were much injured.

FRI AUG 16, 1844
Mrs Fleischman's Seminary for Young Ladies: on E st, between 6th & 7th sts, recommences on the first Mon of Sep next.

Groceries: the subscriber, having opened a store at 6th & H sts. –J Thos Radcliff

Simeon Dutcher, an aged & respectable citizen of Gaines, Orleans Co, N Y, announces in a letter to the Orleans Republican that he shall vote in favor of Clay & against Polk solely on the Texas question.

Col Brodhead, the Historical Agent of the State of N Y, returned on Mon in the ship **Queen of the West**, from Liverpool. He has brought a large number of manscripts copied from the English archives, & another large parcel of French documents are on board the Havre packet daily expected.

The U S schnr **Flirt**, Lt Commanding John A Davis, arrived at Charleston on Sun lat, from Galveston, via Key West. Her ofcrs report that Gen Wm S Murphy, late Charge d'Affaires of the U S at Texas, died at Galveston on Jul 17 of yellow fever, & was buried with all the honors due his station. Just after the **Flirt** anchored in Charleston harbor, acting Lt Hamilton F Porter, one of her ofcrs, died of yellow fever. He was a s/o the late Cmdor Porter. His remains were deposited in the cemetery of St Philip's Church with appropriate honors.

Mr Jas Patterson, of Otisco, Conn, was accidentally killed when he was checking to see if a gun was loaded. The percussion lock slipped.

Alvin Claflin, while blasting at his stone quarry, on Fri, in Framingham, Mass, was so mutilated by an explosion that he lived but 30 minutes after being discovered. He has lain 2 hours with his clothes consuming upon him.

Fatal affray at Jackson, La, on Aug 4, between T B Scott & J C Walker. Walker was instantly killed. Mr Scott is a member elect to the Convention, & Mr Walker a lawyer of some considerable ability. They were both from the parish of Madison.

Died: on Aug 15, after a lingering & painful illness, Lazaro Benvenedo, in his 39th year. His funeral will take place today at 3 o'clock, from his late residence on I st north, near 22nd st.

Capt John Petit, of the schnr **William A Turner**, who took Gen Sentmanat & his men from New Orleans to Tabasco on his ill-fated expedition, & who was made prisoner, together with the crew of his vessel, succeeded in effecting his escape on Jul 3 last, & came passenger in the brig **St Lawrence**, which arrived at N Y on Tue.

Just as the Locofoco procession was leaving Dayton, Ohio, on Thu last, for Liberty, 3 members of the gun squad of the Dayton Artl were seriously injured by a premature discharge of the cannon. Their names are Messrs Smith, Tucker, & Davis. Mr Smith's recovery is extremely doubtful.

The Grand Jury have rejected the bill of indictment against Mr Dyde & Lt D'Arcy, of the 89th Regt, for the alleged murder of Champeau, at the late election. The preferring the indictment was an act of party malice, got up by a few notorious partisans of the ex-Ministry, without a shadow of foundation, as the rejection of it by the Grand Jury fully proves. –Montreal Courier

For rent: 2 new two story frame dwlgs, with basements & garrets completed, each one containing 9 rooms. Apply at 18th & K st, to John C Roemmele.

For rent: large store-room at C & 10th sts. Apply to Edwin Green, 11th st & Pa ave.

SAT AUG 17, 1844
Serious occurrence on board the U S frig **Potomac**, lying at her anchorage off the Navy Yard, Phil, on Tue. One of the seamen returned from liberty intoxicated & Midshipman Bohrer was directed to confine him in the brig. The mutinous sailor knocked Bohrer backwards, fracturing his head when it came in contact with a gun. Mr Bohrer has been removed to the Naval Hospital on the Schuylkill. He is not considered mortally hurt, though the injury may prove fatal. –Phil Gaz

Plattsburg [N Y] Republican of Sat announces the death of Hon Josiah Fisk, of Keeseville, who expired at his residence on Sat, after a short but painful illness.

Hon Wm Brent, jr, Charge to Buenos Ayres, accompanied by his lady & son, sailed from N Y on Tue in the ship **Gaston**, for Rio Janeiro.

A beautiful sword, with elegant scabbard, & silver mountings, has been presented, on behalf of the citizens of Phil, to Capt John Hill, of the City Guards, for his patriotic services in sustaining the supremacy of the laws during the riots in the District of Southwark.

For rent: 3 story brick house on F st, between 13th & 14th sts, opposite the residence of the Hon John Quincy Adams. The key can be had at the bookstore next door, & application to Mr G Ennis, on F st, between 12th & 13th sts, or to the subscriber, at his residence on Capitol Hill, opposite Duff Green's row. –F H Gerdes

By writ of fieri facias, at the suit of Thos T Barnes against Rosa O'Brian: sale of the interest of Rosa O'Brian in sundry articles, some furniture, old carpeting, & stands. Sale on Aug 24, in front of the Centre Market House. –H R Maryman, constable

For rent: dwlg house on I st, near 7th. Keys left at R D Spencer's shoe store, 7th st, between H & I sts.

Tribute of respect: meeting of the ofcrs serving with 6 companies of the 7th Regt of U S Infty, encamped at Pass Christian, Miss, assembled on receiving intelligence of the death of Brevet Capt W K Hanson, U S Army. [1st Lt & Brevet Capt Weightman K Hanson.] Resolutions be transmitted to the father & wife of Brevet Capt Hanson. Signed:

E S Hawkins, Capt 7th Inf
P H Craig, Surgeon U S Army
W Seawell, Brevet Maj 7th Inf
S W Moore, Capt 7th Inf
T H Holmes, Capt 7th Inf
R C Gatlin, Adj 7th Inf

G R Paul, 1st Lt 7th Inf
F Britton, 1st Lt 7th Inf
H Little, 2nd Lt 7th Inf
C H Humber, 2nd Lt 7th Inf
F N Page, 2nd Lt 7th Inf

Mrd: on Jul 31, at Whitesborough, Oneida Co, N Y, by Rev President North, Prof Edw North, of Hamilton College, to Miss Mary Frances, only d/o Hon S Newton Dexter, of the former place.

Mrd: on Aug 15, by Rev Jas Laurie, Jos A Deeble to Eliz G, y/d/o the late Fred'k Tschiffely, all of Wash City.

Mrd: on Aug 6, near Aldie, Loudoun Co, Va, by Rev Mr Masi, Mr Wm I Tabler, of Wash, to Miss Catharine E King.

Died: on Aug 15, Mr Jas Gettys, in his 53rd year. He was long a respectable inhabitant of Gtwn, & was entensively known in this District & elsewhere as one of the Fathers of the benevolent association denominated "The Independent Order of Odd Fellows," of which he was the second Grand Sire, having succeeded in that ofc the Founder of the Order in this country. His funeral is on Sun, at 2 o'clock, at the Odd Fellow's Hall, in Wash City.

Died: on Aug 16, Mrs Eliz Keller, wid/o the late Fred'k Keller, of Wash City, in her 44th year, after a protracted illness of pulmonary disease, leaving 3 interesting children & many friends to lament her loss. Her funeral will take place at 4 o'clock on Aug 18, from the residence of Capt Thos Williams, on E st.

Died: on Aug 15, aged 22, Louisa Jane, d/o Wm G & Sophia Ridgely. Her funeral is from the residence of her father, Cox's row, Gtwn, this afternoon, at 4 o'clock.

Died: on Aug 6, at East Hartford, Conn, Dr Timothy Hall, aged 87. His death was occasioned by being thrown from his wagon. Dr Hall was a Surgeon in the Revolutionary Army, & was beloved & esteemed by all who knew him.

Died: on Aug 2, at his residence in Berkeley Co, Va, after an illness of 6 weeks, Jacob Wever, aged 86 years, 4 months & 13 days. Mr Wever was a native of Cumberland Co, Pa, & served during his youth as a soldier & ofcr in the war of the Revolution.

Died:Jul 17, at his residence at the Cherokee Mission, in the Cherokee nation west, Jesse Bushyhead, Chief Justice of the Supreme Court of the Cherokees. He was attacked with the fever of that climate. He was a correct interpreter & translator, & at his demise he was entensively engaged in translating English into Cherokee. -Chilhowee

Desirable farm at auction: on Sep 10, on the premises, near Bladensburg, adjoining the farms of Geo A Digges & Thos Burch, about 6 miles from the Centre Market-house, Wash. This farm contains about 150 acres, & has a very convenient frame bldg containing 7 rooms, well finished. —Washington Lewis

MON AUG 19, 1844

Died, lately, at Gairlock, Ross-shire, the celebrated Gaelic bard, Alasdair Buidhe Macre Iobhair, at the advanced age of 84. He was poet to the lairds of Gairloch, from whom he had a pension. Some years ago, when a miserly gentleman observed that bards were extinct, No, said Alasdair, but those who rewarded them are gone. —Edinburgh Witness

On Tue Wm Williamson was shutting up Lewis' lead factory, Phil, in which he was employed, when he was struck by one of the levers, & crushed to death.

Capitol Hill Select Classical School: [Number limited.] S M Parsons, from N Y, a graduate of Yale College, assisted by a teacher of Modern Languages, will open on the first Mon in Sep. The school room [the Hall of the Columbia Engine House] is a few rods south of the Capitol.

N Y Commercial Advertiser: announce the death of Wm L Stone, Editor in chief of that paper, which took place, after a prolonged illness, at Saratoga, on Thu last. [Aug 20th newspaper: Col Stone was in his 53rd year; a native of Connecticut, & s/o Rev Wm Stone, who removed nearly 40 years ago to Butternutts, Otsego Co, &from then to Redfield, Oneida Co. He left Redfield about 1809, & footed it to Coopertown, where he obtained a situation with Col John H Prentice, then & now editor of a paper in that village. At the close of the war, he removed to Hudson, where he conducted a paper for 3 years, when he came to this city as editor of the Daily Advertiser. From Albany Col Stone removed to Hartford, Conn, where he edited the Connecticut Mirror, until 1822; connected with Mr Francis Hall, in the N Y Commercial Advertiser. Col Stone married a sister of Pres Wayland, of Brown Univ, who, with one son, survives the loss of a devoted husband & father.]

Mr H B Robertson, the assistant market-master, on Sat last took from a colored man a close-bodied blue cloth coat, which the negro was trying to sell for $5. Any person who has lost such a coat, let him apply at the Watch-house to Capt Goddard.

The Ministerium, or New School, 10th st, between the Baptist Church & Medical College, will admit pupils about Sep 1. –D McCurdy

Mrs Maria Hotchkiss was accidentally drowned a day or two ago, on her way to Albany.

Brookeville Academy, [Md] has induced its Principal, Mr E J Hall, to resume the occupancy of the Boarding House attached thereto. Trustees:
A B Davis, Pres	Remus Riggs	Orlando Hutton
Thos McCormick, Sec	Wm B Magruder	
Thos I Bowie	Basil B Pleasants	

Miss Celia Brooks, aged 20 years, y/d/o Mr Aaron Brooks, of Prospect, Mass, lost her life by leaping from a wagon on Thu last.

Jas Chambers, residing on Butler st, Alleghany city, was seriously, if not fatally, injured at the raising of a Hickory Pole near his residence on Sat. One of his legs was broken & his sides & ribs were crushed.

Died: on Aug 12, at the family residence, in Balt Co, Md, Edw W Wyse.

TUE AUG 20, 1844
The selectmen of Portsmouth, N H, were recently called upon to visit Mr Thos Gammon, a fisherman of about 50 years, who has within a few weeks been suffering under insanity, & had become so wild as to require other care than that of his sister, a few years older, whith whom he has lived in the most parsimonious manner for 20 or 30 years. It was deemed necessary to move him to the Almshouse. Inquiry was made if he had any money, & she led them to the cellar where boxes of silver were buried: about $15,000 in coins that had turned black from exposure . The unfortunate man has been sent to the insane asylum at Concord. -Portsmouth Journal

Vincent Clark, a man deeply implicated in the extensive counterfeiting operations in New Orleans, died in the work-house in New Orleans on Aug 5, after a brief illness.

Stephen Bates, a surviving veteran of the Revolution, residing near Ackron, Ohio, has a family of children & grandchildren amounting in number to 32, who are all zealous, devoted Whigs.

Four men, Rhea, Mitchell, White & Jones, were tried & condemned before Chief Justice Lynch, on Jul 16, at South Sulphur, Texas, for killing 2 men & a boy of the Delaware tribe of friendly Indians. They were executed under said sentence the next day. –Arkansas Intelligencer

Mr Jas Hardin, a planter of Marengo Co, Ala, was killed a few days since by his overseer, Alex'r Deas. The murderer fled & was pursued about 5 miles, when he was caught with dogs, placed in irons, & lodged in the jail at Linden. Deas said he committed the deed in self-defence.

Last week a laborer on the Reading railroad, Patrick Conway, was thrown from a cart, & the train passed over his body. He was taken to the hospital, where he died in about 15 minutes. He was about 23 years of age & a single man.

Died: on Aug 18, Anne Sophia, infant d/o Patrick & Martha McKenna, aged 10 months. Her funeral is this afternoon, at 3 o'clock.

By Divine permission, a Camp Meeting will be held, under the direction of the Meth Prot Church, on the land adjoining the farm of Mr John Adams, near the Old Courthouse, Fairfax Co, Va, to commence on Aug 23. –N Semen, Superintendent Potomac Circuit
+
Notice: the undersigned, having obtained control of the above land, cautions all it may concern not to locate or erect any cart, wagon, tent, booth , or other fixture on any of the said lands for the sale of any article whatsoever. Timber not to be cut without special permission. –Wm C Lipscomb, Fairfax Co, Va

Strayed or stolen on Aug 15, a Buffalo Cow. $5 reward for return of the Cow to me on 6th st, between E & F sts, Wash. –Philip Ennis

Normal School. Mr & Mrs Michard's School for Young Ladies, 19th st, between G & F sts, will re-open on the first Mon of Sep.

By decree of the High Court of Chancery of Md, the subscribers will offer at public sale, on Sep 24, the plantation known as *Collington*, situated in the *Forest of PG Co*, of which the late Dr John Wootton, of Montg Co, died seized: contains about 420 acres . Purchase money payable to the widow & legal reps of John Wootton, dec'd. -Wm t Wootton, Wm D Clagett, Saml Peach, Thos Duckett, Robt Bowie

West Street Academy, Gtwn, D C, will be re-opened on Sep 2. Apply to Wm J Nevius, Beall st, Gtwn.

WED AUG 21, 1844

For rent: 2 story frame house on Capitol Hill adjoining Mr Underwood's. Apply to Mrs Mary Ingle, at Mr John P Ingle's, or to John Underwood, Capitol Hill.

A court-martial has been held at Devonport on Lt Gray, at the instigation of the French Gov't, for alleged misconduct in boarding & searching off the coast of Africa the French vessel **Luiz d'Albuquerque**. The vessel had every appearance of being, & was, in fact, a slaver. The Court sentenced Lt Gray to be severely reprimanded, & cautioned him to be more particular in the future.

Gen Sale, the hero of Jellalabad, & his heroic lady, with their widowed dght, Mrs Stuart, & child, arrived at Lyme Regis, on Jul 22: amid the cheers of a number of persons.

Hong-Kong Gaz of Apr 23: Cmder the Hon Erskine Murray, who had proceeded with a couple of vessels to Borneo to form a settlement there, & to establish friendly relations, was betrayed & treacherously murdered, with several of his party, by the Sultan of Coti.

Louisville Courier of Aug 13: our fellow-citizen, Austin Seymour, went up on the vessel **Little Pike** on Fri, with the intention of bringing his wife home, who was on a visit at Patriot, Indiana. When the **Pike** stopped to put him out, he could not be found. It is probably he slipped or was blown into the river.

Warrant issued by Justice Clark charged that Julia Cross had attempted to poison the family of Mr Aquila Rickette on Aug 10. Bail was set at $1,000 for her appearance at the next Criminal Court.

Appointments by the Pres:
John A Bryan, of Ohio, to be Charge d'Affaires to the Republic of Peru.
Thos D Mosely, to be U S Atty, for the Middlet District of Tenn, vice John M Lea, resigned.
Horatio Ball, to be a Justice of the Peace in Alexandria Co, D C.
Consuls:
Robt Walsh, of Pa, for the City of Paris.
Alex'r Tod, for Alexandria, in Egypt, vice John Gliddon, dec'd.
Robt L McIntosh, for the port of Lufowchou, in China.
John B Williams, of Mass, for the Auckland Islands in the Pacific Ocean, in lieu of his appointment for the Bay of Islands, in New Zealand, revoked.

Mrd: on Aug 19, by Rev Henry Myers, Mr Francis E Parker to Miss Virginia Dorsey, all of Wash City.

Died: yesterday, after a long & painful illness, Mrs Mary Jane Ward, w/o Mr Geo W Ward, aged 24 years. Her funeral is this afternoon from her late residence, on Mass ave, between 4th & 5th sts.

$200 reward for $1,200 stolen from the subscriber, at Mrs Thompson's, on F st.
-Geo Selden, at Galabrun's

THU AUG 22, 1844
Handbill: published by Wm B Clymer & S Maylert, that on Aug 2, while lodging at the house of Wm Cooper in Springfield, Bradford Co, their room was forcibly entered by 12 or 15 men in disguise, who seized their carpet bags, containing title papers & contracts of the Bingham estate to lands in that part of the county. They offered a $300 reward for detection of the thieves & recovery of the property.
-Susquehanna [Pa] Register

Isaac Harris cradled 2 acres & 8 rods of wheat in 2 hours & 10 minutes, & John Salisbury raked & bound it in the same time, in Gorham, Ontario Co, recently.

Rev W N Pendleton, A M, late Rector of the Episcopal High School of Va, will on Sep 9, open a Collegiate School in Balt.

Orphans Court of Wash Co, D C. Letters testamentary on the personal estate of Mauduit Young, late of said county, dec'd. –R Young, exc
+
Public sale on Aug 31, of the goods, chattels, & personal estate of Mauduit Young, late of Wash Co, dec'd, at his late residence, consisting of 2 horses, a wagon & harness, household furniture, farming utensils, & crops. –R Young, exc

Strawberry plants for sale. Orders left at J F Callan's drug & seed store, E & 7th st, Wash, will receive prompt attention. –John H Bayne, near Alexandria, D C

The Virginia Hot Springs for sale: upwards of 800 acres: bldgs can accommodate 150 persons. I will sell two-thirds, three fourths, or the entire property. –Th Goode

Five strayed cows broke into the cornfield on the farm of Mr B M Derringer, 1½ miles north of the Capitol. The subscriber may be seen on the above place, adjoining Mrs Pearson's farm, or at his ofc, Congress st, a few doors above Bridge, Gtwn. –Calhoun M Derringer

Lots for sale in the 5th Ward: lots 23 & 24 in square 795, nearly opposite the Methodist meeting-house. Apply to Jas B Holmead, Auct, corner of 4½ st & Pa ave.

Edw Conway, one of the waiters at the St Chas Hotel, in New Orleans, fell on Aug 9 from one of the upper stories of that bldg & killed himself. He had been at times in the habit of walking in his sleep, or may have sat down on the sill to cool himself.

Fatal accident on Thu last in Rush township, Northumberland Co, Pa. While engaged with a thrashing machine, it burst & so wounded Mr Henry Weaver that he died in a few hours afterwards.

Mrd: on Aug 13, at the residence of Col Wm Worsley, near Waterford, Loudoun Co, Va, by Rev Mr Adie, Thos Mead, of Bedford Co, Va, to Miss Mary Ann, d/o the late John Worsley.

Died: yesterday, at Vandalusia, in this county, of pulmonary consumption, after a long & painful illness, Mrs Eliza Van Horn McCormick, in her 38th year, w/o Alex'r McCormick, leaving a husband & 4 small children. Her funeral is this afternoon at 3 o'clock.

Died: on May 29, 1844, at the residence of Mrs Myra Alexander, in Woodford Co, Ky, Mrs Agatha Madison Marshall, w/o Dr Lewis Marshall, & mother of Hon Thos F Marshall, & numerous other children. Her mortal remains were interred the day but one following her decease at *Buck Pond*, in Woodford Co, the family seat, the home of her whole married life, which lasted more than 44 years, & the last residence of her husband's father, Col Thos Marshall, the father of the late illustrious Chief Justice of the U S.

The corner-stone of the Goethean Hall, of Marshall College, Mercersburg, Pa, is to be laid on Aug 28. An address is to be delivered by David Paul Brown, of Phil.

A young man, Geo D Forbes, formerly of Springfield, but recently a resident of Boston, committed suicide in one of the public street of Boston on Sun, by cutting his throat.

FRI AUG 23, 1844
The steam grist mill belonging to Mr Stephen Gardner, at Columbia, Ill, was lately burned down. The loss is $10,000.

On Aug 9, John Clendenon, an old gentleman of 60, & his nephew Jas Clendenon, an orphan whom he was raising, aged 20, were both instantly killed by lightning at Springfield township, Franklin Co, Indiana, while sitting under a large oak tree.

Mitchel Hersey, of West Bridgewater, at the sitting of the Common Pleas Court in Plymouth last week, had one sentence of 3 days solitary confinement & afterwards hard labor for a term of 9 years in the State Prison, for arson, in burning the ofc of Wm Bayliss, in West Bridgewater, & 1 day of solitary & 9 years hard labor in the State Prison for arson in burning a barn in West Bridgewater.

Mrs Stilson's Boarding House, opposite Gallabrun's Hotel, Pa ave, between 14th & 15th sts, Wash, D C. [Local ad.]

Wash Corp: 1-Resolution for the relief of Jas Frazier: passed. 2-Cmte of Claims: reported a bill for the relief of Isaac Beers. 3-Ptn of the widow of Peter Ham, dec'd, praying to be refunded certain taxes erroneously paid: referred to the Cmte of Claims. 4-Cmte of Claims: bill for the relief of J B Clarke: recommended its indefinite postponement: agreed to.

Mrd: on Aug 20, by Rev T R Owen, Mr J M Black, of Ky, to Miss Ellen H Wailes, d/o Isaac H Wailes, of Wash City.

Died: on Aug 20, in Wash City, aged 3 years & 8 months, Eliza Thomson, y/d/o Mr John Hutchinson.

From Texas: arrival at New Orleans brings dates to Aug 7 from Galveston, the 6th from Houston, & Jul 28 from Matagorda. Yellow fever has been prevailing in a considerable extent in Galveston, being principally confined to the German emigrants. Among the deaths we notice that of Gen Murphy, late Charge d'Affaires of the U S, who died at Galveston on Jul 12; of A M Green, U S Consul at Galveston, who died on Jul 28; & of Mr Richd Drake Sebring, late editor of the News. Considerable sickness in Houston: Judge Patrick C Jack died there on Aug 4. Judge Jack went to Texas in 1832, & shared the labors & privations during the progress of the revolution. Stewart Newell is the acting U S Consul at Galveston since the death of Mr Green.

Wash City Ordinances: 1-Act for the relief of Ann Whitmore: fine imposed for violation of the law for selling spirituous liquors without a license, be remitted: Provided, Whitmore pay the costs of prosecution.

The Church Council of St Paul's Lutheran Church have procured Mr Henry B Robertson, a worthy citizen of Wash, to aid in obtaining donations for the erection of their church. By order of the Church Council, A Noerr, Pres; Jno Sessford, jr, Sec.

Union Hotel in Gtwn, D C, for rent. Apply to W S Nicholls, E M Linthicum, or John Kurtz, Gtwn.

Trustee's sale: deed of trust executed by Henreitta Syrock, Jun 21, 1841, recorded in Liber W B 89 folios 101, 102, & 103, Wash Co: auction on Sep 5, of: lots 12 in square 388; & part of square 353, with the bldgs thereon. –Jas B Holmead, auct

SAT AUG 24, 1844
Martha's Vineyard. This island, with others in the group, was discovered by Gosnold, in 1602. It was granted to Thos Mayhew in 1641; about that time, Mr Folger opened the first English school on the island. A few English families first settled at Great Harbor, now *Edgartown*, in 1642. The first minister was Thos Mayhew, the son & only child of the Govn'r, by whom he was sent, "being then a young scholar about 21 years of age," with some others to form a settlement at Edgartown. The burial grounds of Edgartown are three. One on the land of Grafton Norton, in the village, where are only 3 grave stones, signifying the place of sepulcher of some of the Mayhew family. Tradition gives Thos Mayhew, the first Govn'r, a burial place here, but no stone or hillock marks the spot. Mathew Mayhew is marked on the stone, Gen, died in 1720, aged 45 years. A son of his is recorded as dying in Apr, 1714, & his wife Anna as departing this life Apr 16; the stone having sunk in the earth, the year is not to be seen. The next oldest burial place, probably the most ancient, is a ¼ mile s w, & a half acre, with some 60 or 70 tombstones. I transcribe from one of the stone the memorial of Mrs Eliz Jenkins, who died Jul 27, 1776, aged 21 years. Squire Cook, a lawyer of that period, was the man to whom relatives resorted for epitaphs. Among the monuments is the stone that marks Wiswall's grave, one of the ancient pastors of the Congregational Church:
"Here lyes buried ye body of ye
Rev Mr Samuel Wiswall, late pastor of
ye church of Christ in this town, who departed
this life Dec 28, A D, 1746, aged 67 years."
Some of the oldest graves have stones without any inscription. I saw: Ann Worth, 1724, aged 53 years; John Worth, 1731, aged 65 years.
The third or newest burying-ground is that surrounding the old diplapidated Congressional meeting-house comprising about 2 acres. Mr Collector Thaxter, s/o the venerable clergyman of that name, so long a pastor here, is the man whose

knowledge & taste point him out to effect improvement in the burial place, & I hope the town will employ him. –C C B

Delaware State Journal: Mrs Boulden, the sister of Isaac & Jacob Cannon, of Sussex Co, Dela, & heirs of their great fortune, died on Fri last.

Abraham Smith was taken from jail by force, & executed by a lawless gang at Frederkicktown, Mo, on Aug 5. Smith had been convicted of murder, & was sentenced to be executed on Sep 1. Five men were arrested & committed to take their trial for murder.

Mason & Dixon's Line: this boundary is so termed from the names of Chas Mason & Jeremiah Dixon, the gentlemen appointed to run unfinished lines in 1761, between Pa & Md, on the territories subject to the heirs of Penn & Lord Baltimore.

Murder at the South Sea Islands: from a mail ship recently conveyed to England: At Sippore Island, it was ascertained that the ship **Two Sisters**, a South Sea whaler, commanded by Capt Brend, & every soul of the crew, had been most barbarously murdered.

Louisville Journal: on Fri last, Thos J Welby, of the firm of Lumley & Welby, auctioneers of that city, was charged with passing counterfeit money. He was required to find bail in the sum of $600 to appear at the Circuit Court.

Fatal affray in Sparta, Tenn, on Aug 3, between Joshua Hickey & John H Groaning, in which Hickey received a pistol-shot through the left side. He died on Thu. Mr Groaning was committed to await his trial. The affair was not political.

Southwark, Phil riots: more arrest-Abraham Long was charged on his own admissions, with being one of the most active rebels in the Jul 7 riot. He was committed to prison on the charge of riot, treason, & murder. A boy, Isaac Wilson Taylor was committed in default of $5,000 bail, for setting fire to the house of Patrick Clark, 4th & Masters sts, during the Kensington riots.

Notice: Whereas my wife, Sarah Mankins, having left me without any just cause or provocation, I hereby caution all persons whomsoever not to harbor the said Sarah Mankins, or to trust her on my account under any pretence whatsoever, as I will not be answerable for any debts which she may contract. –John Mankins, [colored]

Copartnership: the subscribers having bought out Darius Clagett's stock of Goods, will continue the Dry Goods business at the old stand, 9th & Pa ave.
–R B Nalley, J B Dodson

Public sale of negroes on Sep 18, 25 to 30 likely negroes, consisting of men, women & children, in Upperville, Fauquier Co, Va. Said slaves will be sold for no fault. –Thos M Latham, agent

MON AUG 26, 1844
Miss M G Meade informs that she has resumed the duties of her Seminary. She has yet room for 4 or 5 children as boarders. Terms made known at her residence on G st, between 21st & 22nd sts, north side.

Washington High School, F & 14th sts, will be resumed on Sep 2. Apply to A M Girault. –Arnold & Girault

Collegiate School, First st, near Capitol Hill, C W Feeks, [successor to S G Bulfinch,] Principal, assisted by W D Miller, a graduate of Amherst College. Will be re-opened on Sep 2.

Young Ladies' Seminary for Day Scholars, F st, between 12th & 13th sts, Wash. M A Tyson & sisters will resume their institution on the 2nd Mon in Sep.

Mrs S Young's Seminary for Young Ladies, F st, below 12th, will resume on Sep 2. Madame Dorman will continue as French teacher.

Information received of the death of Cmdor Alex'r J Dallas, of the U S Navy: died on board the U S frig **Savannah**, in Callao bay, on Jun 3, from a third attack of paralysis. Com Dallas entered the Navy as Midshipman on Nov 22, 1805, & enjoyed an enviable reputation, nearly 39 years. He was the s/o that sterling patriot Alex J Dallas, who distinguished himself at the head of the Treasury Dept at a most critical period, & was the brother of Mr Dallas whose name is now before the people as a candidate for the Vice Presidency.

John O Sargent has published a card denying that he has formed any connexion with the "Republic," as has been stated by a portion of the press of N Y. His brother, Epes, is the Editor of that journal.

The Mobile papers announce the death of Philip McClosky, on Aug 15. He was one of the oldest & most respectable citizens of Mobile. He filled every public station to which he was called with honor to himself & constituents.

Dreadful accident on the Long Island Railroad on Wed, when the engine struck the hind part of a wagon, in which Mrs Southard, w/o Wm Southard, an elderly woman, [residing on the Plains,] was in, killed her instantly. The man driving was injured, but expected to recover.

Fire in Macon, Ga, on Mon, destroyed some of its finest bldgs. Mr Jas Willingham, a printer, & worthy citizen, was instantly killed by the falling of one of the bldgs, which was blow up to arrest the progress of the flames.

A s/o Mr Gotlieb Eckloff, about 14 or 15 years old, fell from a fence on Fri, in his haste to get to the fire, & broke his arm. Surgical aid was immediately rendered & he is doing well.

Balt American, Aug 24. The s/o Hon Thos G Pratt, the Whig candidate for Govn'r of Md, died in this city yesterday. The Patriot states that his child was in his 8th year, & arrived in Balt about 2 weeks ago with his father & mother, on their way to the Berklely Springs. On their arrival here the child was taken ill, & after a most distressing illness of 13 days, yesterday gave up its spirit to Heaven, & its body ceased from suffering.

Capt Berry, of the ship **Vicksburg**, arrived at N Y on Thu from New Orleans, & reports that on Aug 6, a boat was discovered about 3 points forward of the weather beam. On reaching the boat was taken alongside, & 7 persons received on board, who proved to be the capt & crew of the British schnr **Orange**, lost on the voyage from Jamaica to Mantazas: Alex'r McDonald, master; Wm Young, mate; Edw Cook, Richd Evans, & John Brown, seamen; Wm Rozere, ordinary seaman; & Robt Wilkinson, cook; having been 13 days in a boat 14 feet long. Wm Rozere, the youngest of them, was much emaciated & totally insensible, & survived only 3 hours, & at sunrise his body was deposited in the Sailor's Grave, with the solemn service of the Protestant Episcopal Church.

A girl named Catharine Connor attempted to commit suicide by jumping from South Boston new bridge into the water on Sun last. She was rescued by some persons near by, & medical aid soon restored her to consciousness.

TUE AUG 27, 1844
The Whig ticket for N C is now complete, & is as follows:

Wm W Cherry	Danl B Baker	Jas W Osborne
Josiah Collins	Maurice Q Waddel	Col Jonathan Horton
Robt B Gilliam	Jas Kerr	John Baxter
Wm H Washington	Augustine H Shepherd	-Raleigh Register

Salem Gaz: Amos Choate, who lately dec'd in that city, bequesthed $5,000 in trust to the Mayor & Aldermen, to be invested & the proceeds appropriated for the support of the insane poor, at the Worchester Hosp; $1,000 to the Society of the North Church, the interest to be appropriated for the benefit of the Sunday School; & $1,000 to the same Society, the interest to be appropriated in aid of the poor of the Society.

Two promising youths, sons of Mr Hobart, of Conesville, Schoharie Co, N Y, aged 16 & 18 years, were drowned in the mill-pond of Mr John Richmeyer on Aug 3.

Richmond, Va, Aug 26. The great case of the Bank of the U S against Col Andrew Beirne, of Munroe, as endorser for his son-in-law, Mr Steenbergen, [now of N Y,] involving some $650,000, has been decided in Col Beirne's favor, by a special Court of Appeals, at Lewisburg. The case of the appellants [the Bank] was argued by Chapman Johnson & Geo Nicholson Johnson [his son] of this city, & Jas M Mason, of Winchester; that of the appellee by Benj Watkins Leigh & Wm H Macfarland, of Richmond, & Gen Walter Jones, of Wash. The Special Court of Appeals, Judges Stanard, Scott, Leigh, & Fry, were unanimous in the judgment awarded. –Whig

Charleston, S C, Aug 22-as one of Sullivan's Island packets was returning from Morris Island to the city, having been employed on a party of pleasure, whilst tacking, Mrs Sweegan was struck by the boom, knocked overboard & drowned. She was both industrious & respectable, leaving a large & young family. -Patriot

House & lot at private sale: frame house & lot on 7th st, between K & L sts. Call on A B Gladman.

For rent: frame house on 13th st south, between the Canal & Long Bridge. Apply to the subscriber, on Pa ave, between 6th & 7th sts, or to Mr Dale, next door to the house. -Walter Clarke

For rent: large commodious house on K st, late the residence of Wm Hayman, & adjoining that of Mr Jos Smoot. For terms apply to Mr Jos Smoot, or the subscriber, on Pa ave, opposite the late residence of Hon Mr Forsyth, dec'd. –Thos Cissell

Orphans Court of Wash Co, D C. In the case of Noah Drummond, administrator of Clorinda A Thorn, dec'd: the administrator & Court have appointed Sep 17 next for settlement of said estate: so far as collected & turned into money. –Ed N Roach, Reg/o wills

St Louis, Aug 17. Yesterday John McDaniel & Jos Brown, tried & convicted of the murder of the Mexican Charvis, on the Santa Fe road, were executed. -Republican

WED AUG 28, 1844
To rent: 3 story brick house in Granite Row, now occupied by Mrs Lomax: possession on Oct 1. Inquire of Alex McIntire, next door north of St John's Church.

For rent: large 3 story brick house at 10th & Pa ave. Inquire of Michl Sardo, 10th & K sts, or of Mr Michl Combs on the premises.

For rent: two new 2 story frame dwlgs. Apply to the subscriber, 18th & K sts, John C Roemmele.

Most valuable real estate at private sale: the subscriber will sell the Farm on which he now resides, within one mile of Colesville, Montg Co, Md, known as the former residence of Edw Dawes, containing 192 acres: improvements are good.
John Poole

Mrs Mackintosh, a resident of Pottsville, Pa, was found on Fri lying dead with her face in the stream, at the upper end of Market st in that borough. It is supposed she was seized with a fit, fell in the position she was found & so perished.

Imported Hams. Also, 200 Balt cured hams. -Wm Dove, Pa ave, near 9th st.

Sharretts & Brereton have taken the Grocery store recently occupied by Saml Brereton, immediately adjoining their Shoe store, at 7th & F sts. No pains will be spared to procure the most choice articles in their line.

On Thu last, says the Perry [Pa] Freeman, some boys were fowling in Carroll township. Benj Harrison, s/o Francis Gibson, was accidentally shot. Young Gibson survived but one hour & a half.

New Orleans, Aug 19. A son of John Nicholson, Cashier of the Carrollton Bank, went out from Pascagoula on Thu in a skiff. He was found on the lake beach, shot through the head, by accidental discharge of his gun, perhaps the result of carelessness. The ball entered behind one ear. -Tropic

Marion, Miss: dreadful affray between Mr Fisher, who had put up a brickyard on land he thought to be public land. It was found to belong to Mrs Shumacker. Not removing himself from the land, Mr & Mrs Schumacher, loaded with guns & pistols, repaired to the brickyard. Fisher & 2 sons were on one side. Mr S fired first, & then there was general firing from both sides. Mrs Schumacher was mortally & Southey Fisher dangerously wounded. She lived about 12 hours. It is thought Fisher will recover. Schumacher has been committed to jail.

Jas Tooley, jr, the celebrated miniature painter, formerly of Phil, died at Natchez on Aug 12, whither he had gone in the hope that a return to his native air would effect the re-establishment of his health. -Pennsylvanian

Died: on Aug 22, near Bladensburg, Md, Mrs Jane Brashear, w/o Mr Christopher Brashear, & niece of Mrs Jane Hyatt, of Wash City, after a few days' illness, under peculiarly distressing circumstances.

Died: on Aug 24, of scarlet fever, Gwilym Francis, s/o Wm P & Mary Agnes Williams, aged 3 years.

St Vincent's Orphan Asylum: election held on Aug 11 at St Patrick's Church & the following Ladies were duly elected members of the Board of Managers for St Vincent's Female Orphan Asylum:

Mrs Newman	Mrs Hughes	Mrs Graham
Mrs Talbot	Mrs C Hill	Mrs Blake
Mrs Ann S Hill	Mrs Stubbs	Mrs Riggs

Aug 26: Ladies met to elect ofcrs fror the year:
Mrs Newman, 1st Directress   Mrs Ann Hill, Treasurer
Mrs Talbot, 2nd Directress   Mrs Riggs, Sec

THU AUG 29, 1844
Trenton Gaz: Elisha Griggs, of Phil, a young man, while on a gunning expedition, on Aug 20, with friends, near Tulleytown, near Bristol, Pa, had his right arm dreadfully lacerated by the accidental discharge of a gun. He was immediately removed to the Tullytown House, kept by E Scattergood, where the arm was successfully amputated above the elbow joint.

Estray spotted cow came to the residence of the subscriber. Owner is to come forward, prove property, pay charges & take her away. –Thos Adams, F & 12th sts

It is understood that information has reached the Dept of State that Her Britannic Majesty has extended pardon [on the usual condition of good behavior while residents there] to the American prisoners now in the British penal colonies, whose names are embraced in the annexed list:

Jos Stewart	Nelson J Griggs	Saml Newcombe
Elizur Stevens	Jerry Griggs	Jas DeWitt Fers
Gideon A Goodrich	Benj Mott	Luther Darby

Mrd: on Aug 21, at Berlin, Md, by Rev Dr W H Reese, W T Purnell, of Port Gibson, Miss, to Miss Henrietta, d/o the late Hon John S Spence, of the U S Senate.

Mrd: on Aug 27, by Rev Mr Martin, Mr Wm H Yoe, of New Orleans, to Miss Ellen D Maddox, of PG Co, Md.

Died: on Aug 11, at Norfolk, Va, Anna Lee Page, only child of Lt Richd L Page, U S Navy, & Sarah Alexina, his wife.

Died: on Aug 8, at Tampico, in his 50th year, Col Wm Thompson, late a colonel of the Mexican army. He was a native of Md, born near Leonardtown, St Mary's Co: enlisted in the U S Army in 1812. At the close of the war he offered his services to Mexico in the war of independence which she was then waging against Spain.

Wanted: a man & his wife, having no children, as laborer or manager of a farm, & his wife as housekeeper. Apply at Martin Murphy's, Pa ave & 4½ st.

Teacher wanted: a gentleman to reside in his family, to prepare boys for college. Address, postpaid, Wm Clark, near Queen Anne, PG Co, Md.

$5 reward for strayed or stolen from the subscriber, living near the Steamboat Wharf, a light sorrel mare. –Stewart Tuxen

FRI AUG 30, 1844
Chevalier Don Pablo Chacon, Consul General of Spain for the U S, died on Tue, at Bristol, where he had been residing for his health. –Phil U S Gaz

Hon Abbott Lawrence, of Boston, has given Williams College [Mass] $5,000, which relieves it from all pecuniary embarrassments.

Niagara Falls. 1-Mr J Thompson, book-keeper in the commercial house of Carlton R Moore, of Phil, disappeared suddenly at the Falls on Fri last, & is supposed to have perished in the cataract. 2-Last Sat there was another accident at the Falls, the Canadian side, which resulted in the death of Miss Martha K Rugg, a young lady belonging to Lancaster, Mass. At a precipice near the museum, she lost her balance, & with a loud shriek fell. She was taken up alive, but died in about 3 hours.

Nashville Gaz: affray there on Aug 21, between Maj Robt B Turner & Saml Casey. Both shot-Casey in the abdomen, supposed mortally, & Turner in the forehead, dangerously. No particulars are given.

Fratricide. The Montg [Ala] Journal of Aug 21: Jos Armstrong died from the hands of his brother, Tucker Armstrong. The dispute grew out of an old settlement. A knife was plunged into his brother's body 11 times. The aggressor escaped.

Accident at Williamsburg, N Y, from the use of camphine lamp. The lamp overturned, & the wife & child of Mr Meeks, a tailor living in Grand st, were so severely burnt that they are not expected to live.

Judge Jack, who died a few days since at Glaveston, in Texas, of yellow fever, was one of the candidates for the Vice Presidency of the Republic.

Mr Hanford came to his death on Wed last, at the Wissahickon Railroad bridge, when he jumped upon a burden car at Manayunk, missed it, & fell through the bridge, a distance of 60 feet. He was an operative in one of the Wissahickon factories, & was returning to his employment from a visit to his mother, who resides at Haddington, –Germantown Telegraph

Henry, the only s/o Henry F Tallmadge, of N Y, & lately a student of Yale College, was drowned on Tue at a place on Staten Island, about 1 mile back of New Brighton. He was seized with a cramp & drowned. He was 17 years of age.

The Boston Courier states that Pres Tyler has built himself a very elegant house at his Va plantation, on the plan of an English villa, under the superintendenc of that ingenious architect, Mr John Skirving, of Phil, where, with his accomplished lady, he will undoubtedly live much happier than at the White House.

On Sat, a young man, Auguste Scheler, was committed at Phil for stealing at various times from his employers, Messrs Kurlbaum & Co, manufacturing chemists, about 100 pounds of opium, & a quantity of quinine, both of which are very costly.

Mayor's Court of Albany: Thu, Wm Rankin was indicted for threatening to accuse a lady of stealing lace from a store, with intent to extort money. The result was his conviction on trial. -Ledger

A horrid murder was committed in Wash Co, Iowa, on Aug 4. A man named McCaulley fled with the wife & child of Mr Coffman to Indiana. Coffman pursued & brought them back, &, while returning from the house of a neighbor, McCaulley shot both him & his child. The murderer & the wife have been arrested.

Copartnership between Travers & Jackson, has been dissolved by mutual consent. The business will be conducted by Elia Travers. –Elias Travers, R P Jackson

Mrs Eliza Martin, Milliner, on F st, between 6th & 7th sts, has taken the house lately occupied by Mrs Cornock, who disposed her business to Miss Martin.
–Sarah Cornock

On Fri last near the toll-gate on the Phil road, near Balt, at the house of Mrs Decker, her son, Mr L Decker, threw a stone at a cow who had some difficulty. The stone struck the cow & glanced or missed her entirely, & struck Mrs Decker, a lady about 60 years of age, inflicting a head wound. She died on Sun. The son was thus unfortunately the cause of his mother's death.

The Indian Queen Hotel, for many years so well conducted by Mr Jesse Brown, & now so respectably managed by his two sons, Messrs M & T Brown, has lately undergone extensive alterations & improvements. The marble tile flooring was laid by Messrs Berry & Co, of Wash City. The fountain head piece, of silver, were wrought by our fellow citizen, Mr Saml Lewis, a skillful silversmith. Mr S P Franklin is papering all the rooms. A force-pump, manufactured by W & B Douglass, affords cool & refreshing water. Barber Shop: Mr Simpson is an easy shaver & expert shampooist.

SAT AUG 31, 1844
For rent: one of the new brick dwlgs recently erected by him in Gtwn, on Gay st, commanding a beautiful view of the Potomac river & Wash City. For terms apply at the Hardware Store of English & Muncaster, on Bridge st, Gtwn. −D English, jr

Botanico-medical College of Ohio: H W Hill, M D, Dean: Cincinnati, Ohio.

English & Classical Academy: his room near 9th st. −John E Norris

Died: on Aug 29, Mrs Mary Martin, consort of Wm Martin, aged 67 years. Her funeral will take place from her late residence, Navy Yard Hill, Aug 31, at 2 o'clock.

Died: on Aug 16, at the Almshouse of Balt City & County, Patrick McCormick, a native of Longford, Ireland. He was conveyed to the Almshouse on Aug 12 in a state of insensibility, & from documents found in his possession it appears he arrived in N Y about 4 years ago, when he declared his intention to become a citizen of the U S, & that he had recently been employed at the quarry of Mr Donnelly, in Va & vicinity of Alexandria, D C. The relations of the dec'd [some of whom, it is supposed, reside in the neighborhood of Phil] can obtain information to his effects by addressing, post paid, G W Yates, Agent of the Trustees for the Poor of Balt City & County, 121 N Exeter st, Balt, Md.

A boatman, Henry Ochem, belonging to Schuylkill Haven, was drowned in the canal at Reading on Sun last, He has left a wife & 2 children.

Valuable cotton plantation in Louisiana for sale: called *Chaseland*, in the Parish of Rapides, having about 4,400 English acres: fine stock & comfortable cabins. For terms apply, by letter, to Maj Wm H Chase, at Pensacola, or to Wm Flower, at New Orleans.

Household & kitchen furniture at auction: on Sep 16, at the residence of Mrs McCardle, on E st. −Wm Marshall, auctioneer

Wash City lots 9, 10, & 11, in square 408 for sale. Situated in the central part of Wash. -B Mason, Gtwn

Mr Francis Fairbairn, a young gentleman of Balt City, was killed near Carrollton, Ky, on Aug 21, while out gunning in company with his friends. One of them, in shooting at some game, accidentally shot Mr F in the neck, & he soon expired.

MON SEP 2, 1844
Western Academy, 17th st: will be resumed on Sep 2. −G J Abbot

Orphans Court of Wash Co, D C. Letters testamentary on the personal estate of Eliz Keller, of said county, dec'd. –Saml D King, exc

Wash Corp: 1-Ptn of J O P Degges & others, for curbstones & footways on square 122: referred to the Cmte on Improvements. 2-Ptn of John F Callan & others, for curbstone & footways on square 401 & 402: referred to the Cmte on Improvements. 3-Cmte of Claims: bill for the relief of David A Baird: passed.

Lord Mayor of Dublin. The Corp has just given another proof of its liberality in the election of Mr J L Arabin, a Prot Episc, to the ofc of Lord Mayor. Mr Arabin was proposed by Robt McClellan, a volunteer of '82 & seconded by Constantine McLaughlan, one of the sufferers of '98. The honor was offered to Mr O'Connell, but declined. -Chronicle

Alex'r Hoag, the notorious criminal, whose mysterious escape from the Tombs in N Y has created so much excitement, was arrested on Wed at Greenport. He paid the ofcr whom he bribed to let him out $1,800, all of it in bad money.

Utica, Aug 27. On Aug 26, Mr Wm Cattell, formerly of England, now one of our citizens, was accidentally shot & killed by his own gun.

Gtwn Classical & Scientific Academy will be resumed this morning. –Jas McVean, Principal

Coroner's Inquest: the body of a white girl, Mgt Young, was found last Fri floating in the Wash canal, near the wood-yard of Mr P Cazenave, between 9th & 10th sts. Verdict was that she drowned herself. She was about 17 years of age, & had lived for many years as an apprentice with Mr Plant, cabinetmaker in this city.

Fatal accident in Rockville: John Beckwith, who has a wife & numerous family residing in Montg Co, was killed at Rockville last Sat. He was assisting the Democratic party to raise a lofty pole in honor of Polk & Dallas. The pole, which was a very heavy one, snapped in two, & struck Mr Beckwith on the head. He died in about 20 minutes. Another man, Mr Prather, was injured by the fall thereof.

Died: on Aug 30, in Wash City, Mrs Mary Grinder, w/o Mr Antonio Grinder, & d/o Mrs Ann Evans.

Died: on Aug 28, at Davidsonville, Anne Arundel Co, Md, Anna Maria Thumlert, w/o Wm Henry Thumlert. Although the disease was rapid that has deprived a disconsolate husband of a dear & tender wife, & her relatives & neighbors of an affectionate friend, at this moment is basking in the sunshine of her Redeemer.

TUE SEP 3, 1841
Classical Boarding & Day School for Young Ladies: east side of 11th, between F & G sts. Mr & Mrs True, aided by Mrs Bartow, of N Y, as governess, & several masters, will open on Sep 1. Instrumental music by Mr Hewitt.

The birth of another Prince has relieved every solicitude as to the personal welfare of Queen Victoria, besides giving a new security for direct succession to the Crown. This event took place early in the morning of Tue, Aug 6, & was signalized by the firing of salutes at Windsor, at James' Park, & the Tower, & the raising of the flags & ringing of bells in every quarter as the news spread.

Ex-Govn'r Gabriel Moore, of Alabana, [more recently an inhabitant of Louisiana,] is reported to have died recently at his residence in Texas, near the boundary line, where he had removed a few months previously. He was formerly a Rep & then a Senator in Congress from the State of Alabama.

Among the passengers arrived at N Y on Fri in the ship **Mediator**, from London, is Thos Crawford, the American sculptor, who has for the last 10 years been pursuing his studies in Rome.

A public dinner was given in Bedford Co, Va, on Aug 23, to Hon Wm L Goggin, the worthy Whig Rep in Congress from that district. Speeches were delivered by Mr Goggin, John Wills, & Wm S Reid, jr.

The last resting-place of the venerable Noah Webster is now marked by an imposing monument of dark Quincy granite: prepared in Boston at an expense of $400. It stands adjoining the tomb of another illustrious son of New Haven-Eli Whitney. We noticed another monument to the memory of the venerable Jas Hillhouse. Another, erected by the ofcrs & crew of the U S ship **Preble**, in memory of Cmder Voorhees, who died in the East Indies. A neat marble obelish marks the spot where the remains of the ill-fated Tutor Dwight repose, contiguous to the tomb of his illustrious ancestor, the former Pres of Yale College. –Conn Palladium

A fine boy, John Myers, the s/o Mr Josiah Myers, carpenter at the Navy Yard, was yesterday killed by the falling of a heavy gate near the residence of Mr Speisser. We understand the gate was blown open by a sudden gust of wind & fell loose from its hinges. The little sufferer, who is only about 5 years of age, was playing near the gate when it fell upon him & deprived him of life.

For rent: 2½ story brick dwlg on 8th st, between G & H. Inquire of the subscriber, on 11th, between G & H sts. –Mgt Stewart

Mrd: on Sabbath morning, by Rev John C Smith, Mr John Jos White to Miss Eliza Ann Logan, all of Wash City.

Sale of lands at auction, on Sep 10: 300 acres of land on the Rockville & Wash turnpike, & 560 acres on Rock Creek. The first tract is immediately opposite Silver Springs, the farm of F P Blair. The lands lie partly in this District & partly in Montg Co, Md. Sale will take place at the residence of the late Basil Lovelace, on the turnpike near the lands. –Wm Thos Carroll

New Drug Store: on 7th st, between H & I sts. –Saml C Espey, John S Byrne

Estate of Geo Rex, dec'd: Notice is given that the undersighned has been appointed by the Orphans' Court of Montg Co, Pa, auditor to audit & settle the accounts of Geo Rex, Abraham Rex, Theodore Ashmead, & Jacob Dannehower, excs of the last will & testament of Geo Rex, the elder, late of the township of Mooreland, in Montg Co, Pa, dec'd, & to report a distribution of the funds in their hands among the persons legally entitled thereto; & that he will attend at the public house of Danl Shelmire, in Abington township, in said county, on Oct 21, to perform the duties of his appointment. –G H Pawling, auditor

Orphans Court of Wash Co, D C. Letters of administration on the personal estate of Francis Cazeau, late of France, & late merchant of Monterat, dec'd.
–Jacob Bigelow, adm

$100 reward for runaway black man Abraham, about 22 or 23. His father & mother live in Wash, D C. –A C Page, near Good Luck, PG Co, Md

WED SEP 4, 1844
Wash Corp: 1-Bill for the relief of David A Baird: referred to the Cmte of Claims. 2-Ptn of John Barnes, praying remission of a fine: referred to the Cmte of Claims. 3-Ptn of Donald Stewart & others, for a flag footway on 11th st at H: referred to the Cmte on Improvements. 4-Ptn of Geo Savage, praying to be released from the penalty incurred as security for an offender against the laws of the Corp: referred to the Cmte of Claims.

Wholesale & retail grocery store, 8th st, near the Navy Yard. S E Smith has taken into partnership Jas G Smith & the establishment will be conducted hereafter under the firm of S E Smith & Co.

The Corner-stone of the Church of the Ascension, to be erected on H st, will be laid on Sep 5, & the address will be delivered by Rt Rev Wm R Whittingham, Bishop of the Diocese of Md. [Sep 6th newspaper: the lot upon which the Church is to be erected was bequeathed by the late Mrs Van Ness, & immediately adjoins the Mausoleum where her remains are deposited.]

No person will be permitted in future to gun or to hunt with dogs upon my farm *Norway*, on the west side of the Wash & Rockville turnpike, about 4 miles from Wash City. Any person found trespassing after this notice will certainly be prosecuted. --Thos Carbery

F J Bell, mate of the steamer **La Salle**, was stabbd at St Louis on Fri week in a fight with Wm Frothingham, & died in about 20 minutes. Frothingham had been engineer of the same boat. He made no effort to escape, & was taken into custody.

Household & kitchen furniture at auction: on Sep 10, at the residence of Mr F W Manly, on 14th st, near Pa ave. -R W Dyer & Co, aucts

Paints, Oils, & Glass: O Whittlesey, C st, Todd's Bldgs.

Hon Wm S Fulton, U S Senator from Arkansas, died at his residence, about a mile from Little Rock, on Aug 15.

New Almshouse near *Congress Burial Ground*, nearly finished: contractor-Mr Josiah Essex. Mr W G Williams executed the brick work; carpenter's work by Mr Essex; plastering by Mr Jas B Phillips, the painting by Mr W R Lowndes; & the tine roof by Mr Richd Hill.

Harvard Univ: honorary degree of L L D was conferred on Govn'r Riggs & Hon John Sergeant, of Phil. The honorary degree of D D was conferrded on Rev Prof Park, of the Andover Theological Institution, & Rev Andrew Bigelow, of Danvers. -Courier

Thos J Turk, of Polk Co, Mo, was shot & killed on Aug 8, while riding in a prairie, by some person concealed in a thicket. This is the third member of the family who has been assassinated, the father & 2 sons. A young man, Isom Hobbs, has been arrested, charged with the murder.

A boy named Hiram Gilbert was killed in an affray in Dublin township, Huntingdon Co, Pa, on Thu last, by another boy, Saml Thompson. There had been an enmity existing between them for some time. Thompson struck Gilbert below the eye with a stone, felling him to the ground, & then leaving him, where he was found dead in a few hours. Thompson is now in jail.

Mrd: on Aug 29, by Bishop Meade, at the residence of Geo W Blakmore, Clark Co, Va, Col Jas W Irwin, of Logan Co, Ky, to Miss Caroline Augusta Blakmore, d/o Marcus Blakmore, dec'd.

Died: on Sep 1, of scarlet fever, Edw, s/o Peter & Martha McCardle, aged 3 years & 6 months.

Died: yesterday, after a severe & lingering illness, Albert, infant s/o Thos & Caroline Parker, aged 12 months. His funeral is at 10 o'clock this morning, at the residence of Thos Parker, on F st, between 6th & 7th sts.

Died: on Sep 3, at the Navy Yard, of scarlet fever, Margaret Ellen, d/o Dennis & Mary Callaghan.

THU SEP 5, 1844
Janeville Boarding School will commence on Sep 15. –J A Williamson, Janeville, near Berryville, Clarke Co, Va. Refer to:
Rt Rev Wm Meade
Rev Wm G H Jones Millwood, Clarke Co, Va
Rev Wm M Atkinson, D D Winchester, Va
Rev Alex Shirar, Gtwn, D C
Rev Wm Williamson, Warrenton, Va

Trustee's sale. The subscriber, as surviving exc & Trustee of the will of David Peter, dec'd, will offer at auction, on Sep 25, in front of Hayman's Brewery, in square 4 of Wash City, the following: lots 17 & 18 in square 1. All that part of lot 1 in square 2. Lot 1 in square 13. Lots 16, 19, & 21 in square 24. –Geo Peter, exc & trustee
-R W Dyer & Co, aucts

The Sheriff of Albany tarred & feathered. The temporizing course pursued by Gov Bouck in reference to the case of the Rensselaer troubles is beginning to manifest its fruits: we learn from the Albany Citizen of Sat that Sheriff Batterman was violently resisted in the discharge of his duty on Sat, near the village of Rensselaerville. The Sheriff, with ofcrs Leonard, Osterhout, & a man named Baker, arrived on Fri. When he went to serve process on some tenants of the Manor, they were surrounded by about 60 "Indians" with masks. The Sheriff refused to return to the city, & finding him not to be intimidated, he was tarred & feathered.

Jos Bonaparte expired at Florence on Jul 28, at the age of 76. On the assumption of the imperial crown by Napoleon he was offered the kingdom of Lombardy, which he refused. He was made King of Naples in 1806, & in 1808 the will of the Emperor removed him to the throne of Spain, his fall from which we need not relate. On the abdication of Fontainbleau he retired into Switzerland, but on the return of the Emperor in 1815 he came back, & entered Paris on the same day as his brother. After the battle of Waterloo he went to reside in America. In 1817 the State of N J, & in 1825 that of N Y, authorized him to hold lands without becoming an American citizen. In 1832 he left America for England, where he resided for several years, but his impaired health made it necessary for him to live in a milder climate, & he removed to Florence. –Foreign paper

Fatal accident on Mon as one of the trains of cars on the Reading railroad, near Reading, when the boiler suddenly burst. Killed: the engineer Jas Ward, & the conductor John McCabe, both excellent, trustworthy men.

Trial of the Phil Rioters: on Tue. Fred'k Hess, about 17, was first put on trial for arson, in setting fire to a house in Kensington on May 7. Verdict-guilty.

Truste's sale: by virtue of a decree of the Circuit Court of Wash Co, D C, as a Court of Chancery, made in the cause of Rose Ann McGuire against the reps of Wm Hayman, dec'd, et al: auction on Sep 24 of:
Lot 22 in reservation B, with a 2 story brick bldg, fronting on Pa av, & lately in the occupancy of J Boulanger as a restaurant & boarding house.
A lot at the n e corner of square 291, fronting on north E st, with 2 two-story brick tenements. Also, on Sep 25, lots 1, 4, 9, & 10 in square 4. Lot 14 in square 13. Lots 1, 17, & 18, in square 14. Lot 7 in square 40. Lot 13 in square 41. Lot 1 in square 72, & the entire square 149. –Clement Cox, Trustee -R W Dyer & Co, aucts

Mrd: on Sep 3, by Rev Mr Tuston, Mr Edw C Eckloff to Miss Martha Jane Ellis, both of Wash City.

Died: on Wed, Mr John C English. His funeral is this afternoon, from his late residence on 7th st, at 4 o'clock.

Died: on Aug 23, at St James' Island, Florida, Jos R Rowles, of Monticello, Jefferson Co, aged 34 years. He was a merchant well known & respected for his business habits & intelligence. He was a native of Fairfax Co, Va, & emigrated to Florida some years since. He was at St James' Island, a summer retreat on the Gulf, on a visit with some friends, when he was attacked with congestive fever, which caused his death in a few days.

Information wanted of Mr Claudius Jones, who left this city about Nov 1, 1825, & has not been heard from but once since that time, by a gentleman who saw him in Mobile in 1837 or 1838. His friends have had no news of him since. Any information respecting the said Jones will be thankfully received by his only borther, Thos Jones, in Wash City, D C. [Alabama papers please copy.]

FRI SEP 6, 1844
$200 reward for return of a pocket book, containing $785 in notes of Va & Balt. Please leave it with its contents at the ofc of the Nat'l Intell. –Saml Hanauer [Balt sun will coy & send account to this ofc.]

For rent: 2 story frame house, with a basement, on East Capitol st, Capitol Hill. -Isaac Bassett

To let, very desirable dwlg house at G & 22nd sts, recently occupied by Tully R Wise, dec'd. Apply to Mr Chas Eckel, or to W Adler, Gtwn.

The subscriber will sell, in the village of Bladensburg, PG Co, Md, at public sale, on Sep 21, his 2 small frame dwlg houses, on the principal st, immediately opposite the Methodist parsonage. –Thos E Dant, Bladensburg

The w/o Mr J W Burbridge, wholesale grocer, of Pittsburg, was killed on Thu last. As Mr B was approaching the Stone bridge in a carriage, with his lady, the horse took fright & became unmanageable. The carriage was dashed to pieces at the bottom of a precipice some 30 feet high. Mrs Burbridge died before reaching her husband's residence.

$50 reward for runaway negro man Ellis, about 20 years of age. He has a father & mother living at Mr Allen P Bowie's, of this county, near the Long Old Fields. John E Berry, sen, living near Bladensburg, PG Co, Md.

The Hon Judge Morris, of the First Judicial District, died at Galveston on Aug 19.

Roderick McKenzie died at Montreal, Canada, a few days ago, at age 83 years. He became connected with the late Northwest Co at an early age; was 25 years in the Council of the Providence, & was always remarked for the wisdom & moderation of his views & measures.

Brooklyn Advertiser of Mon: a young sailor of this city, Edw Gunning, displayed courage & daring at the fire last evening. The house occupied by Mr Haynes was wrapped in flames, & the screams of a child were heard from the upper story. The young sailor dashed through the flames & in a few minutes the child was safe.

Deaths by lightning: on Aug 22, in Monroe township, Preble Co, Ohio, 2 dghts of Mr Danl Dashers, aged 10 & 13 years, were killed by a flash of lightning. A younger brother was with them, but escaped injury. On the same day, & within 2 hours of the above calamity, the house of Mr G Walker, of Twin township, Drake Co, Ohio, was struck by lightning & his 4 year old son was instantly killed. The arm of a younger brother was broken, & so seriously injured that little hopes were entertained of his recovery. Several members of the family were less injured.

Shocking accident at an ofcr drill in Catskill, N Y, on Wed last, when the gun exploded prematurely. One of the young men, Henry Overbagh, has his left arm so shattered that it will probably be amputated. Wm Overbagh has his left hand severely injured & a part of his thumb had to be taken off. Another young man, named Richards, had the thumb of his left hand blown off, & was seriously wounded in the thigh.

Gen Tilghman A Howard, Charge d'Affaires of the U S to Texas, arrived at Houston on Aug 29.

Died: on Aug 14, at his residence, near Jackson, Miss, Hon Geo Adams, deeply lamented by a large circle of friends. He was one of the oldest & most venerated citizens of that State. A few years since he voluntarily laid down the ofc of Judge of the U S District Court of Miss, & returned to the practice of his profession.

Died: at Cleveland, Ohio, Ashbel Walworth, in his 54th year. On Aug 26, he was standing in the Horticultural Society room conversing with a friend, when suddenly he fell backward & expired without a struggle or a groan. Mr W was one of the earliest pioneers of Northern Ohio, having emigrated there in 1800, & participated largely in the deprivations & hardships of the early settlement of the country. He held various ofcs under the General Govn't, having been Postmaster & Collector of Customs for this district as early as 1812, helidng the latter ofc until 1828.
--Cleveland Herald

Died: on Aug 25, at *Mount Clemens*, Mich, Hon Christian Clemens, age 76. He removed to Detroit from Phil in 1795, & was present at the evacuation of that place by the British the following year. Shortly afterwards he removed to Macomb Co, & founded the present fourishing village of *Mount Clemens*, where he has ever since resided, & where he was emphatically the patriarch of the community.

SAT SEP 7, 1844
Hartwell's Hotel, Phil, Sep 3. John Ross, the celebrated Cherokee chief was married in the President's parlor of this hotel last night to Miss Mary B Stapler, of Wilmington, Dela. He is about 55, & she is only 18 years old; she is a very beautiful girl & highly accomplished. Her father was formerly a highly respectable Quaker merchant of this city. She was given away by her brother, & attended by her sister & a niece of John Ross as bridesmaids. He had collected several of his dghts & nephews from boarding schoold, in N J, to be present at the wedding, &, after the ceremony, a family party of 20 of Ross' [all half breed Indians] sat down to a most sumptuous banquet, for the preparation of which he had given Hartwell a carte blanche, & a most elegant affair it was. Ross is considered to be worth half a million of dollars. He purposes sojourning at this hotel for a short time; then straight to his wild home in the Southwestern prairies.

Rev Mr Andrews, of the Meth Episc Church in 27th st, N Y, lost his life by drowning on Tue last. He was on board the boat **Columbus** on his way to Sing Sing, & on the rupture of one of the steam pipes passing to the cylinder, became alarmed & jumped overboard. He was not missed until the boat reached Tarrytown. He was in feeble health, & has left a family of 5 children to lament his untimely fate.

Rev Ebenezer Patrick, a worthy & eloquent minister of the Methodist Church, attached to the Indiana Conference, recently committed suicide by cutting his throat with a razor, at Princeton, in that State. He was laboring under a fit of temporary insanity, & one of his sons was appointed to superintend his wants. After a while, he asked his son to leave him, as he desired to rest. While thus alone, he inflicted a mortal wound on his throat.

Nicholas Goodwater commited suicide on Tue by throwing himself into the river. A girl in Canada to whom he was enaged to be married recently wrote him that she would soon become the wife of his brother. –Albany Atlas

Mr Potter, of Princeton, N J, has recently built a neat parsonage house, & endowed the Prot Epics church of that town with $10,000 for the support of the cleryman.

Jas Prince, dec'd. Heir at law wanted. Any person who can establish their claim to be Heir at Law of Jas Prince, formerly of Oxford, afterwards of London, Cooper, & who died at Hoxton in 1774, will hear of something greatly to his or her advantage by addressing a letter to J Waterlow, 24 Birchin La, London. Jas Prince's brothers were named Edw, Jos, & John. Edw Prince formerly carried on the business of a Cooper in London, & is supposed to have emigrated to America about 1736, at which period he had 4 children, named Mary, Jas, Edw, & Jos. Any person giving information which may lead to the discovery of the descendants of said Edw Prince will be rewarded for their trouble. Persons reading this advertisement, & acquainted with anyone of the name of Prince, are requested to draw their attention to it.

Farm for sale: lying in Alexandria Co, on the road to Fairfax Court House from Gtwn: contains 239 acres; good barn & stabling. Also, for sale, lots 19, 60, 63, 39, 40, & 72 in square at the s w corner of Wash & Water sts, [now occupied by Messrs Smoot & Ratcliffe,] in Deakin's, Lee's, & Cazenove's addition to Gtwn. Apply to J S Ringgold, at the arsenal.

Trustee's sale of valuable property in Fred'k: by decree of Fred'k Co Court, as Court of equity, the subscriber will sell at public auction, at Zimmerman's Hotel, on Oct 3, the beautiful & spacious Dwlg-house, in East Church st, built by Wm Schley, & now occupied by Mrs E A Lynch. The stable, carriage, & ice house, with the lots fronting on second st, can be had at the desire of the purchaser. Possession will be given on Apr 1, & propably sooner. –M B Luckett, trustee

Trustee's sale: by deed of trust from the late Jos W Hand & Catharine his wife, I shall offer at auction, on Oct 15, 14 acres, 3 roods & 16 perches [more or less] of land running from 7th st about a half a mile from the city line, adjoining the late residence of Mr Hand, & the present residence of Peter G Washington, fronting on the Turnpike. –W Redin, trustee

Durham Cattle for sale. Inquire at Montevideo, near Darnestown, Montg Co, Md.
-John P C Peter

MON SEP 9, 1844
A man named Thos Gansey, charged with riot during the late disturbances in Phil, was found guilty in the Court of Quarter Sessions on Thu. This is the 2nd conviction.

For rent: pleasant dwlg house & premises at 14th & N Y ave, late in the occupancy of Francis H Davidge. Apply to Benj Homans, next door, or to Jas Larned, 13th st.

Canada: Govn'r Metcalf has appointed the following under the new administration in Canada: 1-Wm Henry Draper, to be Atty Gen for the part of the province formerly Upper Canada. 2-Wm Morris, to be a Member of the Exec Council of the Province of Canada; also Receiver Gen. 3-Denis Benj Papineau, to be a Member of the Exec Council of the Province of Canada, & also Com'r of Crown Lands. 4-Jas Smith, to be a Member of the Exec Council of the Province of Canada, & also to be a Queen's Council in & for that part of the Province formerly Lower Canada, & Atty Genr'l for the same.

For sale, a valuable Farm lying in Montg Co, Md, adjoining the farms of Thos Bowie & Wm G Robertson, containing 200 acres of land. It is immediately at the intersection of Goshen rd & the other leading from Wash. The dwlg-house is comfortable & convenient. Apply at the law ofc of the subscribers, attys for the proprietor, on 5th st, or to WmWm Pumphrey, on the premises.
--Swann & Swann, Attys at law

Destructive fire in the village of Laurens, S C, on Aug 27. Fire started in 2 bldgs owned by Saml Vance; other bldgs lost belonged to Saml Fleming; Saml Barksdale; Saxton; J S Osborne; brick house occupied by R Hix as a saddler's shop, owned by Col Irby; storehouse occupied by J R Barksdale as a grocery, owned by Col Irby. No lives were lost.

Woodstock Herald of Aug 24. Caleb Caistor, while engaged in thrashing out grain, got himself entangled in the machine, & his leg was shattered, so that amputation above the knee was necessary.

Mrd: on Sep 1, by Rev Wm T Sprole, Mr Tresley Davis to Miss Sarah Fenesey, all of this county.

Mrd: on Sep 3, by Rev Wm T Sprole, Mr Robt Brown to Miss Mary Ann Guling.

Mrd: on Sep 5, by Rev Wm T Sprole, Mr Robt Speir to Miss Ann Miller, all of Wash City.

Mrd: on Sep 4, inAlexandria, by Rev C B Dana, Mr Wm Dodge, of Wash Co, Md, to Miss Sallie E, eldest d/o the late Richd B Mason, of D C.

Mrd: on Aug 29, in Raleigh, N C, by Rev Dr Mason, Hon J R J Daniel, Rep in Congress from the Halifax district, to Miss Frances Stith, of that city.

Died: on Sep 5, Arthur M Cox, s/o Wm W & Bridget Ann Cox, aged 15 months & 4 days.

Died: on Sep 2, of scarlet fever, George, 2nd s/o Wm & Emily Dalton, in his 4th year.

Deposited in the cavity of the corner stone of the Church of the Ascension by Rev Mr Gillis, rector of the intended church. The Bible, Prayer Book of the Episcopal Church, Canon of the Church, Proceedings of the last Convention of this Diocese, a Parchment with a Latin inscription which is thus translated:
Church of the Ascension.
Instituted A D MDCCCXLIV
This Church, to the Honor of God,
The Great, Amnipotent, & Triune,
Father, Son, & Sacred Spirit,
Was erected
A D MDCCCXLIV,
The Corner Stone being laid by the
Rt Rev W R Whittingham, D C,
Bishop of the Diocese.
Rev L J Gilliss, Rector
Vestry:

W Doughty	W J Darden	S Butt
A Holland	M Johnson	J Reeves
J A M Duncanson	B K Sharretts	

A C Kidwell, G Waters, Wardens.
W J Darden, Register.
J Tyler, President of the U S.
W W Seaton, Mayor.
This lot was presented by Gen J P Van Ness & his late esteemed & lamented wife.
Also, the following newspapers:

Episc Recorder	Globe	Whig Standard
Christian Witness	Nat'l Intell	Balt Sun
Church Advocate	Madisonian	Clipper
Banner of the Cross	Spectator	

List of the Medical Associations of Wash City.
The vocal music was performed by the Musical Assoc, under Mr J L Clubb.

Rozier's Gift for sale: the land I now reside on, in PG Co, & immediately on the road from Broad Creek to Alexandria & Wash: contains 316 acres; 2 story frame dwlg house, kitchen quarters, & other out-houses. Apply to the subscriber residing on the farm, Walter B Brooke.

Wash Livery Stable. The commodious brick stable, built by the subscriber on 8th st, between D & E sts, adjoining the old stand formerly occupied by Golding, near Connolly & Baker's Taverns, will in future be kept by my agent, Wm Kelly, who pledges himself to spare no effort to give general satisfaction. –Geo W Young

TUE SEP 10, 1844
Charlestown Select Female School, Charlestown, Jefferson Co, Va, will commence on the first Mon of Sep. Located in the village of Charlestown. –Mary E Merritt

Teacher wanted: the trustees of Wash Academy, Somerset Co, Md, wish to employ an assistant teacher: salary will be $375 per annum, payable semi-annually. Address applications to the undersigned at Princess Ann, Md. –Jas Polk, Saml W Jones, Jas Stewart, cmte

Household & kitchen furniture at auction: on Sep 12, at the residence of Miss Chisholm, on 4½ st, near Pa ave. -R W Dyer & Co, aucts

For sale: at public auction on Sep 18, on the premises, that large dwlg on **Greenleaf's Point**, formerly the residence of the late Cmdor Rodgers, with the adjacent grounds. -R W Dyer & Co, aucts

For rent: the house & lot lately occupied by Mr Randolph Coyle, Md ave & 12th st west, square 229. Inquire of Mr H Filch, north end of said house, or of Edw Mattingly, near the Navy Yard, Wash.

For rent: 2 story brick bldg on Md ave, near 4½ st. Inquire of John C Harkness at the ofc of Shepherd & Harkness, lumber yard 7th st, or Saml Redfern, near the Seven Bldgs, First Ward.

Died: on Sep 7, of intermittent fever, Mr Wm Hicks, clerk in the Genr'l Land Ofc, in his 30th year, leaving a disconsolate wife & 3 children to mourn their irreparable loss. His funeral is this morning at 10 o'clock, from his late residence on Capitol Hill.

Died: on Aug 9, 1844, in Perry Co, Indiana, Jas Lanman, a native of Fairfax Co, Va, & a soldier of the Revolution, aged 94 years.

Household & kitchen furniture at auction: on Sep 10, at the residence of Mr F W Manez, on 14th st, near Pa ave. -R W Dyer & Co, aucts

Military & Civic picnic at Arlington. The Union Guards annound they will have a picnic excursion on Sep 12. There will be 2 boats running, one leaving 14th st bridge, & the other Easby's wharf. Passage for a gentleman & 2 ladies: $1.25- refreshments, dinner, & supper included. Cmte of Arrangements:

Capt J L Cathcart, jr	Sgt P B Bell	Pvt T F Harkness
Lt S Stott	Cpl F Darnall	Pvt P G Carico
Pioneer T J Boyle	Cpl C Calvert, jr	

WED SEP 11, 1844
Bishop H U Onderonk has resigned his charge as Bishop of the Prot Episc Church, & his resignation has been accepted by a Special Convention of that Church recently convened & held in Phil.

Stock of Groceries & Liquors at auction on Sep 17, belonging to Gen Lambright, near the Railroad depot. –Wm Marshall, auct

The Lowell Advertiser says that Jane Vanvalkenburgh, a colored girl, who has been in that city on exhibition for a few days, died at her lodging last Wed. She was a native of Nassau, N Y, 14 years of age, & weighed 500 pounds.

In Chancery: Geo Bomford, cmplnt, against Chas J Nourse & others, dfndnts. The trustee reported the sale of the real estate decreed by the Court to be sold: Jas F Essex purchased ground in Gtwn on Cherry st, with improvements thereon, for $215.90; Geo Bomford purchased a portion of lot 20 in Gtwn, on Prospect st, for $300; & the west part of lot 6, in square 141, in Wash City, on G st, with dwlg house thereon, occupied by Mr Evelith, for $800; also of the residue of lot 6, & the adjoining portion of lot 7 in the same square, with frame dwlg house thereon, occupied by Capt John Peabody, for $400; that John McCutchen was the purchaser of the residue of lot 7 on G st, with frame dwlg house thereon, for $700; that Jas H Collins was the purchaser of part of lot 10 in square 168, in Wash City, containing 1,216 square feet, for $113.28; that Geo Bomford was the purchaser of part of lot 6 in square 78, in Wash City, with brick dwlg house thereon, occupied by John Barcroft, for $710; that the whole of said property in the said city was sold, subject to the dower of the said Matilda Nourse, the wid/o the late Jos Nourse. The trustee further reported that Jas F Essex, John McCutchen, & Jas H Collins have complied with the terms of the said sales & of the purchases made by them respectively; that he has not yet received from Geo Bomford the cash portions of the purchase moneys agreed to be given by him at said sales, nor any bonds for the credit portions, the whole being greatly less than the amount decreed to be paid & raised to & for said Geo Bomford, & the same appearing to the Court, & therefore that a further compliance with the terms of sale is unnecessary on the part of Geo Bomford: it is ordered that the said sales so made to Essex, McCutchen, Collins, & Bomford be & the same are hereby reatifed & confirmed. –W Brent, clk

Miss M A Cotter still continues to keep her preparatory school for children, on 9th st, near E sts.

Dr I Snell, secured a room on the first floor at Galabrun's Hotel, Pa ave, & offers his services in all that pertains to the health & preservation of the human Teeth.

Wash Corp: 1-The death of Wm Hicks, late a member of the Board of Common Council was announced: the members will attend his funeral tomorrow at 10 o'clock, & will wear the usual badge of mourning for the space of 30 days. 2-Ptn of Mrs Mary M Ellis, praying remission of a fine: referred to the Cmte of Claims.

Mrd: on Tue last, by Rev Mr Tuston, Mr Jos Hyssett to Miss Amy Patchett, both of Wash City.

Mrd: on Sep 5, by Rev F S Evans, Mr Wm A Wilson to Miss Mary Stanton Peckham, all of Wash City.

F A Ruff, of Newberry Village, S C, was accidentally killed there on Aug 22, by being shot with a revolving pistol in the hands of Mr J Y Harris. The dec'd was a young man of great respectability, & his death universally lamented.

For rent: new, pleasant, convenient house lately erected on F st, next door but one east from the house recently occupied by Rev Mr Stringfellow. The key to be had next door to the City Post Ofc. The premises may be occupied immediately.

THU SEP 12, 1844
A boy living at Holley, named Flanders, aged about 12 years, while playing in a warehouse on Tue, jumped into a bin of wheat, & was buried by the wheat which was running in. He died before he could be taken out. –Rochester Democrat

On Mon, in Phil, a watchman observed a man hanging by a rope to an awning post. He cut the cord & found that the man, Saml Rowan, was nearly dead. He recovered under medical aid & was taken to his residence in George st. The rash act was induced by a disappointment in love.

Balt College of Dental Surgery will commence on the first Mon of Nov next, & continue for 4 months. –W K Handy, Dean

Late from Texas: the Caddo Gaz of Aug 24 has intelligence from Shelby Co, Texas, the seat of the difficulties between the Regulators & another party of peace breakers: one of the ring leaders of the Regulators, Davidson, has been killed. Boulware, who, in connexion with Davidson, has for some time been at the head of a party, & is a very determined man. When he left Harrison Co 50 men were in readiness to proceed to the assistance of the Regulators.

Trustee's sale of valuable property in Gtwn: by deed of trust from John T Holtzman, to me, dated May 7, 1841, recorded in Liber W B 85, folios 398 thru 402, of the land records of Wash Co, D C: auction on Oct 25, in front of the tavern on Beall st, now occupied by Geo H Holtzman, all the interest of J T Holtzman & W P Holtzman in & to the real estate of which the late G Holtzman died seized & possessed, being two-sixths of the whole after reserving the widow's [Mrs Eliz Hotlzman] proportion, being one-eighth of the whole, consisting of a 2 story brick house & lots on Beall st, together with the stabling & outhouses thereon, now occupied by Geo H Holtzman as a tavern stand; also, a 2 story brick house & lot on said st, with the outbldg thereunto attached; & also a 2 story brick house with outbldgs, on High st; & also three 2 story brick houses & lots, together with the necessary outbldgs thereon situated, on the same st. –Sam Bacon, trustee

A stray or stolen Horse has been put in my stable for safe-keeping. Owner is to prove property, pay charges, & take him away. –Albert Parker, 18th & G sts, or at the stable of Patrick Casey.

Household & kitchen furniture at auction: on Sep 12, at the residence of Miss Chisholm, on 4½ st, near Pa ave. -R W Dyer & Co, aucts

Gov Bouck, of N Y, has offered a reward of $500 to be paid for information which shall result in the conviction of those who disturbed the public peace, resisted the execution of the laws, & committed violence on Sheriff Batterman, of Albany Co, on Aug 31, & on Deputy Sheriff Lewis, of Rensselaer Co, on Sep 2.

Robbery of the Balt & Wash Stage: last Tue night, a trunk was stolen: John Carter & Jas Elliott, from Balt, were arrested yesterday, charged on the oath of Henry Reval with assaulting with intent to rob & murder said Reval, on the Stage, not far from Beltsville.

Mauch Chunk, Pa, on Tue last, a train of cars & a locomotive were thrown off the track at the Beaver Meadow railroad, burying the brakeman, Wm Arner, in the ruins.

Died: on Sep 10, at her residence, on B st, Miss Mgt E G Wilson. Her funeral service will be at Trinity Church this afternoon at 3 o'clock.

Died: on Mon last, at the residence of J Gales, near Wash City, Josephine Hunter, infant d/o Capt John McClellan, U S A.

FRI SEP 13, 1844
$5 reward for strayed or stolen from the subscriber, a bay Horse. –Michl Talty

We learn that the death of Jos Napoleon, Count de Survilliers, took place at Florence, where he resided, on Aug 28, & was alleviated by the presence of his only 2 surviving brothers, Louis & Jerome. He died like a soldier & a Christian. Jos was born in 1768.

Circuit Court of Wash Co, D C: Eliza Hutchins vs Jacob Holtzman's heirs & others. It is by the Court, Sep 9, 1844, ordered that the papers in this cause be referred to the Auditor, with directions to state the account of the Trustee, & report thereon to this Court. Sep 25 is appointed for the above purpose. –Jos Forrest, auditor

Yarns, children's hose, & trimming goods, for sale. Call at W M Perry's, 2nd door west of 7th st & opposite the Centre Market.

Wood & Coal: apply at 10th & E sts, at Potomac bridge. –J S Harvey & Co

Tobacco, tobacco, tobacco! Reduced prices. –W H Winter, #6 east of Gadsby's, sign of Jim Crow.

For rent: 3 story house on Mo ave, near 4½ st, in complete repair. Apply to Wm Ward.

Notes on the Western Bank of Phil. On Monday ofcr Young, with Messrs Bulkley, Wm Young, & Woodruff, proceeded to the residence of Geo White, in Germantown, & there arrested Mr White & Jas Welsh. They found all the implements for executing counterfeit notes. The men were taken before Mayor Scott, of Phil, & committed to prison.

The great Organ for Trinity Church, in N Y C, now building by Mr Henry Erben, will be by far the largest in this country. The case which is to contain the mechanism will be 53 feet high, 27 feet wide, & 32 feet deep. There are to be four separate organs, known by the names of the Great Organ, the Choir Organ, Swell, & Pedals, respectively. Of draw stops there will be 43, of which 11 are mechanical stops. The gross weight of the whole will be about 40 tons, & the cost will be $10,000.

The Natchitoches [La] Chronicle of Aug 24 noticed the burial of Maj Muhlenburg, U S Army, who died at Grand Ecore. His remains were escorted into Natchitoches on Aug 23 by the 4th Regt of Infty, making a solemn view. The dec'd acted with great gallantry during the last war in the defence of Plattsburg, & was brevetted; he served afterwards with distinction under Gen Jackson, in Florida. The dec'd was a brother of Mr Muhlenburg, the late Democratic candidate for Govn'r of Pa.

The red warehouse on the canal feeder, South St Paul st, occupied by Elisha B Ely, containing 4,000 flour barrels, was destroyed by fire Sep 9. Loss covered by insurance. The fire was doubtless the work of an incendiary. –Rochester Democrat

Household & kitchen furniture at auction: on Sep 14, at the residence of Mr Hedrick, on 1st st, first house in the Burnt Row. –R W Dyer & Co, aucts

J C Wallis, Veterinary Surgeon offers his services to the gentlemen of Wash & neighborhood: 27 years in a very extensive practice; attended the Veterinary College, London. Recommended by:

P W Brown, M D	M J Miller	P P V Daniels
C A Hodges	J Steane	J Breckenborough-M D
Jas Hardin	E McAdams	
W C Tomkins	Thos Sampson	Jacob S Atley
Albert A Morris	Thos G Johnson	John McQuin
J Vessee	Josiah Woodson	Chas Marx
F Lynn	John Staylor	A Bargamin
Jas R Crafton	Alex'r Nott	R W Haxall, M D
Jas Beale, M D	Fred'k Boydon	David W Fisher
Fred'k Woodfin	N Wheat	Jas Schirmirhorn
A C Pleasant	Jos Maye	W Collingworth
John Cullins, M D	Jayes Lyons	Saml Reeve
Fred'k Marx, M D	Wm Smith	Adolph Dill
Valentine Hickler	H Childs	W W Dix
Benj W Green	R K Brock	Geo Trower

Ofc Pa ave, near 4½ st, lately occupied by Mr Bell.

At N Y, on Mon, Edw Leidy was convicted of voting twice at the last city election, & sentenced to the penitentiary for 4 months.

Died: at Pittsburg, Pa, in her 77th year, Mrs Rachel Hollingsworth. She was born at Carlisle, Pa, & resided for many years at Lexington, Ky. She was the d/o John Wilkins, a Capt in the Revolutionary war, & one of the earliest settlers at Pittsburg, of whose numerous family by the frist wife Gen John Wilkins was the eldest son, & Mr Wilkins, the present Sec of War, is now the only survivor. Mrs Hollingsworth was a lady of masculine mind, dignified, & elegant manners, & great goodness of heart. –Pittsburg American [No death date given: current item.]

Died: on Wed last, Susannah Clotilde, infant dght of Richd L & Martha Spalding, aged 10 months.

SAT SEP 14, 1844
Mrs Mead's School, *Shockhoe Hill*, Richmond, Va, will commence on the first day of Oct next. Reference is made to the following gentlemen, all of whom have dghts at Mrs Mead's school: Alexandria: Rev G A Smith. Wash: Hon J Y Mason. Richmond: Rt Rev Bishop Johns, Rev Wm Norwood, Rev Dr Emple, Jas E Heath, Chas J Osborne. Cumberland: Nelson Page. [The Southern Churchman will copy.]

Land in Fairfax Co, Va, for sale at public auction by deed of trust executed by Dr Richmond Johnson & Mgt T Johnson his wife, on Mar 22, 1830, the subscriber, will offer for sale in Wash City, on Oct 1, that portion of a tract of land in said county, called *South Green*, partitioned under a decree of court among the heirs of Andrew Balman, which was allotted to Richmond Johnson & Mgt T Johnson his wife, being half of lots 1, containing 10 acres & 9½ poles in the plat of division; & lot 3 in the same plat, containing 15 acres & 48 poles. -R Smith, trustee
-R W Dyer & Co, aucts

A fire at Bath, Morgan Co, Va, on Tue, consumed the Courthouse & Clerk's Ofc, the boarding house of Mr Jos H Sherrard, a large house belonging to the heirs of Col John Sherrard, Mr A Gustin's dwlg, J W Breatherd's storehouse, & several other bldgs. The public records were saved.

At Edgefield, S C, on Sep 2, after the sheriff's sales were over, a fight ensued between Mr Jos W Glover & Mr Lovett Gomillion, which terminated in the death of Mr Glover. Both parties were armed, & Mr Gomillion with his second pistol shot Mr Glover in the right breast, which killed him instantly. Mr Gomillion surrendered himself to an ofcr. Col Wm H Moss, in attempting to prevent the affair, was very severely but not dangerously shot by one of the parties in the neck & shoulders. Cause of the quarrel is not stated. -Pub Ledger

Mrd: on Sep 10, by Rev J P Donelan, Mr Thos H Stone, of Chas Co, Md, to Miss Eliz Ann Loveless, of this place.

Died: on Sep 10, at Marietta, PG Co, Md, in her 94th year, Miss Sarah Duvall, sister of the late Judge Duvall. She enjoyed all her faculties, her sight only a little impaired. Her funeral was numerously attended by her friends & neighbors.

Died: yesterday, in his 55th year, Borden M Voorhees, of N J, Chief Clerk of the Bureau of Construction, Equipment, & Repairs, Navy Dept. His funeral is this morning, at 10 o'clock, at his late residence on 17th st, between H & I sts.

Died: on Sep 8, Dr Chas G Parsons, [late of the State of Mississippi,] at the residence of his father, Hon John W Parsons, in Rye, N H, aged 36 years.

The family of the late Chauncey Dickerman, of Hamden, numbering in all 11 sons & dghts, met together in the house in which they were born on Thu week. Their ages added together amount to 641 years. The eldest 73, the youngest 45. It is 40 years since they all last met together. –New Haven Herald

Thos wishing to reduce the cost of their Clothing are invited to call at the old stand of J Dixon, La ave, for fit, fashion, & workmanship. –J Riggles, Draper & Tailor

Mr Isaac Cox, his wife, & 4 children, were drowned by the late overflow of the Missouri river. They had moved from Richmond Co, Ky, to Johnson Co, Missouri, where they were living at the time of their misfortune.

MON SEP 16, 1844
N Y Whig Convention at Syracuse on Wed, organized by the choice of Francis Granger Pres, & proceeded to select unanimously the following State ticket:
For Govn'r, Millard Fillmore   For Lt Govn'r, Saml J Wilkin

For Presidential Electors:

Willis Hall	John A Collier
John A King	Henry Van Rensselaer
David Leavitt	Chas E Clarke
Caleb S Woodhull	Jese Matteson
Benj Drake	Wm C Fields
Abraham R Lawrence	Thos G Waterman
Edw D West	Elias Brewster
Pierre Van Cortland	Danl Gott
Thos L Davies	David B Smith
Hiram Bennett	Timothy S Williams
Wm C De Witt	Peter Himrod
Robt A Barnard	Freeman Edson
Saml I McChesney	Jonathan Buell
John Townsend	Martin Butts
Henry H Ross	Timothy H Porter
Billey J Clark	Timothy S Hopkins
Jas Walker	Abel Webster
Harvey W Doolittle	Lorenzo Burrows

Mrd: on Sep 12, by Rev Mr Donelan, Mr Jas A Clarke to Miss Mary Ann Beardsley, both of Wash.

Died: on Sep 12, after an illness of 2 days, of scarlet fever, in her 5th year, Marian, d/o Seth A & Sarah Ann Elliot of Wash City.

Died: on Thus last, in Gtwn, after an illness of 2 days, Horace Hunter, 3rd s/o Thos Woodward, in his 8th year.

For rent: possession given by Oct 1, the house so long occupied by Mrs A Cochran on F st, between 13th & 14th sts: contains 17 rooms. If not applied for during this week, Mrs Cochran will conclude to retain it herself as a boarding house.

Tuition in French: A M Girault, F st, west of 11th st, north side.

Four Indian traders from Chariton Co, Mo, were attacked & plundered about 250 miles above St Peters, a few weeks ago, by a party of Lisiton Sioux Indians. Mr Turner was drowned subsequently, in endeavoring to cross the river, & Mr Bennet was the only one of the four to escape. Col Bruce had left *Fort Snelling* for the purpose of arresting the offenders.

Near Shreveport, a few days since, Mr Battle, father of the editor of the Caddo Gaz, with one of his slaves, met with a most melancholy death. In cleaning the well the negro fell out of the bucket & his master hurried down to his assistance. They were both drowned. The well was indeed foul, but it was from the accumulation of mephitic vapor, which alternately overpowered both. New Orleans Picayune

TUE SEP 17, 1844
Naval Court Martial convened at the Navy Yard in this city yesterday, of which Cmdor Stewart is Pres. The members are: Cmdor Downes, Cmdor Nicholson, Cmdor Read, Cmdor Ridgely, Capt Latimer, & Capt Gwinn. The Court has been ordered for the trial of Capt Newton, late commanding the unfortunate ship **Missouri**, & such other persons as may be brought before it. Others will be tried by the Court. –Madisonian

On Sat Mrs Beatson, w/o Henry Beatson, cabinet-maker, residing in Lombard st, was discovered suspended by the neck from the handrail of the stairway, life extinct. The husband, who showed symptoms of mental derangement, was a week ago placed by his friends in the insane dept of the Md Hospital for medical treatment, where he remains, leaving his wife with 3 children & some workemen in the shop. She did the act with great premeditation by putting her house in order, the young child, about 2, to sleep, & sending the other two, a boy 12 & a girl 14 abroad, with instructions not to return till evening. Henry Beatson & his wife were noted for their temperate, frugal, & industrious habits. They were natives of Sheffield, Eng, & have resided in Balt City some 12 or 14 years.

Mrd: on Wed week, at Gravellyrun, Va, by Rev Theoderick Pryor, Mr Robt Y Jones, s/o Benj Jones, of Petersburg, to Miss E A D Lundy, d/o Col I G Lundy.

Died: on Aug 19 last, at his residence, near Carthage, Tenn, Col Robt Allen. He was bred a merchant, & first settled in Carthage soon after that town was established, nearly 40 years ago, where he continued to live engaged in trade & as clerk of the county court for a great number of years. A number of years since he retired to a beautiful farm on the banks of the Cumberland river, a most industrious farmer. He served as a volunteer & commanded a regt under Gen Jackson with great credit & honor in the South during the late war. He was elected & re-elected to Congress from the Smith & Wilson district, until he chose voluntarily to retire.

Died: on Sep 7, at her residence, near Bryantown, Chas Co, Md, Mrs Dorothy Dyer, wid/o the late Geo A Dyer, in her 53rd year.

Died: on Sep 6, at the residence of his father, Chilton Allan, in Winchester, Ky, Mr Wm Chilton Allan, in his 19th year. This young gentleman bid fair to make one of the most distinguished artist which America has produced. He had already made the most living likeness of Henry Clay which has ever been made. He was also a distinguished sculptor..

Administration notice: the creditors of Henry Grieb, late of Wash City, dec'd, are to produce their claims at the Orphans Court of Wash Co, D C on or before Nov 1 next. –F Grieb, adm of Henry Grieb

For rent: 2 good dwlg houses at H & 6th sts. Also for rent, a small brick house on 6th st. Apply to Jas B Phillips, Mass ave, between 6th & 7th sts.

I certify that Jas Langly, of Wash Co, brought before, as a stray, a white & red steer. –Nath Brady, J P [Owner is to call on me, at Mr Thos Blagden's wharf, prove his property, pay charges, & take him away. –Jas Langly]

WED SEP 18, 1844
Instruction, Vocal, & Instrumental: Madame Eugenie Roget, from Phil. Apply to Madame Roget, at Miss A Young's Seminary, F st, near 12th st.

To let: residence on 3rd st, Gtwn, formerly the property of D Bussard, Gtwn. It is large & commodious. Apply to M Adler, Agent, Gtwn.

Farm for sale: the subscriber will sell his farm containing 231 acres, on the county road leading from Wash to Bladensburg, about 1 mile from Mr Tucker's celebrated peach farm. Improvements are a comfortable dwlg with necessary out houses. The property will be shown by Mr Brashears, who resides on the farm. –C C Hyatt

The Pres has appointed Andrew Jackson Donelson, of Tenn, to be Charge d'Affaires of the U S to Texas, to succeed Mr Howard, dec'd.

Raleigh Independent of Sat last. We announce the death of Col Michl Hoke, late Democratic candidate for Govn'r. Lincoln Courier Extra, Sep 11. He died in Charlotte on Mon, of bilious fever, apart from family & relatives, but in the midst of friends. His body will be interred in this town today. [Sep 21st newspaper: May Heaven temper this heavy affliction to the widow & children of my lost but cherished friend. –R J B -Balt, Md, Sep 19, 1844]

Died: on Sep 13, at the residence of her son in Wash, after a long & painful illness, Mrs Harriet Shott, in her 52nd year. The dec'd was a native of & resident of Balt until within the last 2 months.

Died: on Apr 15, in Wash City, Robt Stephens, of Farnham, Richmond Co, Va. He was an estimable youg mechanic, who but recently came to Wash City to seek a support for himself & a surviving mother. He died of a lingering nervous typhoid affection. Blessed is the death of the poor on earth, but rich in heaven.

Abijah Waters, a young man, s/o Col Reuben Waters, in West Sutton, on Sep 3, while loading a double barreled gun it discharged itself. Both eyes are entirely destroyed & his face badly mangled. His hand has been amputated. –Mass Spy

The Franklin Fire Co thanks Richd Smith for his kindness in furnishing them with refreshments, at the fire in the rear of his house, on Sep 14. –Wm Durr, Sec F F Co

Circuit Court of Wash Co, D C-in Chancery. Esther Hunt & Mary Hunt, Wm Rochester Hunt, & others, heirs at law of Wm Hunt. By decree of said Court, the Trustee appointed, will sell at public auction, on Oct 21 next, all the title & estates of the late Wm Hunt in & to the following: part of lot 1 in square 458, in Wash City, on La ave. –J B H Smith, Trustee -R W Dyer & Co, aucts

Lot for sale at public auction: by deed of trust executed by Mr John S Chaney, on Sep 26, 1842: public auction of the west half of lot 2 in square 256, fronting on north I st, together with improvements. –Richd Smith, Trustee -R W Dyer & Co, aucts

Circuit Court: on Fri last the petition for the freedom of Betsey & Caroline Herbert against Henry Miller, administrator of Geo Miller, was tried. Verdict for petitioners.

Burglary on Mon, to the grocery store of Mr S Tench, 8th & Va ave. The rogues stole fine hams & shoulders out of a lot of bacon that was kept in the warehouse.

Robbery committed last Mon in the boarding house of Miss Janney, 8th & Pa ave. The thief stole a gold thimble, a gold bracelet, & other articles of jewelry.

THU SEP 19, 1844
Stolen from the subsciber's plantation, near Queen Ann, PG Co, Md, on Sep 11, one iron gray Horse. $5 reward if taken within 5 miles of my premises & delivered to me, or $10 if taken up anywhere else & delivered to me. –John Mitchell

Orphans Court of Wash Co, D C. Letters of administration on personal estate of John Paul Jones, late of Virginia, dec'd. –Geo L Lowden, adm, Charleston, S C

Wash City property to be sold for taxes on Dec 11 next, unless the said taxes be previously paid to the Collector, with such expenses & fees as may have accrued at the time of payment. --A Rothwell, Collector

Auld, Jas, heirs of: 1841 thru 43: $17.01
Bealle, Benj B: 41 thru 43: $4.02
Burgess, Richd: 41-43: $1.38
Blackstone, Chas: 41-43: $4.14
Bowen, Geo: 41043: $5.10
Burgess, Henrietta & John E Graig: 41-43: $10.08
Barcroft, John: 41-43: $41.16
Brereton, John: 41-43: $2.55
Burdine, Reuben: 41-43: $104.25
Bush, Wm: 41-43: $17.88
Berry, Wm J: 41-43: $ 12.60
Cazenove, Anthony C: 41-43: $100.53
Carroll, Danl: 37-43: $278.92
Cross, Geo, heirs of: 38-43: $2.24
Cross, H L: 38-43: $75.54
Cromwell, Harriet: 41-43: $4.53
Craven, Isaac, heirs of: 41-43: $60.15
Clephane, Jas: 41-43: $29.06
Conner, Thos: 41-43: $ 11.88
Dyer, Edw: 41-43: $12.09
Davidson, Jas: 34-43: $13.57
Daw, Reuben: 38-43: $8.80
Donaphon, Thornton S: 41-43: $25.59
Dunlop, Eliz: 41-43: $22.14
Dunlop, Jas: 41-43: $89.61
Davidson, Saml, trustees of: 41-43: $4.50
Dougherty, Thos, heirs of: 41-43: $.70
Eckloff, Christian: 41-43: $93.03
Edwards, Jas M: 41-43: $3.12
Edmonson, Nathan: 41-43: $47.64
English & Nevans: 41-43: $5.88
Fowler, Hanson: 41-43: $13.99
Fowler, Chas S: 41-43: $21.87
Fowler, Catharine S: 41-43: $2.19
Foxall, Henry, heirs of: 41-43: $84.18
Grammar, G C: 38-43: $86.09
Greenleaf, Jas: 24-43: $1.147.89
Gratiot, Chas: 41-43: $233.11
Haswell, N B: 41-43: $4.83
Henley, Wm D: 41-43: $7.38
Howison, Henry: 41-43: $74.55

Hilton, John P: 42-43: $15.14
Hoover, John: 41-43: $199.23
Handy, Mary G: 41-43: $29.73
Holland, Saml: 40-43: $8.74
Hayman, Wm heirs of: 38-43: $105.00
Hazel, Zachariah: 40-43: $47.68
Jones, C L: 40-43: $153.03
Jones, John C: 42-43: $22.08
Jeffers, Matthias: 38-43: $309.50
Jarboe, Matthew: 41-43: $25.69
Jones, Sarah: 41-43: $11.41
Keller, Eliz: 42-43: $88.01
Kuhn, J L, heirs: 41-43: $23.01
Kershner, Martin: 40-43: $13.80
Lowe, Barbara: 41-43: $39.84
Lambright, Geo: 41-43: $35.95
Lockrey, Hugh: 40-43: $25.36
Longson, Jos: 41-43: $24.48
Lynch, John: 41-43: $40.08
Leckie, Robt, heirs of: 38-43: $183.26
Lowe, Thos jr, improvements in the name of John Magruder: 41-43: $20.25
Lowe, Wm W: 41-43: $23.85
McGunnigle, Ann, heirs of: 42-43: $87.28
Murphy, Ephraim, heirs of: 42-43: $5.42
McGlue, G T: 41-43: $12.04
Miller, Henry: 41-43: $58.17
Mudd, Ignatius: 41-43: $121.32
McCormick, Jas, heirs of: 42-43: $29,12
Magee, Patrick: 42-43: $13.62
Magill, Thos: 41-43: $23.22
McDuell, John: 38-43: $92.50
McLeod, John: 38-43: $142.42
McDaniel, Wm: 41-43: $192.68
Munro, David: 1841-42: $36.10
Nailor, Allison, jr: 41-43: $48.39
Nevins, John S: 41-43: $3.69
Nourse, Jos, heirs of: 41-43: $146.40
Newell, Wm: 41-43: $4.29
Oden, Benj, heirs of: 41-43: $15. 14
Orme, T T & M A: 42-43: $4.71
Parker & Huntt: 41-43: $100.
Pearson, Martha: 41-43: $33.36
Parker, Nancy: 41-43: $45.89
Pollard, Benj: 41-43: $41.76

Peter, David, heirs of: 38-43: $16.03
Queen, Nicholas L: 39-43: $32.24
Roper, Erasmus H: 41-43: $8.56
Robertson, Mary: 40-43: $19.58
Radcliff, Jos: 40-43: $9.36
Robinson, Saml: 41-43: $93.24
Ratcliff, Sarah: 41-43: $42.84
Randall, John: 1841 & 1843: $100.33
Sanders, Edw J: 41-43: $19.80
Sweeny, Mary: 41-43: $41.55
Sands, R C: 41-43: $12.51
Scott, Upton: 41-43: $1.92
Smith, J B H & others: 41-43: $48.72
Tims, Henry, heirs of: 41-43: $72.81
Thaw, Jos, heirs of: 42-43: $68.04
Thomas, Jas, heirs of: 41-43: 93.76
Thompson, Richd: 41-43: $13.85
Thomas, John H: 41-43: $16.58
Tuel, Patrick: 41-43: $34.17
Thompson, Wm: 37-43: $12.80
Territt, Wm H: 41-43: $6.33
Wood, Ferdinand F, heirs of: 40-43: $37.44
Waters, Henrietta: 40-43: $21.43
Weightman & Webb: 42-43: $51.24
Wertz, Mary E: 41-43: $147.39
Welch, Mary Ann: 41-43: $41.55
Wood, Mary Ann E: 40-43: $53.76
Winder, Levin H: 41-43: $7.68
Young, Eleanor: 37-43: $5.54
Young, Nicholas, heirs: 38-43: $10.20

Household & kitchen furniture at auction: on Sep 26, in the 2 houses occupied by Mr Jos R Thompson, on Missouri ave, between 4½ & 6th sts. –R W Dyer & Co, aucts

Whigs of the Island, attention. The Island Clay Club will meet at the Island Engine house on Sep 19. –D Westefield, jr, sec

A young man, about 17 years of age, named Bartlett, belonging to Amesbury, was accidentally killed last week, while on a gunning excursion.

FRI SEP 20, 1844
Cash Store: great bargains in Ladies & Gentlemen Weat. –S T Wall, Pa ave, between 8th & 9th sts, opposite Centre Market

Naval Gen Court Martial met yesterday at the Nat'l Hotel & the only witness examined was Saml Archbold, 3rd Assist Engineer of the ship **Missouri**. [Sep 21st newspaper: yesterday, Saml Archbold was further examined; Chas H Haswell, formerly Chief Engineer of the **Missouri**, commenced his evidence.

Fatal accident on Mon of last week, just as the Schenectady train left the depot in Saratoga, Chas S Waterman, between 6 & 7 years of age, & s/o Mr Saml Waterman, jumped on the outside of the passenger car to speak to a sister who was leaving with the train, & when attempting to get off, was thrown down, one of his legs falling across the rail, mangling the limb that amputation was necessary. He died a few hours after the accident.

Country Retreat near Wash, for sale. The subscriber offers his present residence, 8 miles from Wash, on the Turnpike to Rockville, Montg Co, Md: comprises a 2 story frame house of 5 rooms, kitchen, pantry, carriage & wood-house, stable, cow sheds, & 50 acres of land under post & rail fence. Proprietor on the premises. –Judson Mitchell, Bridge st, Gtwn, D C

Naval. The U S ship **Erie** arrived in Hampton Roads on Sep 17 from Pacific via Rio de Janeiro. The **Erie** had on board 250 seamen who have been sent home from the different stations. Mr Lewis Merserau, of Portsmouth, Va, died on board the **Erie**, May 12.
List of ofcrs & passengers of the **Erie**:
Lt Commanding: N W Duke
Lts: Murray Mason, Wm H Brown, B Shattuck
Surgeon: Geo Clymer
Acting Master: Wm L Blanton
Acting Purser: John H Poor, jr
Prof of Math: B McGowan
Passed Midshipman: John P Decatur
Midshipmen: Jas Higgins, W F Spicer, Geo M Ransom, Wm Nelson, L B Robinson, F S Conover
Capt's Clerk: H Martin
Boatswain: W A Watson
Passengers: Hon J S Pendleton, Charge d'Affaires to Chili; Purser, Thos E Norris; Mid J L S Beckwith; Messrs Jos Hobson, Geo McLane, Balt; Danl & Saml Haviland, Santiago, Chili; Acting Midshipmen, B G Lindsay & E C Henshaw.

More incendiarism: on Wed last, a frame stable & coach-house occupied by a colored man, Warren Riggs, was set on fire. A valuable horse was destroyed in the flames & another much injured. The stable belonged to Mrs Lear.

Members of the Falcon Boat Club will meet at the Boat House this evening at 4:30 precisely. –W H Topping, Coxswain

The U S sloop-of-war **Jamestown** was launched from the navy yard at Gosport at 12 o'clock on Mon last: built under the sole direction of Foster Rhodes, the naval constuctor at that station. -Beacon

Balt Custom-house: Jos Snyder, Inspector & Storekeeper, removed, & Jas C Berry, appointed. Matthew Kelly, Inspector, removed, & John Patrick appointed. These removals are, perhaps, the most wanton acts of proscription that have ever taken place under any Administration. Mr Snyder by long service had won for himself the character of a most faithful public ofcr. Capt Kelly, is one of the oldest shipmasters in the city; was one of the gallant defenders of the city in the battle of North Point, is the father of a large family, & one of the most estimable & worthy men in Balt. -Patriot

Mr Gibbon, editor of the Bee, in Smithland, Ky, was deliberately shot & killed by Dr Snyder, while walking in the street with his little dght. An article had appeared in the Bee against Snyder, which probably caused the crime. The murderer was immediately arrested. The dec'd was formerly editor of the Louisville Dime.

Wm Rich, whose pardon from the State Prison was obtained by the Washingtonians of Lynn, & who has been officiating as a temperance lecturer, was taken last week in the store of his benefactor, Mr Christopher Robinson, of Lynn. The store had been previously robbed; a watch had been set, & the convict was taken after he had entered the store. –Bunker Hill Aurora

We learn that Gov Bouck has granted a pardon to Dingler, the proprietor of the Broadway Cottage, 312 Broadway, who was sentenced to Sing Sing for an atrocious rape committed at that place to a young girl. The first intimations we believe that a pardon had been granted to him was given by seeing him parading Broadway. -N Y Express

SAT SEP 21, 1844
On Wed last as the sons of Dr Ariel Ballou & Eugene Martin, & a lad named Wm Tilley, were sailing in a skiff on the reservoir pond in Woonsocket, R I, the boat was upset, & Ariel Ballou, jr, & Chas H Martin were drowned. Tilley was saved. The bodies were found in the water in about an hour.

Obit-died: on Aug 19, in the city of St Louis, after a short illness, Lt Francis E Barry, U S N. During 16 years that he had served in the Navy he had spent only 14 months on shore, & he had lately returned to the bosom of his family afer a 5 years' cruise in the Pacific, when he was attacked by the fatal disease, which, in 3 days, terminated his existence. This dispensation of Divine Providence, by removing from them an only son, has inflicted a deep wound on his bereaved parents. -E

Gtwn property to be sold for taxes on Dec 18, 1844. –Wm Jewell, Collector
Lot 291, Beatty & Hawkins' addition, 1½ acres more or less, assessed to Clement Smith: 1840-44.
A lot in Holmead's additon, not numbered, 60 feet on Dunbarton st & 120 feet on Monroe st: assessed to Rachael Steel's heirs: 1844.
Lot 32, & lot 33, Deakins, Lee, & Casanave's addition: assessed to John Lee: 1844.
Lot 213, Beatty & Hawkins' addition, fronting on Fred'k st: assessed to Wm Gadsby: 1844. West half of lot 269, Beall's addition, on Stoddard st: assessed to Wm Gadsby: 1844. East half of lot 274, Beall's addition, on Stoddard st: assessed to Wm Gadsby: 1844.
Parts of lots 7 & 8, old Gtwn, beginning at at point on the west line of Congress st: assessed to Jane Clagett: 1844.

The subscriber will sell at public sale on Oct 29, the Farm on which he now resides, containing 312 acres of land, in PG Co, Md, in the productive region of the county known as the *Forest*; with a small new dwlg-house & all out-bldgs. He will also sell all his stock & farming utensils. –Arundel Smith

Died: on Sep 11, at her residence in Newport, R I, Mrs Sarah Ladd, wid/o & relict of John G Ladd, late merchant of the city of Alexandria. Her past health had been feeble, but her death was sudden & unexpected. -N

Mrd: on Sep 5, at Waterloo, Lamen's District, S C, by Rev S B Leers, Mr Geo E Gates, of Chicksaw Co, Miss, to Miss Arianna B, d/o Capt Geo Bowen, of the former place.
+
Mrd: on Sep 5, at Waterloo, Lamen's District, S C, by Rev S B Leers, Capt Saml P Gates, of the said county of Chickasaw & State of Mississippi, to Miss Antoinette W, d/o the said Capt Geo Bowen.

Mrd: on Sep 19, by Rev John C Smith, Mr Jas Warren, jr, of Phil, to Miss Eliz D Shields, of Wash.

Died: on Sep 17, at his residence in PG Co, Md, Mrs Rebecca S Barron, in her 53rd year. Blessed are the dead who die in the Lord, may our last end be like hers.

Cash for Rags: at the Printing Ofc & Bookbindery of J C McGuire, 10th & Pa ave.

$5 reward for return of 2 Cows lost. Strayed from the subscriber, residing on Capitol Hill, near the Catholic Church. –Jas M Selden

MON SEP 23, 1844
$5 reward for return of strayed sorrel cow. Deliver to Fred'k May, on Capitol Hill.

Kensington Riot Cases of May-Phil: Court of Quarter Sessions at Phil:
Fred'k Hess, a German boy, convicted of rioting & burning St Augustine's Church.
His Brother, John Hess, charged of rioting: jury could not agree.
Richd Gansey, conviced of riot at St Augustine's Church, throwing the books out of the priest's house on to the bonfire in the street.
John Daley, convicted of murder in the 2nd degree, firing upon the Natives, & causing the death of Matthew Hammitt.
Thos Wall, charged with rioting: acquitted.
John O'Neill, Edw Sherry, & Terrence Mullin, each convicted of riot.

Died: on Sep 21, after a long & painful illness, Dr Edw W Clark, aged 56 years. His funeral is this afternoon, at 4 o'clock, from his late residence, Navy Yard.

Died: on Thu last, in Wash City, Eliza Virginia, the y/d/o Robt & Eliza B Mills.

Died: on Sep 22nd, after a few days' illness, Rosanna, eldest d/o Jos & Eliz Smith, in her 7th year. Her funeral is this afternoon, at 4 o'clock, from the residence of her parents, on Mass ave, between 4th & 5th sts.

Destructive conflagration yesterday. The citizens of Gtwn & Wash have to regret the destruction by fire of Col Bomford's valuable & extensive flour & grist mill, which was built not many years since at the south end of the Market Space, between Bridge & Water sts: cost not less than $40,000-insurance $21,000. This does not inclrude contents. Flames spread to the brick bldg belonging to Mr Peter Magruder, & occupied by Mr Thecker; Mr Scott's house caught fire; Mr Smith's brick warehouse caught fire. The watchmen in the mill having fallen asleep, the rubbers caught fire by friction. [Sep 25th newspaper: Mr Vincent Taylor states that there were no rubbers going in that part of the mill, & thinks the fire was not occasioned by friction. It is considered by some few persons to have been caused by an incendiary.]

The Nat'l Hotel has been recently leased to Mr Saml S Colemen, formerly of the Astor House, N Y, & has been undergoing alterations for several weeks. Painting by Mr Benker, of N Y; Mr S P Franklin, of Wash City, has newly papered all the rooms; the portico & capenter's work in front of the bldg has been executed by Mr R H Stewart, of Wash City. The hair-dressing & shaving dept is under the charge of Mr J H Gibbs. The barber's shop is well supplied with cool water, which is continually running into the room from the adjacent spring.

P W Browning, Merchant Tailor: Granite Row, Pa ave, between 3rd & 4½ sts.

For rent: commodious house on G st, at present occupied by the Surgeon General as an ofc. The house is well suited for a large family. Possession can be had in the beginning of Oct. Apply to Mr Rickett's, opposite, or to Louis Vivans.

TUE SEP 24, 1844
Wm F Bokee, 41 North Howard st, between Fayette & Lexington st, Balt: Importer of China, Glass, & Queensware.

Clement Smith returns his thanks to the firemen of Wash for their exertions in the protection of his property on Sun last, which saved his & adjacent property.

Masonic: Columbia Chapter 15: meeting this evening at 7:30 p m. –Wm Greer, sec

WED SEP 25, 1844
Louisville Courier: Alfred Hill, who some time since killed Laura E Delana, age 8 years, had been convicted of murder in the 2nd degree, & sentenced to 30 days' solitary confinement & imprisonment for life in the penitentiary. The girl was bound to him, we believe, & he caused her death by severe whipping.

U S brig **Oregon**, Lt Commanding Sinclair, bound to Chagres, with the U S mail, sailed from Norfolk on Sat. Cmdor Sloat, cmder of the Pacific squadron, & son, Edw Dixon, bearer of dispatches to Bogota, are passengers in the **Oregon**.

The Boston script states that a block of 2 brick houses in Lincoln st, 3 stories high, was safely & successfully removed yesterday 10 feet & 6 inches from their old foundation to the rear. This novel work was accomplished on a plan furnished by Alderman Preston, a member of the cmte for widening streets, & by Mr Moses Parker, who is entitled to great credit for the success of this new enterprise. Concave cast-iron plates are prepared, the foundation of the wall cut away, & 2 plates facing each other inserted, with cannon balls between them. These plates & balls being placed under all the walls, the whole bldg rests upon them. Three screws are applied, & the whole bldg is rolled upon them any distance. These plates & balls are removed one by one, & the brick replaced & the bldg left in the original state, without injury to the structure. This block weighed 700 tons, & was rolled on 120 balls, & accomplished, after the plates were set, in about 2 hours' time.

Mr Saml Carusi, on going by his music store, north Chas st, yesterday, found the front door unlocked, & about $400 worth of instruments had been abstracted therefrom. It is supposed that false keys were used in effecting an entry. -Clipper

A lad named Stillman, about 10 years of age, s/o Peter Stillman, resident in Columbia, near Cave st, Balt, fell off the cars of the Fred'k train, on Mon, his head striking the stones, causing a concussion of the brain. He died about a half an hour afterwards, in the hardware store of Mr Browning, where he had been carried. -Sun

Another Phil Rioter arrested: Wm Franks was bound over on Sat in the sum of $3,000 to answer the charge of riot on May 7 last, in Kensington.

Wm Pritchard, a resident of Portsmouth, Va, was charged on Sat on having caused the death of Danl Fitchett, of that borough, by striking him in the eye with an umbrella, which caused his death. He was committed for further examination.

A s/o Mr & Mrs J R S Van Vleit, 12 Centre st, fell from the window of his room in the 3rd story, breaking his skull. He died in about 2 hours. He was about 4 years old.

Rev Jas Blake Howe, Rector of the Episc Church, Claremont, N H, died suddenly at Albany, N Y, on Tue. He had just taken his seat in the train of cars for the West. He was seized with an apoplectic fit just before the cars started. He was about 60.

While Mr Saml G Martin was repairing a defect in the boiler Wing's steam flouring mill, Paymyra, Wayne Co, N Y, the plug blew out, scalding his whole body. He died in about 10 hours. He was 35 years of age, & has left a wife & 2 children.

A physician named Stadlin, recently from Rome, N Y, lost his life when bitten by a rattlesnake. –Saratoga Whig

I certify that Mrs Eliz Gill, of Wash Co, brought before me, as an estray, a red cow & a male calf about 2 months old. –John L Smith, j p [Owner is to call on me, 14th & C sts south, prove property, pay charges & take them away. –E Gill]

Naval Court Martial: met last Mon. Lt Simon F Blunt & Danl Doharty, fireman, were examined. Jas Faron, jr, chief engineer on board the ship **Missouri**, was also examined.

Bloody tragedies. 1-Rencontre on Sep 6, at Due West Corner, between Saml Miller, of Pontotoc, Miss, & Peter R Thompson, of Anderson, S C, both students of Erskine College, which resulted in the latter receiving 2 stabs, & producing his death in a few minutes. Miller was arrested & committed to jail. The families of each are of the highest respectability. 2-On Aug 25, at Shreveport, La, Isaac Jones was killed by a stab with a bowie knife in the hands of Wm B White.

Mrd: on Sep 17, by Rev Wm T Sprole, Mr E Peddecord to Miss Ann E Gumaer, all of Wash City.

Mrd: on Sep 17, by Rev Mr Boswell, J H D Hall, of Fauquier Co, Va, to Miss Rosa Clay Gunnell, d/o W H Gunnell, of Wash City.

Died: on Thu last, in Charlestown, Va, after an illness of some weeks, Mr Henry F Goertz, Prof of Music, & a most estimable citizen, in his 40th year. He was a native of Saxony, but had resided in Winchester for several years past.

Died: on Sep 21, of hemorrhage, in his 58th year, John Augustus Schneider, a native of Laufen on the Neckar, Kingdom of Wirtemberg, & for the last 12 years a citizen of Wash.

Died: on Thu, at Brooklyn, N Y, Jas H Clark, Purser U S Navy, in his 61st year.

Died: on May 15 last, at Valparaiso, of consumption, Mr Francis E Baker, late Sailingmaster of the U S ship **Cyane**. The U S Counsul reports that he will send him home the personal effects of the dec'd in the store ship **Erie**.

Morgan Riflemen of Gtwn announce a Militrary & Civic Picnic to take place next Fri at the celebrated spring near Arlington. The picnic party calculate on a cordial welcome from the hospitality of G W P Custis, the king proprietor of Arlington.
Cmte of Arrangements:

Capt Duvall	Pvt Poor	Pvt Rodier
Lt Goddard	Lt Robertson	Pioneer Tippett
Sgt Locke	Ensign Fronk	

$5 reward for return of a strayed cow, from the residence of Mrs Potter, on Pa ave.

For rent: the subscriber desires to rent for the remainder of his term, which will expire on May 1, 1845, the house he now occupies at 17th & I sts. –Randolph Coyle

THU SEP 26, 1844
Avondale Farm for sale: the subscriber about to engage in another business, will offer at public sale, on Oct 22, this beautiful, healthy, & productive farm, lying in Montg Co, Md, the turnpike road from Gtwn to Rockville passing through it: contains 212 acres; 2 frame dwlgs, one recently built in cottage style, 2 stories high, with 11 rooms. The other dwlg cotains 6 rooms, kitchen & storeroom. Apply, postage paid, Gtwn, D C, to the subscriber, R Williams.

Runaway was committed to Alleghany Co, Md, jail on Aug 22 last, a negro man Jas Crawford. If said negro is not properly proven by his master, he will be released according to law. –N Bruce, Sheriff of Alleghany Co

Runaway negro man Jas Randall was committed to Alleghany Co, Md, jail, & says he came from near the Point of Rocks, Md. If not properly proven by his master he will be released according to law. –N Bruce, Sheriff of Alleghany Co

The Boston Journal give the names & ages of 25 Revolutionary heroes who were on Thu present at the Whig gathering in that city. Mr Isaac Cazneau, who is past 90 years of age, & was a spectator of the battle of Bunker Hill, appeared on foot in the procession.

A fine boy, 3 years old, s/o Mr Leach, veterinary surgeon, Young st, in this city, met his death from drinking oil of vitriol. An antidote was given, but to no avail. He survived only 3 hours. –Toronto Colonier

For rent: a very nice furnished house on Pa ave, between 9th & 10th sts. -Rosalie Bihler

Riot cases: 1-Robt McQuillan was found guilty on a charge of riot: sentence deferred. 2-Josiah Nicholas was tried on a charge of riot: verdict guilty: sentence deferred.

We find no mention in the will of Jos Bonaparte of his dght by his first wife, whom his brother Napoleon, with his usual disrespect of persons, privileges, & laws, compelled him to divorce. This lady resides at Rossie, N Y, is highly accomplished, & lovely in person, & reflects more credit upon the Bonaparte family than any of the offspring of their ambitious alliances. –Boston Courier

$10 reward for runaway negro woman Sophia Robinson, between 35 & 40 years old. Her husband, as well as all his relatives, are free, & live in Wash City. –Jas C Summers, living near Spalding's old Tavern, commonly called Spalding's district, in PG Co, Md.

$50 reward for runaway negro man Isaac Newton, about 30 or 35 years of age. -Wm P Rennoe, Nanjemoy Post Ofc, Chas Co, Md

Barley Female Seminary: Mrs Eleanor Johnson, Principal: Miss Martha C Annan & Miss Aurelia C Russell, Teachers. Located on the Md Tract, 13 miles from Fred'k city & 6 miles from Harper's Ferry. References:
Rt Rev Bishop Whittingham, Balt, Md   Rev Jas Chisholm, Hedgesville, Va
Rev John Hoff, Fred'k Co, Md   Rev M Holmead, Ellicot's Mills, Md
Rev Jas A Birch, Hancock, Md   Rev O Bulkley, Cumberland Co, Va
Rev Alex'r Shiras, Gtwn, D C
Address to Eleanor Johnson, Petersville, Md.

For sale: brick house on K st north, between 11th & 12th sts. Apply on E st, between 12th & 13th sts, to E H Roper.

Mrd: on Sep 19, at Leeland, Jefferson Co, Va, by Rev C W Andrews, John Simms Powell, of Alexandria, to Sarah Ellen, eldest d/o Edmund I Lee.

Mrd: on Sep 23, by Rev Mr Sprole, Dr Chas G Page to Priscy S Webster, all of Wash City.

The solemnity of laying the corner-stone of Whittingham Chapel took place in the village of Bladensburg, Md, on Sep 9. Rev Wm Pinkney, Rector of this Parish, delivered a truly beautiful & eloquent address.

Died: on Sep 24, Mr Richd Barry, [stone cutter,] a native of the county of Cork, Ireland, aged 43 years. The members of the Wash City Benevolent Society are to attend his funeral from his late residence, on Vt ave, between K & L sts, in the afternoon, at 3 o'clock.

Died: on Sep 15, after a painful illness of 4 weeks, at *Bushwood*, St Mary's Co, Md, in her 25th year, Mrs C G Plowden, consort of E J Plowden.

Died: on Sep 25, from cramps in the breast, Chas Julius, s/o Wm Voss, aged 6 years & 7 months. His funeral is this afternoon, at 4 o'clock, at his residence on Pa ave, between 12th & 13th sts.

Died: on Sep 17, near Eastville, Northampton Co, Va, after a very brief illness of brain fever, Rev Henry Mort. He was a native of England; graduate of Cambridge; bred to the ministry of the Church of England, he passed a few of his earlier years in his own country, & then removed to one of the West India islands, & in a secluded corner of our peninsula devoted his life in conducting a school. –W

Mrs Turpin, Pa ave & 7th st, is now prepared to accommodate permanent & transient boarders on reasonable terms.

FRI SEP 27, 1844
Capt Evans, of the British schnr **Eliza**, from St John, N B, was struck on the head by the boom of his vessel, while in the act of jibing, on Mon, in coming into Boston harbor, & instantly killed.

Henry Ledyard, late Charge d'Affaires of the U S at the Court of Versailles, has returned, with his family, to the U S.

Chenango Telegraph: The d/o Mr Jas H Hughston, of East Guilford, aged 7 years, came to her death, on Sat week. A wagon containing Mrs Hughston, 2 boys & a little girl, was driven to the ferry boat at Sidney Plains, to cross the Delaware. As one of the horses stepped upon the boat it shoved off, not having been fastened. The wagon went into the river. Mrs Hughston & the 2 boys were rescued, but the dght was drowned.

Naval Court Martial: Examined: Lt Winslow; Donald M N Fairfax, Passed Midshipman; Passed Assist Surgeon A J Bowie; Francis Alexander. Acting Master; M Jordan, Naval Storekeeper; & Collin S Throckmorton.

Mrd: on Sep 25, in Wash City, by Rev Dr Laurie, Thos C Amory Dexter, of Boston, to Eliz Marian, d/o Col T Cross, Assist Quartermaster Gen U S Army.

Mrd: on Sep 23, by Rev W Matthews, Mr John Chang, of Bordeaux, France, to Miss Mgt Dubant, of Wash City.

Died: yesterday, in his 22nd year, Richd Thomas, y/s/o Basil & Eliz Warring. His funeral will take place from the residence of his father, I & 18th sts, at 4 p m today.

Just received, a cargo of that superior article Butler [Egg] Coal, suitable for Cooking & Radiator Stoves, which can be delivered to our customers at the shortest notice. -John Pettibone & Co

SAT SEP 28, 1844
On Tue, at Phil, Belby Harris was taken to the hospital with both legs crushed by being run over by the morning train of cars from Balt, on the Phil, Wilmington, & Balt Railroad. He expired about 1 o'clock. The same morning, a boy, John Smith, aged 11 years, whose parents reside in Front st, near Coates, fell from a burden car on the city railroad & was crushed in an awful manner. He expired about 2 o'clock.

Phil Riots: John Daly was held to bail in $5,000 for a further hearing. He is charged with having broken into the Seminary with an axe at the time it was destroyed by fire.

The Western [Missouri] Expositor announces the decease of the following gentlemen, all of St Louis, who left that place a few months ago in Capt Sublett's company for the Rocky Mountians, with the view of recovering their health: Mr Jas H Marshall died on the route to Oregon, on Jun 26; Mr Jas P Ketchum died Jun 28; Mr Jas Brawner, died Jul 7; Mr C C Hayman, died Jul 12.

On Tue, a young man, Chas Bombauer, a resident in Phil, near the Germantown road, while engaged in the dyeing establishment of Mr Boyle, fell into a vat of boiling water, which terminated his life, in great agony, in about 6 hours.

Desirable dwlg for rent: the subscriber offers the dwlg house over Mr Jack's shoe store, on Pa ave, with a 3 story back bldg attached. Apply to G C Grammer.

Desirable farm near Brookville, Md, for sale. The heirs of the late Mr Washington Bowie offer, on Oct 17, the farm recently purchased by him of one of the heirs of the late Wm H Dorsey. It contains about 212 acres; improvements are sufficient for agricultural purposes, consisting of 2 log dwlgs, a corn & tobacco house & stable. [No subscriber name given.]

The Sattinet Factory of Geo Kellogg was destroyed by fire on Mon. The finishing & dye-houses were saved. Insurance on the whole property $10,000.

Instruction in Vocal Music: Monsieur Louis Gibert, brother of the artist Antoine Gibert, well known in this city, left France last month, & is daily expected to take charge of the Vocal Music dept at Mrs Fleischmann's Seminary.

New Boot & Shoe Store, on the west side of 7th st, between D & E sts, recently occupied by Mr Bassett. Remember the place, 7th st, below E. –Chas Pascoe

Fork Patuxent, A A Co, Md. We, voters of the 4th election district of Anne Arundel. Co, have renounced Lococofoism & declare our intention to support Henry Clay & the Tariff. & we go for Whig measures out & out.

Lloyd Murphy	Richd Deaver	Grafton Smith
Hezekiah Whitehead	John Whitehead	Brazilia Whitehead
Wm Turner	Saml Airy, sen	Saml Airy, jr
Jas Snowden	Resin Whitehead	

Naval Gen Court Martial met yester: Albert S Palmer & Naylor C Davis, Assist Engineers, were examined as witnesses. Alfred Clumb, Fireman, was re-examined.

To the voters of the 4th Ward. I learn with pleasure that our fellow-citizen, John Kedgelie, is again brought forward by his friends as a candidate for the City Council. He had resided amongst us for the last 35 years; he fought bravely against the British at the battle of Bladensburg, & has proved himself to be a patriotic citizen. -B

Mrd: on Sep 17, by Rev John Towles, Thos Henderson to Rebecca, 2nd d/o Jas B Beverley, all of Fauquier Co, Va.

For rent: 2 story brick dwlg house on I st, at present in the occupancy of Dr Smoot. Inquire of Maj Geo Bender, near the premises.

MON SEP 30, 1844
On Sat last, Dr Van Dusen, of Troy, in Bradford Co, Pa, was instantly killed. He was assisting in raising a hickory pole; some of the fastenings gave way, & the pole falling struck him on the head & literally dashed him to pieces.

On Sep 20, a young man in North Adams, Mass, drove 2 ladies out towards evening in a buggy, with a spirited horse. The animal became unmanageable & Miss Fletcher, a young lady, was either thrown out or she jumped out of the buggy. She lived but a few minutes. The funeral of Miss Fletcher was attended on Sun by a large number of citizens of North Adams. –Boston Chronicle

Citizens of Wash Co, Ohio, Democrats of the old school of Jefferson, Madison, & Monroe, supporters of Jackson & Van Buren, but not of the modern order of progressive Democracy, have confidence in the Democracy of Henry Clay: we shall give our whole strength for Clay & Frelinghuysen. Our motto is "principles not men."

Geo Templeton	Luciu Cassady	Jacob Rake
J F Dowling	Geo Harris	Jas Ferguson
John Rake	Jonathan T Dye	Geo W Asher
Alex Huntsman	Sampson Cole	Sutton Wards
Heman Judd	Saml Dye	Jas Campbell
Stephen Priest	Wm Caywood, jr	Jas H Dye
John R Thompson	David Goodin	

[This list does not embrace a fourth of the number in the county. Says the Intelligencer.]]

Orphans Court of Wash Co, D C. Letters testamentary on the personal estate of Jos Warren, late of Wash Co, dec'd. –Louisa Warren, excx

Letters from the Oregon Territory announce the death of G W LeBreton, formerly of Newburyport. He was shot by an Indian, & died 2 days afterwards. The Indian was immediately killed by a Mr Winslow.

One of the pleasant features of the news from Mexico is the release of the following who were confined at Perote: Capt Wm Ryon, Col W F Wilson, the famous & efficient old sheriff of Galveston Island, Wallace Jas Armstrong, & Thos Tatem. That same day the news of their release was communicated to them the prison was visted by Hon Mr Shannon, then on his way to Mexico. Of course he was most warmly welcomed.

All the papers from Vera Cruz are clothed in mourning for the wife of Santa Anna. She appears to have been held in the highest personal esteem, independent of her elevated rank.

Obit-died: W Hicks: as a son he was dutiful to his widowed mother; as a husband, ever kind & affectionate; & as a father he loved his 3 dear little children almost to a fault. May he rest in peace! [See Sep 10th newspaper.]

Died: on Mon last, in her 23rd year, Miss Sarah Ann Shott, late of Balt. By her assiduous attentions to an afflicted mother, whose remains were consigned to the tomb but a few days previous, Miss Shott laid the foundation of the disease which has hurried her to an untimely grave.

Died: on Sep 22, at Phil, Rev G W Swan, U S Navy, recently appointed Chaplain to the frig **Potomac**.

Died: on Sep 28, at **Belmont**, near Leesburg, Va, at the residence of Mr John Wilson, Mrs Marcellini Bell, w/o Mr Thos d Bell, of Wash, in her 36th year. The dec'd has for several months suffered from an inveterate cancer in the right breast, for the extirpation of which she had sought the professional aid of Mr Wilson. The disease proved triumpnat, & after months of intense suffering, she meekly surrendered her spirit to the God who gave it. In her relations as a dght, sister, mother, & wife, she filled all with devoted affection. A husband, 2 dghts, & a son, the latter yet young, are left to mourn their irretrievable loss. Her funeral is today at 4 p m, from her late residence, Pa ave, opposite Brown's Hotel.

In his early boyhood Milliard Fillmore was apprenticed to a woolen manufacturer in Cayuga Co. He purchased one year of his time, taught school, & by his unaided efforts acquired the knowledge which has enabled him to earn for himself the fame of a statesmen, & which will have led to his elevation to the high ofc of Govn'r of the state of N Y. How true is the remark that the only aristocracy in this country is the aristocracy of intellect & virtue!

Staple & Fancy Dry Goods: Jas B Clarke, opposite Centre Market.

Naval Court Martial continued last Sat. Examined: Alfred Clumb, Theodore Teller, engineer; John Allen & Wm R Kelly, firemen, & Christopher Jordan, carpenter.

Sunday rioting: two of the accused, Raymond Williams & John Ennis, were apprehended last Fri & examined by Judge Morsell.

The death of Edw W Clark, left a vacancy in the Board of Aldermen, & Geo H Fulmer is recommended to the voters of the 6th Ward as a candidate. He served as a member of the Board of Common Council for the last 5 years. –Many voters

New bldgs & improvements in Wash City: Four storied house, owned & now occupied by Benj F Middleton, on south side of Louisiana ave, opposite 5th st. Bldg erected & work upon & executed by Mr J C Harkness, architect & carpenter; Mr Geo Plant, bricklayer; Mr John Purdy, painter; Mr G W Harkness, plasterer; Mr Jacob Aker, granite cutter; & Mr Caleb Buckingham, whitesmith & bell hanger. Another well finished house, also 4 stories, owned & now occupied by Stanislaus Murray, on 5th st. Bldg was erected & the work executed by Mr Wm Bird, architect & carpenter; Mr John A Cassell, bricklayer; Mr John Purdy, painter; Mr Jas B Phillips, plasterer; & Mr Jacob Aker, granite cutter. The new bldgs now in the course of erection, by Mr Francis Mohun, are 2 handsome brick houses on the east side of 6th st, between D & E sts. Mr Young is also putting up a good brick bldg, to be used by him as a coach factory, near 6th & Louisiana ave.

375 Canisters fresh Salmon & Lobsters. Just received & for sale low by A S Willis, King st, Alexandria.

Cheap stoves: just received from the North, amongst which are Stanley's Coal Burner, Radiators, & Cooking Stoves. Call & examine before you buy, Clem Woodward, Sign of the Stove & Grate, Pa ave, between 10th & 11th sts.

TUE OCT 1, 1844
Wet Nurse. A healthy strong young woman, having lost an infant 4 weeks old, would be glad of a place as West Nurse. Ample vouchers for character can be given. Inquire of Mrs A Richardson, Navy Yard Hill.

Abner Kneeland, well know throughout this country, died at Salubria, Iowa, on Aug 27 last.

We learn that Hon Willie P Mangum is still seriously indisposed at his residence on Flat River. His disease affects his lungs. –Hillsborough [S C] Recorder, Sep 28

Land for sale: the undersigned offers a tract of land, by estimation 330 acres, in Alexandria Co, near the river Potomac & opposite Gtwn. The title is unquestionable. -Francis L Smith, Atty in fact for Richd L T Beale

Two young ladies, dghts of Thos Reynolds, of Wash Co, Ohio, were drowned in the Ohio on Sunday last. They had attempted, with several other persons, to cross the river in a skiff, which sunk with them when nearing the Viginia shore.

Mrd: on Sep 17, at Charlotte Hall, St Mary's Co, Md, by Rev John Claxton, Nathl W Merriam, of Newburyport, to Miss Jane H G Kilgour, of Charlotte Hall.

WED OCT 2, 1844
On Tue, says the Buffalo Gaz, at a stone quarry at Black Rock, a charge prematurely exploded & drove an iron bar nearly through the body of a workman, Jas Malony. He survived the accident but a short time.

Dallas [Ala] Gaz: fatal rencontre on Sep 14, at the house of Capt J A Tait, in Wilcox Co, between Dr Chas Tait & W W Rives, which resulted in the death of Rives. Rives was engaged to be married to the sister of Dr Tait, & on Sep 14, with friends & a clergyman, went to the house of Capt Tait to have the ceremony performed. Tait commenced to assault him with a cane, & when Rives wrested it away from him, he drew a revolving pistol & shot Rives in the stomach, from which wound he died on Mon. After Rives had been carried into the house the marriage ceremony was performed. Tait immediately made his escape. [See Oct 17th newspaper.]

An Ancient Gone. John Carey, one of the early settlers of Wyoming Valley, & a soldier of the Revolution, died at his residence, in Carey town, near Wilkesbarre, Lycoming Co, Pa, on Sunday last, in his 89th year of his age.

Accident at Cobourg, Canada. A few days ago, by the accidental discharge of a fowling piece, the contents passed into the body of Mr Wm Beatty, s/o Rev John Beatty, of Victoria College, formerly of Phil. The youth was 17, & a student in a law ofc at Cobourg. There are but faint hopes of his recovery.

Drownings: 1-Isaac L Hobert, originally from Crown Point, was drowned in the Cuyahoga, at Cleveland, last week. 2-A man named Lewis Woods, on his way to Cincinnati, having in company his aged mother, fell into the canal there & was drowned on Aug 20.

Mrs Julia Terrett can accommodate a few boarders, with or without lodging. Residence on Louisiana ave, near 6th st west.

Household & kitchen furniture at auction: on Oct 8, at the residence of the late Mrs Easton, I & 19th sts. -R W Dyer & Co, aucts

Orphans Court of Wash Co, D C. Letters of administration on the personal estate of John W Duley, late of Wash Co, dec'd. –E M Linthicum, adm, Gtwn

Naval Gen Court Martial: met last Mon: examined: Lt Hunter; Wm Scott, Engineer, Jonathan M Wainwright, Passed Midshipman, & Henry Hunt, Engineer. Donald M N Fairfax was recalled.

For rent, a dwlg, or store & dwlg, both if preferred, on Pa ave, between 9th & 10th sts, opposite Selby Parker's Fancy Store. The Store is at present occupied by Mrs Hamilton as a millinery establishment. Inquire of Wm Hamilton.

Notice: I have this day associated with me in business my brother R J Ryon. The business will be Jno T Ryon & Brother. We have on hand a large assortment of Groceries, Liquors, & Wines.

THU OCT 3, 1844
The U S ship **Vandalia**, Cmder Jno S Chauncey, came up from the navy yard on Mon last, & is now lying at anchor off the town. Gaz

Mr Nathl Hastings, of Caroline, Thompkins Co, N Y, committed suicide on Thu last, by shooting himself through the heart. He was injured in a fight last spring, & it is supposed that he has never been in full possession of his reason since.

Circus rider hurt: Otto Motty, one of the most experienced riders, had some of his ribs broken by a fall from his horse, while riding at Petersham, a few days ago, & was otherwise much injured.

The Mount Vernon races commenced Oct 2 & will continue 5 days. The horses are now at the Course, & will run, to wit: the stables of P R Johnson, Col F Thompson, Maj Thos Doswell, Wm Fields, Col J B Kendall, Pritchart & Beard, Isham Puckett, Towns & Williamson, Newby & Millan, & others. –I Beard, Proprietor

Mrd: on Oct 1, by Rev Mr Wilson, Mr Geo C Jackson to Miss Mary Ann H Carvoe, all of Wash City.

House for rent: on C st, between 11th & 12th sts. Mr Chas H Nourse, the present occupant, will show the premises. Possession may be had Nov 1. –A Shepherd

$100 reward for runaway negro Jack, about 40 years old. –Amelia A Macrae, living near Buckland, Prince Wm Co, Va.

FRI OCT 4, 1844
Naval: Mr Josiah Faxon, sailmaker of the U S, died at Callao on Jun 30, after an illness of 3 months of consumption. He was a young man from Boston, & highly respected by all who knew him.

Buffalo, N Y, Sep 30. Sat last, Maj Geo Zahm, printer, & publisher of Der Weltburger, a German paper of this city, was instantly killed, & Messrs Chas Esslinger & Peter Smith seriously injured. While aiding in erecting a hickory pole, in Cheektowaga, the rope broke & the tree fell in their midst. –Commercial Adv

More reforms in the Custom-House. The following removals have just been made:

Night Inspectors:
Coms Cammeyer	Corns Ulshart-one arm man
Mr Post	Mr Mitland
Arch Ronalds	Danl Houghton
Chas Ridell	G R McLaughlin

Day Inspectors:
R H Thayer	E S McPherson
O M Jenkins	Mr Nagle
John Faulkner	J Morris
Mr Wade	Mr Oatman
Mr Vandewater	

And three others, making 20 removals to begin Oct. Most of thos removed are Whigs. This is a wholesale business, & a worse sort of prescription than we have had for years. Such martyrdom for opinion's sake will made good whigs of many more than those who suffer. –N Y Express

St Louis, Mo. Robt Hamilton, merchant on Market st, was found dead Sep 22nd in his store, & it appears he had locked himself up & then shot himself in the head. He is said to have been in easy circumstances & without family. –New Era

Notice: by 2 writs of fieri facias against the goods & chattels of John Frizzell, at the suits of Thos Vowell & Joshua Hardy, I have seized & taken in execution all the right, title, & claim of Frizzell in one cart & horse, & cart gear, & will expose the said goods to the highest bidder for cash on Oct 8. –H R Maryman, Constable

Mrd: on Oct 1, by Rev Wm J Sprole, Mr C S Whittlesey, of Ohio, to Miss Virginia, d/o Seth Hyatt, of Wash City.

Mrd: on Oct 2, in Alexandria, by Rev C A Davis, Mr John D Lakeman, of Wash City, to Miss Mary Ann Atwell, of the former place.

Mrd: on Sep 26, by Rev John Furgeson, Mr Danl Robertson, s/o Mr H B Robertson, to Miss Eliz Rachel Scott, both of Wash City.

Mrd: on Tue, in Gtwn, by Rev S A Roszel, Mr Thos S Donoho, of Wash City, to Miss Eliz Dunn, of the former place.

The partnership existing under the firm of R France & Co, was dissolved on Aug 1 last, by mutual consent. –R France, T E France. T E France will continue the Lottery & Exchange business at the old stand.

Mr Asabel Cowles, of East Bloomfield, has a valuable mare killed by bees on Sep 17. His son had driven her to a neighbor's & tied her near a bee-house.

$50 reward for return of sorrel horse stolen from my farm near Allen's Fresh, Md, on Oct 1. –Wm D Merrick

Wash Corp: 1-Cmte of Claims: bill for the relief of David A Baird: passed. Same cmte: bill for the relief of Thos J Earhart: passed. 2-Ptn of Wm Gunton & others, praying the improvement of La ave & D st: referred to the Cmte on Improvements. 3-Ptn from Wm McCarty, praying permission to erect a blachsmith's shop on lot 1 in square 730: referred to the Cmte on Improvements. 4-Cmte on Improvements: asking to be discharged from the further consideration of the ptn of Thos Blagden & others, & of Peter F Bacon & others, concerning the graduation of the alley in square 533. Same cmte was referred the ptn of Henry Trueman & others, for a gravel footwalk on 4th st: read twice. 5-Cmte of Claims: asking to be discharged from the further consideration of the ptn of Geo Savage.

Notice: the copartnership existing between Rawlings & Berkeley was dissolved, by mutual consent, on Oct 1. –David Rawlings, Jno T Berkeley
+
Take notice: John T Berkeley's Dyeing & Scouring Establishment, s e corner of 11th & Pa ave. Carpets cleansed at the shortest notice. Reference may be made to F Wheatley, Gtwn.

SAT OCT 5, 1844
Madame Deville, at Balt, will open several cases of Paris Millinery on Oct 5, at 10 o'clock, at 133 Balt st.

Morning Line of Stages: between Balt & Wash. Apply at Brown's Genr'l Stage Ofc, opposite Gadsby's [now Coleman's] Nat'l Hotel, Pa ave. –J Peters & Co, proprietor -J Ackerman, agent

Public sale of pictures at Balt: public auction on Oct 18, at the 2nd story of the house at the s w corner of North & Fayette sts, the choice collection belonging to the estate of the late Cashier of the Bank of Balt, Jas Cox, among which are the works of:

Rubens	Heemskerk	Rousseau	Ross di Tivoli
Solomon	Wecaix	Schaleken	De Heem
Ruysdal	Teniers	Suebach	Doughty
Patamedas	Moucheron	Vander Lew	Shaw
Jan Steen	Johnson	Brenghel	

-J H McCulloh, Saml I Donaldson, excs -Wever, Cannon & Co, auctioneers

Cotton & Sugar Plantation in Florida to lease: called *Bulowville*, about 4,000 acres, near Mosquito Inlet, 40 miles due south from St Augustine East Florida. For further information address W G Bucknor, N Y, or J W Bryant, Jacksonville, East Florida.

Whereas letters of administration on the estate of Geo S Wharton, dec'd, have been granted to the subscriber, all persons indebted are to make immediate payment; claims to be presented, properly authenticated, for settlement, to Jas S Wharton, adm: 76 South 4th st, Phil.

$5 reward for return of a dark bay Mare, of small size. –J C McKelden, 7th st

Jas Williams, one of the old pioneer settlers of Cincinnati, was found dead upon the floor of his lodgings last Sat. He was a single man, originally from England; was in Hull's army, & has been a resident of Cincinnati for above 400 years. He has left considerable property, without any known heirs.

Died: yesterday, Mrs Mary Ann Gather, in her 27th year, leaving a disconsolate husband & 2 small children. Her funeral is from her late residence on Pa ave, 2 doors from Mr Williams' cabinet-maker, at 4 o'clock tomorrow.

Commencement of Columbia College, Oct 2, the degree of A B was conferred upon:

J P Baldwin, Pa
S Cornelius, N J
W J Darden, D C
E T Ingraham, Maine
J W H Lovejoy, D C
Oscar G Mix, Va
L R Smoot, D C
J L Sanders, Miss
T W Tobey, R I
W B Webb, D C

Degree of A M, in Course, was conferred upon:

C L Cocke, Va
S C Clopton, Va
H W Dodge, Va
J B French, D C
J J James, Va
J H C Jones, Md
T J Pearce, S C
J C Welch, N J
J A Wroe, D C

The honorary degree of A M was conferred upon:

P B Spear, N Y
J H Eaton, Tenn
Rev S Cornelius, N J
Rev T Stringfellow, Va
T C Teasdale, Conn

The honorary degree of M D was conferred upon Dr Calvin Howard, N Y

The honorary degree of D D was conferred upon Rev R Fuller, S C; Rev J W Massie, Manchester, England

The degree of A B has been conferred upon the following young gentlemen, graduates of Hamilton Literary & Theological Institution, N Y:

G W Anderson
B F Bronson
S J Bronson
J S Beecher
M H Calkins
S Graves
E C Lord
J Munroe, jr
L Peck
O L Sprague
S S Ainsworth
P C Dayfoot
J A Dixon
J W Fish
A S Devinele
O W Gibbs
S B Grant
E L Haynes
E T Hiscox
W F Purrington
W Roney
D F Twiss
W S Mickels
O Hacket
N Harris
J A Nash
O B Judd
R R Prentice
G B Tenbrook
S Wilder
N M Perkins
Z Smith

Orations were delivered by:

J P Baldwin, Phil, Pa
S Cornelius, jr, Mount Holly, N J
W J Darden, Wash, D C
E T Ingraham, Augusta, Maine
W W Jackson, Clarke Co, Va
J W H Lovejoy, Wash, D C
L R Smoot, Wash, D C
J L Sanders, De Kalb, Miss
T W Tobey, Providence, R I
W B Webb, Wash, D C
J A Wroe, Wash, D C

Died: on Thu, Mrs Mary Ingle, relict of Mr Henry Ingle, in her 79th year. This excellent & beloved "mother in Israel" was sick but a few days. Her funeral will take place from the residence of her son, John P Ingle, this day, at 11 o'clock.

For sale or rent: that well known & established House in Wash, called *Globe Hotel*: south side of Pa ave, formerly occupied & conducted by Mr Azariah Fuller, but has for the last 9 years been conducted by the undersigned. The only reason the undersigned has for offering the above property for sale or lease is his desire to retire from a position which he has for the last 20 years occupied, &, with a large & growing family, retire to a more private life. –Jas Maher, Public Gardener

Clothing! Clothing! Clothing! Fits warranted in all cases. –Wm Egan, Pa ave, south side, between 6th & 7th sts, Wash

MON OCT 7, 1844
The U S frig **United States**, Capt Stribling, arrived at Boston on Thu, from the Pacific, via Rio Janeiro. The Brazilian Minister, Signor Lima, & family, took passage in the **United States**, & were landed at Rio. Ofcrs of the **United States**: Cmder, Capt C K Stribling. Lts: J L Gardner, L B Avery, W Gwathmay, F Winslow, [acting,] J B Randolph, [acting.] Surgeon, Wm Johnson. Purser, Edw Fitzgerald Lt Marines, Geo W Robbins. Chaplain, Theo B Barstow. Prof of Math, H H Lockwood. Acting Master, B S Gavett. Assist Surgeons, Wm A Nelson, M B Beck. Capt's Clerk, H Robertson. Midshipmen: W C West, J J Hanson, H A Colburn, Theo Lee Walker, B W Stevenson, Chas Latimer, John H Russell, H H Key, R W Scott, J H Upshur, Jos L Friend, Wm Sharpe, Wm F Jones, J Armstrong, F P Baldwin. Purser, Wm Hoff. Gunner, Asa Curtis. Carpenter, Jas Meads. Passengers: from Callao, Wm H Caldwell, of New Orleans. From Rio, Passed Midshipman R A Knapp & Mid A F Wailey.

Mrd: on Oct 3, by Rev John G Wilson, Mr Hamilton J Smith to Miss Eleanora Powell, all of Gtwn, D C.

Mr Horatio Abbott, aged 23 years, s/o Gardner Abbott, of Andover, Mass, hung himself on Sun. The unfortunate young man had betrayed slight symptoms of aberration of mind for some time.

The Kensington & Southwark rioters-Phil. John Taggert charged for the murder of Geo Shiffler. Saml Vandergrift for the murder of Cpl Henry C Troutman, of the Germantown Blues. Andrew McClain for the murder of Sgt John Guyer, of the Germantown Blues. Henry Haughey [yet at large] for participating in the murder of Jos Rice. John Taggert for the murder of Chas Stillwell. Peter Devlin, for riot & participating in the murder of Geo Shiffler.

Died: on Sunday, Edw Harvey, a native of England, aged 38 years. His funeral is this morning, at 11 o'clock, from the residence of H S Fox.

Suitable reward for return of a bay horse that strayed from the commons on Sep 30. -Saml Mickum, Navy Dept

The subscriber has this day associated in business with R B Nalley & J B Dodson, & the business will be conducted under the firm of D Clagett & Co. –D Clagett

Naval Gen Court Martial: examination on Tue last of: Lt Simon B Bissell, Lt Geo R Gray, & Alonzo C Wakeman, purser's clerk. Lt Simon Blunt, Wm R Kelly, & Alfred Clum were recalled & re-examined. No witnesses were examined on Thu.

City Ordinance-Wash. 1-Act for the relief of David A Baird: the fine imposed on him for an alleged violation relative to the keeping of dogs, is hereby remitted.

Mrs R M Poulton informs that she still carries on the Dressmaking business at her residence on 10th st, between G & Pa ave.

TUE OCT 8, 1844
For rent: a 2 story brick dwlg house on 9th st, between H & I sts, just vacated by T G Arnold. The key may be found next door south. Apply to Thos Blagden.

Notice is hereby given that all person found trespassing on the lands of the undersigned with dogs & guns will be prosecuted according to law.
–Ed Fenwick, D B Burr, B M Derringer

A fire occurred in Columbia, S C, on Sep 29, which proved quite disastrous. The tenements consumed were occupied as follows: David Ewart, grocer; Mr J Stork, shoestore; J Cooper, jeweler; John Ewart, grocer; J Canle, fruit store; J H Heise, confectioner; A Palmer & Co, tinners. There was also a fire at Pensacola on Sep 25, the work of an incendiary, which consumer the stores of Messrs Siera & La Rud & Mr Campbell, the drug store of Messrs Smith & Catlin, the shoestore of Mr Avery, the coffee-house of Mr J Penny, the Three Unions coffee-house, the dwlg of Mrs Catlin, & several other houses. Most of the bldgs belonged to Capt Forsyth. Mr Campbell was the only one of the sufferers insured.

Valuable lots of ground in square 491, Wash, for sale at auction: by virtue & to answer the purposes of a deed of trust from Wm Gadsby, dated Nov 14, 1842, recorded in the Land Records of Wash Co, D C, in Book W B 98, folio 127-130: sale on Nov 5, of lots 18 thru 21 in square 491, in Wash, & part of lot 22 in said square. The property fronts a part on C st & a part on 4½ st. -R W Dyer & Co, aucts

Trustee's sale: by deed of trust from the late Jos W Hand, to Wm P Elliot, I shall offer at auction on Oct 18, on the premises, lot 11 in square 220 [as subdivided by the heirs of John Davidson,] of the plan of Wash City: fronting on north H st, adjoining the ground upon which St Matthew's Church is erected. —W P Elliot, trustee -R W Dyer & Co, aucts

Balt Clipper: Md Legislature: list of the names of the members elect to the next House of Delegates. Those marked [*] are Democrats.

St Mary's Co
Robt Ford   Wm H Thomas
Jas R Hopewell
Kent Co
Chas B Tilden   Geo W Hollyday
Geo W Spencer
Anne Arundel Co
Chas R Stewart   Nich B Worthington
Robt Garner   John Johnson
Andrew A Lynch
Calvert Co
Richd Hance   Thos J Hellen
Jas S Morsell
Chas Co
John G Chapman   John Hughes
John D Freeman
Balt Co
Jos W Walker*   Carville S Stansbury*
Beale Randall*   J T H Worthington*
N H Ware*
Talbot Co
John Harrington   Chas H Bowdle
H W Goldsborough
Somerset Co
Edw Long   Wm P Williams
Levin Phillips   Benj Lankford
Dorchester Co
Jos E Muse, jr   Wm Frazier
John R Keene   Reuben Tall
Cecil Co
Wm R Maffitt*   Richd C Hollyday*
Chas Harris*   John Bouchell*
PG Co
Chas B Calvert   Wm T Wootton
Osborn Sprigg
Robt Ghieslin

Queen Anne's Co
Saml T Harrison   Thos H Ford
Mathias George
Worcester Co
Wm U Purnell   Jas M Fooks
Zadoc P Henry   Edw Lambden
Fred'k Co
Edw Shriver*   John H Worthington*
Danl S Biser*   Wm Cost Johnson
J E E Poole
Harford Co
Wm J Polk   Fred'k T Amos
Henry W Archer   Geo Yellott
Caroline Co
Robt H McNett   Zabdiel W Potter
John Jump, of E
Balt City
Elijah Stansbury, jr*   Nathl Williams*
David C Springer*   John J Graves*
Francis Gallagher*
Wash Co
Wm B Clarke   Isaac Motter
Hezekiah Boteler   John D Hart
Chas A Fletcher
Montg Co
Wm B Howard   Geo C Patterson
Saml D Waters   Alex'r Kilgour
Allegany Co
Michl C Sprigg*   Patrick Hammill*
John Neff*   Jas Fitzpatrick*
Carroll Co
Jas Raymond   Jos Ebaugh
John P Thompson   Micajah Rogers

The Senate: correct list of the Senators showing the date of the expiration of their respective terms of service:

St Mary's Co: Jas T Blackistone: 1850   Dorchester: Francis P Phelps: 1850
Kent: Wm S Constable: 1850   Cecil: Geo R Howard: 1846
Calvert: John Parran*: 18480   PG: Wm D Bowie*: 1848
Chas: John Matthews: 1848   Queen Anne's: John Palmer: 1846
Anne Arundel: John S Sellman*:1848   Worcester: Teagle Townsend: 1846
Balt: Hugh Ely*:1846   Fred'k: Caspar Quynn*: 1850
Talbot: Saml Hambleton, jr: 1850   Harford: Jas Moores: 1850
Somerset: Wm Williams: 1848   Caroline: Jacob Charles: 1848

Wash: John Newcomer: 1846 Carroll: Wm Roberts: 1850
Montg: Wm Lingan Gaither: 1848 Balt City: Wm Frick*: 1846
Alleghany: John Beall: 1846

Charge of murder. Yesterday, Fenner Ballou & Dr Alex'r A Butler were brought up for examination upon a charge of murdering Maria A Aldrich, whose death is supposed to have been caused by a successful attempt to procure abortion. –Boston Post of Wed

Mrs R Johnston can accommodate a few boarders with comfortable Boarding & Lodging, by the week or month, on moderate terms, on 9th, between D & E sts.

Boarding House: Mrs J Cunningham, opposite the Patriotic Bank, on 7th st. Furnished rooms, with breakfast & tea, to gentlemen desirous of dining out.

Mrd: on Oct 6, by Rev Mr Phelps, Wm T Johnson, formerly of Balt, to Miss Eliz P Dixon, of this place.

Mrd: on Sep 10, at Jefferson Barracks, Missouri, by Rev W Griswold, of St Louis, Lt Geo Deas, of the 5th Regt of Infty, to Eliz Mary, d/o Col John Garland, U S A.

Died: on Oct 4, at Alexandria, of scarlet fever, Eliza Vivian, 2nd d/o Wm H Fowle, aged 8 years & 8 months.

Died: on Oct 1, in Fredericksburg, Miss Catharine Rebecca Lomax, d/o Hon J T Lomax.

Died: on Sep 28, at Phil, while on a visit to her father, [Dr R M Patterson,] Mrs Eliz L Taylor, w/o John Taylor, jr, of Caroline Co, Va.

Died: on Sep 30, at his residence in Spottsylvania, Va, Col Robt Crutchfield, in his 73rd year. He had filled many & various public stations, & all of them with honor & usefulness.

WED OCT 9, 1844
Circuit Court of Wash Co, D C. In the matter of the petition for the division of the real estate of Anne Larken, [formerly McGunnigle,] late of Wash Co, D C, dec'd, the Com'rs appointed by the Court in inquire of & divide the real estate of which said Anne Larkin died seized in said county, if the same, in their judgment could be divided without injury to the parties interested, report that they are of the opinion the real estate cannot be divided without injury, & that the estate is of the value of $6,500; & the Court being of opinion that the report ought to be confirmed; that notice be given to all whom it may concern. –Wm Brent, clk

For rent: new & convenient frame house, with brick bldg, on 12th st, between G & H sts. Inquire next door, or to Richd J Brown, Plasterer.

Stoves & Grates: Jos H Nevett, opposite Fuller's Hotel, Pa ave.

The funeral of Madame Santa Anna took place on Aug 27 near Puebla. A whole page is given in the El Censor to a description of the funeral procession, the ceremonies in the church, & the monument erected to the memory of the dec'd lady.

The trial of Mr Ford, at St Louis, Mo, on a charge of murdering Mr Low, was brought to a close on Sep 28, by a verdict of not guilty from the Jury, after only 5 minutes' consultation. The substantial reason urged for acquittal was that Low had deceived the only d/o Ford by promise of marriage, & refused to comply with his engagement, & deserted her under circumstances well calculated to excite the indignation of a parent. In their attempt to prove Ford's insanity, they brought out the whole history of the intercourse between Low & the d/o Ford.

Balt, Oct 8. More illegal voting: Geo Brown, alleged he moved to Phil with his family 2 months previous & returned here alone prior to the election at which he voted. Chas McDonald, was proven to have voted illegally: fined $20 & costs. Geo Bollman, a resident of Ellicott's Mills, charged with voting illegally: fined $20 & costs. Jas O'Hara, charged with illegally voting, was remanded to jail for a still further hearing. John Fort, charged with illegally voting, was held to bail by Justice Pennington. –American

Mr G M G Wright, formerly of Queen Anne's Co, died on Oct 3 at his residence at Worton, Kent Co, Md, after a brief illness, occasioned by the sting of a spider or some other poisonous insect.

Nashville Whig, Sep 28. At a late hour last evening we were advised that the venerable Robt C Foster, sen, breathed his last at *Mansfield*, the residence of his son, Hon E H Foster, about 4 o'clock. A pioneer citizen of Tenn, he died universally lamented by old & young-by the aged who were his neighbors for more than half a century; by the young, to whom he was singularly endeared. Mr Foster was born in Va, Jul 18, 1769, & therefore had attained the age of 75. His removal to Tenn was contemporary with the admission of the Territory into the Union as a separate State. He lived the patriarch of a large family, & died surrounded by 4 generations of the family name.

Wash Corp elected the following to serve for the ensuing year as police magistrates:

Saml Drury	Wm Thompson	Saml Byington
Saml Smoot	B K Morsell	Nathl Brady
John L Smith	W W Stewart	Jas Crandell
John D Clark	Robt H Clements	Jas Marshall

Geo Warner Holthouse, the keeper of a small tavern in Pittsburg, Pa, was arrested there on Wed last, & held to bail by the Mayor, in the sum of $2,000, for fraudulently procuring naturalization papers for several Germans, who are not entitled by law to receive them.

Mrd: on Oct 6, by Rev Jas Knox, Mr Henry D Bowman to Miss Jennetta Magrath, both of Fredericksburg, Va.

Mrd: yesterday, by Rev John C Smith, Walter H Weed, of Montezuma, N Y, to Miss Mary Gumaer, of Wash City.

Notice: the subscriber has sold out his stock of Boots & Shoes to his son, Malcolm Douglas, by whom the business will hereafter be conducted, on his own account, at the old stand, between 9th & 10th sts, Pa ave. –Wm Douglas

THU OCT 10, 1844
Mr Devore, a minister of the gospel, was murdered in the Choctaw Nation on Sep 6. He had been on a visit to Texas, & was returning to his home in Missouri. He had with him $250 in money, which was all stolen from him with the exception of $60.

The Smithland Bee is now edited by Mrs Gibbon, wid/o the editor who was recently assassinated. Mrs Gibbon, like all the rest of her blessed sex, is a glorious Whig, & enters into the great conflict with the spirit & enthusiasm of a Joan of Arc.
–Louisville Journal

Fall Millinery: on display in her commodious sales room over the grocery store of Messrs Peddecord & Holland, next door to D Clagett & Co. –Miss Jane E Biscoe

Fatal accident on Fri last, as the merchandise train on the Boston & Maine railroad was proceeding to Portland, when near Andover, Mr Danl V Holt, conductor, fell from the cars, injuring him in a shocking manner. He was taken up alive, but no hopes are entertained of his recovery. His death will be a severe affliction to his wife & 5 young children.

$2 reward for return of strayed small red & white Cow. Return to me or give information where I may find her. -Maria Pegg, 11th st, facing the canal.

Trustee's sale of valuable real estate in Gtwn. In pursuance of a decree of Circuit Court of Wash Co, D C, the subscriber offers at public auction, on Oct 24, the following real estate in Gtwn, viz: all parts of lots 13 & 14, of Peter, Beatty, Threlkeld, & Deakin's addition to Gtwn; part of lot 15 in same addition. There is a fine large 3 story brick house, ofc & stable on the premises, for a private residence, it being the same property which was owned by the late Francis S Key.
–John A Smith, trustee -Edw S Wright, auctioneer

Very valuable property in PG Co, Md, for sale: about 200 acres, about 5½ miles from the Centre Market. Also, about 130 acres in D C, adjoining the beautiful farms of Mr A Shepperd & Wm G Sanders. Apply to the subscriber, residing near Bladensburg, Md. -Geo A Digges

By 2 writs of fieri facias, issued by Jas Marshall, against the good & chattels of John L Maddox & Thos M Fugitt, I give notice that I have seized & taken in execution one vessel **Wetipquin**, the property of Thos M Fugit, now lying at the wharf of Griffith Coombs, which will be sold on Oct 12, to the highest bidder, for cash, to satisfy judgments in favor of Danl Kelley. –Thos Plumsill, Constable

By wirt of fieri facias, issued by R H Clement, to me directed, I give notice that I have seized & taken in execution, as the property of John A Lynch, one Hay Scales, lying on East Captiol & 1st sts, which will be sold on Oct 12 to the highest bidder for cash, to satisfy a judgment in favor of Wm M Maddox. –Thos Plumsill, Constable

Capt McLean, late the British Govn'r of Cape Coast Castle, Africa, but better known as the husband of L E L, arrived at Boston, on Thu, in the boat **Pilot**, from Africa.

The U S storeship **Lexington**, Lt Com'r Glendy, arrived at N Y on Sun from Gibraltar. Ofcrs attached to the **Lexington**: W M Glendy, Lt Com'g; C F M Spotswood, 1st Lt; C C Barton, 2nd Lt; D Ammen, Acting Master; S Forrest, Purser; D Egbert, Surgeon; C Gale, Master's Mate; J Magruder, Capt' Clerk. Passengers in the **Lexington**: Lt G Adams, of U S N, lady & 2 children; Mrs C F M Spotswood; Passed Midshipman E F Beale, late of the U S frig **Columbus**.

Mrd: on Oct 8, by Rev Mr Samson, Mr Jas W Lynch to Miss Eliza Ann Gowan, all of Wash City.

Died: on Oct 7, Adam Lindsay, aged 80 years, a native of Scotland. The dec'd emigrated to this country in early life, & was amongst the first settlers of Wash City, in the prosperity & growth of which he ever manifested a lively interest. His funeral is this evening, at 2 o'clock, from his late residence, near the Navy Yard. [Oct 14th newspaper: Adam Lindsay was coeval with our city & identified with its history. Attached to the calm pursuits of agriculture, he devoted much of his time to them, as well as to those of kindred but not less delightful occupation, horticulture. He was a successful cultivator of the grape which led him to establish a Horticultural Society for D C, of which he was the orginator. He was the first to cultivate the silk worm, & to manufacture silk in Wash City, in which he took great pride.]

Died: on Oct 4, at her residence, Park Hall, PG Co, Md, Mrs Sarah Slator, in her 78th year.

Died: yesterday, of consumption, Geo Kleiber, jr. His funeral is this afternoon, at 3 o'clock, from the late residence of the dec'd, Pa ave, between 8th & 9th sts,

Died: on Oct 9, Alice Rebecca, d/o Isaac & Adeline Bassett, aged 2 years. Her funeral is this afernoon at 2 o'clock.

FRI OCT 11, 1844
For rent: comfortable 2 story brick house on I st, near 6th st. Possession given on or about Nov 10. Inquire of Miss E Queen, on 4½ st, near Pa ave, or at the woodyard of Isaac Hill, Canal st, near 7th.

Oakland School, Burlington, N J, by E C Wines: nearly 20 years in the business of teaching. –E C Wines, Principal

Capt John Joiner & Messrs W H Wingate & Richd Drummond were drowned in the bay of Mobile on Sep 28, by the swamping of a sailboat, in which they were on their way to the village of Baldwin Co.

St Louis, Oct 1. The steamer **Monona** towed down the steamer **Potosi** yesterday from Quincy. The **Potosi** collapsed a flue on Fri, by which Mr Perrin, a cabin passenger, was blown among some horses that were fastened on the forecastle, which, being frightened by the report, trampled upon him, & from the injuries he received died the following afternoon. Mr N Perrin resided in N Y, Iowa Territory, & was the head of a large family. His is said to have been the 3rd brother that has lost his life by steamboat accidents. Phillips Miller, a deck-hand, a resident of this city, has not been heard of since the accident, & is supposed to have jumped or been blown overboard & drowned. -Republican

Phil Gaz of Tue: Mrs Fauver, whose funeral took place yesterday, was over 100 years of age. She was only confined to her bed about a week previous to her death. She was a resident of the Northern Liberties. She never had used spectacles, & her hearing was good. She attended religious worship 2 or 3 times on the Sabbath day, & often also once during the week. She was always at work, & on the Fri preceding her sickness she attended to marketing for the family.

On Sep 17, Mr Thos S Talford, a respectable citizen of Tuscaloosa Co, while in pursuit of his horse, fell into a well between 70 & 80 feet deept. No person heard his cries for help until about sunset. Ropes were brought & Mr Jos T Pearce, a worthy mechanic, descended the well & fastened a rope on Mr Talford, & both were drawn up. Mr Talford was unable to stand or to move his legs; the concussion of the spinal nerves had paralyzed him. Mt Talford is 51 years of age, & the father of 6 children. His preservation from a lingering death was truly providential. The well is near the site of the old Eagle Hotel, which was burnt 9 years ago, & known only to a very few individuals, being surrounded by tall weeds. -Picayune

Appointments by the Pres: 1-Vespasian Ellis, of Missouri, to be Charge d'Affaires of the U S to the Republic of Venezuela, in the place of Allen A Hall. 2-Benedict Milburn to be a Justice of the Peace in Wash Co, D C.

Mrd: yesterday, by Rev John C Smith, Mr Jas H Queen to Miss Mary R Ritchie.

Mrd: on Oct 3, at New Rochelle, by Rev E Mason, Capt J Addison Thomas, U S Army, to Catharine, d/o the late Thos A Ronalds, of N Y.

Mrd: on Oct 3, at Newark, N J, by Rev M H Henderson, Capt S M Plummer, U S Army, to Emily H, d/o the late Rev John Brady, of St Mary's, Md.

Died: on Oct 7, Eliza Brightwell, d/o Eliza & Owen H Bestor, aged 9 months & 25 days.

Died: on Oct 7, Catharine Rosanna, d/o Jas & Susan D Bowen, aged 2 years & 3 months.

SAT OCT 12, 1844
Oct 12th newspaper: the protracted trial Capt Newton has terminated. It has not been generally understood that Capt Newton served with distinction in the gallant actions of the **Hornet & Peacock & Hornet & Penguin** as a Lt, under the command of Lawrence & Biddle. Letters addressed to him by Sir Geo Sartorius, of the ship **Malabar 74**, & Sir Robt Wilson, Govn'r & Genr'l of Gilbraltar, were read to the Court, in which these distinguished men awarded this ofcr the highest commendation for his conduct in the conflagration of the steamship **Missouri**. The evidence discloses that Capt Newton was the last man to abandon the devoted ship, & then only when all hope was gone of saving her.

Mrd: on Oct 10, at Alexandria, by Rev Mr Danforth, Mr E Farrell Buckingham, of Wash, to Miss A J A Gertrude, eldest d/o Chas Scott, of the former place.

Mrd: on Oct 10, by Rev Geo W Samson, Mr Saml D Peatross, of Va, to Miss Angelina W Seay, of Wash City.

Died: on Oct 10, at her late residence, Mrs Martha Whaley, aged 50 years. Her funeral is at 3 o'clock, Sunday.

Died: on Thu, after a lingering illness, Wm Eleazer, only child of Rev Henry W & Abigail B Dodge, of Upperville, Va, [formerly of Springfield, Ill,] aged 18 months & 20 days. His funeral is this morning, at 11 o'clock, from the residence of Mr Danl Brown, 18th st.

Mr John Norris, a member of Capt Johnson's company of Springfield Cadets, met a sudden death near Nauvoo on Sep 29. On Sat there was a false alarm in the camp, the sentinels were called in, Mr Norris mistook the order & remained at his post, shots were fired, & a ball passed through his body.

Awful explosion on Mon last of the boilers of the steam engine in the rolling-mill of Messrs Lorenz & Cuddy, in Sligo, opposite Pittsburg, severely scalding Jos Davis, engineer, Jacob Fordling, fireman, & Jacob Poothman, a laboring man. Davis died the next morning. The other two are expected to recover.

$25 reward for 2 fine horses stolen from my residence, on E st, between 3rd & 4th sts, on Oct 10. –Hanson Brooke

Notice: the public are informed that the *Telegraph* is but the instrument of transmitting intelligence, & therefore the operators of the Telegraph have been directed to transmit only such facts & results, in relation to the exciting elections at this season, as are furnishd them at the respective termini at Balt & Wash by responsible men; & they are strictly forbidden to give any partisan character to such facts or results by the expression of individual opinion upon them. –Saml F B Morse, Superintendent of Electro Magnetic Telegraph. Wash, Oct 11, 1844.

Household & kitchen furniture at auction: on Oct 15, at the residence of Mr Randolph Coyle, on 17th st, between H & I sts. -R W Dyer & Co, aucts

Circuit Court of Wash Co, D C-in Chancery. Rose A McGuire, vs Wm Hayman's reps et al. In this cause the trustee, among other sales, reports the following of real estate lying in Wash City, to wit:
In Square 13, lot 14, for $35.43, to Jos Ratcliff
In square 14, lot 18, for $55.33, to Thos Corcoran
In square 40, lot 7, for $59.92, to Thos Corcoran
In square 41, lot 13, for $94.57, to Wm T Dove
In square 72, lot 1, for $54.00, to Jos Abbott
All of square 149, for $9.90, to Jos Abbott
Part of square 291, for $605.00, to Wm H Stewart
Reservation B, lot 22, for $6,000.00, to Andrew Small
-Wm Brent, clerk

MON OCT 14, 1844
Public Sale: of about 50 acres of land, more or less, about 1 mile from Bladensburg, on the Marlborough road, adjoining the land of Mr F Magruder. Mr Thos Baldwin, residing on the premises, will show the land. The sale takes place at Mr Thos Baldwin's Hotel, in Bladensburg, Md, on Nov 9. –Horatio Newman

Naval: 1-The U S ship **Yorktown** was to sail from N Y on Thu for the coast of Africa. List of her ofcrs: Cmder, Chas H Bell; Lts: H A Steele, J A Coyle, M C Masin; Assist Master, John S Neville; Purser, John N Hambleton; Surgeon, Wm L Van Horn; Assist Surgeon, L J Williams; Passed Midshipmen: Saml Edwards, F W Colby, H S Newcomb; Midshipmen: J H Carter, Wm S Cushman, F A Roe; Boatswain, J Lewis; Gunner, T M Crocker; Carpenter, H W Lindsey; Master's Mate, John Lawrence. 2-The U S sloop-of-war **Fairfield**, Saml W Downing, Cmder, arrived at Palermo on Aug 10 from Naples, & was to sail in a short time for Tunis, Tripoli, & Malta, & rendezvous at Port Mahon by the 8th of the present month. Ofcrs & crew all well.

The works of Charlotte Elizabeth, with an introduction by Mrs H B Stowe, just received & for sale at the bookstore of R Farnham, 11th & Pa ave.

J Dixon, Merchant Tailor, has opened in Coleman's Nat'l Hotel, entrance on 6th st, first door from Pa ave.

The true object of the trial of Capt John T Newton was to elicit every fact, & to make the whole matter one of record. The splendid steamship **Missouri**, was destroyed by fire at Gibraltar in Aug, 1843, & which he commanded. Yesterday Capt Newton & his counsel, Philip Hamilton, of N Y, appeared in court. The turpentine was clearly shown to have been carefully concealed from sight & the Captain knew not of its existence was evident to all. On this point the testimony was clear, full, & conclusive. Thus terminated an investigation which cannot but bring out in bolder relief the character & conduct of one who in public or private life has ever been, in the strictest sense, an ofcr & a gentleman. –A Citizen

Piano Fortes: of 5½, 6, 6½ octaves; among them one very fine upright Piano. –J F Kahl, Piano Maker, Pa ave, between 12th & 13th sts, south side.

Circuit Court of Wash Co, D C-in Chancery. David E Twiggs, vs Henry D Hunter, John U Hunter, Alex Hunter, et al. Henry May, appointed trustee for the sale of the property in this cause reported that he did on Sep 10, 1844, sell at public auction, all that piece or parcel of ground in Wash City, being lot 4 in square 533, with the bldgs, improvements, rights, privileges, & appurtances to the same belonging, & that Wm B Kibley, of Wash City, became the purchaser for the sum of $4,350. –W Brent, clk

Michl O'Hanlon has been arrested in Alleghany city, Pa, for perjury, in vouching for his brother, who had only been 2 years in the country. He is a Loco, & was released on bail of $2,000.

Orphans Court of Wash Co, D C. Letters of administration on the personal estate of Wm Hicks, late of Wash Co, dec'd. –J P Pepper, administrator

Wash City Ordinance: 1-Act for the relief of Thos J Earhart: fine imposed for an alleged violation of the act in relation to areas, is remitted: Provided, he pay the costs of prosecution. Approved, Oct 11, 1844.

Notice: all persons are warned not to trespass on my farm on the eastern Branch, or on my farm situated on Oxen Run, with or without guns or dogs, as the law will certainly be rigidly enforced against all offenders. –Jane Woodruff

Singing School: Mr H Morse, Teacher of Music, from Boston, will commence instruction in the lecture room of the new Baptist Church on E st, near 6th, on Mon.

TUE OCT 15, 1844
Providence Journal: John Gordon, convicted at the Mar term of the murder of Amasa Sprague, was sentenced to be executed on Feb 12 next, between 9 & 3 o'clock.

On Oct 2, Mr Moses Crosby, of Tisbury, went out with his gun for the purpose of fowling, & did not return. He was found dead by one of his neighbors, shot with his own gun. It is supposed it accidentally discharged when taking it from a cart he had with him. He was an unusually esteemed as an honest & industrious man, about 60 years of age, & has for many years been considered the most expert gunner in the country. -Boston Atlas

Henry Williams, s/o Nathl F Williams, Collector of the port of Balt, died very suddenly at the residence of his father in Charles, near Franklin st, on Thu. He was discovered in his room in a dying state. He was about 28 years of age, & had for some time past conducted the mercantile business of his father on Bowly's wharf. The dec'd was about to form an alliance with an estimable young lady of Balt City. -Sun

Died: on Oct 13, in Wash City, after a protracted illness, Mrs Maria H Hanson, w/o J K Hanson, in her 50th year. Her funeral is on Tue at 11 o'clock.

Died: on Oct 9, at Allentown, Pa, after a protracted illness of a disease of the heart, Mr P Augustus Sage, printer, formerly of this city, in his 36th year.

Died: on Sep 22, at *Pine Hill*, Rappahannock Co, Va, at the residence of Mrs Wm A Lane, [his eldest child,] Jas Green, far advanced in the 83rd year of his age. He has left behind a numerous posterity to revere his memory & emulate his virtues. [Editors in Ky will please to copy the above.]

Old established Boarding House in Annapolis City: reduced prices. The house is located on Main st, opposite the residence of R W Gill, & the rear opening immediately on the State-house circle. –Mrs Ann Holland

Upholstering: Andrew Reese, in the rooms immediately under Apollo Hall.

Fort Gibson [C N] Sep 6, 1844. Meeting of the ofcrs of the Army stationed at *Fort Gibson*, C N, convened upon receiving intelligence of the death of 1st Lt R H West, 1st Regt Dragoons, Lt Col R B Mason, 1st Dragoons, having ben called to the chair. Lt R H West died on Jul 19, 1844, at the residence of his father, in PG Co, Md.
R B Mason, Lt Col 1st Dragoons
Nathan Boone, Capt 1st Dragoons
A Cady, Capt com'ng Infty
W Scott Ketchum, Capt & A Q M
E Steen, Capt 1st Dragoons
Chas McCormick, Ass't Surg U S A
S Woods, Capt 6th Infty
J B S Todd, Capt 6th Infty
Richd H Coolidge, Ass't Surg U S A
Chas Lovell, 1st Lt 6th Infty
H W Wharton, 1st Lt 6th Infty
Wm Bowman, 1st Lt 1st Dragoons
F F Flint, 2nd Lt 6th Infty
A D Nelson, 2nd Lt 6th Infty
A Buford, 2nd Lt 1st Dragoons
A T M Rust, 2nd Lt 1st Dragoons
H W Stanton, Brevet 2nd Lt 1st Dragoons
R W Kirkham, 2nd Lt 6th Infty
R H Chilton, 1st Lt 1st Dragoons, Sec

WED OCT 16, 1844
Trustee's sale: by deed of trust executed by Henrietta Syrock, dated Jun 21, 1844, recorded in Liber W B 89 folios 101, 102, & 103, land record for Wash Co: sale on Oct 4 of lot 12 in square 388. Also, part of square 353, with improvements.
–Jas B Holmead, auctioneer

N Y Express: Mr Joel Stone, one of the most respectable merchants of N Y died of a disease of the heart, at the age of 50. His death was very sudden. [No date-current item.]

The beautiful residence of the late Jas Cox, "*Cloud Cap*," 5 miles from the city of Balt, on the Fred'k turnpike, was sold on Sat to Robt Taylor, for $10,000: it contained 80 acres.

Valuable property at auction: on Nov 18 next, by deed of trust duly recorded, from John Trescott & wife: west half of lot 5 in square 286, fronting on N Y ave, with improvements. -R W Dyer & Co, aucts

Shocking: New Orleans Crescent City: tragedy in Noxubee Co, Miss, a few days since. Gayton Jones had some difficulty with his brother-in-law, Mr Glenn, in regard to a family dispute, when he, Mr J, struck Glenn with a fence rail, inflicting a mortal wound. Jones made arrangements for legal defence. He returned home, & on the next day, held a pistol to his head & fired, blowing off the top of his head.

Farm for sale: small farm on the turnpike road leading from Wash to Balt, with all necessary houses, such as dwlg, barn, stable, & others. Inquire of John McDuell. Also, for rent: neat 2 story frame house on 14th, between H & I sts.

Orphans Court of Wash Co, D C. Letters of administration on the personal estate of Borden M Voorhees, late of said county, dec'd. –J C Zabriskie, adm [In the absence of the subscriber, claimants will present their accounts to J E Dow.]

Latest from Gibraltar. Capt Thomas, of the brig **Caroline**, arrived at Boston, reports that on Sep 5 a detachment of British soldiers made an unsuccessful attempt to raise the wreck of the steamship **Missouri**, & another attempt was to be made by the crew of the frig **Warspite**, which it was thought would prove successful. –Boston Courier

Mrs Hamilton, relict of Gen Alex'r Hamilton, one of the most distinguished men of our country, is now sojourning in Phil. A seat has been assigned to her in the Convention of the Episcopal Church, now assembled in Phil, & she has been a regular attendant daily. Although nearly 90 years of age, she is lively & cheerful, & relates anecdotes of Revolutionary times with all the fervor & imagination of youth.

Dreadful accident on Sat, during the firing of a feu de joie by the Native American party on Bush Hill. Francis Roberts & Elihu Mathew Foster were charging a gun, when is prematurely discharged. Roberts is in a very precarious situation. Foster had his arm amputated, & is expected to recover. –Phil U S Gaz

Balt Co Court. The case of McClellan & wife, vs Administrator of the estate of Richd C Stockton, involving between fourteen & fifteen thousand dollars, which has been in litigation before Balt Co Court since Tue last, was brought to a close on Sat & given to the jury, who agreed upon a verdict, which was in favor of the dfndnts.

A few evenings since the sloop **Superb**, Capt Ellis, arrived here from West Point, & reported the loss of Jas Lipsey, a young man belonging to Cold Spring, who was knocked overboard by the boom of the sloop between Polopels' Island & Butter Hill. Capt Ellis threw a plank overboard, but was unable to discover Lipsey. Lipsey, being an expert swimmer, succeeded in getting safely ashore-Polopel's Island. After about 2 hours, he took up his board & crossed the island, & again commenced buffeting the waves for the shore. He reached Break Neck safe & sound, much to the surprise of Capt Ellis, & made his appearance on board the boat **Superb** the following day. –Newburgh Courier

Late Paris Papers: The Hanover Gaz announces the death of Baron de Scheele, one of the Ministers of King Ernest.

By virtue of a writ of fieri facias, at the suit of Richd C Washington, against Thos W Thomas: I have seized & taken into possession the right, title, claim, & interest, & estate at law & in equity of the said Thos W Thomas in a lot of ground & premises situated near Good Hope Tavern, Wash Co: public auction of the above will be on Nov 16, 1844. –H R Maryman, constable

Naval Genr'l Court Martial: assembled on Mon last for the trial of John Faron, jr, Chief Engineer of the steamboat **Missouri**, on the charge of negligence. Court consists of the following ofcrs: Cmdor Stewart, Pres; Cmdor Downey, Cmdor Read, Cmdor Nicholson, Capt McCauley, Capt Latimer, & Capt Forrest. Robt Ould, Judge Advocate. Jas Hoban counsel for the accused. Witnesses examined at this sitting: Jon Sutton, coal heaver, Saml Archbold, 3rd assist engineer, & firemen Allen & Kelly. Yesterday the following witness were examined: Fireman Clum, for the prosecuion; Lt Blunt, 3rd Lt Windlow, & 2nd Assist Engineer Davis for the defence.

Circuit Court of Wash Co, D C: cause of the Bank of the Potomac vs Biddy McLaughlin & others. There were 3 issues directed out of chancery to be tried by the jury respecting the validity of 3 deed, covering property which the plntfs claimed to be subject to their debt. Two issues found for the plntfs were upon the deeds of Biddly McLaughlin, purporting to have been made for the consideration of natural love & affection [from the father] & the nominal consideration of $5. The other issue, found for the dfndnt, was upon the deed from Robertson to Biddy McLaughlin.

Mr John Preston, slater, of Wash City, lost his footing while engaged in slating the roof of a 3 story brick house on F st, & fell to the ground. He was immediately conveyed home & surgical assistance obtained. He broke both arms & an ankle, besides other bodily injuries. Strong hopes are entertained for his recovery. [Oct 18th newspaper: Mr Preston had only one arm broken & a sprained ankle. He is doing well.]

Wash Corp: 1-Ptn of the legal reps of the late Peter Ham, dec'd: referred to the Cmte of Claims: passed. 2-Ptn of A Carothers & others, praying for a flag footway across F st at 11th: referred to the Cmte on Improvements. 3-Bill for the relief of Eliz Purcell, reported without amendment.

Died: on Oct 6, at Frankfort, Ky, Josiah Watson, formerly of Alexandria, D C, but for the last 30 years a resident of Ky.

Died: on Oct 15, Matilda Frances, only d/o Eliza & Owen H Bestor, aged 4 years & 6 months.

I lost my pocket-book & was induced to believe, & so believing, to charge, that Mr John M Stewart, of Wash City, had stolen it. This charge was made under circumstances of great excitement & afterwards repeated by me, & I fear may have tended, & may tend, to injure Mr Stewart. I have since recovered the pocket-book, & am fully satisfied that I made the charge without the least cause. I do declare that I know nothing which in any manner derogates from his character & standing as a gentleman & man of honor. Wash, Oct 12, 1844. –John Campbell

THU OCT 17, 1844
Tait, the murderer-$900 reward for his arrest. The reward for the arrest of Dr Tait, the murderer of Thos Rives, of Dallas Co, a relative of the dec'd, has been offered by Govn'r Fitzpatrick, of Alabama. He is a physician by profession. The last account of his is, that he was travelling in the direction of Mississippi. [See Oct 2nd newspaper.]

Died: yesterday, Mrs Mary Andrews, w/o Jos O Andrews, of Wash City, aged 85 years. Her funeral is tomorrow, from the residence of her son-in-law, Dr Thos P Jones, on F st, near 7th st, at 10 o'clock.

Died: on Oct 12, at the residence of his father, in Wash City, Hugo Lawrence Dickins.

Died: on Oct 13, in Gtwn College, Rev A L De Barth, in his 80th year.

Died: on Sep 2, in Wash Co, Ill, after a fever illness of 4 days, Joshua Grimes, in his 48th year.

Died: on Sep 29, in Charlestown, Jefferson Co, Va, of croup, Robt Taylor, 2nd s/o Rev R T Berry, of Gtwn, D C, aged 2 years & 4 days.

Mrs Manning, on 13th st, between E & F sts, has several delightful rooms vacant, & would be pleasee to accommodate either permanent or transient boarders.

For sale: a first rate Mare, Saddle & Bridle. The owner has no further use for her. She can be seen at Mr Sheckle's stable, 9th st, between D & E sts. –Thos Pursell

For rent: 3 story brick house on C st, near 4½ st, now occupied by Gov Bagby. Possession given on oct 21. Apply to E Warner, at the ofc of Donoho & Warner, on D st, near 9th.

Cheap groceries: the undersigned has commenced a Family Grocery Store at the old stand of Mr Geo Lambright, 2 doors west of the Railroad Depot. –Wm B Brashear

Dr Prefontaine, imprisoned at St Louis for one year& fined $1,000 for being concerned in the robbery of Charvis, the Santa Fe trader, remains in jail, though his time had expired, because he is unable to pay his fine.

It is said that a new & very rich gold mine has been discovered on the lands of Col Wm Hancock, in the upper part of Moore Co, N C.

Orphans Court of Wash Co, D C. Letters testamentary on the personal estate of Mary Ingle, late of said county, dec'd. –Jno F Ingle, Jno Underwood, excs

By writ of fieri facias, at the suit of Wm W Lowe, against Albert Henning: I have seized the right, title, & interest of said Henning in & to a 1 story unfinished frame dwlg-house, on 6th st, near East Capitol st: same to be offered for sale on Oct 14. –H R Maryman, Constable

FRI OCT 18, 1844
Household & kitchen furniture at auction: on Oct 22, at the residence lately occupied by Miss Polk, on Pa ave, near 3rd st. –R W Dyer & Co, aucts

Nat'l Theatre for sale: by deed of trust to the subscriber, dated Jul 11, 1835, recorded on Sep 28, 1842, in Liber W B 95 folios 327 thru 333, of the land records of Wash Co, D C: public sale on Nov 2 next, lots 3 & 4 in square 254, in Wash City, or so much of the said lots as are covered by the Theatre erected thereon, together with 7 front feet on each side of the bldg. –Geo Thomas, trustee -R W Dyer & Co, aucts

Chas H Haswell, Chief Engineer, has been promoted to the ofc of Engineer in Chief of the U S Navy, vice G L Thompson, removed. –Balt Sun

Orphans Court of Wash Co, D C. In the case of Lewis G Davidson, widow, & heirs, the trustee having reported the sale made by him on Oct 8,
John K Vernon was the purchaser of: lot 3 in square 127, for $241.31
Jos Schwartz of lot 15 in square 127, for $243.96
Jos Fraser of lots 10 & 11 in square 127, for $406.26
Nicholas Callas of lot 7 in square 163, for $68.10
Jas Carrico of lot 9 in square 163, for $88.14
Hobaart Perriam of lot 9 in square 126, for $363.47
Flodoardo Howard of lot 13 in square 163, for $59.22
Chas Gordon of lot 3 in square 126, & lot 8 in square 163, for *$73.72½.
All in Wash City. –Nathl Pope Causin -Ed N Roach, reg/o wills
[*Paper damaged-best interpretation of the numbers.]

The Utica Baptist Register says that Rev Benj Hovey preached in the Broad st Baptist Chapel in that city on the last Sabbath in Sept. Mr H has attained to the remarkable age of 110 years.

The dwlg-house of Mr Thos G Meredith, on the outskirts of Morley, near Ogdenbury, N Y, was destroyed on fire on Tue, & two of his children, one a boy about 2½ years, & an infant dght about 11 months old, perished in the flames.

Mrd: on Oct 15, by Rev Mr Courtney, Dr Calistus Lancaster to Miss Lucretia Middleton, both of Chas Co, Md.

An affray took place at Burlington, Iowa, on Oct 1, between Mr Andrews, Gen G W Hight, & his son, Geo B Hight. Andrews was seriously injured & died the same day; the matter was under judicial investigation.

SAT OCT 19, 1844
Accident last evening, as one of the locomotives attached to the Long Island Railroad was backing from Bedford, towards the South Ferry, it ran over a woman by the name of Mary McLaughlin, who was crossing the track, severing both her legs from her body. She died in a few minutes. It must have been absolute carelessness that induced the woman to cross the track when the locomotive was in such proximity. –N Y American

Exchange Hotel, Wash City. The subscriber announces this hotel will be opened on Nov 21: situated on C st, near the railroad depot. For many years experienced as keeper of the U S Hotel in Newburgh, N Y. –John M Gilbert

Ladies Select School: Mrs Dr Baker intends opening on Jan 1, 1845, at Providence, Fairfax Co, Va. She has been for many years a successful teacher in a highly respectable Seminary, under the superintendence of her mother, the late Mrs Burgess, in Otsego Co, N Y.

The copartnership existing under the firm of Wilburn & Parker, has been this day dissolved by mutual consent. Jas Parker is alone authorized to collect debts due the late firm. –H Wilburn, Jas Parker [Jas Parker will contine the House Slating business in the future.]

Mrd: on Oct 15, in Wash City, by Rev Wm Matthews, Wm Matthews Merrick, of Fred'k City, Md, to Miss Mary B Wickliffe, d/o Hon Chas A Wickliffe, of Ky.

Mrd: on Oct 17, by Rev Mr French, Mr G W Wheeler to Miss Martha A Knowblock, all of Wash City.

Mrd: on Thu last, by Rev Mr Wilson, Mr John E Bailey, of Wash City, to Miss Rebecca Young, formerly of Balt, Md.

Chancery sale of valuable Wash City property. By decree of the Circuit Court of Wash Co, D C, in Chancery, in the matter of Wm B Stone & Walter Mitchell, excs of Alex'r Greer, dec'd, cmplnts, against Wm D Prout & others, heirs at law, Rachael L Prout, widow, & Chas S Fowler, administrator of Wm Prout, dec'd, dfndnts: Public auction on Nov 22 of the following pieces or parcels of ground in Wash City: lot 3 in square 4, part of lot 1 in square 494, fronting on 4½ st; lots 5, 11, & 12, in square 873; lot 9 in square 877; lots 33, 35, & 36, & part of lot 34 in square 878; lot 10 thru 13 in square 897; lots 3 & 4 in square 899; lots 8 & 9 in square 925; lots 13 thru thru 16 & part of lot 17, in square 926, fronting on 9th st west. All that part of lot 2 in square 926, fronting on south K st; lots 9 thru 11 in square 949; lots 11 thru 15, 17 thru 20 in square 950, fronting on south G st; lot 5 & 6 in square 975; part of lots 11 & 12 in square 975, fronting on 11st st east; lots 3, 6, & 14 in square 1001, & all the estate of the said Wm Prout therein at the time of his decease & which has descended to his heirs at law, & all the interest & estate of Rachael L Prout, his widow, in & to the same. –Richd Wallach, trustee -R W Dyer & Co, aucts

MON OCT 21, 1844
Reported loss of the U S cutter **Vigilant** & 12 of her crew. We learn from Capt Churchill, of the ship **Nathaniel Hooper**, arrived at this port yesterday from Boston, that he spoke on the 14th instant the ship **Ilzaide**, from New Orleans, for London, who requested him to receive on board 3 wrecked seamen, two of them, Michl Driscoll & Henry Hoyt, believed to be the only surviviors of a crew of 14 persons, belonging to the U S revenue cutter **Vigilant**, Capt W B G Taylor, of New Orleans, which vessel was blown from her anchors out of the harbor of Key West, on the 5th instant, during a gale, & capsized. The above name seamen caught hold of a very small canoe, which got loose from the schnr while bottom up; they there retained their hold for 2 days & nights, the sea continually breaking over them. When taken off by the ship **Ilzaide**, they were nearly speechless & quite exhausted.
–Charleston Courier, 18th.

Balt, Oct 17. Balt City Court. Harvey Hevener, found guilty for an assault upon Capt Jos Willey, & ofcr Bowman, & for causing a riot in the streets, was sentenced, for the first offence, to pay a fine of $100 & costs, & 12 months in the Balt city & county jail. For the assault on Bowman he was also sentenced to 6 months; imprisonment, & fined $50 & costs. He was also given 6 additional months imprisonment, fined $50 & costs, & required to stand committed until security could be given in the sum of $500 to keep the peace for 12 months. Thos Stubbens, who was also engaged in the same outrage with Hevener, was found guilty of committing a riot: sentenced to 6 months imprisonment, & to stand committed until $500 security could be given that he would keep the peace 12 months. -Patriot

An ear of corn was raised on the farm of an old friend, Mr Abraham Null, on Moncacy, this season, having on it 1,838 grains, measuring 1½ pint half of shelled corn. –Westminster [Md] Carrolltonian

Worcester [Mass] Aegis contains a full report on the trial [which took place last week,] of Thos Berrett, of Lunenburgh, for the murder of Ruth Houghton of the same place. The indictment charged that the crime was committed by the prisoner by "fixing & fastening both his hands about the neck & throat" of the dec'd, & thereby strangling her. Berrett was found guilty on the charge of murder, & on Thu the Chief Justice pronounced sentence of death.

Household & kitchen furniture at auction: on Oct 24, by order of the Orphans Court of Wash Co, D C, at the residence of the late Wm Hicks, on Capitol Hill. -R W Dyer & Co, aucts

For rent: a 2 story brick house near the Navy Yard. Key is at R H Harrington's Tavern, near the Navy Yard gate, or with the subscriber. –Wm D Acken

Valuable land within ½ mile of Wash for sale: lies about a mile from the city boundary & the Tiber mill, n e of the capitol, & adjoins the lands of Messrs Gales, Derringer, & Brentwood: contains about 60 acres . Apply to Johnson & Callan, Agency Ofc, F st.

Died: on Sat week, in Cincinnati, David Wade, one of the oldest members of the Cincinnati Bar.

Died: on Sep 12, at her residence, 8 miles west of Park Hill, Cherokee Nation, of congestive fever, Mrs Jane, w/o Jos Coody, & eldest sister of John Ross, Principal Chief of the Cherokee Nation, aged 57 years.

Worthington G Snethen, Atty at Law, Wash, D C. [Local ad.]

Naval Genr'l Court Martial: on Fri last: the charge & specifications against Mr Faron were taken up: he was accused of stowing 2 demijohns of turpentine, one of which, through negligence, had been broken & caused the fire of the ship. Mr Faron was also charged with not making such regulations in the engineer dept as the safety of the ship required. The Court re-assembled on Sat, when Richd Muzzleton, seaman on board the U S ship **Potomac**, was put upon his trial under the charge of assaulting Julius S Bohrer, a midshipman of the U S Navy, on Aug 13, 1844, while the said Midshipman Bohrer was in the execution of his duty. Witnesses were examined, & the testimony was closed: Chas Wm Stanway, cpl of marines, private marine Sheeles, Chas Wilson, ordinary seaman, Midshipman Bohrer, & Lt Holcomb. Mr Hoban will make the prisoner's defence on the meeting of the Court this morning.

For rent: a new & delightful house on F st, between 6th & 7th sts, containing 10 rooms, 8 with fire-places. Inquire of Mrs Ann Benning, next door to the Post Ofc.

The Falcon Boat Club has lately been formed in Wash City, & they have procured a splendid boat from Phil, 45 feet in length, & having 8 oars. The uniform of the club is navy blue pantaloons & jacket, with white pearl buttons. The present ofcrs are: Jos B Tate, Pres; John F Coyle, Sec; M Henry Stevens, Treasurer; G McD Burke, Coxswain.

TUE OCT 22, 1844
Balt American of yesterday. We have been furnished by Wm A Shaeffer, Justice of the Peace of this city, with the following list of persons who have been convicted of violating the laws of Md by voting illegally at the election held in Balt City on Oct 2, 1844, for Govn'r of Md & members of the Legislature.
Christopher Atkinson fined $20 & committed to jail for illegally voting. He had been in Balt 2 weeks from the Eastern Shore.
Wm Weir fined $20 & committed to jail. He has a family in Port Deposite.
John Edwards: case filed in Court for the action of the Grand Jury. He was from Port Deposite.
Jos Bevan fined $20 & committed to jail: says he was induced to do so by a Wm Collins.
Walter Hughes, would not state where he belonged. Case file in Court for the action of the Grand Jury.
Lawrence Furlong fined $20 & gave security for the fine & costs. His residence in on the Eastern Shore.
Thos Ryland fined $20 & committed to jail.
Geo Bollman fined $20 & committed to jail. He came from Ellicott's Mills.
Jas O'Hara, who says he was sent from Pittsburg with 14 others, was fined $20 & committed to jail.
Chas McDonald fined $20. Security given for the fine. He was 4 months from Va.
Geo W Brown fined $20, & appealed to the County Court. Says he came from Ellicott's Mills.
Chas W Coleman fined $20 & gave security. He came from the Eastern Shore.
Wm Patrick Kelley, minor, fined $20. Gave security.
Alfred McClaskey fined $20 & committed to jail. He came from Balt Co.
Josiah Keene, who came from the city from Dorchester Co in May last was fined $10. Appealed.
Jas Haslup fined $20, & appealed to Court. He voted at the last Congressional election at Catonsville, Balt Co.
Benj Dove was committed for further examination. He says he came from Washington.
Patrick Brahan fined $20; appealed. Residence in Dorchester Co.
Francis H River, from Phil. He escaped from the custody of the ofcr.

A J Zeller confesses he voted illegally. Says he came from York, Pa, in July, is a shoemaker, went to the Democratic meetings, & was told by some persons there that he could vote any where in the U S where he was at the election time. Fined $20 & committed to jail.

Patrick Finegan fined $20; gave security. Came from Phil, where he lived from spring 1843 to May, 1844, & came to Balt.

Cornelius Hurley fined $20 & committed to jail. Came from Washington; he is not naturalized, not having been a sufficient time in the U S.

Another Phil rioter convicted. Isaac Hahn, indicted for the murder of Jos Rice, came into Court on Sat with a verdict finding the prisoner guilty of Murder in the 2nd Degree. The verdict was accompanied with a recommendation of the prisoner to the mercy of the Court, on account of his youth & inexperience. –Gaz

For rent: a 2 story brick house on D st, near 7th, newly painted & repaired. Inquire of Mr Jas Owner, Va ave, east of Jas Owner, jr, Gen Post Ofc.

Island Drug Store. The subscriber has removed to 10th & Md ave, next door to Mr Wm M Morrison's residence. –Jas Young, jr

Mrd: on Oct 8, at St Louis, Mo, by Rev Mr Lutz, Mr Clement W Coote to Miss Sarah R Beakey, all of that city.

Mrd: on Oct 20, by Rev Mr Myers, Mr John J Morse to Mary Eliz Crussell, all of Wash City.

Mrd: on Oct 10, in Gtwn, by Rev J G Wilson, Mr Chas J Canfield, of Wash, to Miss Mgt J, d/o Wm H Prentiss, of the former place.

Died: on Sep 20, Mr Thos T Parker, in his 38th year. His funeral is from his late residence on G st, at half-past 2 o'clock this day.

Died: on Oct 15, in Wash City, after an illness of 5 weeks, Mrs Catharine Burger, a native of Germany, but for many years past a resident of Alexandria, in this District.

Died: on Sep 10, in Portland, Maine, of consumption, John N Frink, M D, aged 36.

Died: on Oct 8, at her residence in Loudoun Co, Va, Mrs Mary Stovin, in her 72nd year. She has left behind her an affectionate son & many near & dear relatives to weep over the tomb of worth & virtue.

WED OCT 23, 1844
Nicholas Dumser, aged about 24, while walking in Mott st with a friend on Sun, was struck on the breast with a club by some unknown person, & knocked down senseless. He was conveyed to his residence in Houston st, where he died yesterday. –N Y Commercial Advertiser

From the Pittsburg Age: the Flanagans, the 2 persons confined under sentence of death in Cambria Co prison, escaped a few days ago. They were convicted 18 months ago of murdering an old lady for her money.

A traveler named Dodge, supposed to be from Western N Y, was drowned at Quick's Run, on Oct 16. He fell off the steamer **Wilmington**, while walking on her guards. He was bound for Iowa, & had land papers & money about his person. –Cincinnati Gaz

Tremendous gale at Buffalo on Fri: some 40 bodies have been taken from the river. The man who kept the boathouse on the peninsula, we think his name is Gilbert, with his son & a son of the widow Osier, were all drowned. Also, a young man named Ploof, a moulder, from Jefferson Co. Mrs Stalcom & 3 children, recently from Seneca falls, a man named Metot & another named White, who resided at Williamville, are among the number feared drowned. .

Orphans Court of Wash Co, D C. Letters testamentary on the personal estate of Adam Lindsay, late of said county, dec'd. –Maria A Lindsay, excx

$5 reward for return of a double case Silver Watch, left in the out house of the Treasury Bldg, on Sat last. Deliver to Mr Adams, at the door of the Treasury, or to John Sessford.

$50 reward for runaway negro man Stephen Baley, between 22 & 25 years of age. –Wm C Peerce, of Henry, living near the Burnt Mills, Montg Co, Md.

A F Judlin, Practical Upholsterer, just return from Paris. He will be in Wash on Oct 28 to exhibit his magnificent collection of Paris designs. Leave communications at the European House, Wash. Reference, Hon Matthew St Clair Clarke.

THU OCT 24, 1844
Mrs S Hamilton has just returned from the North & has opened her Fall & Winter Millinery at her Store on Pa ave, between 9th & 10th sts.

New Store! On Pa ave, between 10th & 11th sts, 2 doors from King's Lace Store, where I will sell threads, laces, collars, edging, whig bands, bonnet tabs, & a general assortment of articles. –H N Roby

Assignee's sale of 7,490 acres of land in Pa. In the matter of C A Fowler, a bankrupt. Public auction on Nov 15 of the following tracts & parcels of land, lying in Montg , in Indiana Co, Pa, which were conveyed by Patent under the great seal of Pa, in 1835, described by the numbers of the patents, as follows, viz:

3,757 containing 1,000 acres
3,758 containing 1,000 acres
3,762 containing 962½ acres
3,765 containing 962½ acres
3,768 containing 1,000 acres
3,772 containing 1,018+acs
3,774 containing 1,018+acs
3,747 contains for sale 354 acres
3,748 contains for sale 174 acres

These lands lie upon & adjacent to the West Branch of the Susquehanna river. -David A Hall, Assignee of Bankrupts -R W Dyer & Co, aucts

A young man by the name of Kulp, about 18 or 19 years of age, committed suicide last Friday by throwing himself into the Niagara river, at Blackrock. He had been for some time infatuated with the Millerite delusion.

Mrd: on Oct 9, at Ajacio, Loudoun Co, Va, Thos P Bayly, of New Orleans, to Mary E, d/o John Bayly.

Mrd: on Oct 21, at *Mount Pleasant*, Wash, by Rev Mr Hawley, Lt Jas W Abert, of the U S Corps of Topographical Engineers, to Jane L, only d/o W I Stone.

Mrd: on Oct 8, at Providence, R I, by Rev Mr Williams, Trustun D Beale, of Wash City, to Miss Mariana, d/o Hon Jos L Tillinghast.

Died: on Oct 4, at his residence in PG Co, Md, Thos Parker. And on Oct 16, Mary Parker, his widow, in her 76th year. May they rest in peace.

Died: on Oct 16, Ann Caroline, w/o Littleton Dennis, of Accomacre Co, Va, & d/o Wm Fowle, of Alexadnria, in her 22nd year.

Died: on Oct 8, in Wash City, John Edward, only child of Edw & Susannah Hawkins, aged 1 year & 17 days.

FRI OCT 25, 1844
Arrest of Counterfeiters. On Oct 14 the police of St Louis arrested Jerry S Cowden, a boarder at the Arcade Baths, a room-mate named Stintz, & a young man named Keon, a clerk in the employ of Mr Stevens, charged with counterfeiting. The engraving is almost a perfect copy of the genuine plate.

For rent: one of the Seven Bldgs, in which Capt Mordecai resides; also the house on I st, at present occupied by Mr Taggert, & near the residence of Mrs Gen Macomb. Possession may be had on Nov 1. Apply to Saml Stott.

For rent or sale: large 2 story brick house on 17th st, near Mrs Macomb's. Terms moderate. Apply to J H Wailes, agent, at the Capitol.

SAT OCT 26, 1844
For rent & possession immediately. That large & convenient storehouse in Benedict, which was occupied by the late Jas Morton, & to which is attached a large tobacco house. –Wm Morton

Boots & Shoes: A Coyle & Son [Local ad-no address.]

For rent: hose of the 2 brick dwlgs, nearly new, on D st, between 7th & 8th sts. Apply at Mrs Varnum's, on 8th st.

The brig **Saratoga**, Capt Bedell, of & from N Y for Apalachicola was totally lost off Orange Key on Oct 3. Mr Simonton, her 2nd mate, & Saml Smith, passenger have arrived at Boston. The following persons were on board & no doubt perished: Passengers, Capt E G Wood, Capt J Perkins, Donald Campbell, Mrs Larkin & 2 children, Mrs Fitzgerald, Mr Hewins, Mr Markam, Chas McKinney, wife & child, & 2 German steerage passengers. Also, Capt Bedell, 6 colored seamen, steward, & boy, the latter white. The last seen of these passengers by Mr Simonton, 4 or 5 of them were clinging to the stump of the mainmast.

Mrd: on Oct 21, at St Paul's, Chillicothe, by Rev Mr Britton, Wm Peter, H B M Consul for the State of Pa, to Sarah King, d/o the late Gov Worthington, of Ohio.

Mrd: on oct 15, by Rev John O'Brien, Mr Wm McSherry, of Adams Co, Pa, to Miss Eliza Thompson McSherry, d/o Dr Richd McSherry, of Martinsburg, Va.

C H Haven, Atty & Counsellor at Law, St Louis, Missouri. [Ad]

Valuable farm near St Louis, Missouri, for sale: containing 640 acres: 2 miles from Bellefontaine. The whole tract is offered, subject to the mortgage, for $4,220. Address the subscriber at St Louis, Missouri. –Richd Hanson Weightman

MON OCT 28, 1844
City Ordinance: 1-Act for the relief of the legal reps of Peter Ham, dec'd: that the reps be paid $302.90, for over-payment of taxes on parts of lot 1 & 13 in square 118.

One of the Mills belonging to the Hazard Powder Co, in Enfield, Conn, was blown up on Sep 16. Nelson McClester, Gilbert M Durfee, & Wm Prickett, who were in the mill at the time, were so badly injured that death was the consequence.

For rent: 2 story brick dwlg house on I st, at present in the occupancy of Dr Smoot. Inquire of Maj Geo Bender, 4 doors east of the bldg, or at the Ordnance Dept.

Late account from Florida state that besides the U S revenue cutter **Vigilant**-which we have already noticed as having been blown out of the harbor of Key West & wrecked on Sep 4-the schnr **Hudson**, Capt Millen, of N Y, & recently from Wash, D C, drove to sea with 2 anchors dragging, in the early part of the gale, & is supposed to be lost with all on board, viz: Ambrose Cooper, passenger, from St Augustine; Jas Miller, the Capt, of New Orleans; Wm Hellard, mate, of the Eastern Shore of Va; John Saunders, Englishman, & Andy Thompson, Norwegian, crew & owners. The following is a list of the ofcrs of the **Vigilant**: Wm B G Taylor, Cmder; Wm G Taylor, 1st Lt; Mr Cooper, of Dingham, Mass, 2nd Lt; 6 seamen, & the cook & cabin boy. Mr Robt Cooper, one of the Louisiana pilots, & 2 of the negroes who deserted with the pilot boat from the boat **Balize**, were on board. J C Johnson, pilot, belonging to the **Vigilant**, & Mr Robt Armisted, of New Orleans [passenger] were providentially ashore, & saved. The only persons saved from the wreck were Michl Driscoll & Henry Hoyt, seamen, picked up at sea in a canoe belonging to the cutter, which they fortunately fell in with while in the water.

The Genr'l Court of the East India Co have granted to Maj Gen Wm Nott, who has recently returned in bad health from his command in India, an annuity of L1,000. He entered into the service of the company in 1800.

<u>Corp of Wash: List of the ordinaries & taverns in Wash City & of the persons to whom licenses have been granted.</u>
A Favier, square 119, 19th st
Chas Borremans, square 74, Pa ave
Jas B Freer, square 86, 20th st
Benedict Jost, square 168, Pa ave
Andrew Hancock, Pa ave
Jas Davis, square 348, north D & 10th sts
Wm Thomas, square 291, 13th & E sts
Abraham Butler, square 254, north F st
Michl Ward, square 324, corner 12th & E sts
W Creutzfeldt, square 292, Pa ave
E H Fuller, square 225, Pa ave
Jas Maher, square 256, corner E & 13 ½ sts
J H Eberbach, square 291, Pa ave
Geo St Clair, square 327, 11th & Water sts
A Fuller, square 225, Pa ave
Wm Dowling, square 254, north F st
J C Stuart, square 267, Md ave & 13 ½ st
John Purdon, square 226, Paa ve & 14th st
Lewis Gallabrun, square 225, Pa ave
Fritz Creutzfeldt, square 267, Md ave & 13 ½ st
Louis M Gilbert, square 291, E & 13th sts

John T Wright, square 353, 11th st
Wm Samuels, square 457, 7th st
Thos Baker, square 431, 8th st
Christian H Zachman, square 455, 7th st
John West, square 461, Pa ave
John H Clarvoe, square 461, 7th st
Jas Cuthbert, res 10, Pa ave
Jesse Brown, square 460, Pa ave
Jas McGrath, square 380, Pa ave
Michl McDermott, res A, Pa ave
Jas Fitzgerald, res 10, Pa ave
John Emerick, square 459, F st
Michl Talty, square 432, 7th st
Jas Long, square 460, 6th st
Wm Benter, square 491, Pa ave
P A DeSaules, square 431, 7th & E sts
H W Sweeting, square 490, C st
Jos Boulanger, square B, Pa ave
John Foy, square 378, D st
P Moran, square 575, Pa ave
Wm Feeny, square 432, 7th st
Martin Murphy, res 10, Pa ave
King & Hall, square B, Pa ave
Lucy A Lasky, square 461, 7th st
John Douglas, square 490, Louisiana ave
Jas P Gannon, square 461, 7th st
Bonefanti Shadd, res 12, B st
John C Cook, square 461, 7th st
Christopher Schneider, square 408, 9th st
Thompson Tyler, square 490, C st
John H Eberbach, square 407, 8th & E sts
Patrick Quigley, square 492, md ave
John Leary, res 10, B st
Christian, square B, Pa ave
Wm Dipple, square 408, 9th st
Wm Gadsby, square 491, Pa ave
Andrias Ruppert, square 729, East Capitol st
Christopher O'Neale, square 920, L st
Mgt Crane, square 928, 8th st
Alfred Burdine, square 928, 8th st
Richd H Harrington, square 930, 8th st

By whom premises were examined & certified/by whom recommended:

Tho Smith	Saml Redfern	Fred'k Schneider
A Hoover	Geo Krafft	Thos Lundy

John Fister	Wm Evans	Wm Ward
John Mullikin	Geo W Kendrick	Chas Stott
Bernard Kelly	Jas Laurie	S P Franklin
Wm Collins	Jas McClery	Alex'r Provost
Wm Linkins	John C Rives	Walter Lenox
Saml Scott	E Stephens	Jas F Haliday
Ters Godfrey	Nicholas Callan	John T Towers
Henry Walker	J S Harvey	Patrick Moran
Mathieu Bouvet	Dearborn Johnson	Wm H Upperman
Jacob Brodbeck	Peter Cazenave	Stanislaus Murray
Hugh Haney	Thos Berry	Martin Murphy
F A Wagler	Wm B Walker	Francis Mohun
John France	L Thomas	Geo Parker
Abraham Butler	Theodore Harbaugh	Wm H Harrover
Jas McColgan	Raphael Jones	Thos Young
Wm Morrow	Thos Baker	Alex'r Lee
E Simms	J H T Werner	J P Pepper
R E Kerr	Leonard Harbaugh	Columbus Monroe
Wm Orme	Jos Harbaugh	John R Hendly
Jas Clephane	John H Goddard	Richd C Washington
P Kinchy	G Ailier	Levi Pumphrey
Grafton Powell	Thos Macgill	Jas P McKean
Jas Maher	Jos Straub	John W Maury
Chas F Bihler	G W Utermuhle	Chas F Bihler
Michl Nourse	Jacob Sceifferle	Robt Keyworth
Jas Larned	Jas Fossett	Jas C McGinnis
McClintock Young	John Brown	Thos Baker
Allison Nailor	Richd G Briscoe	Owen Connolly
Patrick Green	Jos S Clarke	M McDermott
Wm Dowling	Jas T Clarke	Jos Beasley
J H Eberbach	Saml Bacon	W G W White
C P Sengstack	B O Sheckell	John Emerich
Wm Noell	Peter F Bacon	John H Clarvoe
Wm H Prentiss	I T Ellwood	I T Ellwood
P Kinchy	Thos Pursell	A F Kimmell
Wm Stewart	Seth Hyatt	Edwin Walker
M St Clair Clarke	R Burdine	M Delany
J T Sullivan	B F Middleton	Jacob Acker
W T Dove	Benj Beall	C Utermuhle
N Travers	Chas Bell	Geo Watterston
Wm H Gunnell	John A Donohoo	Cornelius Andree
Lewis Thomas	Thos Cokendorfer	J H T Werner
Jas Mitchell	Henry Howison	W H Campbell
Richd Wimsatt	Abner H Young	Edmund Reily

Z Hazel	Philip Inch	Geo Hartman
D Homans	Thos Bayne	Jas Tucker
J A Lynch	H R Maryman	Andrew Forrest
Vandori Mallion	C O'Neale	Adam Gaddis
R M Combs	Thos Thornley	A F Bulley
Adam Gaddis	Robt Combs	Christopher Weber
John Bohlayer	Geo Sherman	Chas Aug Schneider

Died: on Oct 25, of scarlet fever, Thomas, 4th s/o Saml Coomes, in his 9th year.

TUE OCT 29, 1844
We observe in the list of passengers arrived in the ship **Great Western** the name of M de Bodisco, the very popular Minister of Russia, who left the U S last year on a visit to his own country.

We notice in the English papers the death of Mr Nathan Dunn, founder of the Chinese Museum in Phil, & author of several distinguished charities.

Premptory sale by order of the assignees: *Reading Furnace* & *Charming Forge* properties, known as *Ege's Iron Works*: public sale on Nov 26: long owned & conducted by the late Geo Ege. *Reading Furnace*: about 6,200 acres: large stone mansion house, with the necessary out bldgs. *Charming Forge*: on the Union Canal: 4,700 acres: large substantial stone mansion house & barn, with the necessary out bldgs. –Jas Dundas, Mordecai D Lewis, Saml W Jones, Robt L Pitfiled, Robt Howell, Assignees. M Thomas & Son, auctioneers, 93 Walnut st

Mrd: on Oct 16, by Rev Mr Montgomery, at *Showance Springs*, Mercer Co, Va, Mr Wm L Vance, of Memphis, Tenn, to Miss Letitia H Thompson, y/d/o Col Geo C Thompson.

Mrd: on Mon last, by Rev Mr Danforth, Mr W A Wharton, of Balt, Md, to Miss Virginia, d/o Chas Scott, of Alexandria, D C.

Died: on Sun last, Mrs Ann Maria, w/o Richd G Briscoe, & the eldest d/o Jos S Clarke, in her 34th year, leaving a devoted husband & 5 small children to mourn her loss, to them irreparable. Her funeral is at half past 9 o'clock this morning, at St Patrick's Church.

Died: on Oct 26, Agnes, infant d/o Col T Cross, U S Army.

McGrath's Washington Coffee House, on Pa ave, has been handsomely refitted for the reception & accommodation of the public.

For rent: a 2 story brick house on Md ave & 12th sts, with a good cellar & back bldg adjoining. Inquire of Mr Fitch, next door, or of Edw Mattingly, near the Navy Yard.

WED OCT 30, 1844
At a special term of the Circuit Court, lately held in the town of Washington, Ark, Henry Scaggs was tried for the murder of Wm Oaks, found guilty, & sentenced to be hung on Oct 25.

For rent: a very excellent 2 story brick dwlg on 12th st, between G & H sts. Apply to S Burche.

For rent: 2 furnished rooms, a parlor & a bed room, suitable for a gentleman & lady, or 2 single gentlemen. Board can be furnished if desired. Inquire of A Ricketts, G st, near the War Dept.

$50 reward for runaway mulatto man Danl; about 40 years of age: formerly belonged to the estate of the late Robt Davis, near Charlotte Hall, St Mary's Co, Md. –John D Bowling, Aquasco, PG Co, Md

For sale: pototoes & apples-Ramboy & Pippins. On board schnr **Atlantic**, at P E Sacett's wharf. –Bubbard Scranton, Gtwn

$50 reward for runaway, from my son's place, [Stephny] on the Rockville Turnpike, on Sat last, negro man Battaile Lacy, aged about 46 or 47. –Nathl Pope Causin

Wash Corp: 1-Ptn of Jos Jewett & others, praying for a modification of the law regulating taverns or ordinaries. 2-Bill for the relief of Geo Savage: referred to the Cmte on Improvements. 3-Cmte of Claims: asking to be discharged from the further consideration of the ptn of Wm P Shedd. 4-Nominations by the Mayor for Superintendents of Chimney Sweeps: Wm M Robinson, Geo Y Bowen, J A Keenan, Jas A Breast, N B Wilkerson: considered & confirmed.

More illegal voting. Capt John Goodrich, cmder of a boat hailing from Chas Co, was arrested at Balt on Sat, on a charge of voting illegally at the 7th Ward polls on Oct 2. The Capt had a full hearing before Justice Schaeffer, & notwithstanding he produced the testimony of some of his Locofoco friends, & was fined $20 & costs. The illegalityof his voting was established from admissions of the accused. -Patriot

The stately & elegant packet ship **Thos P Cope** left the port of Phil, for Liverpool, with the following cabin passengers: Rev Chas J Sterling & lady, of St Lucia, W L; Isabella Maclear, of Phil; Mrs J T Gilmer, London; Miss Gilmer, London; Edw A Still; London; Thos Stovell, Phil; Hugh Wrightman, Ohio; Wm Macfarlane, Ohio. Besides these, there are 8 passengers in the 2nd cabin, & 115 in the steerage.

Gen Wm Gibbs McNeil has been appointed engineer of the new Dry Dock to be constructed at the Navy Yard, Brooklyn. –Balt Sun

A Balt man named Armstrong met an awful & sudden death on Wed last, near Whatcoat Chapel, on the Hookstown road, by the instantaneous caving in of a well.

Marie Taglioni, the celebrated danseuse, on Wed appeared before the Civil Tribunal of the Seine to apply for a divorce [separation de corps] from her husband, M le Compte Gilbert des Voisins. In this affair, as in many applications made by distinguished artistes & prime donne, the courious public were left to make their own conjectures as to the real motives to the separation. They were married in 1834. Voisins expressed his desire that his wife should discontinue the theatrical career in which she had already obtained so brilliant a success.

Louisville Courier of Oct 24. Terrible steamboat disaster. The steamboat **Lucy Walker**, Capt Vann, left this place for New Orleans yesterday crowded with passengers. The engine was stopped in order to make repairs, & in about 5 minutes the boiler exploded with tremendous violence. The U S snag-boat **Gopher**, Capt L B Dunham, was about 200 yards distant at the time. He was immediately on the spot, rescuing those in the water. Mr John Hixon & Mr Henry Bebee, passengers in the **Lucy Walker**, deserve notice for their coolness & their efficient exertions in saving the lives of the drowning persons. The following are the names of the dead, missing & wounded, so far as we have been able to learn them. Killed & Missing: Gen J W Pegram, of Richdmond, Va; Saml M Brown, Post Ofc Agent, of Lexington, Ky; J R Cormick, of Va; Chas Donne, of Louisville; Philip Wallis, formerly of Balt; Rebecca, d/o A J Foster, of Greensville, Va: Jas Vanderberg, of Louisville; Mr Hughes, formerly of Lexington, Ky; Mr Matlock, of New Albany, engineer of the steamboat **Mazeppa**; Nicholas Ford, formerly of Louisville; David Vann, the capt; Moses Kirby, pilot; 2nd mate, 2nd clerk, 2nd engineer, barkeeper, & 3 deck hands, names unknown; 4 negro firemen. Wounded: W H Peebles, Mr Raines, of Va, & the 1st Engineer, all very badly hurt; Capt Thompson, pilot, arms fractured; Mr Roberts, of Phil, slightly hurt. It is supposed that John N Johnson & Richd Phillips were on board: if so, they are lost. The boat was owned by Capt Vann, of Arkansas, & was insured.

Criminal Court-Wash: W Cooper, free negro convicted of assaulting John Locke, a county constable, while in the discharge of his duty.

Naval Gen Court Martial: yesterday Mr Hoban read the defence of Lt West, late cmder of the U S brig **Somers**, who was charged with intoxication. The Court went into deliberation & the room was cleared about 2 o'clock.

On Oct 19, the fine ship **Mary Kingsland**, Capt Wear, of N Y, lying at the foot of Esplanade st, in New Orleans, was discovered to be on fire. She had on board 1,700 bales of cotton. The entire loss will hardly fall short of $120,000.

U S brig **Perry**, Macao Roads, Jun 8, 1844. Meeting of the ofcrs of the brig **Perry**, convened for the purpose of passing resolutions relative to the decease of Midshipman Geo W Harrison. We sincerely sympathize with Maj Harrison in his being bereaved of a son whose manifold virtues & accomplishments had endeared him to all who knew him.

E G Tilton, Commanding	R H Wyman, Act'g Master
J C Howell, Act'g Lt	Robt Milligar, Midshipman
H N Harrison, Lt	W W Queen, Midshipman
C Ap R Jones, Act'g Lt	Edw E Stone, Midshipman
Jas Tilton, Act'g Purser	J O Montalant, Capt Clk

Criminal Court-Wash. Grand Jury for the Oct Term:

Thos Carbery, Foreman	Robt White
Wm B Thompson	O M Linthicum
John Cox	Geo Thomas
Joshua Pierce	John W Maury
Geo W Young	John Boyle
John Mason, jr	John F Coxe
Jacob Gideon	Chas R Belt
Lewis Johnson	R C Weightman
Thos Munroe	Thos Blagden
Thos Fenwick	Wm I Stone
Hamilton Luffborough	Levi Sheriff
Jos Forrest	John Lyons

Mr Geo Hoke, of Paradise township, York Co, Pa, was killed a few days since by becoming entwined in a rope place over the horns of a steer, which, taking fright, started off, dragging Mr Hoke a considerable distance, & so injuring him that he died in 2 hours.

Died: Oct 28, Edward Everett, s/o J V N & Meline Throop, aged 3 years & 1 month.

THU OCT 31, 1844
Ebenezer Howland attempted on Fri last to drive his wagon across the track of the Western Railroad at Pittsfield, Mass, while the train was in full sight. His wagon was struck & he was killed on the spot.

On Fri last 4 men were painting the ceiling of the new Post Ofc in N Y, when the scaffold gave way & they fell to the ground. Two of them, one named Davison, the other Jas Lapish, were dreadfully injured.

Boarding: Mrs A Cochran, on F st between 13th & 14th sts. For rent: the adjoining house as soon as finished, which will be about Dec 1.

Boarding: a small family or a few gentlemen, can be accommodated in a private family where there are no small children. Apply to Edmund F Brown, near the Globe Ofc, or Farquhar & Morgan.

Rich & Splendid Dry Goods. –Geo Stettinius

Died: Oct 13, at her residence in Palmyra, Missouri, Mrs Francis T Lane, in her 54th year, consort of the late G W Lane, of that county, & formerly of Fairfax Co, Va.

The Hon Wm Campbell died on Mon at his residence in Cherry Valley, aged 77 years. He was the eldest s/o the late Col Campbell, of Cherry Valley, & the only member of his family who escaped death or captivity in the bloody massacre of that place in Nov, 1778. –N Y Com Adv

The Hon Saml Y Atwell died at his residence at Chepatchet, R I, on Fri last. He was one of the most distinguished members of the legal profession in his State. He was repeatedly elected to the Genr'l Assembly, of which he was a member at the time of his death. –Prov Journal

FRI NOV 1, 1844
The last of the Stuarts. On Jul 15, 1807, the royal faily of the Stuart's became extinct at Rome in the person of Cardinal York. This prince, born at Rome on Mar 6, 1723, was christened the following month of May, by Pope Benedict XIII. He was at first called Duke of York, & afterwards Cardinal of York, which Pope Benedict XIV, conferred on him the Roman Purple in 1747. His father, the Pretender, known under the name of Chevalier de St George, who married Princess Mary Clementine, the grand-dght of Sobieski, the saviour of Vienna, bequeathed all his property, papers, & jewels to his eldest son, Prince Chas Edward, the second Pretender; & at his death, without issue, in 1788, the Cardinal of York, his only surviving brother, took possession of them. On the demise of the Cardinal of York he left his last will.

I certify that Jas A Williams, of Wash Co, brought before me, as an estray trespassing upon his enclosures, a dark bay gelding. –J H Goddard, Justice of the Peace. The owner is to come forward, prove property, pay charges, & take him away. -Jas A Williams, living on 5th st, between H & I sts, Wash.

Mrd: on Oct 20, Dr Lewis W Minor, U S Navy, to Miss Innerarity, of Mobile.

By order to distrain from Jos Scholfield, I shall offer at public sale, on Nov 5, on the premises occupied by Saml Entwistle, near the gate of the turnpike leading from Wash to Bladensburg, for cash: 16 barrels of corn, standing in the fields, 2 tables, 9 chiars, 1 rocking chair, & 1 looking glass, seized & taken to satisfy rent in the arrears due the said Jos Scholfield by the said Entwistle. –H Y Maryman, Bailiff

I have this day associated with me in business my son Richd E Simms: business will hereafter be under the firm of Simms & Son. –Edw Simms [We are daily expecting by the N Y packets a large & well assorted stock of Groceries, Wines, & Liquors.]

Cheap Lumber Yard: at 14th st bridge. –O J Preston

SAT NOV 2, 1844
$100 reward for runaway Michl Wood, about 21 or 22 years old, copper color, & a good looking servant. His father, Cornelius Wood, belongs to R W West, at the Wood Yard, in this county; his grandmother to a Mr Moore, butcher, near Wash; he had a sister belonging to Mr Tobias Nixdorff, in Balt. –Horatio C Scott, Upper Marlborough, PG Co, Md.

Neal McFadon was charged with having voted illegally on Oct 2, in Balt, in Ward 14. Justice Schaeffer yesterday fined him $20 & costs. There is another charge against him for voting illegally in the same ward at the Mayor's election. -Ibid

Changes: 12 laboring men, employed at the Iron works at Stamford, Conn, have renounced the Locofoco party & will proclaim that they will vote for Clay & Protection.

Patrick Rourk	Patrick Barron	Patrick Crowley
John Farnolds	Patrick Shea	Thos Blute
Michl Welch	Wm W Lounsbury	Michl Divine
David Caldwell	Jas Mulcaley	Timothy Crowley

St Louis, Mo, Oct 23. The U S Marshal, Col Ewing, received yesterday a full pardon from the Pres of the U S for David McDaniel, Thos Towson, J F D Pretontaine, Nathl H Morton, John A McCormack, & Wm J Harris. They have been confined in our county jail, under sentence from the U S Circuit Court for participating in the murder & robbery of Chavis, the Santa Fe trader. Jos Brown & John McDaniel were executed on Aug 17 last for the murder. David McDaniel & Thos Towson, both convicted, were respited by the Pres until Jun 17 next. Prefontaine, who was sentenced some time ago to one year's imprisonment, & fined $1,000, has served out the term of his imprisonment, but was held in custody for the payment of the fine. Morton, Harris, & McCormack were sentenced to 9 months in the county jail, & fined $10. Their term had not expired by nearly 2 months. -Repub

Died: on Oct 30, at Springfield, Md, in his 69th year, Richd Brooke, formerly of Chas Co, Md, but for the last 13 years resident of Wash City.

Mr John Porter, merchant at Stephensburg, Ky, was murdered last week by Marquis B Brown, a constable. Mr Porter's house had been entered & his desk robbed of $800. Brown was suspected of the theft. Before the investigation took place, Brown met Porter, shot him, fell upon him with a knife, killed him. & immediately mounted his horse & fled.

Household & kitchen furniture at auction: on Nov 4, at the house on Pa ave, between 1st & 2nd sts, one door est of Patrick Moran's Tavern, [the flag will designate the house.] -Wm Marshall, auctioneer

Property for sale: wishing to sell, I am disposed to give a bargain in my island property, Harper's Ferry, Va. Apply to the subscriber, or to Jos Byrne, Harper's Ferry. -Patrick Byrne

For rent: 2 story frame dwlg house on I st, east of 7th st. Inquire of A Wagoner, the present tenant of the premises.

For rent: 2 story dwlg house on 6th st, between G & H sts. Inquire of Mr Flaherty, next door.

MON NOV 4, 1844
Among those convicted in Balt, Md, of illegal voting & fined is John W Stone, of Wash City.

An extra from the N Y Gaz, dated Sat week, bring the subjoined list of the suffers by the late explosion of the boilers of the steamboat **Lucy Walker**, on the Ohio River.
Killed:
Jacob Nollner, Wash City, residence of his family Petersburg, Va. [He was a clerk on one of the Public Depts]
Mr Norris, residence unknown, supposed to be from Ky.
Mr Cooper, Louisville, 1st engineer
Dght of Dr Webb
J P Harrison
Wm Reed, Louisville
Jacob Meeker, Madison, Indiana
Wm Watt, Starkville, Miss
Jas Doras, Phil, Pa
A E Edwards, Shelbyville, Ky
Rev Jos McCrery, Wilcox, Ala
Mr Mackey, 2nd clerk
Capt David Vann, Arkansas

Saml M Brown, Lexington, Ky
Philip Wallis, Balt
Nicholas Ford, Louisville
Child of A H Foster
Spangler, deck hand
Missing
Jas Vanderburgh, Louisvill
___Dumbar, New Orleans
Peter Hadlock, New Albany, Indiana
John R Cornick, Norfolk, Va
Gen J W Pegram, Richmond, Va
Mr Hughes, Lexington, Ky
Brother-in-law to Dr Webb & servant
Moses Kirby, Pilot
Richd Barnes, Mount Wash, Ky
Wm T Saunders
Chas Donne, Louisville, Ky
Wm Brown, Mayslick, Mason Co, Ky
7 slaves
Wounded:
Alex'r Craton-slightly
Edwards, Shelbyville, Ky-badly
Dr Webb, Princeton, Ky-badly
Col Peter Kintner, Louisville-slightly
Wm R McCain, Portersville, Tenn
Rev D Presley, Starkville, Miss-slightly
Rev Jas Young, Dallas Co, Ala-badly
Capt Thompson, pilot, Jeffersonville: badly
Chas A Rein, Va-badly
Wm H Peebles, Va-slightly
Mrs Taylor & child, Norfolk, Va-slightly
J M Angurea & wife, New Orleans-slightly
Alex'r Martin, New Orleans, slightly
Louis Plout, slightly
5 slaves
Uninjured:
Rev Mr Todd, Louisville
John Hixon, Portland, Ky
Henry Beebe, New Orleans
Chas C Tibbs, Leesburg, Va
G P Sanders, Bullitt Co, Ky
John Allston, Rapides, La
Miss Smith, of Va
A H Foster, wife & 2 children, Greensburg, Va

Mr Brewer, wife, child, & servant, Baton Rouge, La
Mr Amos, wife, 3 children, & servant, Columbus, Miss
W H Peeples, wife, 4 children, & servant
Mr Tilby, wife & 2 children
Rev Mr Wilson & lady
5 slaves belonging to Capt Vann

Naval Genr'l Court Martial met last Wed at the Nat'l Hotel, for the trial of Midshipman A Cook, who is charged with scandalous conduct in purloining 2 pieces of money. Henry McKenzie, Henry D Johnson, W W Bassett, & Thos Phenix, jr, were examined as witnesses for the prosecution. Francis K Murray, Jarvis McDuffie, & Jos M Cardeza were examined for the defence. On Thu, the Court re-assembled, Midshipman John L Nelson was examined on the part of the prosecution; & Midshipmen W W Bassett & C K Graham, & Passed Midshipmen Edw Tatnall & Edw T Nichol for the defence. On Sat the Court-room being opened again, the Court went into the investigation of the case of Midshipman Higgins, who is charged with disobedience of orders.

$60 reward: will be paid for the apprehension & delivery to any military post in the U S of Saml Sanford & Jas Bulger, or $30 for either of then, who deserted fom the Ordnance Corps at Wash Arsenal, D C, on Nov 1, 1844. Sanford is 23 years old, born in Westfield, N J, occupation-blacksmith. Jas Bulger, is 22 years old, born in Richmond Co, Va, occupation-laborer; very illiterate, & cannot write his name.
-Jas Symington, Maj of Ordnance, commanding Additional reward: the undersigned will give an additional $20 for the apprehension of Sanford & Bulger, or $10 for either:

John Balster	Michl Minz	A Fischer
John P M Naesser	J W Jones	Wm Stolker
C White	Henry Brickmann	Cahs Brice
Thos Vickers	Fred'k Whyte	Albert Eiring
Henry Dudley	Auguste Heller	Herman Kaiser
Reuben Clark	Casper Overwater	John H Peerce
Jas May	Antou Pink	-Wash Arsenal
Wm Donovan	John Willson	

Criminal Court-Wash: Saml Scott, a county constable, guilty of assaulting & beating Wm Colson on Capitol Hill.

The partnership between Jas M McKnight & Lewis Clephane, under the firm of McKnight & Clephane, was dissolved by mutual consent on Nov 1. –Jas M McKnight, Lewis Clephane. The Family Groceries will be carried on at the old stand, F st, between 14th & 15th sts, by Jas M McKnight.

For rent: 3 new houses at 8th & L sts, Northern Liberties. Apply to Geo Collard or Thos C Donn, Justice of the Peace, Louisiana ave near 7th st.

TUE NOV 5, 1844
Jos Elder, recently a clerk in the Bank of England, who in Augst last defrauded that institution of L8,000, with which he fled to this country, was arrested on Thu in Boston, where he had passed under the name of Ellis, & committed to prison. He was examined by Solomon Lincoln, U S Marshall, who found certificates in his possession. On Fri he was found dead in his cell, having committed suicide during the night by hanging himself. He was about 60 years of age. A person named Wm Burgess, who was supposed to be an accomplice, for whose arrest a warrant had been issued, was traced last night to Nahant, from which place he escaped in a boat without his hat.

Jas Newman, employed by Horace Pendleton, & Denyse H Denyse, employed by Milford Smith, have been discharged by their employers for walking in the late Whig procession at N Y. -Express

Boarding: Mrs S Masi has several large chambers fronting Pa ave & 4½ st, Wash.

For rent: small farm containing bout 50 acres, near the Long Bridge, with comfortable frame house. Apply to subscriber, residing on 7th st, south of Md ave, or information can be obtained from Capt Edwards, now residing on the farm. --Matilda Radcliff

Household & kitchen furniture at auction: on Nov 11, at the residence of Mr Jas Young, 7th st, in one of Mr Elwood's houses, north of Md ave. --W Marshall, auct

Murder at the Eastern Penitentiary. Jas Gaston, employed there as a nurse, was murdered yesterday by a young man, John Bilman, a prisoner. He tore a piece of board from the floor & killed him, by beating him on the head before assistance could come. Bilman was insane; he had been under sentence for horse stealing & arrested for the murder of his father. This murder he has confessed during his incarceration in Cherry Hill. He has been insane his his committal. --Phil N A

WED NOV 6, 1844
We lately recorded the death of the Rev Henry Francis Cary, whose remains were on Wed last interred in Poet's Corner, Westminster Abbey. At age 15 he published an ode on the death of Kosciusko; at age 18 he was entered as a commoner of Christ Church, Oxford, where he proceeded to the degree of M A. In 1805 he published the Inferno of Dante in English blank verse, with the text of the original.

A young man named Josephs, about 23, committed suicide at Providence, R I, on Sat, by shooting himself through the head. He has recently arrived in this country from England. His relatives here have been informed of his death.

Household & kitchen furniture at auction: on Nov 13, at the residence of Capt Richd France, 5 Franklin Row. –R W Dyer & Co, aucts

On Mon last a colored woman named Ellen Lindsay, often confined in the workhouse, was arrested by R R Burr, constable, under the charge of willfully setting fire to a stable attached to the Wash Almshouse, destroying a horse & carryall, the latter being the property of the Intendent.

Wash Corp: 1-Ptn from J P Hilton & W H Clampit: referred to the Cmte of Claims. 2-Ptn of Chas A Schneider & others, for grading & paving an alley in square 166: referred to the Cmte on Improvements. 3-Ptns of D W Oyster, John Shaw, John Earle, & John Tenant, hucksters, praying remission of fines: referred to the Cmte of Claims. 4-Cmte on Police: asking to be discharged from the further consideration of the ptn of Wm McCarty, praying permission to erect a blacksmith's shop on square 730. 5-Cmte of Claims: asking to be discharged from the further consideration of the ptn of Mary M Ellis.

Illegal voting in Balt: Thos Fillen & John W Bassett, both from Wash, were committed or held to bail, for attempting to vote in the 4th Ward; & Wm Nichols, for the same in the 4th Ward. –Balt American

Chas W Coleman, [Locofoco,] fined for voting illegally in the 5th Ward at the Govn'r election, had his fine remitted on Sat by Gov Thomas.

Lazurus Laronick was arrested on Sat last on a charge of perjury. He is said to have made oath that certain persons had resided 5 years in the U S, knowing they had only been here about 2 years. The object was to secure their naturalization papers. He was released on security for a further hearing. –Balt Patriot

Mrd: on Nov 3, in Gtwn, by Rev J P Moore, Mr Paul Stevens to Miss Miriam E Hurst.

Died: on Nov 2, at *Sligo*, Montg Co, Md, of scarlet fever, Harriet Campbell, da/o Jonathan & Anna L Prout, aged 5 years & 9 months.

Died: on Oct 18 last, in Prince Wm Co, Va, Richard W, s/o Dr R W & Ann L Wheat, in his 5th year.

Died: on Oct 28 last, at the residence of his father, in Prince Wm Co, Va, William E Allen, s/o Wm Allen, in his 25th year.

THU NOV 7, 1844
Orphans Court of Wash Co, D C. Letters of administration on the personal estate of Thos T Parker, late of said county, dec'd. –Barbara A Parker, Jos Fraser, adms

Mrd: on Nov 5, in Wash City, by Rev Mr Sprole, Chas H Raymond, Charge d'Affaires ad interim from the Republic of Texas, to Miss Mary Jane, eldest d/o John Underwood, of the Treasury Dept.

Died: on Nov 2, Mrs Ann Waters, consort of Dr Washington Waters, of Montg Co, Md, whose pious & edifying life while here gives assurance of a happy eternity to her bereaved & numerous friends.

Died: yesterday, in his 70th year, Richd Cropley, a native of Norfolk Co, England, & for 25 years a resident of Gtwn. His funeral is this afternoon, at 3:30 o'clock, from the residence of Mr Robt Barnard, near Gtwn.

An experienced Teacher, a Lady well qualified to instruct in the various branches of an English education, offers her services on very moderate terms. Address Mrs A T Hempstead, King Geo Co, Post Ofc, Va.

FRI NOV 8, 1844
The Brandon [Miss] Advocate says that Gen H G Runnels, formerly Govn'r of Miss, has met a violent death. He was assassinated by a band of lawless rascals, who waylaid & shot him. It was hoped that this report would prove unfounded.

A young man named Chas B Clifford has been arrested in Boston & held to bail to answer to a charge of swindling a number of storekeepers in that city to a considerable amount. His practice was to call at a store in the morning, price & examine goods, say he would call again, & finally leave with some article or another; but at last he was suspected & arrested.

Cincinnati Bulletin: on Tue last, in that city, while the carriage of Mrs Col Davies was descending Sycamore hill, the horses became frightened & ran off. Mr John Armstrong, a young man, was driving, & fell from the carriage, striking the curbstone, with such force, that he died on Thu.

SAT NOV 9, 1844
Dissolution of the partnership between Hitz & Casparis, on Nov 1, by mutual consent. –Florian Hitz, Jas Casparis [Casparis will continue the business.]

Miss Morley: assortment of Millinery: Bonnets, caps, flowers, feathers, bullion trimmings, buches, French Thule, & plain nets. Pa ave, near 9th st, north side.

Letter dated Pensacola, Oct 30th from a naval ofcr: on Oct 23, during a heavy squall, a boat belonging to the U S ship **Falmouth**, on its way from the navy yard to the city, was capsized & 8 persons were drowned, among whom was Lt Ferdinand Piper, of the Navy, & Prof Wm Fox. Midshipman T Cadwalader Harris, & 7 men, were rescued by a small schnr, after remaining on the bottom of the boat between 7 & 8 hours.

The Phil Ledger of Wed says the following were charged with being concerned in the Kensington & Southwark riots, & arraigned Tue for murder: John Paul, for the murder of Lewis Greble, on May 7, in Kensington; Henry Hoy, for the murder of Jos Rice, on May 7, in Kensington. Jas Sherry, for the murder of Wesley Rhinedollar, on May 7, in Kensington. John Campbell for the murder of Lewis Greble, on May 7, in Kensington. David C Hoffman, for the murder of John Guyer, on Jul 7, in Southwark. All the accused pleaded not guilty. [Nov 14th newspaper: John Paul found guilty of murder in the second degree: filing for a new trial.]

Hon Chief Justice John Buchanan died at his residence at Woodland, Wash Co, on Wed, in his 71st year, after a illness of about 4 weeks. Hagerstown Torch Light: He was appointed Assoc Justice of this Judicial this district in 1806, & in 1825 took his seat as Chief Judge of the Court of Appeals. We sympathize with his bereaved family in the loss which they & the public have sustained.

Mrd: on Nov 7, on *Greenleaf's Point*, by Rev R T Nixon, Capt Thos Allen to Miss Louisa Risen, all of Chas Co, Md.

Mrd: on Nov 7, by Rev H Myers, Mr Jas Burke to Miss Tevesa Jackson, both of Wash City. [Tevesa as copied.]

For rent: 2 story brick house on 13th st, between E & F sts, at present occupied by McC Young. Possession can be had Dec 1, or perhaps sooner. –Louis Vivans

MON NOV 11, 1844
American Republican Newspaper, at Wash, D C. The undersigned propose to commence in a short time, the publication of a newspaper in Wash, devoted to the cause of American Republicanism. –J & G S Gideon, Printers: 9th st, Wash, D C

Illegal voting in Balt, Md: 1-John M Bassett fined $20 & costs. Basset had resided neither in the city nor State. He is from Wash City. 2-John Lee fined $20 & costs. 3-Hugh S Boyd, proved to be a resident of Cecil Co, for voting in the Governor's election, in the 7th Ward: fined $20 & costs. Patrick Braham, for illegally voting in the 9th Ward, fined $20 & costs.

Police Intelligence. A colored woman, Susan Marshall, alias Seal, was arrested last Thu in Gtwn, charged with attempting to set on fire the house of Mr Geo Mahorney, &, after examination, was fully committed for trial.

Persons drowned by the upsetting of one of the cutter boats belonging to the U S ship **Falmouth**, in Pensacola Bay, on Oct 28, were Mr Ferdinand Piper, 3rd Lt; Wm S Fox, Prof; Jos Huff, Wm Dixon, Hugh Toner, ordinary seamen; John W Cappo, landsman; Wm Torrington & Wm Wyatt, ship's boys. Peter Brown, ordinary seaman, drifted away from the boat upon her mainmast, & was cast ashore on the island of Santa Rosa & saved. Persons saved by clinging to the boat were Mr Thos C Harris, midshipman, Geo Gray, Peter Martin, seamen; Wm White, Wm Tucker, Edw King & Jas Robinson, ordinary seamen.

TUE NOV 12, 1844
Mr Yeadon, an able & accomplished gentleman, one of the editors of the Charleston Courier, has retired from that paper.

Violent hurricane passed over Jackson, Missouri, on Oct 25, destroyed property & a number of persons were killed. The Western Expositor, printed at Independence, gives the following list of the killed & wounded: Killed: Mrs McGill, Livingston; Mrs Stone; Mr Kerr had 3 children killed, & himself greatly wounded; & Miss Mary Middleton & Dr Martin's son, near Westport. Thos Hedges had all his houses & furniture blown off, & several of his family badly crippled. Saml Lambert, house gone; wife & another person, badly injured. J Beadley, house blown off. J King, house blown off. Mrs Huggins, house blown off, & herself badly crippled. Mrs Ragan, house blown off, & herself & a negro man crippled. Calvin McCoy, house blown off, & several of his family crippled. Dr Martin, Mrs Buckhart, & Thos Smith, all had their houses blown off. C N Hall's steam saw mill, roof blown off, grist mill & houses blown entirely away-damage about $12,000.

Emancipation. The Alexandria Gaz says that Mr Nathl H Hope, of King Geo Co, Va, lately deceased, left by his will nearly all his slaves free, amounting to some two or three hundred, with ample provision to carry them to Liberia. The liberated slaves are to be removed under the direction of the Colonization Society.

Grates for Cumberland & other Bituminous Coal; wire fenders; shovels & tongs, coal hods, & brass castings, made to any pattern. Ebenezer Hubball, 8 north Libery st, Balt, Md.

Desirable improved farm for sale: contains 150 acres, in PG Co, Md. Apply to Jas B Holmead, auct, Wash, or to the subscriber on the premises. –Wallace Kirkwood

Toledo Land Agency. Elisha Whittlesey & Co have associated to establish a land agency at Toledo, Ohio. –Elisha Whittlesey, O H Knapp, J W Scott, J Fitch

Boston Courier: the British forger, Wm Burgess, alias Ellis, was brought before a Com'r at Boston, on Mon, for examination. The Com'r signed a certificate, upon which the Sec of State will issue an order for the delivery of Burgess into the custody of the English ofcr. If convicted in England, he will be transported for life. He spoke feelingly of his late accomplice Elder, [who committed suicide,] & expressed a wish to see where he was buried. He was only 47 years of age, the prisoner thought, & was occasionally engaged in the horse business. His father was an extensive dealer in lumber. [Nov 23rd newspaper: Burgess, the English forger, was among the passengers by the Hibernia to Liverpool.]

Springdale Boarding School for Girls: in Loudoun Co, Va: winter term will commence on Nov 18. –Saml M Janney, Principal Refer to Jonathan Seaver,Wash; Phineas Janney, Alexandria.

Fire in St Louis Oct 29: destroyed the bldgs-the Hope Mills: a flouring-mill, oil-mill, & carding factory. They were owned by Jas C Sutton, Dr Culver, & Mr Black.

WED NOV 13, 1844
Monumental inscriptions. Mount Auburn. Monument has recently been placed in the Cemetery at Mount Auburn to the memory of Rev Dr Channing. It was designed by the late Mr Allston. On the front is this inscription:
In memory of
William Ellery Channing,
honored throughtout Christendom
for his eloquence and courage
in maintaining and advancing
the great cause of
Truth, Religion, and Human Freedom.
This Monument
is gratefully and reverently erected
by the Christian Society
of which, during nearly forty years,
he was Pastor.
On the reverse:
William Ellery Channing,
born, 7th April, 1789,
at Newport, R I.:
Ordained, 1st June, 1802,
as a Minister of Jesus Christ
to the Society worshipping God
in Federal st, Boston;
Died, 2d October, 1842,
while on a journey,
At Bennington, Vermont.

From Mexico. The schnr **Creole** arrived at New Orleans on Mon week, bringing as passengers most of the Texian prisoners who were recently liberated by Pres Santa Anna. The Picayune says: The espousals of Santa Anna & his new bride were celebrated in truly royal style, by proxy, he being upon his estate of *Mango de Clava* & the lady in Mexico City.

Some villains entered the store of Mr Thos Gilpin, at Cincinnati, last week, & blew up his iron safe with gunpowder.

Mrd: on Nov 7, by Rev Mr Wilson, Mr Benj McQuay to Miss Emily Ann Bryan, all of Wash.

Died: on Nov 9, in Wash City, in her 24th year, Letitia Massey, consort of Danl D Davidson, & d/o Alex'r McIntire, leaving an affectionate husband & 3 children to mourn over their sad bereavement. Their loss is her eternal gain.

For rent: 3 story brick house on East Capitol st, only a few steps from the Capitol gate. Inquire of Mrs Rebecca Burch, N J ave, a few doors below the residence of Thos Blagden.

Trustee's sale: Circuit Court of Wash Co, D C, in Chancery. Robt Ramsay, vs Ann McCormick, admx, & the heirs at law of Jas McCormick, dec'd. The undersigned trustee will sell at public auction, on Dec 12, the following: south half of lot 6 in square 345, in Wash City, with the improvements: sold as the real estate whereof Jas McCormick died seized. –J M Carlisle, trustee

THU NOV 14, 1844
The Mayor of Louisville, Ky, recently informed the Common Council that he had taken the responsibility to furnish the survivors of the ill-fated steamboat **Lucy Walker** with clothes & other necessaries required by the sudden & appalling accident. The Common Council, on their first meeting, unanimously appropriated $1,000 to meet the contingencies referred to.

It is all but certain that J K Polk is chosen president of the U S.

At Helena, Ark, on Oct 7, A W Boland killed Lomon B Fisler, with a large bowie knife. Boland was immediately arrested. His trial fixed to take place on Oct 28.

Mrd: on Nov 9, in St Matthew's Church, by Rev J P Donelan, Geo M Grouard to Miss Ellen B Curran, all of Wash City.

Mrd: on Nov 12, by Rev Mr Flanagan, Mr John S Marll to Miss Ursuler A Offutt, all of Gtwn, D C.

Mrd: on Nov 10, by Rev Mr Gilliss, Mr Harvey W Hunt to Mrs Anne Osgood, all of Wash City.

Died: on Tue last, Eugenia Josephine, d/o Henry & Rosa Howard, in her 8th year. Her funeral is this morning, at 10 o'clock, from the residence of her father, on 5th st, between I & K sts.

Notice to the creditors of the bankrupt: Chas S Fowler. Creditors to meet at the ofc of the subscriber, near Brown's Hotel, on Pa ave, on Nov 14, at 7 o'clock, on matters of importance to the assigned estate of the said Fowler. –D A Hall, assignee

Information wanted of Jas Henry Luxen, who left this city in the fall of 1830 with Col Crowell for the State of Alabama, for the purpose of riding a race to come off in that State. From thence he started for Tenn, & since that time has not been heard from. His brothers & sisters still residing in Washington will be thankful for any information that may lead to his discovery, being still under the impression that he is living either in Tenn or Georgia. [Tenn & Georgia papers will please copy.] -Thos J Luxen, Wash

I certify that Mr Bernard Brien, guardian to Wm O'Brien, did, on Apr 16, 1841, settle with the Orphans Court of Wash Co, D C, his 12th & final account as guardian aforesaid, in which he charges himself with the balance due on the last account, & the same is credited to him by a receipt of his ward, produced to the said Court. Test: Ed N Roach, Reg/o wills
+
I have been requested by Mr Bernard Brien, of Gtwn, to state what I recollect of the settlement made by him with Wm O'Brien, whose guardian he has been. So long a time has elapsed that I cannot recollect, & therefore refrain from stating the particulars; but, so far as I do recollect, nothing then occurred which ought to subject Mr Brien to the slightest censure. Mr O'Brien called on me for my professional aid, I think in the summer of 1839, in procuring a settlement with his guardian. I advised him to refer the whole subject to the arbitration of friends. He assented, & selected the late Col Wainwright, & Mr Brien having selected Mr Carbery, these 2 gentlemen met at my ofc, together with Mr Brien & Mr Wm O'Brien. I was entirely satisfied with the results of the meeting. I carefully explaned them to O'Brien so as to make him understand them, & Col Wainwright also explained them to him. My impression then made on my mind, & still remaining is, that Mr Bernard Brien had discharged his ofc with great fidelity, & there was no ground of complaint against him. –Jos H Bradley, Nov 12, 1844

$20 reward for runaway negress Margaret, about 28 years of age. –Thos Williams

FRI NOV 15, 1844
From Africa: in the brig **Francis Lord**, which arrived at N Y from the River Gambia, there came as passengers Rev H Hazlehurst & Rev J Smith, of the Episc mission; Messrs Don Manuel Fernandes, & Mathew Freeman, [colored,] who was sent out some time since by the Board of the American Colonization Society. The Rev Dr Savage, of the Protestant Episcopal mission, arrived at Monrovia on Aug 7 in the brig **Francis Lord**, accompanied by his fellow laborers, Rev Mr Henning & lady, Mrs Patch & Miss Rutherford. The U S brig **Porpoise**, Lt Crann commanding, arrived at Monrovia on Aug 21, & sailed on Aug 23 windward. Rev Mr Connelly, Presbyterian missionary for Settra Kroo, arrived at Monrovia on Aug 29 in the ship **Atlanta**, from N Y, & sailed for Settra Kroo on Sep 2 in the same vessel. The Luminary, in mentioning the death of Rev Mr Campbell, of the A B C F M at Cape Palmas, says: this very fine young man came out in company with the lamented Crocker, of the Baptist mission, in the barque **Palestine**. He was destined for the Gaboon river, to which the Presbyterians have removed their flourishing mission etablishment. Poor man, he did not live to get there. The African fever soon marked him as it prey, & in 6 weeks after he arrived at Palmas he was numbered with the happy dead.

Mrd: on Nov 13, by Rev G W Samson, Mr John Wroe to Miss Lucy Ann Davis, all of Wash City.

Groceries: Wm M Randolph, opposite Brown's Hotel. [Local ad.]

Criminal Court-Wash. 1-Thos Bond, free negro, [an old convict,] found guilty of breaking into the dwlg of Mr F A Dunn, on Aug 25, & stealing a coat, a table cover, & sundry articles of clothing. 2-Henry Ware, alias Wm Beckley, free negro, guilty of stealing from the boarding-house of Miss Janney, on Sep 16, sundry articles of jewelry. He also was found guilty of stealing a coat, 2 pair of pantaloons, & other wearing apparel, the property of Saml S Ashby, a boarder in said house. 3-Jas McKane, alias Oliver, & Richd Morgan, [old offenders,] guilty of stealing a bar of iron & a still, the property of Clement T Coote. 4-Ardinitia Payne, guilty of an assault upon Joanna Edwards, & stabbing her with a knife in 3 places. 5-Wm A Molloy, a county constable, not guilty of resisting H S Wood, another county constable, while in the discharge of his duty. 5-Mary Ann Hall indicted for keeping a house of ill fame-no verdict: jury dismissed. 6-John Carroll, John Luckett, Barney Parsons, Jos Murphy, Thos Green & Jos Anderson: all found guilty for a riot. All found guilty of the assault upon Ann Evans, on Jul 1, 1844. 7-Robt H Davis, free negro, guilty of stealing a $10 note from Mr W H Taylor, who was staying in Hall's Hotel, on Pa ave, in which house the prisoner was a servant. 8-John Smith: guilty of stealing a pair of boots of the value of $3, the property of Jos Kelly. 9-Raphael Davis, free negro, found guilty of stealing 1/3 cord of wood, the property of Robt Widdicumb. 10-John Bryan, alias Brown, guilty of stealing 2 hides belonging to W D Beall, & 2 hides belonging to Aaron Gattrell. 11-Lucy Miles, free negress, found guilty of an assault & battery upon a blind man named Godfrey. [Nov 20th newspaper: Thos Bond to be imprisoned 5 years in the penitentiary. Henry Ware to be imprisoned 3 years in the penitentiary. Robt H Davis: 18 months in the penitentiary. Jas McKane sentenced to 3 years in the penitentiary. John Carroll, John Lucket & Barney Parsons, convited of riot: fined $20 each & 2 months in the county jail. John Carroll, John Lucket, Barney Parsons, Jos Murphy, Thos Green, & John Anderson, convicted of an assault & battery on Ann Evans: each fined $10. Ardinitia Payne: fined $20 & 2 weeks in the county jail. Lucy Miles: fined $10 & 10 days in the county jail. Richd Morgan: 3 years in the penitentiary.]

SAT NOV 16, 1844
The Sandwich Islands: we are indebted to the politeness of Geo Brown, Com'r at the Sandwich Islands for copies of a Hawaiian newspaper [The Friend] for the months of Jun & July. The U S ship **Levant**, Cmder Hugh W Page, arrived at Honolulu on Jun 9, from Tahiti. The number of missionaries present was 54, including 23 females. Among the deaths at the islands, prior to Jul 1, we note the following, for the information of the friends of the dec'd at the North, viz: Miss Sophia R Marshall, of Boston; Mr Elijah Tolman, of Watertown, Mass; Mr Nathl Burton, of Boston. At the U S Hospital, Wm Wells, of Hatfield, Mass. New Orleans Bulletin

Circuit Court of Wash Co, D C-in Equity. Saml Grice, vs Chas F Sibbold. The bill of cmplnt, states that the cmplnt has sustained considerable pecuniary losses & expended large sums of money by reason of the non-execution of a contract on the part of the dfndnt, whereby the dfndnt undertook to furnish certain lands in the Territory of Florida, & did designate as his a large tract of land, upon which the cmplnt proceeded to cut, under said contract, live oak timber; that after the cmplnt had, at great expense& labor, carried his vessels & hands from Phil to Florida, & commenced cutting on the lands thus designated by the dfndnt, the authorities of the U S entered upon these land & forcibly drove the complnt off, claiming the land was the property of the U S & not of the said dfndnt; that the said dfndnt then institued proceedings at law, & the question of the title to said lands was finally decided by the U S Supreme Court to be in said Sibbold, the dfndnt, under certain treaty stipulations, & that the dfndnt then appealed to Congress for relief & indemnity on account of the forcible intrusion made upon his lands by the authority of the U S, & stated as one of the items of his losses the sum of $4,563.31, for which he was responsible to the cmplnt, Saml Grice, & would have to pay to him, the said cmplnt; that Congress thereupon passed an act in 1842 authorizing the 3rd Auditor of the Treasury to adjust & settle the said dfdnt's claims, under the direction of the U S Atty Gen. The bill prays a decree to have this fund paid over to the said cmplnt. -B Thruston, Asst Judge -W Brent, clerk

Died: on Nov 11, at the Univ of Virginia, of consumption, Harriet W, w/o Prof Edw H Courtenay, & d/o the late Capt Benj Rathbone, of Newport, R I, in her 43rd year.

A young clergyman who has traveled abroad wishes to spend the winter at the South, & would be glad to teach during the time. He will teach all the branches taught in our Universities, together with German & Italian. A private family is preferred. References to any extent given. Address Rev M S Vincent, N Y C.

Mrd: on Nov 12, at *Pleasant Ridge*, Montg Co, Md, by Rev Mr French, Edw Swann, of Wash City, to Miss Maria Louisa Thrift, d/o the late Jas Magruder Thrift.

MON NOV 18, 1844

Rencontre near Owingsville, Ky, on Sep 6, between Chas Whittington & John Storms, who came together with knives, both were killed. The cause of the quarrel is not stated.

A young man from Bibb Co, Thos K Fuller, was murdered by Wm Searcy, a resident of this county. The weapon was a pistol, who survived but a few minutes after being shot in the stomach. Searcy fled. A reward of $350 is offered for his apprehension- $150 by the Gov't & $200 by the father of the dec'd. –Milledgeville Journal

$5 reward for recovery of a white pointer Dog, named Duke, lost on Sep 2, in the neighborhood of Good Hope Tavern, PG Co, Md. –Geo C Whiting, Wash, D C

A boy named Wm Scott was very seriously if not fatally injured last Fri, by an accident on the railroad about 1 mile this side of Bladensburg. The boy was riding on one of the mud cars, & fell while jumping to the ground. The car passed over his foot & thigh in a dreadful manner & the car passed over his groin. He was brought home to Wash City yesterday, & is under the care of Dr Washington.

For rent: during the session of Congress. I wish to rent my dwlg house & furniture. It stands on the north side of C st, between 3rd & 4½ sts. –R N Johnson

Criminal Court-Wash. 1-U S vs Richd Burnett: dfndnt was indicted for resisting J M Wright, a police constable, while in the discharge of his duty. The jury found him not guilty. 2-Wm T Turten, was found guilty of assault & battery upon John Wilson. 3-U S vs Geo Tyler: guilty of assault & battery; not guilty of assault with intent to kill Henry Greenfield, alias Belt, free negro . The prisoner remains in custody.

TUE NOV 19, 1844

The U S revenue steamship **Legare** sailed from N Y on Wed last for Key West, Florida. List of her ofcrs: Henry B Nones, Cmder; Lts-Douglas, 1st; Nicholas Austin, 2nd; John A Webster, 3rd; E T Hyatt, 4th; Thos H Faron, Chief Engineer; John Dougherty, Assist Engineer.

Rev Wilson Conner, a Baptist minister in Georgia, fell dead in the pulpit on the 5th Sabbath in Jun last, after preaching.

On Sat last, a 12 year old son of Judge Sturgis lost his life, when some boys had been projecting a sham-fight, with toy cannons, when a large buck-shot struck the unfortunate boy in the neck, causing his death in a few moments. —Columbus [Ga] Enquirer

Meeting on Oct 23, 1844, of the ofcrs stationed at *Fort Gibson*, Cherokee Country, Lt Col R B Mason, 1st Dragoons, called to the chair, & Lt Flint, 6th Infty, appointed sec: tribute to the memory of the late 1st Lt Wm Bowman. Lt Bowman was in the full flesh of health & happiness, suddenly stricken from among us by apoplexy, while engaged on an errand of love in hastening to the relief of a sick brother. Copy of the proceedings be sent to the widow & brother of the dec'd.

R B Mason, Lt Col 1st Dragoons H W Wharton, 1st Lt 6th Infty
A Cady, Capt 6th Infty F F Flint, 2nd Lt 6th Infty
W S Ketchum, Capt 6th Infty A D Nelson, 2nd Lt 6th Infty
Chas McCormick, Assist Surg, U S A A S M Rust, 2nd Lt 1st Dragoons
E Steen, Capt 1st Dragoons Geo W Lay, 2nd Lt 6th Infty
Chas S Lovell, 1st Lt 6th Infty

Mr John L Haines, of Concord, N H, was mangled by the premature discharge of a field-piece at the Polk & Dallas carousal on Sep 8. One of his arms had been amputated; & if he recovers he will be otherwise disfigured.

$5 reward for return of strayed or stolen, from Lewis Carusi's lot, a dark sorrel mare. Return her to Levi Pumphrey's stable, 6th & C sts, Wash, or to the subscriber in PG Co, near Brandywine, Md. —Catharine Townsend

Teachers wanted: the Board of Visiters of Palmetto Lodge School, Columbia, S C, are authorized to employ 2 Teachers for said School, one Principal & one Usher. Address, post paid, John L Manning or John S Preston, Columbia, S C.
R H Goodwyn J S Scott J C Clifton
John McKenzie John L Manning

Died: on Sep 11, at Raleigh, N C, in her 44th year, Mrs Caroline M West, relict of the late Maj Thos L West, & d/o the late Jos Gales.

Died: on Sep 17, Eliza Melvina, infant d/o Henry & Melvina Grey, aged 3 months & 13 days.

By virtue of 3 writs of fieri facias issued against the goods & chattels of John E Dement: I have seized one black horse & wagon, which will be sold on Nov 23, to satisfy judgments in favor of Thos Blagden, Mary Ball, & R H Maryman.
—T Plumsill, Constable

By virtue of 2 writs of fieri facias, at the suits of Mary Ball, & Mary Ball, admx of Isaac Ball, dec'd, against the goods & chattels, lands & tenements, rights & credits of Ignatius W Atcherson, to me directed, I have seized of said Atcherson, furniture & sundry articles, to be sold on Nov 23, in front of the Centre Market, Wash City, for cash. –T Plumsill, Constable

WED NOV 20, 1844
For rent: new 3 story brick house, on F st, between 13th & 14th sts. Apply to F H Gerdes, on Capitol Hill, opposite Duff Green's Row. The key can be had next door.

All persons having claims against Geo W Hinton previous to Aug 15 last, are to present them immediately to the subscriber, so that he can made a distribution of the assets in his hands. -R W Dyer & Co, aucts

Circuit Court of Wash Co, D C-in Chancery. Geo Kirby, exc of John B Kirby, vs Barbara S Young, admx, & Sarah Ann Young et al, heirs at law of Ignatius F Young, dec'd. Trustee's sale of real estate, in the above cause: one undivided fifth part of & in all & singular the following real estate lying in Wash City:
Lots 9 thru 14 in square 353
Square 709
Lots 1, 2, 9 thru 12, in square 776
Lots 3 thru 9 in square 777
Square north of square 931
Squares 932 & 933
Lots 13 & 14 in square 959
Lots 1 thru 4, 11 thru 14, in square 1002
Square 1049
Lots 1, 2, & 6 in square 1060
As the said lots & squares are marked & laid down on the plat of Wash City..
By virtue of same decree: sale of real estate lying in Wash Co & PG Co, Md: tract of land called *Nonsuch*, in Wash Co, containing about 10 acres; & another tract in PG Co, containing 50 acres . –J M Carlisle, trustee -Clement Cox, atty for the owners

Wash Corp: 1-Ptn of Mrs Anne Cochran: referred to the Cmte of Claims. 2-Act for the relief of J Broadbeck, jr: referred to the Cmte of Claims.

Mrd: on Nov 19, in Wash City, by Rev H Stringfellow, Mr Benj Harrison to Miss Eliz Higgins.

Died: on Nov 16, in Wash City, in her 28th year, Mrs Serena Cary, consort of J N Cary, after a lingering & painful illness, which she bore with Christian fortitude.

THU NOV 21, 1844
Dry Goods Store: cloths, cassimeres, flannels & alpacas.
–Wm M Perry, 7th st opposite the Centre Market

Fred'k Osborne, a Norwegian, was injured on Mon last on the Utica & Schenectady railroad, at Herkimer, when he was thrown from the train crossing the hydraulic bridge, & from the bridge fell into the waer. When taken up he was so much injured that he died in a few minutes.

In the Court of Oyer & Terminer, at Phil, on Mon, the Jury in the case of Andrew McLain, charged with the murder of Sgt John Guyer during the Southwark riots, rendered a verdict of not guilty.

Ohio paper: it did our heart good to see Rev Jos Badger, of this town, now in his 88th year, deposit his vote for Clay & Frelinghuysen. He was a soldier of the Revolution in 1776, chaplain at *Fort Meigs* under Gen Harrison in 1813, & where, the Hon Elisha Whittlesey of this State says, he saved his life.

A letter from Constantinople, dated Sep 20, reports the release of Dr Wolff, [celebrated missionary,] by the Khan of Bokhara. He was daily expected at the Persian frontier. –Journal of Commerce

$10 reward for Geo Washington Mockbee, about 19, formerly of Bladensburg & lately of Wash, as he is supposed to have entered the house of John Mills, Nov 14 & 17th, & took from the trunk of Richd Purdy one black Frock Coat, lined through with silk & quilted; one pair of new plaid cassimere Pantaloons, main color brown. Apply to Richd Purdy or John Mills, 10th & Pa ave.

Mr Geo P Hathaway, of Beford, Mich, was married on Oct 9 to Miss Harriet Cornell, of Erie, Mich. On the Sat following they left to visit his friends in Farmington, Ontario Co, N Y, & on Oct 22 left on their return home. When about 18 miles west of Rochester, the stage was overset & Mr Hathaway was so severely injured that he died on Oct 28. He was in his 25th year, & highly respected & esteemed.

Mrd: on Nov 14, at St Thomas' Church, by Rev Mr Kroes, Jos Stone to Miss Sarah A, eldet d/o Gustavus Simpson, all of Chas Co, Md.

Mrd: on Nov 19, in Balt, by Rev Dr Dorsey, the Rev Thos Sewall to Miss Julia E Waters, d/o Freeborn Garretson Waters, all of Balt.

Mrd: on Nov 14, by Rev Norval Wilson, J Ross Brown, of Louisville, Ky, to Lucy Anna, d/o Dr Spencer Mitchell, of Wash City.

Died: on Nov 15, in Balt, Md, Mr John Booth, in his 77th year. He was a native of St Mary's Co, Md, but was a long respected resident for 50 years of Wash City & Gtwn, & for the past 9 years a resident of Balt. May he rest in peace!

For rent: 2 story brick house, with basement, 6th & H sts. Inquire of John Sexsmith.

FRI NOV 22, 1844
There is now in Pittsburg a black glass bottle manufactory, owned by Mr C Ihmsen, which supplies all the markets in the West & South with wine & porter bottles, demijohns, acid jars & flasks. There is no manufactory of the kind in the Union west of the Alleghanies, & but a few in the East.

The great 10 miles race: N Y Morning News: came off on Tue over the Beacon Course, & Barlow, the English pedestrian, beat all competitiors in the short space of 54 minutes & 21 seconds. Purse of $700 to the first, $250 to the second, $150 to the third, $75 to the fourth, & $25 to the fifth. The following entries were made:
1-John Gildersleeve, the winner of the last race [Though defeated Gildersleeve's honors are not diminished.]
2-John Barlow [age 22]
3-Thos Greenhalgh [age 24]
4-J P Taylor
5-John Underhill
6-Wm Carles
7-Jas Bradley
8-Thos McCabe
9-J L T Smith
10-Thos Ryan
11-John Steeprock, Indian
Barlow & Greenhalgh appeared in short linen drawers, silk caps, socks & light shoes, the upper part of their bodies & their legs entirely uncovered. Several hundred spectators had come from Albany & Rochester, many disposed to speculate on the Englishman.

Late from Africa: the U S brig **Porpoise** arrived at N Y on Tue, from the west coast of Africa, via Port Praya. List of her ofcrs:

Thos T Craven, Lt Com'g	G Maalsby, Assist Surgeon
H S Stillwager & E C Ward, 1st Lts	R Pettit, Purser
G W Podgee, Acting Master	
B Randolph, J M Ford, G M Dibble, J B Stewart: Midshipmen	
C C Williamson, Capt's Clerk	H C Baker, Purser's Stewart
J Gatchell, Master's Mate	J G Cary, Surgeon's Steward

Mr McNaughton, of St John, New Brunswick, was sitting next to a person having a loaded pistol in his breeches pocket which went off, the ball lodging in the knee. Amputation was necessary, & the man died from his sufferings.

Md Historical Society: meeting held Nov 14, at the Historical Rooms, the chair was taken by Brante Mayer. Donations of documents, works, & coins were given by Messrs Brantz Mayer, Jas Lucas, Wm Minifie, J S Sumner, & Hon Louis McLane. Robt Gilmor sent an original document, the Book of Field Notes taken by the surveyors who ran the line between Md & Pa about 1751, certified each day by the surveyors, & at the close by the Com'rs of the 2 States. With this were letters of Mason & Dixon, who ran the remainder of the boundary; & several letters from the Com'rs & others, a sketch of the tangent line, on a letter from John Emory, one of the surveyors in 1751. Gilmor also sent a copy of the map made by Col Cresap of the river Potomac-& the original map accompanied it. [Sent to S F Streeter, Sec Md Historical Society.] Mr Gilmor being present, made some remarks in reference to the papers: Letter from the Com'rs on the part of Richd Penn, Oct 20, 1760. Letter from Thos Garrett, one of the surveyors, Sep 5, 1761. Letter of C Mason & J Dixon to Mr Ridout, Apr 14, 1766. Letters from Mason & Dixon to Gov Sharpe, dated Jun 10, Aug 12, & Oct 1, 1766. These valuable papers excited much interest. For the safe-keeping of the original documents, the Treasurer, John I Donaldson, offered the use of the vault of the Franklin Bank, in the immediate vicinity of the Rooms, which was accepted. Gentlemen elected honorary members: Monsieur Alex'r Vattemare, of Paris, & Gulian C Verplanck, of N Y. Following gentlemen were nominate for membership, to be balloted for at the next meeting:
Corresponding member: J Bosman Kerr, of Talbot Co
Active members: Jonathan Meredith, & Fred'k Von Kapff.
Dr S Collins offered his resignation of the ofc of Librarian, which, after some discussion, was accepted. Dr Graves asked to be supplied with copies of the Constitution & By-laws to be presented to members of the State Legislature. Mr Gilmor read an amusing letter from Rev Bennet Allen to Gov Sharpe, detailing the particulars connected with his induction into a living presented to him by Lord Baltimore, & proving him to have been quite as expert in handling carnal weapons as in wielding the sword of the Lord. Society adjouned to the first Thu in Dec.

Wm Davis, the under-keeper of the N Y C prison, on trial in the Sessions on a charge of surreptitiously liberating the notorious Alex'r Hoag, from that prison, has been pronounced guilty by the jury, & the accused remanded to prison to await his sentence.

Frankfort [Ken] Commonwealth of Nov 12: Asa Young, late Senator from Barren, was stabbed at one of the election precincts on yesterday week. He received 11 wounds in the side & abdomen, & his condition, though not quite hopeless, is represented to be very critical.

A friend residing at Phoenixville informs that an Englishman, Wm Palmer, aged 21, was found in a ravine, shot in the neck & dead. He had been missed for about 3 weeks, but it was supposed he had clandestinely left. The man he boarded with has been arrested & committed for trial. –Phil Inquirer

Died: on Thu last, at Albany, Mrs Eliz Van Buren, w/o Mr John Van Buren, & d/o the late Judge Vanderpoel. She had passed the winter at Madeira for the benefit of her health, & it was hoped it was re-established, but these hopes have been blasted, & she is now the early tenant of the tomb.

Boarding: Mrs Hepburn, corner of 4½ st & Missousi ave, Wash.

Boarding: the subscriber has a house adjoining Holtzman's Hotel, Beall st, Gtwn, with 4 or 5 excellent chambers. –Geo H Holtzman

Household & kitchen furniture at public sale on Nov 25. –D S Waters, auct

SAT NOV 23, 1844
E Graves, a brakeman on the freight train of the Western railway, fell from one of the cars as the train was leaving Pittsfield on Wed for the East, & killed on the spot.

A young man, John Russell, was instantly killed at Zanesville, Ohio, on Nov 14, by the premature discharge of a cannon, which he, with others, was firing as a salute in honor of a political victory. He leaves a wife & 3 children.

The Ladies of Cincinnati [says the Gaz] intend presenting a silver pitcher to Thos Corwin. It is massive & beautifully wrought-Messrs E & D Kinsey, the makers. The pitcher bears on it the following inscription:
                    Presented
                    By the
      Whig Ladies of Cincinnati
                    To
          Thomas Corwin,
            of Ohio,
In testimony of their respect and gratitude
   for his disinterested services in the
         Political Contest of
             1844.

$500 reward for runaways, negro men, Anthony Chase-28; Ned Dodson-23; Tom Vermillion-21; Henry Buchanan-23; & Hanson Shaw-16. Dodson was purchased of Dr Edelen's estate, near Piscataway, where I think he will attempt to go. Shaw's mother is owned by Mr Wm Coats, who resides on the plantation of Thos B Craufurd. –Roderick McGregor, near Upper Marlborough, PG Co, Md

The Connecticut Historical Society has had a recent windfall in the shape of the identical Deal Chest formerly owned by Elder Brewster, the celebrated companion of Rev Dr Robinson & the rest of the Pilgrims who landed at Plymouth in 1620. The chest was brought over in the ship **May Flower**, & is identified not only by its original marks, but by other satisfactory testimony. It has remained in the possession of the lineal descendants of the Elder. It passed from him into the hands of his son Wm Brewster, thence into the possession of his grandson Jos Brewster, & afterwards into the possession of his great grand-dght, Ruth Brewster, who married Mr Wm Sampson, & removed to West Springfield, Mass, where she died, a few years since, at a great age, in the family of Henry Day, from whom Dr Robbins procured it. It is made of Norway Pine, & was probably procured in Holland.

For sale: 2 story frame house & lot on I st, between 22nd & 23rd sts, in Wash City, belonging to the estate of Eliz D Stillings, dec'd. Inquire at J McCutchen's Wood Yard, corner of G & 19th sts.

To Dairy-men & others, using Brewer's grains, can be obtained at Harman's, late Hayman's, Wash Brewery, 3 times per week, during the winter season.
–L C Harman, jr.

Valuable farm at auction: on Dec 18 next, on the premises, the farm lately occupied by Washington Lewis, in PG Co, Md, adjoining the Farms of Geo A Digges & Thos Burch. Contains 148 acres of choice land, with a new dwlg-house, barn, corn crib & other necessary out-bldgs. –Washington Lewis. -R W Dyer & Co, aucts

The subscriber has just opened a new Dry Goods store, Pa ave, between 8th & 9th sts. -G W Adams

Household & kitchen furniture at auction on Dec 2, at the residence of Wm A Bradley, 7th & Md ave. -R W Dyer & Co, aucts

MON NOV 25, 1844
Inauguration Ball: in honor of the Pres & Vice President elect, Jas K Polk & Geo M Dallas: to be given on Mar 4, 1845. Cmte appointed: Maj A A Nicholson, Col C K Gardner, Maj G W Cambloss, Dr J L Heiskell, & Jas G Berret. –T P Andrews, C J McNulty, Robt J Brent, Presiding ofcrs. Secs: R A Lacy, & John B Blake. Mr Murdock tendered his list of subscribers to the Ball he had intended to give at Carusi's Saloon, which could be obtained for the Ball.

For rent, & possession immediately, the large dwlg house at G & 22nd sts, recently occupied by the late T R Wise Apply to Chas E Eckel, or M Adler, Gtwn.

Circuit Court of Wash Co, D C-in Chancery-Mar Term, 1844. Priscilla Hardy, vs Danl Renner, John Lipscomb, Wm C Lipscomb, & others. Rule on the cmplnt to employ new counsel. –Wm Brent, clerk

Died: on Nov 17, at Airville, Gloucester Co, Va, Mrs Martha L, w/o Jno T Catlett, of the firm of Estep & Catlett, Wash.

The Censor of Vera Cruz announced the departure of Pres Santa Anna from his hacienda of *Mango de Clavo* to meet his bride at Encero.

This is to certify that Richd T Hazel, of Wash Co, on Nov 23, brought before me a trespassing sorrel mare. –J W Beck, J P Owner is to come forward, prove property, pay charges, & take her away. –Richd T Hazel

For sale or rent: large 3 story brick house at *Greenleaf's Point*, at present occupied by Mason Piggott. This house has upwards of ½ acre of ground attached to it. Apply to Francis A Dickins.

TUE NOV 16, 1844
Presidential Election: It is now certain that at the late elections held for the Electors of Pres & Vice Pres of the U S, Electors have chosen of whom a majority will cast their votes for Mr Polk for the first, & Mr Dallas, for the second of these ofcs. So that, in effect, Jas K Polk, of Tenn, has been chosen Pres, & Geo M Dallas, of Pa, Vice Pres of the U S, for 4 years from & after Mar 4 next.

Md: S M Semmes, of Alleghany Co, has been appointed, by the Exec of Md, to fill the vacancy in the judiciary of Md, whoch has lately become vacant by the death of Judge Buchanan, & Mr Semmes has accepted the appointment.

Mr Haight, the late American Consul at Antwerp, arrived at N Y a few days ago in a Swedish ship. On the passage home, he had the misfortune to lose his wife by death.

Gen Wm H Marriott has been appointed Collector of the Port of Balt, in place of Nathl F Williams, removed. This removal is made on purely party grounds. Mr Williams has faithfully discharged the duties of the ofc, & retires without any complaint against him. –Balt Pat

Red River Republican. The Hon Isaac Van Zandt, late Minister from Texas, in passing through Alexandria on is return home, was tendered the compliment of a dinner by the citizens of the place, which was given on Nov 7.

Alabama Monitor: New & improved Cotton Gin, the inventor is John H Sherrard, a wealthy planter of Sumter Co, Ala, & it is in full operation. A 50 saw gin, the size of that Mr Sherrard now has, will gin 4 bales per day.

Two men, Jos & Jeremiah James, left their homes in Canaan, Vt, on Nov 4, to examine sable traps they had set up in the wilderness. Not returning in due time, a search was made for them. They were found on Nov 14, both dead, probably on account of cold & hunger.

Geo Leisler, a native of Darmstadt, who came in the ship **Frederick Jacob**, Capt Warneken, from Bremen, which arrived at New Orleans at few days ago, committed suicide on Thu, by shooting himself through the head with a rifle. It appeared he was desperatedly in love with a young lady, a fellow-passenger on board the ship, who was engaged to marry a gentleman now living in Arkansas. -Picayune

Constable's sale: by 2 writs of fieri facias, at the suit of Peter Little, sr, against Chas H Brown: I have seized & taken into execution the right, title, & interest of said Brown in lots 7 thru 9 in square 897, with an unfinished frame house. –Thos Plumsell, constable

On Nov 13, as the steam tow-bow **Tiger** was taking the ship **Marcia**, bound to Liverpool, from the port of New Orleans over the Southwest Bar, she burst all her 6 boilers, destroying everthing over the guards. Killed: Capt Danl B Clark, pilot, of New Orleans; David Brown, 1st engineer, of N Y; & Abraham Snyder, 2nd engineer, of Canada.

The dwlg house of Rev Mr Elliott was destroyed by fire yesterday, from a stove in one of the upper rooms. St Louis Republican

At Wiscasset, Eleazer Master has been married to Miss Ellen Trade. If the old proverb holds good, that he who is master of a trade is the owner of an estate, Eleazer has married a fortune.

Mrd: on Nov 21, by Rev Wm Matthews, S B Boarman to Miss Maria Louisa, 2nd d/o Capt Geo Morgan, late of St Mary's Co, Md.

Died: on Nov 13, at *Fort Johnson*, Smithville, N C, Ann Eliza Childs, aged 16 years, 2nd d/o Lt Col Thos Childs, U S Army.

Stray mare came to the subscriber's farm, on Nov 18. Owner is to come forward, prove property, pay charges, & take her away. –Jane Woodruff

Rev A Biewend, minister of the German Lutheran Church, offers his services to those who want to learn the German language. Apply at his residence in Gtwn, Gay st, between Wash & Green sts.

For rent: a 2 story frame dwlg-house, on E st. Apply to G F Eckloff, now occupying the premises.

WED NOV 27, 1844
For rent: the dwlg house in Franklin Row, now occupied by Richd France. For terms apply to John France, on Pa ave, near 12th st.

Boarding: Mrs E T Argueles, on Pa ave, nearly opposite Coleman's. [Local ad.]

Dissolution of the partnership under the firm of Upperman, Hotchkiss, & Mix, this day, by mutual consent. Leonard S Hotckiss is alone authorized to settle the business. –Chas E Upperman, Leonard S Hotchkiss, Jos Mix

The Appalachicola Advertiser records the death of Col Latham Babcock, keeper of the East Pass light-house. He was with 2 other men hunting on Crooked river in a small boat, when some of the rigging caught in a double-barrel gun & the contents discharged into Mr Babcock. He was a native of R I, & was esteemed by all who knew him.

Dennis M Stephens attended the polls at Wash, Ga, on the day of the Pres election, got very drunk, & was found dead the next morning, sacrificed to his love of rum.

Owen McGee was arrested at Balt on Mon charged with stealing $1,000 from his uncle, Patrick McGee, of this city. The money was found in his trunk. [Dec 27th newspaper: Owen McGee was yesterday committed by Justice Thompson for trial on the charge of robbing Patrick McGee of gold & silver money amounting to upwards of $750.]

Fatal accident on Sat, as a wagon with 2 men was crossing the reading railroad near Schuykill, the train ran into it, & the men were thrown upon the road. J P Service had his spine & thigh broken & died almost instantly. McClintock received some severe internal injuries.

Wash Corp: 1-Ptn of John Y Bryant & others, for the establishment of a free school in the northern part of the 3rd Ward: to lie on the table. 2-Ptn from W Marshall & others: referred to the Cmte on Improvements. 3-Cmte on Improvements: asking to be discharged from the further consideration of the ptn of Jas Fraser, sen, of Wm Easby, & of G A W Randall & others: discharged accordingly. 4-Ptn of J H Kirkpatrick & others: referred to the Cmte on Improvements. 5-Ptn of Geo Hercus, praying that stock may be issued for a claim for repairing pumps in the 4th Ward: referred to the Cmte of Claims.

On Nov 3, Mr Silas Beckwith, of New Lyme, Ohio, terminated his existence by hanging himself. He was a man of property, & has a respectable & agreeable family. —Ashtabula Sentinel

Mrd: on Tue, by Rev John C Smith, Jas B Clarke to Miss Eliz W, 2nd d/o Col Wm P Young, all of Wash City.

Mrd: on Nov 21, at N Y, by Rev A Rogers, Mr John H Gibbs, of Wash, to Miss Emma Batchelor, late of London, England.

Died: on Nov 26, Miss Mary Jane French, in her 24th year. Her funeral is from the residence of her mother, 2nd st east, at 3 o'clock tomorrow.

Miss E B Scott, having removed from her former residence on Indiana ave to Missouri ave, 2nd door east of 4½ st, can accommodate boarders, gentlemen with or without their families. Her terms are moderate.

For rent, that very desirable & extensive house & premises, the property of Dr Davis, on E st. Apply to Chas A Davis, near the Seven Bldgs.

$50 reward: for lost small calfskin Pocket Book, containing some various bank notes, amounting to $328, with other papers. Deliver to Mr Vincent Taylor, at Gtwn. —Isaac Rogers

Trustee's sale of stock, under a decree of Circuit Court of Wash Co, D C, sitting in Chancery, passed Oct 11, 1844, in the case of the Pres & Dirs of the Bank of the Metropolis vs John A Breckenridge, exc of John Breckenridge, dec'd, & Robt E Kerr, adm of Alex'r Kerr, dec'd: public auction on Dec 19, of 56 shares of the stock of the Bank of the Metropolis, on each of which $25 has been paid.
—Richd Smith, trustee -R W Dyer & Co, aucts

THU NOV 28, 1844
We learn from the N Y American the death of Capt C H Camplin, late cmder of the London packet ship **Toronto**. He arrived at N Y from London only a few days since, & while on a visit to his family at Lynn, Conn, had a sudden & severe attack of inflammation on the bowels, which carried him off in a very short time. He was one of our most popular & accomplished packet masters, & his death will be very sincerely lamented.

The subscriber offers for sale Scott's Fire-proof Chests, which are immediately from the manufactory. Address John H Pennington, Wash Post Ofc.

We hear, by way of Paris, that G W Featherstonhaugh, formerly a resident for many years in this country, has been appointed British Consul at Havre.

We learn by arrival of the U S brig **Porpoise**, Capt Craven, at N Y, from Port Praya & Monrovia, that Dr Woffley, late Surgeon of the U S ship **Decatur**, recently fell from a cliff of rocks & so injured himself as to cause his death in 4 hours.

Phil rioter: Eaton Harwood's case was finally disposed of on Mon. He has been in prison since Jul 17. Judge Parsons administered to him some excellent advice, & sentenced him to pay a fine of $1 & costs.

Mrd: on Nov 26, by Rev Wm Hawley, Mr Francis Lombardi to Miss Caroline Eckloff, all of Wash City.

Obit-died: on Nov 19, at the going down of the sun, at the Rockhill Institute, Elkridge, in his 17th year, Louis McLane Saunders, s/o Hon R M Saunders, of Raleigh, N C, & grandson of Wm Johnson, of Charleston, late of the Bench of the Supreme Court of the U S. In his prolonged suffering, near 50 days, he has had all that medical aid & skill could proffer at his bedside. He father & mother, with his beloved sister, came from the far South to mingle with us & watch by him in his sufferings & when he died. –Howard District Press

FRI NOV 29, 1844
Chattanooga Gaz of Nov 16: announces the death, at Pikesville, Tenn, of the notorious John A Murrell, whose name as a land pirate figured so frequently in the press some years since, died of consumption, & denied to the last moment of his life that he was guilty of the principal charges against him.

On Sun, one of the Phil watchmen observed a fire in a dwlg house in Callowhill st. It was occupied by Mitchel Finnigan [shoemaker,] & his wife Matilda, who had gone to bed intoxicated, & left the lamp burning near some clothes, which took fire. They were found burnt to a crisp. He was 37 & she was 26. –U S Gaz

Mr Upton Duvall, of Fred'k, was killed last Mon by the premature discharge of a cannon, which was being fired in honor of the election of Mr Polk.

The N Y papers announce the death of Saml Stevens, in his 61st year. His death appears to be universally lamented. He was the s/o Gen Ebenezer Stevens, a distinguished ofcr of the Revolutionary war. He was a lawyer of eminence, & for several years a member of the Common Council, & one of the com'rs appointed to direct the construction of the Croton aqueduct, with which it is said his name will ever be associated.

Knitting Yarns: this day received 150 pounds of white, black, & colored Knitting Yarns. –Wm Egan, south side of Pa ave, between 6th & 7th sts.

Miss Heany's Academy, I st, opposite Pres' square, Wash. Miss Heany, of Boston, Mass, principal instructress, is resuming the education of Young Ladies in Wash City in the former family residence of Col Bomford.

Died: on Nov 26, in N Y, in his 61st year, Saml Stevens, a distinguished member of the N Y Bar. The civil law courts adjourned in token of respect to his memory.

Died: on Nov 6, at the residence of his son, Standish Barry, jr, in Newport, N Y, after a long & painful illness, Col Standish Barry, formerly of Balt, aged 81 years. He maintained through a long life an unblemished character. Though but a stripling at the time, he joined the gallant band of patriots who rallied around Washington towards the close of our Revolutionary struggle, & contributed towards the achievement of our liberty & struggle. At the time of the Whiskey Insurrection, as 1st Lt of the Independent Blues [in the absence of the Capt] he marched that fine company, in conjunction with other volunteer companies from Balt, to place them under the command of Washington, who, as cmder-in-chief, had taken the field to assert the majesty of the laws over the rebellious spirits who had conspired to bid defiance to them. In the war of 1812 Col Barry was a Major in the 5th Regt of Balt Volunteer Militia, & was in the battles of Bladensburg & North Point, In the walks of private life he was as exemplary in the discharge of the duties of husband, father, relative, neighbor, & friend.

Mrs Mary Ann Whitehill, from Pa, has opened a Boarding-house on 12th st, first door from E st. Refer to Dr Laurie & Rev S Tustin, Chaplain of the U S Senate.

SAT NOV 30, 1844
Mobile Advertiser, Nov 14, from Clairorne, Ala: A lad, H C Steele, was amusing himself by swinging on a rope suspended from the limb of a tree near the dwlg of his parents. The day he came to his death, he accidentally strangled himself before help could arrive. He was 11 years & 4 months old, the y/c/o Stephen & Eliz Steele.

Mrd: on Thu, by Rev John C Smith, Mr Robt McGowan to Miss Rachel A Rote, all of Wash City.

Died: yesterday, after an extreme illness of 9 days, in her 17th year, Miss Frances Ann Hampton, eldest d/o Thos R Hampton, of the 3rd Auditor's Ofc, formerly of Fauquier Co, Va. Her funeral is from the residence of her father on 10th st, south of Pa ave, this afternoon, at 3 o'clock.

Died: on Nov 28, of scarlet fever, Mildred, infant d/o R J & Ellen Pollard, aged 1 year, 9 months & 25 days. Her funeral is at 10 o'clock, today, from her father's residence on B st south, between 6th & 7th sts.

$5 reward for strayed from the subscriber, in Bladensburg, PG Co, Md, on Nov 26, a dark bay Mare. Above reward for her recovery. –Jas B Brooke

Orphans Court of Wash Co, D C. Letters of administration on the personal estate of the personal estate of Eliza Ross, late of said county, dec'd. –Wm [x] Ross, adm [x his mark]

MON DEC 2, 1844
Geo D Flanders, a boy of about 14 years, was run over on the Lynn double track by the Salem train for Boston on Wed, & was killed instantly.

Mr Henry Hurlbert, a brakeman on the eastern freight train, was killed instantly near Worcester, Mass, on Mon last. In passing under a bridge he was knocked off & fell under the wheels. His age was about 25 years.

Appointments by the Pres of Marshals of the U S: Isaac O Bates, for the State of Mass; Andrew S Pond, for the Northern District of N Y; & Alex'r Porter, for the State of Delaware.

Board of Naval Surgeons convened in Phil on Oct 7 last, & on Oct 25, report the following Assist Surgeons as having been examined & found qualified for promotion:
Of the date of Jun, 1838-Wm B Sinclair & Stephen A McCeery.
Of date of Oct & Dec, 1838-Jas B Gould, Chas H Wheelright, & John H Wright.
Of the candidates examined for admission into the Navy as Assist Surgeons, 16 were found qualified in the following order of relative merit:

1-Bernard Henry, jr	9-Philip Lansdale
2-Robt T Maccoun	10-P Benson De Lany
3-Wm A Harris	11-Alex'r J Rice
4-Robt E Wall	12-S Allen Paddock
5-Washington Sherman	13-John A Pettit
6-Henry O Mayo	14-Thos B Steele
7-John Rudenstein	15-J F Harrison
8-Randolph F Mason	16-A N Bell

Pres Tyler, we learn, has removed Mr McNier, the Postmaster at Annapolis, & appointed in his stead Martin Revel, a Tyler-Locofoco.

Thirty years ago the people of the Sandwich Islands were savages & cannibals. Now tuition on the piano is advertised in the newspaper printed at the Sandwich Islands, by M J A Presenent, maker & repairer of piano fortes.

Fashionable Tailoring Establishment. Saml Fowler has removed from his old established stand to the store room immediately adjoining the Temperance Hotel, [Beers'] between 3rd 4½ sts, north side of Pa ave.

Groceries: F & J Hitz, Capitol Hill, Wash. [Local ad.]

I am a Friar of Order Grey. The Rev Sydney Smith thus pleasantly discourses of himself: I am 74 years old; & being a Canon of St Pauls in London & Rector of a parish in the country, my time is divided between them. I dine with the rich in London & physic the poor in the country.

Died: on Dec 1, Miss Eliz Carbery, aged 19 years, y/d/o Jas Carbery. Her funeral will take place at 11 o'clock today.

Boarding: 1-Mrs A Cochran, on F, between 13th & 14th sts. 2-Miss Shonnard's Boarding House, south side of Pa ave, nearly opposite the U S Hotel. 3-Mrs Timms, at her old residence, south side of Capitol Square. 4-Mrs J C Turner, Indiana ave. 5-Mrs D Galvin, C st, between 3rd & 4½ sts. 6-Mrs Preuss, on Pa ave, opposite F Taylor's bookstore. 7-Miss Gurley, C st, near 4½ st.

To the humane: Wm Grubb, aged 16 years, s/o Curtis Grubb, of Loudoun Co, Va, absented himself Sep 16, 1844, without any known cause to his parents, & they are greatly distressed & desire some information of him. Should this meet his eye he is requested either to return to his parents or write to them. His mother in particular is in great distress at his indiscretion, & will be relieved much on hearing from him. Editors throughout the country will serve the cause of humanity by publishing this, & his father will compensate them if called upon. His residence is Waterford, Loudoun Co, Va.

On Nov 12, in the New Lane, off the Coal Quay, Sally, the w/o Patrick Donoghue, at the age of over 60 years, gave birth to a son. The mother & child are both well. -Cork Examiner

Mr Sgt Bompas, who died suddenly a short time since, left a widow & a large family in somewhat indifferent circumstances; but his professional brethren esteemed him so highly that a subscription was entered into for the benefit of the family, to which Sir Thos Wilde contributed the princely sum of 1,000 guineas. -Derby Reporter

Paris Confectionary & Depot of Comestibles. -C Gautier, 11th & Pa ave, Wash

Choice Wines & Liquors: Geo & Thos Parker, Centre Market Space

Orphans Court of Wash Co, D C. In the case of Alex'r McIntyre, adm of Danl H Haskell, dec'd: the Court & administrator appoint Dec 20 for settlement of the estate with the assets as far as collected, now in the administrator's hands.
–Ed N Roach, Reg/o wills

TUE DEC 3, 1844
Exchange Hotel, Exchange Place, Balt, Md. The subscriber informs he has purchased Mr Erastus Coleman's interest, & became sole lessee of the above mentioned hotel. -John West

To Land Owners: wanted, from 3,000 to 5,000 acres of first rate Land in one compact body either in Pa or Va. Address, post paid, Wm B Anderson, Pittsburg, Pa.

Chief ofcrs of the 2 Houses, heretofore appointed, who yesterday took their seats & officiated as such are as follows: in the Senate: Pres, [pro tem] Hon Willis P Mangum, of N C. Sec: Asbury Dickins. In the House of Reps: Speaker, Hon John W Jones, of Va. Clerk: Caleb J McNulty.

Wash Assemblies, 1845, Managers:

Hon Wm Wilkins	Hon W P Mangum
Hon E W Hubard	Hon Jas Buchanan
Hon Hamilton Fish	Hon Chas M Reed
Hon S A Douglass	Com W B Shubrick
Gen Geo Gibson	Capt J H Aulick
Gen N Towson	Dr J M Thomas
W W Seaton	Gen Alex Hunter
Thos H Blake	Maj W B Scott
Lt J R Goldsborough	Lt Overton Carr
Dr H L Heiskell	Richd D Cutts
Thos R Quimby	John W Butler
Thos H Patterson	Dr R A Lacy
Aug L McCrea	Chas P Wilkins
Lt P Calhoun	Lt W W Russel

The first Assemby will take place on Jan 2nd, 1845.

Hon Ratcliff Boone, formerly a member of Congress from Indiana, died at his residence in Louisiana on the Dec 20th, in his 64th year.

For rent: dwlg house on 9th st, between L & M sts, directly north of Col Doughty's brick row. Inquire of Jos Downing, 8th st.

Isaac Hough, 21, & Isaac Clark, 22, were both killed at Mesopotamia, Ohio, on Dec 19, by the bursting of a gun which was being fired in honor of the late Locofoco victory. They were the persons who had thus charged the instrument of their death.

Wm Tyler, of Dorchest Co, Md, an aged man, was tried before Talbot Co Court last week for the murder of Wm W Graham, of Dorchester Co, & found guilty of murder in the first degree.

Geo Dunn, recently convicted in Pittsurg of the murder of John Anderson, was sentenced on Tue last to be hanged.

Nashville papers announce the death of Robt White, aged 78 years, late one of the Judges of the Supreme Court of Error & Appeals of Tenn. He was a native of the Shire of Galloway in the Kingdom of Scotland. He emigrated to the U S some 50 years ago, & settled in Va.

Notice to Teachers. The undersigned, at the request of others equally interested with himself, take this method of making it known that a highly favorable opportunity for establishing a permanent institution of the instruction of both sexes now presents itself at this place. Thos disposed to embark in the business are requested to address H B Powell, Middleburg, Loudoun Co, Va.

Most valuable real estate at private sale: a tract of land in Jefferson Co, Va, containing 835 acres: 3½ miles from Charlestown: comfortable dwgl houses, barn, stabling, & all necessary out bldgs. The tract is divided into 2 farms one of 384 acres, & the other 451 acres. Apply to the subscriber on the premises, or by letter directed to Charlestown. –Jas M Ranson

Public sale: by order of the Orphan's Court of PG Co, Md, the subscriber will sell at the late residence of Mrs Sarah Slater, near Bladensburg, on Dec 12, all the personal estate of said dec'd, consisting of 14 valuable negroes; horses, cattle, sheep, hogs, crop of tobacco, corn, wheat, rye, oats & hay; household & kitchen furniture, & farming utensils. –W B C Worthington, adm C I A of Sarah Slater

For sale: a most valuable farm of Loudoun. I offer for sale the whole of my landed estate, within one mile of Hillsborough, the country seat consisting of 606 acres, divided into 2 parts; one of 206 acres, the other contains about 400 acres, with a 2 story dwlg house, 75 feet in length, with a cellar 50 feet long. Apply to the undersigned, or in his absence to Theodore N Davisson. –T M McIlhany, Hillsborough, Loudoun Co, Va.

Mrd: on Nov 20, in Phil, by Rev Mr Clemson, Mr Richd B Washington to Miss Christene Maria Washington, d/o the late Dr Saml Washington, of Harwood, Jefferson Co, Va.

Public sale of land: the legatees of Stephen Beard, dec'd, offer on Dec 10, on the premises, the Farm on which he resided at his death, lying on both sides of the Little River Turnpike Road, 3 miles below Aldie Loudoun Co, Va. The farm contains about 330 acres: the dwlg house is large & convenient, built of brick. There is also a house occupied as a wagon tavern. Call on John Moore, in Aldie, or Jonathan Beard, Gum Spring, who will show the land.

Rev Chas T Torrey, whose trial commenced before the Balt City Court on Fri last, on a charge of aiding in the abduction of slaves, has been found guilty. The offence is punishable by confinement in the State Penitentiary. The counsel for the accused gave notice they they would move the Court for an arrest of judgment & a new trial.

Mrd: on Nov 28, by Rev H Myers, Mr Thos Feller to Miss Eliz Slateman, both of this place.

Mrd: on Nov 26, by Rev Mr Saunders, Wm W Hill to Mary T, d/o the late Thos Magruder, of PG Co, Md.

Died: on Nov 26, at Raleigh, N C, John L Foreman, Senator in the State Legislature [now in session] from Pitt Co.

Died: on Nov 16, at **Belle Air**, Jefferson Co, Va, after a short illness, in the bloom of life, Mrs Mary Ann Washington, the beloved w/o Lewis W Washington, & d/o Jas Barroll, of Balt.

The Object of Life: the Rev Thos H Stockton, of Phil, will deliver a Lecture on the subject, in the Methodist Protestant Church on 9th st, Wash, on Wed at 7 o'clock.

Pleasant rooms for rent: 3rd st near Pa ave. Good board within a few doors.
–W W Birth

Boarding: Mrs Holdsworth, opposite the American Hotel. Also, several rooms for rent adjoining, over Mr Edw Simms' new grocery store, either furnished or not.

WED DEC 4, 1844
$50 reward for 4 men who ranaway from the barque **Madeline**, taking the ship's boat with them. Their names are Chas Hopkins, Jas Gould, Alfred Andon, & Robt D Pain. Pain can easily be detected by a large red scar on the left side of his face. Apply to Capt Chas H Shankland on board, or to Clement Smith, Water st, Gtwn.

Died: on Nov 9, at Buffalo, N Y, Mrs Eliza, w/o Ira Germain, & d/o the late Maj C Vandeventer.

Cherokee Difficulties. Arkansas Intelligencer: Gen Roger Jones, Adj Gen of the U S Army, Gov'r P M Butler, Cherokee Agent, & Lt Col Mason, of the U S Army, who were appointed the Com'rs to inquire into the difficulties heretofore & now existing among the Cherokee Indians, have arrived in that country.

Jonathan Burr died in Wash Co, N Y, a few days since, leaving property to the amount of some $500,000 to his son, a hopelessly insane man, 53 years old, who has not for many years received a cent from his father, but has supported himself by selling pamphlets about the streets of Albany. Next to him are 36 heirs. Old Burr's widow is still living, having long since been divorced from her miserly husband.

The store-house occupied by Capt Elijah W Day, in Port Tobacco, Chas Co, Md, was destroyed by fire, with its contents, on Wed last. The loss is some $6,000 or $8,000, & no insurance. The house was owned by Mr Basil Spaulding, of Balt.

The slaughter-house of Mrs S C Burton, of Ohio City, Ohio, was destroyed by fire on Nov 25, together with a large quantity of provisions belonging to Mr N C Baldwin. Loss from $4,000 to $7,000.

Orphans Court of Wash Co, D C. Letters of administration de bonis non on the personal estate of Henry L Coombs, late of PG Co, Md, dec'd. –Jas Lusby, J C Dawes, Adms de bonis non

Yesterday, a little son of Mr McGee, who resides near the Steamboat Wharf, in going with his sister to the pump, was kicked by a horse, & is so badly hurt that it is feared he will not survive the injury.

Union Guards meeting on Dec 4, at 7 o'clock. –Saml E Douglass, sec

THU DEC 5, 1844
Henry A Foster has been appointed by the Govn'r of the State of N Y a U S Senator, to supply the vacancy occasioned by the resignation of Mr Wright. Danl S Dickinson to supply the vacancy occasioned by the resignation of Mr Tallmadge.

The Milwaukie [Wisc] Courier announces the arrival of Gov Tallmadge in that city, having located his family at Fond du Lac.

On Nov 27 the dwlg house of Mr Geo Wyrick, 13 miles from Greensborough, N C, was burnt down & 3 of his children perished-a son about 16, & 2 dghts still younger. Mr Wyrick is a widower, & slept in one end of his house, while his children slept in the other end. He was not awakened in time to save them or to save anything else.

Mrd: on Nov 28, at Marcus Hook, Pa, by Rev A V Hard, Edw R Crosby, of Delaware Co, to Amanda E, d/o the late Benj Berry, jr, of PG Co, Md.

The Jury who sat at the coroner's inquest on the body of Miss Almeda Smith, who was killed on the Long Island Railroad last week, attributed the calamity to the negligence of said Railroad Co in not stopping their train at the regular stopping place on Pa ave.

Died: on Dec 3, Catharine M Hill, d/o Wm B & Catherine Hill, of PG Co, Md, aged 3 years & 7 months. [Note 2 spellings of Catharine/Catherine.]

The U S frig **Potomac**, Capt Gwynn, dropped down to Hampton Roads on Sun, preparatory to sailing on Wed. Wm Crump, of Va, U S Charge d'Affaires to Chili, & J H Bryan, of Ohio, U S Charge d'Affaires to Peru, go out as passengers.

Stop the Thief. $60 reward. Was stolen on Nov 30, from Jesse Gregg, living in the State of Delaware, a large Bay Mare. Also, from Peter Gregg, a new square built Carriage with light trimmings & lamps. The reward will be paid by the Treasurer of the Centerville Assoc. –Jas Delaplane, Treas

Congress Hall & Eating Saloon: in the establishment lately occupied by Mr Boulanger, will open on Dec 2, for reception of visiters. –Jos Jewett, P H King

Mrs Turpin, 7th & Pa ave, prepared to accommodate Members of Congress & permanent & transient boarders. Terms moderate.

Wine Store: John H Buthman, Pa ave, between $4\frac{1}{2}$ & 6th sts, Wash.

Mrs Mary A Mount's boarding house, east of the Capitol, in Duff Green's row, has been newly painted, papered, & put in thorough repair.

FRI DEC 6, 1844
Mail of yesterday brought us news of the death, at his residence, in Swanton, Vt, of the Hon Jas Fisk, in his 82nd year. He came into Congress in 1805; retired after the close of the war of 1812. The last ofc he filled was Collector of the Revenue of the U S for the District in which he lived.

Miss Mary E Bullock accidentally lost her life last Wed at the Pokanoket steam mill, in Bristol, R I. While she was passing an upright shaft in the carding-room, her clothes touched the shaft, by which she was carried round with great velocity until the engine was stopped. Her skull was badly fractured & she died almost immediately.

Gen Simon Perkins, one of the oldest & most distinguished citizens of the Western Reserve, died at his residence in Warren, Trumbull Co, Ohio, on Nov 19, in his 74th year.

At Newburyport, Mass, on Nov 28, Mr Thos Davidson broke his neck by falling down a flight of stairs. He was about 65 years old, & came from England several years ago.

Dreadful accident at Webster's Flour Mill, near Cockeysville, Balt Co, by which a young man, Jas Hanson, was suddenly hurried into eternity. He accidently fell upon some wheels while they were in motion, & was drawn in among them in such a manner that his body was dreadfully mangled.

New Printing Ofc: on Pa ave, corner of 11th st. –T Barnard

Cincinnati Times of Nov 25 says: a gentleman of this city, just from Greenville, Darke Co, Ohio, informs us that on Tue last a Mrs Stephens, the 2nd w/o a farmer near Greenville, murdered her husband, his son, & dreadfully mangled his dght, after which she fled & hung herself. The domestic discords arose from the settlement of the estate of the woman's first husband, a dispute growing out of the disposition of the proceeds. The boy was 12 years of age & the girl 14.

On Wed last, as the Long Island train of freight cars were on their way from Greenport to N Y, a young man named John Rogers, employed as brakeman, fell between the cars & was instantly killed. He was a sober & industrious young man.

Obit-died: Jos Taney, the uncle of the present Chief Justice of the U S, died at his residence near Emmitsburg on Nov 24, in his 90th year. For more than 50 years was he known to the writer of this feeble tribute to his memory. During the greater part of that time he acted as a Justice of the Peace, was for many years a Com'r of the Tax for Fred'k Co, & repeatedly elected a member of the House of Delegates. He has left 4 sons & 4 dghts to mourn the loss of a kind affectionate parent. His remains were interred in the cemetery at Mount St Mary's College. –Fred'k [Md] Herald [No death date-current item.]

Two men, John Darrah & Chas P Darrah, father & son, of Hookset, N H, have been committed to prison, charged with the murder of Esther Darrah, w/o one of the prisoners, & mother of the other. They are both intemperate men. [Dec 9th newspaper: John & Chas Darrah were discharged. The murder should be laid with the great heap at the door of rum. It is a relief to be able to acquit the husband & son of a crime so monstrous.]

Religious & Juvenile Books, at N Y & Boston prices, for sale by Wm Q Force, 10th st, near Pa ave.

New Jewelry Establishment: on Pa ave, between 4 ½ & 3rd st. –Christian Gessler, Jeweller, lately from Phil.

Household & kitchen furniture at auction: on Dec 10, at the residence of Robt N Johnson, on C, between 3rd & 4½ sts. –R W Dyer & Co, aucts

Wash Corp: 1-Ptn from W M Maddox: referred to the Cmte of Claims. 2-Cmte of Claims: reported a bill for the relief of John P Hilton & W H Clampit: passed. 3-Bill for the relief of J Broadbeck, jr: passed.

Boarding: Mrs Mary A Bordley Cummin, late of Md, has opened a Boarding house on N J ave, 2 squares south of the Capitol.

A mess of 4 or 5 members can be accommodated with board, at the Cottage, north Capitol st. –Jno Skirving

SAT DEC 7, 1844
For rent: comfortable 2 story brick house on Gay, near the corner of Montg st, Gtwn, & possession immediately. –David English, jr, Bridge st, Gtwn

Valuable residence for sale: large & commodious brick house on square 764, being near the residence of Danl Carroll of Duddington, in Wash City. Apply to W Hickey, Friendly agent of the proprietors.

The Public are cautioned against receiving the draft of Edmund Key on the Treasurer for the Western Shore of Md in favor of Michl B Carroll, & endorsed by said Carroll & myself, for the sum of $350, dated Nov 8, 1844. The draft has not come to hand, & no doubt has been purloined. –C C Magruder

N Y Tribune: a pair of silver pitchers were, "presented to Thos Sewall, M D, by J Phillips Phoenix." Dr Sewall was Mr Phoenix's physician last winter, during his severe illness at Wash, & these pitchers are a testimonial of the patient's sense of obligation to the doctor. They are of a large size, beautifully executed, with choice devices & rich casting by Ald Adams, 185 Church St, at a cost of some $250.

Trustee's sale: by deed of trust from Francis Hill et al, dated Jan 6, 1843, recorded in Liber B #3, page 502, of the records of deeds for Alexandria Co, D C. Auction on Dec 30 of that property in said county, adjoining the Little Falls Bridge across the Potomac, & now occupied by said Hill. Property includes about 15 acres of land, improved by a large stone mill. Also, will be included in the sale, a quantity of machinery, now set up in the bldg, for the manufature of paper. –Clement Cox, trustee -R W Dyer & Co, aucts At the same time & place, will be sold, in virtue of a deed of trust from Geo Hill to the subscriber, dated Jan 20, 1843, all the machinery mentioned in a schedule attached to the said deed, recorded in Liber W B #97, folio 25, of the land records of Wash Co. –D A Hall, trustee -R W Dyer & Co, aucts

Mrd: on Dec 3, at Norfolk, Va, by Rev Mr Miller, Saml Forrest, Purser U S Navy, to Anna Maria, d/o Dr Thos Henderson, U S Army.

Mrd: on Dec 3, by Rev Wm Hawley, Passed Midshipman Wm H Jamesson, of the U S Navy, to Miss Cornelia Lee, d/o the late Wm Taliaferro, of Peccatone, Westmoreland Co, Va.

Mrd: on Thu last, by Rev Mr Owens, Mr Henry T Smith to Miss Sarah Jane Erers, all of Wash City.

Mrd: on Dec 5, by Rev G W Samson, Mr Alex'r Johnson to Miss Mary Ellen Collason, all of Wash City.

Mrd: on Dec 5, by Rev Mr Taring, Mr Wm Thos Selby to Miss Eliz Rodburn, all of Wash City.

Died: on Nov 22, at her residence in Cabarras Co, N C, in her 62nd year, Mrs Eliz Barringer, relict of the late Gen Paul Barringer, & mother of the Hon D M Barringer. A large circle of relations & friends are left to mourn her loss.

Died: on Nov 14, at **Fort Towson**, Mrs Virginia L Bacon, in her 19th year, w/o Lt J D Bacon, U S Army, & d/o Maj Benj L Beall, 2nd Dragoons. Her death has caused anguish to her affectionate husband & parents, & a large circle of friends.

Died: on Dec 6, in his 66th year, Mr Henry Smith, for 45 years a resident of Wash City, & formerly of Southampton, Long Island, N Y. His funeral will take place from the residence of his family, on 11th st, tomorrow, at 2 o'clock.

Rev Mr Quigley, from N C, will preach in St Patrick's Church tomorrow at 11 o'clock, & take up a collection for the benefit of his Church at Raleigh.

MON DEC 9, 1844
Mutton! For sale at his stall, in the old Centre Market on Dec 10, grazed & fatted by John T Bury, of P G Co, Md. He has also purchased from E J Smith, of Clark Co, Va, a very large lot of most superior Mutton every offered in the District.
–Philip Otterback

Orphans Court of Wash Co, D C. Letters of administration on the personal estate of Jos Caloit, late of the State of Mississippi, dec'd. –Francis A Dickins, adm

Mrd: on Nov 26, at Charlotte Hall, Md, by Rev Mr Wyatt, Danl N Washington to Martha M Keech.

Died: on Sabbath, Mrs Eliz Fales, consort of Nathan W Fales, in her 48th year. Her funeral is from her late residence, H & 9th sts, on Tue at 3 o'clock.

Died: on Nov 8, of scarlet fever, Lois Margaretta, y/d/o Abm B & Sarah J T Lindsley, in her 6th year.

For rent: two new & comfortable frame dwlg-houses on M st, between 5th & 6th sts. For particulars, inquire of Thos Jarboe, 6th & Massaa ve.

Mrs Stevenson, w/o Mr Elan Stevenson, a respectable farmer of Darke Co, residing about 9 miles north of Greenville, Ohio, murdered her husband & 2 children, then committed suicide herself. There is confirmation of the horrible story, noticed a day or two since.

Taking the veil. On Nov 22, feat of the presentation, sisters Mary Rose Mudd, of Chas Co, Md, Mary Pulcheria Gibbons, of Wash, & Mary Pelagia Byrnes, of Phil, were admitted to their religious vows, in the convent of the visitation, Gtwn, D C. The Most Rev Archbishop presided & preached on the occasion. –Balt Sun

Moses Dawson, an aged citizen, well known in the community, died suddenly on Mon. He was sitting conversing with neighbor in his usual health, when he was seized with an apoplectic fit, & in a few minutes expired. He was for many years connected with the public press of this city as editor of the Daily Advertiser, before it was merged into the Enquirer. –Cincinnati Republican

City Ordinance-Wash. 1-Act for the relief of J Broadbeck, jr, that the sum of $2.10 be paid to him being an excess paid by him for a license to sell confectionary. Approved: Dec 6, 1844.

Washington Clothing Establishment: large & extensive assortment on hand. -Christopher Cammack, F st, near 15th st.

TUE DEC 10, 1844
New Orleans, Nov 29. Saml Marshall was yesterday arrested by the First Municipality police on the charge of murder. About 2 weeks ago a small party of U S discharged soldiers were on their way to this city from *Fort Jesup*, among them was one named Miller, who had a few hundred dollars in his possession. Miller's body was subsequently found & Marshall was arrected for the murder. A loaded pistol was found in his possession. He will probably be conveyed to that part of the State where the murder was committed. -Picayune

The residence of Capt J S Pickett, at Fruit Farm, Fauquier Co, Va, was found on fire on Dec 1. The bldg was entirely consumed. The family & neighbors saved nearly all the furniture & articles of value. How the fire originated was unknown.

House of Reps: 1-Memorial of the widow & admx of Jas Reeside, dec'd, formerly a great mail contractor, who claims a large balance due from the U S on the verdict of a jury: referred to the Cmte on the Post Ofc & Post Roads. 2-The heirs of Rignal Hilleary had leave to withdraw their memorial & papers.

Senate: 1-Ptn of Noah Miller: referred to the Cmte on Commerce. 2-Ptn of Smith Crain, a Revolutionary soldier, praying a pension: referred to the Cmte on Pensions. 3-Ptn of Albert A Muller: referred to the Cmte on Revolutionary Claims. 4-The documents on file relating to the claims of Jas Duffy: referred to the Cmte on Naval Affairs. 5-Ptn of Stephen Steele & Jas Daniel: referred to the Cmte on Private Land Claims. 6-Ptn of Jameson & Williamson: referred to the Cmte on the Post Ofc. 7-Ptn of Lucy Roberts, asking a pension: referred to the Cmte on Pensions. 8-Memorial of the heirs of Wm Fisher: referred to the Cmte on Private Land Claims. 9-Mr Buchanan obtained leave to withdraw from the files the papers of Joshua Shaw. 10-Ptn of Eliz Fitch: referred to the Cmte on Revolutionary Claims. 11-Ptn of Jane Clark, asking a pension: referred to the Cmte on Pensions. 12-Bill introduced for the relief of the heirs of the late Robt Fulton: referred to the Cmte on Naval Affairs. 13-Bill for the relief of Mark Simpson: referred to the Cmte on Pensions.

Constable's sale: 2 writs of fieri facias, at the suit of E M Linthicum, against Wm W Stewart & Richd H Stewart: public sale of all the right, title, & interest of Wm W Stewart in & unto lot 1 in Burche's & Stewart's subdivision of lot numbered 5 in square 518. Sale on Jan 7 next, in front of the premises. –John Adams, constable

Constable's sale: writ of fieri facias at the suit of E M Linthicum, against Mathias Jeffers: public sale of all the right, title, & interest of Jeffers in lot 1 in square 757, with a 2 story brick house. Sale on Jan 10, in front of the premises.
–John Adams, constable

Valuable paper-mill & farm at auction: by 2 deeds of trust from Geo Broadrup, dated Sep 30, 1835, recorded in Liber W B 54, folios 473 to 476, of the land records of Wash Co, D C, & the other dated Aug 18, 1844, recorded in Liber W B 90, folios 58 to 66 of said land records: sale on Mar 17, all that valuable property on Rock Creek, now in the occupancy of said Broadrup, embracing 75 acres of land, with an extensive Paper-mill. All conveyancing to be done at the cost of the purchaser.
–John McClelland, trustee -R W Dyer & Co, aucts

Trustee's public sale: by decree of Chas Co Court, in Equity: sale on Dec 17, in Port Tobacco, that tract of land lying in said county, of which the late Jas B Pye, of said county, died seized, containing by survey 664 acres, & called *Glymont*. This farm is on the banks of the Potomac river, 10 miles from the village of Port Tobacco.
-N Stonestreet, trustee

The Govn'r of Md has appointed Augustus R Sollers, Clerk of Calvert Co Court, in place of Wm Hance, dec'd.

WED DEC 11, 1844
The Hon Francis Xavier Martin, presiding Judge of the Supreme Court of the State of Louisiana, who went to Paris some months ago to obtain from the medical men of that capital relief for a disorder in his eyes, has returned to New Orleans. The papers of that city express great regret that no effectual remedy has been found, & his eyes are in no better state then they were before.

Two unfortunate persons, a man & his wife, came to Upper Marlborough, Md, on foot last Thu, in a destitute condition, & while here the woman became sick & died. We learn that her maiden name was Maria Funk, & that her relatives live in Perry Co, N Y, where she was married to Patrick Leonard, the man who came with her, & who is a native of Ireland. They were taken in by Doct Harper & his kind lady. –Upper Marlboro Gaz

On Mon last two 12 year old boys, a s/o Mr Erastus Goodwin, & a s/o Wm J Denslow, broke through the ice in Mill river & were saved by the heroic efforts of Col Nathan M Waterman, who broke through himself, but resolved on saving the lads at all hazards. Boats & planks were then brought to their rescue, & the trio was quite exhausted when brought to shore. –Hartford Courant, Wed

Another Cincinnati artist. The Queen City appears to be the mother of artist in the West. She boasts of her Powers, her Clevenger, & her Kellogg, & now presents another citizen, John L Whetstone, for a niche in the temple of fame as a self-taught sculptor. Mr Whetstone is now 23 years old.

Senate: 1-Ptn of Col Nathl Hoggatt, for confirmation of certain sales of the public lands in Louisiana: presented. 2-Ptn of Robt Poindexter, filed at the last session: presented. 3-Ptn of Catherine Leavitt: presented. 4-Memorial of Thos M Bryan, asking Congress to purchase the fossil remains of the Mastodon in his possession, [deposited at present at the Patent Ofc,] presented. 5-Ptn of Hezekiah Hamlett: presented. 6-Ptn of A Brainard, praying a pension: presented. 6-Bill for the relief of the legal reps of Pierre Menard, dec'd: presented. 7-Bill for the relief of Wm Elliott, of Fulton Co, Ill: presented. 8-Cmte on naval Affairs: bill to place Jas Duffy on the pension list: presented.

Coroner Woodward held an inquest last Mon in view of the body of a free colored woman, Maria Proctor, who was burnt to death in a hut situated near the Old Mansion House. She had a quantity of friction matches in her pocket, which ignited her clothes. She was a person of intemperate habits.

House of Reps: 1-Mr J Q Adams gave notice of a motion for leave to introduce a bill for the relief of Jos Holmes & others, owners & reps of the crew of the fishing schnr **Industry**. 2-Ptn of Seth Chapin, for a pension: referred to the Cmte on Revolutionary Pensions. 3-Ptn of Sarah C Wenwood, for compensation for Revolutionary services rendered by her father: referred to the Cmte on Commerce. 4-Ptn of Elisha Dyer & others, for an appropriation to clear out & deepen Providence Harbor: referred to the Cmte on Commerce. 5-Ptn of Saml Gladding, for drawback duties on sugar: referred to the Cmte on Commerce. 6-Ptn of Audley Clarke & others, asking indemnity for French spoliations: referred to the Cmte on Foreign Affairs. Same fo Philip Allen & others. 7-Ptn of David Melville, administrator of Benj Fry, dec'd, for a claim against the U S on the certificate of a jury: referred to the Cmte on the Judiciary. 8-Ptn of Wm H S Bayley & others, for the reduction of postage: referred to the Cmte on the Post Ofc & Post Roads. 9-Ptn of Jas McAvoy, for pay for work on the Cumberland road, with additional documents: referred to the Cmte of Claims. 10-Ptn of Wm B Stokes, surviving copartner of J N C Stockton & Co, late mail contractors: referred to the Cmte on the Post Ofc & Post Roads. 11-Ptn of Lathrop Allen. [No other information.] 12-Memorial of Capt Thos Ap Catesby Jones, asking compensation for services of a diplomatic character with chiefs of the Sandwich & other South Sea Islands, in the years 1826 & 1827, & for extra expenditures incurred in promoting the interest of the Gov't whilst recently in command of a U S squadron on a foreign station. 13-Ptn of Geo Taylor, in relation to French spoliations prior to 1800. 14-Ptn of Jas G Mackall & others, heirs of Capt John G Mackall. 15-Ptn of Stephen Beard & others. 16-Ptn of Wm Norman. 17-Ptn of Esther Standish, wid/o Amos Standish, dec'd, for a pension. 18-Ptn of the heirs of Philip R Rice, praying to be paid the value of a vessel belonging to him & impressed into the public service in the Revolutionary war, & thereby lost, was withdrawn from the files in the Clerk's ofc & referred to the Cmte on Revolutionary Claims. 18-Ptn of Abner E Van Ness, of Cass Co, Indian, praying indemnification for losses sustained by him in a contract for surveying Public lands in the State of Michigan. 19-Ptn of Mrs Nancy Haggard, of Cumberland Co, Ky. 20-Ptn of Thos Emerson, administrator & heirs of John Emerson, dec'd, of Cumberland Co, Ky. 21-Ptn of the widow F B De Bellevue, of the parish of Avoyelles, Louisiana, for pension money.

Wash, Dec 6, 1844. Cmte to take up a subscription of books for a library to be placed in the Navy Yard Fire Co Hall:

Lemuel Townend	Wm E Howard	Wm M Ellis
John R Queen	Hugh Pritchard	Wm D Acken
John F Tucker	Jonas B Ellis	Danl Quigley
Jas Marshall	Thos Thornly	Abel G Davis
John Davis, of Abel	Jas A Gordon	Chas Gordon
Richd Barry	Thos Blagden	

Mrd: on Dec 10, by Rev Mr Wilson, of Gtwn, Parker P Clark, of N Y, to Mary E, only chilled of Wm D Acken, of Wash City.

Mrd: on Dec 4, at Christs' Church, N Y, by Rev Dr Lyell, Douglass Vass, of Wash, to Miss Mary Shaw Fyfe, recently from Scotland, 2nd d/o the late Lawrence Fyfe, of Jamaica, West Indies.

Died: on Nov 21, in Robertson Co, Tenn, Mrs Margaret Washington, w/o Geo A Washington, & d/o Maj Wm B Lewis, of Washington, aged 21.

Died: on Dec 10, in Gtwn, after a short & painful illness, Mrs Sarah H Lipscomb, aged 45 years, w/o Jesse Lipscomb. Her funeral is tomorrow at 3½ o'clock, from the residence of her brother, John H King.

For rent: the house of Edw Fitzgerald, corner of 18th & I sts, at present occupied by Mr Chas W Forrest. Possession may be had on Jan 1 next. –Thos Carbery, agent

Orphans Court of Wash Co, D C. Letters testamentary on the personal estate of Jas T Davis, late of said county, dec'd. Persons having claims are to exhibit the same, with vouchers, to the subscriber on or before Dec 6 next. –Catharine S Davis, excx

Splendid property for sale: those 2 new & beautiful 3 story brick dwlg houses on H near 7th st. In each yard is a brick woodhouse & pump of fine water. Apply a few doors from the premises to Isaac Clarke.

N Y: on Sat evening John R Willis, an old & most estimable citizen, lost his life. Having been attached to the fire dept in his younger days, on hearing the bells, he ascended through the scuttle to the top of his house. But, in moving about, he unfortunately stepped backwards & fell through the skylight of the house of his next door neighbor, upon the 2nd flight of stairs. His head was so fractured by the fall, that he died in 5 minutes without any sign of consciousness. Mr Willis was Pres of our Board of Almshouse Commissioners. He was universally beloved.

THU DEC 12, 1844

Private letter from Montevideo, giving the particulars of the melancholy death of Cmder Newman, of the U S Navy, state that when the brig **Bainbridge** first arrived at Montevideo, in Sept, two of three shots were fired into her by a little Buenos Ayrean schnr, which Capt Newman did not return, under the impression that the act was committed through mistake. This conduct, however, gave rise to much comment, which so preyed upon his mind that he committed suicide by jumping overboard, unobserved at the time, during the night of Oct 9. His body was recovered the next day, & buried with the honors of war in the English burying-ground, outside the walls of Montevideo, attended by a lare concourse, besides his own countrymen, of foreign ofcrs & others.

Senate: 1-Ptn of Mary Reeside, excx of Jas Reeside, praying for the adjustment of the account of her late husband with the Gov't, & asked for its reference to the Cmte on the Judiciary. 2-Bill for the relief of the legal reps of Pierre Menard.

The Hon Wm Prescott died on Sun of an attack of apoplexy. He occupied for many years a prominent station as a member of the bar of this Commonwealth, as a sound lawyer & able advocate, frequently called to fill some of the most important ofcs. –Boston Daily Adv

German Universal Gaz: a conspiracy by the nuns of the convent of Varaten against the Princess Breakovaz, who, after relinquishing an immense fortune, took the veil in that convent. At the death of the late superior, these 1,100 nuns refused to accept the princess as her successor, she having excited their animosity by her determination to make a reform in their conduct, which she considered to have been much too free. The rebellious nuns carried their opposition so far as to break all the windows of the convent.

Mrd: on Dec 10, by Rev G W Samson, Mr Philip R Jones, of Balt, to Miss Eliza M Jeffers, of Wash City.

Lithography: Geo Hiring, [from N Y.] Maps, charts, & plans done in the neatest style & with the utmost despatch. All orders thankfully received.
–Geo Hiring, East Capitol st, Capitol Hill

Notice: the subscriber, at a public sale held on Dec 4, 1841, by the Collector of Taxes for Wash City, became the purchaser of lot 4 in square 38, also of the east half of lot 6 in square 660, for which certificates were issued, which are believed to be lost or mislaid; & notice is given that application will be made for the issuing of others to supply the place of the originals. –Jas Carrico

House of Reps: 1-Ptn of Harrison Whitson, asking Congress to pay him for provisions, & forage, furnished Capt Gilliam's company of mounted Florida volunteers in 1837, under contract made with said Gilliam. 2-Ptn & papers of John Stone, praying a pension; the ptn & papers in the case of J W Hackett; the ptn of Peter Shaffer; the ptn of Robt Seybold, praying a grant of land: presented. 3-Ptn of Barbara Burnham, wid/o Capt John Burnham, a Revoltuionary pensioner, praying for a pension. 4-Papers of Reuben Taylor, of Luzerne Co, Pa, for a pension on account of services as a privateersman. 5-Ptn of Roswell Woodworth for an increase of pension. 6-Ptn of Eliz James & others, & of Thompson Hutchinson, for pensions.

Constable's sale; by virtue of 2 writs of fieri facias, at the suits of D Bowen, use of E E Sterke, use of John France, & Jas Owner, jr, against the goods & chattels, lands & tements, rights & credits of Mathias Jeffers in & to lot 1, in square 757, with a 2 story brick house. –Thos Plumsill, constable

Fine farm for sale: 260 acres of choice land, in PG Co, & in the beautiful valley of the Northwest Branch, 1½ miles west of Bladensburg. It has a new dwlg house with the necessary bldgs attached. Also, a lot of 34 acres of woodland, 2 miles north of Rock Creek Church, adjoining the District line. Apply to the subscriber on the premises, or by letter, post paid, to Bladensburg post-ofc. –N M McGregor

FRI DEC 13, 1844
Senate: 1-Memorial of the heirs of Jos Watson, praying compensation for services rendered in the Territory of Michigan from 1806 to 1812. 2-Memorial of Thos McClellan & other citizens of Maine praying indemnity for French spoliations prior to 1800. 3-Bill for the relief of Wm Elliott, of Fulton, Ill: referred. 4-Bill for the relief of the legal reps of Pierre Menard: referred. 5-Bill for the relief of Jas Duffy: to be engrossed.

R H Belt, U S Consul at Matamoras, died at that port on Oct 11, of the fever which prevailed there as an epidemic.

The Hon Anson Jones, the new Pres of Texas, was to assume the reins of Gov't on Dec 2.

David J Hancock, late Postmaster at Cairo, Henderson Co, Ky, has been convicted of robbing letters of money, & sentenced to 10 years' imprisonment, by the U S Circuit Court sitting in Frankfort. –Shelby News

House of Reps: 1-Ptn of Elias Carpenter, of Sturbridge, Mass, praying for the arrears of a pension for loss of health produced by services rendered in the late war with Great Britain. 2-The claims of Jeremiah Moors, of Detroit; of the administrators of John Anderson, dec'd; of Catharine Knaffe; of Francis Cicote; & of Guy Carpenter: presented. 3-Ptn & papers of Jas S Campbell, praying compensation for property of his father, Danl Campbell, destroyed in the service of the Gov't during the Revolutionary war: presented. 4-Memorial of Wm Saunders & Co, sureties of Wm Estis, late paymaster of the 4th Virginia Regt, asking to be released from the payment of certain liabilities. 5-Ptn of Nathl Shiftell, of Albemarle Co, Va, asking for a pension. 6-Ptn of Geo Hall, of Albemarle Co, Va, for a pension. 7-Several ptns of Geo Easler; Andrew McLaughlin; Geo Langley; Francis Davidson; & Fred'k Christman, for pensions. 8-Memorial & other papers of Saml Colt, praying Congress to inquire into & test the utitlity of his water-proof cartridges. 9-Ptn of Geo D Spencer, of the State of Md. 10-Ptn of Andrew Waggonner, of Mason Co, Va, praying compensation for a negro man, the property of said Waggonner, lost in the public service, at Craney Island, during the war with Great Britain in 1813. 11-Ptn of Jacob Addison, of Muskingum Co, Ohio, praying for an increase of pension.

The mail robber, Capt *Bowers, who was tried & convicted for his crime some 2 or 3 years since, & has been confined in the Ky penitentiary, has had some 4 or 5 years of his sentence remitted, & been pardoned by Capt Tyler. *Powers is known to be a grand scamp, & there is full proof of his guilty. –Shelby News [*Bowers/Powers- copied as written.]

Circuit Court-Wash: the case Burr & others vs Keyworth, was tried last Tue, & the jury returned a verdict for the plntfs, who sued the dfndnt for $100, which he offered the plntfs for the recovery of his runaway servant, & which he [the dfndnt] afterwards refused to pay.

John Weston, an old convict, noticed reconnoitering houses in Wash City, as it was suspected, for the purpose of depredation, was committed by Justice Morsell to the workhouse for 90 days.

Large sale of very superior piano fortes, at Balt, from the manufactory of Loud, Phil. Public sale on Dec 14, at 9 South Charles, near Balt st. –Jos E Loud, agent for the manufacturers. –Wm Ward, auctioneer, Balt, Md

Mr John P Wake manufactures Piano Fortes, in Fulton st, very near the west side of Broadway, N Y. A specimen of his instruments can be seen by inquiring of the Postmaster of the House of Reps.

Died: on Sun, of consumption, Mrs Mary J White, in her 32nd year.

Died: week before last, in Middleburg, Va, Col Noble Beveridge, of that place, highly esteemed by a large circle of friends & relations.

Died: on Dec 11, at Olney, his residence in Montg Co, Md, Dr Chas Farquhar, of bilious pleurisy. To the large circle of his friends & acquaintances the stroke is as distressing as it was unexpected. But to his most interesting family the bereavement is overwhelming, & none but He who gave can heal the wound. -L G R

Large Newfoundland dog pup, nearly all white, srayed from the residence of the undersigned, on 9t st, near the Northern Liberties Engine-house, on Mon last. Whoever will return said dog will be liberally rewarded. –Danl Gold

The Mississippi "Southron" of Nov 27 says that the report of the death of ex-Govn'r Runnells, late of that State, is entirely erroneous. At the latest accounts from Texas, received through his own son, Mr Runnells was in the enjoyment of remarkably good health.

SAT DEC 14, 1844
Orphans Court of Wash Co, D C. Letters of administration on the personal estate of Margaret Atkinson, late of Wash Co, dec'd. –Barbara Baswill, admx

Furnished house for rent: on 19th st, near Pa ave. At the request of many physicians, the subscriber will keep on hand during the winter a constant supply of his celebrated Mineral Waters. –A Favier

Beallair at Private Sale: this desirable estate, 3½ miles from Charlestown, containing about 530 acres, considered one of the most desirable farms in Jefferson Co. Improvements consist of a stone dwlg-house, stone stable, stone smoke-house, [with cement floor,] stone dairy, [with cement floor,] frame stable & carriage-house, [stabling 24 horses,] superior corn-crib with granary attached, overseer's house-new, ice house, blacksmith & carpenter's shops, & bath house. Address the subscriber on the premises, near Halltown, Jefferson Co, Va. –Lewis W Washington

MON DEC 16, 1844
The Delhi Gaz of Wed: in Delaware Co, N Y, on Sun, the house & barn of Mr Seymour F Benedict, a few miles from the village of Walton, was destroyed by fire on Dec 8, & his wife & 6 children perished in the flames. Mr Benedict, his wife, & the youngest child slept below, & the other children in the chamber. The three below escaped, but Mrs Benedict went back into the house to rescue some of the others, & was followed unconsciously by the child, when the chamber floor gave way & buried them in the ruins. The oldest dght, aged 18 years, escaped through the chamber window, but was so badly burnt that she died the following night.

Gen Simon Perkins, one of the oldest settlers of the Western Reserve, in Ohio, died at his residence in Warren on Nov 15. He was a native of Norwich, Conn, but removed to Western N Y in 1795, & to Northern Ohio in 1798, & became a land surveyor & agent. He resided at Warren from 1801 till his death.

The trial of Abner Parke for the murder of John Castner, [the old Warren tragedy, for participation in which Carter stands convicted,] has just commenced before Judge Nevins, in the Oyer & Terminer of Warren Co, N J. About 70 witnesses are in attendance on the part of the State.

Loss of the ship **Massasoit**, Capt Barry, from Calcutta for Boston, having on board a valuable cargo, was wrecked on Alderton Bar, at the entrance of Boston harbor, on Wed night. Of three of her crew who attempted to swim ashore, 2 were drowned: Mr Stpehen C Holbrok, of Jamaica Plains, a passenger, was lost in consequence of falling down the main hatch. The vessel belonged to Messrs Russell & Co of Plymouth, & was insured for $16,500. The cargo was insured for $57,200.

Mr Winans, of Balt, & Messrs Harrison & Estwick, of Phil, who are in Russia constructing railroads, under a contract with the Emperor, are doing very well. Their contract with the Russian Gov't exceeds three millions of dollars, & they expect to make a great deal of money.

Hon Thos Morris, the candidate of the Libery party for the Vice Presidency at the late election, died suddenly at his residence near Bethel, Clermont Co, Ohio, on Dec 7. He was apparently in vigorous health before his decease. He has been a member of the Legislature, Judge, & U S Senator.

Washington Seminary, N Y ave, between 17th & 18th sts, Wash. Alex'r H Evans, Principal, has associated with him, in teaching, Mr A A Hopkins, of N Y.
References:
House of Reps::Hon Andrew Stewart, Hon Robt Dale Owen, & Hon Wm Lucas.
Wash City: Rev Wm Hawley, Maj Wm B Scott, Capt Hetzell, U S A; Wm Speiden, U S N; Alex'r Ray, John D Wilson, Chas B Penrose, Doct J S Gunnell; Saml Potts, & Alex'r Suter.
Va: Rt Rev Wm Meade, Gen J H Carson, Hon John Scott, Hon J R Douglass, & Hon R J Field

House of Reps: 1-Ptn of Wm Simpson, for compensation for damages done by troops in the year 814. 2-Ptn of Wm Depens, for a reduction of the duties imposed on Canary wine by the tariff act of 1842. 3-Ptn of Mary Martin, late of N Y, formerly Mary Lindsley, praying compensation for a negro man captured by the British during the last war. 4-Ptn of Eliza Trenchard & 13 others, widows, of ofcrs of the navy, praying that provision be made to restore to the Navy Pension Fund the amount lost by depreciation or other causes.

City Hotel for rent. Apply to H Wilson, at Mrs Eliz Irwin's, on Cameron st, Alexandria.

Mrd: on Dec 12, by Rev G W Samson, Mr Wm W Whitmore to Miss Catharine P Collason, all of Wash City.

Mrd: on Dec 12, by Rev Dr Laurie, Lt A A Harwood, U S Navy, to Margaret B, d/o Vinal Luce, of Wash City.

Mrd: on Dec 10, in N Y, by Rev J W Alexander, D D, Z Chandler to Miss Letitia Grace, d/o Geo Douglass, all of N Y.

Mrd: on Nov 10 last, by Rev Mr Cruse, Mr Saml H Cox to Mrs Eliz J Nash, both of Chas Co, Md.

Died: on Dec 6, in Alexandria, Isaac Kell, in his 74th year, one of the oldest & most respectable citizens. Mr Kell has left a large family & numerous friends & connexions to mourn his death. He had been for a number of years one of the Justices of the Peace for the city, & performed his duties with the esteem of his fellow citizens.

Police Intelligence-Wash. On Sat last ofcr Burr arrested Robt Johnson, alias Williams, & Anthony Linsley, free negroes, charged with stealing a gold watch & chain of the value of $100, the property of Mary Heisler.

TUE DEC 17, 1844
House of Reps: 1-Ptn for the relief of the heirs of Sgt Maj John Champ, dec'd: referred. 2-Ptn of Geo Alford, of Monroe, Mich, to be reinstated on the pension roll. 3-Ptn of Capt John Martin for arrears of pension. 4-Ptn of the heirs of Capt Danl Mills, for compensation due for Revolutionary services. 5-Ptn of Jesse Campbell, of Mason Co, Ky, a soldier in the late war with Great Britain, one of the captives confined in the Dartmouth prison in England, praying that Congress may pass a law for his relief, he now being poor & an invalid, aged & infirm. 6-Ptn of Saml Goodwin & others, of Marblehead. 7-Memorial of Job Dennen, of Rockport. 8-Ptn of Ebenezer Wheelright, of Newburyport. 9-Ptn of Eliz Russell, of Marblehead. 10-Ptn of Moses Noyes. 11-Ptn of S Riley Knight, for compensation for losses & injuries sustained while in the service of the U S as keeper of a light-house in Louisiana. 12-Ptn of Eliz H Dickson, praying for the recognition of a certain pre-emption claim.

By writ of fieri facias, I shall offer at public sale, on Dec 24, in Wash City, opposite the Centre Market-house, one bay horse, seized & taken as the property of John Goings, & will be sold to satisfy a judgment due Levi Underhill.
–Lambert S Beck, constable

Senate: 1-Memorial of Geo Taylor, for indemnity for French spoliations prior to 1800. 2-Ptn of Thos Dyer & others, asking remuneration for losses sustained in the naval service. 3-Ptn of Nathl Phillips, praying to be placed on the pension list of invalid seamen. 4-Memorial of Henry Williams, praying that a provision may be made in the bill for the relief of the heirs of Jas Reeside, to recompense him for losses. 5-Bill for the relief of Wm Russell. 6-Judiciary Cmte reported a bill for the relief of Mary Reeside, wid/o excx of Jas Reeside.

For sale or rent: commodious & well-finished house near the Steamboat Wharf, with a good stable & all necessary out-bldgs, recently occupied by Col Nourse. Also, that handsome little dwlg on Md ave, near 7th st, now occupied by Mr Dorsey, would be sold, & good time given to a purchaser. –J Van Reswick, at the Planing Mills

Marshal's sale: in virtue of a writ of fieri facias, public sale on Jan 16, of the following property: lots 6 & 7 in square 216, in Wash City, duly made & recorded by a certain Saml Davidson, in the ofc of the Surveyor of Wash City, being the same lots purchased by Henry C Slade of Col Geo Bomford, as per deed bearing date Mar 19, 1836, with the improvements thereon, being an unfinished 2 story frame house. Seized & levied upon as the property of Saml Holland, & sold to satisfy judicials 127, to Nov term, 1844, in favor of Louisa Levy. –Alex'r Hunter, Marshal of D C

A little boy, s/o Peter S Van Zandt, near Titusville, was attacked one day last week by a ram, which butted him on the head, & fractured his skull so that he died in half an hour. –Trenton State Gaz

Household & kitchen furniture at auction: on Dec 19, at the residence of John Williamson, late Recorder in the Land Ofc. -R W Dyer & Co, aucts

I hereby forewarn the citizens of Wash City or elsewhere from crediting or in any manner harboring or encouraging my wife, Margaret Smith, alias Margaret Wachter, who had, without cause or provocation, left my bed & board. Said Margaret has no justifiable reason for her immoral conduct, she having received, previous to her absconding, that treatment which an honest & laborious husband administers to a faithful & industrious wife. I further state that the full extent of the law will be put in force should it be disregarded. –Jacob Wachter

WED DEC 18, 1844
Henry Moore & wife have recovered $2,000 in an action in the Supreme Court against the city of Lowell, for injury to Mrs M by falling into a cellar through the sidewalk.

Wm F Gooding, one of the oldest settlers of Goderich, together with Isaac G Clark & Randall Gooding, were unfortunately drowned in Lake Huron a few days since. Their sailboat upset. Mr Gooding was extensively kown & highly respected. –London [Can] Enquirer

Senate: 1-Ptn of Thos A Russell, asking compensation for a horse taken during the Revolution: referred. 2-Ptn of Wm Bradstreet, praying for an allowance of bounty: referred. 3-Ptn of Jas Sanders, late an ofcr in the Navy, praying to be restored to the pension roll: referred. 4-Ptn of Mary Blakesel, asking a pension: referred. 5-Ptn of Elliston Williams, of Kenton Co, Ky, praying a pension: referred. 6-Ptn of Jacob Fowler, praying a pension: referred. 7-Ptn of Jas Smalles, praying remuneration for Revolutioary services. 8-Ptn of Henry Hatch, for French spoliations prior to 1800.

Farm for sale: 52 acres, within 3 miles of Gtwn Ferry, in Alexandria, D C. Apply to J D King, F st.

House of Reps: 1-Cmte of Claims: to inquire into paying Saml Perry the amount deducted from a freight bill under a contract with McClure & Co for transportation of Indian stores, & an additional amount claimed for detention & the expenses incurred thereby. 2-Bill for the relief of Joshua Kennedy: passed. 3-Resolved, that the Cmte on Revolutionary Pensions inquire into granting a pension to Wm Gump, of Greene Co, Pa.

Public Sale: on Dec 23, on 27th st, Wash, near the old stone house, all the personal property of the late Thos Herbert, dec'd. Also, a large quantitiy of house-joiner's & carpenter's tools. They are worthy of the attention of mechanics.
--Geo F Kidwell, for the heirs

One Cent Reward: for my indented apprentice, Basil Baden, to the cabinet-making business, who ran away on Oct 20 last. He is about 18 years of age, 5 feet 6 inches high, inclined to be dressy, but uncommonly lazy. Any person returning said runaway apprentice shall receive the above reward, but no extra charges, nor the thanks of the subscriber. I hereby forewarn all persons from harboring or employing said boy, under the law respecting runaway apprentices, as it will be rigidly enforced. --Peter Callan

Elected Trustees of the Public Schools-Wash:
Robt Farnham	Thos Donoho	Wm M Ellis
Geo J Abbott	John C McKeldon	Isaac S Miller
John T Hartley	John P Ingle	Ignatius Mudd
Peter Force	Noble Young	Thos Blagden

Mrd: on Nov 12, at Mount Verde, Essex Co, Va, by Rev John Duvall, Mr A O Yerby to Mrs Betty Smith.

Died: on Dec 8, at his residence in Middleburg, Loudoun Co, Va, Col Noble Beveridge, in his 67th year. He was one of the oldest citizens of that village, in which he settled as a merchant in very early life, & where he pursued his occupation until a few years past with an industry & perservaerance which were crowned by signal success. He left a very large fortune, the fruits of his well-directed enterprise.

Microscope found a few days ago, about a mile from Wash City. Owner to apply to Geo Nietzey, North Capitol & G sts.

The remains of the late Prof Fred'k Hall, of Wash, who died so suddenly in the West about a year since, while on a geological exploring tour, have been brought to Balt under the direction of his brother, David W Hall, & were deposited in his lot in *Green Mount Cemetery*, on Wed last. The funeral rites were performed by Rev Dr Morris. Prof Hall was for a number of years the proprietor & principal of Mount Hope College. -Patriot

Confectionary: Wm Emmert, Bridge st, Gtwn.

On Fri last a son of Mr Mittens, of Schuylkill Haven, was knocked down by the cars of the railroad & died shrtly after. He was standing at the end of the train talking to his mother, when the train was backed, which caused the accident.

Reading [Pa] Gaz: the Reading Furnace, about 12 miles from this town, & owned by the assignees of the U S Bank, were last week sold, with all the landed property attached, to Govn'r D R Porter & Co, of Harrisburg, for $50,000.

THU DEC 19, 1844
Senate: 1-Memorial of Levin Wethered, of Balt, praying a remission of duties. 2-Bill for the relief of Asa Andrews: referred. 3-The bill for the relief of the heirs of late Robt Fulton was taken up a 3rd time & was passed, & went to the House of Reps: for concurrence.

House of Reps: 1-Bill for the relief of the legal reps of Joshua Kennedy, of Indiana: referred to the Cmte on Indian Affairs. 2-Bill for the relief of the heirs of Robt Fulton: referred to the Cmte on Claims. 3-Bill granting a pension to Jas Duffey: referred to the Cmte on Naval Affairs. 4-Cmte of Claims reported a bill for the relief of Thos Allen: referred to the Cmte of the Whole House.

A great deal of excitement prevailed in our community yesterday, in consequence of an attack being made at the Capitol on the person of the Hon John Quincy Adams, by an individual named Thos Sangster, who, either in a fit of insanity, or under the influence of intoxication, attempted to commit an act of outrageous violence on the ex-Pres. When Sangster attempted to strike Mr Adams in the face, he was prevented from doing so by 2 or 2 bystanders & witnesses of the outrage. Sangster was arrested. We learn that Thos Sangster keeps an agency ofc near the western termination of Pa ave, & is a native of Va. [Dec 25th newspaper: Sangster was admitted to bail by the committing magistrate last night, the latter having first received the certificate of a physician that he had examined Mr Sangster & considered him to be of "sane mind."]

Chatsworth Mansion for sale or rent: formerly occupied by the late Jeremiah Hoffman, situated on Franklin st, in the city of Balt, it occupies a front on Franklin st. It constitutes as one of the most eligible residences in the U S. Apply to Danl B Banks, 49 Balt st.

For rent: a 2 story brick house, with back bldg, near the Navy Yard. Inquire of the subscriber on I st north, between 9th & 10th sts wst, or of R H Harrington, near the Navy Yard gate. –W D Acken

For rent: the 2 sotry brick house he now occupies, on I st, between 9th & 10th sts. It is new & in good order. Apply as above. –Wm D Acken

The Edinburgh papers announce the sudden death of Dr Abercrombie, of that city. He was found by his servant lying dead in his own room. It is supposed he was carried off in a fit of apoplexy. He was upwards of 60 years of age.

Died: on Dec 9, at his residence, Montg Co, Md, Mr Richd Piles, aged 73 years. His last sickness was short but of the most painful kind. He died as he had lived, an honest, upright man, the noblest work of god's creation. He has left a large circle of relatives & friends to mourn his loss.

Mrs Preuss has a large & commodious house for the reception of permanent or transient boarders or members of Congress, with or without families. Her house is on Pa ave, opposite F Taylor's bookstore.

FRI DEC 20, 1844
Senate: 1-Ptn of Mrs Francis Edwards, of Phil: referred. 2-Cmte of Claims: unfavorable report on the bill for the relief of T A Russell. Same cmte, reported a bill for the relief of Wm Rich. 2-Bills to be engrossed: bill for the relief of Jas Ritchie; of J McFarlane; of Wm Rice; settlement of the accounts of Purser Thornton; of Gideon Batchelor; of the legal reps of Pierre Menard, & others; & in favor of David Shaw & Solomon T Corser.

Deacon Saml P Cowles, of Marcellus, N Y, died very suddenly in that village on Thu last. While shaking hands with a friend, near the Salina St Bridge, he was struck with a fit of apoplexy, fell & died almost instantly. He was 53 years of age, & has left a family to mourn his sudden exit.

Rencontre at Murfresborough, Rutherford Co, from a communication dated Dec 4. The rencontre took place on the public square of that town, between J Climer & J McKissick, 2 young men of the place, which resulted in the death of McKissick. –Nashville Banner

On Dec 8, Mrs Lydia Vann, d/o Mr Barnet Sipley, in the township of Hardwick, Warren Co, N J, put an end to her life by means of a rope. She was found by her father soon after the fatal deed was perpetrated. The cause is supposed to have been the cruel treatment of a drunken husband. She has left behind 3 infant children. -Sussex Register

Horace Bartlett, s/o Chas E Bartlett, of Berwick, Me, was drowned last Wed, by falling into a hole in the ice while skating. His body was recovered about 2 hours afterwards.

House of Reps: 1-Memorial or Richd Wells, sr, of Carroll Co, Md, praying for a pension. 2-Ptn of Isaac Davenport, of Philips, Maine, for a pension. 3-Ptn of Saml Butler, praying for a pension. 4-Ptn of the executors of Col John Taylor, dec'd, praying for compensation for damages done to their property, known as Fuller's Hotel, whilst in the occupancy of the Post Ofc Dept. 5-Ptn of Thos Jett & others, for a Revolutionary claim. 6-Ptn of Sally W Griffith, excx of Eliz Thompson, dec'd, for compensation for houses & other propery destroyed by the enemy during the late war with Great Britain. 7-Ptn of John L Harris, for confirmation of fractional lot number 16, township 16, range 14, on the river Mississippi, in Madison parish, Louisiana. 8-Ptn of Jos Paxton, now of the State of Missouri, praying remuneration for arms & clothing lost by him during the late war, while in the service of the U S. 9-Memorial of Geo J Green to be reinstated upon the pension roll. 10-Ptn fo Jos de la Francis, praying the settlement of his claim for payment for arms sold to the Conventional Gov't of Florida in 1810. 11-Ptn of Alanson Phinney, praying that a land patent may be issued to him. 12-Memorial of Chas H Todd, of N Y C, praying to be refunded duties that have been erroneously paid. 13-Ptn of the heirs of the Rev David Avery, dec'd, for a pension. 14-Ptn of Laura Redington, praying for a payment to her of the pension to which her husband, John Redington, a Revolutionary soldier, was entitled.

Frontier Journal: Mr J D Balmat, of Fowler, while out deer stalking in the woods, killed a boy named Geo Newton, whose grey dress he mistook for a deer. The lad was about 13 years of age, & died half an hour after being wounded.

Grand Lodge of Free & Accepted Masons of D C: the following were elected ofcrs for the ensuing year:

Wm B Magruder, M D, Grand Master
Robt Boyd, Deputy G Master for Wash
A E Eliasson, Deputy F Master for Gtwn
H B Robertson, Grand Senior Warden
Robt Clark, Grand Jr Warden
H C Williams, Grand Sec
Geo Thompson, Grand Treasurer
Marinus Willitt, Grand Visiter & Lecturer
A A Muller, D D, Grand Chaplain
Wm H Sloane, Grand Senior Deacon
Chas Venable, Grand Jr deacon
B M Deringer, Grand Marshal
Jos K Boyd, Grand Sword Bearer
John Robertson, Grand Pursuvint
John G Stock, Grand Tyler

The Hagerstown [Md] News states that in Wash Co Court on Wed last, Miss Susan Startzman, in an action for breach of promise brought against Mr Conrad Smith, received a verdict in her favor to the full amount of damages claimed-$2,000.

Wash Corp: 1-Ptn of M J Peerce, praying remission of a fine: referred to the Cmte of Claims. Same for J Visser; & same for J H Eberbach. 2-Cmte of Claims: asking to be discharged from the further consideration of the ptns of Geo Hunter, of Allen Matthews, of Smith & Tucker, & of Geo Hercus. 3-Cmte of Claims: ptn of Wm Dalton, reported a resolution that the prayer of the petitioner ought not to be granted.

John Hanna, a farmer living in the neighborhood of Montreal, was killed there on Sat week, by the falling of a large body of ice & snow from the roof of a house.

Died: on Dec 18, of scarlet fever, Wm Eleazer, y/s/o Abm B & Sarah J T Lindsley, aged near 4 years, being the 2nd child they have lost within 10 days of the same disease. "Suffer little children to come unto me, saith the Lord, for of such is the kingdom of Heaven."

Died: on Dec 19, at the residence of her son-in-law, Mrs Catharine Ramsay, aged 67 years, the wid/o the late Andrew Ramsay, universally & deservedly beloved & lamented by her numerous relatives & friends. Her funeral is tomorrow, at 12 o'clock.

Died: on Dec 11, after a protracted illness, at Honeywood, Berkeley Co, Va, the residence of her brother, Edw Colston, Mrs Mary I Thomas, relict of the late John Hanson Thomas, of Fredericktown, Md, in her 56th year.

SAT DEC 21, 1844
House of Reps: 1-Ptn of Josiah Dillon, praying for the repayment of money furnished by him for the use of the U S Army during the late war as Assist Deputy Quartermaster Gern'l. 2-Ptn of the reps of Gustavus B Horner, a surgeon's mate in the Revolutionary army, for bounty land or other compensation for his services & for commutation. 3-Additional evidence in the case of the heirs of Rev David Avery, dec'd, praying for a pension: presented. 4-Ptn of Danl Bailey, jr, & others, praying that slavery may be oblished in D C & Florida. 5-Ptn of Justin Jacobs, for a pension. 6-Ptn of Edw J Heard, of the parish of St Martin, La, praying to be allowed to purchase a fraction of Gov't land for the reasons set forth in the petition. 7-Ptn of J L Kimberly & Co & 110 commission merchants & ship-owners of the city of Buffalo, asking Congress to make an appropriation for improving the harbor of Manitowoe, on Lake Michigan.

Hon Heman Allen, formerly a member of Congress from Vt & Minister to Chili, died at his residence in Burlington on Wed week, aged 58 years. He was one of the most distinguished men in the State of Vt.

Z D Gilman gives notice to his customers that their annual bills are now ready for distribution, & would invite all those indebted to him to call, with as little delay as possible, & hand in their respective amounts.

By writ of fieri facias, at the suit of John Priven, use of John H Wilson, against the goods & chattels, lands & tenements, rights & credits of Ebenezer E Stark, to me directed, I have seized 24 window sash, 16 window-blinds, 7 doors, & 2 unfinished doors; & will offer them for sale on Dec 28, in front of the Centre Market.
-H R Maryman, constable

In consequence of an advertisement from my unworthy husband, "whom 'twere gross flattery to call even a coward," I am reluctantly compelled, in justice to myself, to reply to it, & leave the public to judge if I had not a justifiable reason for my conduct. I had submitted, & patiently suffered inhuman & barbarous treatment at his hands, [alias Jacob Wachter's] till forbearance ceased to be a virtue, & was left no alternative for personal safety but precipitate flight. I had been induced by his concessions & promises of amendment under like circumstances once before, to return to him only to be treated worse than at first, & therefore feared to venture my life again under his roof, although earnestly solicited by him so to do on the very evening previous to which his notice first appeared in the Intelligencer.
–Margaret Wachter

Ofcrs attached to the U S ship **St Mary's**, now lying at Norfolk, furnished by Lt Simms, of the Marine Corps. Cmder John L Saunders; 1st Lt C H Kennedy; 2nd, Wm R K Taylor; 3rd Chas R Stedman; 4th Chas Morris; Master, Joshua D Todd; Lt of Marines, John D Simms; Purser, Z L T Waller; Surgeon, J C Palmer; Prof of Mathematics, J McDuffie; Assist Surgeon, W A Harris; Passed Midshipmen, J B Clitz & R H Getty; Midshipmen, Robt Selden, J H Russell, W Van Wyck, W V Gilliss, J H Sharpe, & J N Upshur.

Mrd: on Dec 19, by Rev G W Samson, Thornton A Doniphan, M D, to Mrs Ann Faithful, all of Wash City.

Died: on Nov 28, at Alexandria, D C, Wm C Gardner, merchant, a highly respected resident of that city. [The notice of this gentleman's death ought to have been published at the time of his decease, but was inadvertently omitted.]

Died: on Dec 20, at her residence, near Wash City, in her 27th year, Cordelia Ellen, w/o Wm Holmead. By her death her husband has become bereft of an affectionate & confiding wife, & 3 little girls [too young to know their loss] have lost a doting & indulgent mother. In all the varied relations of mother, dght, sister, friend, & wife, she was a model of admiration & of imitation. During an illness of several weeks, her suffering, which at times were excruciating, were born with a degree of patience & resignation almost incredible. Her funeral wil take place from her late residence, on Dec 22, at 2 o'clock.

Died: yesterday, Geo M Kendall, jr, in his 6th year. His funeral will take place tomorrow at 2 o'clock, at the residence of Gen M Kendall.

Orphans Court of Wash Co, D C. Letters of administration on the personal estate of Edw Harvey, late of said county, dec'd. –Saml Redfern, adm

MON DEC 23, 1844
The Mobile papers announce the death of Martin Durand, one of the oldest & most respected merchants of that city. [No date-current item.]

Isaac Joyner, Whig, has been elected to the Senate of the State of N C from Pitt Co, in place of Mr Foreman, dec'd.

Destructive fire in Salem, Mass, on Dec 18, broke out in that town, originating in the steam sawing & planning establishement of Jas N Buffum, on Front st, & spread with unparalleled rapidity. Some 40 or 50 bldgs of all descriptions are totally destroyed. The entire loss of property is estimated at $100,000.

For rent: desirable residence on 3rd st, near Pa ave, adjoining the residence of Judge Thruston. For terms apply to F Black.

$10 reward for return of a sorrel Horse, stolen from the subscriber, living at Rossburg. Additional reward of $20 for the detection & arrest of the thief.
-Richd Batts, Rossburg

U S District Court, sitting in admiralty at New Orleans, Hon T H McCaleb, Judge, a decree was given on Thu week in favor of Geo H Caldwell & owners of the steamer **Buckeye**, [which boat was sunk by collision wiht the steamer **De Soto** in Mar last,] against the owners of the **De Soto** for $5,500 & costs.

Anti-Rent party of N Y meeting at the village of Smokey Hollow, in Columbia Co, resulted in the death of a man from Hillsdale, a spectator, named Rizenburgh. He had spoken against the proceedings, & was required by one of the "Indians" to cry "down with the rent." He refused, & the Indian shot him with his pistol, & he expired immediately.

Mr Matthew C Field, formerly attached to the New Orleans Picayune, & recently the editor of the St Louis Reveille, died a few days ago on his passage from Boston to Pensacola, whither he was going for the benefit of his health.

In a recent trial at Talladega, Ala, in the case of Hammock & wife against Hay & wife, for slander a verdict was rendered for the plntf for $10,000.

Cumberland Civilian: Wm Price has given Dr Fitzpatrick notice of his intention to contest his seat as a member of the House of Delegates of Md from Alleghany Co, on ground of being returned upon fraudulent & illegal votes.

The undersigned is provided with a complete assortment of Confectionary & Toys, & other articles suited for Christmas presents. His store is on the north side of Pa ave, a few doors west of 4½ st. –W Grupe

House of Reps: 1-Ptn of Gideon Walker, praying compensation for services rendered the U S as an enlisted soldier from the eyar 1792 to 1795. 2-Memorial of the administrator of Robt Carroll Brent, for a pension due the father of said Robt. 3-Ptn of Frances Swann & others, for compensation for 5 hogsheads of tobacco destroyed by the British during the late war. 4-Ptn of Fleming Wood, praying to be indemnified for property seized by ofcrs of the U S for an alleged violation of the laws regulating trade & intercourse with the Indians.

Circuit Court of Wash Co, D C-in Equity. Thos Dunlap & Jos R Ingersoll, vs, Saml Grice, Chas F Sibbald, Danl Mann, Geo M Bibb, [Sec of the Treasury,] & others interested. Bill of cmplnt: Chas F Sibbald, of Phil City, in 1837, was a petitioner to Congress for relief & indemnity, in consequence of damages & injuries sustained by him by reason of the interference of agents of the U S with his rights & property in the territory of Florida; & that in 1842 an act was passed by Congress for his relief; that the said Sibbald executed an assignment of part of the moneys which might be awarded under said act to the cmplnts upon trusts set forth in said assignment; that before the said act had passed the said Sibbald issued certificates of loan, which certificates were to be paid out of the portion of the award which your cmplnts, as trustees, were to receive & pay to the certificate holders; that an award had been made under the said act, which falls far short of the amount of the certificates issued. The cmplnts deemed it their duty to call upon the Sec of the Treasury for payment of the amount so awarded in behalf of the said certificate holders, they having no other object or interest in the present proceeding than to protect the interests of the said certificate holders. But a certain Saml Grice claims to have a prior lien upon the said fund, & has filed a bill in equity against the said Chas F Sibbald for the purpose of sustaining his claim. A certain Wm L Jaudon, by virtue of a deed of assignment, in trust, executed by the said Sibbald, & in behalf of such assignee, or of Ashbel G Jaudon, or some other person substituted for such assignee, claims that the said fund should be paid to him as agent & atty of said assignee, or substitute of such assignee, or otherwise. A certain Danl Mann, alleging himself to be one of the said certificate holders, has also claimed a part of said fund; & divers other parties unknown to the cmplnts, claiming the said fund, or parts thereof, have exhibited their claims to the Treasury Dept & demanded payment thereof. The cmplnts aver that the Sec of the Treasury is without jurisdiction in the case, & has request & advised the parties to present the subject before this Court, & to invoke its aid by a bill in the nature of a bill of interpleader, praying that they may be paid the amount justly represented by them, or such part thereof as to the Court may seem reasonable & just, & such further relief in the premises as may be deemed just & equitable. The bill also states that several of said dfndnts reside out of the jurisdiction of the said Court-to wit, in the city of Phil. Said dfndnts to appear at the Circuit Court on the 4th Mon of Mar next. —Wm Brent, clerk

Land for sale: his tract of land, within less than 1 mile of Gtwn: bounded on its whole southern line by the new free road leading from 7th st to the Little, Falls Bridge, & on its entire eastern side by the county road, commonly called the ridge road. An undisputed title will be given. –John W Murdock, residence at Wm Collins', near Hayman's Brewery, Wash.

Public Sale: on Dec 30, at the late residence of Basil Loveless, dec'd, on the Wash & Rockville Turnpike, in Wash Co, D C, the following personal property, to wit, 4 head of horses, 3 colts, 6 cows, 2 shoats, & poultry, a small lot of pork, farming utensils, household & kitchen furniture. –Charlotte Loveless, Benoni Loveless, administrators of Basil Loveless, dec'd

Local News: Church Directory:
Catholic Churches:
St Patrick's Church, F st, between 9th & 10th sts. Very Rev Dr Matthews, Pastor; Rev Jas B Donelan, Assist Pastor. Service 7½ o'clock, 11 o'clock A M & 4 o'clock P M.
St Matthew's Church, at the corner of 15th & G sts. Rev J P Donelan, Pastor; Rev Jas Myers, Assist. Services 7½ o'clock A M, 11 o'clock A M, & 4 o'clock P M
St Peter's, Capitol Hill, 3rd st east. Rev Jas Van Horseigh, Pastor. Services 7½ o'clock A M, 11 o'clock A M, & 4 o'clock P M.
Protestant Episcopal Churches:
St John's Church, President's Square. Rev Wm Hawley, Rector; Rev Smith Pyne, Assist Rector. Service 11 o'clock A M & 3 o'clock P M.
Christ's Church, Navy Yard. Rev Mr Bean, Rector. Service 11 o'clock A M & 3 o'clock P M.
Trinity Church, 5th st, between D & E sts. Rev H Stringfellow, Rector. Service 11 o'clock A m & 7 o'clock P M.
Church of the Epiphany, G st, between 12th & 13th sts. Rev John W French, Rector. Service 11 o'clock & 3 o'clock P M.
Church of the Ascension, H st, between 9th & 10th sts. Rev L J Gilliss, Rector. The congregation meet for worship at Mr McLeod's Academy in 9th st. Service 11 o'clock A M & 3 o'clock P M.
Methodist Episcopal Churches:
Foundry Church, corner of G & 14th sts. Rev H Tarring & Rev E D Owens, Pastors. Service 11 o'clock & 6½ o'clock P M.
Wesley Chapel, corner of F & 5th sts. Rev Norval Wilson, Pastor. Service 11 o'clock & 6½ o'clock P M.
Ebenezer Church, 4th st east, between G & E sts. Rev E P Phelps, Pastor. Service 11 o'clock & 6½ o'clock P M.
Ryland Chapel, [unfinished,] corner of 10th & Md ave.
Methodist Church, [unfinished,] Mass ave, between 9th & 10th sts.

Methodist Protestant Churches:
Methodist Protestant Church, 9th st. Rev U Ward, officiating minister. Service 11 o'clock A M & 7 o'clock P M.
Methodist Protestant Church, 6th st east. Rev Mr Murray, officiating minister. Service 11 o'clock A M & 7 o'clock P M.
Baptist Churches:
Baptist Church, 10 st, near E. Rev O B Brown, Pastor. Service 11 o'clock A M & 3 o'clock P M.
Baptist Church, E st near 6th st. Rev G W Samson, Pastor. Service 11 o'clock A M & 7 o'clock P M.
Baptist Church, near the Navy Yard. Service 11 o'clock, A M, & 7 o'clock, P M.
Baptist Church [Shiloh,] Virginia ave, between 4½ & 6th sts. Rev Mr Leechman, Pastor. Service first Sun in every month at 11 o'clock A M.
Presbyterian Churches:
Presbyterian Church, F st. Rev Dr Laurie & Rev Septimus Tuston, Pastors. Service at 11 o'clock A M & 3½ o'clock P M.
First Presbyterian Church, 4½ st. Rev Wm T Sprole, Pastor. Service at 11 o'clock A M & 3½ o'clock P M.
Second Presbyterian Church, N Y ave, between 13th & 14th sts. Rev Jas Knox, Pastor. Service at 11 o'clock A M & 3½ o'clock P M.
Fourth Presbyterian Church, 9th st, between G & H sts. Rev John C Smith, Pastor. Service at 11 o'clock A M & 3½ o'clock P M.
Unitarian Church:
Corner of D & 6th sts. Rev Mr Hale, officiating Minister. Service 11 o'clock A M & 7 o'clock P M.
St Paul's English Lutheran Church:
Corner of 11th & H sts. Rev A A Muller, D D, Pastor. Service at 11 o'clock A M & 3 o'clock P M. [As this new church edifice is not yet in a condition to be occupied, 2 or 3 weeks may elapse before meetings can be held in it.]
Swedenborgian Church:
Meet at the Council Chamber, City Hall. Service at 11 o'clock A M.
German Evangelical Church:
Corner of G & 21st sts. Rev A Biervand, Pastor. Service at 11 o'clock A M.
Friends' Meeting House:
On I st, between, 18th & 19th sts. Service First day at 11 o'clock, & Fourth day at 3 o'clock.
[Dec 30th newspaper: correction-Of the Presbyterian Church, F st, we learn that Rev Dr Laurie is Pastor, & Rev Septimus Tuston, Assist Pastor. The service in the Fourth Presbyterian Church, Rev John C Smith, commenced at 3: 30 P M, should have been at 7 o'clock P M.]

Mrd: on Dec 19, by Rev Norval Wilson, Mr Saml Bond to Mrs Ann Hendley, all of Wash City.

Died: on Dec 20, at Balt, Mrs Sophonisba Breckenridge, consort of Rev Dr Breckenridge, after a long & painful illness.

TUE DEC 24, 1844
Persons wishing to make Christmas presents would do well to call & examine my stock of Perfumery, corner of 4½ st & the avenue. –M Delany

Watches, jewelry, silver spoons, & spectacles. –Jas Galt, between 9th & 10th st, Pa ave, Wash

Senate: 1-Ptn of Robt Ramsay, asking a pension. 2-Ptn of Mary Colton, asking a pension. 3-Ptn of Jas Mitchell, praying the right of pre-emption to a tract of land in Missouri. 4-Ptn of Philip Ward, asking a pension. 5-Two memorials of Wm H Thomas, praying compensation for corn, provisons, & clothing furnished the Cherokee Indians in the year 1836. 6-Ptn of S D Marchand, of Arkansas, praying indemnity for French spoliations prior to 1800. 7-Cmte on the Judiciary: reported a bill for the relief of Asa Andrews, without amendment. 8-Cmte on Military Affairs: reported a bill for the relief of Joshua Shaw. 9-Cmte on Private Land Claims: reported a bill for the relief of the heirs of Wm Fisher. 10-Cmte on Pensions: reported without amendment a bill for the relief of Mark Simpson. 11-Engrossed bills passed: relief of Gideon Batchelor; of Jas McFarlane; of Jas Ritchie; of Pierre Menard, Edw Roberts, & others. 12-Joint resolution allowing Purser Thornton an allowance in the settlement of his accounts.

Mrd: on Dec 22, in Gtwn, by Rev Mr Flanegan, French S Johnson, of Va, to Miss Emily Crow, of the former place.

Died: on Nov 18, on his estate near the Chesapeake Bay, Anne Arundel Co, Md, Jos Galloway Harrison, aged 58 years. This estimable gentleman was the last male occupant of one of the most ancient family seats in Md. By his industry & enterprise he added largely to his paternal estate, & his exemplary & pious life gave a happy assurance that he had exchanged his earthly inheritance for one far better & brighter, & that fadeth not away.

The Wheeling Gaz & Times, 2 respectable newspapers at Wheeling, have become united, & for the future will be under the proprietorship of J E Wharton, of the Times. Mr W has long been connected with the public press.

From Europe: The Princess Sophia Matilda, sister of the late Duke of Glouceser, & cousin of the Kings Geo IV, & Wm, & of Queen Victoria's father, died Nov 29, in her 72nd year.

For rent: 2 story brick house immediately fronting the east wing of the City Hall. For the key & further particulars apply to Mr A Baldwin, a short distance east of the house.

To the Public: I have transferred all my professional business in the Circuit Court of Wash Co, D C to Henry May, who will be found at my late Ofc, in the east wing of the City Hall, & where my clients will please to call upon him. My son, Robt J Brent, of Balt, will aid in the trial of such cases as his services may be required in. Having removed from Wash City, to pursue my profession in the South, all those having unsettled business with me in my profession as an Atty, will please to communicate with H May, & such as have business connected with private affairs will please to address themselves to R J Brent, of Balt, Md. –Wm L Brent

The subscriber will render all accounts on Jun 1, 1845, & hopes this notice will be sufficient to induce all to settle their accounts. –C H James, 14th & E sts

WED DEC 25. 1844
On Dec 14, as the steamboat **Belle of Clarksville**, from New Orleans for Nashville, was rounding the bar below the Horseshoe Cut-off, she came in collision with the steamboat **Louisiana**, from Memphis on her way to New Orleans. The **Belle of Clarksville** did not obey her helm, but sheered off, by which she came directly across the bow of the **Louisiana**. List of those who lost their lives, nearly all were residents of West Tenn.

Wm Tabb	Wm Jones	Son of J W Hull
P Linn	T Whitley	J Peay
W Linn	N T Allen	Jno Holliday, assist-
J Ryan	A Kirkland	engineer
R Malisle	J Askew	
N Sills	G Hyer	

House of Reps: 1-Ptn of the heirs of Wm Cohen: presented. 2-Ptn of Simeon Butterfield, of Chelsea, Mass, for a reduction of postage. 3-Ptn of Alex'r Hebert & others, praying that the said Hebert may be allowed to bring into the U S a certain family of negroes taken into Texas by his ancestor, aged 90 years, which negroes have left a large number of friends & relations in the State of Louisiana. 4-Ptn of Lydia Baker, wid/o Josiah Baker, asking for a pension. 5-Ptn of Saml Larrabee, for a pension for Revolutionary services. 6-Ptn of Wm Allen, asking for a pension. 7-Ptn of Nice Berry, wid/o Beletiah Berry, asking for a pension. 8-Ptn of Holt Ingraham, of Portland, Maine, asking compensation for services rendered the U S. 9-Ptn of Jos Lawrence, praying that certain duties by him paid may be refunded.

A Mr Starrett, who resided about 6 miles from Fairmount, Marion Co, Va, was murdered on Dec 10 by 2 young men named Coon & Boober.

Appointments by the Pres:
J P Schatzel, to be U S Consul for the port of Matamoras, vice R H Belt, dec'd.
Jas Miller, to be Collector of Customs for the District of Salem & Beverly, Mass.
Cornelius P Van Ness, to be Collector of Customs for the District of N Y.
Lorenzo F Lee, to be Collector of Customs for the District of Bridgetown, N J.
Wm H Marriott, to be Collector of Customs for the District of Balt, Md.
Reuben T Thom, re-appointed Deputy Postmaster at Fredericksburg, Va.
Pleasant S Ward, to be Postmaster, Shawneetown, Ill, vice John Stickney, removed.

Promotions in the Navy:
Promotions:

Wm Jameson, to be a Capt   Chas A Hassler, to be a Surgeon
Henry Eagle, to be a Cmder

To be Lts:
John Cassin Henry   Jas Withers Read
Wm A Wayne   Washington A Bartlett
Jas S Riddle   Francis Winslow
C R Perry Rodgers

Appointments:
To be Assist Surgeons:
Jas Hamilton   Robt T Maccoun
Chas H Oakley   Wm A Harris
Bernard Henry, jr   Robt E Wall

To be Pursers:
Jas A Semple   Jas H Watmough

Mrs E Turance has just arrived from Balt with a splendid assortment of French & other Millinery. Her stay in this city is limited, & she asks an early call at Mrs Marshall's store, Pa ave, south side, between 9th & 10th st.

Died: on Nov 19, in Wash, Jas T Davis, in his 42nd year. His sudden call from this life is a dispensation so afflictive, that to Him alone who dealt the blow the bereaved must look for solace.

Died: on Mon last, after a painful illness of 2 months, Mr Peter McCaffrey, a native of the county of Fermannagh, Ireland, in his 45th year. His funeral will take place from his late residence, on Md ave near B st, at 3 o'clock this afternoon.

Died: on Dec 22, at her residence, near Balt, in her 77th year, Mrs Eliz Clark, wid/o Mr Francis Clark, dec'd, formerly of Wash City. Mrs C was a native of the county Angrim, Ireland; but for many years had been a valuable & respected member of our community, before her removal to Balt. Her death will be keenly felt by her bereaved family, & deeply mourned by many friends. Her funeral will take place from Dr Laurie's Church, F st, tomorrow, at 12 o'clock.

Wash Corp: 1-Ptn of John F Grimes, praying the remission of a fine: referred to the Cmte of Claims. Same for R C Washington & others. 2-Ptn of Jos Peek, praying to be released from the payment of a certain bond: referred to the Cmte of Claims. 3-Ptn of J B Mills & others, praying for a gravel foot-walk on 9th st west: referred to the Cmte on Improvements. 4-Cmte of Claims: asking to be discharged from the further consideration of the ptn of Philip Ennis.

House of Reps: 1-Cmte of Claims: bill for the relief of Wm P Zantzinger. 2-Cmte of Claims: the bill form the Senate for the relief of the heirs of Robt Fulton: presented. 3-Cmte of Claims: adverse report on the case of Sally W Griffith, excx of Eliz Thompson. 4-Cmte on Indian Affairs: asking to be discharged from the further consideration of the Senate bill for the relief of the legal reps of Joshua Kennedy, dec'd, & that it be referred to the Cmte of Claims. Agreed to. 5-Cmte on Naval Affairs: asking to be discharged from the further consideration of the case of Reuben Taylor: & that it be referred to the Cmte on Revolutionary Pensions. Agreed to. 6-Cmte on Revolutionary Pensions: bill for the relief of Richd Elliot; a bill for the relief of Susannah Scott; a bill for the relief of Eliz Jones & others, heirs of John Carr. Same cmte: bill for the relief of Eliz Fitch. 7-Cmte on Invalid Pensions: report adverse to the ptn of Jos Bowlen. Also, asking to be discharged from the further consideration of the ptn of John Farnham, & that it be laid on the table. Same cmte: bill for the relief of Isaac Allen. Same cmte; asking to be discharged from the further consideration of the memorial of Alex'r Gutheridge, & that it lie on the table. Agreed to. Same cmte: bill for the relief of Eliz Blodgett.

Paul Beck, of Phil, died on Sat. He had attained to a very advanced age, &, owing to blindness & other infirmities of declining life, had for a year or two past mingled very little with the public. He was formerly one of the most enterprising merchants of Phil, & had acquired a large fortune. His death will be mourned by thousands, & his good deeds held in continued grateful remembrance. –U S Gaz

FRI DEC 27, 1844
House of Reps: 1-Ptn of McHatten & Herdon, praying compensation for carrying the U S mail. 2-Ptn of Jonathan Cowdery & others, surgeons & assist surgeons in the navy at the Norfolk station, praying for assimilated or correlative rank with the other ofcrs of the navy. 3-Memorial of A D Foster & others of Worcester, Mass, praying for a modification of the laws on the subject of postage & the carrying of the mail. 4-Ptn of Sam L Breese, capt, & 30 others, commissioned & warrant ofcrs on board U S frig **Cumberland**, on the Mediterranean station, praying that the spirit portion of the navy ration may be abolished. 5-Memorial of Mrs Ann J Ross, of Va, praying for a pension on account of the services of her dec'd husband.

$30 reward for strayed or stolen from Josiah Suit's farm, 4 miles below Bladensburg, PG Co, Md, a bright bay Mare. $15 for the conviction of the thief. Address: Bladensburg, Md-Grafton Suit.

For rent: dwlg & store on A st, Capitol Hill, south side, opposite Capitol yard. Apply to Eliz Barron, or Wm W Stewart, Agent.

Superior piano forte for sale: one of the best instruments of that celebrated maker, Rosenkrantz. -R W Dyer & Co, aucts

To the Editors; Messrs Gales & Seaton. As a duty I owe to the citizens of Wash, I take the liberty to inform you that I came on here from Balt, with my wife, in search of an orphan female child, about age 14 years, who was abducted from her home on the Eastern Shore of Md by a base woman, Mary Berry, alias Lackey Berry, alias Coyle. Said base woman is a fugitive from justice, as there are criminal indictments now on the docket of the City Court of Balt for which she has not been tried. Said base woman, in the early part of last Oct, abducted 2 orphan female children from the Eastern Shore. We succeeded in finding one of them in Balt. The oldest of the two we found in this city this morning, in a house kept by the said base woman Mary Berry, alias Lackey Berry, alias Coyle. The house is on C st, near 13th, & has a sign on the side of the door,"Mrs Coyle, Dress Maker." This is for a cloak. After many weeks of making search & inquiry in different places, we at last found her as above stated. We, that is my wife & myself, came on to this city & made cmplnt to the U S District Atty, & that gentleman, together with Counsellor Carlisle, instituted the legal warrants for the arrest of said base woman & her own dght, who did aid in the abduction of the 2 poor orphan females, & in particular the one we found in this city. Mrs McKnight is the aunt of the child, being the mother's sister & the next of kin to the child. We had the base woman & her dght brought before Judge Cranch, & he decided that the child should be placed in the hands of her aunt, out of the possession of said base woman. The next step was that the base woman & her dght were found guilty of the abduction of the child we found in her house, which was proved to be a house of infamy, & the base woman & her dght were committed to prison to await the requistion of the Executive of Md. Now, Messrs Editors, will the citizens of this city say that said base woman should go free or be dealt with by the law as she richly deserves? I hope no gentleman will be found that will approve of her base conduct. Said base woman has been guilty of prostituting her own dght, & is it any wonder she would now abduct poor orphan females with the intention of said base purposes? But, thank God, we rescued her this day. We return our thanks to P R Fendall, Counselor Carlisle, Esquire Thompson, & also of ofcrs Burr, Dexter, Mills, & other gentlemen who aided us to arrest said base woman & her dght; & now we feel grateful, & return our sincere thanks to Chief Judge Cranch for his kindness & righteous decision; & we thank the witnesses who testified to the base course of said woman, & their knowledge of how she had this child in durance; &, in conclusion, trust that every such den of iniquity will be broken up. And now we leave the city with the poor child. Her own aunt is happy in rescuing the child, & only wishes that this circumstance will put an end to her base career. Very respectfully, your obedient servant, Jas H McKnight, Wash, Dec 24, 1844.

Fire broke out on Christmas Day in the rear of 2 confectionary stores occupied by Mr Norbeck & Mr Jeremiah Murphy, on Pa ave, between 9th & 10th sts. The fire seems to have originated in the chimney. The bldgs were owned by Mr N Travers, who is insured. Mr Norbeck's stock in trade was not insured. Mr Murphy is partially insured. Mr Griffin's shoe store also caught fire, & was pretty burnt.

Oxford, Nov 2. The Rev Chas Penny, M A, student of Christ Church, & curate of Ashendon, has resigned his studentship on conforming to the Roman Catholic Faith. A letter has been received from Rev J H Newman, of Littlemore, addressed to Rev Isaac Williams, author of the famous tract "On Reserve," & intimating that he can no longer continue a member of the English Church. The intelligence has created a great sensation, as it is supposed Mr Newman' secession will be followed by that of several others.

Circuit Court of Wash Co, D C-in Chancery. John Easter of John et al, composing the firm of Easter, Brother & Co, vs Wm W Orme, Chas E Orme, Emily B Orme, Frances D Orme, et al. This bill is filed by the cmplnts in behalf of themselves & other creditors of Wm C Orme, one of the dfndnts. The bill charges that on Nov 18, 1842, said Wm C Orme was largely indebted to the cmplnts & others in several debts yet remaining unpaid, & was then greatly embarrassed & unable to pay his debts at maturity, if not actually insolvent; that he was then seized of the west half of lot 11 in square A of Wash City, with valuable improvements thereon, worth $3,500 or more, & constituting a large protion of his entire property; & being so seized thereof, on said date, he made a voluntary settlement & conveyance thereof to the dfndnt Wm Ward, in trust for certain infant children of said Wm C Orme, of whom the dfndnts named in the titling of this order are the only survivors & parties entitled; that the said conveyance left the said W C Orme wholly insolvent & unable to pay his debts; that said Wm C Orme afterwards, on Apr 20, 1843, without having in the interval increased his debts or diminished his assets, except as aforesaid, made a general conveyance of all his remaining assets, of every description, to John N Brown, as trustee for the equal benefit of all the creditors of said Wm C Orme, & said trust has been duly & faithfully administered by said trustee; & it is certainly ascertained that the trust fund is greatly insufficient to pay said debts, & a large portion of the debts to the cmplnts & others will remain wholly unsatisfied from that source; & said Wm C Orme is entirely without other property out of which the deficiency can be satisfied. The objects of the bill are to have the said conveyance to Wm Ward set aside & annulled, & the said half lot & premises subjected to the payment of the remaining debts owing to the cmplnts & others who may become parties to this suit, according to their respective right of priority or quality, & for general relief. And forasmuch as it is represented that the dfndnts, Wm W Orme, Chas E Orme, Emily B Orme, & Frances D Orme, reside & are out of D C, it is by the Court this 19th day of Dec, 1844, ordered that said dfndnts do, on or before the first Mon of May next, appear in Court & show cause, if any they have, why a decree should not pass as prayed. –Wm Brent, clk

Circuit Court of Wash Co, D C-in Equity. John Baldwin vs Chas Ely. The bill of cmplnt in this case in substance states that the cmplnt was one of the citizens of the U S who had claims upon the Mexican Gov't provided for by the convention between the U S & Mexico; that his claims were presented to the Board of Com'rs organized under said convention, & a large sum of money was awarded to the cmplnt by the said Board; that, after said awards were made, the Treasury Dept of the U S, by virtue of authority conferred upon it by Congress, made & issued to the cmplnt & other claimants certificates for the amount so awarded, in & by which the U S promised to pay to the cmplnt or his assigns the sum specified in said certificates whenever the same should be received from the Mexican Gov't. The cmplnt shows that, among the certificates thus made & issued to him, there were three numbered as follows, viz Nos 989, 990, & 991, which were the sole & exclusive property of the cmplnt, & that as such he had them in his possession, & that there has been received from the Mexican Gov't at the Treasury Dept of the U S large sums of money for & on account of said awards, whereof the cmplnt is entitled to receive his ratable proportion; & that each of said certificates is for the sum of $1,000. And the bill further shows that while the cmplnt was in possession of the said certificates, he wrote his name on the back of them, but without any word of transfer or assignment, & still continued to hold the same as the lawful owner thereof; & that while the said certificates were thus held by him, the said 3 above certificates were either lost by him or as he believes stolen from his possession; that the cmplnt on discovering the said abstraction notified the Treasury Dept of the fact, with a request that payment might be stopped on them; that the Sec of the Treasury agreed to suspend their payment until the cmplnt should have an opportunity to obtain possession of them, or assert his right to the same by some legal proceedings; that the cmplnt, after diligent inquiries, was unable to ascertain where said certificates were or by whom held; but that in Jan last application was made to the Treasury Dept by Hon Osmyn Baker in behalf of Chas Ely, of N Y C, stating that he held the 3 certificates so as aforesaid lost or purloined from the cmplnt, & claiming payment for the same. The bill further states that as the said Osmyn Baker is a member of Congress & not amenable to the process of this Court, & that as Ely is a non-resident, the cmplnt is remediless in the premises save in this Court; therefore he prays that said dfndnt may be required to prove & show to this Court how the certificates were procured from the cmplnt, & that he be required to produce the same before this Court, & be decreed to deliver up the same to the cmplnt, & that the cmplnt may have such other relief in the premises as may be agreeable to equity & good conscience. Said dfndnt to appear at the Circuit Court of Wash Co, D C on the 4th Mon of Mar next, to answer said bill.
–W Cranch, Chief Judge -W Brent, clerk

Mrd: on Sun last, by Rev O B Brown, Mr Saml Kelly to Eliz, y/d/o Mr John Sessford.

Mrd: on Dec 25, by Rev Mr Tarring, Mr E E Brown, of Md, to Miss Mary A Moore, of Wash City.

There is great reason to fear that the steamboat **Mount Pleasant** is lost, & all on board have perished-says the N Y Commercial Advertiser. She sailed from N Y on the 10th, for Phil. The boat had been purchased by Messrs McMain & Schober, of Phil, to run to Lewistown, Delaware. Mr McMain was on board with a crew which he brought on from Phil. We can only learn the name of one of them, Capt Clifton, the pilot. The engineer, Erastus Hilton, was from Albany, where he has left a wife & 2 children.

Senate: 1-Ptn of the wid/o the late Jos Nourse. 2-Ptn from the heirs of Elijah Hall, asking indemnity for French spoliations prior to 1800: referred. 3-Ptn of Dr C Taylor, a Surgeon in the Revolutionary army, asking a pension. 4-Ptn of Richd Phillips, for an order of survey. 5-Ptn of John McClennahan, claiming back pay for services in the army during the Western wars. 6-Ptn of John Youngman & other citizens of Arkansas, asking for a post route. 7-Bills to be engrosses-relief of: Wm Ritch; of David Shaw & others; & of Wm Russell. 8-Bill for the relief of the sureties of Saml Swartwout: passed. 9-Memorial of Wm Couch, a colored man, of Fairfield, Conn, who is now free, claiming a pension for services rendered in the Revolutionary war while he was a slave: referred to the Cmte on Revolutionary Pensions. 10-Bill for the relief of Jos Holmes & others, owners & legal reps of the crew of the schnr Industry: referred to the Cmte on Commerce. 11-Resolved, that the Clerk of the House be authorized to grant leave of absence for 6 weeks to Mr R M Lusk, an assistant clerk in his ofc, whose health is now such as to render him unable to perform his duties, & that he be also authorized to employ an assistant in Mr Lusk's place, at the same rate of compensation, to be paid out of the contingent fund, during the sickness of Mr Lusk.

Died: on Dec 25, Thomas Chase, twin son of Wm G Ridgely, in his 19th year. His funeral is from the residence of his father in Gtwn, today at 12 o'clock.

Died: on Dec 11, at her residence, near Upper Marlborough, PG Co, Md, after a short & painful illness, Mrs Pamela Chesley, w/o Zadox C Chesley, & eldest d/o the late Tobias Belt. The decease of this estimable lady has caused an irreparable loss to her distressed husband & 2 infant children, as well as to many near relatives.

Died: on Dec 26, after a lingering & painful illness, Jas Robertson, infant s/o Edwin S & Anna Maria L Arnold.

An estray female Mule, of black color, came to my premises about 4 days ago. Owner is to call on the subscriber, near the Congressional Burying Ground, & pay for this advertisement, to obtain her. –Wm Clarke

$5 reward: sold by an unauthorized person, or stolen from the public space opposite the Centre Market, a small sheet-iron cylinder Stove. I will give the above reward for any information that shall lead to the detection of the offender & the recovery of the stove. --T M Milburn

SAT DEC 28, 1844
Mr Wm Calder, of Wilmington N C, was lost overboard from the steamer **Govn'r Dudley**, on his way from Charleston, Dec 20. He was standing near the wheelhouse conversing with the capt when his hat blew off, &, in the effort to recover it, he was precipitated overboard, directly under one of the paddlewheels. He was a native of Charlestown, Mass.

By 2 writs of fieri facias, at the suit of Walter Clarke sen, & Walter M Clarke, trading the the firm of Walter Clarke & Son, use of Richd L Walton, at the suit of A McMakin & E Holden, trading under the firm of McMakin & Holden, against the goods & chattels, lands & tenements, rights & credits of John Evans, & to me directed, I have seized furniture, the property of said Evans, & will offer the same for sale on Jan 4, 1845, for cash. --H R Maryman, constable

Mr Mills, of Wheeling, Va, having been repeatedly robbed lately, he prepared a pistol so that when the door was opened it would go off. He forgot the contrivance, & was himself the first to enter the store, when the contents entered his chest. He lies in a critical condition.

House of Reps: 1-Bill for the relief of J McFarland: referred to the Cmte of Claims. 2-Bill for the relief of Gideon Batchelder & others: referred to the Cmte of Claims. 3-Bill for the relief of the legal reps of Pierre Menard, Josiah T Betts, Jacob Feaman, & Edmund Roberts, sureties of Felix St Vrain, dec'd, late an Indian agent: referred to the Cmte on the Judiciary. 4-Bill for the relief of Jas Ritchie: referred to the Cmte of Claims. 5-Ptn of Thos Thornley & John R Queen, a cmte on behalf of the Anacostia Navy Yard Fire Co, Wash City. 6-Ptn of Francis Dodge, for a pension. 7-Ptn of Mrs Lydia Bartoll, of Mass, for a pension. 8-Ptn of Isaac Johnson, of Cass Co, Indiana, praying relief. 9-Ptn of Wm Scott, of Beaver Co, Pa, for a pension.

Died: yesterday, of congestion on the brain, Jas S Ringgold, of the State Dept. His funeral will take place on Sun at 1 o'clock, at his late residence on Gay st, Gtwn.

Died: on Dec 19, in Raleigh, N C, in her 18th year, Sarah E Saunders, d/o the Hon R M Saunders. Following within a month the loss of a brother who was the hope & pride of his parents, the death of the sister has excited a feeling & sympathy, which it is scarcely an exaggeration to say, makes it seem to all as if "there was not a house in which there was not one dead." Raleigh Register

Died: on Dec 19, at his residence, a few miles below Warrenton, Fauquier Co, Va, Dr Aldridge James, after an illness of a few days.

MON DEC 30, 1844
Troy Whig of Thu: the Sheriff of Rensselaer Co, accompanied by the under sheriff & 2 police ofcrs, proceed to Grafton on Tue to arrest the murderers of Elisha Smith. Norman Gager & Henry Lund were arrested without difficulty or resistance. They were both lodged in jail, to await their trial.

Wesley Flavel, convicted at Phil of murder in the 2nd degree in killing his niece, a young girl named McMurray, was on Sat sentenced to be imprisoned in the Cherry Hill Penitentiary for 12 years-the extent of punishment fixed by the statute for the crime. Flavel was once a highly respectable man, but he took to the rum bottle & became a degraded demon.

The schnr **Caledonia**, Capt Brown, of Norfolk, was capsized between the Rip Raps & Sewall's Point on Mon, & every soul on board, 7 in number, perished. Capt Isaac Pugh, of Phil, was on board, & his body, the only one found, was discovered entangled in the ropes.

City Ordinances-Wash. 1-Act for the relief of Anne Cochran: that the fine imposed on her for the alleged violation of the law respecting the excavation of areas, be remitted: provided Cochran pay the costs of prosecution.

Mrd: on Dec 22, by Rev Mr Wilson, Mr Geo L Gillchrest, formerly of Maine, to Miss Clotilde M J Sherlock, of Wash City.

Criminal Court at Phil, Fri last, sentences passed on some of the convicted rioters:
John O'Neil: $1 fine & costs, & 9 months imprisonment.
John Taggart & John McLear: each fined $1 & costs, & 1 month imprisonment.
Patrick Murray: $1 fine & costs, & 6 months imprisonment.
John Bennett: riot at the Nunnery: $1 fine & 4 months imprisonment. Sentence to take effect after the expiration of another sentence for assaulting a police ofcr while arresting him for beating his wife. Bennett pleaded guilty to the charge of riot.
Fred'k Hess-a lad of German birth. Arson on May 7. $1 fine & costs, & 1 year in the Eastern Penitentiary.

$500 reward: was stolen on Nov 10, a female servant, named Mary Frances, about 16 or 17 years old, white, with straight black hair. Reward will be paid for the apprehension & conviction of the thief & delivery of said girl to the subscriber at Thompsonville, Culpeper Co, Va. She calls herself sometimes Mary Frances Lightfoot Roberson. She was suspected of being in the family way. --Geo Ficklin, Thompsonville, Culpeper Co, Va

A lamentable accident at Worcester depot, in Boston, on Mon. Mr Ellingwood, of Boston, was imprudently crossing the track at the moment, & was run over by the train & his body completely severed in two.

TUE DEC 31, 1844
McCormick's Reaper. As the undersigned will at times be absent from home, & as Robt McCormick, sen [his father] will be associated with him in the manufacture of the Reaper, address R & C H McCormick, Steele's Tavern P O, Augusta Co, Va. He will get his Reaper introduced as far as he can in the States of Md & Pa next harvest. –C H McCormick

The case of Rev Chas T Torrey, convicted at Balt of abducting slaves, was disposed of by Balt City Court on Sat, when the motion which had been previously submitted for a new trial, & in arrest of judgment, was overruled, & the prisoner was sentenced, on 3 different indictments, to 6 years & 3 months imprisonment in the penitentiary.

Senate: 1-Ptn of the heirs of Moses White, praying for arrears of pension.
2-Memorial of Capt John Stockton, praying compensation for losses in the late war.
3-Ptn of Saml Merrill & other citizens of Maine, protesting against the annexation of Texas.

Miss Julia A Webster, who was some time ago arrested at Lexington, Ky, on a charge of being an agent of the Abolitionists, sent there to assist slaves in escaping from their masters, has had her trial & been found guilty. The jury returned the verdict of guilty & fixed her punishment at 2 years' confinement in the penitentiary. The members of the jury, in consideration of her sex, signed a petition to the Govn'r for her pardon.

On Sun last W H Tayloe's splendid mansion, at *Mount Airy*, in Richmond Co, Va, was entirely destroyed by fire. Mr Tayloe is at the South, & his family were at church at the time. It is supposed the house was set on fire by a negro woman. The iron chest containing plate & valuable papers was found after the fire bursted open & contents gone. –Alex Gaz

Natchex, Miss, Dec 19. Rencontre took place a few evenings since in Woodville, between Mr B F Herbert, sheriff of Wilkinson Co, & Mr Fenner, a lawyer, which resulted in the death of Mr Herbert from a pistol shot wound received in the fight. Mr Fenner, we learn, acted on the defensive, & will no doubt be acquitted.
–Free Trader

Bristol, Conn: yesterday, Robt Free, a workingman in the knife & fork manufactory of Geo W Bartholomew, in Bristol, was killed instantly by the bursting of a grindstone.

For rent: 3 story brick house on F st, between 13th & 14th sts, at present occupied by Mr Ferguson. Possession about Feb 1. –Apply to Jos Abbott, living on G st.

Overseer & gardener wanted: for my farm, in Fairfax Co, Va. –Francis A Dickins

House of Reps: 1-Hon Wm S Fulton, a Senator from the State of Arkansas, dec'd. Senator Fulton left this city at the close of the last session in good health. Now his remains rest in the sleep of death, beneath the sod of his adopted State. He died at *Rosemont*, his residence, near the city of Little Rock, Arkansas, on Aug 15 last, in his 50th year. He was a native of Cecil Co, Md. He leaves an afflicted widow & bereaved children. 2-Ptn of Bernice McKinstry, of Great Barrington, Mass, for a pension. 3-Ptn of J Warren Newcomb.

Mrd: on Dec 26, by Rev Mr Gasaway, Geo Beall Balch, U S Navy, to Miss Julia Grace Vinson, of Gtwn.

Mrd: on Thu last, by Rev H Stringfellow, Augustus E Perry, [of the firm of Perry & Ashby] to Miss Mary J Ross, all of Wash City.

Died: yesterday, suddenly, in Gtwn, Joseph, 2nd s/o Mrs E H Brawner, aged 10 years. His funeral is from the residence of his mother, at 4 o'clock this afternoon.

Died: on Dec 20, in Alexandria, D C, Rev Dr Benj A Young, S J. The dec'd was a descendant of the early settlers of Md, & was connected with the most respectable families of that State & the District of Columbia. He was for many years Professor of Rhetoric & Philosophy at St John's College, Fredericktown, & was well known as a gentleman & scholar of profound worth, eminent in learning, & in his social relations respected & esteemed by all.

A

Abbot, 16, 233, 386
Abbott, 63, 113, 127, 238, 431, 441, 515, 536
Abell, 344
Abercrombie, 326, 517
Abert, 148, 455
Abott, 206
Abrams, 340
Acken, 23, 206, 249, 451, 506, 516, 517
Acker, 459
Ackerman, 429
Ackey, 313
Ackley, 315
Acklin, 134
Acton, 185, 301
Adams, 2, 5, 13, 21, 63, 69, 71, 74, 81, 91, 108, 135, 142, 173, 177, 191, 206, 214, 246, 254, 256, 262, 288, 313, 323, 341, 353, 366, 369, 372, 383, 394, 438, 454, 486, 501, 504, 506, 516
Addams, 267
Addison, 62, 112, 351, 509
Addition, 170
Adie, 35, 206, 375
Adkins, 31
Adler, 393, 407, 486
Adriance, 313
Agate, 216
Agnew, 156
Ailier, 459
Ainsworth, 132, 430
Airy, 422
Akenson, 18, 120, 272
Aker, 424
Akison, 244, 256
Alabatcha, 81
Alberger, 105
Albert, 352
Albright, 221

Alden, 101
Aldrich, 27, 71, 435
Alesbury, 196
Alexander, 106, 140, 151, 206, 212, 270, 271, 281, 291, 337, 358, 361, 375, 420, 512
Alford, 513
Alfred, 309
Alien wife, 152
Aliwinn, 36
All the Chances, 170
Allan, 89, 345, 407
Allcott, 39
Allen, 35, 44, 54, 55, 56, 57, 60, 94, 107, 121, 136, 141, 157, 158, 175, 178, 196, 206, 210, 220, 228, 281, 292, 296, 320, 330, 344, 351, 365, 406, 424, 446, 470, 472, 484, 506, 516, 519, 526, 528
Allens, 116
Alliance, 197
Allis, 57
Allison, 31
Allsberger, 337
Allspach, 244, 256, 281, 298
Allston, 467, 474
Almonte, 239
Almy, 27
Alpack, 139
Alricks, 142
Alvey, 81, 97
Alward, 26
Ambler, 107, 206, 245, 257, 270
Ame, 283
American pay, 238
Ames, 72, 179, 367
Amesbury, 411
Amie, 65, 125
Ammen, 438
Amos, 212, 434, 468
Ancrum, 165
Anderson, 7, 34, 41, 63, 70, 78, 80, 108, 133, 147, 189, 195, 199, 201,

206, 211, 249, 276, 282, 286, 296,
303, 354, 356, 363, 430, 477, 478,
495, 496, 509
Andon, 497
Andrae, 289
Andre, 247
Andree, 459
Andrews, 27, 137, 146, 155, 283, 361,
394, 419, 447, 449, 486, 516, 525
Andry, 344
Angurea, 467
Angus, 24
Anna, 313
Annan, 15, 212, 419
Anthony, 206
Antumes, 335
Antunez, 335
Appleton, 52, 229, 317
Arabin, 387
Archbold, 412, 446
Archer, 95, 101, 106, 113, 212, 215,
230, 274, 434
Ardon Corrected, 168
Argueles, 489
Argyle, 277
Aristotle, 167
Armand, 291
Armfield, 284
Armistead, 278, 326
Armisted, 457
Armor, 187
Armstead, 167, 170
Armstrong, 19, 51, 81, 84, 97, 133,
277, 384, 423, 431, 462, 471
Arner, 401
Arney, 347
Arnold, 32, 176, 212, 288, 363, 432,
532
Arns, 314
arnum, 214
Arraro, 230
Arsenal, 468
Arsenith, 272
Arthur, 15, 27

Artis, 221
Artot, 199
Asbury, 39
Asby, 12, 277
Aschley, 279
Aschon, 146
Ashburner, 318
Ashby, 206, 477, 536
Ashdown, 95
Asher, 423
Ashley, 279
Ashmead, 389
Askew, 526
Aspinwall, 338
Astley, 93
Astor, 142, 272
Atcherson, 481
Atchison, 153, 155, 230, 245, 281,
305
Atkins, 177
Atkinson, 114, 149, 150, 358, 391,
452, 511
Atlee, 18, 94, 132, 159
Atley, 403
Atwell, 428, 464
Auboyneau, 234
Auld, 409
Aulick, 319, 495
Ausment, 153
Austin, 12, 15, 363, 479
Avery, 23, 354, 431, 432, 518, 519
Avondale Farm, 418
Aylwin, 90

B

Babbitt, 31
Babcock, 489
Babe, 11, 109, 136
Baber, 275
Bach, 148
Bache, 20, 250
Bachelder, 88

Bacon, 23, 73, 102, 113, 117, 121, 145, 206, 229, 241, 260, 290, 401, 428, 459, 502
Bacon's Castle, 150
Baden, 515
Badger, 120, 331, 482
Badolett, 23
Baer, 104, 212
Bagby, 250, 447
Baggs, 318
Bailey, 67, 70, 134, 180, 206, 229, 266, 312, 351, 450, 519
Baily, 296
Bainbridge, 175, 201, 264
Baird, 387, 389, 428, 432
Baker, 20, 110, 121, 153, 158, 173, 177, 215, 244, 246, 251, 256, 257, 265, 278, 282, 285, 296, 303, 326, 360, 380, 391, 398, 418, 449, 458, 459, 483, 526, 531
Bakewell, 97
Balance, 10
Balch, 180, 212, 362, 536
Baldridge, 266
Baldsin, 145
Baldwin, 2, 57, 67, 72, 116, 123, 160, 186, 198, 206, 267, 323, 430, 431, 441, 526, 531
Baley, 454
Ball, 14, 58, 80, 206, 312, 374, 480, 481
Ballard, 40, 72, 158, 212, 351
Ballintine, 313
Ballou, 248, 413, 435
Balman, 404
Balmat, 518
Balster, 468
Baltimore, 378, 484
Banister, 334
Banker, 150, 177
Bankhead, 31, 173, 180, 241
Banks, 200, 516
Banter, 206
Bar Landing, 357

Barber, 24, 72, 149, 280
Barbot, 241
Barbour, 68, 87, 171, 300, 346
Barclay, 68, 117, 121, 148, 323
Barcroft, 399, 409
Barefoot, 241
Bareta, 173
Bargamin, 403
Bargy, 232, 266
Baring, 286
Barker, 8, 22, 88, 106, 162, 270, 272, 354, 366
Barksdale, 396
Barlow, 214, 483
Barnard, 185, 358, 361, 405, 471, 500
Barnes, 47, 136, 243, 307, 313, 315, 345, 361, 369, 389, 467
Barney, 45, 84, 204, 246
Barnhart, 204
Barnicoat, 250
Barnitz, 204
Barnum, 99, 225, 319
barque **Bacchus**, 127
barque **Elizabeth**, 112
barque **Emma**, 179
barque **Madeline**, 497
barque **Palestine**, 477
barque **Pearl**, 178
barque **Saladin**, 356
Barr, 18, 34, 88
Barragan, 150
Barrett, 43, 91, 165, 183, 282, 314, 351
Barringer, 314, 502
Barroll, 497
Barron, 307, 414, 465, 529
Barrow, 27, 68, 319
Barry, 153, 258, 277, 326, 347, 348, 420, 492, 506, 511
Barstow, 431
Bartholomew, 535
Bartlet, 37
Bartlett, 35, 57, 180, 342, 351, 411, 517, 527

Bartley, 198
Bartolini, 50
Bartoll, 533
Barton, 2, 69, 72, 102, 123, 351, 438
Bartow, 111, 276, 388
Bartram, 39
Bascom, 215
Basnett, 274
Bassett, 2, 8, 28, 40, 46, 206, 309, 392, 422, 439, 468, 470, 472
Baswill, 511
Batchelder, 230, 231, 266, 533
Batchelor, 490, 517, 525
Bates, 29, 69, 206, 240, 343, 351, 372, 493
Battaile, 299, 300
Battell, 319
Batterman, 391, 401
Battle, 406
Batts, 521
Baxter, 156, 215, 380
Bay, 35
Bayard, 37, 40, 84, 91, 265
Bayles, 194
Bayley, 65, 506
Bayliss, 376
Baylor, 299
Bayly, 193, 206, 455
Bayne, 375, 460
Beach, 57, 113, 222, 230
Beadley, 473
Beakey, 453
Beale, 20, 81, 351, 403, 425, 438, 455
Beall, 40, 47, 203, 230, 242, 288, 365, 435, 459, 477, 502
Beallair, 511
Bealle, 409
Beam, 19
Bean, 11, 28, 63, 85, 89, 100, 149, 184, 201, 244, 354, 366, 523
Bear Camp, 168
Beard, 122, 427, 497, 506
Beardsley, 86, 96, 177, 206, 319, 330, 405

Beasley, 459
Beason, 296
Beatson, 406
Beattee, 170
Beatty, 168, 169, 274, 288, 344, 426
Beaumont, 241
Beaura, 349
Bebee, 462
Bechnell, 60
Beck, 81, 196, 206, 260, 275, 431, 487, 513, 528
Becker, 206
Beckford, 262
Beckham, 144, 187
Beckley, 477
Beckner, 70
Beckwith, 387, 412, 490
Becraft, 177
Bedell, 140, 456
Bedford, 284
Bedinger, 346
Bedwell, 144
Bee, 327
Beebe, 179, 467
Beecher, 430
Beef & Chickens, 169
Beeler, 16, 310, 363
Beercraft, 8
Beers, 23, 53, 159, 189, 191, 206, 218, 366, 376, 494
Beggs, 26
Begnette, 84
Beinvenue, 263
Beirne, 381
Belin, 250
Belknap, 171
Bell, 45, 69, 102, 108, 120, 142, 158, 159, 176, 187, 202, 206, 217, 218, 242, 288, 364, 390, 399, 403, 424, 442, 459, 493
Belle Air, 80, 333, 497
Belmont, 424
Belt, 31, 96, 116, 203, 212, 215, 224, 234, 268, 463, 479, 509, 527, 532

Belton, 159
Bender, 206, 422, 456
Benedict, 511
Benjamin, 15, 206
Benker, 415
Bennel, 94
Bennell, 281
Bennet, 31, 316, 334, 347, 406
Bennett, 100, 117, 123, 146, 212, 258, 334, 405, 534
Benning, 135, 270, 452
Bentel, 156
Benter, 458
Benton, 29, 100
Benvenedo, 368
Benzett, 333
Beorncasle, 313
Berard, 213, 245, 257, 274, 282, 304
Berkeley, 429
Berley, 215
Bernadotte, 200
Bernard, 206
Berret, 486
Berrett, 75, 451
Berrick, 352
Berrien, 94, 215, 340
Berry, 21, 27, 129, 131, 206, 222, 253, 258, 259, 269, 299, 318, 361, 380, 393, 409, 413, 447, 459, 498, 526, 529
Berryman, 295
Bertand, 154
Bertrand, 314
Beryon, 314
Besiah, 266
Bestor, 206, 440, 447
Bethel, 305
Betsey's Delight, 185, 301
Betts, 11, 188, 236, 533
Betty, 167
Betty's Plains, 168
Bevan, 323, 452
Beveridge, 510, 515
Beverley, 68, 79, 422

Beverly, 74
Beyer, 147
Beziah, 101
Biays, 212
Bibb, 282, 328, 522
Bickerill, 27
Bicknell, 327
Bickner, 47
Biddle, 51, 102, 109, 323, 440
Biennial Register, 95
Biervand, 524
Biewend, 488
Bigelow, 153, 189, 363, 389, 390
Bigham, 150, 187
Bihler, 234, 242, 419, 459
Billingalie, 260
Billings, 152, 225
Billingsgate, 267
Bills, 165
Bilman, 469
Binge, 211
Bingham, 46, 95, 266, 374
Binney, 229
Birch, 117, 121, 141, 206, 259, 267, 278, 286, 419
Birchett, 262
Birchmore, 84
Bird, 15, 89, 206, 313, 343, 355, 424
Birth, 156, 206, 231, 256, 497
Biscoe, 146, 176, 437
Biser, 434
Bishop, 36, 72, 90, 206, 214, 222, 271
Bispham, 97
Bissel, 78
Bissell, 20, 241, 432
Bizouard, 335
Black, 11, 76, 156, 332, 376, 474, 521
Black Oak Ridge, 167, 169
Blackemore, 115, 145, 147, 251
Blackenship, 178
Blackford, 46
Blackistone, 434
Blackmore, 233, 281
Blackstone, 409

Blackwell, 77, 174
Blagden, 106, 206, 240, 259, 288, 407, 428, 432, 463, 475, 480, 506, 515
Blair, 47, 78, 133, 134, 144, 389
Blake, 23, 206, 342, 383, 486, 495
Blakemore, 177
Blakesel, 514
Blakesly, 32
Blakistone, 146
Blakmore, 390
Blanc, 343
Blanchard, 149, 206
Bland, 299
Blaney, 221
Blankenship, 194
Blannerhassett, 22
Blanton, 412
Blantyre, 204
Bleek, 309
Bliss, 108, 351, 355
Blodget, 107, 145, 147
Blodgett, 528
Blood, 41, 270
Bloomfield, 19
Bloomingdale, 198
Bloomsbury, 349
Blue, 195, 202, 204, 277
Blunt, 77, 122, 151, 417, 432, 446
Blute, 465
Blythe, 87
Boardman, 215
Boarman, 43, 157, 275, 347, 488
boat **Columbus**, 394
boat **Pilot**, 438
boat **Superb**, 445
Bocanegra, 62
Bodine, 7, 20, 315
Bodisco, 343, 460
Bodley, 120, 274
Bodly, 244, 256
Bodwett, 27
Boerum, 74
Bogan, 255
Bogard, 43

Boger, 167
Bogue, 307, 347
Bohlayer, 460
Bohrer, 340, 347, 362, 368, 451
Boislarge, 154
Bokee, 416
Boland, 475
Bollman, 436, 452
Bolton, 115, 126, 171, 294
Bombauer, 421
Bomford, 13, 80, 103, 179, 223, 399, 415, 492, 514
Bompas, 494
Bonaparte, 391, 419
Bond, 212, 234, 477, 524
Bondurant, 165
Bonnel, 136
Bonnell, 57, 236, 251
Bonsall, 313
Boober, 526
Bookstaver, 99
Boone, 59, 190, 220, 310, 444, 495
Bootes, 206
Booth, 91, 483
Boozer, 219
Boqua, 42
Bordelon, 263
Bordman, 351
Borie, 323
Borland, 56, 99
Borremans, 457
Borrows, 23, 144, 206
Bosher, 250
Boss, 206
Bossier, 137, 202, 203, 204
Bostar, 100
Bostwick, 193
Boswell, 417
Bosworth, 13
Boteler, 157, 205, 206, 350, 356, 434
Botts, 36, 340, 343
Bottsford, 64, 351
Bouchell, 433
Boucher, 15, 344

Bouck, 391, 401, 413
Boulanger, 135, 361, 392, 458, 499
Boulden, 378
Bouldin, 260
Boulware, 400
Bourgeois, 118
Bourguin, 296
Bouvet, 459
Bowden, 324
Bowdle, 433
Bowen, 66, 94, 141, 177, 206, 299, 346, 409, 414, 440, 461, 508
Bowers, 115, 151, 510
Bowie, 20, 49, 61, 62, 194, 212, 276, 290, 334, 371, 373, 393, 396, 420, 421, 434
Bowlen, 528
Bowling, 461
Bowman, 76, 437, 444, 450, 480
Bowne, 91
Boyce, 271
Boyd, 248, 264, 296, 316, 336, 472, 518
Boydon, 403
Boyle, 95, 96, 112, 137, 143, 198, 206, 259, 335, 342, 345, 356, 399, 421, 463
Brackenridge, 7, 51
Bradburn, 90
Bradbury, 276
Braddock, 26, 135, 288
Bradds, 152
Bradford, 119, 163, 182, 212, 248
Bradish, 58, 151
Bradley, 23, 95, 106, 117, 128, 129, 135, 142, 148, 203, 206, 271, 320, 476, 483, 486
Bradstreet, 514
Brady, 95, 110, 143, 213, 314, 328, 330, 347, 407, 436, 440
Bragg, 158
Braham, 472
Brahan, 452
Brainard, 236, 282, 505

Brainen, 107
Brainer, 145
Brainerd, 158, 297
Brainers, 147
Braly, 309
Branch, 57, 133, 262, 282, 347
Brannan, 4
Branson, 165
Brashear, 84, 382, 448
Brashears, 407
Brawner, 22, 157, 271, 284, 309, 342, 364, 421, 536
Brayman, 139
Breakovaz, 508
Breast, 461
Breatherd, 404
Breckenborough, 403
Breckenridge, 490, 525
Breedlove, 110, 181, 284, 323
Breese, 528
Breevort, 250
Brempton, 167
Brend, 378
Brenghel, 429
Brengle, 56, 166, 212
Brenner, 69, 94
Brent, 7, 41, 43, 61, 148, 181, 197, 199, 206, 234, 276, 277, 343, 369, 399, 478, 486, 522, 526, 530
Brentwood, 451
Brereton, 14, 22, 382, 409
Brevett, 206
Brevitt, 322
Brew, 204
Brewer, 468
Brewster, 262, 313, 405, 486
Brian, 122
Briars, 78
Brice, 167, 468
Brickerhoff, 250
Brickmann, 468
Bridge, 100, 351
Bridges, 302
Brien, 96, 122, 476

brig **Bainbridge**, 196, 507
brig **Boxer**, 1
brig **Caroline**, 445
brig **Emily**, 140
brig **Francis Lord**, 477
brig **Georgiana**, 287
brig **Henry**, 220
brig **Lawrence**, 68, 70, 364
brig of war **Griffon**, 199
brig of war **Mercure**, 364
brig of war **Rapid**, 85
brig **Oregon**, 416
brig **Pearl**, 354
brig **Perry**, 463
brig **Porpoise**, 477, 483, 491
brig **Powhatan**, 294
brig **Saratoga**, 456
brig **Somers**, 42, 86, 104, 173, 199, 462
brig **St Lawrence**, 368
brig **Truxton**, 298
brig **Washington**, 246
brig **Wasp**, 85
Briggs, 28, 117, 234, 305, 306, 355
Bright, 133
Brighthart, 330
Brightwell, 440
Brinker, 92
Brinkerhoff, 222
Brinley, 283
Briscoe, 128, 197, 459, 460
Bristoll, 352
British pay, 238
Brittingham, 119, 212
Britton, 369, 456
Broadbeck, 481, 501, 503
Broadbent, 335
Broadrup, 504
Brochin, 13
Brock, 403
Brockett, 178
Brodbeck, 459
Brodhead, 367
Bromaghin, 188

Bronaugh, 5, 171, 179
Bronson, 132, 256, 430
Brook, 122, 133
Brooke, 59, 109, 111, 124, 166, 178, 190, 197, 263, 269, 331, 343, 344, 365, 398, 441, 466, 493
Brooks, 28, 206, 266, 313, 348, 371
Brotherton, 197
Broughton, 1
Brown, 8, 9, 11, 12, 14, 17, 20, 22, 26, 35, 41, 44, 57, 72, 78, 81, 83, 88, 91, 101, 107, 116, 119, 122, 126, 135, 138, 148, 150, 152, 155, 156, 159, 163, 175, 177, 182, 183, 189, 194, 196, 202, 206, 212, 217, 218, 219, 236, 248, 251, 253, 255, 266, 271, 273, 276, 278, 283, 288, 291, 296, 306, 307, 308, 310, 311, 321, 332, 333, 346, 350, 359, 363, 375, 380, 381, 385, 396, 403, 412, 436, 440, 452, 458, 459, 462, 464, 465, 466, 467, 473, 477, 478, 482, 488, 524, 530, 531, 532, 534
Browne, 34, 158, 277
Brownel, 355
Brownell, 276
Browning, 31, 124, 183, 206, 415, 416
Brownlow, 115
Brownson, 296
Brua, 145
Bruce, 19, 49, 132, 139, 166, 212, 298, 406, 418
Bruel, 161
Bruff, 289
Brum, 188
Brummett, 185
Bruner, 107
Brunet, 266
Brunot, 192
Brunson, 113, 313
Bryan, 10, 23, 117, 121, 132, 152, 153, 206, 230, 231, 244, 262, 266, 277, 280, 281, 313, 353, 374, 475, 477, 499, 505

Bryant, 15, 54, 88, 191, 308, 429, 489
Bryson, 215
Bt Yard, 168
Bube, 98
Buchanan, 199, 212, 472, 485, 487, 495, 504
Buchard, 132
Buck, 148, 331
Buck Pond, 375
Buck's Bones, 170
Buckener, 123
Buckhart, 473
Buckingham, 3, 4, 5, 92, 124, 172, 206, 424, 440
Buckner, 47, 327
Bucknor, 429
Budd, 193
Buehler, 187
Buell, 58, 405
Buffington, 166
Buffum, 521
Buford, 444
Bugg, 196
Buist, 212, 225, 277, 327
Bulfinch, 14, 28, 195, 233, 379
Bulger, 468
Bulher, 84
Bulkley, 402, 419
Bull, 28, 158, 221, 290
Bullard, 62
Bullen, 283
Bulley, 460
Bullitt, 114
Bullock, 499
Bullus, 1
Bully, 69
Bulowville, 429
Bulwer, 105
Bumbard, 309
Bunner, 138
Bunting, 152
Burbank, 57, 215
Burbridge, 393
Burch, 17, 206, 370, 475, 486

Burche, 117, 121, 206, 260, 350, 461
Burdett, 90
Burdick, 72
Burdine, 409, 458, 459
Burger, 4, 117, 206, 453
Burgess, 365, 409, 449, 469, 474
Burke, 144, 168, 276, 341, 452, 472
Burkpyrt, 267
Burlin, 57
Burlison, 32
Burn, 275
Burnet, 215
Burnett, 10, 96, 137, 479
Burnham, 205, 508
Burns, 25, 87, 101, 206
Burnt Mill Seat, 168
Burr, 116, 206, 214, 230, 341, 432, 470, 498, 510, 513, 529
Burris, 78
Burritt, 84
Burrough, 97
Burroughs, 44, 69, 177, 206
Burrows, 17, 243, 405
Burrus, 108
Burson, 242
Burtis, 77
Burton, 250, 478, 498
Burtt, 276
Burwell, 3, 327
Bury, 502
Bush, 285, 288, 409
Bushwood, 420
Bushyhead, 370
Bussard, 407
Buthman, 499
Butler, 21, 22, 31, 57, 63, 66, 107, 109, 119, 144, 147, 151, 155, 206, 215, 240, 244, 256, 270, 286, 288, 435, 457, 459, 495, 498, 518
Butt, 206, 211, 255, 397
Butterfield, 38, 526
Butterworth, 52
Butts, 405
Byington, 113, 117, 260, 436

Byrne, 40, 389, 466
Byrnes, 503
Bythwood, 285

C

Cadens, 135
Cadwalader, 20, 250, 351
Cady, 444, 480
Cain, 134, 278
Caistor, 396
Calaghen, 96
Calahan, 178
Calder, 533
Caldwell, 10, 16, 44, 55, 57, 84, 107, 145, 150, 179, 239, 245, 282, 287, 302, 313, 324, 332, 352, 431, 465, 521
Calhoun, 5, 24, 107, 115, 120, 126, 147, 186, 236, 252, 282, 495
Calkins, 430
Call, 22, 282
Callaghan, 391
Callahan, 189
Callan, 6, 13, 25, 113, 134, 181, 193, 194, 206, 229, 315, 319, 375, 387, 451, 459, 515
Callas, 448
Calley, 238
Calnan, 96
Caloit, 502
Calvert, 31, 124, 177, 279, 399, 433
Camanche, 98, 337
Camapu, 211, 291
Cambloss, 73, 486
Cammack, 90, 206, 503
Cammeyer, 427
Campau, 69, 210, 211, 242, 274, 281, 282, 291, 305
Campbell, 27, 81, 89, 96, 97, 108, 144, 166, 195, 206, 211, 213, 218, 233, 238, 274, 313, 314, 335, 351, 423, 432, 447, 456, 459, 464, 470, 472, 477, 509, 513
Campfield, 38

Camplin, 490
Canalizo, 123, 150
Canfield, 27, 173, 311, 453
Canle, 432
Canning, 108
Cannon, 319, 378, 429
Canon, 126
Capen, 31
Cappo, 473
Capron, 315
Carbery, 27, 96, 220, 224, 259, 390, 463, 476, 494, 507
Cardeza, 468
Cardoza, 164
Carey, 205, 426
Carico, 399
Carignan, 90
Carles, 483
Carleton, 81
Carlin, 6
Carlisle, 7, 27, 206, 475, 481, 529
Carlist party, 341
Carman, 46, 260
Carmel, 170
Carnahan, 337
Carnes, 13
Carns, 221
Caro, 81
Carothers, 213, 354, 446
Caroudelet, 160
Carpenter, 32, 107, 276, 311, 509
Carr, 27, 38, 297, 354, 356, 495, 528
Carrico, 343, 353, 448, 508
Carroll, 27, 93, 96, 148, 159, 214, 242, 248, 289, 346, 389, 409, 477, 478, 501
Carson, 96, 111, 224, 512
Carter, 21, 42, 79, 138, 176, 182, 206, 210, 223, 238, 254, 295, 312, 313, 401, 442
Carusi, 3, 130, 416, 480, 486
Carvoe, 427
Cary, 469, 481, 483
Casanave, 104

Cascade, 170
Casewell, 177
Casey, 327, 384, 401
Cason, 4
Casparis, 471
Cass, 30
Cassady, 423
Cassell, 424
Cassin, 19, 344
Castein, 186
Castellanos, 344
Castelnau, 27
Castle Hill, 166
Castner, 295, 511
Caswell, 57, 136, 233
Catalani, 99, 201
Catalano, 201
Catalini, 43
Cathcart, 54, 98, 121, 399
Catlett, 206, 300, 487
Catlin, 314, 432
Caton, 235, 264
Cator, 2
Catron, 13, 319
Cattell, 387
Catts, 142
Caulfield, 344
Causin, 20, 146, 212, 273, 336, 448, 461
Causine, 169
Causten, 148
Cavelier, 109
Caywood, 423
Cazea, 244
Cazeau, 282, 292, 363, 389
Cazenave, 387, 459
Cazenove, 409
Cazneau, 418
Cenas, 342
Cent, 237
Ceohe, 205
Chacon, 384
Chaffee, 71
Chamberlain, 344

Chamberlane, 100
Chambers, 142, 215, 217, 280, 319, 371
Champ, 513
Champeau, 368
Champion, 364
Chance, 170
Chandler, 15, 134, 276, 278, 361, 512
Chandona, 121
Chandonai, 114
Chaney, 408
Chang, 421
Channing, 474
Chapin, 71, 133, 266, 278, 279, 506
Chapman, 37, 88, 133, 157, 167, 170, 245, 278, 279, 285, 336, 364, 433
Chappell, 9, 252
Charles, 206, 434
Charlotte Elizabeth, 442
Charlotte Hall, 262
Charming Forge, 460
Charter, 79
Charvis, 216, 219, 333, 381, 448
Chase, 186, 250, 313, 356, 359, 485
Chaseland, 386
Chatard, 164, 250
Chatfield, 272
Chatsworth Mansion, 516
Chauncey, 196, 364, 426
Chavis, 465
Cheatham, 108
Cheddick, 204
Cheek, 153
Cheever, 139, 230
Cheney, 238
Chenino, 139
Chenoworth, 20
Cherino, 245, 257
Cherokee, 66, 102, 116, 177, 199, 210, 247, 297, 305
Cherokee Advocate, 199
Cherry, 156, 223, 380
Cherry Tree Meadow, 166
Cherry Tree Meadows, 166

Cheshire, 232
Chesley, 532
Chester, 133, 166
Chesterfield, 116
Chevalier, 336
Chew, 42, 55, 81, 107, 148, 194, 253, 333
Chezum, 206
Chichester, 213
Child, 335
Childs, 35, 248, 323, 403, 488
Chile, 335
Chilton, 312, 444
Ching, 48, 73
Chinn, 109, 358
Chipman, 351
Chirley, 250
Chisholm, 398, 401, 419
Chisole, 351
Choate, 148, 380
Chouteau, 160
Chretian, 245
Chretien, 257
Chriss, 26
Christen, 304
Christian, 40, 272, 274, 282, 283, 337, 458
Christien, 213, 304
Christman, 509
Christopher, 17
Church, 82, 180, 184, 244, 249, 257, 270, 281, 298
Churchhill, 133
Churchill, 174, 450
Cicote, 509
Cissell, 129, 135, 381
Clack, 126
Claflin, 368
Clagett, 2, 87, 141, 155, 176, 183, 206, 231, 240, 248, 342, 366, 373, 378, 414, 432, 437
Claiborne, 87, 134
Clampit, 470, 501
Clapp, 3, 107, 145, 147, 270

Clare, 148
Clark, 19, 29, 34, 49, 51, 70, 78, 81, 84, 129, 142, 146, 185, 231, 241, 247, 254, 276, 314, 327, 332, 340, 352, 362, 365, 372, 373, 378, 384, 405, 415, 418, 424, 436, 468, 488, 496, 504, 506, 514, 518, 527
Clarke, 4, 31, 42, 65, 107, 145, 147, 153, 158, 180, 186, 189, 204, 206, 207, 250, 255, 275, 282, 288, 296, 297, 343, 347, 348, 376, 381, 405, 424, 434, 454, 459, 460, 490, 506, 507, 532, 533
Clarkson, 32, 119, 269, 273, 362
Clarvoe, 458, 459
Clary, 279, 283
Claude, 30
Clavers, 15
Claxton, 206, 425
Clay, 89, 108, 146, 235, 330, 336, 367, 407, 422, 465, 482
Claypoole, 355
Clayton, 6, 23, 215, 340
Cleary, 144, 206
Clemens, 394
Clement, 438
Clements, 83, 113, 117, 138, 172, 198, 206, 344, 348, 362, 436
Clemson, 286, 496
Clendenon, 376
Clephane, 206, 409, 459, 468
Cleveland, 224
Clevenger, 505
Clifford, 471
Clifton, 480, 532
Climer, 517
Cline, 184, 289
Clinton, 29, 33, 239, 252, 322
Clitch, 22
Clitherall, 130, 160, 213
Clitz, 520
Clopton, 430
Cloud, 164, 181, 220
Cloud Cap, 444

Cloutier, 335
Cloutman, 324
Clover, 54
Clubb, 397
Clum, 432, 446
Clumb, 422, 424
Clymer, 374, 412
Coad, 94, 132, 146, 212, 335
Coal in Store, 168
Coale, 152, 212, 267, 336
Coates, 116, 230, 231, 266
Coats, 485
Cobb, 127
Cobban, 174
Cobey, 183
Coburn, 129, 135
Cochran, 27, 60, 191, 206, 405, 464, 481, 494, 534
Cochrane, 47, 84, 86, 255
Cocke, 210, 355, 430
Cockey, 212
Coddeback, 21
Coddington, 339
Codrick, 155
Coe, 169, 335
Coffee, 133, 297
Coffin, 115
Coffman, 248, 385
Cogdell, 211
Cogswell, 35
Cohen, 526
Coit, 67, 160
Cokely, 117
Cokendorfer, 459
Col Fenwick's bar, 357
Colburn, 431
Colby, 241, 442
Cole, 133, 164, 263, 290, 423
Coleman, 21, 42, 108, 133, 274, 452, 470, 495
Colemen, 415
Colen, 313
Colgate, 315
Collard, 206, 469

Collason, 502, 512
Collier, 25, 44, 283, 329, 405
Collington, 373
Collingworth, 403
Collins, 51, 107, 129, 130, 135, 206, 263, 274, 380, 399, 452, 459, 484
Collins', 523
Collins' Adventure, 170
Collinson, 135
Collison, 224
Collum, 108
Colmer, 187
Colmus, 57, 94, 136, 236, 251, 281
colored citizens, 172
Colquhon, 94
Colquhoun, 195, 196, 207
Colson, 468
Colston, 519
Colt, 138, 140, 194, 235, 509
Coltman, 40, 117
Colton, 61, 130, 211, 314, 525
Columbus, 12
Colvocoressis, 75
Combs, 95, 139, 207, 381, 460
Comegar, 279, 283
Commager, 181, 244, 256, 270, 281, 298
Common Sense, 170
Compton, 220
Conant, 71
Conard, 325
Conger, 99
Congressional burying ground, 226
Conly, 347
Conn, 130
Connell, 141, 159, 268
Connelly, 93, 477
Conner, 5, 166, 169, 197, 199, 236, 409, 479
Connolly, 143, 398, 459
Connor, 44, 66, 380
Conolly, 239
Conover, 37, 53, 65, 250, 412
Conrad, 172, 323

Conradt, 76
Constable, 212, 434
Constitution Vale, 170
Contee, 20, 104
convent of Varaten, 508
Converse, 139, 244, 256
Conway, 300, 372, 375
Coody, 451
Cook, 46, 57, 88, 107, 111, 145, 154, 157, 158, 166, 263, 269, 282, 286, 297, 317, 327, 330, 377, 380, 458, 468
Cooke, 27, 107, 349
Cookman, 139, 160
Coolidge, 103, 444
Coombe, 358
Coombs, 92, 438, 498
Coomes, 89, 460
Coon, 526
Cooney, 51
Cooper, 14, 20, 32, 44, 114, 118, 143, 206, 250, 276, 296, 314, 365, 374, 432, 457, 462, 466
Coote, 132, 453, 477
Cope, 169
Copeland, 101
Copen, 38
Copley, 51
Copper, 314
Corbin, 241
Corbit, 255
Corcoran, 148, 259, 441
Cordiel, 143
Cordis, 144
Cordoza, 218
Cormick, 462
Cornelius, 430
Cornell, 70, 482
Cornick, 467
Cornock, 385
Coromandel, 169
Corrett, 240
Corser, 517
corvette **Fairfield**, 50

corvette **La Brillante**, 199
corvette **La Brillants**, 364
Corwin, 247, 340, 485
Coryell, 277
Costen, 287
Coster, 364, 365
Costigan, 1, 146
Costin, 288
Cotter, 400
Cotton, 122
Couch, 532
Coulter, 166
Count of Nassau, 43
Course, 16
Courtenay, 176, 478
Courtney, 49, 58, 353, 449
Couthoy, 228
Covall, 122
Covent Garden, 170
Cover, 350
Cow Island, 9
Cowan, 81
Cowden, 455
Cowdery, 528
Cowen, 82
Cowles, 428, 517
Cowperwait, 169
Cox, 27, 41, 43, 96, 157, 197, 213, 215, 218, 219, 224, 259, 313, 325, 347, 348, 392, 397, 405, 429, 444, 463, 481, 501, 512
Coxan, 337
Coxe, 7, 15, 46, 73, 126, 148, 277, 326, 328, 463
Coy, 114
Coyle, 4, 12, 131, 162, 206, 223, 259, 335, 398, 418, 441, 442, 452, 456, 529
Cozeau, 153
Crabb, 95, 127, 351
Crabtree, 263
Craddock, 26, 33
Crafton, 403
Craig, 164, 165, 212, 369

Crain, 43, 157, 212, 269, 504
Cralle, 186
Cramer, 323
Cramphin, 41
Crampton, 69
Cranch, 28, 317, 529, 531
Crandall, 206
Crandell, 436
Crandle, 113
Crane, 31, 65, 101, 165, 246, 458
Craney Island, 197
Crann, 477
Craton, 467
Crauford, 13
Craufurd, 485
Craven, 207, 409, 483, 491
Crawford, 78, 91, 115, 145, 147, 217, 265, 329, 388, 418
Creamer, 262
Creighton, 241
Crenshaw, 26, 33
Cresap, 484
Creson, 234
Creutzfeldt, 18, 457
Crews, 31
Crim, 311
Cripps, 55, 219, 273, 356
Crittenden, 114, 120, 161, 340
Crocker, 17, 71, 241, 276, 279, 442, 477
Crockford, 338
Croggon, 40
Croill, 145
Croix, 344
Crommelin, 174
Cromwell, 409
Cronk, 84, 281
Cronkhite, 145, 261, 281, 295
Cronkite, 84
Crook, 144
Crooker, 228
Cropley, 320, 471
Crosby, 68, 218, 241, 313, 443, 498
Croskey, 27

Croson, 203
Cross, 116, 139, 206, 246, 296, 373, 409, 421, 460
Crossfield, 206
Crosswell, 40
Crouk, 94
Croukhite, 94
Croul, 225
Croule, 236
Croull, 261
Crouse, 27
Crow, 85, 402, 525
Crowell, 319, 476
Crowley, 28, 206, 465
Crown, 266
Crozier, 115, 156, 317
Cruger, 45, 114, 116, 147, 294
Cruit, 207
Crump, 83, 183, 499
Cruse, 512
Crussell, 453
Crutchfield, 435
Cruthett, 163
Cruttenden, 206
Cryder, 188
Crysal, 149
Cuculla, 171
Cucullu, 264
Cuddy, 441
Cudliff, 62
Culbertson, 125, 339
Culget, 4
Cull, 260
Cullins, 403
Cullum, 206
Culver, 474
Culwek, 57
Cummin, 179, 251, 343, 501
Cummings, 70, 80, 276, 347
Cummiskey, 343
Cunningham, 19, 435
Curd, 327
Curley, 280
Curran, 475

Currier, 56
Curson, 81
Curtain, 134
Curtis, 182, 279, 305, 306, 431
Curwen, 232
Cushing, 120, 121, 286
Cushman, 442
Cushwa, 154
Custer, 107
Custin, 149
Custis, 137, 143, 418
Cuthbert, 458
Cutler, 318
Cutter, 276
cutter **Morris**, 86
cutter **Vigilant**, 450, 457
Cutting, 74
Cutts, 96, 106, 260, 348, 495
Cuvillier, 222
Cuyler, 74

D

D'Arcy, 368
D'Meza, 27
Da Costa, 234
Dade, 142, 199, 299, 300
Dagget, 41, 141
Daggett, 65, 187
Daily, 269
Daingerfield, 9, 52, 145
Dairy, 274
Dale, 381
Daley, 415
Dallam, 124
Dallas, 20, 74, 187, 250, 295, 337, 351, 379, 387, 480, 486
Dallinar, 138
Dallinger, 207
Dallman, 207
Dally, 269
Dalton, 18, 362, 397, 518
Daly, 421
Dame, 238
Damoreau, 199

Dan's Mountain, 169
Dana, 15, 21, 122, 174, 397
Dance, 20, 241
Danels, 334
Danenhower, 90
Danforth, 26, 238, 250, 440, 460
Daniel, 2, 63, 157, 187, 236, 397, 504
Daniels, 32, 116, 334, 403
Dannehower, 389
Dant, 393
Darby, 383
Darden, 397, 430
Darling, 187
Darlington, 256
Darnall, 399
Darne, 9, 232, 252, 267
Darnoldson, 67
Darragh, 171
Darrah, 500
Dashers, 393
Datcher, 43
Davenant, 15
Davenport, 22, 88, 120, 145, 181, 241, 281, 518
David, 166, 207, 281, 313, 359
Davidge, 106, 148, 322, 396
Davidson, 265, 400, 409, 433, 448, 475, 500, 509, 514
Davies, 37, 180, 313, 405, 471
Davis, 21, 22, 23, 25, 26, 42, 90, 94, 98, 102, 107, 110, 113, 117, 121, 135, 144, 158, 166, 167, 175, 184, 196, 200, 201, 202, 204, 207, 210, 211, 212, 213, 214, 215, 220, 244, 245, 246, 256, 260, 270, 281, 290, 296, 304, 367, 368, 371, 396, 422, 428, 441, 446, 457, 461, 477, 484, 490, 506, 507, 527
Davison, 463
Davisson, 496
Daw, 409
Dawes, 15, 92, 207, 382, 498
Dawsett, 290

Dawson, 29, 42, 215, 248, 277, 344, 350, 503
Day, 4, 299, 486, 498
Dayfoot, 430
Dayton, 21, 320
De Barth, 447
De Bellevue, 506
De Buys, 141, 186, 193
De Camp, 34, 226
De Felding, 103
de Figaniere, 335
De Ford, 318
De Forest, 15
De Grass, 71
De Grost, 313
De Haven, 234
De Kalb, 71, 242, 313, 430
De Krafft, 90
De Kraft, 36
De Lany, 493
De Peyster, 45, 147, 244, 294
De Russy, 159
de Sandrans, 337
de Silver, 234
De Vaughan, 12
De Veaux, 44
De Vos, 136
De Witt, 151, 405
Deal, 212
Deale, 207
Dean, 31, 32, 56, 94, 117, 129, 132, 135, 136
Dearing, 346
Deas, 217, 241, 372, 435
Deatty, 59
Deaver, 422
Deblanc, 344
Debuys, 161
Decatur, 80, 179, 201, 249, 412
Decatur tract, 80
Decker, 106, 133, 385
Dedrick, 220
Deeble, 207, 369
Deep Creek Farm, 170

Defiance, 168
Degges, 22, 207, 387
Deitz, 178
DeKrafft, 6
Delana, 416
Delano, 295
Delany, 191, 207, 459, 525
Delaplane, 499
Dell, 52, 177, 266
Deloro, 331
Dement, 8, 41, 69, 138, 220, 240, 271, 284, 364, 366, 480
Deming, 37
Demmon, 81
Denby, 343
Denford, 296
Denham, 207, 211
Denike, 8
Denison, 31, 94
Denman, 155, 327
Denmead, 335
Dennen, 513
Dennett, 279
Dennin, 145, 282, 303
Dennin., 84
Denning, 129
Dennis, 455
Dennison, 42, 119, 132, 207
Denslow, 505
Dent, 43, 56, 273, 291, 347
Denyse, 469
Depas, 155
Depens, 512
Depew, 195
Derbanne, 83, 145, 281, 304
Deringer, 518
Deritt, 207
Dermott, 38, 69, 85, 98
Derr, 17
Derrick, 61
Derringer, 375, 432, 451
DeRussy, 180
DeSaules, 361, 458
Deselding, 30

553

Deshler, 40
Deslonde, 347
Desobry, 335
Deunnin, 236
Devaney, 352
Devaughan, 25
Devaughn, 207
Devecmon, 166
Devereux, 136
Deville, 429
Devin, 57
Devinele, 430
Devlin, 50, 144, 431
Devoe, 367
Devore, 437
Dexter, 182, 242, 278, 321, 369, 421, 529
Dey, 283, 286
Dibble, 193, 266, 483
Dickerman, 404
Dickey, 60, 132, 190, 223, 245, 257, 265, 282, 298
Dickins, 13, 258, 286, 447, 487, 495, 502, 536
Dickinson, 152, 498
Dickson, 210, 211, 214, 230, 245, 277, 281, 297, 513
Diel, 165
Dierkes, 333
Dietz, 273
Digges, 194, 352, 370, 438, 486
Diggs, 344
Dill, 57, 403
Dillard, 98
Dillon, 195, 244, 256, 271, 278, 282, 283, 298, 519
Dines, 135
Dingler, 413
Dipple, 458
Divine, 465
Dix, 128, 403
Dixon, 6, 25, 36, 67, 69, 89, 90, 138, 150, 181, 182, 243, 322, 338, 378, 404, 416, 430, 435, 442, 473, 484

Dobbin, 215
Dobbins, 71, 144
Dobbs, 79
Dobbyn, 25, 179
Dod, 337
Dodd, 76
Dodge, 67, 181, 347, 397, 430, 440, 454, 533
Dodson, 186, 378, 432, 485
Doescher, 93
Doggett, 24, 38
Dogherty, 271
Doharty, 417
Doig, 189
Dolce, 141
Dollman, 253
Dolson, 10
Dominick, 242
Donabay, 69
Donaldson, 198, 219, 429, 484
Donaphon, 409
Donavan, 335
Donelan, 25, 30, 60, 137, 222, 241, 348, 404, 405, 475, 523
Donelson, 407
Doniphan, 105, 520
Donn, 98, 197, 198, 205, 207, 309, 350, 469
Donne, 462, 467
Donnegan, 343, 344
Donnell, 37, 70, 109
Donnelly, 343, 386
Donoghue, 347, 348, 494
Donohay, 107
Donoho, 113, 123, 127, 207, 224, 247, 428, 447, 515
Donohoo, 459
Donovan, 468
Doolittle, 405
Dooly, 95
Door, 224, 330
Doras, 466
Dorman, 379
Dorr, 109, 115, 124, 224, 295

Dorset, 76
Dorsett, 207
Dorsey, 59, 85, 91, 105, 155, 171, 183, 185, 201, 204, 212, 237, 278, 301, 374, 421, 482, 513
Doswell, 427
Dothard, 314
Doty, 52, 282
Dougherty, 245, 256, 281, 302, 409, 479
Doughty, 162, 231, 397, 429
Douglas, 312, 437, 458, 479
Douglas' Bottoms, 361
Douglass, 197, 207, 240, 385, 495, 498, 512
Dourd, 349
Douthats, 216
Douty, 288
Dove, 207, 289, 356, 382, 441, 452, 459
Dow, 95, 199, 200, 445
Dowden, 7
Dowey, 32
Dowling, 143, 423, 457, 459
Downer, 133, 138, 207, 332
Downes, 22, 75, 406
Downey, 446
Downing, 10, 207, 360, 442, 495
Downingville, 360
Downman, 290
Downs, 260, 276
Downs', 233
Doyle, 17, 105, 116, 215, 275, 343, 346
Drain, 343
Drake, 207, 240, 293, 405
Draper, 151, 396
Drayton, 91, 243
Dress, 93
Drew, 84, 149
Dreyfoos, 130
Drinker, 81, 119
Driscoll, 151, 450, 457
Drouet, 344

Drowt, 238
Drummond, 167, 265, 381, 439
Drury, 56, 92, 207, 235, 240, 247, 275, 288, 436
Dry Hill, 169
Drysdale, 74
Dubant, 207, 421
Dubois, 219
Duboise, 230, 245, 257
Dubosq, 313
Dubuque, 160, 258
Duck, 48
Duckett, 28, 373
Ducoing, 107
Dudley, 212, 300, 468
Dudley Springs, 312
Duer, 36, 90, 334
Duffey, 248, 266, 516
Duffy, 198, 254, 504, 505, 509
Dufief, 207
Duke, 412
Duke of Glouceser, 525
Dulaney, 105
Dulany, 118, 202, 218
Duley, 23, 149, 426
Dulin, 214
Dumbar, 467
Dumlap, 169
Dumser, 454
Dunbar, 73, 146
Duncan, 15, 51, 211, 313, 344
Duncanson, 397
Dundas, 460
Dunham, 57, 84, 145, 296, 462
Dunhan, 187
Dunlap, 355, 522
Dunlop, 73, 100, 409
Dunn, 51, 108, 118, 428, 460, 477, 496
Dunning, 193
Dunnington, 183
Dunnock, 334
Dupie, 109
Duponceau, 161

Dupuy, 15
Durald, 218
Durand, 521
Durasso, 45
Durezzo, 77
Durfee, 456
Durff, 207
Durham, 93, 236
Durling, 165
Durr, 105, 207, 408
Dutch, 258
Dutcher, 250, 295, 367
Dutton, 54, 237
Duval, 210, 211, 274, 281, 303
Duvall, 5, 22, 35, 53, 92, 96, 102, 119, 125, 153, 207, 212, 244, 256, 271, 404, 418, 491, 515
Dwight, 223, 284, 388
Dyde, 368
Dye, 423
Dyer, 4, 13, 14, 29, 36, 37, 43, 90, 125, 146, 162, 190, 207, 271, 288, 346, 354, 360, 361, 407, 409, 450, 506, 513
Dyett, 74
Dykers, 343
Dyot, 57

E

Eaches, 117
Eakin, 249
Eames, 158
Earhart, 263, 340, 428, 443
Earle, 253, 470
Earnes, 153
Easby, 13, 84, 189, 207, 329, 332, 399, 489
Easler, 509
Easter, 335, 530
Eastman, 102, 163
Easton, 10, 41, 139, 176, 189, 426
Eaton, 22, 27, 107, 116, 207, 430
Eaxridge, 225
Ebaugh, 340, 434

Eberbach, 457, 458, 459, 518
Eccles, 236
Eccleston, 212
Eckel, 393, 486
Eckles, 167
Eckley, 234
Eckloff, 103, 207, 380, 392, 409, 489, 491
Eckright, 92
Eddy, 124, 260, 327
Edelen, 347, 353, 485
Edelin, 132, 354
Eden Spring, 167
Eden's Paradise Regained, 167
Edes, 205, 278, 326, 328
Edgar, 224
Edgartown, 377
Edgerton, 220
Edmarson, 139
Edmonds, 300
Edmonson, 244, 256, 281, 292, 409
Edmonston, 207
Edmunds, 142
Edsall, 276
Edsell, 248
Edson, 405
Edward, 73
Edwards, 7, 118, 157, 168, 215, 241, 312, 350, 409, 442, 452, 466, 467, 469, 477, 517
Egan, 431, 491
Egbert, 438
Ege, 460
Ege's Iron Works, 460
Eggleston, 189
Egnew, 147
Eiring, 468
Elder, 469
Eldred, 17
Eldridge, 81, 94, 184, 296
Eliasson, 518
Eliot, 207, 359
Eliovitch, 58
Elk Lick, 170

Eller, 130
Ellery, 43, 94, 122, 272, 474
Ellet, 15
Elli, 313
Ellicott, 166
Ellingwood, 535
Elliot, 258, 332, 362, 405, 433
Elliott, 84, 94, 129, 145, 177, 228, 233, 238, 239, 313, 401, 488, 505, 509
Ellis, 100, 123, 207, 232, 240, 248, 264, 296, 392, 400, 440, 445, 469, 470, 474, 506, 515
Ellsworth, 25, 89, 138, 148
Ellwell, 34
Ellwood, 459
Elly, 196
Elmer, 85, 314
Elmes, 314
Elney, 31
Elridge, 272
Elwood, 9, 46, 469
Elwyn, 120, 229
Ely, 402, 434, 531
Elzey, 328
Emack, 135
Emancipation, 170
Embury, 15
Emerich, 360, 459
Emerick, 4, 128, 458
Emerson, 307, 506
Emery, 68, 89, 153, 207
Emmert, 516
Emmons, 94, 150
Emory, 148, 248, 259, 333, 335, 355, 484
Emple, 403
Emrick, 105
Engle, 78
English, 126, 262, 317, 386, 392, 409, 501
Enlow, 167
Ennalls, 353

Ennis, 16, 46, 95, 143, 276, 343, 369, 373, 424, 528
Enoch, 165
Enos, 242
Entwistle, 465
Erben, 402
Erers, 502
Ericson, 239
Ermerick, 128
Esban, 313
Eskridge, 152
Esling, 15
Esmoil, 259
Espey, 389
Espy, 138, 207
Essex, 65, 207, 390, 399
Esslinger, 427
Estep, 207, 487
Estes, 242
Estis, 509
Estrada, 27
Estwick, 512
Eustis, 194, 234
Evans, 2, 4, 24, 49, 58, 73, 112, 120, 138, 145, 152, 156, 169, 184, 203, 207, 218, 235, 238, 263, 264, 266, 270, 296, 380, 387, 400, 420, 459, 477, 478, 512, 533
Evans' Purchase, 169
Evards, 76
Evelith, 399
Everly, 166, 325
Eves, 78
Evinger, 26
Ewart, 432
Ewing, 85, 108, 120, 304, 340, 349, 465
Ex Post Facto, 167
Eynaud, 361

F

Factories, 168
Fagan, 52, 221, 307
Faherty, 143

Fahnestock, 124
Faidley, 245
Fair, 77
Fairbairn, 386
Fairchild, 313
Fairfax, 184, 420, 426
Fairfax Beall, 2
Fairfield, 136
Fairman, 15, 44
Faisan, 196
Faithful, 520
Fales, 207, 503
Falkner, 318
Fallansbee, 207
Falman, 283
Fant, 345
Far Enough, 170
Faris, 76
Farkin, 262
Farmer, 225
Farnam, 207
Farnham, 23, 57, 94, 95, 136, 177, 207, 233, 286, 442, 515, 528
Farnolds, 465
Faron, 417, 446, 451, 479
Farquhar, 4, 207, 357, 359, 464, 510
Farquharson, 166
Farrand, 364
Farrar, 135
Farrington, 57, 84
Farrow, 27, 46
Fastnaugh, 197
Faub Park, 170
Faulconer, 93
Faulkner, 427
Fauns, 20
Fauntleroy, 7, 136, 241
Fauver, 439
Favier, 289, 457, 511
Fawcett, 44, 196
Faxon, 427
Fay, 3, 15
Feach, 167
Feaman, 188, 236, 533

Fearer, 167
Featherstonhaugh, 37, 490
Febiger, 241
Feeks, 379
Feeny, 458
Felger, 167
Feller, 497
Fellows, 238, 295
Felton, 114, 216, 266
Fenby, 212
Fendall, 529
Fenesey, 396
Fenner, 255, 535
Fenno, 359
Fenwick, 68, 96, 243, 432, 463
Ferguson, 31, 43, 87, 95, 153, 157, 189, 207, 236, 238, 240, 244, 256, 261, 281, 293, 351, 423, 536
Fernandes, 477
Fernandez, 335
Ferrall, 2, 31
Ferretan, 46
Ferreton, 18, 79
Ferris, 127, 143, 182, 240, 279
ferry-boat **Icelander**, 26
Fers, 383
Fessenden, 56, 94, 136, 149, 281, 292, 341
Fetterman, 334
Fewell, 203
Fichlie, 130
Ficklin, 534
Field, 40, 262, 277, 300, 326, 512, 521
Fielding, 346
Fields, 405, 427
Filch, 398
Fill, 207
Fillebrown, 141
Fillen, 470
Fillmore, 46, 66, 405, 424
Finch, 37
Findley, 308
Finegan, 274, 453
Finlay, 286

Finn, 296
Finnegan, 207, 314
Finney, 28, 101, 183
Finnigan, 491
Fischel, 53
Fischer, 34, 183, 329, 468
Fish, 54, 151, 430, 495
Fisher, 26, 27, 140, 219, 223, 236, 238, 314, 323, 324, 382, 403, 504, 525
Fisk, 51, 219, 368, 499
Fisler, 475
Fister, 207, 459
Fisterer, 137
Fitch, 30, 84, 107, 145, 147, 162, 177, 348, 461, 473, 504, 528
Fitchett, 417
Fitnam, 344
Fitsgerald, 283
Fitzgerald, 140, 143, 241, 348, 362, 431, 456, 458, 507
Fitzhugh, 87, 166, 207, 288, 299, 300
Fitzpatrick, 113, 434, 447, 521
Flagg, 250, 353
Flaherty, 4, 466
Flamborough, 169
Flanagan, 358, 475
Flanagans, 454
Flanders, 400, 493
Flanegan, 525
Flavel, 534
Fleanor, 81
Fleischman, 367
Fleischmann, 422
Fleming, 396
Fletcher, 24, 158, 346, 347, 348, 422, 434
Flinn, 85, 210, 313
Flint, 444, 480
Flora's Goodwill, 169
Flower, 386
Flowers, 237
Flowery Mead, 168
Flowery Meads, 169

Floyd, 40, 132, 329, 335
Flye, 250, 322
Focsett, 81
Foley, 135, 335
Folger, 44, 94, 132, 148, 210, 281, 292, 377
Follansbee, 75, 158
Follins, 27
Folson, 151
Foltz, 36, 90
Fontainbleau, 391
Fontenot, 40
Fooks, 434
Foot, 174
Foote, 56, 94, 114, 132, 136, 149, 281, 292
Fop, 238
Forbes, 187, 234, 376
Force, 117, 121, 148, 211, 259, 500, 515
Ford, 10, 58, 110, 146, 207, 284, 316, 338, 433, 434, 436, 462, 467, 483
Fordling, 441
Fordyce, 352
Foreman, 497, 521
Forest, 96, 414
Forest of PG Co, 373
Forrest, 27, 86, 88, 103, 121, 259, 319, 358, 402, 438, 446, 460, 463, 502, 507
Forstall, 4, 343, 344
Forsyth, 34, 115, 283, 381, 432
Fort, 236, 436
Fort Adams, 297
Fort Delhi, 294
Fort Erie, 65
Fort George, 3
Fort Gibson, 444, 480
Fort Jesup, 136, 503
Fort Johnson, 488
Fort Leavenworth, 157, 354
Fort Lyttleton, 60
Fort Meigs, 482
Fort Monroe, 159, 328

Fort Moultrie, 32, 158, 341
Fort Pierce, 38
Fort Smith, 47
Fort Snelling, 406
Fort Sullivan, 47
Fort Towson, 242, 502
Fort Washington, 100
Fort Washita, 242
Fort Wayne, 276, 307
Fortier, 343
Forward, 120
Fosdick, 155
Fossett, 111, 207, 265, 459
Foster, 6, 78, 108, 116, 145, 147, 158, 169, 199, 231, 236, 241, 281, 298, 299, 324, 436, 445, 462, 467, 498, 528
Fowle, 140, 435, 455
Fowler, 40, 57, 67, 106, 137, 168, 176, 189, 207, 229, 296, 409, 455, 476, 494, 514
Fowler's Lot, 168
Fox, 241, 259, 287, 337, 365, 432, 472, 473
Fox Chase, 169
Foxall, 409
Foxwell, 1
Foy, 143, 362, 458
France, 5, 92, 105, 112, 117, 121, 140, 162, 178, 207, 296, 428, 459, 470, 489, 508
Frances, 534
Francis, 15, 151, 250, 304, 518
Franciscan monks, 128
Frank, 159
Franklin, 68, 92, 95, 145, 147, 207, 346, 385, 415, 459
Franks, 416
Frasee, 141
Fraser, 117, 120, 184, 191, 221, 332, 448, 471, 489
Frazee, 270
Frazer, 46, 145, 147, 282, 294, 316, 326, 328, 341

Frazier, 55, 113, 324, 353, 376, 433
Frederick, 43, 178
Free, 535
Freeland, 333
Freeman, 27, 54, 94, 98, 101, 145, 177, 203, 215, 219, 233, 235, 321, 323, 336, 433, 477
Freer, 457
Frelinghusen, 330
Frelinghuysen, 31, 78, 217, 229, 235, 330, 423, 482
Freman, 84
French, 24, 37, 113, 123, 131, 148, 166, 183, 188, 238, 265, 430, 449, 479, 490, 523
Frere, 288
Frescati, 87
Frick, 106, 110, 119, 154, 248, 335, 435
Friend, 167, 431
Friendship, 169, 197, 223
frig **Columbia**, 20, 247, 265, 351
frig **Columbus**, 438
frig **Confederacy**, 339, 343
frig **Congress**, 12, 250
frig **Cumberland**, 528
frig **Hudson**, 306
frig **Macedonian**, 127
frig **Mississippi**, 13
frig **Philadelphia**, 201
frig **Potomac**, 143, 199, 368, 423, 499
frig **Raritan**, 36, 90
frig **Savannah**, 379
frig **United States**, 187, 431
frig **Warspite**, 445
Frink, 453
Frizzel, 94
Frizzell, 428
Frogge, 57, 136, 187, 236
Fronk, 418
Frosser, 72
Frost, 148, 240, 258, 327
Frothingham, 390
Fry, 35, 86, 153, 195, 323, 381, 506

Frye, 87, 157, 231
Fugitt, 146, 438
Fuller, 4, 28, 101, 107, 108, 161, 207, 232, 245, 257, 271, 430, 431, 457, 479
Fullslove, 5
Fulmer, 260, 424
Fulton, 37, 49, 81, 86, 155, 181, 246, 248, 275, 288, 390, 504, 516, 528, 536
Funk, 289, 505
Furgeson, 428
Furlong, 188, 452
Furman, 37, 242, 349
Furtney, 7
Fyfe, 507

G

Gaddis, 460
Gadsby, 4, 16, 46, 77, 85, 124, 128, 232, 249, 269, 311, 332, 414, 432, 458
Gage, 24, 64, 182
Gage's hill, 29
Gager, 534
Gahn, 187
Gaines, 4, 55, 134, 158, 203, 263
Gaither, 10, 168, 175, 212, 435
Gale, 19, 150, 161, 188, 351, 438
Gales, 25, 179, 401, 451, 480, 529
Gallabrun, 376, 457
Gallagher, 122, 347, 434
Gallaher, 53, 118
Gallatin, 151, 252
Gallaway, 335
Gallebrun, 108
Galloway, 166, 356
Galpin, 174
Galt, 133, 308, 525
Galvin, 357, 494
Gamble, 358
Gammon, 372
Gannon, 458
Gansevoort, 75

Gansey, 396, 415
Gantt, 188, 212
Garallan Farm, 361
Gardiner, 43, 49, 58, 104, 106, 113, 152, 157, 181, 185, 207, 301, 302
Gardner, 9, 55, 57, 68, 85, 90, 100, 104, 230, 231, 299, 310, 311, 354, 364, 376, 431, 486, 520
Garesche, 334, 335
Garey, 352
Garland, 35, 435
Garlick, 144
Garner, 105, 122, 131, 433
Garret, 73, 240
Garrett, 5, 132
Garrison, 295
Garvin, 118
Gasaway, 536
Gaskill, 313
Gasquett, 199
Gassaway, 178, 232, 252
Gaston, 63, 242, 469
Gatch, 212
Gatchell, 124, 483
Gates, 53, 145, 288, 314, 414
Gatewood, 234
Gather, 429
Gatlin, 369
Gattrell, 477
Gautier, 494
Gavett, 431
Gawronski, 82
Gawsey, 133
Gay, 35
Gaylord, 308
Gedney, 246
Gee, 154
Geesey, 291
Geesy, 271
Geisinger, 265
Geisler, 273
Geist, 101
Geller, 189

Gen Duff Green's iron & ore lands, 168
Gengenback, 36
Genin, 18
George, 7, 87, 212, 434
George Washington, 17
Gerdes, 369, 481
Gerding, 27
Gerhard, 11
Germain, 497
German, 313
Gessler, 500
Getty, 335, 520
Gettys, 370
Getzendanner, 252
Geurin, 64
Ghieslin, 433
Gibbon, 413, 437
Gibbons, 141, 503
Gibbs, 55, 65, 207, 415, 430, 490
Gibert, 137, 422
Gibson, 42, 57, 67, 73, 81, 87, 107, 145, 147, 177, 233, 236, 261, 281, 283, 313, 326, 331, 347, 382, 495
Gideon, 11, 13, 21, 29, 95, 96, 117, 121, 135, 172, 207, 246, 463, 472
Gier, 11
Giesborough Manor, 258
Giesey, 156, 244, 256
Giesler, 231
Giger, 337
Gihon, 313, 314
Gilbert, 24, 66, 154, 155, 277, 282, 289, 309, 332, 362, 390, 449, 454, 457
Gilchrist, 70
Gild, 84
Gildersleeve, 483
Giles, 101
Gill, 125, 232, 327, 417, 443
Gillam, 77
Gillchrest, 534
Gillespie, 337
Gilleylen, 227

Gilli, 193
Gilliam, 27, 380, 508
Gillis, 42, 88, 250, 397
Gilliss, 397, 476, 520, 523
Gilman, 88, 184, 207, 519
Gilmer, 46, 81, 100, 104, 106, 119, 120, 133, 137, 461
Gilmor, 484
Gilmore, 44
Gilpey, 313
Gilpin, 210, 238, 475
Gilson, 248
Gingles, 118
Girard, 124
Girault, 91, 379, 405
Gist, 212
Given, 207
Giveny, 95, 340
Gizor, 223
Gladding, 506
Gladman, 381
Glascock, 108
Glasscock, 263
Gleanings, 167
Gleason, 4, 238
Glendy, 438
Glenlyon, 332
Glenn, 20, 162, 196, 445
Glenn Ross, 118, 328
Glenn Ross Farm, 213
Gliddon, 361, 374
Globe Hotel, 431
Glover, 85, 120, 177, 207, 233, 261, 281, 312, 404
Glymont, 504
Goddard, 200, 207, 354, 371, 418, 459, 464
Godey, 3, 5
Godfrey, 459, 478
Godon, 250
Goertz, 417
Goff, 252
Goforth, 160
Goggin, 388

Goings, 129, 202, 513
Gold, 343, 510
Golding, 398
Goldman, 78
Goldsborough, 20, 74, 131, 157, 247, 295, 347, 351, 433, 495
Goldsby, 57
Goldsmith, 288
Gomez, 335, 336
Gomillion, 404
Good, 40, 53
Good Hope, 170
Goodall, 308
Goode, 257, 375
Goodenow, 266
Goodfellow, 234
Goodin, 423
Gooding, 514
Goodly Lands, 167
Goodman, 189
Goodrich, 169, 180, 383, 461
Goodright, 144
Goodsell, 57, 276
Goodwater, 395
Goodwin, 23, 54, 139, 174, 232, 244, 335, 505, 513
Goodwyn, 480
Gordon, 10, 13, 27, 54, 90, 106, 109, 116, 133, 179, 197, 224, 300, 443, 448, 506
Gore, 204
Gosnold, 377
Gott, 69, 405
Gough, 125, 146, 174, 204
Gould, 15, 38, 322, 349, 493, 497
Gow, 119, 125
Gowan, 438
Graebe, 319
Graeff, 192
Graeme, 35
Grafton, 20
Graham, 20, 54, 137, 218, 232, 237, 241, 276, 313, 383, 468
Grammar, 166, 409

Grammer, 96, 167, 240, 347, 421
Grammer's Discovery, 166
Grandison, 364
Granger, 120, 227, 405
Grannis, 44
Grant, 8, 81, 95, 131, 177, 184, 231, 272, 322, 355, 430
Grasse, 41, 65
Grasshopper, 168
Gratiot, 409
Grattan, 15
Graves, 46, 69, 134, 223, 430, 434, 484, 485
Gray, 43, 68, 72, 79, 108, 117, 122, 132, 157, 187, 361, 373, 432, 473
Grayson, 41, 80, 98, 114, 149, 266, 327
Greble, 472
Greely, 305
Green, 12, 19, 26, 27, 33, 45, 71, 108, 134, 140, 168, 169, 200, 204, 233, 283, 347, 351, 368, 376, 403, 443, 459, 477, 478, 518
Green Hill, 282
Green Mount Cemetery, 225, 515
Greene, 133, 250
Greenfield, 207, 479
Greenhalgh, 483
Greenhow, 30, 34, 133
Greening, 276
Greenleaf, 25, 238, 331, 409
Greenleaf's Point, 115, 398, 472, 487
Greenwood Cemetery, 322
Greer, 57, 160, 416, 450
Gregg, 66, 499
Gregory, 36, 90, 169, 253
Grelaud, 194
Gresham, 115, 145, 198, 236, 252
Grevel, 221
Grey, 68, 174, 480
Grice, 478, 522
Grider, 143
Grieb, 407
Grier, 210

563

Griffin, 174, 217, 307, 530
Griffith, 92, 127, 152, 167, 175, 207, 518, 528
Grigg, 270
Griggs, 322, 383
Grignon, 142
Grimes, 75, 207, 331, 447, 528
Grindage, 259
Grinder, 82, 387
Grinnell, 140
Griswold, 15, 313, 435
Groaning, 378
Grogge, 94
Groome, 290
Gross, 343
Grossman, 313
Grouard, 475
Grove, 167
Grover, 350
Groves, 363
Grubb, 146, 311, 494
Grund, 275
Grupe, 521
Grymes, 18
Gtwn College, 245, 257, 280
Guest, 83
Guiles, 22, 67
Guilford, 119, 153
Guion, 109
Guling, 396
Gumaer, 40, 417, 437
Gummey, 313
Gump, 164, 515
Gunnell, 95, 121, 162, 207, 343, 348, 417, 459, 512
Gunning, 393
Gunton, 13, 148, 259, 309, 428
Gurley, 21, 148, 494
Gustin, 88, 404
Gustine, 130, 280
Gutheridge, 528
Guthrie, 23, 173, 181, 244, 257, 281, 297
Guttslich, 344

Guy, 121, 318, 363
Guyer, 431, 472, 482
Gwathmay, 431
Gwathmey, 74
Gwatkins, 272
Gwinn, 406
Gwynn, 499
Gwynne, 347

H

Haas, 137
Hack, 143
Hacket, 430
Hackett, 313, 508
Hackworth, 96
Haddock, 133
Hadley, 65
Hadlock, 467
Hadman, 246
Hagan, 121, 214, 323
Haggard, 54, 506
Haggerty, 75, 246
Hagner, 358
Hahn, 453
Haight, 487
Hail, 144
Haile, 52
Haines, 17, 119, 480
Hair, 219
Haire, 115
Haldeman, 228
Hale, 178, 524
Halford, 190
Haliday, 113, 117, 207, 211, 260, 459
Halkerson, 168
Hall, 9, 20, 25, 43, 55, 56, 74, 101, 105, 111, 112, 129, 133, 140, 144, 145, 167, 171, 177, 205, 207, 208, 216, 229, 246, 247, 262, 264, 266, 271, 278, 283, 284, 288, 290, 327, 335, 351, 356, 370, 371, 405, 417, 440, 455, 458, 473, 476, 477, 501, 509, 515, 532
Halleck, 14

Hallett, 313
Halliday, 290, 323
Hallock, 31, 94, 121, 158, 236, 251, 281
Halloway, 192
Hallowell, 154, 319, 359
Hallyburton, 282
Halsted, 191
Ham, 29, 376, 446, 456
Hambleton, 434, 442
Hamel, 335
Hamilton, 28, 34, 97, 136, 142, 165, 235, 252, 258, 262, 276, 279, 290, 313, 321, 426, 428, 442, 445, 454, 527
Hamlet, 42, 158
Hamlett, 505
Hamlin, 77, 349
Hamm, 313
Hammett, 121, 221
Hammill, 434
Hammock, 521
Hammond, 99, 168, 182, 207, 242
Hamon, 41
Hamot, 131
Hampson, 144
Hampton, 247, 492
Hanauer, 392
Hance, 343, 433, 505
Hancock, 81, 182, 196, 291, 327, 448, 457, 509
Hand, 9, 207, 245, 280, 287, 395, 433
Handy, 188, 207, 208, 212, 276, 353, 400, 410
Hanegan, 123, 184
Hanes, 58
Haney, 459
Hanford, 384
Hanly, 13
Hanna, 323, 519
Hannold, 355
Hannon, 280
Hansbury, 296
Hansford, 62

Hanson, 208, 269, 278, 326, 334, 354, 369, 431, 443, 500
Harbaugh, 23, 117, 121, 172, 207, 314, 459
Harbert, 196
Hard, 498
Hardcastle, 212
Hardel, 149
Harder, 158
Hardesty, 10
Hardin, 107, 133, 168, 215, 283, 340, 372, 403
Harding, 88, 354
Hardisty, 135
Hardy, 235, 366, 428, 487
Hare, 289, 351
Harender, 141
Harford, 208
Haring, 247
Harkness, 5, 23, 92, 95, 148, 207, 211, 240, 398, 399, 424
Harman, 486
Harmer, 28
Harne, 340
Harper, 100, 117, 123, 153, 212, 275, 505
Harpers' Ferry, 145
Harpole, 24
Harrell, 143, 196, 217
Harriman, 324
Harrington, 15, 212, 255, 308, 433, 451, 458, 516
Harris, 2, 22, 46, 47, 99, 118, 133, 180, 181, 205, 313, 349, 374, 400, 421, 423, 430, 433, 465, 472, 473, 493, 518, 520, 527
Harrison, 10, 21, 32, 38, 53, 64, 86, 94, 117, 121, 122, 139, 170, 171, 177, 189, 200, 207, 210, 230, 241, 260, 268, 281, 297, 306, 336, 434, 463, 466, 481, 482, 493, 512, 525
Harriss, 207
Harrover, 459
Harry, 62, 112

Hart, 27, 181, 245, 257, 307, 323, 335, 434
Hartley, 515
Hartman, 208, 243, 460
Hartshorn, 119
Hartstene, 68
Hartt, 207
Hartwell, 68, 354
Harvey, 38, 207, 247, 344, 402, 432, 459, 520
Harwell, 38
Harwood, 325, 491, 512
Haskell, 146, 308, 495
Haslup, 183, 329, 452
Hassler, 45, 279, 527
Hastings, 20, 250, 426
Haswell, 120, 409, 412, 448
Hatch, 514
Hatfield, 65
Hathaway, 60, 112, 482
Hatherington, 167
Haughey, 431
Haven, 456
Havener, 30
Havenner, 207, 208
Havens, 18
Haviland, 345, 412
Hawes, 131
Hawkins, 5, 57, 65, 91, 157, 189, 237, 240, 258, 265, 328, 369, 455
Hawley, 12, 21, 40, 46, 71, 73, 88, 114, 290, 455, 491, 502, 512, 523
Hawthorne, 15
Haxall, 403
Haxtun, 36, 90
Hay, 38, 132, 207, 521
Hayden, 54, 279, 282
Hayes, 36, 73, 229
Hayman, 131, 215, 381, 391, 410, 421, 441, 486, 523
Haynes, 155, 393, 430
Hayre, 17
Hays, 90, 99, 100, 152, 229, 241, 327, 335, 337

Hazard, 129
Hazel, 410, 460, 487
Hazel Plain, 203
Hazell, 113
Hazelon, 356
Hazlehurst, 477
Hazzy Offutt's farm, 9
Head, 279
Head of Frazier, 336
Heakes, 37
Healey, 270
Healy, 104, 107, 145, 147, 305
Heany, 492
Heard, 146, 212, 519
Heartt, 107
Heath, 125, 186, 403
Heaton, 260
Hebard, 54
Hebert, 526
Hedges, 34, 473
Hedrick, 403
Heem, 429
Heemskerk, 429
Heerman, 201
Heise, 432
Heiskell, 115, 226, 486, 495
Heisler, 513
Heitmuller, 289
Helen, 212
Helfenstein, 133
Hellard, 457
Hellen, 65, 207, 274, 340, 354, 433
Heller, 167, 468
Hellert, 336
Helton, 79
Heminway, 84
Hempstead, 340, 471
Hempstone, 317
Hemrill, 158
Henche's Discovery, 170
Henderson, 13, 44, 46, 116, 162, 171, 204, 207, 229, 330, 348, 422, 440, 502
Hendley, 524

Hendly, 459
Hendon, 230
Hening, 103
Henley, 409
Henning, 207, 258, 286, 448, 477
Henry, 26, 212, 237, 327, 337, 363, 434, 493, 527
Henshaw, 23, 36, 81, 90, 95, 120, 207, 278, 412
Henson, 58, 153, 155, 245, 281, 297
Hepburn, 207, 352, 485
Hepeline, 169
Herbert, 14, 71, 118, 149, 313, 408, 515, 535
Hercus, 489, 518
Herdon, 528
Herman, 121
Hernandez, 38, 44, 180, 347
Herreta, 335
Herrick, 154, 200, 231, 271
Herring, 55, 57, 313
Herrington, 123
Herron, 5
Hersey, 376
Hess, 142, 392, 415, 534
Hesselbaugh, 221
Heth, 101, 156, 244, 265, 281, 298
Hettick, 169
Hetzell, 512
Heustis, 295
Hevener, 450
Hewett, 15
Hewins, 456
Hewitt, 23, 28, 105, 110, 207, 388
Heyl, 24
Hibbart, 71
Hibbert, 61, 79
Hickey, 378, 501
Hickler, 403
Hickley, 336
Hicks, 19, 46, 160, 260, 295, 398, 400, 423, 442, 451
Hidden, 107, 293
Hiddon, 244, 256

Hiester, 119
Higgins, 235, 270, 283, 358, 366, 412, 468, 481
Highgate, 175
Hight, 449
Hilaire, 332
Hiles, 313
Hill, 5, 28, 34, 43, 81, 93, 98, 100, 148, 152, 172, 194, 208, 212, 218, 225, 246, 258, 278, 288, 325, 335, 350, 369, 383, 386, 390, 416, 439, 497, 499, 501
Hill & Dale, 169
Hilleary, 9, 504
Hillhouse, 277, 326, 388
Hilliard, 235, 286
Hillman, 221
Hilton, 410, 470, 501, 532
Himrod, 405
Hindes, 165
Hinds, 115
Hinebread, 58
Hines, 3, 95, 330
Hinkle, 154
Hinsdell, 277
Hinshaw, 71
Hinton, 207, 365, 481
Hiring, 508
Hiscox, 430
Hitchcock, 228
Hitz, 471, 494
Hix, 396
Hixon, 462, 467
Hoa, 97
Hoag, 31, 72, 81, 94, 136, 149, 281, 293, 387, 484
Hoban, 19, 143, 181, 446, 451, 462
Hobart, 71, 238, 381
Hobbie, 347
Hobbs, 390
Hobert, 426
Hoblitzel, 104
Hoblitzell, 212
Hobson, 412

Hockett, 88
Hockley, 21, 176
Hodge, 129, 208, 337
Hodges, 189, 199, 357, 403
Hodgkin, 230
Hodgson, 208
Hoe, 8
Hoff, 253, 419, 431
Hoffa, 108
Hoffman, 15, 16, 64, 104, 148, 204, 277, 326, 328, 472, 516
Hoffman's Delight, 169
Hoffmans, 130
Hoffner, 355
Hogan, 27, 133
Hoggatt, 505
Hogmire, 250
Hogshead, 156
Hoke, 407, 463
Holbrok, 511
Holbrook, 147, 337
Holcomb, 451
Holden, 533
Holdsworth, 497
Hollady, 363
Holland, 96, 118, 123, 141, 176, 296, 355, 397, 410, 437, 443, 514
Holleman, 357
Holliday, 296, 526
Hollige, 208
Hollingshead, 208
Hollingsworth, 56, 94, 136, 403
Hollinsworth, 28
Hollis, 197
Holly, 366
Hollyday, 433
Holmead, 34, 93, 103, 146, 161, 207, 208, 222, 225, 237, 269, 320, 360, 367, 375, 377, 419, 444, 473, 520
Holmes, 23, 40, 51, 63, 71, 98, 104, 107, 156, 207, 244, 275, 322, 354, 369, 506, 532
Holroyd, 186

Holt, 107, 145, 147, 238, 281, 285, 306, 437
Holthouse, 437
Holtzman, 220, 401, 402, 485
Holzman, 364
Homans, 74, 95, 240, 284, 396, 460
Hooe, 27, 203, 300
Hook, 169
Hoomes, 345, 360
Hoover, 105, 145, 204, 207, 208, 218, 250, 288, 311, 325, 410, 458
Hope, 4, 260, 276, 473
Hopewell, 433
Hopkins, 8, 36, 52, 57, 90, 94, 123, 136, 259, 313, 323, 340, 405, 497, 512
Hopkinson, 109, 201
Hopper, 20
Hopson, 308
Horn, 28, 308
Horner, 6, 25, 54, 195, 264, 519
Hornet, 440
Hornor, 25
Hornsby, 159, 316, 333
Hornsley, 115
Horton, 324, 380
Horvey, 242
Hosack, 252
Hosier, 54
Hoskins, 112, 168, 366
Hotchkiss, 283, 371, 489
Hough, 30, 58, 308, 496
Houghton, 71, 228, 427, 451
House, 276, 295
Houseman, 7, 315
Houston, 87, 98, 150, 250, 265
Houx, 310
Hovey, 449
Howard, 15, 26, 77, 97, 111, 168, 169, 183, 189, 198, 207, 232, 248, 269, 275, 324, 330, 335, 336, 354, 394, 407, 430, 434, 448, 476, 506
Howe, 138, 198, 417

Howell, 20, 26, 33, 169, 201, 210, 228, 244, 460, 463
Howie, 347
Howinson, 76
Howison, 153, 203, 409, 459
Howland, 28, 463
Howle, 65, 343, 347
Hoy, 130, 310, 472
Hoye, 212, 346
Hoye's coal, 168
Hoye's Fortune, 169
Hoyt, 238, 450, 457
Hubard, 495
Hubball, 473
Hubbard, 72, 228, 248
Hubbell, 181, 323
Huber, 221
Huchins, 65
Hudson, 25, 94, 181, 203, 241, 332
Huff, 62, 473
Huger, 159, 277
Huggins, 473
Hughes, 43, 112, 148, 157, 210, 212, 336, 383, 433, 452, 462, 467
Hughston, 420
Hugsham, 313
Huguenots, 119
Hugunin, 81
Hull, 98, 158, 361, 429
Hultz, 3
Humber, 369
Humes, 207
Hummer, 295, 302
Humphrey, 77, 319, 340
Humphries, 36, 90, 348
Hungerford, 14, 190
Hunt, 100, 126, 248, 312, 340, 408, 426, 476
Hunter, 2, 16, 20, 36, 37, 49, 57, 66, 68, 90, 102, 103, 107, 128, 131, 145, 147, 148, 150, 242, 245, 250, 257, 274, 282, 302, 303, 336, 356, 366, 401, 405, 426, 442, 495, 514, 518

Hunting Ground, 170
Huntington, 17, 113, 139, 272
Hunton, 299
Huntsman, 423
Huntt, 208, 347, 354, 410
Hurat, 130
Hurdle, 204, 208
Hurlbert, 493
Hurley, 453
Huron, 167
Hurst, 470
Hurt, 237
Huston, 270
Hutchins, 98, 402
Hutchinson, 38, 65, 94, 120, 125, 177, 242, 243, 319, 376, 508
Hutton, 371
Hyams, 122
Hyatt, 23, 39, 207, 382, 407, 428, 459, 479
Hyde, 21, 234, 268
Hyer, 526
Hyneman, 144
Hyssett, 400

I

Iardella, 4, 284
Icard, 205, 266
Iddins, 208
Iglehart, 174, 343
Ihmsen, 483
Ilsley, 6
Improvements, 168
Inakep, 45
Inba & Lyphase, 169
Inch, 55, 60, 79, 460
Ineheart, 13
Ingalls, 107, 145, 147, 236
Ingersoll, 106, 148, 217, 248, 522
Ingle, 13, 21, 61, 193, 229, 259, 267, 366, 373, 431, 448, 515
Ingles, 258
Ingolla, 225
Ingraham, 208, 430, 526

Ingres, 109
Ington, 167
Inman, 14
Innerarity, 464
Internal Improvements, 167
Iobhair, 370
Irby, 396
Iron Mine, 169
Irvine, 119
Irving, 180
Irwin, 34, 142, 390, 512
Isaacks, 251
Ives, 153
Ivy, 37
Izard, 201

J

Jack, 376, 384, 421
Jacksen, 165
Jackson, 31, 42, 48, 55, 71, 88, 101, 111, 116, 129, 154, 168, 223, 285, 316, 352, 367, 385, 402, 406, 423, 427, 430, 472
Jacob's Kindness to Jacob, 168
Jacobs, 519
Jacobson, 309
Jacre, 313
Jamar, 212
James, 18, 114, 124, 208, 286, 320, 430, 488, 508, 526, 534
Jameson, 504, 527
Jamesson, 241, 502
Jamieson, 21
Janieson, 309
Janner, 238
Janney, 57, 208, 212, 408, 474, 477
Jaquith, 105
Jarboe, 410, 503
Jarnagin, 29, 69
Jarvis, 88, 296
Jasper, 153, 182
Jaudon, 522
Jauregui, 176
Jay, 35, 72, 144

Jaynes, 334
Jeffers, 105, 110, 131, 198, 410, 504, 508
Jefferson, 8, 119, 221, 352, 423
Jeffries, 133, 313
Jellison, 268
Jenifer, 2, 47, 235
Jenkins, 43, 49, 58, 98, 120, 157, 168, 212, 244, 257, 266, 270, 302, 313, 334, 343, 344, 347, 348, 377, 427
Jennings, 55, 254
Jepso, 167
Jesap, 101
Jesse, 300
Jester, 333
Jesuits, 203
Jett, 518
Jewell, 18, 93, 168, 414
Jewelry, 168
Jewett, 71, 330, 461, 499
Jillard, 322
Jingle, 105
Jno Michael, jr lands, 168
Johnes, 89
Johns, 48, 142, 279, 403
Johnson, 8, 18, 20, 24, 29, 40, 53, 57, 74, 78, 96, 101, 111, 116, 117, 123, 124, 138, 140, 154, 161, 162, 164, 166, 167, 170, 178, 194, 196, 198, 203, 208, 225, 228, 230, 231, 235, 240, 245, 248, 250, 260, 266, 277, 278, 284, 286, 290, 296, 314, 326, 338, 340, 381, 397, 403, 404, 419, 427, 429, 431, 433, 434, 435, 441, 451, 459, 462, 463, 468, 479, 491, 501, 502, 513, 525, 533
Johnsonn, 152
Johnston, 21, 30, 42, 74, 219, 296, 356, 435
Johnstone, 150
Joiner, 439
Joines, 257
Jones, 10, 11, 17, 30, 38, 44, 57, 65, 67, 77, 78, 85, 86, 90, 93, 94, 98,

103, 108, 112, 120, 132, 148, 156,
159, 166, 187, 188, 208, 210, 215,
256, 260, 269, 275, 279, 288, 289,
292, 296, 309, 313, 317, 318, 328,
330, 333, 339, 343, 356, 362, 372,
381, 391, 392, 398, 406, 408, 410,
417, 430, 431, 445, 447, 459, 460,
463, 468, 495, 498, 506, 508, 509,
526, 528
Jonffroy, 363
Jordan, 81, 95, 143, 173, 213, 277,
313, 314, 326, 327, 420, 424
Josephs, 470
Jost, 147, 457
Journey, 107, 145, 147
Joyce, 89
Joyne, 244
Joyner, 521
Joynes, 120
Judd, 423, 430
Judge, 45, 253
Judkins, 314
Judlin, 454
Judson, 49
Julian, 231
Julien, 225
Jump, 212, 434
Justice, 57, 94, 136, 177, 233, 251,
281
Justus, 317

K

Kahl, 442
Kain, 193
Kaine, 210
Kaiser, 468
Kalklaser, 191
Kane, 106, 183
Kavanagh, 48
Kavasales, 351
Kealey, 208
Kean, 211
Kearney, 148, 157, 246
Kearny, 358

Kearsly, 283
Kedgelie, 422
Kedgely, 250
Keech, 9, 502
Keenan, 335, 461
Keene, 212, 433, 452
Keerl, 155
Keevil, 73
Keim, 40
Keith, 42, 138, 272, 358
Kell, 5, 513
Kellenberger, 80
Keller, 84, 188, 224, 289, 322, 347,
348, 370, 387, 410
Kelley, 28, 100, 335, 438, 452
Kellogg, 307, 422, 505
Kelly, 31, 66, 81, 84, 143, 168, 216,
265, 296, 313, 320, 335, 348, 362,
398, 413, 424, 432, 446, 459, 477,
531
Kelton, 155, 225
Kemball, 63
Kemble, 346
Kemp, 335
Kendall, 24, 220, 310, 427, 520
Kendig, 164, 223
Kendrick, 142, 459
Kendy, 221
Kengla, 197
Kennard, 4, 22, 107, 244, 256, 280,
281
Kennede, 313
Kennedy, 63, 122, 157, 167, 168, 171,
208, 234, 259, 264, 515, 516, 520,
528
Kennon, 100, 104, 106, 127, 160, 276
Kenrick, 316
Kent, 20, 152
Kenton, 4, 53
Keon, 455
Kepler, 152
Kerby, 86
Kerley, 236
Kerlinger, 204

Kern, 127, 314
Kerr, 7, 17, 53, 98, 128, 130, 153, 213, 245, 281, 305, 380, 459, 473, 484, 490
Kershner, 410
Ketcham, 182
Ketchum, 181, 245, 257, 271, 277, 282, 294, 326, 328, 421, 444, 480
Keteltas, 15
Key, 11, 51, 342, 431, 437, 501
Keyser, 91, 212
Keyworth, 203, 347, 459, 510
Kibbey, 208
Kibbie, 149
Kibby, 135
Kibley, 442
Kidd, 145
Kidwell, 4, 5, 322, 397, 515
Kiernan, 202
Kifer, 102
Kiger, 42
Kilbourne, 212
Kilburn, 326
Kilgore, 81
Kilgour, 262, 330, 336, 425, 434
Killinger, 119
Kilman, 123
Kimball, 28, 57
Kimberly, 160, 519
Kimmell, 99, 336, 459
Kincaid, 131
Kinchy, 213, 459
Kinder, 266
King, 5, 9, 18, 55, 65, 76, 77, 117, 122, 126, 132, 139, 140, 146, 160, 176, 180, 187, 195, 208, 211, 213, 226, 228, 260, 262, 264, 267, 295, 313, 329, 331, 334, 347, 369, 387, 405, 454, 456, 458, 473, 499, 507, 514
King's Sorrow, 170
Kingness, 170
Kingsberry, 33
Kingsby, 114
Kingsley, 17, 83, 180
Kington, 123
Kinkade, 32
Kinney, 40
Kinnicutt, 91
Kinsey, 485
Kinsley, 180, 208
Kintner, 467
Kinzer, 319
Kirby, 248, 336, 462, 467, 481
Kirk, 184
Kirkham, 444
Kirkland, 73, 526
Kirkpatrick, 489
Kirkwood, 31, 194, 208, 473
Kissich, 108
Kitty, 250
Klady, 193
Kleiber, 439
Kleppart, 12
Klopfer, 208, 285, 286
Klopper, 135
Klunk, 208
Knaffe, 509
Knaggs, 112
Knapp, 152, 284, 286, 431, 473
Kneeland, 425
Knickerbocker, 32
Knight, 211, 348, 513
Knighton, 343
Knopp, 264
Knott, 8, 57, 335
Knowblock, 449
Knowle, 329
Knowles, 108, 272
Knowlton, 41
Knox, 21, 61, 335, 347, 437, 524
Kohler, 94
Kohn, 155
Koontz, 170
Kosciusko, 469
Krafft, 458
Kraffts, 191
Kraitsir, 338

Krantz, 204
Kreemer, 60
Kreightbaum, 170
Kroes, 482
Kuhn, 410
Kulp, 455
Kurlbaum, 385
Kurtz, 57, 96, 131, 197, 201, 259, 289, 377
Kusman, 81
Kuykendall, 266

L

La Rud, 432
Lachner, 33
Lacon, 69
Lacroix, 335
Lacy, 461, 486, 495
Lad, 250
Ladd, 414
Ladiga, 142
Lafayette, 44
Lafille, 271
Lafon, 137, 143
Laforest, 210
Laidlow, 81
Laighton, 90
Laird, 211
Lake, 75
Lakeman, 428
Lambden, 434
Lambdin, 212
Lambert, 241, 274, 473
Lamborn, 141
Lambright, 45, 336, 399, 410, 448
Lamontt, 296
Lamuade, 296
Lanahan, 335
Lancaster, 19, 20, 157, 284, 449
Land, 39
Land Flowing with Milk & Honey, 170
Lander, 182
Landeras, 176

Landernau, 75
Landry, 344
Lane, 26, 51, 61, 140, 158, 160, 184, 308, 443, 464
Lang, 36, 153
Langdon, 288
Langley, 344, 509
Langly, 185, 301, 407
Langreen, 84
Langrey, 244
Langtree, 120, 265
Langtry, 257
Langworthy, 276
Lanham, 85
Lankford, 433
Lanman, 398
Lansdale, 342, 349, 493
Lapher, 96
Lapish, 463
Lapwing, 167
Larcomb, 222
Larer, 164
Larken, 435
Larkin, 4, 17, 27, 37, 351, 435, 456
Larnards, 70
Larned, 46, 148, 322, 396, 459
Laronick, 470
Laroque, 335
Larr, 143
Larrabee, 101, 526
Lasell, 313
Lasher, 46
Lasky, 458
Lassell, 101, 266
Lasselle, 281, 304
Lassiter, 307
Latham, 13, 67, 100, 312, 379
Lathrop, 3, 279
Latimer, 48, 73, 74, 265, 406, 431, 446
Latore, 265
Latshaw, 54
Lauck, 5
Lauderman, 107

573

Laughlin, 2
Launitz, 226
Laurie, 21, 46, 249, 369, 421, 459, 492, 512, 524, 527
Lausing, 91
Law, 127, 135
Lawrence, 25, 37, 41, 106, 148, 151, 201, 215, 216, 221, 222, 274, 384, 405, 440, 442, 526
Lawrenson, 285
Laws, 201, 242
Lawson, 110, 126, 154
Lay, 480
Lazenby, 208
Lea, 115, 374
Leach, 208, 419
Leadrum, 238
Leakin, 167
Lear, 46, 412
Learned, 268
Leary, 458
Leas, 27, 60
Leatherman, 108
Leatherwood Bottom, 168
Leaths, 174
Leavenworth, 114
Leavitt, 27, 405, 505
Lebengood, 69
LeBreton, 423
Leckie, 410
Ledoux, 111
Ledyard, 420
Lee, 32, 41, 52, 78, 79, 83, 91, 125, 144, 153, 181, 208, 228, 246, 268, 330, 414, 419, 459, 472, 527
Leebavenan, 313
Leech, 164, 334
Leechman, 524
Leed's Manor, 216
Leeds, 114
Leers, 414
Leet, 49, 280
Lefler, 40
Legare, 97, 120

Lehi, 177
Lehman, 196
Leib, 285
Leidy, 403
Leigh, 340, 381
Leighton, 36
Leiper, 283
Leisler, 488
Lelson, 142
Lemer, 26
Lemmon, 195
Lemon, 262
Lemosey, 35
Lenox, 117, 121, 148, 208, 260, 459
Lenthall, 212
Lentner, 252
Leon, 173
Leonard, 79, 347, 505
Leonards, 296
Lepine, 349
Lepretre, 344
Leroy, 75
Leslie, 15, 196
Lester, 45, 276
Lesueurs, 259
Levi, 33
Levin, 314, 323
Levy, 275, 319, 514
Lew, 429
Lewis, 6, 8, 15, 18, 25, 46, 100, 108, 121, 122, 139, 172, 182, 208, 225, 234, 240, 248, 252, 254, 257, 308, 313, 320, 323, 331, 340, 355, 357, 370, 385, 401, 442, 460, 486, 507
Libengood, 116
Lieber, 50
Ligon, 63
Lilly, 186, 280
Lima, 431
Limestone, 168
Lincoln, 68, 84, 101, 239, 469
Lindenberger, 260
Lindsay, 15, 29, 36, 90, 142, 162, 330, 412, 438, 454, 470

Lindsey, 348, 442
Lindsley, 180, 217, 322, 503, 512, 519
Lindsly, 271
Linguiar, 296
Linkins, 45, 208, 459
Linn, 223, 526
Linsey, 26
Linsley, 513
Linthicum, 158, 259, 377, 426, 463, 504
Linton, 139, 208, 244, 281, 296, 298
Linvill, 330
Lipscomb, 134, 160, 346, 372, 487, 507
Lipsey, 445
Lister, 313
Lithbridge, 224
Littell, 119, 144, 310
Little, 28, 31, 35, 44, 77, 96, 267, 332, 350, 369, 488
Little Bull Run, 203
Little Worth, 166
Litton, 31
Livingston, 37, 191, 276, 283, 344, 473
Lloyd, 66, 113, 117, 121, 135, 314
Lochrey, 325
Lock, 311
Lock Isle, 170
Locke, 273, 418, 462
Lockerman, 212, 295
Lockett, 3
Lockhart, 165
Lockrey, 410
Locks, 228
Lockwood, 82, 431
Locust Hill, 38
Loder, 51
Logan, 277, 388
Logsdon, 167
Lomax, 29, 55, 262, 381, 435
Lombardi, 491
Long, 79, 212, 270, 314, 378, 433, 458

Long Boat, 167
Long Meadows, 179
Longfellow, 15
Longley, 167
Longson, 410
Longwood, 254
Loomis, 35, 119, 139, 244, 256, 271, 330
Lord, 132, 182, 208, 285, 430
Lorenz, 441
Loring, 330
Losey, 72
Lost Glove, 169
Lott, 314
Louallier, 48
Loud, 15, 510
Loughborough, 111
Lounsbury, 17, 465
Love, 142, 348
Lovejoy, 430
Lovelace, 389
Loveless, 404, 523
Lovell, 63, 85, 144, 187, 226, 444, 480
Lovely, 169
Low, 8, 45, 114, 284, 316, 436
Lowden, 408
Lowe, 70, 261, 282, 302, 410, 448
Lowndes, 151, 390
Lowrey, 136
Lowry, 75, 355
Loyd, 144
Lozier, 36, 90
Lubin, 143
Lubrick, 55
Luby, 96
Lucas, 22, 108, 114, 288, 360, 484, 512
Luce, 46, 512
Lucker, 263
Lucket, 478
Luckett, 32, 328, 395, 477
Lucky Discovery, 223
Ludlow, 10, 107

Lufborough, 73, 96, 347
Luffborough, 463
Luforough, 259
Lumley, 378
Lund, 534
Lundy, 406, 458
Lusby, 92, 170, 222, 498
Lusher, 221
Lusk, 195, 532
Luther, 140, 289
Lutz, 99, 218, 453
Luxen, 62, 476
Luynes, 109
Luzenberg, 364
Lyell, 507
Lyle, 84, 318
Lynch, 24, 46, 57, 76, 95, 143, 150, 155, 313, 343, 347, 372, 395, 410, 433, 438, 460
Lynd, 39
Lynn, 133, 403
Lyon, 171, 189, 363
Lyons, 215, 275, 344, 403, 463
Lytle, 166

M

Maalsby, 483
Mabbett, 101
Macalester, 323
Macauley, 115
Maccoun, 493, 527
Macfarland, 381
Macfarlane, 461
Macgill, 459
Macguire, 80
Machen, 103
Machlin, 137
Mackall, 212, 506
Mackenheimer, 104
Mackenzie, 122
Mackey, 466
Mackintosh, 382
Macklin, 233
Maclean, 337
Maclear, 461
Macomb, 49, 139, 159, 277, 289, 327, 328, 455, 456
Macrae, 427
Maddox, 47, 117, 153, 161, 218, 240, 334, 335, 383, 438, 501
Madeiras, 229
Madison, 2, 3, 221, 321, 352, 423
Maffit, 74
Maffitt, 212, 433
Magar, 121
Magaw, 250
Magee, 4, 348, 350, 410
Magill, 12, 410
Maglennan, 177
Magnum, 289
Magoffin, 21
Magrath, 174, 437
Magruder, 23, 69, 76, 106, 117, 148, 157, 167, 175, 208, 228, 260, 315, 355, 363, 366, 371, 410, 415, 438, 441, 479, 497, 501, 518
Maguire, 116, 143, 145, 147, 233, 252, 282
Mahan, 180
Maher, 95, 96, 143, 208, 431, 457, 459
Mahew, 10
Mahool, 336
Mahorney, 473
Maines, 116
Maitland, 262
Major, 156
Malby, 173
Malisle, 526
Mallet, 277
Mallion, 460
Mallory, 302
Malon, 110
Malony, 164, 425
Manard, 41
Manez, 398
Mangett, 186, 200
Mango de Clava, 475

576

Mango de Clavo, 487
Mangum, 187, 296, 425, 495
Manhattan, 47
Mankin, 42, 208, 330
Mankins, 378
Manly, 390
Mann, 1, 10, 13, 47, 172, 340, 522
Manning, 74, 75, 110, 192, 447, 480
Mansfield, 436
Manson, 3
Mantom, 196
Mantz, 66
Manypeny, 51
Marberry, 167, 168
Marbury, 75, 364
March, 6, 36, 90, 210, 211
Marchand, 525
Marche, 1
Marcy, 241
Marin, 275
Mark Amended, 169, 233
Markam, 456
Markoe, 46, 106, 148, 151
Markon, 50
Marks, 186, 222
Markward, 18, 100, 316
Markwood, 288
Marll, 475
Marmillion, 335
Maron, 187
Marquis, 102
Marr, 56
Marriott, 487, 527
Marsden, 139, 245, 257
Marsh, 204, 212, 295, 355
Marshall, 10, 18, 27, 28, 50, 51, 59, 68, 93, 112, 141, 155, 173, 198, 208, 213, 216, 217, 240, 263, 291, 312, 343, 350, 375, 386, 421, 436, 438, 466, 469, 473, 478, 489, 503, 506, 527
Marshfield, 81
Marstelle, 203
Martha's Vineyard, 377

Martin, 13, 44, 53, 58, 108, 118, 120, 122, 133, 136, 170, 172, 173, 177, 188, 192, 208, 212, 253, 286, 329, 339, 355, 360, 383, 385, 386, 412, 413, 417, 467, 473, 505, 512, 513
Martin's Freehold, 185
Martorel, 164
Marvin, 171
Marx, 403
Maryman, 50, 83, 135, 146, 246, 268, 369, 428, 446, 448, 460, 465, 480, 519, 533
Masi, 183, 347, 348, 369, 469
Masin, 442
Mason, 5, 16, 56, 63, 88, 92, 96, 128, 133, 151, 163, 168, 174, 177, 180, 190, 200, 210, 214, 230, 235, 247, 250, 295, 312, 332, 378, 381, 386, 397, 403, 412, 440, 444, 463, 480, 484, 493, 498
Massey, 236, 367
Massie, 33, 287, 430
Masson, 313, 344
Master, 488
Masterson, 244, 256, 272
Masterton, 153
Mastin, 364
Mather, 228, 230
Mathers, 119
Matheson, 153
Mathews, 136, 173, 241
Matlock, 340, 462
Matson, 51
Matteson, 189, 405
Matthews, 69, 82, 124, 137, 148, 177, 262, 347, 348, 421, 434, 449, 488, 518, 523
Mattingley, 350
Mattingly, 27, 82, 162, 205, 208, 264, 301, 348, 398, 461
Mattison, 196
Maurice, 45, 258
Maury, 20, 45, 96, 117, 121, 124, 148, 183, 241, 259, 459, 463

577

Mauzy, 250
Maver, 107
Maxcy, 100, 104, 106, 112, 169
Maxwell, 250
May, 16, 76, 81, 84, 139, 208, 251, 255, 301, 347, 348, 356, 414, 442, 468, 526
Maye, 403
Mayer, 27, 484
Mayfield, 261
Mayhew, 377
Maylert, 374
Maynadier, 191
Maynard, 20, 35, 63, 75, 250, 356
Mayo, 221, 225, 234, 493
Mays, 35
McAdams, 403
McAfee, 5
McAlpin, 41
McAvery, 130
McAvoy, 101, 506
McCabe, 164, 242, 392, 483
McCaffrey, 527
McCain, 467
McCaleb, 323, 521
McCall, 65, 286
McCallum, 250
McCammon, 6
McCardle, 319, 321, 386, 390
McCarthey, 203
McCarthy, 43, 96, 143, 208, 344
McCartney, 152
McCarty, 25, 76, 212, 234, 247, 328, 428, 470
McCaughan, 29
McCaughen, 184
McCauley, 15, 113, 195, 244, 256, 260, 272, 290, 446
McCaulley, 385
McCeery, 493
McCella, 144
McCeney, 235
McChesney, 405
McClain, 431

McClaskey, 452
McClellan, 5, 250, 319, 387, 401, 445, 509
McClelland, 14, 20, 92, 105, 117, 121, 208, 240, 504
McClennahan, 532
McClery, 148, 459
McClester, 456
McClintock, 489
McClosky, 379
McClure, 152, 515
McCobb, 96
McColgan, 261, 459
McComas, 16
McConnell, 102, 126, 143, 239
McCormack, 465
McCormick, 8, 32, 95, 108, 118, 157, 179, 184, 208, 240, 313, 366, 371, 375, 386, 410, 444, 475, 480, 535
McCorry, 134
McCoy, 186, 473
McCracken, 169
McCrady, 224
McCrain, 147
McCraw, 145, 188, 236
McCrea, 495
McCreery, 75
McCrery, 466
McCubbin, 8
McCue, 64, 316, 367
McCullock, 26
McCulloh, 106, 429
McCurdy, 314, 371
McCutchen, 399, 486
McDanial, 317
McDaniel, 94, 122, 130, 216, 219, 321, 333, 381, 410, 465
McDermot, 351
McDermott, 4, 138, 143, 320, 458, 459
McDonald, 38, 79, 150, 299, 320, 335, 338, 353, 380, 436, 452
McDonough, 201
McDougal, 250

McDowell, 119
McDuell, 129, 152, 410, 445
McDuffie, 250, 468, 520
McElfresh, 208
McFaddon, 8
McFadon, 465
McFarland, 533
McFarlane, 83, 517, 525
McFate, 313
McGarry, 96
McGee, 117, 240, 489, 498
McGill, 473
McGinnis, 178, 285, 459
McGlue, 18, 89, 92, 202, 213, 410
McGoon, 80, 160
McGowan, 268, 412, 492
McGown, 246
McGrath, 105, 143, 458, 460
McGregor, 485, 509
McGuffin, 341
McGuire, 28, 63, 76, 88, 138, 143, 148, 177, 211, 215, 228, 259, 306, 307, 392, 414, 441
McGunnigle, 410, 435
McHardy, 265
McHatten, 528
McIlhany, 496
McIlyar, 129
McIntire, 12, 53, 249, 381, 475
McIntosh, 53, 147, 151, 213, 224, 374
McIntyre, 190, 495
McKane, 477, 478
McKavett, 139
McKay, 6, 196
McKean, 200, 239, 290, 354, 360, 459
McKee, 269
McKeetran, 86
McKelden, 95, 208, 240, 429
McKeldon, 515
McKenna, 219, 246, 372
McKennan, 215
McKenney, 21, 51, 203
McKenny, 208
McKenzie, 346, 393, 468, 480

McKessie, 160
McKew, 335
McKibbon, 278
McKie, 158
McKinley, 13, 68
McKinney, 456
McKinstry, 536
McKissick, 517
McKnight, 468, 529
McLain, 482
McLane, 412, 484
McLaughlan, 387
McLaughlin, 28, 51, 63, 67, 109, 115, 117, 140, 148, 170, 204, 253, 427, 446, 449, 509
McLauren, 354
McLaws, 278, 326
McLean, 5, 13, 27, 128, 270, 277, 326, 438
McLear, 534
McLellan, 79
McLelland, 208
McLeod, 143, 208, 265, 316, 348, 410, 523
McLosky, 335
McLure, 285
McMahon, 367
McMain, 532
McMakin, 533
McMan, 174
McManus, 47, 110
McMullin, 313
McMurray, 534
McMurtie, 323
McMurtrie, 67, 116, 230, 231, 266, 314
McNair, 8, 92, 224
McNamara, 212, 239, 316
McNamee, 107, 133, 208
McNamer, 44
McNaughton, 484
McNeil, 462
McNerhany, 347
McNett, 434

McNiel, 60
McNier, 493
McNulty, 486, 495
McNutt, 15
McPhail, 262
McPharian, 158
McPherson, 75, 96, 105, 114, 125, 134, 151, 187, 195, 208, 243, 244, 281, 305, 349, 427
McQuay, 475
McQuillan, 419
McQuin, 403
McRae, 277, 341
McSherry, 456
McVain, 65
McVean, 21, 387
McWhorter, 234
McWilliams, 163, 208
Meachan, 210
Meachum, 350
Mead, 283, 375, 403
Meade, 137, 285, 347, 379, 390, 391, 512
Meads, 431
Mealey, 167
Means, 220
Mecham, 260
Mechlin, 155
Meckerson, 27
Meehan, 36, 90, 366
Meeker, 186, 187, 275, 288, 466
Meeks, 384
Mehegan, 5
Meigs, 214, 287, 293
Melcher, 203
Melville, 86, 153, 506
Menard, 18, 188, 236, 505, 508, 509, 517, 525, 533
Mercer, 62, 78, 112, 182, 245
Meredith, 35, 42, 290, 449, 484
Merriam, 425
Merrick, 6, 34, 286, 428, 449
Merrill, 535
Merritt, 218, 247, 398

Merryman, 159, 204
Merserau, 412
Mertland, 202
Metcalf, 396
Metcalfe, 84, 340
Metot, 454
Metoyer, 344
Michael, 168
Michard, 373
Michler, 83
Mickels, 430
Mickles, 55, 115
Mickum, 432
Middleton, 4, 13, 19, 64, 208, 217, 221, 230, 315, 347, 348, 424, 449, 459, 473
Mierden, 313
Mighels, 229
Mikener, 313
Milburn, 208, 311, 440, 533
Miles, 70, 313, 334, 477
Mill, 31
Mill seat, 167, 169
Mill Seat, 167, 169, 211
Mill Seat Improvement, 166
Millan, 427
Millen, 457
Miller, 6, 29, 36, 43, 44, 62, 66, 82, 83, 94, 99, 107, 108, 117, 133, 145, 147, 157, 158, 159, 161, 164, 168, 187, 189, 200, 205, 208, 210, 211, 212, 215, 228, 236, 244, 247, 252, 281, 287, 288, 296, 305, 323, 329, 333, 379, 396, 403, 408, 410, 417, 439, 457, 502, 504, 515, 527
Miller's Chance, 169
Milles, 210, 238
Millet, 18
Millete, 313
Millford, 353
Milligar, 463
Milliken, 149
Millington, 124, 314

Mills, 15, 19, 94, 147, 222, 228, 242, 261, 281, 415, 482, 513, 528, 529, 533
Millspaughor, 293
Millstone Point, 169
Millville Mills, 172
Milly, 84, 304
Miln, 365
Milner, 242
Milstead, 162, 163, 318
Milsted, 244, 256
Mines, 73
Minge, 132
Miniette, 142
Minifie, 484
Minkler, 26
Minor, 217, 224, 275, 464
Minz, 468
Miskell, 302
Mitchel, 243
Mitchell, 41, 47, 116, 135, 144, 174, 185, 229, 237, 248, 274, 301, 349, 372, 408, 412, 450, 459, 482, 525
Mitland, 427
Mitten, 26
Mittens, 516
Mix, 285, 430, 489
Mockbee, 482
Moffat, 233
Mohun, 4, 213, 356, 424, 459
Molineaux, 63
Molleson, 241
Molley, 299
Molloy, 477
Moncure, 58
Mongazida, 30
Monroe, 36, 90, 123, 166, 177, 178, 184, 195, 196, 271, 281, 293, 302, 352, 423, 459
Montalant, 463
Montcalm, 30
Montevideo, 190
Montgomery, 21, 57, 212, 310, 460
Monticello, 221

Montpelier, 221
Moody, 143, 189, 198, 247, 275, 288
Moon, 128
Mooney, 358
Moony, 54
Moor, 250
Moore, 27, 30, 65, 72, 92, 100, 146, 153, 172, 175, 200, 208, 214, 235, 238, 241, 244, 245, 256, 258, 271, 281, 298, 308, 313, 353, 361, 364, 369, 384, 388, 465, 470, 497, 514, 532
Moores, 434
Moorhead, 29
Moorlands, 242
Moors, 509
Moran, 16, 113, 122, 210, 228, 234, 458, 459, 466
Morcoe, 208
Mordecai, 158, 455
More, 218
Morehouse, 15, 187
Moreland, 305
Morfit, 160
Morgan, 4, 29, 37, 69, 109, 140, 148, 168, 196, 208, 224, 242, 245, 281, 296, 297, 302, 332, 344, 354, 357, 464, 477, 478, 488
Morigles, 141
Morley, 449, 471
Mormon, 315
Mormons, 13, 89, 315
Morr, 27
Morrell, 196, 205, 266
Morrelly, 316
Morrice, 254
Morrill, 238
Morris, 15, 32, 34, 46, 81, 115, 183, 201, 289, 323, 393, 396, 403, 427, 512, 515, 520
Morrison, 25, 84, 105, 131, 227, 242, 286, 453
Morrow, 129, 459

Morse, 177, 208, 216, 331, 441, 443, 453
Morsell, 20, 30, 104, 213, 215, 259, 306, 317, 340, 424, 433, 436, 510
Mort, 420
Morton, 23, 133, 242, 456, 465
Mosely, 62, 374
Mosher, 118
Moss, 404
Motherwill, 308
Mott, 17, 213, 285, 383
Motter, 434
Motty, 427
Moucheron, 429
Moulder, 208, 313
Mount, 499
Mount Aetna, 168
Mount Airy, 166, 223, 320, 535
Mount Clemens, 394
Mount Hermon, 231
Mount Misery, 170
Mount Nebo, 166
Mount Pleasant, 267, 455
Mount Zion, 192
Mountjoy, 238
Mower, 226
Mowry, 132
Moxley, 353
Much ado about Nothing, 166
Mudd, 157, 185, 301, 410, 503, 515
Muhlenberg, 364
Muhlenburg, 137, 402
Muiler, 314
Muir, 26
Mulcaley, 465
Muldoon, 233
Mulford, 42
Mullany, 183
Mulledy, 131
Mullen, 54
Muller, 92, 224, 289, 504, 518, 524
Mullett, 276, 278
Mullikin, 61, 110, 459
Mullin, 155, 415

Mullings, 31, 121, 144, 154, 281
Mumford, 48, 141
Munchs, 335
Mundell, 155
Munding, 273
Munro, 410
Munroe, 108, 151, 244, 256, 336, 430, 463
Munson, 73
Muphy, 313
Murch, 68, 230, 245, 281, 305
Murdock, 167, 486, 523
Murphy, 34, 118, 152, 229, 244, 278, 281, 305, 325, 367, 376, 384, 410, 422, 458, 459, 477, 478, 530
Murrans, 253
Murray, 13, 134, 173, 217, 220, 250, 254, 271, 301, 310, 312, 373, 424, 459, 468, 524, 534
Murrell, 491
Murry, 185
Muse, 277, 326, 328, 433
Musgrove, 296
Muzzey, 223
Muzzleton, 451
Myerle, 44, 127, 138, 145
Myerlee, 67
Myers, 40, 84, 133, 178, 204, 241, 278, 296, 362, 365, 367, 374, 388, 453, 472, 497, 523
Myers', 35

N

Naesser, 468
Nagle, 427
Nailor, 208, 246, 410, 459
Nalley, 158, 189, 378, 432
Nance, 107, 281
Nancrede, 221
Naner, 293
Napoleon, 70, 200, 391, 402, 419
Narrow Escape, 167
Nash, 324, 430, 512
Nason, 250

Naudain, 251
Naull, 258
Navarro, 173
Naylor, 14, 45, 146, 178, 224, 239, 363
Neal, 15, 163, 308, 359
Neale, 76, 125, 150, 260, 320, 335
Neall, 313
Needham, 212
Neely, 249
Neff, 434
Neighbors, 196
Neill, 141
Neilson, 28
Neinsteel, 119
Nellis, 157
Nelson, 27, 84, 103, 115, 120, 124, 138, 170, 243, 412, 431, 444, 468, 480
Nesbit, 363
Nesbitt, 81
Netherland, 141, 170, 187
Netherlands, 149
Nettleton, 287
Nevans, 409
Nevett, 436
Neville, 442
Nevins, 268, 339, 343, 347, 410, 511
Nevius, 373
Newbury, 57
Newby, 427
Newcomb, 69, 241, 442, 536
Newcombe, 383
Newcome, 213
Newcomer, 435
Newell, 27, 376, 410
Newingham, 244, 256, 261, 281, 291
Newington, 162
Newland, 294
Newman, 36, 90, 95, 169, 210, 211, 266, 296, 300, 313, 333, 355, 383, 441, 469, 507, 530
Newsman, 69

Newton, 5, 40, 68, 116, 174, 216, 276, 406, 419, 440, 442, 518
Nichol, 468
Nicholas, 124, 130, 250, 419
Nicholl, 296
Nicholls, 377
Nichols, 212, 283, 326, 470
Nicholson, 50, 71, 107, 241, 313, 382, 406, 446, 486
Nickles, 165
Nickolls, 346
Nicoil, 144
Nicoll, 11, 81
Nietzey, 515
Niles, 161
Nixdorff, 465
Nixon, 152, 319, 365, 472
Noble, 55, 84, 89, 196, 283
Nobles, 138
Nock, 242
Nodding, 338
Noel, 57, 133
Noell, 125, 134, 459
Noerr, 289, 377
Nokes, 208
Nollner, 466
Nones, 20, 351, 479
Nonsuch, 481
Noonan, 349
Norbeck, 251, 530
Norman, 40, 506
Norris, 111, 386, 412, 441, 466
North, 113, 196, 223, 254, 369
Northam, 272
Norton, 15, 377
Norvell, 224
Norville, 312
Norway, 390
Norwood, 403
Nott, 403, 457
Nottingham, 85
Nourse, 89, 103, 168, 181, 223, 266, 329, 354, 399, 410, 427, 459, 513, 532

Noyes, 208, 317, 318, 321, 347, 513
Nuckerson, 125
Null, 451
Nunens, 129
Nunnamaker, 321
Nutt, 106, 284
Nye, 9, 232, 266, 274, 314

O

O'Brian, 369
O'Brien, 95, 175, 456, 476
O'Conner, 143
O'Connor, 63, 348
O'Donaghue, 95, 96
O'Hanlon, 442
O'Hannagin, 307
O'Hara, 40, 171, 436, 452
O'Neal, 51, 100, 350
O'Neale, 66, 79, 95, 208, 458, 460
O'Neil, 534
O'Neill, 415
O'Reilly, 255, 330
O'Rielly, 230
O'Riely, 95, 96
O'Sullivan, 150
Oakey, 323, 341
Oakley, 201, 527
Oaks, 461
Oakville, 68
Oat, 313
Oathondt, 116
Oatland, 290
Oatman, 427
Obear, 250
Ober, 208
Ocean House, 163
Ochem, 386
Oden, 410
Odenheimer, 11
Odthoudt, 60
Offerd,, 348
Offley, 21
Offutt, 9, 30, 252, 253, 475
Ogden, 173

Ogle, 76, 96, 119, 171, 320
Oglebay, 169
Ogleton, 124
Olds, 213, 244, 256, 270, 281, 303
Olingary, 67
Olive, 1
Oliver, 10, 118, 122, 170, 477
Ollinger, 4
Olmsted, 229
Olney, 39
Onderdonk, 25, 302
Onderonk, 399
Opdyke, 33
Orchard, 144
Ord, 76, 120, 145
Organ for Trinity Church, 402
Orm's Mill Seat, 167
Orm's Mistake, 167
Orm's Trouble, 167
Orme, 21, 169, 208, 260, 290, 410, 459, 530
Orr, 32, 222
Orte, 221
Orvis, 245, 257
Osborn, 59, 144, 203
Osborne, 12, 380, 396, 403, 482
Osburn, 178
Osgood, 15, 337, 476
Osier, 454
Ossian Hall, 258
Osterhout, 391
Ostrander, 256
Ostraunder, 244
Otis, 40, 132, 162, 351
Otterback, 28, 61, 171, 502
Otto, 302
Ould, 16, 209, 446
Ousley, 95, 143
Ovear, 159
Overbagh, 393
Overwater, 468
Owen, 4, 132, 160, 183, 263, 376, 512
Owens, 26, 55, 87, 144, 208, 502, 523

Owner, 95, 134, 184, 214, 240, 311, 359, 453, 508
Oyster, 18, 354, 365, 470
Ozias, 122

P

Pa_ne, 364
Paca, 170
Packenham, 80
packet-boat Kentucky, 307
Paddock, 295, 493
Paerson, 362
Page, 18, 27, 66, 78, 89, 116, 154, 156, 162, 237, 250, 286, 287, 329, 369, 383, 389, 403, 419, 478
Pageot, 31, 299, 344
Pain, 63, 497
Paine, 19, 32, 271
Painter, 81
Pairo, 88, 215
Palen, 217
Palmer, 57, 63, 114, 132, 149, 171, 208, 213, 285, 313, 422, 432, 434, 485, 520
Pancoast, 313
Papineau, 396
Paradise, 170
Parham, 4
Parish, 156
Park, 390
Park & the Rights of Man, 170
Parke, 114, 139, 256, 511
Parker, 20, 51, 74, 84, 86, 94, 100, 105, 114, 132, 138, 145, 168, 177, 208, 222, 251, 296, 314, 348, 366, 374, 391, 401, 410, 416, 426, 449, 453, 455, 459, 471, 494
Parkeson, 127
Parkhill, 151, 344
Parkinson, 5, 28
Parks, 40, 133, 178, 180, 219
Parks & Rights of Man, 166
Parr, 156, 354
Parran, 434

Parrot, 193
Parrott, 88, 280
Parsons, 45, 342, 364, 371, 404, 477, 478, 491
Partnership, 169
Pascoe, 2, 422
Passet, 320
Passett, 128
Patamedas, 429
Patch, 477
Patchett, 313, 400
Patrick, 5, 395, 413
Patten, 208
Patterson, 5, 14, 23, 24, 68, 93, 107, 208, 316, 330, 334, 336, 367, 434, 435, 495
Patton, 49, 215
Paul, 54, 237, 256, 323, 369, 472
Paulding, 15, 183
Pauley, 34
Paullin, 153, 191, 218
Paullind, 138
Pawling, 67, 98, 114, 389
Paxton, 518
Payne, 35, 48, 61, 194, 201, 299, 313, 348, 477, 478
Payson, 296
Pea Patch Island, 19
Peabody, 18, 33, 208, 399
Peach, 373
Peachy, 114, 124, 234
Peacock, 277, 440
Peak, 74
Peake, 244
Peale, 221, 291
Pearce, 3, 107, 133, 245, 257, 270, 306, 344, 430, 439
Pearson, 32, 35, 74, 75, 153, 165, 173, 260, 268, 337, 375, 410
Peatross, 440
Peay, 526
Peck, 75, 84, 94, 245, 288, 327, 430
Peckham, 241, 400
Peddecord, 141, 176, 417, 437

Pedrick, 156, 244
Peebles, 462, 467
Peek, 528
Peeples, 468
Peerce, 454, 468, 518
Pegg, 437
Pegram, 462, 467
Peirce, 28, 362
Peltier, 18, 41
Pendergrast, 250, 344
Pendlemon, 286
Pendleton, 10, 119, 283, 360, 374, 412, 469
Penguin, 440
Penn, 311, 378, 484
Pennington, 34, 36, 53, 58, 90, 436, 490
Pennock, 158, 232, 257
Penny, 163, 178, 432, 530
Penrose, 21, 512
Pepper, 66, 107, 108, 145, 147, 183, 248, 281, 303, 442, 459
Percival, 107
Perham, 156, 244, 256, 281, 302
Perkins, 52, 61, 122, 144, 186, 208, 322, 339, 430, 456, 499, 511
Perrault, 60
Perriam, 448
Perrin, 296, 439
Perrine, 132
Perry, 41, 70, 127, 139, 184, 196, 208, 217, 230, 244, 256, 270, 402, 482, 515, 536
Persico, 12, 287
Peter, 79, 169, 190, 211, 215, 233, 267, 391, 396, 411, 456
Peters, 65, 245, 330, 429
Peterson, 92, 196, 314, 335, 351
Petit, 313, 335, 368
Pettibone, 6, 98, 259, 421
Pettit, 483, 493
Pew, 248
Pews, 258
Peyster, 114, 116

Peyton, 263, 340
Pfeil, 314
Phalen, 142
Pheatt, 285
Phelps, 32, 58, 322, 434, 435, 523
Phenix, 468
Philip, 351
Philips, 218, 260, 330
Phillips, 19, 52, 177, 194, 208, 239, 301, 323, 359, 366, 390, 407, 424, 433, 462, 513, 532
Phillipsburg, 187
Philpot, 336
Phinney, 518
Phoenix, 501
Pickard, 149
Pickering, 126, 285
Pickett, 503
Pickman, 163
Pickrell, 3, 22, 332, 347
Pierce, 10, 35, 119, 154, 208, 224, 244, 257, 259, 271, 347, 463
Piercy, 275
Pierrepont, 358
Pierson, 15, 266
Pig Iron, 168
Piggott, 231, 487
Pike, 84, 283
Pilcher, 37
Piles, 517
Pilling, 208
Pinckney, 59
Pine, 159
Pine Hill, 443
Piney Plains, 169
Piney Point, 309
Pink, 468
Pink of Alleghany, 166, 170
Pinkham, 74, 95, 184
Pinkney, 254, 314, 420
Pinn, 203
Piper, 208, 472, 473
Pistorius, 208
Pitfiled, 460

Pitkin, 283, 326
Pitkin,, 328
Pitman, 216, 272
Pitts, 11, 124, 182, 212
Place, 241
Placy, 18, 41
Plant, 208, 322, 387, 424
Pleasant, 403
Pleasant Hill, 49, 58
Pleasant Ridge, 168, 479
Pleasanton, 327, 331
Pleasants, 111, 208, 269, 371
Pleasontor, 318
Ploof, 454
Plout, 467
Plowden, 347, 357, 420
Plume, 286
Plummer, 63, 88, 187, 236, 440
Plumsell, 488
Plumsill, 438, 480, 481, 508
Pochon, 335
Podgee, 483
Poe, 329
Poindexter, 109, 222, 225, 505
Point Addition, 170
Point Pleasant Valley, 166
Points, 40
Poland's Sugar Camp, 168
Polk, 148, 155, 252, 276, 299, 330, 367, 387, 398, 434, 448, 475, 480, 486, 487, 491
Pollard, 122, 189, 410, 492
Pollock, 58, 119
Polly, 166
Pomeroy, 8, 33, 324
Pomonkey, 197
Pond, 493
Pool, 212
Poole, 62, 382, 434
Poole,, 212
Pooler, 99, 255, 260
Poor, 84, 348, 412, 418
Poothman, 441
Pope, 59, 74, 324, 363, 448, 461

Pope Benedict XIII, 464
Pope Benedict XIV, 464
Pope's creek, 190
Poplar Grove, 259
Porche, 344
Port Tobacco Times, 199
Porter, 27, 44, 56, 58, 61, 76, 83, 120, 124, 141, 147, 149, 151, 189, 208, 278, 287, 288, 313, 314, 367, 405, 466, 493, 516
Porterfield, 142
Posey, 43, 157, 266
Post, 102, 427
Posten, 208
Potato Garden, 170
Pottawatamie, 116, 294
Potter, 36, 61, 63, 90, 108, 208, 395, 418, 434
Potts, 167, 169, 512
Poulson, 355
Poulton, 432
Powell, 69, 74, 203, 278, 419, 431, 459, 496
Power, 119, 242, 343
Powers, 8, 36, 90, 126, 141, 505, 510
Prain, 111
Prather, 96, 387
Pratt, 57, 63, 101, 307, 380
Pray, 174
Preble, 201
Prefontaine, 448, 465
Prentice, 180, 313, 371, 430
Prentiss, 109, 174, 233, 276, 340, 453, 459
Prescott, 292, 508
Presenent, 493
Presley, 467
Preston, 91, 125, 148, 215, 340, 416, 446, 465, 480
Pretontaine, 465
Pretty Prospect, 168, 223
Prettyman, 286
Preuss, 494, 517
Prevost, 27, 63, 76

Price, 43, 65, 107, 149, 204, 267, 349, 521
Prickett, 456
Priest, 254, 423
Prince, 395
Prince Albert, 90
Princess Sophia, 525
Pringle, 130
prisons, 345
Pritchard, 417, 506
Pritchart, 427
Priven, 519
Proctor, 208, 230, 256, 261, 281, 306, 505
Profit, 278
Prophet Joe, 13
Prospect Hall, 243
Proud, 339
Prout, 450, 470
Provest, 208
Provost, 459
Prudhomme, 335
Pryor, 406
Puckett, 427
Pue, 260
Puffer, 66
Pugh, 156, 534
Pulcifer, 61, 138
Pulsifer, 338
Pulvermacher, 103, 134
Pumphrey, 4, 396, 459, 480
Purcell, 446
Purdon, 457
Purdy, 117, 121, 183, 208, 424, 482
Purgett, 169
Purnell, 383, 434
Purrell, 202
Purrington, 430
Purrinton, 256
Pursell, 302, 447, 459
Pursuvint, 518
Pussy, 311
Putnam, 126
Putney, 120, 145, 147, 158, 297

Pye, 504
Pyncheon, 108
Pynchou, 144
Pyne, 523

Q

Quackenbush, 36, 90
Quantrill, 34, 57
Quarto, 169
Queen, 96, 178, 260, 411, 439, 440, 463, 506, 533
Queen Victoria, 388
Quigley, 150, 458, 502, 506
Quimby, 13, 239, 495
Quincy, 248
Quinn, 99, 314
Quynn, 434

R

Rabbits Walk, 169
Rabineau, 365
Radcliff, 37, 367, 411, 469
Ragan, 218, 473
Ragsdale, 152
Raines, 462
Rainey, 96, 179, 263, 343
Rake, 423
Ramsay, 111, 475, 519, 525
Ramsey, 61, 94, 124, 136, 163, 168, 219
Ramson, 74
Rand, 15
Randall, 148, 208, 212, 214, 240, 411, 418, 433, 489
Randolph, 4, 36, 79, 82, 88, 90, 106, 111, 134, 205, 208, 219, 431, 477, 483
Range, 170
Rankin, 385
Ransom, 412
Ranson, 51, 246, 496
Rantoul, 128, 134, 278, 279
Rapelje, 64
Raper, 196

Raquet, 138
Ratcliff, 66, 200, 411, 441
Ratcliffe, 209, 395
Rathbone, 19, 478
Rathbun, 200
Rawdon, 90
Rawle, 323
Rawlings, 360, 429
Ray, 512
Ray's Discovery, 168
Rayall, 73
Raymond, 33, 54, 158, 167, 168, 234, 340, 434, 471
Rayner, 338
Read, 10, 174, 267, 296, 327, 360, 406, 446, 527
Reading Furnace, 460
Rearden, 152
Rector, 40
Redding, 186
Reddington, 13
Redfern, 398, 458, 520
Redfield, 228, 270
Redin, 103, 223, 288, 395
Reding, 55
Redington, 518
Redrow, 64
Redwood, 35
Reed, 12, 35, 72, 81, 84, 112, 119, 123, 149, 208, 262, 281, 334, 335, 466, 495
Reedy, 347
Reepe, 296
Reese, 94, 168, 325, 345, 383, 444
Reeside, 83, 119, 258, 504, 508, 513
Reeve, 84, 403
Reeves, 204, 218, 397
Regnard, 364
Regnaud, 199
Reich, 104
Reid, 75, 94, 122, 236, 241, 281, 293, 362, 388
Reiley, 84
Reilly, 50, 57, 143, 189, 336

Reily, 95, 459
Rein, 467
Reitz, 209
Rencher, 27
Renehan, 143
Rennell, 313
Renner, 487
Rennock, 245
Rennoe, 419
Renshaw, 241, 335
Rensselaer, 391
Renwick, 148
Request, 169
Rescorl, 152
Resurvey, 223
Reval, 401
Revel, 493
Revenue Cutter **Woodbury**, 199
Reverton, 168
Rex, 389
Rey, 280
Reynier, 90
Reynold, 178
Reynolds, 28, 141, 159, 215, 341, 425
Reynolds' farm, 349
Rhea, 266, 372
Rhind, 46
Rhinedollar, 221, 472
Rhodes, 28, 59, 69, 70, 142, 197, 263, 413
Ricaud, 175, 212, 335
Rice, 74, 124, 177, 221, 316, 337, 431, 453, 472, 493, 506, 517
Rich, 31, 35, 150, 261, 262, 335, 413, 517
Rich Bottom, 166
Rich Glades, 170
Richards, 9, 123, 139, 314, 336, 393
Richardson, 80, 91, 161, 188, 266, 425
Richcreek, 181, 257, 282, 303
Riche, 323
Richey, 143, 170
Richie, 170
Richmeyer, 381

Richmond, 32, 208
Rickets, 365
Rickett, 365, 415
Rickette, 373
Ricketts, 461
Riddle, 120, 145, 158, 297, 527
Ridell, 427
Rider, 212, 324
Ridgaway, 184
Ridge, 37
Ridgeley, 21
Ridgely, 99, 370, 406, 532
Ridgway, 5, 79
Ridout, 41, 484
Riebaud, 194
Ried, 251
Rigden, 34
Rigg, 111
Riggles, 404
Riggs, 143, 148, 259, 269, 315, 371, 383, 390, 412
Rights of Man, 166
Riley, 30, 95, 99, 140, 314, 326
Ringgold, 208, 353, 395, 533
Rinker, 10
Riordan, 208, 273, 334
Ripp, 198, 200
Risen, 472
Risinger, 6
Risler, 184
Risley, 212
Ritch, 532
Ritchie, 37, 125, 242, 243, 248, 274, 440, 517, 525, 533
Ritter, 123, 248, 322
River, 452
Rives, 95, 117, 148, 183, 340, 425, 447, 459
Rivieres, 344
Rivinus, 27
Rizenburgh, 521
Roach, 96, 106, 128, 132, 208, 289, 316, 363, 381, 476, 495
Roach, reg/o wills, 448

Roane, 248
Roanoke, 168
Robb, 36, 88, 90, 210, 266, 283
Robbins, 80, 107, 218, 233, 313, 431, 486
Roberson, 534
Roberts, 3, 43, 107, 111, 142, 165, 185, 188, 236, 254, 255, 272, 274, 301, 310, 313, 319, 323, 340, 367, 435, 445, 462, 504, 525, 533
Robertson, 11, 22, 42, 53, 75, 111, 119, 150, 157, 293, 353, 371, 377, 396, 411, 418, 428, 431, 446, 518, 532
Robeson, 101
Robey, 156, 157
Robey's Adventure, 167
Robillard, 349
Robinson, 3, 5, 65, 68, 100, 104, 108, 139, 151, 154, 159, 171, 184, 196, 199, 203, 208, 242, 260, 296, 313, 334, 335, 350, 353, 358, 411, 412, 413, 419, 461, 473, 486
Robison, 123
Roby, 61, 454
Rochambeau, 71
Roche, 24, 344, 347
Rochford, 343
Rockwell, 237
Rodbird, 208
Rodburn, 502
Roden, 311
Rodgers, 1, 80, 88, 331, 351, 398, 527
Rodgers tract, 80
Rodier, 418
Rodman, 11, 286
Rodney, 78
Roe, 250, 442
Roebling, 238
Roebock, 219
Roemmele, 289, 368, 382
Rogers, 40, 41, 57, 63, 68, 72, 85, 102, 156, 197, 228, 239, 244, 257, 262, 325, 340, 366, 434, 490, 500

Roget, 407
Rohrer, 333
Rokhill, 334
Roland, 142
Rollins, 33
Rollston, 215
Romain, 212
Romaine, 64
Roman, 109, 243
Ronalds, 427, 440
Ronckendorff, 74
Roney, 313, 430
Root, 215, 283
Roper, 411, 419
Rosas, 20
Rosborough, 108
Rose, 77, 81, 84, 87, 145, 231, 236, 312
Rose Bud, 168
Rose Cottage, 363
Rose Hill, 36
Roseberry, 18
Rosemont, 77, 111, 536
Rosenkrantz, 529
Rosenkranz, 76
Ross, 32, 77, 118, 149, 189, 199, 204, 212, 213, 236, 324, 328, 394, 405, 451, 493, 528, 536
Ross di Tivoli, 429
Rossignal, 276
Rossignol, 335
Roszel, 262, 263, 428
Roszell, 152
Rote, 492
Rothwell, 21, 86, 409
Roulet, 205
Rourk, 465
Rousseau, 429
Rowan, 133, 400
Rowe, 107, 201, 245, 257, 270
Rowland, 72, 77, 248, 270, 348
Rowles, 129, 392
Royal Charter, 170
Royston, 12, 40, 299, 340

Rozere, 380
Rozier's Gift, 398
Rubens, 429
Rucker, 357
Rudenstein, 493
Ruff, 400
Ruffner, 192
Rugg, 384
Ruggs, 122
Rule, 360
Rumnell, 202, 240
Rundlet, 158, 177
Rundlett, 94
Runnells, 510
Runnels, 471
Runyon, 323
Ruppert, 458
Rush, 133, 134
Russel, 347, 495
Russell, 27, 33, 39, 54, 69, 75, 136, 156, 218, 226, 244, 257, 272, 347, 419, 431, 485, 511, 513, 514, 517, 520, 532
Russell's Planetarium, 116
Russuam, 76
Russworm, 149
Rust, 444, 480
Rustic Hat, 169
Rutherford, 188, 224, 477
Rutledge, 59
Rutlidge, 260
Rutzell, 339
Ruysdal, 429
Ryan, 121, 483, 526
Ryder, 118, 137, 195, 204, 280
Ryland, 310, 452
Ryon, 423, 426

S

Sacett, 461
Sackrider, 70
Saffarrans, 319
Sage, 443
Sailor's Rest, 87, 231

Salaignao, 314
Sale, 360, 373
Salisbury, 357, 374
Saltmarsh, 107, 232, 245, 257, 271, 276
Sammons, 332
Sampson, 365, 403, 486
Samson, 11, 57, 62, 100, 142, 155, 172, 186, 438, 440, 477, 502, 508, 512, 520, 524
Samuels, 209, 458
Sand, 93
Sanders, 162, 174, 194, 229, 246, 255, 285, 311, 335, 411, 430, 438, 467, 514
Sanderson, 175
Sands, 103, 195, 244, 250, 256, 263, 281, 306, 411
Sanford, 468
Sangster, 516
Sanno, 338
Santa Anna, 43, 62, 423, 436, 475, 487
Santmanat, 194
Sardo, 139, 381
Sargeant, 152
Sargent, 15, 361, 379
Sartorius, 440
Sasscer, 209
Saulsbury, 46
Saunders, 6, 7, 47, 109, 119, 248, 457, 467, 491, 497, 509, 520, 533
Sautell, 68
Savage, 37, 39, 48, 209, 242, 389, 428, 461, 477
Sawtell, 158
Sawyer, 82, 127
Saxton, 71, 396
Scaggs, 461
Scarburg, 193
Scattergood, 383
Sceifferle, 459
Schaeffer, 313, 461, 465
Schaghen, 47

Schaleken, 429
Schatzel, 527
Scheele, 446
Schekell, 348
Scheler, 385
Schenck, 48, 218
Schirmirhorn, 403
Schley, 277, 395
Schneider, 418, 458, 460, 470
Schnell, 44, 73
schnr **Ann**, 151
schnr **Atlantic**, 461
schnr **Caledonia**, 534
schnr **Creole**, 475
schnr **Dove**, 156, 245, 257, 272
schnr **Eagle**, 110
schnr **Eliza**, 420
schnr **Enterprise**, 20
schnr **Exchange**, 85
schnr **Farmer & Mechanic**, 34
schnr **Flirt**, 367
schnr **Florilla**, 108, 245, 257, 272
schnr **Freedom**, 231
schnr **Gallatin**, 250
schnr **Gannet**, 272
schnr **Garnet**, 108
schnr **Garnett**, 245, 257
schnr **Gen Wm Washington**, 38
schnr **Grampus**, 22, 51, 75, 114, 124, 320
schnr **Hudson**, 457
schnr **Illinois**, 285
schnr **Industry**, 506
schnr **James & Henry**, 95, 184, 272
schnr **John Barr**, 173
schnr **Mary Carver**, 127
schnr **Mary Frances**, 108
schnr **Mary Francis**, 245, 257, 272, 282, 293
schnr **N Biddle**, 231
schnr **Orange**, 380
schnr **Pauline**, 184
schnr **Pearl**, 292

schnr **Privado**, 84, 156, 245, 257, 272, 282, 297
schnr **Sarah Lavinia**, 11
schnr **Shamrock**, 231
schnr **Shark**, 295
schnr **State**, 140
schnr **Success**, 132, 272
schnr **Thomas**, 56
schnr **Two Brothers**, 156, 245, 257, 272
schnr **Union**, 177, 245, 257, 272
schnr **Vanderbilt**, 250
schnr **Virginian**, 140
schnr **William A Turner**, 368
schnrs **James & Henry**, 81
schnrs **Sevo & Ida**, 43
Schober, 532
Scholfield, 172, 465
Schoolcraft, 151
Schoonhoven, 180
Schrack, 196
Schroader, 328
Schumacker, 248
Schureman, 277, 326
Schussler, 360
Schuyler, 6, 28, 63, 85, 120, 132, 177, 233
Schwartz, 448
Schwartztrawber, 244, 256
Scipio, 361
Scott, 9, 76, 88, 107, 112, 116, 120, 133, 142, 144, 171, 174, 178, 221, 230, 244, 246, 257, 270, 277, 295, 296, 306, 308, 309, 318, 328, 344, 347, 350, 368, 381, 402, 411, 415, 426, 428, 431, 440, 459, 460, 465, 468, 473, 479, 480, 490, 495, 512, 528, 533
Scovell, 16
Scranton, 461
Seals, 258
Seaman, 184
Search, 352
Searcy, 479

Searight, 233
Searle, 328
Searls, 248
Seaton, 4, 95, 113, 137, 148, 289, 397, 495, 529
Seaver, 113, 474
Seawell, 369
Seay, 440
Sebring, 376
Second Thought, 2
Secor, 71
Sedgwick, 5, 15
Seeley, 211
Seigert, 15
Seigle, 159
Seiler, 296
Selby, 134, 193, 210, 212, 502
Selden, 134, 250, 374, 414, 520
Selfridge, 285
Sellers, 232, 245, 257
Sellman, 212, 434
Semen, 372
Semmes, 5, 134, 199, 209, 233, 242, 250, 254, 336, 347, 348, 487
Semple, 91, 527
Sengstack, 139, 244, 256, 271, 281, 459
Sentman, 289
Sentmanat, 341, 368
Sergeant, 11, 123, 193, 390
Servant, 91
Service, 489
Sessford, 209, 211, 289, 377, 454, 531
Sessions, 164, 310
Settle, 5
Seven Springs, 169
Severeux, 325
Sevier, 17
Sewall, 75, 107, 146, 148, 165, 224, 322, 482, 501
Seward, 180
Sewell, 124
Sexsmith, 34, 483
Seybold, 508

Seymour, 130, 373
Shadd, 458
Shadernah, 292
Shaeffer, 196, 452
Shaffer, 313, 508
Shaler, 279
Shamrock Hill, 342
Shankland, 497
Shanklin, 12
Shanks, 39, 350
Shannon, 107, 115, 145, 147, 158, 176, 198, 251, 282, 423
Shannon Hill Farm, 184
Shard, 196
Sharp, 155, 330, 351
Sharp's Island, 359
Sharpe, 20, 431, 484, 520
Sharretts, 382, 397
Shattuck, 412
Shaw, 44, 66, 213, 235, 263, 313, 429, 470, 485, 517, 525, 532
Shawnee Indians, 22, 222
Shea, 465
Sheahan, 4, 143, 357
Sheckell, 459
Sheckle, 447
Shedd, 340, 461
Sheehan, 96
Sheehy, 143
Sheeles, 451
Sheid, 310
Shekells, 209
Shelby, 67
Sheldon, 295, 353
Shelmire, 389
Shelton, 209
Sheme, 256
Shepard, 81, 212
Shephard, 90, 273
Shepherd, 185, 200, 283, 296, 380, 398, 427
Shepherd's Park, 168
Sheppard, 36, 183
Shepperd, 194, 438

Sheriff, 31, 179, 463
Sherlock, 130, 534
Sherman, 79, 133, 209, 230, 313, 460, 493
Sherrard, 404, 487
Sherry, 415, 472
Shield, 248
Shields, 209, 414
Shiffen, 81
Shiffler, 431
Shifler, 219
Shiftell, 509
Shinn, 61
ship **Alexandria**, 75
ship **Boston**, 250
ship **Carlos**, 205
ship **Champion**, 178
ship **Charles Carroll**, 51
ship **Clematis**, 179
ship **Columbus**, 36
ship **Columbus 74**, 20
ship **Constellation**, 59
ship **Cyane**, 187, 418
ship **Decatur**, 491
ship **Delaware**, 115, 151
ship **Erie**, 29, 187, 412, 418
ship **Falmouth**, 472, 473
ship **Frederick Jacob**, 488
ship **Gaston**, 369
ship **Grampus**, 276
ship **Great Western**, 460
ship **Herald**, 20
ship **Hornet**, 306
ship **Ilzaide**, 450
ship **Johannes**, 333
ship **Johannis**, 275
ship **John Adams**, 250
ship **Levant**, 478
ship **Malabar 74**, 440
ship **Marcia**, 488
ship **Mary Kingsland**, 463
ship **Massasoit**, 511
ship **May Flower**, 486
ship **Mediator**, 388

ship **Missouri**, 406, 412, 417
ship **Nassau**, 178
ship **Nathaniel Hooper**, 450
ship of the line **Delaware**, 12
ship of the line **Pennsylvania**, 157
ship **Ohio**, 287
ship **Oxford**, 145
ship **Palestine**, 228
ship **Peacock**, 107, 181
ship **Pennsylvania**, 19
ship **Phenix**, 355
ship **Plymouth**, 363
ship **Potomac**, 451
ship **Preble**, 388
ship **Princeton**, 100, 104, 105
ship **Queen of the West**, 367
ship **Roebuck**, 343
ship **Saladin**, 346
ship **Saratoga**, 127
ship **Savannah**, 295
ship **Siddons**, 214
ship **St Mary's**, 520
ship **Styx**, 194
ship **Thos P Cope**, 461
ship **Toronto**, 490
ship **Two Sisters**, 378
ship **Vandalia**, 364, 426
ship **Venture**, 216
ship **Vicksburg**, 380
ship **Vincennes**, 19, 199
ship **Yorktown**, 442
Shipley, 104
ship-of-the-line **Columbus**, 20, 250
Shirar, 391
Shiras, 419
Shircliff, 212
Shirk, 25
Shirley, 36, 90
Shittenden, 302
Shivers, 181
Shockhoe Hill, 403
Shoemaker, 39, 197
Sholar, 156
Shonnard, 494

Short, 44, 92
Shott, 408, 423
Showance Springs, 460
Shower, 204
Showers, 305
Shreve, 37, 184, 266
Shrieves, 221
Shriver, 434
Shroeder, 335
Shrofe, 145, 147, 282, 305
Shrofer, 258
Shubrick, 20, 36, 60, 74, 90, 155, 247, 265, 275, 351, 495
Shultz, 309
Shumacker, 382
Shumenberg, 275
Shurts, 362
Sibbald, 522
Sibbold, 478
Siddons, 313
Sideling Hill Improved, 169
Siera, 432
Sigler, 168
Sigoigne, 137
Sigourney, 15
Silby, 318
Silence, 5
Silliman, 35, 180, 228
Sills, 526
Simmes, 106, 356
Simmons, 67, 313
Simms, 15, 36, 90, 96, 165, 209, 212, 241, 259, 284, 332, 459, 465, 497, 520
Simonds, 142
Simons, 181
Simonton, 456
Simpkins' Kindness, 167
Simpson, 37, 80, 91, 104, 137, 258, 263, 313, 325, 385, 482, 504, 512, 525
Sinclair, 96, 119, 153, 416, 493
Singleton, 167
Singley, 139, 244, 256

Singly, 116
Sipley, 517
Sisson, 285
Sister Clotilda, 255
Sisters of Charity, 143, 160
Skiller, 281
Skinner, 4, 6, 19, 25, 31, 53, 114, 116, 147, 210, 228, 244, 273, 280
Skippon, 145
Skipton, 169
Skirvin, 200
Skirving, 209, 385, 501
Slack, 317
Slacum, 27, 232
Slade, 514
Slagg, 242
Slamm, 311
Slateman, 497
Slater, 287, 335, 496
Slator, 438
Slaughter, 353
Slavin, 116
Sleeman, 174
Slevin, 347
Slicer, 351
Sligo, 470
Slinkard, 32
Sloane, 518
Sloansker, 314
Sloat, 416
Slocum, 28, 119
Slone, 54
sloop **Decatur**, 127
sloop **Marion**, 13
sloop of war **Peacock**, 81
sloop of war **Saratoga**, 341
sloop **Saratoga**, 127
sloop **Superb**, 445
sloop-of-war **Fairfield**, 442
sloop-of-war **Jamestown**, 413
sloop-of-war **Vestal**, 80
Slye, 279
Small, 441
Smalles, 514

Smalley, 41
Smallwood, 285
Smead, 341
Smedes, 153, 215
Smidley, 159
Smith, 4, 5, 13, 15, 18, 25, 26, 29, 40, 41, 44, 46, 54, 56, 76, 82, 98, 108, 122, 133, 136, 139, 144, 148, 150, 163, 173, 176, 178, 181, 186, 190, 196, 200, 204, 209, 210, 213, 216, 218, 222, 223, 224, 227, 229, 231, 234, 241, 244, 246, 250, 255, 265, 266, 267, 270, 273, 279, 287, 289, 296, 306, 308, 313, 315, 324, 328, 329, 342, 343, 354, 359, 368, 378, 388, 389, 396, 403, 404, 405, 408, 411, 414, 415, 416, 417, 421, 422, 425, 427, 430, 431, 432, 436, 437, 440, 456, 458, 467, 469, 473, 477, 483, 490, 492, 494, 497, 499, 502, 514, 515, 518, 524, 534
Smiths, 315
Smithson, 62
Smitt, 1
smoking, 357
Smoot, 96, 98, 194, 209, 232, 237, 250, 381, 395, 422, 430, 436, 456
Smyser, 119
Smyth, 95
snag-boat **Gopher**, 462
Snead, 153, 244, 256
Sneed, 265, 281
Snell, 26, 33, 400
Snethen, 278, 364, 451
Snively, 157
Snodgrass, 308
Snow, 119, 138, 234, 248, 266, 295, 329
Snowden, 194, 343, 344, 422
Snyder, 5, 163, 172, 321, 413, 488
Sobieski, 464
Soldier's lot, 169
Sollers, 158, 212, 348, 505
Solomon, 114, 429

Somerley, 57
Somers, 173, 214
Somerville, 190
Sommerance, 23
Sommeraner, 244, 256
Sommeroner, 120
Soper, 59, 334
Sothoron, 5
Soult, 200
South Green,, 404
Southall, 173
Southard, 217, 379
Southworth, 115
Sower, 349
Spalding, 5, 22, 43, 181, 251, 272, 299, 344, 403, 419
Spangler, 467
Sparrow, 109
Spaulding, 195, 250
Speakes, 3
Spear, 430
Spedden, 21
Speiden, 81, 512
Speir, 396
Speiser, 61
Speisser, 28, 388
Spence, 33, 383
Spencer, 11, 14, 74, 97, 120, 148, 212, 272, 276, 278, 306, 311, 347, 365, 369, 433, 509
Sperey, 71
Spicer, 209, 412
Spies, 25
Sportman's Field, 170
Spotswood, 438
Spotts, 68
Sprague, 6, 10, 72, 154, 197, 294, 338, 430, 443
Spratt, 143
Sprigg, 97, 433, 434
Spring, 87
Spring Hill, 189
Springer, 238, 290, 325, 434

Sprole, 34, 122, 189, 332, 396, 417, 419, 428, 471, 524
Squier, 202
Squire, 93
Squirrel Range, 167
St Augustine, 51
St Clair, 457
St George, 464
St John, 41, 190
St Joseph's Park, 41
St Vrain, 236, 254, 256, 533
Stacy, 133, 278, 279
Stadlin, 417
Stalcom, 454
Stallings, 143
Stanard, 381
Standford, 347
Standish, 69, 506
Stanhope, 180
Stanley, 39, 150, 209, 258
Stanly, 215, 338
Stansbury, 328, 433, 434
Stanton, 49, 149, 400, 444
Stanway, 451
Stapler, 394
Staples, 1
Stark, 3, 519
Starke, 198
Starr, 102, 345
Starrett, 526
Startzman, 518
Staylor, 403
steamboat **Augusta**, 197
steamboat **Belle of Clarksville**, 526
steamboat **Cleveland**, 285, 306
steamboat **Clipper**, 138
steamboat **Diamond**, 162
steamboat **Farmer**, 64
steamboat **General Vance**, 308
steamboat **Hempstead**, 87
steamboat **Henry Bry**, 26
steamboat **Louisiana**, 526
steamboat **Lucy Walker**, 462, 466, 475

steamboat **Mazeppa**, 462
steamboat **Missouri**, 446
steamboat **Mount Pleasant**, 532
steamboat **New Haven**, 85
steamboat **Oceola**, 131
steamboat **Phoenix**, 61
steamboat **Portsmouth**, 367
steamboat **Shepherdess**, 26, 33, 47, 53, 94
steamboat **Sydney**, 63
steamer **Acadia**, 314
steamer **Buckeye**, 122, 193, 521
steamer **Caledonia**, 263
steamer **Columbia**, 309
steamer **De Soto**, 122, 193, 521
steamer **Gen Morgan**, 263
steamer **Gen Taylor**, 364
steamer **Govn'r Dudley**, 533
steamer **La Salle**, 390
steamer **Missouri**, 36
steamer **Monona**, 439
steamer **Palestine**, 308
steamer **Phenix**, 363
steamer **Poinsett**, 199
steamer **Potosi**, 439
steamer **President**, 139
steamer **Princeton**, 3, 108, 110, 112, 113, 239, 299
steamer **Princeton** was, 109
steamer **Rhode Island**, 352
steamer **Shepherdess**, 84
steamer **St Matthews**, 82
steamer **Troy**, 308
steamer **Union**, 217, 364
steamer **Wilmington**, 454
steamship **Acadia**, 310
steamship **Legare**, 479
steamship **Missouri**, 440, 442, 445
Steane, 403
Stedman, 520
Steedman, 246
Steel, 93, 260, 414
Steele, 58, 214, 242, 442, 492, 493, 504

Steen, 429, 444, 480
Steenbergen, 381
Steenrod, 56
Steeprock, 483
Steever, 225
Steeves, 353
Stegagnini, 209
Stelle, 201
Stembel, 75, 246
Stenson, 68
Stephen, 31, 299, 342
Stephens, 14, 15, 21, 57, 101, 329, 340, 408, 459, 489, 500
Stepper, 11
Sterke, 508
Sterling, 68, 193, 290, 337, 461
Sterrett, 31
Stetson, 361
Stettinius, 132, 209, 246, 464
Steuart, 114
Steuben, 161
Steven, 36
Stevens, 90, 103, 144, 164, 172, 209, 242, 250, 276, 296, 308, 351, 367, 383, 452, 455, 470, 491, 492
Stevenson, 21, 313, 431, 503
Stewart, 13, 23, 51, 55, 62, 69, 98, 122, 128, 138, 161, 174, 209, 212, 213, 232, 266, 288, 290, 347, 383, 388, 389, 398, 406, 415, 433, 436, 441, 446, 447, 459, 483, 504, 512
Stewart's Delight, 170
Stibel, 221
Stickney, 238, 527
Stiles, 52, 200
Still, 461
Stillings, 486
Stillman, 416
Stillwager, 483
Stillwell, 431
Stilson, 61, 376
Stinson, 56
Stintz, 455
Stith, 209, 397

Stock, 518
Stocking, 81
Stockton, 100, 109, 110, 126, 148, 205, 217, 445, 497, 506, 535
Stoddard, 4, 19, 44, 75, 142, 250
Stoker, 139
Stokes, 86, 506
Stolker, 468
Stone, 4, 14, 15, 38, 46, 67, 71, 95, 122, 126, 132, 184, 196, 197, 214, 218, 272, 311, 347, 348, 371, 404, 444, 450, 455, 463, 466, 473, 482, 508
Stonestreet, 253, 282, 504
Stoops, 348
Store, 57
Storer, 10
storeship **Lexington**, 438
Stork, 432
Storke, 126
Storm, 37
Storms, 479
Story, 72, 331
Stott, 95, 209, 240, 399, 455, 459
Stouse, 294
Stout, 75, 147
Stouton, 43
Stovell, 461
Stovin, 453
Stowe, 15, 442
Stowell, 279
Stratford, 126
Straub, 459
Street, 314, 318
Streets, 124
Stretch, 88, 350
Stribling, 63, 431
Strickland, 110
Strine, 313
Stringer, 365
Stringfellow, 218, 220, 400, 430, 481, 523, 536
Strohm, 112, 119

Strong, 44, 83, 145, 215, 274, 287, 294, 327
Strong,, 276
Struller, 15
Stuart, 185, 209, 250, 254, 300, 301, 303, 373, 457
Stuarts, 93, 464
Stubbens, 450
Stubblefield, 92
Stubbs, 95, 143, 383
Stufflebeau, 202
Stull, 27, 92, 107
Stupe, 169
Sturges, 245, 257, 282, 303, 304
Sturgess, 181, 293
Sturgis, 480
Sturns, 44
Sublett, 421
Suebach, 429
Suit, 528
Sullivan, 95, 148, 459
Sullivant, 107
Sultan of Coti, 373
Summeraner, 270
Summers, 16, 419
Sumner, 136, 308, 484
Suter, 512
Sutton, 248, 335, 446, 474
Suydam, 315
Swaggart, 100
Swallow, 195
Swan, 27, 283, 423
Swanberg, 295
Swann, 68, 75, 98, 133, 177, 361, 396, 479, 522
Swanton, 9
Swartwout, 327, 532
Swartzwauver, 177
Sweegan, 381
Sweeney, 184, 308
Sweeny, 411
Sweepstates, 169
Sweet, 295
Sweeting, 209, 458

Swift, 198, 214
Swinger, 23
Swingrison, 314
Swink, 313
Sylvester, 8
Symington, 307, 358, 468
Symmes, 268
Syrock, 225, 377, 444

T

Tabb, 526
Taber, 116
Tabler, 209, 331, 369
Tache, 334, 335
Tagart, 212
Taggart, 221, 534
Taggert, 217, 431, 455
Taglioni, 462
Taibor, 313
Tait, 425, 447
Taking the veil, 503
Talbot, 153, 383
Talburt, 82, 176
Talcott, 246
Talfair, 213
Talford, 439
Taliaferro, 7, 25, 75, 171, 329, 502
Taliferro, 153
Tall, 433
Talley, 28
Talliaferro, 221
Tallmadge, 158, 282, 385, 498
Talty, 401, 458
Tandy, 26
Taney, 13, 500
Tanner, 129, 135
Tappan, 71, 141, 324
Taring, 502
Tarlton, 135
Tarr, 81, 313
Tarring, 152, 310, 325, 523, 532
Tate, 209, 268, 452
Tatem, 11, 423
Taten, 147

Tatman, 81
Tatnall, 468
Tattnall, 241
Taul, 108
Taw-cum-e-go-qua, 291
Tayloe, 96, 148, 209, 535
Taylor, 5, 15, 19, 30, 60, 77, 90, 92, 99, 108, 109, 118, 123, 135, 136, 150, 162, 181, 187, 209, 212, 213, 230, 231, 250, 293, 296, 314, 320, 327, 328, 330, 378, 415, 435, 444, 447, 450, 467, 477, 483, 490, 506, 508, 513, 517, 518, 520, 528, 532
Tayman, 4
Teal, 317
Teale, 72
Teas, 54
Teasdale, 430
Tedman, 287
Tefts, 143
Tegan, 26
Telegraph, 441
Telfair, 72, 244, 257, 281, 305
Teller, 424
Templeman, 161, 168, 347
Templeton, 423
Ten Eick, 74, 161
Ten Eyck, 193
Tenant, 470
Tenbrook, 430
Tench, 209, 408
Teniers, 429
Tennant, 319
Tennent, 242
Tenney, 313, 366
Terrett, 426
Territt, 411
Terry, 284
Test, 24, 168
Tete, 344
Tewksbury, 164
Thatcher, 173, 247, 276
Thaw, 411
Thaxter, 377

600

Thayer, 71, 180, 427
Thecker, 415
Theobold, 168
Theriot, 128, 320
Thom, 527
Thomas, 6, 24, 26, 33, 48, 60, 67, 72, 73, 81, 96, 109, 112, 118, 135, 140, 146, 148, 175, 209, 218, 246, 251, 277, 288, 291, 305, 326, 327, 342, 353, 411, 433, 440, 445, 446, 448, 457, 459, 460, 463, 470, 495, 519, 525
Thomas & Ann, 170
Thomasson, 25
Thompson, 1, 8, 13, 14, 23, 25, 27, 51, 56, 62, 75, 80, 114, 128, 132, 138, 148, 173, 176, 191, 196, 197, 209, 212, 214, 242, 245, 257, 259, 260, 265, 266, 278, 282, 283, 295, 298, 318, 340, 349, 374, 383, 384, 390, 411, 417, 423, 427, 434, 436, 448, 456, 457, 460, 462, 463, 467, 489, 518, 528, 529
Thomson, 109, 314, 376
Thorn, 209, 331, 381
Thornberger, 173
Thornley, 113, 460, 533
Thornly, 260, 506
Thornton, 11, 23, 29, 111, 153, 227, 230, 231, 244, 299, 300, 307, 351, 517, 525
Thorpe, 89, 218, 240, 248
Thorwaldsen, 200
Thrift, 479
Throckmorton, 420
Throop, 463
Thruston, 128, 248, 478, 521
Thume, 63
Thumlert, 387
Thurman, 72
Thurston, 209, 295
Tibbats, 182
Tibbatts, 12
Tibbetts, 65

Tibbits, 41
Tibbs, 467
Tidball, 312
Tiernan, 173
Tilby, 468
Tilden, 276, 278, 433
Tilghamn, 323
Tilghman, 212, 267
Tillard, 56
Tillaston, 250
Tilley, 277, 320, 413
Tillinghast, 455
Tillotson, 313
Tilton, 20, 238, 463
Timms, 295, 494
Timothy Level, 168
Tims, 411
Tinckle, 84
Tindall, 128
Tinsdall, 127
Tinslar, 161
Tippett, 320
Tipton, 124, 138
to, 40
Tobey, 430
Tod, 374
Todd, 20, 25, 103, 205, 209, 212, 250, 319, 444, 467, 520
Toland, 313
Tolbortt, 296
Toledana, 335
Toledano, 335
Tolman, 478
Tolson, 309
Tomb, 227, 242
Tomkins, 403
Tomlinson, 2
Tompkins, 275
Toner, 182, 473
Tonge, 209
Toole, 115
Tooley, 382
Toombs, 329
Topping, 337, 412

Tornel, 43
Torrance, 152
Torrey, 337, 497, 535
Torrington, 473
Tortoise Shell, 185
Totten, 148, 180
Toutant, 109
towboat **Pilot**, 125
tow-bow **Tiger**, 488
Towers, 23, 209, 260, 459
Towle, 113, 285
Towles, 422
Town, 284
Towne, 37
Townend, 506
Towns, 182, 427
Townsend, 5, 24, 36, 90, 132, 133, 148, 212, 285, 319, 405, 434, 480
Towson, 63, 219, 321, 465, 495
Tracy, 214, 334
Trade, 488
Traisol, 108
Trammell, 79
Trane, 96
Trapier, 155
Travers, 93, 189, 209, 335, 385, 459, 530
Tree, 225
Trenchard, 512
Trenholm, 120, 221, 282, 294
Trenk, 184
Trescott, 444
Tressler, 37
Trevit, 327
Triggel, 237
Trio, 169
Tripler, 226
Triplett, 47, 141, 151, 301, 353
Tripp, 8
Trippe, 31
Trippelette, 264
Troutman, 431
Trower, 403
Troxel, 253

Truax, 308
True, 388
Truehat, 196
Trueheart, 29, 55, 65
Trueman, 428
Truitehell, 32
Truman, 294
Trumbull, 35, 252
Trunnel, 38
Trunnell, 274
Tschiffely, 369
Tuck, 59, 94, 132, 148, 210, 281, 292
Tucker, 5, 44, 46, 63, 92, 105, 118, 209, 332, 368, 407, 460, 473, 506, 518
Tuckerman, 15
Tudor, 98, 332
Tuel, 411
Tuley, 42
Tulip Hill, 112
Tuomey, 229
Turance, 527
Turk, 390
Turnbull, 148, 347, 348
Turner, 20, 75, 111, 160, 169, 204, 209, 212, 217, 224, 300, 356, 384, 406, 422, 494
Turney, 195
Turpin, 108, 420, 499
Turrington, 279
Turten, 479
Turton, 289
Tustin, 492
Tuston, 1, 288, 392, 400, 524
Tutt, 299
Tuxen, 384
Tweedy, 240
Twigg, 114
Twiggs, 16, 36, 90, 356, 442
Twiss, 430
Two Yankees, 169
Twogood, 115, 159, 316, 333
Twomey, 54, 344
Two-third Republic, 170

Tyler, 68, 93, 104, 142, 176, 183, 191, 195, 264, 271, 286, 289, 299, 302, 306, 309, 310, 331, 385, 397, 458, 479, 493, 496, 510
Tyree, 273
Tyrer, 35
Tyson, 48, 296, 379

U

Ufford, 86
Ullmann, 187
Ulrick, 322
Ulshart, 427
Umberger, 67
Umble, 167
Underhill, 483, 513
Underwood, 62, 263, 284, 329, 354, 366, 373, 448, 471
Updegraff, 205
Updyke, 20
Upham, 4
Upperman, 5, 209, 259, 459, 489
Upshur, 86, 100, 104, 106, 120, 126, 156, 252, 276, 299, 431, 520
Usher, 65, 244, 256, 281, 293
Ushur, 270
Utermuhle, 459

V

Vail, 75
Valade, 304
Van Alatine, 266
Van Alstyne, 241
Van Bibber, 363
Van Buren, 51, 126, 352, 423, 485
Van Campen, 352
Van Cleve, 75
Van Cortland, 405
Van Dieman, 93, 101
Van Dieman's Land, 213, 295
Van Dusen, 422
Van Dyke, 313
Van Horn, 101, 375, 442
Van Horne, 327

Van Horseigh, 69, 82, 189, 203, 523
Van Ness, 46, 66, 106, 113, 135, 148, 199, 238, 271, 288, 289, 389, 397, 506, 527
Van Rensselaer, 99, 362, 405
Van Reswick, 240, 513
Van Riswick, 348
Van Schmidt, 148
Van Tyne, 105
Van Vechten, 173
Van Vleit, 417
Van Voast, 52, 256
Van Wyck, 520
Van Zandt, 225, 351, 487, 514
Vanbibber, 167, 168
Vance, 6, 97, 308, 344, 396, 460
Vandeford, 19
Vanderberg, 462
Vanderburgh, 467
Vandergrift, 431
Vanderpoel, 485
Vanderslice, 296
Vandeusen, 57
Vandeventer, 497
Vandevoort, 149
Vandewater, 427
Vanleer, 119
Vanmeter, 167
Vann, 209, 288, 462, 466, 468, 517
Vansant, 170
Vanstavoren, 219
Vanuxem, 229
Vanuxen, 67
Vanvalkenburgh, 399
Vanvleek, 309
Vanzant, 21
Varnum, 456
Vasques, 145
Vasquez, 107
Vass, 299, 507
Vattemare, 484
Vaughan, 31, 141
Vaux, 323
Veazey, 159

Veazie, 13
Veazy, 170
Vecklin, 50
Venable, 108, 220, 518
Venderburg, 140
Verdan, 209
Vermillion, 54, 94, 485
Vernet, 109
Vernon, 448
Verplanck, 151, 484
Verrell, 331
Vessee, 403
vessel **Brig Tweed**, 1
vessel **Gen Lincoln**, 367
vessel **Little Pike**, 373
vessel **Luiz d'Albuquerque**, 373
vessel **West Wind**, 309
vessel **Wetipquin**, 438
Vick, 274
Vickers, 212, 468
Vigo, 22
Vincent, 2, 41, 479
Vineyard, 39
Vinson, 354, 536
Visser, 53, 77, 518
Viti, 112, 141
Vivans, 209, 415, 472
Voisins, 462
Von Kapff, 484
Von Schmidt, 55, 161, 230, 231, 238, 249, 266
Voorhees, 107, 250, 347, 388, 404, 445
Vose, 31, 157
Voss, 196, 420
Vowell, 169, 428
Vroom, 248

W

Wachter, 514, 520
Waco, 337
Waddel, 380
Waddington, 110
Wade, 137, 188, 427, 451
Wadlow, 212
Wadsworth, 272
Waggaman, 246, 335
Waggoner, 350
Waggonner, 509
Wagler, 459
Wagner, 313
Wagoner, 166, 466
Wailes, 359, 376, 456
Wailey, 431
Wainwright, 78, 328, 426, 476
Waite, 7
Wake, 510
Wakeman, 25, 242, 432
Waldron, 234
Walker, 6, 28, 31, 69, 99, 148, 188, 209, 230, 251, 265, 274, 275, 309, 313, 332, 337, 347, 351, 368, 393, 405, 431, 433, 459, 522
Wall, 36, 96, 118, 129, 143, 411, 415, 493, 527
Wallace, 24, 72, 126, 151, 205, 277, 326
Wallach, 16, 159, 209, 213, 356, 360, 450
Waller, 520
Walling, 175
Wallingsford, 209
Wallis, 94, 99, 124, 143, 209, 281, 293, 403, 462, 467
Walls, 305
Wally, 91
Walmsley, 91
Walnut Botton, 166
Walnut Grove, 353
Walnut Ridge, 166
Walsh, 35, 137, 215, 246, 374
Walter, 170, 335
Walton, 187, 533
Walworth, 128, 394
Wambersie, 27
Wannal, 249
Wannall, 209
Wants, 313

War, 340
War of Independence, 168
Ward, 17, 18, 19, 29, 36, 39, 53, 62, 83, 87, 90, 94, 133, 145, 186, 200, 209, 238, 274, 300, 314, 332, 374, 392, 402, 457, 459, 483, 510, 524, 525, 527, 530
Warder, 103
Wards, 423
Ware, 30, 43, 276, 433, 477
Warfield, 56, 170
Waring, 99, 350
Warley, 36
Warneken, 488
Warner, 77, 123, 133, 209, 213, 244, 271, 447
Warren, 72, 123, 124, 216, 247, 259, 287, 414, 423
Warring, 148, 170, 421
Warrington, 103, 107, 202, 241
Warwick, 105
Wash Canal, 290
Washabaugh, 119
Washington, 23, 29, 30, 40, 46, 69, 109, 131, 141, 156, 191, 198, 209, 247, 249, 254, 256, 267, 281, 282, 303, 321, 380, 395, 446, 459, 479, 492, 496, 497, 502, 507, 511, 528
Wasson, 171
Waterlow, 395
Waterman, 405, 412, 505
Waters, 31, 35, 89, 130, 209, 306, 330, 334, 336, 397, 408, 411, 434, 471, 482, 485
Waters' Wharf, 130
Watkins, 41, 259
Watmough, 36, 323, 527
Watmouth, 90
Watson, 20, 29, 36, 57, 81, 90, 94, 136, 148, 159, 240, 242, 290, 312, 323, 343, 360, 412, 446, 509
Watt, 466
Watterson, 276, 278
Watterston, 23, 148, 209, 214, 259, 459
Watts, 119, 152, 200
Waugh, 5, 366
Waverley Academy, 9
Wayland, 371
Waylen, 233
Wayman, 26
Wayne, 13, 29, 161, 527
Wealsh, 170
Wear, 463
Weaver, 58, 65, 130, 163, 319, 375
Webb, 107, 124, 411, 430, 466, 467
Weber, 460
Webster, 18, 79, 120, 125, 154, 180, 213, 214, 218, 254, 289, 296, 356, 388, 405, 419, 479, 535
Wecaix, 429
Wedel, 289
Weed, 98, 114, 222, 236, 437
Weeks, 238
Weems, 212, 237, 352
Weightman, 4, 96, 124, 148, 180, 209, 215, 259, 363, 411, 456, 463
Weims, 312
Weir, 101, 452
Welby, 378
Welch, 411, 430, 465
Welcome Here, 169
Weld, 15
Wellesley, 358
Wellford, 262
Wellingcamp, 26
Wells, 66, 159, 184, 199, 242, 319, 325, 334, 339, 343, 478, 518
Welsh, 218, 240, 402
Wenthing, 139
Wentling, 244, 256
Wentworth, 3
Wenwood, 506
Werkmeister, 45
Werner, 209, 459
Wertz, 411
Wesson, 74

West, 20, 97, 209, 211, 225, 242, 250, 258, 325, 338, 339, 405, 431, 444, 458, 462, 465, 480, 495
West Point, 160
Westake, 306
Westefield, 411
Western Connexion, 166
Weston, 25, 40, 52, 134, 278, 510
Wethered, 110, 191, 516
Wetherill, 119
Wetherlee, 77
Wetmore, 84, 151, 279, 315
Wever, 370, 429
Whaley, 440
Whaly, 143
Wharton, 157, 267, 313, 357, 362, 429, 444, 460, 480, 525
What you please, 169
What you Will, 169
What-Cheer, 255
Wheat, 21, 43, 403, 470
Wheatley, 264, 347
Wheaton, 226
Wheelan, 334
Wheeler, 152, 277, 326, 328, 449
Wheelright, 493, 513
Wheelwright, 19
Wherry, 219
Whetstone, 505
Whetten, 27
Whitaker, 39, 214, 218
White, 4, 11, 12, 67, 89, 91, 96, 101, 108, 109, 114, 122, 123, 138, 144, 147, 150, 152, 177, 200, 209, 211, 213, 224, 234, 236, 286, 299, 323, 333, 339, 347, 348, 355, 372, 388, 402, 417, 454, 459, 463, 468, 473, 496, 510, 535
White Hall, 295
White Oak Flat, 166
White Oak Point, 170
White,, 347
Whiteford, 177
Whitehead, 361, 422
Whitehill, 492
Whitehurst, 133
Whiteley, 334
Whiteside, 108
Whitesides, 266
Whiting, 223, 241, 250, 295, 358, 479
Whitley, 526
Whitman, 144
Whitmore, 202, 240, 377, 512
Whitney, 24, 36, 57, 158, 161, 209, 260, 388
Whitridge, 124
Whitson, 508
Whittaker, 221
Whitten, 111, 230, 231
Whittier, 266
Whittingham, 363, 389, 397, 419
Whittington, 479
Whittlesey, 327, 390, 428, 473, 482
Whitton, 8
Whitwell, 366
Whyte, 468
Wickliffe, 120, 135, 215, 275, 449
Wicks, 152
Widdicumb, 477
Wilbur, 276
Wilburn, 5, 449
Wilcocks, 249
Wilcox, 113
Wild Cherry Tree Meadow, 166
Wilde, 494
Wilder, 228, 430
Wilds, 15
Wileman, 72
Wilkerson, 461
Wilkes, 74, 75, 229
Wilkeson, 27
Wilkin, 405
Wilkins, 6, 25, 32, 81, 120, 217, 230, 246, 330, 403, 495
Wilkinson, 156, 204, 343, 380
Willaims, 123
Willams, 93
Willer, 295

Willett, 168, 252
Willetts, 276
Willey, 101, 450
William & Mary, 170
Williams, 5, 30, 39, 72, 76, 87, 100, 115, 117, 123, 132, 138, 160, 163, 165, 176, 183, 184, 189, 191, 195, 202, 209, 211, 215, 236, 247, 248, 259, 261, 262, 275, 276, 282, 284, 296, 300, 310, 314, 323, 342, 353, 370, 374, 383, 390, 405, 418, 424, 429, 433, 434, 442, 443, 455, 464, 476, 487, 513, 514, 518, 530
Williams', 5
Williamson, 20, 76, 205, 209, 217, 278, 312, 324, 326, 342, 370, 391, 427, 483, 504, 514
Willing, 232, 323
Willingham, 319, 380
Willis, 425, 507
Willitt, 518
Willitts, 278
Willock, 132
Willow Bank, 169
Wills, 388
Willson, 172, 468
Wilmer, 11
Wilson, 13, 46, 66, 95, 98, 103, 113, 114, 115, 117, 121, 128, 130, 139, 148, 152, 159, 164, 202, 209, 212, 218, 222, 227, 231, 242, 244, 245, 249, 256, 257, 260, 270, 273, 307, 310, 315, 331, 340, 343, 349, 400, 401, 423, 424, 427, 431, 440, 450, 451, 453, 468, 475, 479, 482, 506, 512, 519, 523, 524, 534
Wilson's Risk, 169
Wiltberger, 209, 311
Wiltherger, 229
Wimbish, 121
Wimer, 224
Wimsatt, 118, 459
Winans, 86, 512
Winchester, 277

Winder, 117, 126, 191, 243, 323, 360, 411
Windlow, 446
Windsor, 54
Wines, 144, 439
Wingate, 158, 439
Wingerd, 80
Winifrey, 122
Winne, 148
Winslow, 95, 112, 133, 278, 283, 420, 423, 431, 527
Winston, 299
Winter, 209, 235, 277, 278, 279, 282, 313, 402
Winters, 85, 323
Winting, 54
Wirt, 34, 200
Wise, 70, 85, 113, 209, 291, 307, 338, 359, 393, 486
Wiswall, 377
Withers, 21, 299
Witler, 283
Woffley, 491
Wolcott, 214, 290
Wolf, 218
Wolff, 482
Woll, 176
Womack, 277
Wontling, 272
Wood, 43, 83, 135, 157, 177, 209, 212, 226, 241, 268, 314, 315, 318, 332, 411, 456, 465, 477, 522
Wood Lawn, 203
Wood Park, 221
Woodbury, 6, 35, 252, 286
Woodfin, 403
Woodhouse, 74
Woodhull, 36, 75, 90, 405
Woodland Plains, 156
Woodlands Estate, 249
Woodley, 338
Woodruff, 72, 402, 443, 488
Woods, 101, 168, 313, 327, 426, 444
Woodside, 18, 190

Woodson, 49, 403
Woodward, 9, 93, 106, 209, 265, 354, 405, 425, 505
Woodworth, 241, 308, 508
Woodyard, 203, 338
Wool, 230
Woolford, 107
Woolsey, 217
Wootton, 63, 373, 433
Worden, 209
Wordsworth, 262
Worley, 130
Wormley, 94, 95, 122, 145, 236
Wormly, 38, 248
Worsham, 231
Worsley, 375
Worth, 246, 377
Worthington, 165, 172, 260, 433, 434, 456, 496
Wray, 81
Wren, 107, 135, 145, 147, 274, 277, 281, 292
Wright, 10, 22, 26, 31, 33, 34, 49, 56, 68, 72, 73, 84, 93, 96, 100, 101, 103, 112, 134, 147, 153, 160, 190, 209, 219, 222, 223, 225, 231, 248, 269, 271, 277, 288, 320, 327, 339, 345, 364, 367, 436, 437, 458, 479, 493, 498
Wrightman, 209, 461
Wrine, 238
Wroe, 34, 186, 209, 365, 430, 477
Wurton, 58
Wyatt, 98, 315, 473, 502
Wyche, 75
Wyman, 463
Wynn, 22, 124, 243
Wyrick, 498
Wyse, 371
Wysham, 335, 336

Y

Yantis, 133
Yard, 250
Yarnall, 212, 351
Yarnell, 144
Yates, 17, 45, 79, 132, 250, 386
Yeadon, 473
Yeager, 358
Yellott, 434
Yerby, 515
Yerrington, 212
Yoast, 156, 244
Yoe, 383
York, 118, 464
York Springs, 311
Yost, 311
Young, 1, 9, 23, 25, 32, 43, 50, 53, 72, 86, 88, 116, 138, 148, 168, 179, 191, 196, 201, 204, 209, 217, 221, 230, 231, 236, 240, 248, 258, 266, 280, 281, 320, 323, 340, 341, 347, 348, 351, 363, 374, 379, 380, 387, 398, 402, 407, 411, 424, 450, 453, 459, 463, 467, 469, 472, 481, 484, 490, 515, 536
Youngman, 532
Youngs, 22

Z

Zabriskie, 445
Zachman, 458
Zahm, 427
Zales, 312
Zantzinger, 34, 130, 194, 272, 276, 306, 528
Zeilin, 351
Zell, 99
Zeller, 453
Zieber, 314

Other Heritage Books by the author:

National Intelligencer *Newspaper Abstracts, Special Edition: The Civil War Years, 1861-1863*

National Intelligencer *Newspaper Abstracts 1846*
National Intelligencer *Newspaper Abstracts 1845*
National Intelligencer *Newspaper Abstracts 1844*
National Intelligencer *Newspaper Abstracts 1843*
National Intelligencer *Newspaper Abstracts 1842*
National Intelligencer *Newspaper Abstracts 1841*
National Intelligencer *Newspaper Abstracts 1840*
National Intelligencer *Newspaper Abstracts, 1838-1839*
National Intelligencer *Newspaper Abstracts, 1836-1837*
National Intelligencer *Newspaper Abstracts, 1834-1835*
National Intelligencer *Newspaper Abstracts, 1832-1833*
National Intelligencer *Newspaper Abstracts, 1830-1831*
National Intelligencer *Newspaper Abstracts, 1827-1829*
National Intelligencer *Newspaper Abstracts, 1824-1826*
National Intelligencer *Newspaper Abstracts, 1821-1823*
National Intelligencer *Newspaper Abstracts, 1818-1820*
National Intelligencer *Newspaper Abstracts, 1814-1817*
National Intelligencer *Newspaper Abstracts, 1811-1813*
National Intelligencer *Newspaper Abstracts, 1806-1810*
National Intelligencer *Newspaper Abstracts, 1800-1805*

www.ingramcontent.com/pod-product-compliance
Lightning Source LLC
Chambersburg PA
CBHW071132300426
44113CB00009B/949